SCHAUM'S OUTLINE OF

THEORY AND PROBLEMS

of

OPERATIONS
MANAGEMENT

•

by

JOSEPH G. MONKS, Ph.D.
Professor of Operations Management
Gonzaga University

SCHAUM'S OUTLINE SERIES
McGRAW-HILL BOOK COMPANY

New York   St. Louis   San Francisco   Auckland   Bogotá   Hamburg   London
Madrid   Mexico   Milan   Montreal   New Delhi   Panama   Paris
São Paulo   Singapore   Sydney   Tokyo   **Toronto**

To Clara

JOSEPH G. MONKS is a professional mechanical and industrial engineer with a Ph.D. in Business Administration from the University of Washington. His experience includes positions with Westinghouse, General Electric, and the U.S. government in addition to consulting work. Dr. Monks taught at Oregon State University and in Europe prior to joining Gonzaga University. He holds professional certification in Production and Inventory Management (CPIM) and has written articles and other books in the areas of statistics and operations management.

Schaum's Outline of Theory and Problems of
OPERATIONS MANAGEMENT

3 4 5 6 7 8 9 10 11 12 13 14 15 16 17 18 19 20 SHP SHP 8 9 8

ISBN 0-07-042726-7

Sponsoring Editor, Barbara Brooks
Editing Supervisor, Marthe Grice
Production Manager, Nick Monti

Library of Congress Cataloging in Publication Data

Monks, Joseph G.
    Schaum's outline of theory and problems of operations
management.

    (Schaum's outline series)
    Includes index.
    1. Production management.   2. Industrial engineering.
I. Title.
TS155.M674   1985   658.5   84-781
ISBN 0-07-042726-7

Preface

This Outline has three major uses: (1) as a supplement to current texts in production and operations management, (2) as a text in its own right, (3) as a study guide for practicing professionals who are preparing for the American Production and Inventory Control Society (APICS) certification examinations. Key features of the Outline are its comprehensive coverage, condensed theory, and multitude of examples and solved problems.

As a supplement and/or text for production and operations management courses, the Outline presents materials normally taught at the upper college or introductory graduate (MBA) level. Although it covers all topics generally included in AACSB accredited courses, the interesting but nonessential descriptive materials are minimized. Instead, theory is straightforward, precise, and somewhat concentrated. Emphasis is on applications and examples, which are worked out in a systematic fashion.

As a reference guide for practicing managers, the Outline has independent chapters which offer relatively complete coverage of a given topic area. In addition, Chapters 9 through 14 cover production and inventory control topics of special importance to production and inventory control managers. These materials can be used as one (of many) references for preparation to take the APICS certification examinations.

The Outline makes extensive use of quantitative techniques. However, a background in college algebra is sufficient for general understanding throughout. Statistical, calculus, and management science techniques are explained largely by example as the needs for them arise. The quantitative topic shown in smaller type after a chapter title indicates that a more detailed explanation of that quantitative method is contained in the chapter. Designed for quantitative support, the Outline tends to favor simplicity and clarity of presentation over mathematical sophistication.

My thanks to all the staff at Gonzaga University and at McGraw-Hill who helped bring this project to completion.

JOSEPH G. MONKS

Contents

CONTENTS

CONTENTS

Chapter 1

Operations Management Functions

HISTORY

Production activities are the foundation of a nation's economic system. They transform human, material, and capital resources into higher-valued goods and services. Figure 1-1 identifies some key individuals and events in the development of productive systems over the past 200 years.

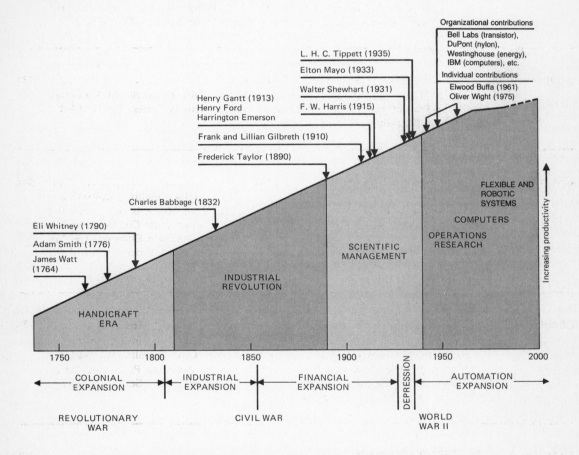

Fig. 1-1 Key individuals and events in the development of production systems

James Watt's steam engine (1764) advanced the use of mechanical power and Adam Smith (1776) publicized the advantages of the division of labor. The United States Constitution (1789) encouraged capital investment and trade, and the Civil War, along with the expanding railroad system, spurred early industrial development. Growth of the factory system was rapid for there was no well-established production system to supplant, and unskilled labor was available. In the early 1900s Frederick Taylor's work then ushered in the scientific management era, and endowed him with the title of "Father of Scientific Management." As better machinery and automatic controls were developed, much of the heavy manufacturing effort was directed toward mass production of similar products.

1

Example 1.1   Table 1-1 lists some of the major contributors to scientific management and their contributions.

Table 1-1

Contributor	Major Contribution
Frederick Taylor	Philosophy of scientific management, use of training, time study, and standards
Henry Ford	Assembly-line mass production
Harrington Emerson	Improvement of organizational efficiency
F.W. Harris	First economic order quantity (EOQ) model
Henry Grant	Use of scheduling systems
Walter Shewhart	Statistical quality control
Elton Mayo	Attention to behavioral factors
L.H.C. Tippett	Work sampling

CURRENT STATUS OF PRODUCTIVE SYSTEMS

In the mid-1900s, as operations research techniques were developed and as computers became economical, industry entered an unparalleled age of automation. Computers then came along to give managers up-to-the-minute information about markets, costs, production levels, and inventories. Manufacturers began installing logic units in equipment so that machines could receive and carry out preprogrammed instructions. The grouping of computer-controlled machines and the development of industrial robots has now given production systems the flexibility to receive and respond to online information. Robots can sense a need and rapidly perform individualized tasks. With robots, flexible manufacturing systems can deliver customized products at volumes that were previously available only under "hard-wired" mass-production automation.

Mass-production activities that involve substantial amounts of labor are now gradually being transferred from developed to less-developed countries to reduce costs. This shift creates employment in Asian and South American industries at the expense of employment in industries such as textile and steel in the United States and Western Europe. Meanwhile, robots and flexible production systems are further reducing the demand for low-skilled direct labor in the United States. Offsetting this surplus of untrained workers in the United States is the growing need for more technically trained control and maintenance personnel. Retraining is needed to prepare low-skilled workers for these emerging, more sophisticated fields of work.

The productive emphasis in the United States is also shifting from an industrial (manufacturing) to an informational (knowledge) economy. This is one of the most significant changes of the twentieth century. Businesses of the future will be more active in fields involving specialty items (e.g., high-tech metals) and advanced information and communications services. By the year 2000, about 80 percent of our work force will most likely be engaged in nonmanufacturing activities. Here again, high-technology systems (e.g., electronic, microwave, fiber optics, lasers) will play a major role.

MANAGEMENT

Numerous approaches have been developed to explain the role of managers. Three of the most prominent are the (1) functional, (2) behavioral, and (3) decision-making (systems) approaches.

Example 1.2   Briefly describe the three approaches to management.

    (1)   *Functional* is the traditional (classical) approach that holds that managers plan, organize, direct, and control the activities of an organization.

(2) *Behavioral* is a human relations approach that emphasizes interpersonal relationships and organizational behavior. Under it, managers work through other people to lead the activities of an organization.

(3) *Decision-making* (*systems*) is an approach that focuses upon the use of data and quantitative techniques for making decisions that facilitate system goals. Managers are primarily decision makers within an operating system.

Management is the process of developing decisions and taking actions to direct the activities of people within an organization toward common objectives. Objectives differ, but most organizations have multiple goals that include:

● welfare of employees
● service to customers
● returns to stockholders
● responsibility to society

To accomplish the organizational objectives, managers formulate policies, operating plans, procedures, and rules. Figure 1-2 uses the upside-down pyramid concept to illustrate how broad-based objectives (e.g., good customer service) are eventually operationalized via specific rules (e.g., maintain a safety stock of 50 units). It also shows how the organization's database forms a foundation for decision-making at all levels. Note that managerial values influence objectives, policies, plans, procedures, and rules by filtering down through the organizational structure—perhaps in a subtle way. Values can influence the database, and factual data can modify values.

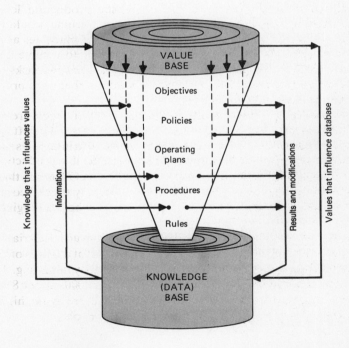

Fig. 1-2 Information flows for decision-making

OPERATIONS MANAGEMENT

Operations management is that activity whereby resources, flowing within a defined system, are combined and transformed in a controlled manner to add value in accordance with organizational objectives. Figure 1-3 depicts this process.

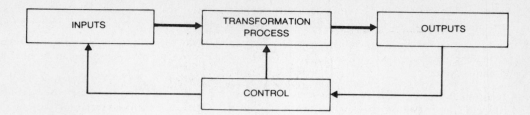

Fig. 1-3 A simplified production system

Operations management responsibilities include bringing the inputs together under an acceptable production plan that effectively utilizes the materials, capacity, and knowledge available in the production facility. Given a demand on the system, work is scheduled and controlled to produce the goods and services required. Meanwhile, control must be exercised over inventory, quality, and costs. In addition the facility itself must be maintained.

Example 1.3 Illustrate the operations management responsibilities in the form of a schematic diagram.

See Fig. 1-4. Operations managers are responsible for *planning*, *organizing*, and *controlling* the transformation activities. These duties interface closely with personnel, engineering, finance, legal, marketing, and accounting functions.

The definition of operations management contains the key concepts of (1) resources, (2) systems, and (3) transformation and value-adding activities.

Resources are the human, material, and capital inputs. *Human* inputs (both physical and intellectual) are often the key asset. *Material* inputs include plant, equipment, inventories, and supplies such as energy. *Capital* inputs, in the form of equity, debt, taxes, and contributions, are a store of values which regulate the flow of other resources.

Systems are arrangements of components designed to achieve objectives according to plans. Our social and economic environment contains many levels of systems and subsystems, which are in turn components of larger systems. We have a free-enterprise economic system. Business firms, which are components of that system, contain personnel, engineering, finance, operations, and marketing functions, all of which are subsystems within the individual firms.

A *systems approach* emphasizes the integrative nature of all system activities and stresses the relationship and cooperation that should exist within the total system. A consistent and integrative approach can lead to *optimization* of the overall (macro) system goals. If the subsystem goals are pursued independently, *suboptimization* may result.

The ability of a system to accomplish its objectives depends upon its design and control. *Systems design* is a predetermined arrangement of components. The more structured the design, the less decision-making is involved in its operation. *Systems control* is the conformance of activities to plans or goals.

Example 1.4 Identify four essential elements of control.

(1) *Measurement* by an accurate sensory device
(2) *Feedback* of information in a timely manner
(3) *Comparison with standards* such as time and cost standards
(4) *Corrective action* by one with authority and ability

Transformation and value-adding activities combine and transform the resources using some form of technology (mechanical, chemical, medical, electronic, etc.). This transformation creates new goods and services that have a higher value to consumers than the acquisition and processing costs of the inputs

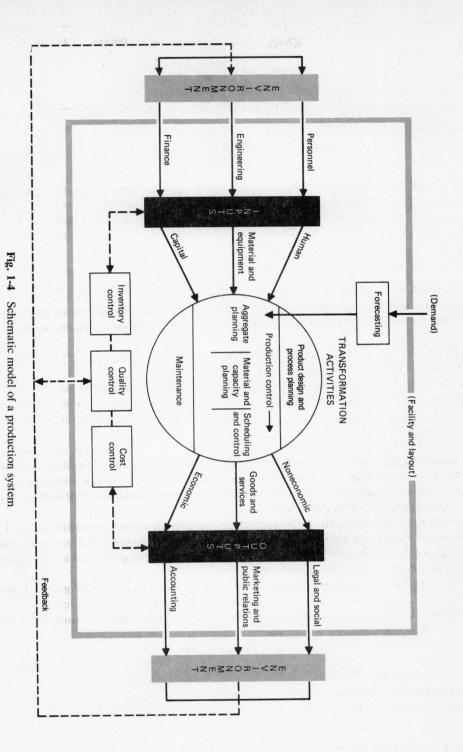

Fig. 1-4 Schematic model of a production system

have to the organization. *Productivity* is a measure of the effectiveness of the use of resources to produce goods and services. The ratio of output value to input cost should be greater than 1.

$$\text{Productivity} = \frac{\text{value of outputs}}{\text{cost of inputs}}. \qquad (1.1)$$

Example 1.5 An accounting firm generates services valued at $8,000 per day and has total costs of $5,000 per day. What is a measure of its productivity?

$$\text{Productivity} = \frac{\text{value of outputs}}{\text{cost of inputs}} = \frac{\$8,000}{\$5,000} = 1.6$$

Note that the value of the outputs is established by consumers in the marketplace, and the cost of inputs is dictated largely by what the firm must pay its suppliers (accountants in the example above). Management often focuses upon the efficiency of the transformation activities.

FACTORS AFFECTING PRODUCTIVITY

After increasing at an annual rate of about 3 percent until the mid-1960s, the United States rate of increase in productivity dropped to about 2 percent until 1973 and averaged less than 1 percent for the next 10 years. Some of the principal factors influencing productivity changes are:

● capital/labor ratio

● resource scarcity

● work force changes

● innovation and technology

● regulatory and bargaining effects

● quality of work life

A declining *capital/labor ratio* reflects the fact that many of the plants and much of the equipment in the United States is over 20 years old. The decreased level of capital investment signals a short-term perspective that is characteristic of many firms. However, the use of automation and robots in some industries will tend to improve this ratio. *Resources* are increasingly scarce, especially energy, metals, and water. Emphasis is shifting toward the use of renewable resources. *Work force changes* include a steady shift away from blue-collar occupations, which are estimated to account for only about one-third of the work force in 1990. Unfortunately, education and retraining for new jobs are inadequate to maintain full employment. Service occupations are the fastest-growing segment. Productivity in service activities is difficult to measure, but is generally assumed to be lower than in goods-producing activities.

A reduction in *research and development* (R&D) *expenditures* explains some of the decline in productivity, as does the deluge of *regulations* in the early 1980s. The power of *organized labor* to command wage increases in excess of output increases has also had a detrimental impact. However, union membership has dropped from about 30 percent of the work force (1950) to less than 20 percent. *Quality of work life* is perhaps the most encompassing reason, for it reflects the entire work environment. Many United States firms have moved toward participative management approaches designed to foster loyalty, teamwork, and commitment of employees, as much Japanese industry has stressed.

MANUFACTURING AND NONMANUFACTURING SYSTEMS

Whereas manufacturing produces tangible goods that can be measured, stored, and consumed at a later date, most services provide intangible products that convey value directly to the consumer as they are produced. *Manufacturing systems* are often classified as being for either make-to-stock goods (such as appliances) or make-to-order goods (such as power transformers). Some *nonmanufactur-*

ing systems deal with tangible goods (warehousing, distribution, auto repair), whereas others involve intangible services (tax assistance, counseling services). In service activities, when the customer is a participant, production and consumption occur simultaneously and no inventory accrues.

Example 1.6 Identify characteristics of most service systems.

- Locations are decentralized.
- Demand is highly variable.
- Inputs are often variable.
- No inventory is accumulated.
- Outputs are often customized.
- Output quality is often variable.

Services employ about two-thirds of United States workers and generate over half the gross national product (GNP). Many services (entertainers, travel agents, stockbrokers, lawyers) depend largely upon the performance of people, while others (phone companies, utilities) rely more heavily upon the use of equipment or facilities. The people-equipment mix is significant because *people* can learn better ways of doing jobs, but most machines cannot. However, machines are more predictable and measurable. Of most significance, however, is that manufacturing systems deal primarily with planning, scheduling, and controlling *materials*. With services, the production-control efforts concentrate upon the flow of *customers*.

Example 1.7 Use a sketch to illustrate a significant difference in goods-producing versus services-producing facilities.
See Fig. 1-5.

INTERNATIONAL OPERATIONS

Operations managers hold various titles (vice-president of operations, general manager, production manager, plant superintendent) and work in widely diversified industries (manufacturing, food service, transportation, government). Because United States firms are increasingly faced with global rather than national competition, they often have multinational operations. Thus operations managers may find themselves in any locality (Europe, China, South America). The problems the operations managers face in their work are similar regardless of location, but the organizational and national cultures differ. Activities and behavior that are appropriate in a free-enterprise society such as the United States may not be acceptable in a more socialist environment such as France, or in a closed society such as the Soviet Union, and vice versa.

When production operations cross international borders, special attention must be given to all aspects of those operations, from the acquisition of human, material, and capital resources to the eventual delivery of products to the market. Firms expanding into a foreign country should have a thorough knowledge of that country's political, economic, and legal systems and must be prepared to adapt to the educational and cultural values of the new environment.

Example 1.8 Identify characteristics of Japanese firms that differ from characteristics of some United States firms.

(1) *Corporate objectives.* Employees and customers are given priority over shareholders.

(2) *Financing.* More use of debt capital, and less use (approximately 25 percent) of equity capital.

(3) *Long-term perspective.* Viability in the long run is more important than short-term profits. Employees are evaluated on *long*-term performance.

(4) *Emphasis on training.* Employees are thoroughly trained and rotated to learn a diversity of skills; less emphasis on job descriptions.

(5) *Employment relations.* Long-term employment of loyal workers. Employees are paid on the basis of employee worth and needs. Unions cooperate to benefit firms.

(6) *Worker participation.* Direct involvement of employees in productivity improvements via suggestions, quality circles, consultation.

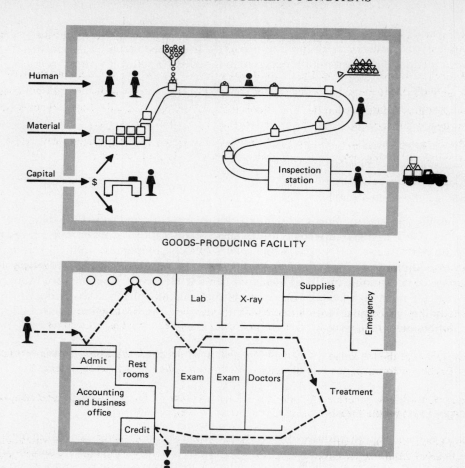

Fig. 1-5   Goods- and services-producing facilities

Solved Problems

1.1   In what way did Adam Smith contribute to the development of productive systems?

Adam Smith's book, *The Wealth of Nations* (1776), publicized the advantages of the division of labor, which included skill development, time savings, and the use of specialized machines.

1.2   Which approach to management describes the managerial function in terms of planning and staffing activities?

The functional approach.

1.3   In what sense is a hospital a "productive" activity?

Hospitals combine the resources of doctors, nurses, and staff with facilities and equipment to provide health care (service) to patients in a controlled environment. The medical care adds value (and enhanced existence) to the patients' lives.

1.4   Identify some major changes that have recently influenced productive activities in the United States.

(a)   A decline in productivity and a renewed concern over the factors affecting productivity

(b)   A gradual shift from mass production of identical items to mass production of customized items

(c)   A continued shift in employment from the production of goods (steel, textiles, etc.) to the production of services (health care, transportation, repair services, etc.)

(d)   An increased emphasis on the production of knowledge-based services such as education and training, counseling, consulting, financial and legal advice, and the like

Supplementary Problems

1.5   Describe the approach to management that tends to be most "analytic" by virtue of relying upon the use of data.   *Ans.*   Decision-making (systems)

1.6   Explain the key concepts included in the definition of operations management.
Ans.   Include resources, systems, transformation, value-added activities, objectives

1.7   In what sense are the following "production" activities?   (a) airline (b) farm (c) restaurant (d) university.
Ans.   Each transforms inputs into higher-valued outputs within a controlled system.

1.8   If a restaurant were to generate food services valued at $4,000 per day and to incur total costs of $3,000 per day, what would be the measure of its productivity?   *Ans.*   1.33

1.9   Explain how a key characteristic of the French economy makes the managerial environment of French firms different from that of United States firms.   *Ans.*   Much French industry is nationalized.

Chapter 2

Operations Decision Making

Break-Even, Statistical Methods, and Decision Trees

DECISION CHARACTERISTICS

Making decisions about how to plan, organize, direct, and control business activities is a major responsibility of operations managers. The amount and type of analysis given to the decision depend upon: (1) the *significance* of the decision, (2) the *time* and *cost* limitations, and (3) the *complexity* of the problem. Trivial or routine problems may best be handled by simple judgmental choices. Complex problems that involve many interdependent variables and significant cash flow or personnel changes usually require more sophisticated methods. Similarly, decisions made under conditions of uncertainty often require statistical analysis.

DECISION SCIENCE

Decision scientists hold that people need not be "born managers" to do a good job. Education, scientific training, and experience can enhance one's ability to make good, logical decisions. The basis for viewing management as a science rests upon the following similarities with other sciences:

(1) Organized principles of knowledge

(2) Use of empirical data

(3) Systematic analysis of data

(4) Repeatable results

The fundamental principles of organization and control form a knowledge base. Use of the scientific method then rests largely upon the quantification and analysis of business *data*. Computers are very helpful to management today because they can easily perform sophisticated mathematical and statistical analysis. But not all variables are quantifiable, and decision makers must still supply critical value-based judgments to the decision process.

THE DECISION-MAKING PROCESS

Table 2-1 lists the steps in a systematic decision-making process. (Not all decisions follow these formal steps.)

Table 2-1   The Decision-Making Process

1. *Define* the problem and its parameters (relevant variables).
2. Establish the decision *criteria* (objectives).
3. Relate the parameters to the criteria (i.e., *model* the problem).
4. Generate *alternatives* by varying the values of the parameters.
5. *Evaluate* the alternatives and choose the one that best satisfies the criteria.
6. *Implement* the decision and *monitor* the results.

MODEL BUILDING

Model building (Step 3) is the heart of the scientific decision-making process. Models describe the essence of a problem or relationship by abstracting the relevant variables from the real-world situation and expressing them in a simplified form so the decision maker can study the underlying relationships in isolation. The reconstructed problem (model) is then used for analysis and testing of alternative outcomes. Some useful models are:

(1) Verbal (words and descriptions)

(2) Physical (modified scale)

(3) Schematic (diagrams and charts)

(4) Mathematical (equations and numbers)

Mathematical (and statistical) models are the most abstract—and often the most useful. They can succinctly describe a problem, are readily computerized, and are easily manipulated to test different outcomes.

Example 2.1 Zag Corp. uses a simple linear model to estimate next period's production requirements.

$$P_{t+1} = D_t - (I + P_{t-1})$$

where P_{t+1} = units of production (P) required next period ($t + 1$)

D_t = estimated current period demand (an unknown and uncontrollable variable)

I = present inventory level

P_{t-1} = units produced in previous period

Last period's production was 20 units, the present inventory level is 5 units, and the current period demand is estimated at 40 units plus or minus 10 percent. Use the model to develop an interval estimate of next period's production requirements.

For the *minimum* estimate, let $D_t = 40 - .10\,(40) = 36$ units.

$$P_{t+1} = 36 - (5 + 20) = 11 \text{ units}$$

For the *maximum* estimate, let $D_t = 40 + .10\,(40) = 44$ units.

$$P_{t+1} = 44 - (5 + 20) = 19 \text{ units}$$

Using this model, the estimated production required will be from 11 to 19 units.

In business situations, the validity of a model is judged by how useful it is in predicting the real-world situation. Some advantages of models are that they:

(1) Necessitate a good understanding of the problem

(2) Require a recognition of all relevant (controllable and uncontrollable) variables

(3) Facilitate an understanding of the relationship, costs, and tradeoffs existent among the variables

(4) Permit manipulation of variables and testing of alternative courses of action

DECISION METHODOLOGY

The choice of a model depends upon the characteristics of the decision (i.e., significance, time and cost, and complexity). Decisions are more complex when the data describing the variables are incomplete or uncertain. The degree of certainty is classified as:

(1) *Complete certainty.* All relevant information about the decision variables and outcomes is known (or assumed).

(2) *Risk and uncertainty.* Information about the decision variables or the outcomes is probabilistic. Objective data (from large samples) lend more certainty than subjective data.

(3) *Extreme uncertainty.* No information is available to assess the likelihood of alternative outcomes.

Figure 2-1 illustrates some useful quantitative methods that are classified according to the amount of certainty that exists with respect to the decision variables and possible outcomes. These analytical techniques often serve as the basis for formulating models to help reach operational decisions.

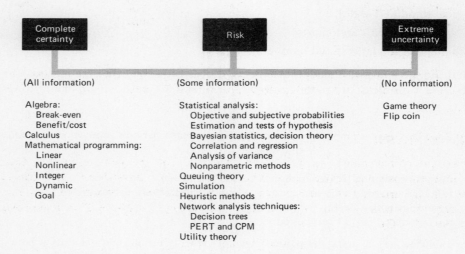

Fig. 2-1   Quantitative methods as a function of degree of certainty

Example 2.2   *Complete Certainty*: Security Storage Inc. leases document storage facilities to county governments on a three-year contract basis. They are considering three potential locations for a new facility. The leasing revenues and installation costs shown below are all guaranteed by contract and are paid in advance.

County Location	Gross Revenue	Installation and Maintenance Costs
A	$4,000	$2,750
B	3,600	2,540
C	4,200	2,900

Which choice of location will maximize the net return?

Net return = gross revenue − installation and maintenance costs

A = $4,000 − $2,750 = $1,250

B = $3,600 − $2,540 = $1,060

C = $4,200 − $2,900 = $1,300

Therefore, C is optimal.

Whereas complete certainty problems are typically solved in an algebraic (or deterministic) manner, risk situations often involve probabilities. When probability values $P(X)$ are used to weight the alternative outcomes of X, and the values times their probabilities are summed, i.e., $\Sigma X \cdot P(X)$, the result is an expected value, $E(X)$. The $E(X)$ is an average, or mean, of the distributions of values.

$$E(X) = \Sigma [X \cdot P(X)] \qquad (2.1)$$

Example 2.3 *Risk*: Ohsaka Games Ltd. is evaluating the cost of producing electronic toys in Philadelphia. Analysts are uncertain about the variable costs (VC) and have developed *low*, *most likely*, and *high* estimates to which they have assigned probabilities of .2, .5, and .3, respectively. Develop an expected-value estimate of the cost.

Variable Cost Component	Low	Most Likely	High
Labor cost/unit	$4.10	$4.40	$4.85
Material cost/unit	2.65	2.95	3.10
Variable OH cost/unit	1.80	1.85	2.00
Total VC/unit	$8.55	$9.20	$9.95

$$E(X) = \Sigma\,[X \cdot P(X)]$$

$$E(\text{cost}) = (\text{low \$}) \cdot P(\text{low}) + (\text{most likely \$}) \cdot P(\text{most likely}) + (\text{high \$}) \cdot P(\text{high})$$
$$= \$8.55(.2) + \$9.20(.5) + \$9.95(.3) = \$9.30$$

BREAK-EVEN ANALYSIS

Break-even (*or cost-volume*) *analysis* is an algebraic and graphic model for describing the relationship between costs and revenues for different volumes of production. Costs are classified as either fixed (FC), or variable (VC), depending upon whether they vary with the volume of output (Q). Profits occur when total revenues (TR) exceed total costs (TC), where TC = fixed costs (FC) plus total variable costs (TVC).

$$\text{Profits} = \text{TR} - (\text{FC} + \text{TVC}) \tag{2.2}$$

Figure 2-2a illustrates the profit concept and Fig. 2-2b identifies the quantity at the break-even point, Q_{BEP}. At the break-even point (BEP), the profit is zero and TR = TC. Recognizing that revenues reflect the selling price per unit (P) times the quantity sold (Q), we restate the TR = TC expression as:

$$PQ = \text{FC} + \text{VC} \cdot Q$$

where VC is the variable cost per unit. The quantity at the break-even point is then

$$Q_{\text{BEP}} = \frac{\text{FC}}{P - \text{VC}} \tag{2.3}$$

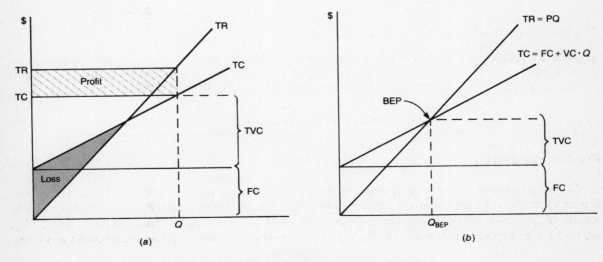

Fig. 2-2 Profit and break-even point analysis

Example 2.4 Annual fixed costs at a small textile shop are \$46,000, and variable costs are estimated at 50 percent of the \$40-per-unit selling price. (*a*) Find the BEP. (*b*) What profit (or loss) would result from a volume of 3,000 units?

(*a*)
$$Q_{BEP} = \frac{FC}{P - VC} = \frac{\$46,000}{\$40 - (.50)(40)} = 2,300 \text{ units}$$

(*b*)
$$\text{Profit} = TR - (FC + TVC) = PQ - (FC + VC \cdot Q)$$
$$= (\$40)(3,000) - [\$46,000 + \$20(3,000)] = \$14,000$$

Break-even analysis is a useful model, especially for a single product. But it usually assumes certainty conditions, which limits its applicability.

Table 2-2 Assumptions and Advantages of Break-Even Analysis

Assumptions	Advantages
1. All costs and volumes are known.	1. Is simple and easy to visualize.
2. Cost-volume relationships are linear.	2. Focuses upon profitability.
3. All output can be sold.	3. Uses both algebraic and graphic display.

Contribution is a companion measure of economic value that tells how much of the revenue from the sale of one unit will contribute to cover fixed costs with the remainder going to profit. The per-unit contribution C of a product is determined by subtracting the variable cost per unit (VC) from the price (P).

$$C = P - VC \tag{2.4}$$

Example 2.5 Find the contribution for the textile shop of Example 2.4.

$$C = P - VC = \$40 - (.50)(\$40) = \$20 \text{ per unit}$$

All of the contribution from a product is absorbed in paying for fixed costs up to the break-even point. Beyond that, the contribution is all profit.

STATISTICAL MODELS

Business decisions that must rely upon limited or incomplete information often utilize probabilities and other statistical models. Probability is the most basic measure of uncertainty, for it attaches a quantitative value (between 0 and 1) to the occurrence of an event. See Table 2-3.

Table 2-3 Probability Rules

Complement	$P(A) = 1 - P(\bar{A})$	(2.5)
Multiplication	$P(A \text{ and } B) = P(A)P(B\|A)$	
	$\qquad = P(A)P(B)$ (if independent)	(2.6)
Addition	$P(A \text{ or } B) = P(A) + P(B) - P(A \text{ and } B)$	
	$\qquad = P(A) + P(B)$ (if mutually exclusive)	(2.7)
Bayes' rule	$P(A\|B) = \dfrac{P(A \text{ and } B)}{P(B)}$	
	$\qquad = \dfrac{P(A)P(B\|A)}{P(A)P(B\|A) + P(\bar{A})P(B\|\bar{A})}$	(2.8)

Two types of probabilities are commonly used:

(1) *Empirical probabilities* are based upon observed data and express the relative frequency of an event in the long run.

(2) *Subjective probabilities* are based upon personal experience or judgment and are sometimes used to analyze one-time occurrences.

Example 2.6 Market research data on a company's product has shown that during the first three years of use, 10 percent of the products had a mechanical difficulty and 40 percent had an electrical problem. The probability of an electrical problem, given some mechanical difficulty, is .6. What is the probability that a product will have either a mechanical difficulty or an electrical problem, or both?

$$P(M) = .10 \qquad P(E) = .40 \qquad P(E|M) = .60$$
$$P(M \text{ or } E) = P(M) + P(E) - P(M \text{ and } E)$$

where $P(M \text{ and } E) = P(M)P(E|M) = (.10)(.60) = .06$

$$P(M \text{ or } E) = .10 + .40 - .06 = .44$$

Two key concepts underlying statistical inference are those of sampling distributions and the central limit theorem.

(1) *Sampling distribution.* This is a theoretical distribution of all sample proportions (p's), or all sample means ($\bar{x}$'s) of a given size. The distribution includes all possible values that can occur, along with their probabilities of occurrence.

(2) *Central limit theorem.* This states that for sufficiently large samples, the distribution of both sample proportions and sample means tends to follow a smooth, bell-shaped normal curve.

DISCRETE AND CONTINUOUS DATA DISTRIBUTIONS

Frequency data that are grouped into classes and used to express probabilities are either discrete or continuous. *Discrete* data stem from countable populations and are often expressed in terms of proportions (p's). *Continuous* data are obtained from measurable populations and are often classified

Table 2-4   Statistical Equations for Discrete and Continuous Data

	Discrete (countable: attributes data)	Continuous (measurable: variables data)

Population
  Central value
 	
  Standard deviation
	Proportion π
	
	$\sigma = \sqrt{\pi(1-\pi)}$ (2.9)
		Mean μ
		
		$\sigma = \sqrt{\dfrac{\Sigma(X-\mu)^2}{N}}$ (2.10)

Sample
  Central value
 	
  Standard deviation
	Proportion p
	
	$s = \sqrt{pq}$
	where $q = 1 - p$ (2.11)
		Mean $\bar{X}$
		
		$s = \sqrt{\dfrac{\Sigma(X-\bar{X})^2}{n-1}}$ (2.12)

Sampling distribution
  Central value
 	
  Standard error
	Average proportion $\bar{p}$
	
	$s_{\bar{p}} = \sqrt{\dfrac{pq}{n}}$ (2.13)
		Average mean $\bar{\bar{X}}$
		
		$s_{\bar{x}} = \dfrac{s}{\sqrt{n}}$ (2.14)

as variables data, (designated x). Discrete probabilities result from summations (Σ) of individual event probabilities, whereas continuous probabilities are obtained from an integration ($\int$) of the area under a continuous probability function. The distinction between discrete and continuous distributions is important because it affects the sample sizes and the risks of error associated with work sampling, quality control, and other productive activities.

Table 2-4 summarizes some statistical equations for computing measures of central value and dispersion for populations, samples, and sampling distributions.

Example 2.7 (Discrete) In 400 observations of a computer operator, an analyst found him idle 32 times. Find (a) the sample proportion, and (b) the standard error of proportion.

(a)
$$\bar{p} = \frac{\text{no. idle}}{\text{total no.}} = \frac{32}{400} = .08$$

(b)
$$s_{\bar{p}} = \sqrt{\frac{pq}{n}} = \sqrt{\frac{(.08)(.92)}{400}} = .014$$

Example 2.8 (Continuous) In a study to find the time to service customers, a bank teller worked 60 minutes and served 36 customers. A record of the individual service times showed $\Sigma (X - \bar{X})^2 = (.79 \text{ minutes})^2$. Find ($a$) the sample mean time, and (b) the standard error of the mean.

(a)
$$\bar{X} = \frac{\Sigma x}{n} = \frac{60}{36} = 1.67 \text{ min per customer}$$

(b)
$$s_{\bar{x}} = \frac{s}{\sqrt{n}}$$

where
$$s = \sqrt{\frac{\Sigma (X - \bar{X})^2}{n - 1}} = \sqrt{\frac{.79}{36 - 1}} = .15 \text{ min}$$

Therefore,
$$s_{\bar{x}} = \frac{.15}{\sqrt{36}} = .025 \text{ min}$$

DECISION TREES

Decision trees are schematic diagrams that show the alternative outcomes and interdependence of choices in a multiphase, or sequential, decision process. The treelike diagram is constructed from left to right, using square boxes for controllable (decision) points and circles for uncontrollable (chance) events. Each branch leads to a payoff that is stated in monetary (or utility) terms on the right.

Decision trees are analyzed backward (from right to left) by multiplying the payoffs by their respective probabilities (which are assigned to each chance event). The highest expected value then identifies the best course of action and is entered at the preceding decision point.

$$E(X) = \Sigma [XP(X)]$$

This then becomes the expected value for the next higher-order expectation, as the analyst continues to work back to the trunk of the tree.

Example 2.9 A manufacturer of small power tools is faced with foreign competition, which necessitates that she either modify (automate) her existing product or abandon it and market a new product. Regardless of which course of action she follows, she will have the opportunity to drop or raise prices if she experiences a low initial demand.

Payoff and probability values associated with the alternative courses of action are shown in Fig. 2-3. Analyze the decision tree and determine which course of action should be chosen to maximize the expected monetary value. (Assume monetary amounts are present-value profits.)

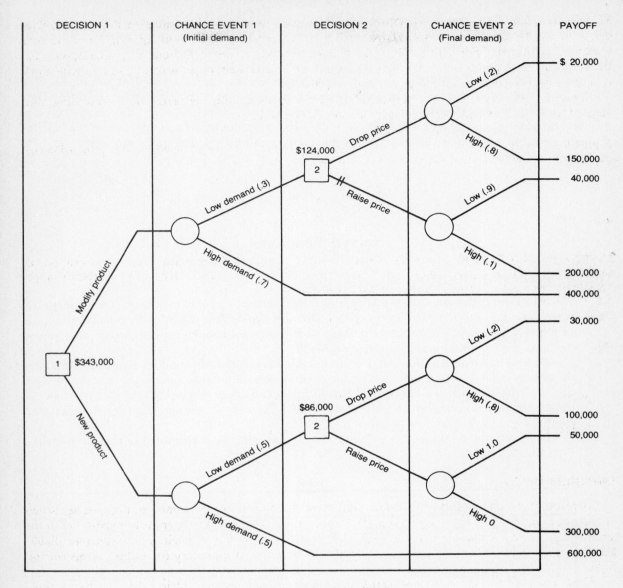

Fig. 2-3 Decision tree diagram

Analyze the tree from right to left by calculating the expected values for all possible courses of action and choosing the branch with the highest expected value. Begin with the top (modify product) branch.

At chance event 2

Drop price branch: $E(X) = \$20,000\ (.2) + \$150,000\ (.8) = \$124,000$

Raise price branch: $E(X) = \$40,000\ (.9) + \$200,000\ (.1) = \$56,000$

Therefore, choose to drop price and use $124,000 as the value of this branch at Decision 2. *Note*: The $124,000 is an expected monetary value (EMV) and can be entered above the square box under Decision 2. Place slash marks through the other (nonusable) alternative.

At chance event 1

If low demand: $\$124,000\ (.3) = \$\ 37,200$

If high demand: $400,000\ (.7) = \underline{\ 280,000}$

$E(X) = \$317,200$

Therefore, use \$317,200 as value of this branch at Decision 1. Similarly, for the bottom (new product) branch, the values are \$86,000 at Decision 2 and \$343,000 at Decision 1. The new product branch thus has a higher expected value and is selected as the best course of action under the expected value criteria.

Decision trees help to structure decisions in an objective way, force an explicit identification of alternatives, and foster a clear distinction between controllable and uncontrollable variables. They also permit us to incorporate uncertainty in a systematic, objective way. But monetary and probability values must still be estimated. Also, the expected-value approach may not be the best for a given situation; other approaches, such as maximax, maximin, or maximum probability may be preferred.

Solved Problems

THE DECISION-MAKING PROCESS

2.1 Mike Jackson is the operations manager of Supermarket Suppliers Inc., which runs a large old warehouse that services 80 delivery trucks. He must decide how many loading docks to include in a new warehouse. He decided that they should plan on enough capacity to handle average demand plus about 25 percent extra for growth.

To help make his decision, Mike collects some data on the current dock usage and simulates the unloading and loading activities on the company computer. The simulation generates values ranging from 7 to 14 docks. However, 12 loading docks handle average demand, and Mike tells the design engineer to plan for 15. Two weeks later Mike calls the design engineer to make sure everything is working out satisfactorily.

List the sequential steps in the decision process and the corresponding activity from the situation described.

Table 2-5

Decision Process Step	Corresponding Activity in Situation
1. Define the problem and its parameters.	1. Problem is to determine number of loading docks required. Parameters are demand and load-unload time.
2. Establish decision criteria.	2. Criterion is capacity to meet average demand plus 25 percent.
3. Construct a model.	3. Model is a simulation model on computer.
4. Generate alternatives.	4. Alternatives range from 7 to 14 docks.
5. Evaluate and choose best alternative.	5. Best alternative is to plan for 15 docks (12 plus 25 percent).
6. Implement and monitor solution.	6. Tell design engineer and follow up 2 weeks later.

DECISION METHODOLOGY

2.2 An automobile company is evaluating the prospect of developing fuel cells for cars. As an alternative to financing the research and development (R&D) by itself, the firm is considering joining with an engineering consulting firm. Depending upon the success of the R&D, the automobile company estimates its 10-year, present-value profits (millions \$) as shown in Table 2-6.

Table 2-6   Success of R&D

	θ_1	θ_2	θ_3
	Highly Successful	Moderately Successful	Not Successful
D = Develop on own	300	40	−60
J = Joint venture	200	30	−20

Based upon feasibility studies and consultations with development and marketing groups, the operations vice-president has assigned subjective probabilities of $\theta_1 = .2$, $\theta_2 = .4$, $\theta_3 = .4$. The vice-president feels that some prototype studies by his firm could perhaps give a better indication of success and thus modify these probabilities.

(a)   Determine the expected profit of each course of action and the optimal expected monetary value, EMV*.

(b)   Determine the expected value of perfect information (EVPI).

(c)   Explain the meaning of your EVPI figure.

(d)   Depict this decision situation in the form of a decision tree.

(a)   Using the data in Table 2-7, the expected value of each action, $E(A)$, can be determined by:

$$E(A) = \sum \theta_{ij} P(\theta_j)$$

where i = row and j = column.

$$E(D) = \$300(.2) + 40(.4) - 60(.4) = \$52 \text{ million}$$
$$E(J) = \$200(.2) + 30(.4) - 20(.4) = \$44 \text{ million}$$

D is the optimal course and is designated EMV*.

Table 2-7

	$\theta_1 = .2$	$\theta_2 = .4$	$\theta_3 = .4$
D	300	40	−60
J	200	30	−20

(b)   The expected value of perfect information, EVPI, is the incremental amount that can be justified to remove uncertainty about the feasibility of the project. It is the excess of value over the EMV* up to what would be expected if no uncertainty existed with respect to the state of nature (i.e., the outcome of the fuel-cell development effort). This is referred to as the expected profit under certainty, EPC. Thus the EVPI is:

$$EVPI = EPC - EMV^* \qquad (2.15)$$

The EPC is the best course of action under each state, weighted by the probability of occurrence of the state. See Table 2-8. (*Note*: Each state is presumed to exist in proportion to the probability of its occurrence.)

Expected profit with perfect information (EPC)	$68 million
Expected monetary value of optional act (EMV*)	−52 million
Expected value of perfect information (EVPI)	$16 million

Table 2-8

(1) If state is known to be	(2) Then the best action and profit would be	(3) And percent of time this occurs is	(4) Expected profit (2) × (3)
θ_1	$D = 300$	.2	$60
θ_2	$D = 40$	.4	16
θ_3	$J = -20$	.4	$\underline{-8}$
			EPC = $68

(c) This means it would be worth up to $16 million to know how successful the R&D is likely to be before deciding between *D* or *J*. The firm's *expected profit* would increase by $16 million if it had a perfect forecast of the success of the project. Note, however, that this is a long-range, expected-value concept and that the actual profitability may be more or less than $16 million. Furthermore, perfect information may be unattainable in this situation.

(d) See Fig. 2-4.

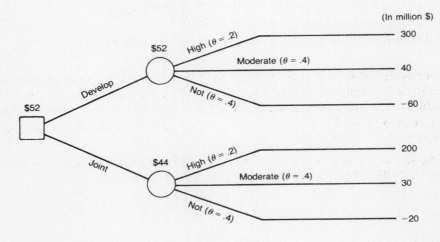

Fig. 2-4

BREAK-EVEN ANALYSIS

2.3 A professional sports promoter leases a 40,000-seat stadium for football games. Tickets sell for an average of $14 each. If fixed costs per season (four games) are $720,000 and variable costs are $2 per spectator, what is the break-even point in number of seats filled per game?

$$Q_{BEP} = \frac{FC}{P - VC} = \frac{\$720,000/\text{season}}{\$14/\text{seat} - \$2/\text{seat}} = 60,000 \text{ seats/season}$$

$$BEP = \frac{60,000 \text{ seats}}{4 \text{ games}} = 15,000 \text{ seats/game}$$

2.4 Process X has fixed costs of $20,000 per year and variable costs of $12 per unit, whereas process Y has fixed costs of $8,000 per year and variable costs of $22 per unit. At what production quantity (*Q*) are the total costs of X and Y equal?

$$X = Y$$

where
$$FC_X + VC_X \cdot Q = FC_Y + VC_Y \cdot Q$$
$$\$20,000 + \$12Q = \$8,000 + \$22Q$$
$$\$10Q = \$12,000$$
$$Q = 1,200 \text{ units}$$

2.5   Cover-the-Globe Paint Co. produces 9,000 paint sprayers per year and obtains \$675,000 revenue from them. Fixed costs are \$210,000 per year and total costs are \$354,000 per year. How much does each sprayer contribute to fixed costs and profit?

$$C = P - VC$$

where
$$P = \frac{\$675,000 \text{ revenue}}{9,000 \text{ units}} = \$75/\text{unit}$$

and
$$VC = \frac{TVC}{Q}$$

with
$$TVC = TC - FC = \$354,000 - \$210,000 = \$144,000$$

We can find the value for VC:

$$VC = \frac{\$144,000}{9,000 \text{ units}} = \$16/\text{unit}$$

Therefore,
$$C = \$75 - \$16 = \$59/\text{unit}$$

2.6   A firm has annual fixed costs of \$3.2 million and variable costs of \$7 per unit. It is considering an additional investment of \$800,000, which will increase the fixed costs by \$150,000 per year and will increase the contribution by \$2 per unit. No change is anticipated in the sales volume or the sales price of \$15 per unit. What is the break-even quantity if the new investment is made?

The \$2 increase in C will decrease VC to \$7 − \$2 = \$5/unit. The addition to FC makes them \$3.2 million + \$150,000 = \$3,350,000.

$$Q_{BEP} = \frac{FC}{P - VC} = \frac{\$3,350,000}{\$15/\text{unit} - \$5/\text{unit}} = 335,000 \text{ units}$$

2.7   *Two-Volume, Break-Even Analysis.* A producer of air conditioners sells the industrial model for \$175 each. The production costs at volumes of 2,000 and 4,000 units are as shown in Table 2-9. The company does not know the FC at zero volume and realizes that some of its costs are "semi-variable." Nevertheless, it wishes to prepare a break-even chart and determine the BEP.

Table 2-9

	2,000 Units	4,000 Units
Labor	\$ 40,000	\$ 80,000
Materials	90,000	180,000
Overhead	70,000	80,000
Selling and administrative	80,000	90,000
Depreciation and other FC	70,000	70,000
Total	\$350,000	\$500,000

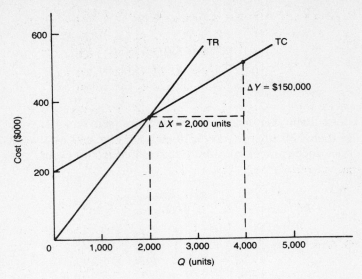

Fig. 2-5

This is a more realistic situation, because the FC and VC are determined from actual production volumes. Plot the TC at both volumes as seen in Fig. 2-5. The slope of the TC line $(\Delta Y/\Delta X)$ is the estimated VC per unit.

$$VC = \frac{\text{change in } Y}{\text{change in } X} = \frac{\Delta Y}{\Delta X} = \frac{\$500,000 - \$350,000}{4,000 \text{ units} - 2,000 \text{ units}} = \$75/\text{unit}$$

By subtracting 2,000 units of variable cost from the total cost at 2,000 units, we can evaluate the implied fixed costs as follows:

$$FC = \text{total cost @ 2,000 volume} - (2,000 \text{ units}) (\text{variable cost/unit})$$

$$= \$350,000 - 2,000 \text{ units} (\$75/\text{unit}) = \$200,000$$

$$Q_{\text{BEP}} = \frac{FC}{P - VC} = \frac{\$200,000}{\$175/\text{unit} - \$75/\text{unit}} = 2,000 \text{ units}$$

STATISTICAL MODELS AND DISTRIBUTIONS

2.8   Three molding machines (X, Y, and Z) are used to produce 600 computer terminal keys that are rushed (without inspection) to a customer. The number of good (G) and defective ($\bar{G}$) keys from each machine are as shown in Table 2-10.

Table 2-10

	Machine X	Machine Y	Machine Z	Row Total
Good (G)	45	225	270	540
Not good ($\bar{G}$)	5	25	30	60
Total	50	250	300	600

When the customer receives the keys, they are randomly selected for installation in CRTs. What is the probability that a key selected (*a*) is defective, (*b*) was produced by machine Z and good, (*c*) was either produced by machine Z or is good? (*d*) Is the probability of selecting a good key independent of the machine from which the key was made?

Given the data we can estimate the empirical probabilities as follows:

$$P(G) = \frac{\text{number of good}}{\text{total number keys}} = \frac{540}{600} = .900$$

$$P(Z) = \frac{\text{number from Z}}{\text{total number keys}} = \frac{300}{600} = .500$$

$P(G|Z)$, which is read "Good, given it is from Z," is found as follows:

$$P(G|Z) = \frac{\text{number from Z that are good}}{\text{total number from Z}} = \frac{270}{300} = .90$$

Now, using the rules of probability we have:

(a) $\qquad\qquad\qquad P(\bar{G}) = 1 - P(G) = 1 - .90 = .10$

(b) $\qquad\qquad P(Z \text{ and } G) = P(Z)P(G|Z) = (.50)(.90) = .45$

(c) $\qquad P(Z \text{ or } G) = P(Z) + P(G) - P(Z \text{ and } G) = .50 + .90 - .45 = .95$

(d) The $P(G)$ does not depend on whether the key is from machine X, Y, or Z:

$$P(G) = P(G|X) = P(G|Y) = P(G|Z) = \frac{540}{600} = \frac{225}{250} = \frac{45}{50} = .90$$

2.9 *Bayes' Rule.* Let θ represent the probability of defective wiring and A represent an accidental fire. In a large old factory, spot checks have established that $P(\theta) = .20$. Given that a plant has defective wiring, the probability of a fire occurring at some time during the year is .7 (that is, $P(A|\theta) = .7$), and if the wiring is not defective, the chance of a fire is reduced to .1 (that is, $P(A|\bar{\theta}) = .1$). A recent fire burned one employee severely and caused \$90,000 damage. Although evidence is destroyed, the operations manager has been asked by an insurance company to estimate the likelihood that the fire was caused by defective wiring.

$$P(\theta) = .2 \qquad \text{thus} \qquad P(\bar{\theta}) = 1 - .2 = .8$$
$$P(A|\theta) = .7 \qquad \text{thus} \qquad P(\bar{A}|\theta) = 1 - .7 = .3$$
$$P(A|\bar{\theta}) = .1 \qquad \text{thus} \qquad P(\bar{A}|\bar{\theta}) = 1 - .1 = .9$$

We wish to find the probability of defective wiring θ given the occurrence of the recent fire A. Using Bayes' rule we have:

$$P(\theta|A) = \frac{P(\theta)P(A|\theta)}{P(\theta)P(A|\theta) + P(\bar{\theta})P(A|\bar{\theta})} = \frac{(.2)(.7)}{(.2)(.7) + (.8)(.1)} = .64 \text{ or } 64 \text{ percent chance}$$

Table 2-11

Observation	$X - \bar{X}$	$(X - \bar{X})^2$
4.7	−.3	.09
4.2	−.8	.64
5.1	.1	.01
4.8	−.2	.04
5.5	.5	.25
5.4	.4	.16
5.8	.8	.64
4.8	−.2	.04
5.0	0	0
4.7	−.3	.09
50.0		1.96

2.10 *Continuous Data.* Ten observations were taken of the time required to assemble a sofa frame in a furniture plant (as shown in Table 2-11). Find (*a*) the mean time, (*b*) the standard deviation, and (*c*) the standard error of the mean.

(*a*)
$$\bar{X} = \frac{\Sigma X}{n} = \frac{50}{10} = 5.0$$

(*b*)
$$s = \sqrt{\frac{\Sigma (X - \bar{X})^2}{n - 1}} = \sqrt{\frac{1.96}{9}} = .47$$

Note: An equivalent equation is

$$s = \sqrt{\frac{\Sigma X^2 - (\Sigma X)^2/n}{n - 1}} = \sqrt{\frac{252 - (50)^2/10}{10 - 1}} = .47$$

(*c*)
$$s_{\bar{X}} = \frac{s}{\sqrt{n}} = \frac{.47}{\sqrt{10}} = .15$$

2.11 *Normal Distribution.* Samples show that the time required to stain a sofa is normally distributed with a mean of 10 minutes and standard deviation of 2 minutes. What is the probability that a sofa, selected at random, will require more than 13.5 minutes?

First

Determine how many standard normal deviates (Z units) 13.5 minutes is from the mean

$$Z = \frac{X - \bar{X}}{s} = \frac{13.5 - 10.0}{2} = 1.75$$

See Fig. 2-6.

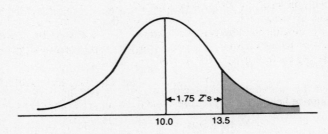

Fig. 2-6

Second

Look up the Z value in the normal distribution table from Appendix B to find the area between the mean and Z = 1.75. The area is .4599.

Third

Because we seek the probability *above* 13.5, subtract the value of .4599 from .5000, which is one-half of the area of the distribution.

$$P(X > 13.5) = .5000 - .4599 = .0401, \text{ say 4 percent}$$

DECISION TREES

2.12 A glass factory specializing in crystal is experiencing a substantial backlog, and the firm's management is considering three courses of action: (*A*) arrange for subcontracting, (*B*) begin overtime production or (*C*) construct new facilities. The correct choice depends largely upon future demand, which may be low, medium, or high. By consensus, management ranks the respective probabilities as .10, .50, and .40. A cost analysis reveals the effect upon profits that is shown in Table 2-12.

Table 2-12

	Profit ($000) If Demand Is		
	Low (P = .10)	Medium (P = .50)	High (P = .40)
A = Arrange subcontracting	10	50	50
B = Begin overtime	−20	60	100
C = Construct facilities	−150	20	200

(*a*)   State which course of action would be taken under a criterion of: (1) maximax, (2) maximin, (3) maximum probability, (4) maximum expected value.

(*b*)   Show this decision situation schematically in the form of a decision tree.

(*a*)   *Maximax.* Maximize the maximum profit. Choose *C* in hopes that demand will be high.
Maximin. Maximize the minimum profit. Choose *A*, where the least profit is $10,000.
Maximum probability. Maximize under the most likely state. Choose *B* as the highest payoff under medium demand where *P* = .50.
Maximum expected value. Choose the act with the highest expected value.

$$E(X) = \Sigma \, XP(X)$$
$$E(A) = 10(.10) + 50(.50) + 50(.40) = 46,000$$
$$E(B) = -20(.10) + 60(.50) + 100(.40) = 68,000$$
$$E(C) = -150(.10) + 20(.50) + 200(.40) = 75,000$$

Therefore choose *C*, with expected value of $75,000 profit.

(*b*)   For the decision tree, Fig. 2-7, the controllable (choice) decision variables are *A*, *B*, and *C*, and the uncontrollable variable is demand. We begin on the left by showing the decision choices first, followed by the chance alternatives of demand. The payoff value under each alternative is shown at the right. The expected value of each branch is then computed by summing the profit times the probability for each. For example, for *A*

$$E(A) = 10(.10) + 50(.50) + 50(.40) = \$46(000)$$

The best choice here, based upon the expected-value criteria is the construction of new facilities, *C*.

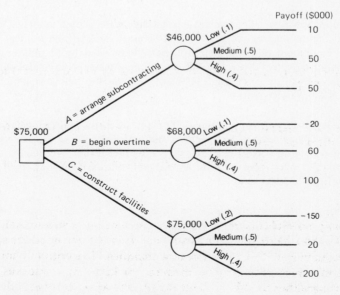

Fig. 2-7

Supplementary Problems

2.13   What analytical technique would be appropriate for modeling the following situations? (a) An oil company seeks to maximize its profits subject to limitations in the number of drilling rigs available, the overtime cost of working its exploration crews double shifts, and the storage capacity available for refined distilates. (b) The manager of a railroad yard is concerned about the number of rail cars waiting to be loaded or unloaded, and the overall utilization of the loading crews. She would like to decrease the idle-time costs (and improve service) if possible. (c) Computer Stores Northeast is planning to open a new computer center in Bangor. This involves finding a site, hiring a manager and technican, advertising, ordering inventory, etc. They hope to plan and control the project so that it is finished on time and within the agreed-upon budget.
Ans.   (a) linear programming (b) queuing theory and simulation (c) CPM or PERT

2.14   Frozen Pizza Co. is considering whether it should allocate funds for research on an instant freeze-dry process for home use. If the research is successful (and the R&D manager feels there is a 75-percent chance it will be), the firm could market the product at a \$4-million profit. However, if the research is unsuccessful, the firm will incur a \$6-million loss. What is the expected monetary value (EMV) of proceeding with the research?   *Ans.*   \$1.5 million

2.15   Fixed costs are \$40,000 per year, variable costs are \$50 per unit, and the selling price is \$90 each. Find the BEP.   *Ans.*   1,000 units

2.16   Nationwide Survey Co. has fixed costs of \$20,000 per year, variable costs of \$3 per survey, and charges \$5 per survey. What is the break-even point in number of surveys?   *Ans.*   10,000 surveys

2.17   Florida Citrus produced 40,000 boxes of fruit that sold for \$3 per box. The total variable costs for the 40,000 boxes were \$60,000, and the fixed costs were \$75,000. (a) What was the break-even quantity? (b) How much profit (or loss) resulted?   *Ans.*   (a) 50,000 boxes (b) \$15,000 loss

2.18   If the sales price of a product is \$8 and the variable cost is \$2, what is the contribution?   *Ans.*   \$6

2.19   A travel agency has an excursion package that sells for \$125. Fixed costs are \$80,000, and at the present volume of 1,000 customers, variable costs are \$25,000, and profits are \$20,000. (a) What is the break-even point volume? (b) Assuming that fixed costs remain constant, how many additional customers will be required for the agency to increase profit by \$1,000?
Ans.   (a) 800 units (b) 10 customers

2.20   A nonprofit municipal water department has variable costs (direct labor) of \$5 million per year. Current revenue, based upon the service of 200,000 accounts, is \$20 million. The water-production manager wishes to add equipment that will raise the yearly fixed costs by \$1 million and reduce the current and future direct labor costs by 20 percent. What volume of account services would be required to justify the change economically? The price paid per customer is to be held constant.
Ans.   At least 200,000 accounts

2.21   Last year, Dever Furniture Co. produced 200 maple dressers (pattern 427) that sold for \$210 each. The company incurred labor costs of \$42 per unit and material costs of \$18 per unit, and it allocated \$80 per unit of overhead costs to each dresser. Cost records reveal that overhead costs are 60 percent fixed and 40 percent variable. What was the total annual contribution from pattern 427?
Ans.   \$118/unit, or \$23,600 total

2.22   Madison Industries has the following data (Table 2-13) on costs at two volumes of production for a product that sells for \$50. (a) Construct a two-volume, break-even chart. (b) Compute the variable cost, the contribution, and the BEP. (c) Using the contribution from (b), estimate the profit at a volume of 8,000 units.
Ans.   (a) TC line is plotted through $X = 6,000$, $Y = \$230,000$, and $X = 10,000$, $Y = \$300,000$ (b) \$17.50/unit, \$32.50/unit, 3,846 units (c) \$135,005

Table 2-13

	6,000 Units	10,000 Units
Labor	$ 60,000	$100,000
Material	36,000	60,000
Overhead	54,000	60,000
Other FC	80,000	80,000
	$230,000	$300,000

2.23   Company safety records show that 40 percent of all accidents occur when new employees (those with less than one year's service) are operating equipment, and 60 percent occur when the more-experienced employees are operating it. The firm averages six accidents over a 300-workday year. What is the chance that on any given day during the year an accident will happen to (*a*) a new employee, (*b*) an experienced employee?   *Ans.*   (*a*) .008 (*b*) .012

2.24   A stockroom clerk at an auto assembly plant has absentmindedly mixed the stock of arm-support brackets for the left- and right-front doors of automobiles, and cannot readily tell them apart, nor can she distinguish the type of mounting (that is, A, B, or C). She receives an urgent request for a right-front bracket, type A, randomly selects one, and rushes it to the assembly area.

   Suppose the stock records show that she has 500 brackets (total) on hand, in the quantities shown in Table 2-14.

Table 2-14

	Right Front	Left Front
Type A mount	274	146
Type B mount	0	50
Type C mount	26	4

(*a*) What is the probability that she chose a correct bracket? (*b*) Suppose she could identify the type of mounting but not whether it was for a right or left door. What would be the probability of a correct choice in this case?   *Ans.*   (*a*) .55 (*b*) .65

2.25   In a chemical plant, the probability of any employee being injured from a fall is $P(F) = .005$ and from chemical inhalation is $P(C) = .020$. If a worker falls, the probability of injury from chemical inhalation increases to $P(C|F) = .100$. What is the probability that an employee will be injured (*a*) by *both* a fall and chemical inhalation, and (*b*) by *either* a fall or chemical inhalation?   *Ans.*   (*a*) .0005 (*b*) .0245

2.26   The operations manager of a large airport is concerned with the problem of having adequate personnel to offer individual assistance to handicapped passengers during rush hours. Data were collected on the number of requests for assistance during 20 randomly selected rush hours and revealed the information shown in Table 2-15.

Table 2-15

Hour no.	1	2	3	4	5	6	7	8	9	10
No. of requests	40	42	42	30	38	48	42	44	37	38
Hour no.	11	12	13	14	15	16	17	18	19	20
No. of requests	49	47	34	57	42	52	56	44	50	48

Determine (*a*) $\bar{X}$, (*b*) s, and (*c*) $s_{\bar{x}}$.   *Ans.*   (*a*) 44 requests per hour (*b*) 7 requests per hour (*c*) 1.57

2.27   Long-range planners of Desert Power Co. have forecasted the need to add 400 megawatts of power to their system in year 5. They must decide between a solar plant that will cost about $150 million and a coal-fired plant that will cost 20 percent less. Both plants would have a 20-year life. Construction of a solar plant would require public approval, but management feels there is a good probability (.9) of obtaining this. If the plant is not approved, the utility will still have incurred an engineering fee of 5 percent of the estimated plant cost in the second year and will have to purchase the necessary power from another utility at a cost of $12 million a year.

   If power demand is heavy and the solar plant can operate at base load, operating costs (not including depreciation) are estimated at $4 million a year. However, planners feel that there is a 40 percent chance the plant will have to operate at cycle load, which will increase operating costs by 10 percent.

   Should the firm decide on a coal-fired plant, operating costs are expected to be $5 million a year, unless additional costs for pollution control prove inevitable. If the air filters are unsatisfactory and public concern is strong, it could cost the utility an additional $10 million in the third year after the plant comes online. Management feels that there is a fifty-fifty chance this will occur, and requests some guidance in making this decision.

   Utilize a decision tree with accompanying financial data to help identify the appropriate decision, based upon expected-value criteria. (Do not convert to present-value figures for this exercise.)

   Ans. E(solar) = $234.6 million and E(coal) = $225.0 million, so the coal is less costly by $9.7 million.

Chapter 3

Capital Budgeting and Analysis

Present-Value Criteria

FRAMEWORK

Capital is a resource of funds owned or used by an organization. A *capital budget* is a financial plan that shows the sources and uses of funds for a specified time period in the future. Funds come from equity (capital stock), from debt, and from earnings retained from past profits. Taxes are a source of funds for public organizations. Stockholders receive *dividends*, which are the rewards of profits to the owners of the firm. Holders of debt financing require *interest*, which is the cost of money, or rental rate for funds. The interest rate is determined by (1) the *availability* of money in the economy (e.g., the prime rate), (2) the *alternative opportunities* investors have for the use of funds, and (3) the *risk of loss* the lenders must take.

The cost of capital to an organization depends on the mix of equity and debt. Debt financing is often less expensive, unless the proportion of debt is so high that the organization risks becoming insolvent. In United States firms, equity often constitutes well over 50 percent of the source of funds, whereas in large Japanese firms, for example, it may average only 30 percent.

Major capital allocation within an organization typically follows a thorough review process including:

(1) Capital proposal (by an originating department)

(2) Initial policy review (by a budget committee)

(3) Technical and market evaluation (by engineering, production, marketing)

(4) Quotations and financial evaluation (by purchasing, accounting, finance)

(5) Approval or disapproval (by general manager, vice-president, president)

Evaluation of investment alternatives typically requires consideration of the initial investment, plus cash flows, depreciation, and taxes over the economic life of the proposed asset. The *economic life* is the useful service life of the asset and may differ from the *accounting life*, which is governed by Internal Revenue Service regulations and corporate tax policies.

CASH FLOWS

Both the *timing* and *quantity* of cash flows are important. Timing is important because of the time value of money concept; that is, cash available today is more valuable than the same quantity of cash available later. This is because funds have an earning power and can buy factors of production that may create value and generate greater revenues over time. The quantity of cash flow is also important. *Net cash flow* is the difference between incoming (revenues) and outgoing (expenses) flows and is often expressed in present-value terms.

The difference between present values P and future sums F of money is due to accumulated interest i over the number of periods n. For example, the interest due on $1,000 borrowed at 10 percent for one year would be equal to the (principal)(rate)(time), or ($1,000)(.10)(1) = $100. The total amount due at the end of one time period, F_1, consists of the principal amount borrowed P plus the interest on that principal i.

29

$$F_1 = P + P(i) = P(1 + i)$$

The total amount due at the end of two time periods consists of the amount due at the end of the first period, $P(1 + i)$, plus interest on that amount for the second period.

$$F_2 = P(1 + i) + P(1 + i)i = P(1 + i)(1 + i) = P(1 + i)^2$$

Similarly, at the end of three periods, $F_3 = P(1 + i)^3$, and for n years, the future sum F is:

$$F = P(1 + i)^n \qquad (3.1)$$

Example 3.1   Find the principal and the interest due at the end of two years if $1,000 is borrowed at a rate of 10 percent (Fig. 3-1).

$$F_2 = P(1 + i)^n = \$1,000(1 + .10)^2 = \$1,210$$

The accumulation of interest with capital to future values is referred to as *compounding*. Conversely, the present value P of the future sum F *discounted* (reduced in value back to the present) at interest rate i for n periods is

$$P = F \frac{1}{(1 + i)^n} \qquad (3.2)$$

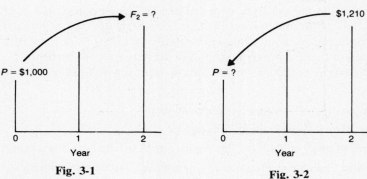

Fig. 3-1   Fig. 3-2

Example 3.2   What is the present value of $1,210 received two years from now if the sum is discounted at 10 percent (Fig. 3-2)?

$$P = F \frac{1}{(1 + i)^n} = \$1,210 \frac{1}{(1 + .10)^2} = \$1,000$$

The above expression can be restated in a general formula:

$$P = F \frac{1}{(1 + i)^n} = F(\text{PV factor}) = F(\text{PV}_{sp})_{i\%}^{n\text{yr}} \qquad (3.3)$$

where PV_{sp} is a tabled factor for the present value of a single payment made in n years if the interest rate is i percent. This PV_{sp} factor, when multiplied by the amount of the future payment F will yield a discounted present-value amount P. Appendix E contains PV_{sp} factors for payments of $1 over a commonly used range of interest rate i and period n values. Many business calculators are programmed to produce and use these factors directly, once i and n values, along with either a P or F value, are specified. Simply assign values to three of the four variables, and the calculator will compute the unknown value.

Example 3.3   What is the present value of the salvage on a robot if the salvage price 10 years from now is $9,000 and if the discount rate is 12 percent?

$$P = F(\text{PV}_{sp})_{12\%}^{10\text{yr}} = \$9,000(.322) = \$2,898$$

On other occasions, one must determine the present value of a series of equal payments made over n years when they are discounted or compounded at an interest rate i. These equal sums paid or received regularly are annuities and are usually designated by an R or an A. Appendix F contains present-value factors for annuities (PV_a) of \$1. The present value of an annuity is determined in a manner like that used for single payments, except the factor differs.

$$P = A(PV_a)^{n\,yr}_{i\%} \qquad (3.4)$$

Example 3.4 Find the present value of a series of \$200 payments, paid at the end of each of four years, when the interest rate is 14 percent (Fig. 3-3).

$$P = (PV_a)^{4\,yr}_{14\%} = \$200(2.914) = \$583$$

This means that the sum of \$583 now is equivalent to annual payments of \$200 at the end of each of four years if the interest rate is 14 percent. That is, if \$583 were placed in a bank at 14 percent interest, sums of \$200 could be withdrawn at the end of each of four years. With the fourth-year withdrawal of \$200, the balance would be exactly \$0.

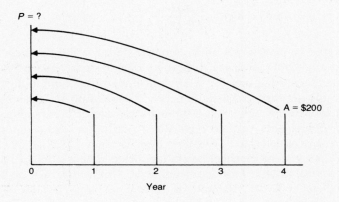

Fig. 3-3

Calculators that have present value (P) and future sum (F) keys also have a key for annuities (A or PMT). Appendix G shows the equations used to find F given P, P given F, A given F, A given P, F given A, and P given A when $i = 10$ percent.

DEPRECIATION

When an investment is made in new equipment, cash is paid "up front" at the time of purchase. However, the equipment is typically used (and helps generate revenues) over many years. *Depreciation* is an accounting procedure for reducing the value of an asset by charging it off as an expense over time (that is, in annual increments). No cash actually flows out in later periods as a result of this accounting entry, but the depreciation expense does reduce the reported profits and therefore affects the amount of taxes paid. Although the total amount of depreciation write-off is ultimately the same, a faster (accelerated) write-off in early years reduces taxes in early years and releases cash that can be invested elsewhere. In this sense depreciation is sometimes referred to as a *tax shield*.

Because depreciation is an accounting expense only, it does not reduce the cash position of the firm as a material or labor expense would. As a matter of fact, if a company's cash flow is computed from its net profits, the depreciation amount must be added back because no cash actually leaves the firm to cover the depreciation expense (which was actually expended earlier as a capital investment).

Example 3.5   Let revenues equal \$100, and let labor (\$40), materials (\$20), and depreciation (\$20) be the only expenses. Compute (a) the profit and (b) the net cash flow.

(a)
$$\text{Profit} = \text{revenues} - (\text{expenses, including depreciation})$$
$$= \text{revenues} - (\text{labor} + \text{material} + \text{depreciation})$$
$$= \$100 - (\$40 + \$20 + \$20) = \$100 - \$80 = \$20$$

(b)
$$\text{Net cash flow} = \text{revenues} - (\text{expenses, not including depreciation})$$
$$= \text{revenues} - (\text{labor} + \text{material})$$
$$= \$100 - (\$40 + \$20) = \$100 - \$60 = \$40$$

For internal purposes of measuring the decline in value of production equipment, both *use* and *time* methods of depreciation are useful to a company. Use methods are typically based upon the number of service hours expected from an asset.

Example 3.6   *Use Method*: A \$140,000 molding machine is expected to be capable of producing 400,000 units. What would be the depreciation rate under the use concept?

$$\text{Depreciation} = \frac{\$140,000 \text{ cost}}{400,000 \text{ units}} = \$.35 \text{ per unit}$$

For calculating taxable income, firms must compute depreciation on their plant and equipment in accordance with the applicable Internal Revenue Code. Property placed in service before 1981 may still be depreciated according to (1) a straight-line, (2) a double-declining balance, (3) a sum-of-years digits, or (4) another consistent method, depending on the choice made when the property was placed in service. Problems 3.6–3.9 illustrate some of these methods.

For most tangible depreciable property placed in use after 1980, the capital cost must be recovered according to the Accelerated Cost Recovery System (ACRS) specified by the Internal Revenue Code. The ACRS system specifies percentages that reflect a 150 percent declining-balance depreciation that changes to straight-line depreciation at a time that will maximize the deduction. Property is assigned a 3-year, 5-year, 10-year, or 15-year recovery period, as specified by the tax code. Many items are designated 5-year property (unless otherwise specified) with 10-year and 15-year property being largely public utility (PU) property, or real estate (15-year property). Salvage values are disregarded, but no recovery deduction is allowed in the year of disposition of the property. Table 3-1 gives the applicable percentage to be deducted each year for property placed in service from 1981 through 1984, in 1985, and for 1986 and beyond; the last values are, of course, subject to change.

Table 3-1   ACRS Percentage for Property Classes of 3-, 5-, 10-, and 15-Year Recovery Periods

Recovery Year of the Property	(1981–1984)				(1985)				(1986 and beyond)			
	3 yr	5 yr	10 yr	15 yr* (PU)	3 yr	5 yr	10 yr	15 yr* (PU)	3 yr	5 yr	10 yr	15 yr* (PU)
1	25	15	8	5	29	18	9	6	33	20	10	7
2	38	22	14	10	47	33	19	12	45	32	18	12
3	37	21	12	9	24	25	16	12	22	24	16	12
4		21	10	8		16	14	11		16	14	11
5		21	10	7		8	12	10		8	12	10
6			10	7			10	9			10	9
7			9	6			8	8			8	8
8			9	6			6	7			6	7
9			9	6			4	6			4	6
10			9	6			2	5			2	5
11				6				4				4
12				6				4				3
13				6				3				3
14				6				2				2
15				6				1				1

*PU = public utility.

Example 3.7 A communications company purchased $80,000 worth of equipment (five-year property class) and installed it in 1984. It is expected to have a $10,000 salvage value when it is retired from service in 1990. How much depreciation will apply to the fifth year of service?

As found in Table 3-1, for equipment purchased in 1984 under the 5-year property class, 21 percent of the cost is depreciated in recovery year 5. Therefore,

$$\text{Depreciation in fifth year} = (.21)\,(\$80,000) = \$16,800$$

Note: Salvage value is disregarded.

Special provisions apply to leased property, real property (real estate), and physical property whose life is shortened by technological changes, industry developments, changes in laws and regulations, and so forth. In addition, firms may elect (with IRS consent) to use a straight-line or a fixed-percentage method of computing depreciation, so that the cost deducted is uniform over the useful life of the equipment. Simply divide the investment by the allowable recovery period. (See Table 3-2.) Note also that the salvage value is not deducted from the investment amount.

Table 3-2 Straight-Line Depreciation Time Periods Allowable under ACRS

Property Class	3 yr	5 yr	10 yr	15 yr (PU)*
Allowable recovery periods for straight-line depreciation	3, 5, or 12 yrs	5, 12, or 25 yrs	10, 25, or 35 yrs	15, 35, or 45 yrs

*PU = public utility.

Example 3.8 An electric utility installed major plant facilities in 1980 at a cost of $2.8 million. The equipment will have an estimated $500,000 salvage value after an estimated useful life of 35 years. The utility has elected to depreciate the plant facilities on a straight-line basis over a 35-year recovery period. How much depreciation is allowed each year?

Note: Thirty-five years is an allowable recovery period.

$$\text{Depreciation/yr} = \frac{\$2,800,000}{35 \text{ yrs}} = \$80,000/\text{yr}$$

TAX CONSIDERATIONS

Federal income taxes are an important consideration because they can consume close to 50 percent of the profit from an investment. Nevertheless, many investment decisions can be adequately evaluated on a before-tax (BT) basis because the question becomes which of several comparable alternatives to choose, and not whether or not to invest. The effect of taxes, then, is not a deciding factor.

Taxes are levied against profits on the basis of rates specified by federal and state governments.

$$\text{Tax} = \text{tax-rate percentage (income} - \text{expense)} \qquad (3.5)$$

Insofar as the depreciation class determines the amount of depreciation expense, the class also affects the taxes owed in any given year.

Example 3.9 Daily Delivery Service Co. purchased a light-duty truck for $15,000 in 1985. It generated an income of $9,000 per year, until sold for $6,000 in 1987. Assuming a tax rate of 42 percent, find the after-tax cash available for each of the three years of service.

Note: We determine from the tax code (or IRS) that the light, general-purpose truck is classified as 3-year property.

		Year 1	Year 2	Year 3
(a)	Income	$ 9,000	$ 9,000	$11,400*
(b)	Truck (property) cost basis	15,000	15,000	15,000
(c)	ACRS percentage (Table 3-1 for 3-yr property)	29%	47%	0%
(d)	Depreciation expense $[(b) \times (c)]$	$ 4,350	$ 7,050	$ 0
(e)	Income − expense $[(a) - (d)]$	4,650	1,950	11,400
(f)	Tax [at 42% $\times (e)$]	1,953	819	4,788
(g)	Cash available $[(a) - (f)]$	7,047	8,181	6,612

*No recovery allowed during year of property disposition, but the excess of the $6,000 salvage over the undepreciated amount (24 percent of $15,000 or $3,600) constitutes additional income during year 3 in the amount of $6,000 − $3,600 = $2,400. This makes a year-3 income of $9,000 + $2,400 = $11,400.

PAYBACK

Payback (payoff) tells the number of years that an investment takes to pay for itself. Dollar amounts in the payback formula are not normally discounted.

$$\text{Payback} = \frac{\text{investment} - \text{salvage}}{\text{operating advantage/yr}} = \frac{I - S}{\text{OA/yr}} \qquad (3.6)$$

The *operating advantage* reflects the improvement in cash flows from increased income (e.g., higher volume or prices) or from decreased expenses (e.g., lower labor, material, overhead cost) or both. Thus the denominator is a net cash-flow figure resulting from improved earnings, but does not have depreciation expense deducted from it. Payback measures how quickly the savings resulting from the investment will recoup the cost of the investment.

In its simplest form, payback does not consider salvage values or taxes. However, they can be included in the analysis by reducing the investment I by the value of any salvage S and subtracting any tax amounts from the operating advantage.

Example 3.10 Security Insurance Co. is considering the purchase of an information-processing system that will cost $27,000, last for six years, and have a guaranteed $3,000 salvage value. It will generate savings of $11,000 per year (before depreciation) but necessitates that $3,000 of the savings be paid in taxes. If management insists on a 4-year, after-tax payback period, does this investment qualify?

$$\text{Payback} = \frac{I - S}{\text{OA/yr} - \text{tax}} = \frac{\$27,000 - \$3,000}{\$11,000 - \$3,000} = 3.0 \text{ yr}$$

The investment does meet the management criteria.

Payback is simple and quick to calculate, easy to understand, and a useful measure of the time required to return an original investment. However, it does not consider the economic life of the investment, the total return on investment, or the time value of money.

PRESENT VALUE

Present value tells the worth of future income or expense flows in terms of present dollars. These cash flows are typically the investment value, the maintenance and operating costs, and the income flows. The initial investment is usually already in present-value terms, so there is no need to consider its depreciation and interest charges. Operating expenses, however, do involve cash outlays in the future and must be discounted (reduced) to present values.

$$\text{Present-value cost} = \text{PV investment} + \text{PV other costs} - \text{PV salvage}$$

$$\text{PV}_{\text{cost}} = I(\text{PV}_{\text{sp}}) + \Sigma \, \text{OC}(\text{PV}_{\text{sp}}) - S(\text{PV}_{\text{sp}}) \qquad (3.7)$$

Example 3.11 Sunshine Smelter is considering an investment of $40,000 in a stack filter that is expected to have a salvage value of $10,000 after an economic life of five years. Maintenance and operating costs are estimated to be $5,000 the first year and to increase by $1,000 per year thereafter. The firm's cost of capital is 14 percent. Find the present-value cost of this investment.

$$PV_{cost} = I(PV_{sp}) + \Sigma\, OC(PV_{sp}) - S(PV_{sp})$$

where

$$I(PV_{sp})^{0\ yr}_{14\%} = \$40,000(1.00) = \qquad \$\ 40,000$$

$$
\begin{aligned}
OC(PV_{sp})\text{: year 1} &= (5,000)(.877) = \ \$4,385 \\
\text{year 2} &= (6,000)(.769) = \ \ \ 4,614 \\
\text{year 3} &= (7,000)(.675) = \ \ \ 4,725 \\
\text{year 4} &= (8,000)(.592) = \ \ \ 4,736 \\
\text{year 5} &= (9,000)(.519) = \ \underline{\ \ \ 4,671} \\
&\qquad\qquad\qquad\quad \$23,131 \quad \underline{\$+23,131}
\end{aligned}
$$

$$
\begin{aligned}
&\qquad\qquad\qquad\qquad\qquad\qquad\quad \$\ 63,131 \\
\text{Less } S(PV_{sp})^{5}_{14} &= 10,000(.519) = \quad \underline{-5,190} \\
PV_{cost} &= \ \$\ 57,941
\end{aligned}
$$

Present value considers the total return, includes time-value considerations, easily handles fluctuations in costs or revenues, and includes the effect of taxes, if applicable. However, it does not consider the rate of return or time for an investment to be paid off, and it assumes that cash inflows can be reinvested at the cost of capital. It is widely used.

EQUIVALENT ANNUAL COST

Equivalent annual cost is a time-adjusted method of calculating an equal annual cost over the life of an investment. It permits nonuniform costs to be apportioned equally over the life of the investment, as depicted in Fig. 3-4. Thus it is especially useful for comparing projects with different economic lives because it offers comparable per-year figures.

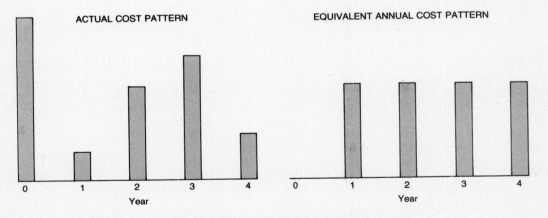

Fig. 3-4 Actual versus equivalent annual costs

The equivalent annual-cost method discounts and compounds cost amounts at a specified interest rate in such a way as to convert them all into annuity amounts. It includes three components: (1) capital recovery and return on the investment, less any salvage, (2) interest on the salvage, and (3) other annual maintenance and operating costs.

$$\frac{\text{Equivalent}}{\text{annual cost}} = \frac{\text{capital recovery}}{\text{and return}} + \frac{\text{interest}}{\text{on salvage}} + \frac{\text{other}}{\text{costs}}$$

$$EAC = (CR \text{ and } R) + i(S) + OC \tag{3.8}$$

Apportioning the present-value investment amount into an annuity is the reverse of converting an annuity into a present value, so we use $(1/PV_a)$, which is known as the capital recovery factor (CRF). Thus the CR and R is $(\text{investment} - \text{salvage})(1/PV_a)$.

Example 3.12   Sunshine Smelter (of Example 3.11) has received a bid for a stack filter from a second vendor. This proposal would cost \$45,000 and have an estimated salvage value of \$8,000 after an estimated useful life of six years. Maintenance and operating costs are expected to be \$6,000 per year. Use 14 percent as the cost of capital and find the equivalent annual cost of this investment.

The equivalent annual cost consists of:

$$CR \text{ and } R = (\text{investment} - \text{salvage})\left(\frac{1}{PV_a}\right)$$

$$= (\$45{,}000 - \$8{,}000)\left(\frac{1}{3.889}\right) = \quad \$\ 9{,}514/\text{yr}$$

$$i(S) = (.14)(\$8{,}000) = \quad\quad\quad\quad 1{,}120/\text{yr}$$

$$OC = \text{maintenance and operation} = \quad\quad \underline{6{,}000/\text{yr}}$$

$$\$16{,}634/\text{yr}$$

Example 3.13   Compare the two stack-filter costs from Examples 3.11 and 3.12. Which appears to be the most economical?

Proposal II (Example 3.12) costs \$5,000 more initially and has a salvage value of \$2,000 less, but the equipment lasts one year longer and has a lower average maintenance-and-operation cost. It is difficult to decide which proposal is less costly on the basis of these individual variables, especially with the different lifetimes. However, we can compare the two on an equal basis by converting the first proposal into an equivalent annual cost.

$$\text{Proposal I, equivalent annual cost} = PV\left(\frac{1}{PV_a}\right)_{14\%}^{5\,\text{yr}}$$

$$= \$57{,}941\left(\frac{1}{3.433}\right) = \$16{,}878/\text{yr}$$

$$\text{Proposal II, equivalent annual cost} = \quad\quad \underline{16{,}634/\text{yr}}$$

$$\text{Proposal II advantage} \quad = \quad\quad \$\quad 244/\text{yr}$$

The equivalent annual cost has many of the same advantages as present value, for it is readily convertible into a present-value amount (and vice versa). It is especially useful for comparing projects of different lifetimes, but it does not consider the total-cost or income aspects of a project.

INTERNAL RATE OF RETURN (IRR)

The internal rate of return (IRR) is the discount rate that equates an investment cost with its projected earnings. When discounted at the IRR, the present value of cash outflow will equal the present value of cash inflow.

$$IRR = i \text{ rate, where } PV(\text{cash outflow}) = PV(\text{cash inflow}) \tag{3.9}$$

Figure 3-5 depicts the concept of IRR. The problem of finding the IRR is essentially one of finding what interest rate i is realized from an investment I over n years.

If the annual cash inflows are equal annuities A and there is no salvage value, the IRR can easily be determined by using the PV_a table (Appendix F) because:

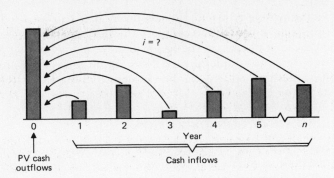

Fig. 3-5 Internal rate of return

$$PV_a = \frac{\text{initial investment}}{\text{annuity cash flow}} = \frac{I}{A} \qquad\qquad (3.10)$$

Example 3.14 A baggage-handling device will cost $18,000, but will generate savings (positive cash flow) of $4,000 per year for eight years (no salvage). Find the IRR.

The PV_a ratio associated with this return is:

$$PV_a = \frac{I}{A} = \frac{\$18,000}{\$4,000} = 4.50$$

Referring to the PV table for the row $n = 8$ years, we find the factor $i = 4.639$ for $i = 14$ percent and 4.487 for $i = 15$ percent. The IRR is thus very close to 15 percent.

For nonuniform cash flows, as depicted in Fig. 3-5, the IRR is more difficult to calculate because the PV_{sp} factor must be used, and it differs for each year. The calculation technique involves trial and error, starting first at some arbitrarily selected i rate. If on first try the present value of future earnings is less than the present value of the investment, the true IRR must be lower than that initially tried. With a lower i rate, the present value of a series of earnings will be more—and vice versa.

Example 3.15 A proposed machine costing $20,000 is expected to generate cash inflows of $4,000 in year 1, $6,000 in year 2, $10,000 in year 3, and a salvage value of $10,000 in year 4. Find the IRR.

Try several i rates (for example, 10 percent, 15 percent, and others) until the PA of cash inflow is approximately equal to the PV of cash outflow ($20,000), as shown in Table 3-3.

Table 3-3

Year	Cash Flow	10 Percent		15 Percent		16 Percent	
		PV_{sp} Factor	PV Amount	PV_{sp} Factor	PV Amount	PV_{sp} Factor	PV Amount
1	4,000	.909	$ 3,636	.870	$ 3,480	.862	$ 3,448
2	6,000	.826	4,956	.756	4,536	.743	4,458
3	10,000	.751	7,510	.658	6,580	.641	6,410
4	10,000	.683	6,830	.572	5,720	.552	5,520
			$22,932		$20,316		$19,836

The IRR appears to be a little closer to 16 percent than to 15 percent, but in view of the many uncertainties that accompany such calculations, either value (or perhaps $15\frac{1}{2}$ percent) would be a reasonable estimate.

In addition to providing a time-adjusted rate of profit that can be used for comparison with similar rates from other projects, it is useful to compare the IRR against the cost of capital. If an IRR does not equal or exceed the cost of capital, the firm will loose money on the project. The IRR does not, however, consider the total magnitude of cash flows, and it always requires estimates of returns as well as costs. It also assumes that returns can be reinvested at the same IRR.

INFLATION AND UNCERTAINTY CONSIDERATIONS

Inflation has the effect of reducing the future values of cash flows beyond whatever discount rate the firm is using. For example, assume that a rate of return (in today's present-value dollars) is expected to be 16 percent. If 6 percent of the return is due to inflation, the effective rate is only 10 percent.

Inflation makes current investments (and inventories) worth more, and future investments worth less. This works both ways, however. Costs that are already fixed into the future will be paid more easily with inflated dollars, but revenues fixed in the future are also worth less.

Future cash flows are also affected by other uncertainties, such as changes in (1) fixed or operating costs, (2) the useful life of the investment, (3) market size and share, (4) selling price, (5) market growth rate, and (6) obsolescence and salvage values. If reasonable probabilities can be assigned to the key determinants of cash flow, expected values may be used to develop expected cash flows. Decision trees and computer simulations have also proven to be effective tools to analyze cash flows under conditions of risk and uncertainty. For example, if the expected economic life of proposed equipment is very uncertain, empirical estimates (such as 5 years or 15 years) can be built into a *simulation model*. Then, a computer can be programmed to simulate hundreds of different IRR calculations, randomly assigning an economic life in accordance with whatever likelihood (or probability) is specified. The result is a probability distribution of IRR's that provides the decision maker with not only an expected value for the IRR, but also a measure of risk (dispersion).

Solved Problems

CASH FLOWS

3.1 Let $n = 12$ years and $i = 15$ percent. Find (a) the discounted present value of a future sum of $20,000, and (b) the discounted present value of an annuity of $5,000 per year.

(a) $$P = F(PV_{sp})_{15\%}^{12\,yr} = \$20,000(.187) = \$3,740$$

(b) $$P = A(PV_a)_{15\%}^{12\,yr} = \$5,000(5.421) = \$27,105$$

3.2 Find (a) the future value of $10,000 compounded at 15 percent over a 12-year period, and (b) the annuity amount that could be obtained for 12 years from a present value of $30,000 invested at 15 percent.

(a) $$F = P(1 + i)^n = \$10,000(1 + .15)^{12} = \$10,000(5.35) = \$53,500$$

also $$F = P\left(\frac{1}{PV_{sp}}\right) \qquad\qquad (3.11)$$

$$= \$10,000\left(\frac{1}{.187}\right) = \$53,476 \text{ (accurate to three decimals)}$$

(b) $$A \doteq CR \text{ and } R = P\left(\frac{1}{PV_a}\right) = \$30,000\left(\frac{1}{5.421}\right) = \$5,535$$

3.3   Operating costs for a machine are estimated at $500 per year for 10 years, plus an additional $1,000 for overhaul at the end of the fifth year. Assuming a 10-percent cost of capital, convert the maintenance and operating cost of the machine to a total present-value amount.

We can depict the problem on the accompanying time-cost diagram (Fig. 3-6).

$$\text{PV of M and O cost} = \text{PV annual operating costs} + \text{PV maintenance cost}$$
$$= \$500\,(PV_a)^{10\,yr}_{10\%} + \$1,000\,(PV_{sp})^{5\,yr}_{10\%}$$
$$= \$500\,(6.145) + \$1,000\,(0.621) = \$3,072 + \$621 = \$3,693$$

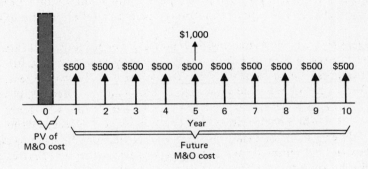

Fig. 3-6

3.4   Let $P = \$30,000$, $n = 5$ years, and $i = 10$ percent. Use Appendixes E, F, and G to find (a) F given P, (b) P given F, (c) A given F, (d) A given P, (e) F given A, and (f) P given A.

See Table 3-4 and Appendix G.

Table 3-4

Compound Interest Factors	Calculations for $n = 5$ yr, $i = 10\%$
To find	
F given P $\quad F = P(1+i)^n \quad = P(F\|P)^n_i$	If $P = \$30,000 \quad F = \$30,000(1.611) \ = \$48,315$
P given F $\quad P = F\dfrac{1}{(1+i)^n} \quad = F(P\|F)^n_i$	If $F = \$48,315 \quad P = \$48,315(.6209) \ = \$30,000$
A given F $\quad A = F\dfrac{i}{(1+i)^n - 1} = F(A\|F)^n_i$	If $F = \$48,315 \quad A = \$48,315(.16380) = \$7,914$
A given P $\quad A = P\dfrac{i(1+i)^n}{(1+i)^n - 1} = P(A\|P)^n_i$	If $P = \$30,000 \quad A = \$30,000(.26380) = \$7,914$
F given A $\quad F = A\dfrac{(1+i)^n - 1}{i} = A(F\|A)^n_i$	If $A = \$7,914 \quad F = \$7,914(6.105) \ = \$48,315$
P given A $\quad P = A\dfrac{(1+i)^n - 1}{i(1+i)^n} = A(P\|A)^n_i$	If $A = \$7,914 \quad P = \$7,914(3.791) \ = \$30,000$

3.5   Depict the P, F, and A values from Prob. 3.4 in schematic form.

See Fig. 3-7.

The annuity payments A at the end of each year necessary to accumulate a future value F (of \$48,135) are

$$A = F(A \mid F)^5_{10} = \$48,315\ (.1638) = \$7,914$$

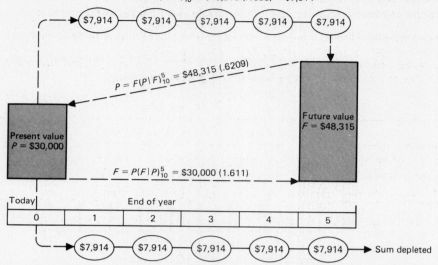

The annuity payments A that could be made at the end of each year from a present value P (of \$30,000) are

$$A = P(A \mid P)^5_{10} = \$30,000\ (.2638) = \$7,914$$

Fig. 3-7

DEPRECIATION

3.6 *Straight Line (Prior to 1981).* An investment of \$12,000 in new equipment, made prior to 1981, was expected to have a salvage value of 2,000 after a 5-year life. Find the straight-line depreciation expense per year allowed if pre-ACRS standards are followed.

See Fig. 3-8.

$$\text{Depreciation} = \frac{I - S}{n} = \frac{\$12,000 - \$2,000}{5\ \text{yr}}$$
$$= \$2,000/\text{yr} \quad \text{(same each year)}$$

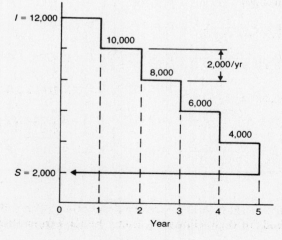

Fig. 3-8

3.7   *Declining Balance* (*Prior to 1981*). An investment of $12,000 in new equipment prior to 1981 is expected to have a salvage value of $2,000 after a 5-year life. Find the declining-balance depreciation expense per year if pre-ACRS standards are followed.

Under declining balance, a fixed percentage of the book value of the asset is deducted each year. The rate may not exceed 200 percent of the straight-line rate.

The straight-line rate is $2,000/$10,000 = 20 percent per year. We shall assume (for illustrative purposes) that double this rate (40 percent) is satisfactory. (See Table 3-5.)

Table 3-5

	Year 1	Year 2	Year 3	Year 4	Year 5
Asset's book value	$12,000	$7,200	$4,320	$2,592	$2,000
Less depreciation @ 40%	4,800	2,880	1,728	592*	0
Next year's book value	$ 7,200	$4,320	$2,592	$2,000	$2,000

* Depreciation is terminated at a salvage value of $2,000, so the recorded depreciation for the fourth year would be $2,592 − $2,000 = $592.

3.8   *Sum-of-Years Digits* (*Prior to 1981*). An investment of $12,000 in new equipment prior to 1981 is expected to have a salvage value of $2,000 after a 5-year life. Find the sum-of-years digits depreciation expense per year if pre-ACRS standards are followed.

Under the sum-of-years digits depreciation, the digits representing each year of life of the asset are summed, and the total serves as the denominator of a fraction that is multiplied by the value of investment minus salvage. The numerator represents the remaining useful life of the investment and varies each period beginning with the largest-year digit down to the smallest-year digit, as seen in Fig. 3-9.

The amount to be depreciated is (investment − salvage) = $12,000 − $2,000 = $10,000 per year. The sum-of-years digits is $N = 1 + 2 + 3 + 4 + 5 = 15$.

Depreciation Amount

Year $1 = \dfrac{5}{15}(10,000) = \$\ 3,333$

Year $2 = \dfrac{4}{15}(10,000) =\ \ 2,667$

Year $3 = \dfrac{3}{15}(10,000) =\ \ 2,000$

Year $4 = \dfrac{2}{15}(10,000) =\ \ 1,333$

Year $5 = \dfrac{1}{15}(10,000) =\ \ \ \ \ 667$

Total $\qquad\qquad\qquad \$10,000$

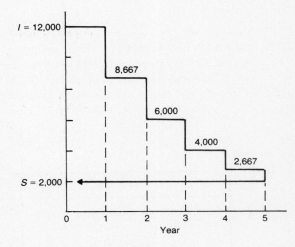

Fig. 3-9

3.9   *Comparison* (*Prior to 1981 Basis*). Compare the straight-line, declining-balance, and sum-of-years digits methods of depreciation by using the data from Probs. 3.6, 3.7, and 3.8.

See Table 3-6.

Table 3-6

	Straight Line	Declining Balance	Sum-of-Years Digits
Year 1	$ 2,000	$ 4,800	$ 3,333
Year 2	2,000	2,880	2,667
Year 3	2,000	1,728	2,000
Year 4	2,000	592	1,333
Year 5	2,000	0	667
	$10,000	$10,000	$10,000

Declining-balance and sum-of-years digits methods are both accelerated methods, with the declining-balance method yielding the fastest write-off.

3.10 *ACRS Method* (*Post 1985*). Using a 5-year property class, compute the ACRS depreciation allowed on the $12,000 investment in Probs. 3.6–3.9. (Assume a 5-year life and $2,000 salvage value *after* the fifth year.)

Table 3-7

	Year 1	Year 2	Year 3	Year 4	Year 5
(a) Cost basis	$12,000	$12,000	$12,000	$12,000	$12,000
(b) ACRS percentage (Table 3-1)	20%	32%	24%	16%	8%
(c) Depreciation expense $[(a) \times (b)]$	$ 2,400	$ 3,840	$ 2,880	$ 1,920	$ 960

Note in Table 3-7 that the first year depreciation is reduced (from pre-1981 declining-balance rates) to reflect a half-year convention during the first year of service. Salvage *after* year 5 would be reported as income.

3.11 Hawthorn Restaurants Inc. has purchased a $7,000 oven that is expected to yield a before-tax operating advantage of $4,000 per year, for five years. It will be salvaged during the fifth year for $750, and will be depreciated on an ACRS rate for 5-year property (beyond 1986). Compute the yearly tax amounts, assuming that a 46-percent tax bracket applies.

See Table 3-8.

Table 3-8

	Year 1	Year 2	Year 3	Year 4	Year 5
(a) Operating advantage	$4,000	$4,000	$4,000	$4,000	$4,190*
(b) Cost basis	7,000	7,000	7,000	7,000	7,000
(c) Depreciation $[\text{ACRS}\% \times (b)]$	1,400	2,240	1,680	1,120	0
(d) Income − expense $[(a) - (c)]$	$2,600	$1,760	$2,320	$2,880	$4,190
(e) Tax @ 46% $\times (d)$	1,196	810	1,067	1,325	1,927

*If the 5-year property class for 1986 and beyond is used, 92 percent of the asset's value is depreciated in years 1–4. This leaves (.08)($7,000) = $560 undepreciated. The excess of salvage value over the remaining depreciation ($750 − $560 = $190) is taxable income, and for convenience, is included in the year 5 operating advantage.

3.12 Find the net present value of cash flow after tax (AT) for Prob. 3.11. Use a discount rate of 12 percent and assume that next year is year 1.

See Table 3-9.

Table 3-9

	Year 1	Year 2	Year 3	Year 4	Year 5
Operating advantage	$4,000	$4,000	$4,000	$4,000	$4,000
Less: Tax	1,196	810	1,067	1,325	1,927
Cash flow AT	$2,804	$3,190	$2,933	$2,675	$2,263
PV_{sp} factor	.893	.797	.712	.636	.567
PV amount	$2,504	$2,542	$2,088	$1,701	$1,283

Net PV of Cash Flow AT = $2,504 + $2,542 + $2,088 + $1,701 + $1,283 = $10,118

PAYBACK

3.13 A $40,000 extrusion machine is expected to be obsolete after 10 years, with no salvage value. During its lifetime, it should generate an $8,000-per-year operating advantage, $3,000 of which must be paid in taxes. What is the payoff period?

$$\text{Payoff} = \frac{I - S}{\text{OA/yr}} = \frac{\$40,000 - 0}{\$8,000 - \$3,000} = 8 \text{ years}$$

3.14 A $30,000 investment can be made in either X, Y, or Z, and will yield the estimated cash flows shown in Table 3-10. Find the payback period for each.

Table 3-10

Year	X	Y	Z
1	$20,000	$10,000	$ 0
2	10,000	10,000	5,000
3	5,000	10,000	10,000
4	2,000	10,000	12,000
5	1,000	10,000	10,000

Cumulate the cash flow for each alternative, until the cash flow equals the investment amount of $30,000 as shown in Table 3-11.

Table 3-11

Year	X	Y	Z
1	$20,000	$10,000	$ 0
2	30,000	20,000	5,000
3		30,000	15,000
4			27,000
5			37,000

X's payback is 2 years, Y's is 3 years, and Z's is early in the fifth year. Therefore X appears best, based on payback.

3.15 A proposed new $16,400 automatic machine will have operating costs of $.30 per unit produced, whereas the existing machine costs are $.70 per unit. The existing machine has a market value of $8,700 now and has another five years of life. It would cost $500 to remove the existing machine and install the new one. If the firm requires a 3-year payout period, how many units must be produced annually to justify the new machine? Disregard taxes.

$$\text{Payout} = \frac{\text{investment}}{\text{OA/yr}}$$

We have

$$\text{Payout} = 3 \text{ yr}$$

$$\Delta \text{ investment} = \$16{,}400 - \$8{,}700 = \$7{,}700$$

$$\text{Add installation cost: } \underline{\quad 500}$$

$$\text{Total } \$8{,}200$$

$$\text{OA/unit} = \$.70 - \$.30 = \$.40/\text{unit}$$

$$\text{OA(total)} = \$.40 \ (N \text{ units/yr})$$

Therefore

$$3 \text{ yr} = \frac{\$8{,}200}{\$.40(N)}$$

and

$$N = \frac{\$8{,}200}{\$1.20/\text{unit}} = 6{,}833 \text{ units/yr}$$

PRESENT VALUE

3.16 Computer Services, Inc., offers maintenance services at $1,000 per year for five years plus an additional $2,000 at the end of the third year for overhaul. If a firm contracts for five years of services, what is the net present-value cost to the firm? The firm estimates its capital cost at 14 percent and has sales of $3.5 million per year.

The sales data are not relevant to computing the present-value cost.

$$\text{Present-value cost} = \text{PV other costs} = \text{PV (maintenance cost)} + \text{PV (overhaul cost)}$$

$$= \$1{,}000(\text{PV}_a)_{14\%}^{5\,\text{yr}} + \$2{,}000(\text{PV}_{\text{sp}})_{14\%}^{3\,\text{yr}}$$

$$= \$1{,}000(3.433) + \$2{,}000(.675) = \$3{,}433 + \$1{,}350 = \$4{,}783$$

3.17 An instrument transformer manufacturer in Long Island is considering purchase of an ultrasonic welding machine to replace an existing manually operated machine. The existing machine cost $12,000 two years ago and has been depreciated down to a $10,000 book value, using a 12-year life and no salvage. However, the market value of the machine is only about $4,000 now. The ultrasonic welder would improve product quality enough to boost revenue from an existing $80,000 per year to $100,000 per year. It would cost $44,000 and have a 10-year life. Any salvage value on it would be consumed in the removal expense. An advantage of the ultrasonic machine is that by reducing annual labor costs, it would cut operating expenses from $8,000 to $3,000 annually. Use a 50-percent tax bracket and estimate the firm's cost of capital at 12 percent. Should the manufacturer purchase the ultrasonic welder?

Determine the after-tax profit under each alternative and select the most favorable one. It will be most convenient to do calculations on an annual basis and then convert to present value.

Existing machine:

Revenue	$80,000
Less:	
Operating costs	8,000
Depreciation	1,000
Income subject to tax	$71,000
Income tax (@ 50%)	$35,000

$$\text{Cash inflow} = \text{revenue} - \text{operating costs} - \text{taxes}$$
$$= \$80,000 - \$8,000 - \$35,500 = \$36,500/\text{yr}$$

$$\text{Present value of cash inflow (AT)} = R(PV_a)_{12\%}^{10\,\text{yr}} = \$36,500(5.65) = \$206,225$$

$$\text{Net PV gain after taxes} = \text{PV (cash inflow)} - \text{PV}(I)$$
$$= \$206,225 - \$4,000 = \$202,225$$

New ultrasonic machine:

Revenue	$100,000
Less:	
Operating costs	3,000
Depreciation	4,400
Income subject to tax	$92,600
Income tax (@ 50%)	$46,300

$$\text{Cash inflow} = \$100,000 - \$3,000 - \$46,300 = \$50,700$$

$$\text{Present value of cash inflow (AT)} = \$50,700(5.65) = \$286,455$$

$$\text{Net PV gain after taxes} = \$286,455 - \$44,000 = \$242,455$$

Note the net PV gain AT from the ultrasonic machine installation exceeds the existing arrangement by $40,230 and thus the new machine should be installed. Note also that the relevant investment cost of the existing machine is the market value, *not the book value*. There is no relevant advantage to be gained from writing off some of the existing machine as a loss, since this write-off should take place whether the new machine is purchased or not. The write-off advantage is not relevant to the decision problem.

EQUIVALENT ANNUAL COST

3.18 Alaska Construction Co. is purchasing a portable generator from Lyon Electric for $5,026 and plans to finance the purchase from a local bank at 8-percent interest. The contract stipulates that Lyon Electric will pay the construction company $1,000 for the used machine after 10 years. What is the equivalent annual purchase cost to Alaska Construction Company?

$$CR \text{ and } R = (I - S)\left[\frac{1}{(PV_a)_{8\%}^{10\,\text{yr}}}\right]$$

$$= (\$5,026 - \$1,000)\left[\frac{1}{6.71}\right] = \$600/\text{yr}$$

$$(i)S = (0.08)(\$1,000) = \qquad\qquad 80/\text{yr}$$

$$\text{Other costs (none considered):} \qquad \underline{\quad 00/\text{yr}}$$

$$\text{Total} \quad \$680/\text{yr}$$

3.19 Porter & Fisher Ltd. plans to sign a 3-year lease for automobiles for its production supervisors at a seafood plant in Norway. The company can obtain car A for $2,000 plus $.15/mile or car B for $1,200 plus $.30/mile. If funds cost 18 percent, how many miles must be driven before the use of car A is justified? Use the equivalent annual-cost method.

$$CR \text{ and } R = (I - S)\left[\frac{1}{(PV_a)_{18\%}^{3\,\text{yr}}}\right]$$

	Car A	Car B
CR and *R*:	($2,000)(1/2.174) = $920/yr	($1200)(1/2.174) = $552/yr
Interest on salvage:	no salvage	no salvage
Mileage charges:	$.15N	$.30N
Total	$920 + $.15N	$552 + $.30N

Setting the total costs for car A equal to the total costs for car B:

$$TC_A = TC_B$$
$$\$920 + \$.15N = \$552 + .30N$$
$$\$.15N = \$368$$
$$N = 2,453 \text{ miles}$$

INTERNAL RATE OF RETURN

3.20   An investment of \$5,650 is expected to yield an operating advantage (before depreciation and taxes) of \$4,000 at the end of the first year, \$2,000 at the end of the second year, and \$1,000 at the end of the third. What is the time-adjusted rate of return?

Set PV(income) = PV(I) = \$5,560.

Try 14 percent: 1st-yr earnings = $F(\text{PV}_{sp})_{14\%}^{1\,yr}$ = \$4,000(.877) = \$3,508

2d-yr earnings = $F(\text{PV}_{sp})_{14\%}^{2\,yr}$ =   2,000(.769) =   1,538

3d-yr earnings = $F(\text{PV}_{sp})_{14\%}^{3\,yr}$ =   1,000(.675) =   675

\$5,721

Since PV(income) > PV(I), try a higher rate.

Try 16 percent: 1st yr = \$4,000(.862) = \$3,448

2d yr =   2,000(.743) =   1,486

3d yr =   1,000(.641) =   641

\$5,575

Since PV (income) is less than PV(I), try a lower rate. Note that the 16-percent rate yields a PV (income) figure \$75 below the investment amount, whereas the 14-percent rate yields a figure \$71 above. Thus the correct value should be about midway between, or 15 percent.

Try 15 percent: 1st yr = \$4,000(.870) = \$3,480

2d yr =   2,000(.756) =   1,512

3d yr =   1,000(.658) =   658

\$5,650

The (BT)IRR is 15 percent.

Supplementary Problems

3.21   Bradley Enterprises borrows \$60,000 from Suffolk Bank at 14-percent interest per year. How much must the firm repay two years later?   *Ans.*   \$78,000 (rounded)

3.22   The maintenance expense on a printing press is expected to be \$300 per year over the next six years. If the owner must pay 12 percent to borrow money, what is the present-value cost of the maintenance expense?   *Ans.*   \$1,233

3.23   Cascade Wines invests \$16,000 in 1986 in a tank that has a 5-year recovery period under ACRS guidelines. The investment is expected to yield a before-tax operating advantage of \$5,000 per year for the first year and \$7,000 per year for the next four years. It will probably continue in service after five years, even though it is fully depreciated. (*a*) Compute the depreciation expense per year for each year. (*b*) What is the after-tax cash flow per year, assuming a 40 percent tax rate?
Ans.   (*a*) \$3,200, \$5,120, \$3,840, \$2,560, \$1,280 (*b*) \$4,280, \$6,248, \$5,728, \$5,224, \$4,712

3.24 Find the net present value of cash flow after tax in Prob. 3.23 if all values are discounted back to 1985 at a 16 percent rate.   *Ans.* $17,130

3.25 A $20,000 machine will last 10 years, have no salvage, and will generate a $4,000-per-year operating advantage, $1,000 of which must be paid in taxes. Find the payoff period.   *Ans.*   6.7 years

3.26 A new lead-casting furnace costs $30,000 installed and is expected to have a $4,000 salvage value at the end of an 8-year economic life. Operation and maintenance costs will run about $7,000 per year. Using 12-percent interest, what is the present-value cost of the furnace?   *Ans.* $63,160

3.27 Rochester Shoe Co. wishes to decide between two automatic clicker machines. Machine X has a net-present-value cost of $25,000 (all costs considered). Machine Y has an initial cost of $14,000 and will have a salvage value of $1,000. The annual labor cost is $3,300, and annual taxes, insurance, and other costs are estimated at 5 percent of the initial cost. Both machines would have the same 4-year life under the heavy use expected. If Rochester Shoe Co. uses an 8-percent interest rate and uses the declining-balance method of depreciation, how would the net present-value cost of machine Y compare with that of machine X?   *Ans.*   Machine Y is $1,513 more.

3.28 A leather-goods producer in New Orleans plans to modify his shop layout and is considering the alternatives shown in Table 3-12.

Table 3-12

	Plan 1	Plan 2
New machinery cost	$22,000	$20,000
Installation labor cost	3,000	2,000
Annual savings expected (in operating costs)	8,000	7,000

The new layout is expected to be suitable for five years of operation, with no salvage. (*a*) If the producer has a 12-percent cost of capital, what is the equivalent annual cost (or savings) for plan 1 and plan 2? (*b*) Which plan should be adopted?   *Ans.*   (*a*) Plan 1 = $1,065 savings   Plan 2 = $897 savings (*b*) Plan 1

3.29 Lowell Corp. has an opportunity to invest $7,680 in a plant modification that is expected to yield an operating advantage of $5,000 at the end of the first year and $1,000 at the end of each of the next 5 years. What is the before-tax internal rate of return?   *Ans.*   12 percent

3.30 Directors of Convalescent Care of Chicago, Inc., are considering a capital-expansion program to meet the increased demand for health care facilities. They are proposing an expansion of either $A = 100$, $B = 200$, or $C = 300$ beds and have estimated profits (losses) as shown in Table 3-13. Their estimate of demand for the various expansion alternatives is:

   $P(100 \text{ beds required}) = .2$ $P(200 \text{ beds required}) = .5$ $P(300 \text{ beds required}) = .3$

Table 3-13

Expansion Alternatives	Profit ($000) for Demand of		
	100 Beds	200 Beds	300 Beds
$A = 100$	200	200	200
$B = 200$	000	400	400
$C = 300$	(200)	200	600

(a) How large of an expansion should be planned under (1) maximax, (2) maximin, (3) maximum probability, (4) expected-value criteria?   (b) Assume the profit figures are yearly annuity values that will continue for 5 years only. What is the net expected present value of the best alternative, assuming funds cost 10 percent?

Ans.   (a) (1) choose 300 (2) choose 100 (3) choose 200 (4) choose 200 (b) 200-bed expansion is still best choice, with an expected present value of $1,213,220

3.31   Forest Paper Co. is considering the purchase of a $10,000 paperbox press which would be used for three years and sold for $1,000 in salvage value. Operating costs are $400 per year. Maintenance costs are $500 the first year and increase by $500 each year thereafter. Production volume is 1,000 units per year, and the firm operates on a three-shift-per-day basis. It uses straight-line depreciation, is in a 40-percent tax bracket, and estimates the cost of capital at 10 percent. (a) Determine the present-value cost of owning and using the machine before tax is considered. (b) Determine what effect taxes have on the present-value cost. (c) Assume that the maintenance costs remain constant at $1,000 per year and that all sales and administrative costs are included in the operating costs of $400 per year. If the firm achieves a paperbox sales revenue of $12,000 per year from the press, what is the after-tax payoff period?

Ans.   (a) $12,651, (b) Taxes reduce the net profit, but depreciation expenses can be deducted before taxes are computed. If depreciation = $3,000 per year and taxes = 40 percent, then tax = .40 (OA before depreciation −$3,000) = $1,200 less that is paid each year because of the depreciation expense. This $1,200 per year has a present value of ($1,200) (2.487) = $2,984, (c) 1.2 years

3.32   The Synco Steel production manager is evaluating two machines to determine which would be most economical. Both machines are capable of generating the same revenue. The firm's cost of capital is 14 percent. Data on the two machines are shown in Table 3-14.

Table 3-14

	Machine A	Machine B
Initial cost	$20,000	$30,000
Maintenance and operating cost/yr	2,000	3,000
Economic life	4 yrs	4 yrs
Salvage value (estimated)	$ 2,000	$15,000

For machine A find (a) the net present value cost and (b) the equivalent annual cost.

Ans.   (a) $24,650 (b) $8,457 per year

3.33   Solve Prob. 2.27 using an expected-value criteria with all figures converted to present values for the current year, year zero, using a 10 percent discount rate.

Ans.   E (Solar) = $128.1 million and E (Coal) = $119.0 million, so the coal is less costly by $9.1 million.

Chapter 4

Facility Location

Transportation Linear Programming

LOCATION PLANNING

Location decisions are crucial to both new and existing facilities because they commit the organization to long-lasting cost, employment, and marketing patterns. Location (and relocation) opportunities should be reviewed as labor conditions, raw-material supplies, or market demands change. Firms can respond to the change by maintaining their status quo, by expanding or closing existing facilities, or by developing new ones.

No locational procedures can ensure that an optimal location is chosen. Avoiding a troublesome (or disastrous) location is perhaps more important than finding an *ideal* site. Numerous firms have encountered unexpected problems with zoning restrictions, water supply, waste disposal, labor unions, transportation costs, tax laws, community attitudes about pollution, etc. that should have been foreseen. Avoiding such problems is why a systematic analysis (including the use of a comprehensive checklist) is strongly recommended. Firms often do a quantitative analysis first to establish the feasibility of alternative locations, then follow with an exhaustive review of qualitative (less tangible) factors.

TYPE OF FACILITY: GOODS VERSUS SERVICES

A review of facilities ranging from mining and heavy manufacturing, through warehousing and retailing, to government and professional services reveals two key determinants of location:

(1) The source of *inputs* and the market for *outputs*

(2) The type of processing (especially whether goods or service)

Material resources (e.g., bulky resources from mines and forests) and concentration of labor supply (e.g., workers skilled in electronics) strongly influence locations. Similarly, the market dictates the location of retail outlets, hospitals, and a wide range of public services.

Environmental (and zoning) controls restrict the location of goods-producing facilities. But goods are often standardized and can be stored and transported to customers for use at a later date. Services are produced and consumed simultaneously, so service industries are highly dependent upon the location of their customers. Figure 4-1 illustrates the flexibility of location for facilities producing

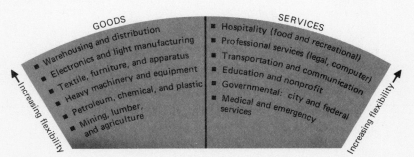

Fig. 4-1 Locational flexibility of facilities producing goods and services

goods and services. The increasing flexibility for goods coincides with processing activities that bring the refined or finished product closer to the consumer. For services, the life-support need (medical, fire, police) is the strongest determinant, and flexibility increases as the proliferation and competitive nature of the service increases. Information services tend to be highly flexible because of the ease of electronic communications.

LOCATION DECISION PROCESS

Table 4-1 lists possible formal steps in a facility location decision process. The actual approach varies with the size and scope of operations.

Table 4-1   Steps in a Facility Location Decision

1. Define the location *objectives* and associated variables.
2. Identify the relevant decision *criteria*.
   (*a*) Quantitative—economic
   (*b*) Qualitative—less tangible
3. Relate the objectives to the criteria in the form of a *model*, or models (such as break-even, linear-programming, qualitative factor analysis).
4. Generate necessary data and use the models to evaluate the *alternative* locations.
5. *Select* the location that best satisfies the criteria.

The objectives are influenced by owners, suppliers, employees, and customers of the organization. They may stem from opportunities (or concerns) with respect to any phase of the production system (i.e., inputs, processing, or outputs). The following sections describe some of the variables, criteria, and models relevant to the location decision process.

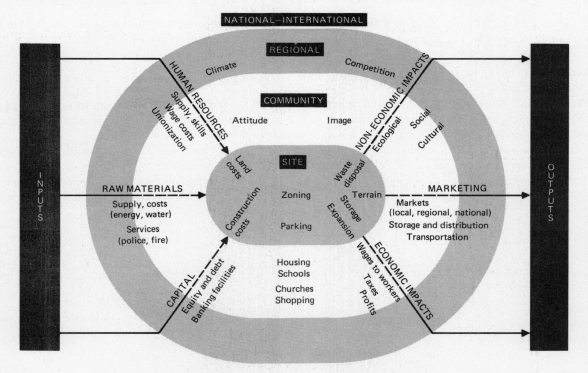

Fig. 4-2 Factors affecting location decisions

FACTORS AFFECTING LOCATION DECISIONS

Location decisions involve so many factors that a systematic approach (or checklist) is essential. Figure 4-2 shows the use of a standard systems framework in combination with a geographical overlay. It calls for systematic attention to inputs, processing, and outputs, while recognizing that the geographic scope of the decision typically converges from national and regional (macro) evaluations. The choices are often reduced to three or four communities—site locations that are evaluated in detail—before the final choice is made.

LOCATIONAL BREAK-EVEN ANALYSIS

Both profit and not-for-profit organizations work from limited budgets; they are economically pressured to control costs. Potential locations can be compared on an economic basis by estimating the fixed and variable costs and then graphing (or computing) them for a representative volume at each location. Assuming equal revenues from all locations, the graphic method for locational break-even analysis is as listed in Table 4-2.

Table 4-2   Method for Locational Break-Even Analysis

1. Determine all relevant costs that vary with the locations.
2. Categorize the costs for each location into annual fixed costs (FC) and per-unit variable costs (VC).
3. Plot the costs associated with each location on a single chart of annual cost versus annual volume.
4. Select the location with the lowest total cost (TC) at the expected production volume (V).

If revenues per unit vary from one location to another, revenue values must also be included, and comparisons should be made on the basis of TR minus TC at each location.

Example 4.1 Potential locations at Albany, Baker, and Casper have the cost structures shown in Table 4-3 for a product expected to sell for \$130. (a) Find the most economical location for an expected volume of 6,000 units per year. (b) What is the expected profit if the site selected in (a) is used? (c) For what output range is each location best?

Table 4-3

Potential Location	Fixed Cost/Yr	Variable Cost/Unit
Albany (A)	\$150,000	\$75.00
Baker (B)	200,000	50.00
Casper (C)	400,000	25.00

For each set, plot the fixed costs (costs at zero volume) and total costs (FC + TVC) at the expected volume of output. See Fig. 4-3.

(a)
$$TC = FC + VC(V)$$
$$A: \quad TC = \$150,000 + \$75\,(6,000) = \$600,000$$
$$B: \quad TC = \$200,000 + \$50\,(6,000) = \$500,000$$
$$C: \quad TC = \$400,000 + \$25\,(6,000) = \$550,000$$

Therefore the most economical location is B.

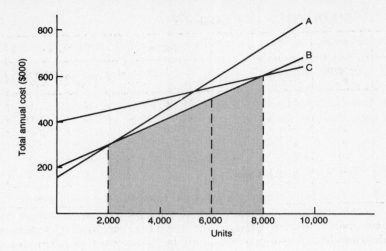

Fig. 4-3

(*b*) Expected profit (using B)

$$\text{Profit} = TR - TC = (\$130/\text{unit}) (6,000 \text{ units}) - \$500,000 = \$280,000/\text{yr}$$

(*c*) From the graph (Fig. 4-3), use A for volumes up to 2,000, B for 2,000–8,000, and C for volumes greater than 8,000 units.

Locational break-even analysis applies to one-product (or product-line) situations, so if multi-products are involved, their respective cost and volume effects must be appropriately weighted. It also assumes that fixed costs hold constant and that variable costs remain linear. If the expected volume is very close to the crossover point between two locations, other factors may be more influential than costs.

QUALITATIVE FACTOR RATING

Factor rating is a means of assigning quantitative values to all the factors related to each decision alternative, and deriving a composite score that can be used for comparison. It allows the decision maker to inject his or her own preferences (values) into a location decision, and it can accommodate both quantitative and qualitative factors.

Table 4-4   Procedure for Qualitative Factor Rating

1. *Develop a list* of *relevant factors* (e.g., use a checklist or a graph such as Fig. 4-2).
2. *Assign a weight* to *each factor to* indicate its relative importance (weights may total 1.00).
3. *Assign a common scale* to *each factor* (e.g., 0–100 points), and *designate any minimum*.
4. *Score each potential location* according to the designated scale, and *multiply the scores* by the weights.
5. *Total the points* for each location, and *choose the location* with the maximum points.

Example 4.2 National Glass Co. is evaluating four locations for a new plant and has weighted the relevant factors as shown on Table 4-5. Scores have been assigned with higher values indicative of preferred conditions. Using these scores, develop a qualitative factor comparison for the four locations.

Table 4-5

Relevant Factor	Assigned Weight	Atlanta		Baltimore		Chicago		Denver	
		Score	Weighted Score	Score	Weighted Score	Score	Weighted Score	Score	Weighted Score
Production cost	.33	50	16.50	40	13.20	35	11.55	30	9.90
Raw material supply	.25	70	17.50	80	20.00	75	18.75	80	20.00
Labor availability	.20	55	11.00	70	14.00	60	12.00	45	9.00
Cost of living	.05	80	4.00	70	3.50	40	2.00	50	2.50
Environment	.02	60	1.20	60	1.20	60	1.20	90	1.80
Markets	.15	80	12.00	90	13.50	85	12.75	50	7.50
Total location score			62.20		65.40		58.25		50.70

Weighted scores are computed by multiplying the score times the assigned weight (for example, $50 \times .33 = 16.50$) and summing those products. Based on this data, Baltimore is the preferred location.

TRANSPORTATION LINEAR PROGRAMMING

Transportation adds no value to a product other than place utility. However, the transportation costs for raw materials and finished goods are often significant and merit special analysis. Before deciding on a plant location, management may want to know which plants will be used to produce what quantities and to which distribution warehouses all quantities should be shipped.

If the location problem can be formulated as one of minimizing a transportation cost, subject to satisfying overall supply and demand requirements, the transportation linear-programming (LP) method may be useful. The transportation model is a variation of the standard linear-programming approach and assumes the following:

(1) The objective is to minimize total transportation costs.

(2) Transportation costs are a linear function of the number of units shipped.

(3) All supply and demand are expressed in homogeneous units.

(4) Shipping costs per unit do not vary with the quantity shipped.

(5) Total supply must equal total demand.

   (a) If *demand* is larger than *supply*, create a dummy supply and assign a zero transportation cost to it so that excess demand is satisfied.

   (b) If *supply* is larger than *demand* create a dummy demand and assign a zero transportation cost to it so that excess supply is absorbed.

To use the transportation (also called *distribution*) linear-programming format, the demand requirements and supply availabilities are formulated in a rectangular matrix. The transportation costs between the supply and demand points are placed in the upper corner of each cell.

Supply is then allocated to meet demand by placing entries, which express the number of units shipped from a supply source to a demand destination, into the cells. The solution procedure is an iterative one that begins with an initial solution that is feasible, but not necessarily optimal. The solution is progressively tested and improved upon until an optimal solution is reached. The optimal solution satisfies demand at the lowest total cost.

Several methods of obtaining initial and optimal solutions have been developed:

Initial Solutions
(1) Minimum cost (intuitive)
(2) Northwest corner
(3) Vogel's approximation (VAM)

Optimal Solutions
(1) Stepping-stone
(2) Modified distribution (MODI)

The minimum cost method works well for simple problems, but VAM is likely to yield a better initial solution, which is often also the optimal solution. VAM works by sequentially zeroing in on the most cost-advantageous row-and-column combinations. The northwest-corner method does not usually yield as good an initial solution as VAM, but it is extremely easy to apply.

When used in conjunction with the stepping-stone method, VAM is useful for hand calculation of relatively large-scale problems. However, most large problems are solved by computer, and numerous computer programs are available. The MODI method is well-suited to computer applications. It is a modified stepping-stone algorithm that uses index numbers to systematically reach an optimum solution. Example 4.3 uses the northwest-corner method for the initial solution and the stepping-stone method for the final solution.

Example 4.3 (*Describes distribution linear programming methods*) The Milltex Co. has production plants in Albany, Bend, and Corvallis, all of which manufacture similar paneling for the housing market. The products are currently distributed through plants in Seattle and Portland. The company is considering adding another distribution plant in San Francisco and has developed the transportation costs in dollars per unit, shown in Table 4-6:

Table 4-6

Production Plants	Cost to Ship to Distribution Plant in:		
	Seattle	Portland	San Francisco
Albany	$10	$14	$ 8
Bend	12	10	12
Corvallis	8	12	10

The production capabilities at the Albany, Bend, and Corvallis plants are 20-, 30-, and 40-unit loads per week, respectively. Management feels that a San Francisco plant could absorb 20 units per week, with Seattle and Portland claiming 40 and 30 units per week, respectively. Determine the optimal distribution arrangement and cost if the San Francisco site is selected.

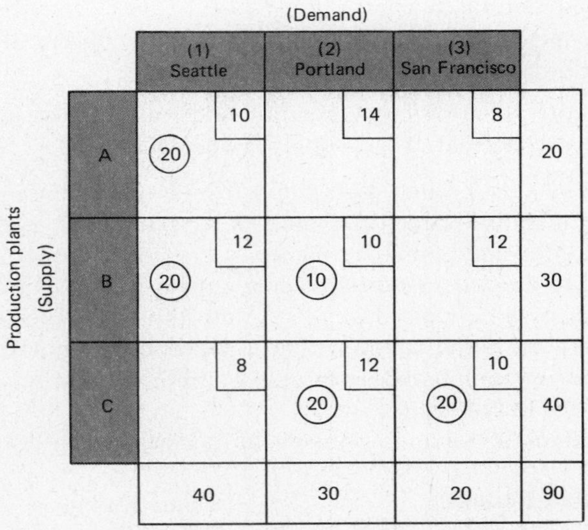

Fig. 4-4 Initial solution to distribution linear-programming matrix

We will use the northwest-corner method for the initial allocation and the stepping-stone method for the final solution. To do this requires that the data be arranged in a matrix. Figure 4-4 shows supply on the horizontal rows, demand on the columns, and unit transportation costs ($) in the small boxes of the matrix. The initial allocation via the northwest (NW)-corner method is made as follows.

(a) Assign as many units as possible to the NW-corner cell A1 from the total available in row A. Given the 20-unit available supply in row A and the 40-unit demand in column 1, the maximum number of units that can be assigned to cell A1 is 20. This is shown as ⑳, indicating an initial allocation.

(b) Assign additional units of supply from row B (or additional rows) until the demand in column 1 is satisfied. This requires 20 additional units in cell B1 and leaves 10 units of B's unassigned.

(c) Assign remaining units in the subject row to the next column, continuing as above until its demand requirements are satisfied. This means the 10 units left in B are assigned to cell B2. Since this does not satisfy demand in column 2, an additional 20 units are allocated from row C.

(d) Continue down from the NW corner until the whole supply has been allocated to demand. The initial assignment is completed by assigning the 20 units remaining in row C to cell C3.

(e) Check allocations to verify that all supply and demand conditions are satisfied. Since all row and column totals agree, the initial assignment is correct. Also, the number of entries is five, which satisfies the $R + C - 1$ (rows plus columns minus one) requirement for $3 + 3 - 1 = 5$.

The initial solution is, perhaps obviously, not an optimal (or least-cost) allocation scheme. The transportation cost for this arrangement is:

20 units	A to Seattle @ $10/unit =	$200
20 units	B to Seattle @ $12/unit =	240
10 units	B to Portland @ $10/unit =	100
20 units	C to Portland @ $12/unit =	240
20 units	C to San Francisco @ $10/unit =	200
		Total $980

An optimal solution can be obtained by following a stepping-stone approach, which requires calculation of the net monetary gain or loss that can be obtained by shifting an allocation from one supply source to another. The important rule to keep in mind is that every increase (or decrease) in supply at one location must be accompanied by a decrease (or increase) in supply at another. The same holds true for demand. Thus there must be two changes in every row or column that is changed—one change increasing the quantity and one change decreasing it. This is easily done by evaluating reallocations in a closed-path sequence with only right-angle turns permitted and only on occupied cells. Of course, a cell must have an initial entry before it can be reduced in favor of another, but *empty (or filled) cells may be skipped over to get to a corner cell.* To be sure that all reallocation possibilities are considered, it is best to proceed systematically, evaluating each empty cell. When any changes are made, cells vacated earlier must be rechecked.

Only unused transportation paths (vacant cells) need to be evaluated, and there is only one available pattern of moves to evaluate each vacant cell. This is because moves are restricted to occupied cells. Every time a vacant cell is filled, *one* previously occupied cell must become vacant. The initial (and continuing) number of entries is always maintained at $R+C-1$. When a move happens to cause fewer entries (for example, when two cells become vacant at the same time but only one is filled), a "zero" entry must be retained in one of the cells to avoid what is termed a *degeneracy* situation.

The zero entry (or Greek letter ε) assigned to either cell should ensure that a closed path exists for all filled cells. The cell with the zero entry is then considered to be an occupied and potentially usable cell. If a cell evaluation reveals an improvement potential in a given cell, but no units are available because of a zero entry in the path to that cell, the zero (zero units) should be transported to the vacant cell, just as any other units would be shipped. Then the matrix should be reevaluated. Improvements may still be possible until the zero entries are relocated to where evaluations of all vacant cells are greater than or equal to 0.

The criterion for making a reallocation is simply the desired effect upon costs. The net loss or gain is determined by listing the unit costs associated with each cell (which is used as a corner in the evaluation path) and then summing over the path to find the net effect. Signs alternate from + to − depending upon whether shipments are being added or reduced at a given point. A negative sign on the net result indicates that cost can be reduced by making the change. The total savings are, of course, limited to the least number of units available for reallocation at any negative cell on the path.

Evaluate cell A2:

Path: A2 to B2 to B1 to A1 (designated as I in Fig. 4-5)

Cost: $+14 - 10 + 12 - 10 = +6$ (cost increase)

Therefore, make no change.

Evaluate cell C1:

Path: C1 to B1 to B2 to C2 (designated as II in Fig. 4-6)

Cost: $+8 - 12 + 10 - 12 = -6$ (cost savings)

Therefore, this is a potential change. Evaluate remaining empty cells to see if other changes are more profitable.

Evaluate cell A3:

Path: A3 to C3 to C2 to B2 to B1 to A1 (not shown in Fig. 4-5)

Cost: $+8 - 10 + 12 - 10 + 12 - 10 = +2$ (cost increase)

Therefore, make no change.

Evaluate cell B3:

Path: B3 to C3 to C2 to B2 (not shown in Fig. 4-5)

Cost: $+12 - 10 + 12 - 10 = +4$ (cost increase)

Therefore, make no change.

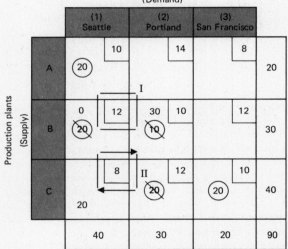

Fig. 4-5 Revision of matrix

Cell C1 presents the best (only) opportunity for improvement. For each unit from C reallocated to Seattle and from B reallocated to Portland, a $6 savings results. Change the maximum number available in the loop (20) for a net savings of ($6)(20) = $120. (The maximum number will always be the smallest number in the cells where shipments are being reduced, that is, cells with negative coefficients.) The crossed circles and arrows on loop II of Fig. 4-5 show that transformations have been made. Note that cells B1 and C2 have both become vacant (a degenerate situation), so a zero has been assigned to one of the vacant cells (B1) to maintain the $R + C - 1$ requirement of 5.

Because a reallocation was made, the empty cells are again evaluated for further improvement:

Cell A2:   A2–B2–B1–A1 = +6 (no change)

Cell C2:   C2–C1–B1–B2 = +6 (no change)

Cell A3:   A3–C3–C1–A1 = −4 (a possibility)

Cell B3:   B3–C3–C1–B1 = −2 (a possibility)

Cell A3 has the greatest potential for improvement. (Note that the loop evaluating cell B3 has zero units available for transfer from cell B1, so no reallocation could take place without first locating another route to B3. This would be done by relocating the zero. However, in this example cell A3 offers the best improvement, so we capitalize upon the opportunity to load cell A3.) A reallocation of 20 units to cell A3 results in the matrix shown in Fig. 4-6. Note that a zero has again been retained in one of the vacated cells (C3) to satisfy the $R + C - 1$ constraint.

Distribution plants
(Demand)

	(1) Seattle	(2) Portland	(3) San Francisco	
A	10	14	8 20	20
B	12 0	10 30	12	30
C	8 40	12 0	10	40
	40	30	20	90

Fig. 4-6 Optimal solution

Further evaluation of the cells reveals that no additional savings can be achieved. The optimal solution is shown in Fig. 4-6. The transportation cost for this arrangement is:

40 units	C to Seattle @ $8/unit = $320
30 units	B to Portland @ $10/unit = 300
20 units	A to San Francisco @ $8/unit = 160
	Total $780

Net savings over the initial allocation is $980 - $780 = $200/week.

Solved Problems

LOCATION PLANNING AND ANALYSIS

4.1   Briefly describe a logical approach to locating a new facility.

(a) Follow a systematic decision procedure involving (1) objectives, (2) criteria, (3) a model, (4) alternatives, and (5) selection.

(b) Evaluate relevant factors in a systematic manner. For example, use an

$$\boxed{\text{input}} \longrightarrow \boxed{\text{processing}} \longrightarrow \boxed{\text{output}}$$

format with sequential attention to national, regional, community, and site considerations.

(c) Determine the economic feasibility first, then follow up with consideration of less tangible factors.

4.2   Distinguish between (*a*) locational break-even analysis and (*b*) qualitative factor rating.

(*a*)   *Locational break-even analysis* is an economic comparison of total costs (FC + TVC) at an expected volume. The location having the lowest total cost can be selected.

(*b*)   *Qualitative factor analysis* yields a composite score that reflects all factors relevant to a location alternative (qualitative and quantitative). From this, the preferred location can be selected.

LOCATIONAL BREAK-EVEN ANALYSIS

4.3   A firm is considering four alternative locations for a new plant. It has attempted to study all costs at the various locations and finds that the production costs of the items shown in Table 4-7 vary from one location to another. The firm will finance the new plant from bonds bearing 10-percent interest.

Table 4-7

	A	B	C	D
Labor (per unit)	$ .75	$ 1.10	$ .80	$ .90
Plant construction cost (million $)	4.60	3.90	4.00	4.80
Materials and equipment* (per unit)	.43	.60	.40	.55
Electricity (per yr)	30,000	26,000	30,000	28,000
Water (per yr)	7,000	6,000	7,000	7,000
Transportation (per unit)	.02	.10	.10	.05
Taxes (per yr)	33,000	28,000	63,000	35,000

*This cost includes a projected depreciation expense, but no interest cost.

Determine the most suitable location (economically) for output volumes in the range of 50,000 to 130,000 units per year.

See Table 4-8.

Table 4-8

Costs	A	B	C	D
Fixed costs (per yr):				
10% of investment	$460,000	$390,000	$400,000	$480,000
Electricity	30,000	26,000	30,000	28,000
Water	7,000	6,000	7,000	7,000
Taxes	33,000	28,000	63,000	35,000
Total	$530,000	$450,000	$500,000	$550,000
Variable costs (per unit):				
Labor	$ .75	$ 1.10	$ .80	$ .90
Materials and equipment	.43	.60	.40	.55
Transportation	.02	.10	.10	.05
Total	$ 1.20	$ 1.80	$ 1.30	$ 1.50
Total costs	$530,000+ $1.20/unit	$450,000+ $1.80/unit	$500,000+ $1.30/unit	$550,000+ $1.50/unit

The points for a plant location break-even analysis chart are as follows. At zero units of output, use fixed-cost values. At 100,000 units of output,

$$A = \$530,000 + 100,000(\$1.20) = \$650,000$$
$$B = \$450,000 + 100,000(\$1.80) = \$630,000$$
$$C = \$500,000 + 100,000(\$1.30) = \$630,000$$
$$D = \$550,000 + 100,000(\$1.50) = \$700,000$$

For minimum cost, use site B for a volume of 50,000 to 100,000 units; use site C for a volume of 100,000 to 130,000 units, as shown in Fig. 4-7.

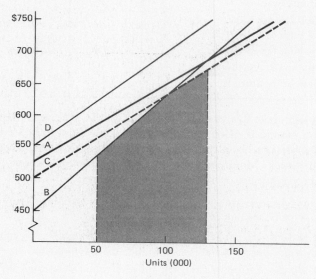

Fig. 4-7

4.4   Using the data from Prob. 4.3, assume that the market research department of the firm has estimated the market volume for the product per year over the next 10 years. For volumes (in thousands) of 50, 75, 100, and 200 units, the probabilities are .4, .2, .1, and .3, respectively. What is the most suitable location on the basis of an expected-value criterion?

Set up Table 4-9 as shown to determine the expected volume.

Table 4-9

Volume X	Probability $P(X)$	Expected Value $XP(X)$
50,000	.40	20,000
75,000	.20	15,000
100,000	.10	10,000
200,000	.30	60,000
Expected demand 105,000		

Select site C.

QUALITATIVE FACTOR RATING

4.5   The Miltex Company, which has distribution plants in Syracuse and Philadelphia, is considering adding a third assembly and distribution plant in either Athens, Baltimore, or Chapel Hill.
The company has collected the economic and noneconomic data shown in Table 4-10.

Table 4-10

Factor	Athens	Baltimore	Chapel Hill
Transportation cost/week	$ 780	$ 640	$ 560
Labor cost/week	$1,200	$1,020	$1,180
Selected criteria scores (based on a scale of 0–100 points):			
Finishing material supply	35	85	70
Maintenance facilities	60	25	30
Community attitude	50	85	70

Company management has preestablished weights for various factors, ranging from 0 to 1.0.
They include a standard of .2 for each $10 per week of economic advantage. Other weights
that are applicable are .3 on finishing material supply .1 on maintenance facilities, and .4 on
community attitudes. Maintenance also has a minimum acceptable score of 30. Develop a
qualitative factor comparison for the three locations.

(1)   The relevant factors are (a) relative economic advantage, (b) finishing material supply, (c)
       maintenance facilities, and (d) community attitude.

(2)   Factor weights for (a), (b), (c), and (d) are .2 per $10 weekly advantage, .3, .1, and .4, respectively.

(3)   Evaluation scales are all 0–100 points. Maintenance minimum = 30.

(4)   Weighted scores = Σ (score) (weight). First we must determine the relative economic advantage
       score as shown in Table 4-11.

Table 4-11

	Athens	Baltimore	Chapel Hill
Cost/week (transportation + labor)	$1,980	$1,660	$1,740
Relative economic advantage (highest cost − cost/week)	0	320	240
Economic advantage score in $10 units	0	32	24

(5)   The Baltimore site (Table 4-10), with a score of 25, does not meet the maintenance minimum (or
       threshold) of 30. Chapel Hill has the highest total points (see Table 4-12) and so would be
       recommended on the basis of this limited analysis (even though Baltimore has a lower cost structure).

Table 4-12

Factors	Athens	Baltimore	Chapel Hill
Economic	0(.2)= 0	32(.2)= 6.4	24(.2)= 4.8
Material supply	35(.3)=10.5	85(.3)=25.5	70(.3)=21.0
Maintenance	60(.1)= 6.0	25(.1)= 2.5	30(.1)= 3.0
Community	50(.4)=20.0	65(.4)=26.0	70(.4)=28.0
Total	36.5	60.4	56.8

TRANSPORTATION LINEAR PROGRAMMING

4.6 A tire-producing firm is considering locating two warehouses capable of absorbing 80 units (total) per week from the firm's plants. If unit transportation costs are as shown ($), what is the total transportation cost for an optimal allocation? Apply the northwest-corner and stepping-stone methods to Fig. 4-8.

Warehouse Site

Production Plant	SF	SL	
1	10	12	40
2	12	15	40
	30	50	80

Fig. 4-8

(a) Beginning in the NW corner of Fig. 4-8, we assign 30 units to 1 SF and the remaining 10 to 1 SL. This exhausts our supply from Plant 1.

(b) Going to row 2 we assign all 40 units to 2 SL. This completes the initial allocation. All row and column totals agree, and we have $R + C - 1 = 2 + 2 - 1 = 3$ entries.

(c) Evaluate cell 2 SF:

Path: 2 SF to 1 SF to 1 SL to 2 SL

Cost: $+12 - 10 + 12 - 15 = -1$ ($1 cost decrease)

Therefore, change 30 units, as shown in Fig. 4-9.

(d) No other changes can be made to improve the allocation. Cost of the optimal solution is:

$$40 \text{ units } 1 \text{ to SL @ } \$12 = \$480$$
$$30 \text{ units } 2 \text{ to SF @ } 12 = 360$$
$$10 \text{ units } 2 \text{ to SL @ } 15 = \underline{150}$$
$$\text{Total cost} = \$990$$

Warehouse Site

Production Plant	SF	SL	
1	10 ㉚	12 ⑩ 40	40
2	12 30	15 ㊵ 10	40
	30	50	80

Fig. 4-9

4.7 The transportation LP cost analysis for a plant-location study covering possible sites X, Y, and Z is complete except for final evaluation of cell AY in Fig. 4-10. Complete the evaluation of cell AY, make any changes justified, and compute the optimal cost.

Demand

		X		Y		Z		
		− 5		+ 2		9		
A	10							10
			10	− 6		+ 3		
B				15		3		18
		+ 9		8		− 6		
C	5				7			12
		15		15		10		40

Supply

Fig. 4-10

Evaluate cell AY as shown in Fig. 4-11.

Path: AY to BY to BZ to CZ to CX to AX to AY

Cost: $+2 - 6 + 3 - 6 + 9 - 5 = -3$ ($3 cost savings)

Therefore, change 7 units (the smallest entry in the negative cells).

Cost: $3(5) + 12(9) + 7(2) + 8(6) + 10(3) = \$215$

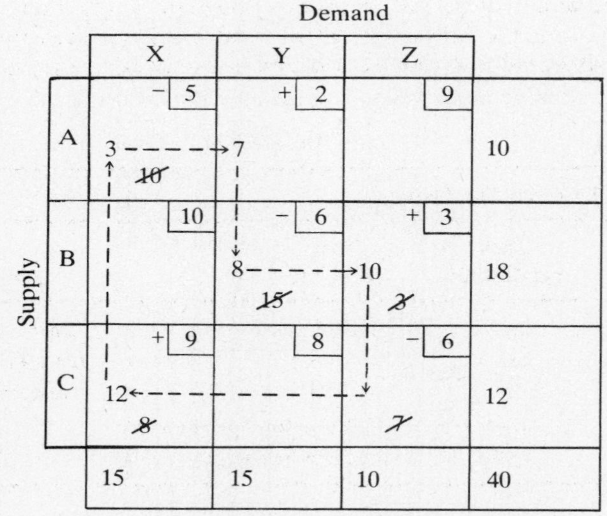

Demand

Fig. 4-11

4.8   A plant-location study yielded the matrix shown in Fig. 4-12 as one iteration in a stepping-stone solution. (*a*) Evaluate the empty cells, make whatever improvements are possible, and show the optimal solution in the matrix on the right. (*b*) Compute the optimal matrix cost.

(*a*)   Evaluation of all vacant cells is not shown. However, for cell D1 the costs are:
$$+4 - 6 + 6 - 16 + 8 - 10 = -14 \text{ (a cost savings)}$$
Therefore, change = 40 units. The solution is shown in Fig. 4-13.

(*b*) $\text{Cost} = 30(6) + 80(4) + 40(4) + 80(6) + 20(16) + 100(8) = \$2,260$

Distribution Plant

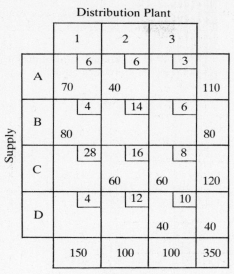

Fig. 4-12

Distribution Plant

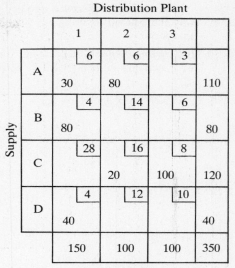

Fig. 4-13

4.9   Plastic Cabinet Supply Company (PCS) is a wholly owned subsidiary of an international conglomerate firm that has major interests in the housing industry. PCS has cabinet plants located in Boston, Seattle, and Miami. The plants produce prefabricated housing components that are delivered to other company assembly plants in Chicago, Denver, and Nashville. Demand has grown to the point where PCS can justify construction of another plant. The immediate problem is determining a location that will minimize production and transportation costs to the existing assembly plants. In order to be close to raw material supply and to service other potential markets, the alternative plant locations have been narrowed down to Omaha and Phoenix. Cost, demand, and production data on the various alternatives are shown in Tables 4-13*a* and *b*.

Table 4-13*a*

	PCS Production Data			Assemblies Demand	
Plants	Units per Month	Cost per Unit		Plant	Units per Month
Boston (B)	2,000	$7.00		Chicago (C)	6,000
Seattle (S)	6,000	7.08		Denver(D)	5,000
Miami (M)	5,000	6.90		Nashville (N)	6,000
Omaha (O)	4,000	6.90	(anticipated)		
Phoenix (P)	4,000	6.20	(anticipated)		

Table 4-13*b*   Transportation Cost, $/unit

To	Boston	Seattle	From Miami	Omaha	Phoenix
Chicago	$5.00	$7.00	$5.00	$4.00	$6.00
Denver	6.00	4.00	7.00	3.00	4.50
Nashville	5.50	7.00	3.00	5.00	5.00

Which of the two plant locations (Omaha or Phoenix) is more desirable from an economic standpoint?

It makes no difference whether supply is on the horizontal or vertical axis. The major concern is that row and column totals agree. Since the data are given with demand on the horizontal axis, let us use it that way.

(a) *Using Omaha.* Allocating via the northwest-corner method and making adjustments by the stepping-stone method, we arrive at the matrix in Fig. 4-14 (omitting any zero adjustments).

	Boston	Seattle	Miami	Omaha	Demand
Chicago	$5.00 2,000	$7.00	$5.00	$4.00 4,000	6,000
Denver	6.00	4.00 5,000	7.00	3.00	5,000
Nashville	5.50	7.00 1,000	3.00 5,000	5.00	6,000
Supply	2,000	6,000	5,000	4,000	17,000

Fig. 4-14

Transportation cost calculation:

$$2,000 \times 5.00 = \$10,000$$
$$4,000 \times 4.00 = 16,000$$
$$5,000 \times 4.00 = 20,000$$
$$1,000 \times 7.00 = 7,000$$
$$5,000 \times 3.00 = \underline{15,000}$$
$$\$68,000 \longrightarrow \$68,000$$

Add production costs (Omaha): $6.90/unit $\times$ 4,000 = $\underline{27,600}$

$$\$95,600$$

(b) *Using Phoenix.* Figure 4-15 gives the information for Phoenix.

	Boston	Seattle	Miami	Phoenix	Demand
Chicago	$5.00 2,000	$7.00 1,000	$5.00	$6.00 3,000	6,000
Denver	6.00	4.00 5,000	7.00	4.50	5,000
Nashville	5.50	7.00	3.00 5,000	5.00 1,000	6,000
Supply	2,000	6,000	5,000	4,000	17,000

Fig. 4-15

Cost calculation:

$$2,000 \times 5.00 = \$10,000$$
$$1,000 \times 7.00 = 7,000$$
$$3,000 \times 6.00 = 18,000$$
$$5,000 \times 4.00 = 20,000$$
$$5,000 \times 3.00 = 15,000$$
$$1,000 \times 5.00 = \underline{5,000}$$
$$\$75,000 \longrightarrow \$75,000$$

Add production costs (Phoenix): \$6.20/unit $\times$ 4,000 = $\underline{24,800}$
$$\$99,800$$

Omaha is the best choice since it shows the least cost per month.

DUMMY VARIABLE, DEGENERATE SOLUTION, AND REQUIRED SHIFTING ZEROS

4.10 A transportation LP problem has the rim requirements (supply and demand) and cost coefficients shown in Fig. 4-16. Use the northwest-corner and stepping-stone methods to obtain an optimal solution.

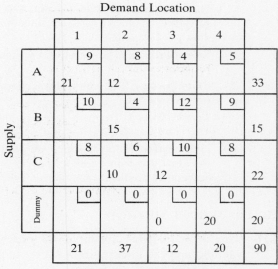

Fig. 4-16

Fig. 4-17   Initial Allocation

(*a*) First note that the demand exceeds the supply, so add a dummy supply and assign zero transportation costs to it as shown in Fig. 4-17.

(*b*) Allocate the units via northwest corner beginning with 21 units in cell A1, 12 in A2, etc.

(*c*) Check the $R + C - 1$ constraint; we should have $4 + 4 - 1 = 7$ entries. Because we have only 6 (a *degenerate* situation), assign a zero to one of the cells that could normally have an allocation under the northwest-corner method, such as D3.

(*d*) *First iteration*

B1: $+10 - 9 + 8 - 4 = +5$	B3: $+12 - 10 + 6 - 4 = +4$
C1: $+8 - 9 + 8 - 6 = +1$	A4: $+5 - 0 + 0 - 10 + 6 - 8 = -7$
D1: $+0 - 9 + 8 - 6 + 10 - 0 = +3$	B4: $+9 - 0 + 0 - 10 + 6 - 4 = +1$
D2: $+0 - 6 + 10 - 0 = +4$	C4: $+8 - 0 + 0 - 10 = -2$
A3: $+4 - 10 + 6 - 8 = -8$ (most negative)	

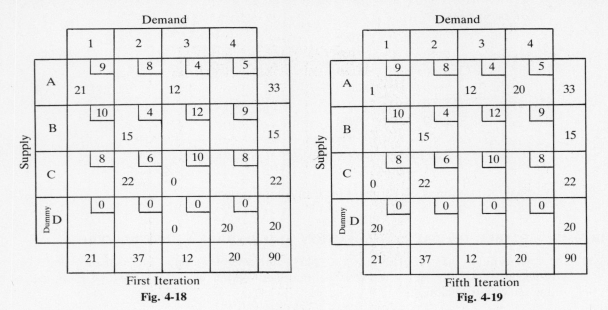

First Iteration
Fig. 4-18

Fifth Iteration
Fig. 4-19

Therefore, transfer 12 units to A3. *Note:* When 12 units are transferred to A3, both cells A2 and C3 go vacant (another *degenerate* situation). Add a zero to either one of those two cells, e.g., C3 as shown in Fig. 4-18.

(e) *Second iteration.* The path to C1 is most negative (-7). Therefore transfer a zero into C1, and C3 becomes vacant.

(f) *Third iteration.* The path to D1 is most negative (-5). Therefore, transfer a zero into D1, and D3 becomes vacant.

(g) *Fourth iteration.* The path to A4 on the loop A4 $-$ D4 $-$ D1 $-$ A1 is the only negative path (-4). Therefore transfer 20 units into A4, and D4 becomes vacant.

(h) *Fifth iteration.* All evaluations are positive, therefore the solution shown in Fig. 14-19 is optimal. Note that it was necessary to transfer some zeros and that one of the zeros (put in to overcome the degeneracy problem) eventually left the solution.

MINIMUM-COST METHOD

4.11 Use the data from Example 4.3 except make the initial allocation via the minimum-cost method and the final solution via the stepping-stone method.

The minimum-cost method is simple: the lowest-cost cell is located, and as many units as possible are assigned to it. The next-lowest-cost cell is then located and again filled up. This continues until all supply and demand conditions (that is, rim conditions) are satisfied. In the case of two boxes having equally low costs, the best choice is to fill the one that can absorb the most units. Then fill the other if possible. See Fig. 4-20.

(a) Cells C1 and A3 both have equally low costs of $8 per unit. First put 40 units into C1 to meet its supply and demand conditions of 40 and 40. Then fill A3 with 20 units to meet its requirements of 20 and 20.

(b) The next-lowest transportation cost is $10 per unit, which occurs in cells A1, B2, and C3. However, the supply conditions of rows A and C have already been satisfied (exhausted), so only B2 needs to be considered. Put 30 units in B2 to meet its rim conditions.

(c) The initial solution appears to be correct, but the normal checks of row and column totals must be made.

Row A   20 = 20, OK   Col. 1   40 = 40, OK
Row B   30 = 30, OK   Col. 2   30 = 30, OK
Row C   40 = 40, OK   Col. 3   20 = 20, OK

Distribution plants (Demand)

Production plants (Supply)	(1) Seattle	(2) Portland	(3) San Francisco	
A	10	14	8 (20)	20
B	12 0	10 (30)	12	30
C	8 (40)	12	10 0	40
	40	30	20	

Fig. 4-20

(*d*) The initial solution is now complete. [It is, however, degenerate in that (no. rows) + (no. cols.) − 1 ≠ (no. entries); that is, $3 + 3 - 1 \neq 3$. Zeros may be assigned to two empty cells, say B1 and C3, so that the constraint is satisfied.]

Note that the initial solution happened to be the same as the final, optimal solution as arrived at in Example 4.3 via the stepping-stone method. This will not always be the case, although the initial solution is likely to be better than the initial solution as arrived at via the northwest-corner method. Since the optimal solution has already been achieved, no additional stepping-stone-method calculations will be carried out.

VOGEL'S APPROXIMATION METHOD (VAM)

4.12 Given the following demand-supply matrix (Fig. 4-21), use VAM for the initial allocation and, if necessary, the stepping-stone method for the final solution.

Demand

Supply	W	X	Y	Z	
A	6	8	2	7	12
B	10	9	9	6	35
C	2	4	12	12	23
	20	10	18	22	70

Fig. 4-21

Steps for Vogel's Approximation Method (VAM)

1. Calculate the difference between the two smallest costs in each row and each column. (Write the resulting numbers at the right side/bottom of each row and column.)
2. Select the row or column with the largest cost difference, and allocate as many units as possible to the lowest-cost cell. (In the event of a tie, use the row or column that has the lowest-cost cell.)
3. Eliminate from further consideration (or cross out with x's) the row or column that has been satisfied.
4. Using the reduced matrix, repeat steps 1–3 until all of the supply has been allocated to meet the demand.

First VAM iteration (*Fig. 4-22*)

(*a*) The differences are shown as Δ's.

(*b*) The largest cost difference is in Column Y. Allocate 12 units (maximum available) to cell AY.

(*c*) Eliminate row A and form a new matrix. (*Note*: The Y-column requirements are now 18 − 12 = 6.)

Demand

Supply	W	X	Y	Z		Δ row
A	[6]	[8]	[2] 12	[7]	12	4
B	[10]	[9]	[9]	[6]	35	3
C	[2]	[4]	[12]	[12]	23	2
	20	10	18	22	70 / 70	
Δ col.	4	4	7	1		

Fig. 4-22

Second VAM iteration (*Fig. 4-23*)

(*a*) The differences are as shown.

(*b*) The largest cost difference is in column W. Allocate 20 units (maximum possible) to cell CW.

(*c*) Eliminate column W and form a new matrix.

Demand

Supply	W	X	Y	Z		Δ row
B	[10]	[9]	[9]	[6]	35	3
C	[2] 20	[4]	[12]	[12]	23	2
	20	10	6	22		
Δ col.	8	5	3	6		

Fig. 4-23

Third VAM iteration (*Fig. 4-24*)

(*a*) The differences are as shown.

(*b*) The largest cost difference is in Row C. Allocate 3 units (maximum available) to cell CX.

(*c*) Eliminate row C and form a new matrix.

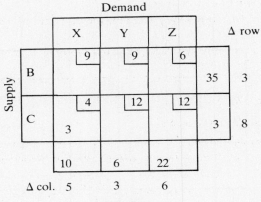

Supply \ Demand	X	Y	Z		Δ row
B	[9]	[9]	[6]	35	3
C	[4] 3	[12]	[12]	3	8
	10	6	22		
Δ col.	5	3	6		

Fig. 4-24

Supply \ Demand	X	Y	Z	
B	[9] 7	[9] 6	[6] 22	35
	7	6	22	

Fig. 4-25

Supply \ Demand	W	X	Y	Z	
A	[6]	[8]	[2] 12	[7]	12
B	[10]	[9] 7	[9] 6	[6] 22	35
C	[2] 20	[4] 3	[12]	[12]	23
	20	10	18	22	70

Fig. 4-26

Fourth VAM iteration (*Fig. 4-25*)

The remaining values are determined by the demand requirements. The resultant VAM allocation is as follows and as shown in Fig. 4-26.

AW: $+6-2+9-9+4-2=6$

BW: $+10-9+4-2=3$

AX: $+8-2+9-9=6$

CY: $+12-4+9-9=8$

AZ: $+7-6+9-2=8$

CZ: $+12-4+9-6=11$

All evaluations are positive, therefore, the solution shown in Fig. 4-26 is optimal.

4.13 Solve the previous problem using a condensed-solution format that utilizes a new set of difference (or penalty-cost, PC) rows and columns for each iteration.

The solution procedure is the same. We simply add a new penalty-cost row and column for each iteration, and use that outermost row or column as shown in Fig. 4-27. The largest cost difference for each iteration is circled for identification only.

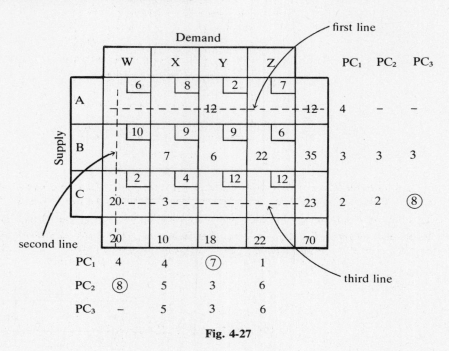

Fig. 4-27

4.14 Use the data from Example 4.3, except make the initial allocation via VAM. If necessary, use the stepping-stone method for the final solution.

(*a*) The differences between the two lowest costs in each row and column each equal 2 (an unusual situation), as shown in Fig. 4-28.

	Demand			
	1	2	3	Row Difference
A	10	14	8	20 2
B	12	10	12	30 2
C	8	12	10	40 2
	40	30	20	90
Column Difference	2	2	2	

Fig. 4-28

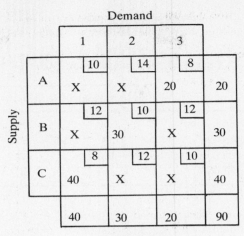

Fig. 4-29

(b) Given the tied situation, pick rows A and C, which have the lowest-cost cells (A3 and C1). Allocate 20 units to A3, and 40 units to C1 (since both have $8 costs) as shown in Fig. 4-29

(c) Cross out the remaining cells in the rows (A and C) and columns (1 and 3) that have been satisfied.

(d) Repeat until all supply has been allocated. The only remaining allocation is 30 units to B2. This yields the same optimal solution as Example 4.3, so the solution is complete.

Supplementary Problems

4.15 Tractorboy Products Company is evaluating three different cities for a new plant designed to produce lawn mowers that will sell for $145 each. The economic portion of a plant-location study shows the cost and market data in Tables 4-14a and b.

Table 4-14a

Cost Data	City A	City B	City C
Fixed costs/yr	$300,000	$200,000	$75,000
Variable costs/unit	30	45	70

Table 4-14b

Market Data	
Volume X	$P(X)$
4,500	.10
5,500	.30
6,500	.60

(a) On the basis of maximizing an economic expected value, graph the plant-location cost curve using appropriate scales. (b) Which city should be selected on the basis of the given volume estimate? (Use your graph.) (c) What is the break-even volume for the city selected?

Ans.   (a) Volume range 0–10,000; Dollar range $0–$800,000 (b) City B (c) 2,000 units

4.16 Coombes Container Co. is considering three potential locations for a new aluminum can plant, and management has assigned the scores shown in Table 4-15 to the relevant factors on a 0–100 basis (100 is best).

Table 4-15   Score of Relevant Factor for Plant Location

	Hong Kong	Manila	Honolulu
Material supply	50	90	80
Labor cost	90	80	40
Regulations	100	60	30
Distribution	30	80	70

The relevant factors have been assigned the following weights: material supply = .3, labor cost = .3, regulations = .2, distribution = .2. Using a qualitative factor-rating analysis, which location would be prefered?   *Ans.*   Manila (with 79 points)

4.17 A firm producing appliances at plants #1 and #2 is considering locating distribution centers at San Francisco and New York. If transportation costs are as shown (in $) in Fig. 4-30, what is the total transportation cost for an optimal allocation?   *Ans.* $6,360

	SF	NY	
#1	40	50	60
#2	50	62	60
	30	90	

Fig. 4-30

4.18 A materials manager is considering locating warehouses in Knoxville and Jersey City capable of absorbing 30 and 60 units per day, respectively, from the firm's two plants, each of which can produce 45 units per day. Unit transportation costs ($) are shown in Table 4-16.

Table 4-16

	To Knoxville	To Jersey City
From Plant #1	$ 9	$11
From Plant #2	11	14

(*a*) Show the northwest-corner allocation in an initial matrix. (*b*) Show the optimal allocation in a final matrix. (*c*) Compute the optimal transportation cost.
Ans.   (*a*) #1K = 30, #1JC = 15, #2JC = 45 (*b*) Allocations are #1JC = 45, #2K = 30, #2JC = 15 (*c*) $1035/day

4.19 A building-materials firm with production plants in Reno, Spokane, and Tacoma ships freight cartons to three distribution centers with costs per carton as shown in Table 4-17.

Table 4-17   Cost per Carton ($00) to Ship to Three Centers

From:	Center 1 (30-carton monthly demand)	Center 2 (30-carton monthly demand)	Center 3 (35-carton monthly demand)
Reno (25-carton monthly productive capacity)	$3	$3	$2
Spokane (40-carton monthly productive capacity)	4	2	3
Tacoma (30-carton monthly productive capacity)	3	2	3

Use the northwest-corner and stepping-stone methods to determine the optimal allocation to minimize costs. Find the optimal cost.   *Ans.* $23,000

4.20   A large copper producer has refineries in Magna, Utah; Yuma, Arizona; and Grants, New Mexico—all of which receive ore from mines identified as MX-1, MX-2, MX-3, and MX-4—located in the Four Corners Area. The mine supply and mill capacities (units per day) and shipping cost (dollars per unit-load) data are shown in Table 4-18.

Table 4-18

	Refineries			Supply
	Magna	Yuma	Grants	
MX-1	3	5	5	400
MX-2	5	7	8	500
MX-3	2	9	5	200
MX-4	10	7	3	700
Capacity	500	500	800	1,800 units/day

The vice-president of operations has asked you to analyze the transportation costs and determine an optimal distribution.   *Ans.*   More than one solution may be optimal at a transportation cost = $7,400.

4.21   Suppose that in Prob. 4.20 the variable production costs (in dollars per unit-load) for mines MX-1, MX-2, MX-3, and MX-4 are $2, $1, $3, and $1, respectively. What is the optimal distribution, taking production as well as distribution costs into account?
Ans.   More than one solution may be optimal at a production and transportation cost equal to $10,000.

4.22   Dayfresh Bakery has plants at A, B, and C that have capacities of 20, 30, and 40 truckloads of bread per day, respectively. Production costs are the same at each plant, but the bread must be trucked to distribution centers at X, Y, and Z, and trucking costs per load (in dollars) vary as shown in Fig. 4-31. The distribution centers currently absorb most of the capacity, with X, Y, and Z taking 30, 30, and 20 loads per day, respectively. Use the distribution method of linear programming, to (*a*) show the optimal allocation scheme, and (*b*) find the cost of the optimal distribution plan.
Ans.   (*a*) Dummy demand is required to supply 10 units. (*b*) $700

Distribution center

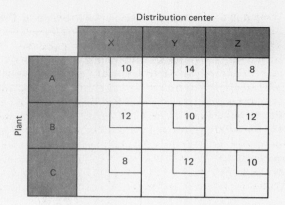

Fig. 4-31

4.23 Comfort Zone Furniture has plants in Boston, Dallas, and Seattle, which ship to four demand locations, with transportation costs as shown in Fig. 4-32. Use the northwest-corner and stepping-stone methods to determine the optimal transportation cost. Show your initial and final solutions.

    Ans.   The northwest-corner allocation is shown in Fig. 4-32. The final solution is not shown in Fig. 4-33, but has an optimal cost of $610.

Initial Matrix
Demand Location

		1	2	3	4	
Boston		3	5	7	4	50
		20	30			
Dallas		6	8	5	2	50
			30	20		
Seattle		1	9	7	3	50
				10	40	
		20	60	30	40	150

Fig.4-32

Final Matrix
Demand Location

		1	2	3	4	
Boston		3	5	7	4	50
Dallas		6	8	5	2	50
Seattle		1	9	7	3	50
		20	60	30	40	150

Fig. 4-33

4.24 Use Vogel's Approximation Method (VAM) and the stepping-stone method to solve Prob. 4.23.
    Ans.   The optimal solution (after VAM and stepping-stone) is as shown in Fig. 4-34.

	1	2	3	4
Boston		50		
Dallas			30	20
Seattle	20	10		20

Fig. 4-34

4.25 Complete the second, third, fourth, and fifth iteration of Prob. 4.10.
    Ans.   Optimal solution is the last matrix shown.

4.26   A Forest Service ranger has the responsibility for extinguishing fires in a large national forest in Washington State. Each time equipment is air-lifted into a remote area to fight a forest fire, the cost averages $22,000. The ranger is considering locating some equipment storage bunkers in the wilderness area and must determine whether they are economically feasible, and if so, how large an area to serve by each bunker. The number of fires per season averages one per 400 square miles, and the timber loss from each fire averages $25,000. (*a*) An equipment storage bunker is being considered that would eliminate air lifts and reduce timber losses within a 40-mile radius to 60 percent. Would its cost of $310,000 per season be justified?   (*b*) For an additional $200,000, the equipment bunker could service an additional 10-mile radius. Air lifts in the extended service area would also be eliminated, but losses in the outer service ring would be held down to only 80 percent. Is the additional investment justified?

   Ans.   (*a*) The service area of 5,027 square miles averages 12.57 fires at an existing cost of $590,790. The cost with bunkers = $498,550. Therefore, yes. (*b*) The existing cost of serving additional area = $332,290. The cost with bunkers = $341,400. Therefore, the additional cost is not justified.

Chapter 5

Facility Design, Capacity, and Layout

DESIGN AND SYSTEM CAPACITY

Design and capacity decisions link the location and layout considerations, as depicted in Fig. 5-1. The facility design must *fit* the location, and the location in turn affects capacity. Capacities should be stated in physical units, service times, or work-center hours rather than in dollar volume of sales.

The *design capacity* of a facility is the engineered rate of output of standardized products under normal operating conditions. It stems from a knowledge of consumer demand and from having a policy for meeting that demand. Firms do not necessarily plan to satisfy all the demand. However, they may adjust to seasonal variations in the short run and economic trends over the long run.

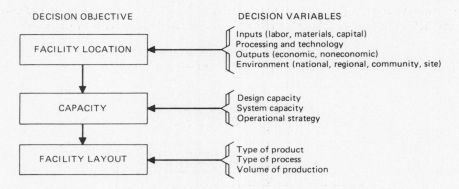

Fig. 5-1 Variables for location, capacity, and layout decisions

Facility design is often contracted to engineering consultants or architects. In addition to work centers, the facility will probably require water, electricity, heating and ventilation, restrooms, a cafeteria, stockrooms, loading docks, computer stations, and a multitude of service facilities. Designers work within specified cost budgets to provide the design capacity required in an efficient (and, it is hoped, attractive) work environment.

Example 5.1 A bank operations manager estimates the peak hourly demand at a planned drive-up facility as shown. She is considering two options. What capacity is required to (*a*) meet 90 percent of the estimated peak hourly demand, and (*b*) accommodate 120 percent of the estimated average demand plus a 25 percent allowance for growth? Assume that each carport can serve 30 cars per hour.

No. of Cars	Chance, %	Cumulative %
$0 < 50$	5	5
$50 < 100$	55	60
$100 < 150$	30	90
$150 < 200$	10	100

(*a*) From the cumulative percent column, 90 percent of the estimated demand is less than 150 cars. Therefore

$$\frac{150 \text{ cars/hr}}{30 \text{ cars/hr-carport}} = 5 \text{ carports}$$

(b)

Number of Cars		Probability	
Interval	Midpoint X	$P(X)$	$X \cdot P(X)$
$0 < 50$	25	.05	1.25
$50 < 100$	75	.55	41.25
$100 < 150$	125	.30	37.50
$150 < 200$	175	.10	17.50
			97.50

Expected value of demand $= E(X) = \Sigma[X \cdot P(X)] = 97.5$ cars

Base-level capacity $= 120\%$ $(97.5) = 117$ cars

Add for 25 percent allowance: $117 + .25\ (117) = 146.25$ cars

Therefore, $\dfrac{146.25\ \text{cars/hr}}{30\ \text{cars/hr-carport}} = 4.87 \cong 5$ carports

It appears that 5 carports will satisfy both criteria.

System capacity is the maximum output of a specific product or product mix that the system of workers and machines is capable of producing as an integrated whole. Figure 5-2 illustrates the relationship between design capacity, system capacity, and actual output. The *system efficiency* (SE) is a measure of the actual output of goods or services as a percentage of system capacity.

$$\text{SE} = \frac{\text{actual output}}{\text{system capacity}} \qquad\qquad (5.1)$$

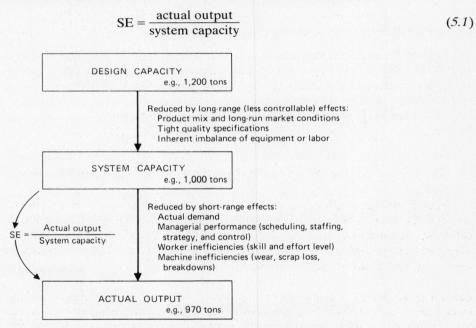

Fig. 5-2   Relationship between capacities and output

Example 5.2 A large title insurance company processes all titles sequentially through four centers (A, B, C, D), which handle the search and recording activities. The individual work center capacities and actual average output in titles processed per day are as shown. Find (a) the system capacity, and (b) the system efficiency.

(a)   System capacity = capacity of most limited component in the line = 22 titles/day

(b) $\text{SE} = \dfrac{\text{actual output}}{\text{system capacity}} = \dfrac{18}{22} = .82 = 82\%$

COMPUTATION OF EQUIPMENT REQUIREMENTS

If the actual output is specified (e.g., by design), the amount or size of equipment required to deliver that output can often best be determined by working backward to allow for system losses and inefficiencies.

Example 5.3 An automobile equipment supplier wishes to install a sufficient number of ovens to produce 400,000 good castings per year. The baking operation takes 2.0 minutes per casting, but the oven output is typically about 6 percent defective. How many ovens will be required if each one is available for 1800 hours (of capacity) per year?

$$\text{Required system capacity} = \frac{\text{actual (good) output}}{\text{SE}}$$

$$= \frac{400,000}{.94} = 425,532 \text{ units/yr}$$

Converting to units/hr, $\dfrac{425,532 \text{ units/yr}}{1,800 \text{ hrs/yr}} = 236 \text{ units/hr}$

$$\text{Individual oven capacity} = \frac{60 \text{ min/hr}}{2.0 \text{ oven-min/unit}} = 30 \text{ units/oven-hr}$$

$$\text{Number of ovens required} = \frac{236 \text{ units/hr}}{30 \text{ units/oven-hr}} = 7.9 \text{ (8) ovens}$$

LAYOUT OBJECTIVES AND DETERMINANTS

Layout decisions are concerned with the arrangement of production, support, customer service, and other facilities. Layouts can be costly investments, but they affect materials handling, capital equipment utilization, inventory storage levels, worker productivity, and even group communications and employee morale. Any significant change in operations (e.g., new product, new process, change in product mix) may warrant a revision of an existing layout. The type of layout is largely determined by the:

(1) Type of product (i.e., whether a good or service, product design, and quality standards)

(2) Type of production process (i.e., technology, type of materials or service)

(3) Volume of production (i.e., high-volume continuous versus low-volume, intermittent)

A good layout will enable materials, people, and information to flow in a safe and efficient manner.

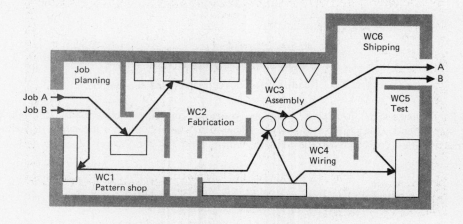

Fig. 5-3 Process layout for sign production

TYPES OF LAYOUTS

The basic types of layouts are (1) process (functional) layouts, (2) product (line) layouts, and (3) fixed-position layouts; there are many combinations of these. Flexible production systems are line layouts that use microprocessors and robots to gain some of the advantages of functional layouts.

Process layouts group the people and equipment performing similar functions, such as x-raying, typing, or electroplating. They lend themselves to low volumes of customized jobs and use a variety of general-purpose equipment. Work flow is typically intermittent and guided by individual work orders. Figure 5-3 illustrates a process layout.

Process layouts tend to rely heavily on the planning and professional skills of employees at all levels. Table 5-1 lists some advantages and disadvantages of process layouts.

Table 5-1   Advantages and Disadvantages of Process (Functional) Layouts

Advantages	Disadvantages
1. Flexible systems for custom work	1. Costly materials handling
2. Less costly general-purpose equipment	2. High-cost skilled labor
3. Less vulnerability from breakdowns	3. Higher supervision cost per employee
4. Enhances job satisfaction (more diversity and challenge)	4. Low equipment utilization
	5. More complex production control (for instance, scheduling, inventory control)

Product layouts group the workers and equipment according to the sequence of operations performed on the product or customer. They lend themselves to the use of (assembly line) conveyors and automated equipment to produce large volumes of relatively few items (for instance, refrigerators and freezers). Work flow is typically continuous and guided by standardized instructions.

Product layouts are used in both discrete manufacturing and in process industry plants. It is important to distinguish process layouts from process industries. Process industries add value by mixing, separating, forming, or combining inputs. For example, oil, chemical, and food processing plants are process-industry facilities that usually have product (line) layouts.

Products such as cars and tractors, which offer consumers a wide range of options, must be manufactured according to specific instructions. Manufacturers are able to produce these customized products at assembly-line volumes by using flexible production systems. Flexible systems are

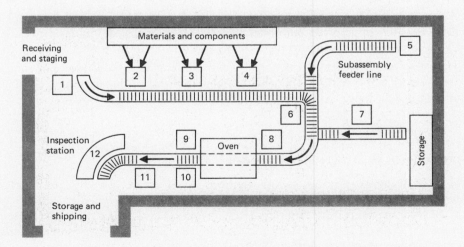

Fig. 5-4   Product layout for electronic toy manufacturing

enhanced line layouts that produce to order in lot sizes as small as one. Production is guided by individualized instructions often made possible by computer-assisted manufacturing (CAM) systems.

Traditional product layouts are often highly structured (i.e., hard automation), leaving workers with mundane and repetitive tasks. Flexible production systems relegate the more repetitive tasks to numerically controlled machines and robots. This sometimes means fewer workers; however, they are left with more challenging planning and control tasks. Figure 5-4 shows a typical product layout.

Product layouts are more heavily structured from a design standpoint, and require little innovation or decision skills from the employees operating on the line. Table 5-2 describes several advantages and disadvantages of product layouts.

Table 5-2 Advantages and Disadvantages of Product (Line) Layouts

Advantages	Disadvantages
1. High utilization of people and equipment	1. Inflexible system (unless designed for flexibility)
2. Low materials-handling cost	2. High-cost specialized equipment
3. Low-cost unskilled labor	3. Interdependent operations
4. Less work-in-process inventory	4. Dull, monotonous jobs (unless products are customized or system is flexible)
5. Simplified production control	

Fixed-position layouts are arrangements where labor, materials, and equipment are brought to the work site. They apply to construction, farming, mining, and other activities that must be completed in a particular place. Project activities can take advantage of network techniques (CPM and PERT) for work planning and control.

LAYOUT SELECTION CONSIDERATIONS

Facility layouts must integrate numerous interdependent variables (materials-handling equipment, work-center locations, storage space, toolrooms, washrooms, offices), and no single technique will yield an optimal layout. Good layouts minimize nonproductive costs such as materials handling and storage, while maximizing worker effectiveness. Layout analysis has focused primarily upon these two concerns:

(1) *Process Layouts* attempt to minimize materials-handling costs by arranging departmental sizes and locations according to the volume and flow rate of products.

(2) *Product Layouts* attempt to maximize worker effectiveness by grouping sequential work activities into work stations that yield a high utilization of labor and equipment with a minimum of idle time.

PROCESS (FUNCTIONAL) LAYOUT METHODS

The objective of many process layout methods is to locate work centers that have high interaction near to each other, resulting in a minimum flow of material (or personnel) to nonadjacent work centers. Several methods of designing process layouts focus on the amount of material moved and the distance it is moved. Other methods incorporate less quantitative goals by utilizing a *nearness* criteria. Four methods of layout design illustrated below are (1) simple graphic approach, (2) operations sequence analysis, (3) load-distance analysis, and (4) systematic layout planning.

A *simple graphic approach* uses a trial-and-error process which attempts to minimize nonadjacent flows by centrally locating the active departments. A travel chart is first developed to show the number of moves made between departments and identify the active departments. Then a trial solution is developed using circles to depict work centers and connecting lines to represent the loads transported per time period. Departments next to each other or diagonally across from each other are regarded as adjacent.

Example 5.4 Valley Electronics has leased a facility with six production areas as shown in the outline below (Fig. 5-5). They propose to locate six departments (A, B, C, D, E, F), which have the number of moves per day between departments as shown in the accompanying travel chart, Table 5-3. Develop a layout of the six departments which minimizes the nonadjacent flows.

1	2	3
4	5	6

Fig. 5-5 Facility outline

Table 5-3   Travel Chart

		Number of Moves to					
		A	B	C	D	E	F
From	A	—	5	10	—	3	2
	B	—	—	—	12	—	—
	C	10	4	—	8	—	—
	D	—	—	16	—	—	—
	E	—	—	7	—	—	—
	F	—	—	8	—	—	—

First, determine which departments have the most frequent links with other departments. This can be done by totaling the *number of entries* in each row and column. Thus, A has four row entries (B, C, E, and F) and one column entry, for a total of five links.

Department	A	B	C	D	E	F
Number of links	5	3	7	3	2	2

Second, try to locate the most active departments in central positions. Thus, we place departments A and C in locations 2 and 5.

Third, use trial and error to locate the other departments so that nonadjacent flows will be minimized.

Fourth, if all nonadjacent flows are eliminated, the solution is complete (as shown in Fig. 5-6). If nonadjacent flows still exist, try to minimize the *number of units* flowing to nonadjacent areas. In this instance you would weight the number of flows by the number of distance units, as discussed next.

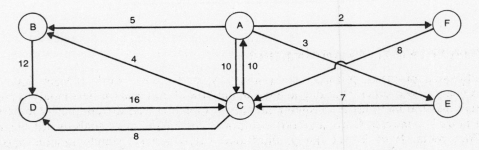

Fig. 5-6

Operations sequence analysis is a refinement over the simple graphic approach by using a weighted load-distance measure. Adjacent departments are assigned a distance factor of 1, and others take on successively higher integer values, depending upon how many rows or columns they are from each other. Departments are then shifted in an effort to minimize the sum of the load times the distance for the entire matrix. The selection of which departments to shift is done by visual inspection.

Load-distance analysis evaluates alternative layouts on the basis of the sum of actual distance (feet) times the load (units) for each alternative. A variation of this is to compute the materials-handling cost directly by multiplying the number of loads by the materials-handling cost per load. The layout with the lowest load times distance total or load times cost total is the best choice. Costs are usually a linear function of distance, unless pickup and unload costs are considered separately.

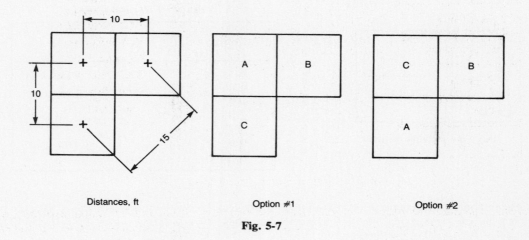

Distances, ft   Option #1   Option #2

Fig. 5-7

Example 5.5 A facility that will be used to produce a single product has three departments (A, B, C) that must be housed in the configuration shown in Fig. 5-7. The interdepartmental workload flows and travel distances between work centers are given in Table 5-4 below. In addition, two trial-and-error optional layouts are shown. Evaluate the two layouts on a load-distance basis and identify the preferred layout. Assume that the cost to transport this product is $1 per load-foot.

Table 5-4   Interdepartmental Workload per Week

	To: A	B	C
From: A	—	30	25
B	20	—	40
C	15	50	—

	Option #1 (load)(distance)	Option #2 (load)(distance)
No. Loads per Week (both directions)		
A to B and B to A = 30 + 20 = 50	(50)(10) = 500	(50)(14) = 700
A to C and C to A = 25 + 15 = 40	(40)(10) = 400	(40)(10) = 400
B to C and C to B = 40 + 50 = 90	(90)(14) = 1,260	(90)(10) = 900
	Total 2,160	= 2,000

At $1 per load-foot option #2 would be preferred at a total cost of $2,000. However, 3 factorial (!) or $3 \cdot 2 \cdot 1 = 6$, options are possible, and a different arrangement may be less costly.

Systematic layout planning is a generalized approach to layout, developed by Richard Muther, that utilizes a grid matrix to display ratings of the relative importance of the distance between departments. The importance ratings are indicated by code letters (a, e, i, o, u, and x) in the matrix, and range from absolutely necessary (a) to undesirable (x). A reason code (usually a number) can also be assigned. For example, reason 1 might be the use of common personnel, 2 might be noise isolation, and 3 might be safety. Figure 5-8 illustrates the systematic layout planning (SLP) approach as applied to the sign production (process) layout of Fig. 5-3.

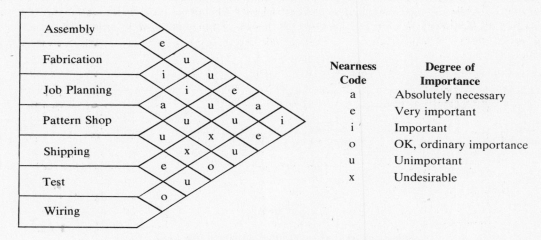

Nearness Code	Degree of Importance
a	Absolutely necessary
e	Very important
i	Important
o	OK, ordinary importance
u	Unimportant
x	Undesirable

Fig. 5-8   Nearness codes for process layout of Fig. 5-3

Several *computerized approaches* are available for developing and analyzing process layouts. Some computer systems such as the Apple Lisa have very flexible, easy-to-use drawing and layout programs. The analytical (software) packages are primarily heuristic, step-by-step (iterative) methods. The ALDEP (automated layout design programs) and CORELAP (computerized relationship layout planning) programs attempt to maximize a nearness rating within the facility dimension constraints. The CRAFT (computerized relative allocation of facilities technique) program attempts to minimize materials-handling costs by calculating costs, exchanging departments, and calculating more costs until a good solution is obtained. None of the methods guarantees optimality.

LINE BALANCING IN PRODUCT LAYOUTS

Line balancing is the apportionment of sequential work activities into work stations in order to gain a high utilization of labor and equipment and therefore minimize idle time. Compatible work activities are combined into approximately equal time groupings that do not violate precedence relationships. The length of work (or operating) time that a component is available at each work station is the cycle time, CT.

$$CT = \frac{\text{available time/period}}{\text{output units required/period}} = \frac{AT}{\text{output}} \tag{5.2}$$

From Equation 5.2, we can see that CT is also the time interval at which completed products leave the production line. If the time required at any station exceeds that which is available to one worker, additional workers have to be added to the station.

The theoretical (ideal) number of workers needed on the assembly line is the product of the time it takes one worker to complete one unit and the number of output units required, divided by the available time.

$$\text{Theoretical minimum} \atop \text{number of workers} = \frac{(\text{worker time/unit})(\text{output units/period})}{\text{available time/period}}$$

$$= \frac{\Sigma t}{\text{CT}} \tag{5.3}$$

where Σt is the sum of the actual worker time required to complete one unit.

Example 5.6 The precedence diagram (Fig. 5-9) for assembly activities A through G is shown below, with the element time requirements shown in minutes. The line operates 7 hours per day, and an output of 600 units per day is desired. Compute (*a*) the cycle time, and (*b*) the theoretical minimum number of workers.

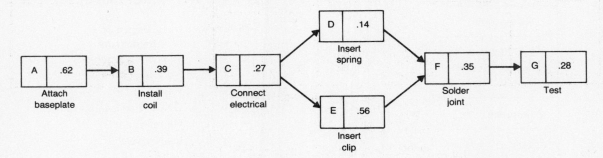

Fig. 5-9

$$\text{CT} = \frac{\text{available time/period}}{\text{output units reqd/period}} = \frac{(7 \text{ hrs/day})(60 \text{ min/hr})}{600 \text{ units/day}} = \frac{420}{600} = .70 \text{ min/unit}$$

$$\text{Theoretical minimum} = \frac{\Sigma t}{\text{CT}}$$

where
$$\Sigma t = .62 + .39 + .27 + .14 + .56 + .35 + .28 = 2.61$$

$$\text{Theoretical minimum} = \frac{2.61}{.70} = 3.73 \text{ workers}$$

(*Note*: This is theoretical—not actual.)

The procedure for analyzing line balancing problems involves (*a*) determining the number of stations and time available at each station, (*b*) grouping the individual tasks into amounts of work at each station, and (*c*) evaluating the efficiency of the grouping. An efficient balance will minimize the amount of idle time. The balance efficiency (Eff_B) can be computed in either of two ways:

$$\text{Eff}_B = \frac{\text{output of task times}}{\text{input of station times}} = \frac{\Sigma t}{\text{CT}(n)} \tag{5.4}$$

$$\text{Eff}_B = \frac{\text{theoretical minimum number of workers}}{\text{actual number of workers}} \tag{5.5}$$

where CT is the cycle time per station and n is the number of stations. The grouping of tasks is done heuristically with the aid of a precedence diagram. Designate work zones on the precedence diagram and move appropriate activities into preceding zones (i.e., to the left) until the cycle time is as fully used as possible.

Example 5.7 Using the data and precedence diagram from Example 5.6, (*a*) group the assembly-line tasks into an appropriate number of work stations, and (*b*) compute the balance efficiency. (*Note*: CT = .70 minute, $\Sigma t = 2.61$ minutes)

The CT of .70 means that .70 minute is available at each work station. Activity A consumes .62 of the .70 minute available at the first station, but the next downstream activity (B) is too large to combine with A. Activities B and C can be combined, however, for they total only .66 minute. Similarly D and E and F and G can be combined as shown in Fig. 5-10.

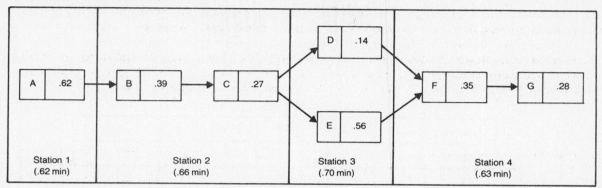

Fig. 5-10

$$\text{Eff}_B = \frac{\Sigma t}{(\text{CT})n} = \frac{2.61}{(.70)(4)} = 93\%$$

Also

$$\text{Eff}_B = \frac{\text{theoretical minimum number of workers}}{\text{actual number of workers}} = \frac{3.73}{4} = 93\%$$

Computerized routines are available for testing the multitude of potential work-station configurations that exist for realistic large-scale, line-balancing problems. Although they utilize heuristic decision rules, they can rapidly converge on a reasonably good balance. One commonly used heuristic is to move down the network diagram, selecting first those tasks that have the longest activity times, but that still fit within the cycle time available at the work station, while meeting precedence requirements.

In the preceding examples, the output and activity times specified the production-line output, and determined the number of work stations. If, instead of output, the number of work stations n is specified, production-line output can be used to define a target cycle time, CT_t:

$$\text{CT}_t = \frac{\Sigma t}{n} \tag{5.6}$$

where Σt is the summation of activity times. The target cycle time represents the minimum average time necessary at a work station and must be greater than or equal to the longest activity time.

Example 5.8 Suppose the activities shown in Fig. 5-9 are to be grouped into a three-station assembly line. (a) What is the target cycle time? (b) Which grouping of activities results in the largest output per hour? (c) What output will result in a 7-hour day?

(a)
$$\text{CT}_t = \frac{\Sigma t}{n} = \frac{2.61 \text{ min}}{3 \text{ stations}} = .87 \text{ min/station}$$

(b)   The largest output will result from the smallest CT.

Trial	Station #1	Station #2	Station #3	CT
1	.62	.39 + .27 = .66	.14 + .56 + .35 + .28 = 1.33	1.33
2	.62	.39 + .27 + .14 = .80	.56 + .35 + .28 = 1.19	1.19
3	.62 + .39 = 1.01	.27 + .56 = .83	.14 + .35 + .28 = .77	1.01

The third grouping is best.

(c)
$$\text{Output} = \frac{(7 \text{ hr/day})(60 \text{ min/hr})}{1.01 \text{ min/unit}} = 416 \text{ units/day}$$

Solved Problems

DESIGN AND SYSTEM CAPACITY

5.1   A forest ranger in charge of constructing a new campground has been instructed to provide enough campsites to accommodate 10 percent more than the average summer weekend demand at the nearby Fall Creek site. The ranger obtains the following estimate (Table 5-5) from an employee who patrols the Fall Creek area. For what capacity should the ranger design the new campground?

Table 5-5

Campsite demand	0–10	10–20	20–50	50–80	80–100
Percentage of time	5	30	50	10	5

The employee has provided the ranger with a distribution which has unequal class sizes and overlapping class limits—that is, we do not know into which class the 20, the 50, and the 80 fall. Nevertheless, if this is the best information available, we should use it. See Table 5-6.

Table 5-6

Midpoint X	$P(X)$	$XP(X)$
5	.05	.25
15	.30	4.50
35	.50	17.50
65	.10	6.50
90	.05	4.50
		33.25

$$E(D) = \Sigma\,[XP(X)] = 33.25 \text{ campsites}$$
$$\text{Add } 10\% \quad \underline{3.32} \text{ campsites}$$
$$\text{Design capacity} \quad 36.57 \text{ campsites}$$
$$\text{Best estimate} = 37 \quad \text{campsites}$$

5.2   A common-stock transfer operation of a large New York brokerage firm has been automated so that each of four workers (A = Alice, B = Bob, C = Carol, and D = Dan) performs a sequential task, such as typing names on certificates or recording ownership. The maximum number of certificates per hour that each worker is capable of handling is 75, 50, 70, and 60, respectively. However, workers A and D operate at 70-percent efficiency, and workers B and C operate at 90-percent efficiency.

   (*a*)   What is the effective capacity of the system?

   (*b*)   What is the expected output of the system? (Assume workload is greater than capacity.)

   A schematic representation of the system is shown in Fig. 5-11.

   (*a*)   The effective capacity of the system is limited by the individual capacity of B. Therefore, system capacity equals 50 units per hour.

   (*b*)   If, in this human system, each worker's efficiency were judged in relation to his or her own individual capability, the potential output from each worker would be:

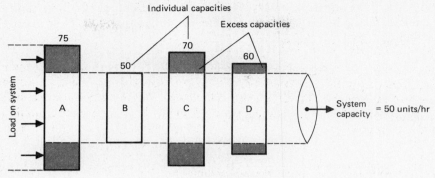

Fig. 5-11

A: (75 units/hr)(.70) = 52.5 units/hr
B: (50 units/hr)(.90) = 45.0 units/hr
C: (70 units/hr)(.90) = 63.0 units/hr
D: (60 units/hr)(.70) = 42.0 units/hr

Thus D would be the limiting component at 42 units per hour. Notice, however, that if B produced only 45 units per hour for D to work on, and if D's efficiency of 70 percent were applied to that input, the actual output would be only 31.5 units per hour.

COMPUTATION OF EQUIPMENT REQUIREMENTS

5.3   Rocket Propulsion Co. is considering the expansion of a solid-propellant manufacturing process by adding more 1-ton-capacity curing furnaces. Each batch (1 ton) of propellant must undergo 30 minutes of furnace time, including load and unload operations. However, the furnace is used only 80 percent of the time due to power restrictions in other parts of the system. The required output for the new layout is to be 16 tons per shift (8 hours). Plant (system) efficiency is estimated at 50 percent of system capacity. (*a*) Determine the number of furnaces required. (*b*) Estimate the percentage of time the furnaces will be idle.

(*a*) $$\text{Required system capacity} = \frac{\text{actual output}}{\text{SE}} = \frac{16 \text{ tons/shift}}{.50} = 32 \text{ tons/shift}$$

or, expressed differently,

$$\text{Required system capacity} = \frac{32 \text{ tons/shift}}{(.8)(8 \text{ hr/shift})} = 5 \text{ tons/hr}$$

$$\text{Individual furnace capacity} = \frac{1 \text{ ton}}{.5 \text{ hr}} = 2 \text{ tons/hr per furnace}$$

$$\text{Number of furnaces required} = \frac{5 \text{ tons/hr}}{2 \text{ tons/hr per furnace}} = 2.5 \; (3) \text{ furnaces}$$

(*b*)   Total hours available per shift = 3 furnaces @ 8 hours = 24 furnace hours
Total hours of actual use per shift = 16 tons(.5 hr/ton) = 8 furnace hours
Idle time = 16 hours

$$\text{Percentage of idle time} = \frac{16 \text{ hours idle}}{24 \text{ hours total}} = 67\% \text{ idle time}$$

5.4   A film developing agency must determine how many photo-enlarger cubicles are required to maintain an output of 200 good prints per hour. The set up and exposure can theoretically be done in 2 minutes per print, but operators are on the average only 90 percent efficient and, in addition, 5 percent of the prints must be scrapped and redone. Also, the cubicles can be utilized for enlarging only 70 percent of the time. (*a*) What is the required system capacity in prints per hour? (*b*) What average output per hour can be expected from each cubicle, taking its use factor and efficiency into account? (*c*) How many enlarger cubicles are required?

(*a*)
$$\text{System capacity} = \frac{\text{good output}}{\text{SE}} = \frac{200}{.95} = 210.5 \text{ prints/hr}$$

(*b*)
$$\text{Output/hr} = (\text{unit capacity})(\text{utilization}\%)(\text{efficiency})$$

where
$$\text{Unit capacity} = \frac{60 \text{ min/hr}}{2 \text{ min/print}} = 30 \text{ prints/hr}$$

$$\text{Output/hr} = (30 \text{ prints/hr})(.70)(.90) = 18.9 \text{ prints/hr}$$

(*c*)
$$\text{Number cubicles} = \frac{210.5 \text{ prints/hr required}}{18.9 \text{ prints/hr-cubicle}} = 11.14 \text{ cubicles (use either 11 or 12)}$$

PROCESS (FUNCTIONAL) LAYOUT METHODS

5.5   *Operations Sequence Analysis.* Shown at the left in Fig. 5-12 is an initial solution in a plant layout operations sequence analysis. The numbers shown on the lines connecting work centers (circles) represent the number of loads transported between centers (in either direction). Develop any improvements in the layout that you can, and show your improved layout by lettering the work centers. Note that work centers F and G are fixed.

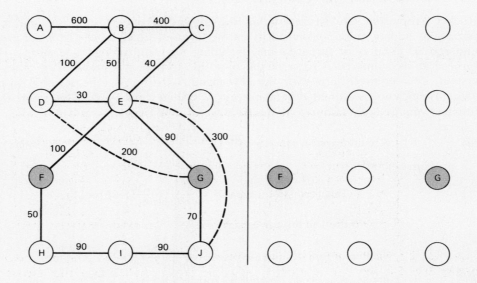

Fig. 5-12

(*a*)   Regard departments as adjacent if they are next to each other or diagonally across from each other.

(*b*)   Minimize the nonadjacent (distance) × (load). This layout has two nonadjacent loads, each going to two columns (or rows) beyond the starting point:

$$2(200) + 2(300) = 1,000 \text{ unit distances}$$

(*c*)   Improve the layout by visual inspection and calculation check. Some solutions are shown in Fig. 5-13. (There are additional layouts that are equally optimal.) Note that all solutions given are equally satisfactory and cannot be improved upon because no loads are transported to nonadjacent work centers.

A	B	C		A	B			C	B	A			A
	E	D		C	E	D			E	D		C	B	D
F	J	G		F	J	G		F	J	G		F	E	G
H		I		H		I		H		I		H	I	J

Fig. 5-13

5.6 *Load-Distance Analysis with Multiple Products.* Assume that a second product (Table 5-7) is to be produced in the facility described in Example 5.5. Recalculate the load-distance analysis for the two options.

Table 5-7   Product #2 Workloads/Week

	To: A	B	C
From: A	—	40	5
B	25	—	7
C	10	8	—

No. Loads/Week Product #2 (both directions)	Option #1 (load)(distance)	Option #2 (load)(distance)
A to B and B to A = 40 + 25 = 65	(65)(10) = 650	(65)(15) = 975
A to C and C to A = 5 + 10 = 15	(15)(10) = 150	(15)(10) = 150
B to C and C to B = 7 + 8 = 15	(15)(15) = _225_	(15)(10) = _150_
	1,025	1,275

Given this second product, also at $1 per load-foot cost, option #1 is now the lesser cost as seen in Table 5-8.

Table 5-8

Product	Load-Distance Total under	
	Option #1	Option #2
No. 1 (Example 5.5)	2,250	2,050
No. 2 (This example)	_1,025_	_1,275_
Total	3,275	3,325

5.7 *Systematic Layout Planning.* Using the critical links concept, which departments in the Muther grid of Fig. 5-8 will (*a*) be used to form the initial clusters of a trial layout, and (*b*) be separated.

(*a*) Critical links are the a links: job planning–pattern shop, testing–assembly

(*b*) Critical separations are the x links: pattern shop–testing, job planning–testing

Note: The major criteria for the sign production layout is likely to be a smooth flow (material handling) of the job. However, the nearness codes refine that.

5.8 *Systematic Layout Planning.* A chemical fertilizer facility has eight work centers that must be arranged into a 2 row by 4 column facility. The closeness ratings for absolutely necessary (a), very important (e), and undesirable (x) indexes are given in Fig. 5-14. Assign the critical work centers (i.e., a and x) first, and develop a suitable layout.

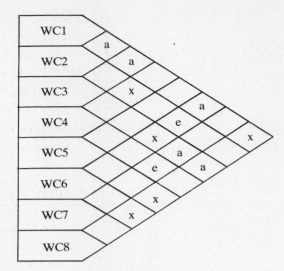

Fig. 5-14

First: List the critical (a and x) links, and identify the work centers that should be centrally located (have the most links) and those that should be separated.

> a links: 1-2, 1-3, 1-6, 3-7, 3-8 (WC3 and WC1 are most common)
>
> x links: 1-8, 2-4, 3-6, 5-8, 6-8 (WC8 is most common)

Second: Form a cluster (or clusters) of the a links beginning with the most common (WC3 and WC1). Also graph the x links (Fig. 5-15).

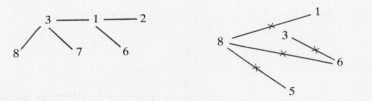

Fig. 5-15

Third: Add on to the cluster to meet other nearness criteria and rearrange as necessary to fit into the specified 2 × 4 matrix.

> *Note*: The matrix shown (Fig. 5-16) satisfies all requirements, including the 1–6 linkage because of the corner-to-corner contact.

8	3	1	5
4	7	2	6

Fig. 5-16

LINE BALANCING IN PRODUCT LAYOUTS

5.9   A Los Angeles producer of electronic equipment needs to add a component subassembly operation that can produce 80 units during a regular 8 hour shift. The operations have been designed for three activities with times as shown in Table 5-9:

Table 5-9

Operation	Activity	Standard Time (min)
A	Mechanical assembly	12
B	Electric wiring	16
C	Test	3

(a)   How many work stations (in parallel) will be required for each activity?

(b)   Assuming that the workers at each station cannot be used for other activities in the plant, what is the appropriate percentage of idle time for this subassembly operation?

(a)   With 480 minutes per day available to each activity, the output capacities per single work station would be as shown in the accompanying diagram.

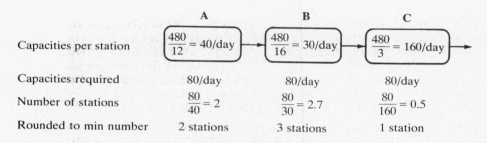

	A	B	C
Capacities per station	$\frac{480}{12} = 40$/day	$\frac{480}{16} = 30$/day	$\frac{480}{3} = 160$/day
Capacities required	80/day	80/day	80/day
Number of stations	$\frac{80}{40} = 2$	$\frac{80}{30} = 2.7$	$\frac{80}{160} = 0.5$
Rounded to min number	2 stations	3 stations	1 station

(b)   Idle time can be determined by comparing the total time available with the standard time found in Table 5-10.

Table 5-10

Time Available (at 480 min/day)	Standard Time for 80 Units
A: 2 stations = 960	A: 80 units at 12 min = 960
B: 3 stations = 1,440	B: 80 units at 16 min = 1,280
C: 1 station = 480	C: 80 units at 3 min = 240
2,880	2,480

$$\text{Percent idle time} = \frac{\text{total available} - \text{standard}}{\text{total available}} = \frac{2,880 - 2,480}{2,880} = 14\%$$

5.10   An electric appliance assembly area is as shown in Fig. 5-17 with potential work stations A through F. The tasks that must be done, along with their respective times, are indicated in the precedence diagram.

   The machine scan is automatic and can come anytime after task 2. The manufacturer desires an output of 367 units per 8-hour day and stops the line for a 20-minute break in the middle of the morning and the afternoon. (a) Group the assembly-line tasks into appropriate work stations, and (b) compute the balance efficiency.

(a)
$$CT = \frac{AT}{\text{output}} = \frac{480 \text{ min/day} - 2(20) \text{ min/day}}{367 \text{ units/day}} = 1.20 \text{ min/unit}$$

Each worker can be scheduled for up to 1.2 minutes of work at a work station. Grouping the tasks into the maximum amounts of work that can be done at a work station, we obtain one arrangement as shown in Fig. 5-18. Potential work stations are marked off with dashed lines. Notice that task 7 requires 3.4

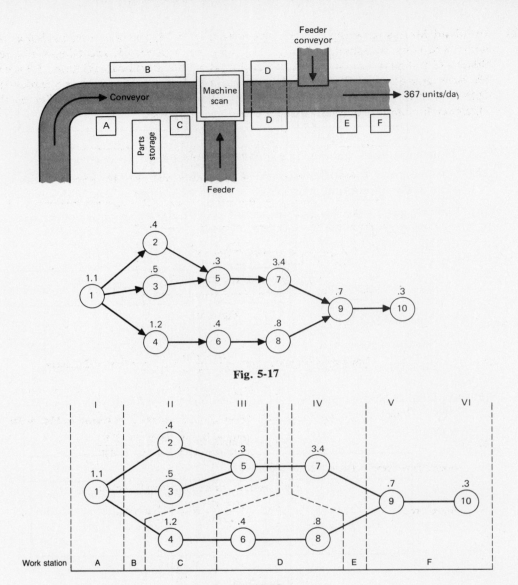

Fig. 5-17

Fig. 5-18

minutes of work (Table 5-11). Because the nearest multiple of cycle time is 3.6 (i.e., 3×1.2), this station will require three workers. The addition of two extra workers makes the equivalent number of work stations (or number of workers) eight rather than six, so we will use that for our calculations.

Table 5-11

Work Station	A	B	C	D	E	F	
Tasks	1	2, 3, 5	4	6, 8	7	9, 10	
Actual time (min)	1.1	1.2	1.2	1.2	3.4	1.0	$\Sigma t = 9.1$

(b)

$$\text{Eff}_B = \frac{\Sigma t}{(\text{CT})n} = \frac{9.1}{(1.2)(8)} = 94.8\%$$

5.11 Overland Motors produces 50 cars per hour (Fig. 5-19) and has a transmission feeder shop with three work stations (A, B, C), which take times of 55, 45, and 60 seconds, respectively. Station C assembly time is normally distributed, with a standard deviation of 5 seconds. (*a*) If all work arrived at C on time, what proportion of the time would the feeder shop fail to deliver transmissions on time to the main auto assembly line?   (*b*) What is the balance efficiency for the transmission feeder shop?

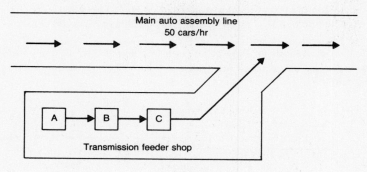

Fig. 5-19

(*a*)

$$\text{Main assembly line rate} = \frac{60 \text{ min/hr}}{50 \text{ cars/hr}} = 1.2 \text{ min/car} = 72 \text{ sec/car}$$

$$Z = \frac{x - \mu}{\sigma} = \frac{72 - 60}{5} = 2.4 \text{ sec}$$

$$P(x > 72) = .008 \cong .01 = 1\% \text{ (from normal distribution shown in Fig. 5-20)}$$

(*b*)

$$\text{Eff}_B = \frac{\text{output of task times}}{\text{input of station times}} = \frac{\Sigma t}{(\text{CT})n}$$

where cycle time CT is governed by

$$\text{Main assembly line output} = 72 \text{ sec/car}$$

Therefore,

$$\text{Eff}_B = \frac{55 + 45 + 60}{(72)(3)} = \frac{160}{216} = 74\%$$

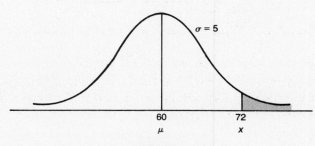

Fig. 5-20

Supplementary Problems

5.12 A manufacturer of television-watches uses three TR87 electronic chips in each television-watch produced. Demand estimates for the number of television-watches that could be sold next year are shown in Table 5-12.

Table 5-12

Demand X	20,000	40,000	50,000
$P(X)$	.30	.50	.20

(*a*) Assuming the firm decides to produce on an expected-value basis, how many TR87 chips should it plan to produce for next year's television-watch sales? (*b*) What capacity is required to meet 150 percent of expected demand?   *Ans.*   (*a*) 108,000 chips (*b*) 162,000 chips

5.13   The individual work stations in a toy production line layout have design capacities (units/day) as shown in Fig. 5-21. If the actual output of the system is 80 toys per day, what is the system efficiency?
Ans.   53 percent

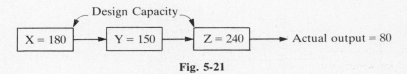

Fig. 5-21

5.14   An existing factory has the equipment arrangement shown in Fig. 5-22. Manufactured fittings must be processed through each of three operations in sequence, but it does not matter which lathe or mill is used. Each lathe is capable of handling 30 fittings per hour, each mill can handle 45 per hour, and the grinder can handle 80 per hour. A different operator runs each group of machines, and due to the workload, the lathe operator can handle an output of 25 fittings per hour from each lathe when they are all operating. The mill and grinder operators can produce 45 per hour (per mill) and 80 per hour (per grinder), respectively. During the past 40-hour week, actual production from this department was 1,000 fittings. Find (*a*) the system capacity and (*b*) the system efficiency.
Ans.   (*a*) 75 per hour (*b*) 33.3 percent

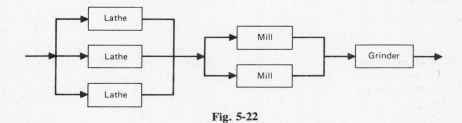

Fig. 5-22

5.15   Your firm must purchase some new plating machines capable of producing 160,000 *good* parts per year. They will become part of a processing line, and you expect that 20 percent of the production will have to be scrapped because of defects. What is the required system capacity in parts per year?
Ans.   200,000 parts per year.

5.16   Use the data from Prob. 5.15, and assume that plating one part takes 90 seconds. The plant in which the machines will be installed operates 2,000 hours per year. However, the plating machines are used only 50 percent of the time. If the plating machines are 90 percent efficient, what actual plating machine output per hour is achieved?   *Ans.*   18 parts per hour

5.17   Using the data from Probs. 5.15 and 5.16, how many plating machines are required?
Ans.   5.6 (6) machines

5.18   A textile firm wishes to acquire enough stamping machines to produce 30,000 good T-shirts per month. They operate 200 hours per month, but the stamping machines will be used for T-shirts only 70 percent of the time, and the output is 4 percent defective. The stamping operation takes 1 minute per T-shirt. Allowing for adjustments, clean out, and unavoidable downtime, the stamping machines are 90 percent efficient. How many stamping machines are required?   *Ans.*   4.13 (4) machines

5.19   Mohawk Valley Furniture has purchased a plant with six production areas as shown in Fig. 5-23 facility outline. The firm proposes to locate six departments (A, B, C, D, E, F), which have the number of moves per day between departments as shown in Table 5-13's travel chart.

Table 5-13   Travel Chart

		A	B	C	D	E	F
		Number of Moves to					
From	A	—	7	—	—	—	5
	B	—	—	—	4	10	—
	C	—	7	—	—	2	—
	D	—	—	8	—	—	—
	E	4	—	—	—	—	3
	F	—	6	—	—	10	—

1	2	3
4	5	6

Fig. 5-23   Facility outline

Develop a layout of the six departments which minimizes the nonadjacent flows. *Ans.*   One arrangement is shown in Fig. 5-24.

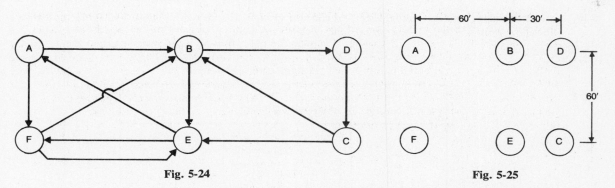

Fig. 5-24   **Fig. 5-25**

5.20   The distances between centers of departments for one solution of Prob. 5.19 (above) are shown in Fig. 5-25. Diagonal moves are permissible. (*a*) Using daily totals, compute the (load) (distance). (*b*) Compute the materials-handling cost if the cost to move a load is $.025 per foot. (*c*) Use a trial-and-error approach to develop a less costly layout. (*d*) How much does your new layout save?
Ans.   (*a*) 4,078 foot-loads per day. (*b*) $102 per day. (*c*) More than one answer is possible. (*d*) A savings of over $3,000 per year is possible.

5.21   In the operations sequence chart shown in Fig. 5-26, circles represent work centers, and numbers represent the units of load transported. Develop improvements in the layout, and show the best one you can.
Ans.   There are at least six possible solutions involving no nonadjacent loads. Each is correct.

5.22   Arrange six work centers into a 2(row) × 3(column) grid in a layout that satisfies the following: WC1 must adjoin WC4, WC1 must adjoin WC5, WC5 must adjoin WC6, WC2 and WC5 must be separated.
Ans.   One arrangement is

$$\begin{bmatrix} 3 - 4 - 1 \\ 2 - 6 - 5 \end{bmatrix}$$

5.23   Using only the nearness codes a, o, and x, develop a Muther grid for Prob. 5.22. Assume unspecified relationships are all of ordinary importance.
Ans.   Show a's in intersections 1 and 4, 5 and 6, 1 and 5, and x in 2 and 5; others are all o.

5.24   Arrange the six work centers into a 3(row) × 2(column) grid that satisfies the nearness criteria shown on the Muther grid in Fig. 5-27.   *Ans.*   Departments 3 and 6 must be in the middle row.

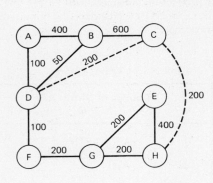

Fig. 5-26   Fig. 5-27

5.25   A line-balancing problem involves 10 work stations having a Σ times = 24.0 minutes (where the shortest is 2.1 minutes and the longest is 3.0 minutes). Assuming only one worker is located at each station, and using the longest time as the cycle time, what would be the balance efficiency?   *Ans.*   80 percent

5.26   A line-balancing analysis resulted in a precedence grouping as shown in Table 5-14. Find the balance efficiency, assuming the longest actual time is the cycle time.   *Ans.*   CT = 1.5, so Eff_B = 84 percent

Table 5-14

Work Center	Activity Numbers	Actual Time (min)
A	1, 2	1.2
B	3, 5, 6	1.4
C	4, 7	.9
D	8, 10, 11	1.3
E	9	1.5

5.27   A furniture-manufacturing activity requires the times shown in Fig. 5-28 to perform five tasks in an assembly line. Operations are to be scheduled for producing six units per hour and each employee can contribute 48 minutes per hour of productive work. (*a*) What is the cycle time in minutes per unit?   (*b*) What is the theoretical minimum number of personnel?   (*c*) Combine the tasks into the most efficient grouping of work stations. What is the resulting efficiency of balance?
Ans.   (*a*) 8 minutes per unit (*b*) 3.78 employees (*c*) 94.5 percent

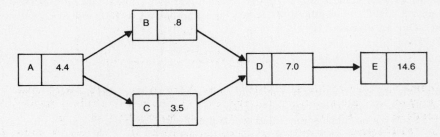

Fig. 5-28

5.28   A toy manufacturer produces doll houses on a product line geared to an output of one per minute. The assembly precedence relationships and activity times (in minutes) are as shown in Fig. 5-29.

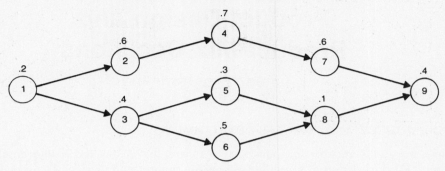

Fig. 5-29

(*a*) Group the activities into the most efficient arrangement. (*b*) What is the balance efficiency (Eff_B)?
Ans.   (*a*) One solution is shown in Table 5-15. (*b*) 76 percent

Table 5-15

Work Station	A	B	C	D	E
Tasks	1, 2	3, 6	4, 5	7, 8	9
Actual times	.8	.9	1.0	.7	.4

5.29   Robotic Controls Corp. uses a robotic-controlled flexible production system to assemble the robots it sells. Five robots are available and must complete the tasks specified in Table 5-16.

Table 5-16

Task	Time (sec)	Preceding Task(s)
A	10	None
B	24	None
C	17	A
D	49	A
E	12	C
F	14	C
G	27	B
H	9	E
I	20	F, G
J	23	D, H, I
K	36	I
L	18	J, K

(*a*) Draw a precedence diagram. (*b*) What is the theoretical minimum (target) cycle time if all five robots are fully utilized in a five-station assembly line? (*c*) Group the tasks into the most efficient five-station assembly line. (*d*) What is the cycle time? (*e*) What is the balance efficiency?
Ans.   (*a*) Diagram must meet precedence requirements. (*b*) 51.8 seconds/station (*c*) I = A, C, E, F
     II = B, G   III = D   IV = H, I, J   V = K, L(*d*) 54 seconds (from station V) (*e*) 96 percent

Chapter 6

Product-Design and Product-Mix Decisions

Linear Programming

STAGES IN PRODUCT AND PROCESS DEVELOPMENT

Products are goods and services, and *processes* are the means (skills and equipment) used to produce them. Product decisions are discussed in this chapter and process decisions in the next.

Figure 6-1 illustrates one of many possible paths from an idea to a finished good or service.

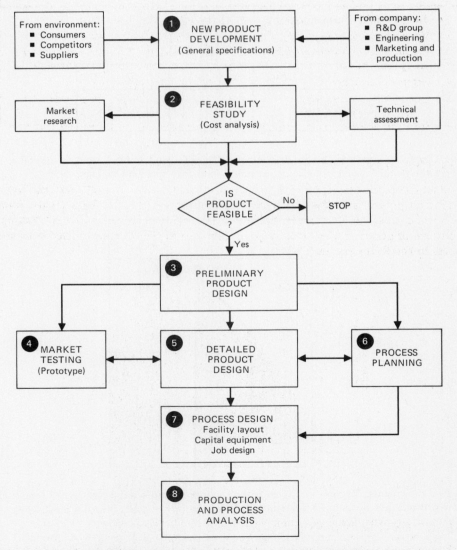

Fig. 6-1 Product and process design and analysis

Inputs come from both the external—*market*—environment (shown on the left) and the internal—*technical*—environment (shown on the right). Management must develop and meet the customer's needs by using the available resources and the technological capabilities of the organization.

PLANNING FOR GOODS AND SERVICES

Planning for goods and services must allow for differences such as those listed in Table 6-1. Planning for goods is often more formalized because designs, engineering drawings, and quality standards tend to be more thoroughly specified. In addition, the manufacturing environment is typically separated from the consumer. This means that scheduling, assembly, and production-control activities can be tightly controlled. Service activities tend to be more flexible, and production usually takes place in the presence of the consumer.

Table 6-1   Differences in Planning for Goods versus Services

Goods	Services
1. *Tangible* (physical) product	1. *Less tangible* product
2. Value stored *in product*	2. Value conveyed *as used*
3. Produced in *industrial environment* (away from customers)	3. Produced in *market* environment (in conjunction with customer)
4. Often *standardized*	4. Often *customized*
5. Quality inherent in *product* (a function of materials)	5. Quality inherent in *process* (a function of personnel)

PRODUCT LIFE CYCLES

Most products pass through the stages of introduction, growth, maturity, and decline, as depicted in Fig. 6-2. Not all products follow the same pattern (for instance, fashion items, foods, building materials) and some goods don't seem to decline at all (for instance, paper clips). But knowledge of the general pattern of goods and services helps planners to forecast demand and to maintain a viable mix of products in the firm's product line.

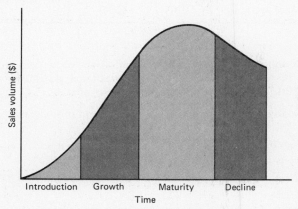

Fig. 6-2 Typical good or service life cycle

RESEARCH AND DEVELOPMENT (R&D)

Research is a consciously directed investigation to find new knowledge. *Basic research* is a search for new knowledge without regard to any specific use, such as that done by universities and foundations. *Applied research* is investigative or experimental work directed toward specific problems, products, or processes. Developmental efforts often consume the bulk of R&D funds. *Development* is the activity of converting research results into commercially viable products.

Research often involves a good deal of uncertainty about the technological and economic success of a project. Bayesian statistics offers managers one measure of how much money is justified for market studies, pilot projects, etc. to reduce or remove uncertainty about the outcome of research. *Uncertainty* refers to the decision maker's ignorance about which outcome, or *state of nature*, will prevail. The incremental amount that can be justified to remove this uncertainty is called the *expected value of perfect information*, EVPI.

$$\text{EVPI} = \text{EPC} - \text{EMV}^* \qquad (6.1)$$

In Eq. 6.1, EPC is the *expected profit under certainty*, which is the maximum profit that would result if no uncertainty existed about the state of nature. In the computation of EPC, each state is presumed to exist in proportion to its probability of occurrence, and the best act under a given state is always chosen. EMV* is the *expected monetary value* (EMV) of the course of action offering the *highest* average when payoffs are weighed by their probabilities of occurrence.

Example 6.1 Automated Service Systems Inc. has spent $200,000 on design and prototype work for a computerized self-service ticketing system for airlines. Customers simply punch in their destination and desired departure time. The system then automatically scans available flights, reserves the space, and computes the fare, which is shown on a video monitor. Once a credit card is inserted for payment, the ticket emerges.

The firm must decide whether to produce the system for a regional market, a national market, or not at all. Success will depend on the level of customer acceptance. Market researchers have categorized this as poor, moderate, good, or high, with associated probabilities of .3, .1, .4, and .2, respectively. The three-year, present-value, before-tax profits ($000) are estimated as shown in Table 6-2.

Table 6-2

Course of Action	Level of Customer Acceptance			
	θ_1 Low	θ_2 Moderate	θ_3 Good	θ_4 High
A: Do not produce	(200)	(200)	(200)	(200)
B: Regional market	(280)	80	310	650
C: National market	(910)	(350)	760	2,800

(a) Which course of action should be followed if the firm wishes to be very conservative, i.e., a *maximin* strategy? (b) What is the best course of action under a *maximum probability* strategy? (c) Compute the EMV*. (d) What is the EVPI? (e) Evaluate the results of your analysis.

(a) Under maximin, choose to minimize the maximum loss. Do not produce the product, so the loss is held to $200,000.

(b) Under maximum probability, the most likely state of nature is "good" (with $\theta_3 = .4$), and within this category the best choice is to market nationally for a profit of $760,000.

(c) $$E(A) = (\text{all values are the same amount of loss}) \qquad = (200)$$
$$E(B) = (-280)(.3) + 80(.1) + 310(.4) + 650(.2) \qquad = 178$$
$$E(C) = (-910)(.3) + (-350)(.1) + 760(.4) + 2{,}800(.2) = 556$$

Therefore, EMV* = $556,000, and the choice is to market nationally.

(d) EVPI = EPC − EMV*, where EPC is the expected profit under certainty and is the best course of action under each state, weighted by the probability of the occurrence of that state as shown in Table 6-3.

$$\text{EVPI} = \text{EPC} - \text{EMV}^* = \$812{,}000 - 556{,}000 = \$256{,}000$$

Table 6-3

(1)	(2)	(3)	(4)
If state is known to be:	Then best action and profit would be to choose:	Percent of time this occurs is:	Expected profit [(2) × (3)]:
θ_1	$A = (200)$	.3	(60)
θ_2	$B = 80$	.1	8
θ_3	$C = 760$	.4	304
θ_4	$C = 2,800$	.2	560
			EPC = 812

The firm could justify spending a maximum of $256,000 to do studies that would increase the probability of a positive outcome.

(*e*) The proper choice depends on factors such as the asset level of the firm and the risk attitude of management. Other firms are already in this market. The EMV* choice of marketing nationally may not be the best choice, because it is biased by the large payoff that results from high customer acceptance, where the probability is only $\theta_4 = .2$. The expected value from the other states under a national market strategy is even a loss, that is, $(-910)(.3) + (-350)(.1) + 760(.4) = -4$, or a $4,000 loss.

PRODUCT DESIGN AND STANDARDIZATION

Product design is the structuring of component parts or activities so that as a unit they can provide a specified value. Product specification is typically an engineering function; detailed drawings or specifications are prepared which give dimensions, weights, colors, and other physical characteristics. In service industries, product specification often consists of an environmental requirement to be maintained or a procedure to be followed, such as operating room procedures in a hospital.

Design, production, and marketing costs are reduced by standardizing and simplifying the product. *Standardization* involves producing items to a commonly accepted standard to assure the interchangeability and/or the quality level of the product. The use of a limited number of uniform parts reduces the sizes and number of items to be purchased, cuts inventory storage and handling costs, and enables firms to work with larger (and more economical) quantities of fewer items. Standardization makes both mass production and maintenance much easier. However, standardization of design at an early stage can forestall improvements which might otherwise be made to those products (for example, typewriter keyboards have a standard, though inefficient, placement of letters). It also limits the options available to consumers.

Modular designs also facilitate production and maintenance. Modules are common components grouped into interchangeable subassemblies, and they range in size from microelectronics to prefabricated houses.

Once developed, many products also undergo *value engineering* or *value analysis*. This is an attempt to see if any materials or components can be substituted or redesigned in such a way as to continue to perform the desired function, but at a lower cost. After prototype units are designed and produced, the products are further analyzed and tested to see how well the quality, performance, and costs conform to the design objectives. *Simplification* may take place to reduce unnecessary variety in the *product line* by discussing the number and variety of products produced.

CAD/CAM

CAD and CAM activities reflect the trend toward a fully automated manufacturing facility, which may ultimately link product design and manufacturing activities with material and capacity planning, scheduling, materials handling, and finished inventory control. The potential for such an integrated factory rests upon the use of computers and a carefully designed database. In the common database, each element (e.g., a part number) exists only once, but the relevant characteristics of the elements (e.g., size, composition, number in stock) are available to many functional users such as engineering and marketing department personnel.

Computer-aided design (CAD) is the use of computerized work stations, complete with database and computer graphics, to rapidly develop and analyze a product's design. The designer can input specifications, then watch the system create a three-dimensional geometric model of the product. That image can be rotated on the screen to totally display the product's characteristics even before it is manufactured. In addition, designers can obtain and test such factors as stress, tolerances, product reliability, serviceability, and costs.

Computer-aided manufacturing (CAM) follows CAD. It is the extensive use of computers to accomplish and control production operations. Some major uses of computers here are in (1) numerically controlled (NC) machines, (2) process controllers, (3) systems that are linked by group technology, (4) automatic assembly operations, and (5) computer-aided inspection and testing.

NC machines and group technology applications may link CAD and CAM. The computerized *NC machines* convert CAD specifications into precise machine commands that will produce a given part. In addition, groups of NC machines can be linked in a hierarchical network that communicates production, scheduling, downtime, quality, and other information that can improve productivity.

Group technology (GT) is a method of grouping similar parts or products into families to facilitate both design and manufacturing activities. This grouping minimizes the differences due to individual designs, routings, etc., in favor of standardized processes. By reducing set-up and changeover times, GT concepts help firms produce customized products at medium to high volumes.

PRODUCT SELECTION

Product selection decisions are influenced by (1) the firm's resource and technology base, (2) the market environment, and (3) the firm's motivation to use its capabilities to meet the needs of the marketplace. Motivation is often economic, but it can also be social, political, religious, or other. Figure 6-3 depicts the three factors named and suggests that successful organizations match their resource capabilities against market demands to produce at an economic or social advantage.

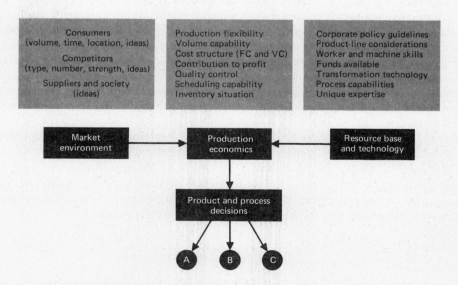

Fig. 6-3 Factors relevant to product selection decisions

PRODUCT-MIX DECISIONS VIA LINEAR PROGRAMMING (GRAPHIC)

Within the product-line groupings, decisions must be made to select which mix of products to produce (or which processes to use) in view of cost, capacity, and other limitations. Linear programming is a useful technique for assisting in the product-mix (and numerous other) decisions. It applies to situations where the firm has a demand for whatever quantities of two or more products it can produce. Another typical application is for the selection of the least costly mix of raw materials or processes to use when several are available.

Linear programming is a mathematical technique for maximizing or minimizing a linear objective function, subject to linear constraints. It assumes that cost and revenue values are known (*certainty*) and that profits from various activities are additive (*additivity*), and it does not allow negative production values (*non-negativity*). We review linear programming here in the context of a product-mix decision. However, it has widespread application to other problems such as capital budgeting, line balancing, planning, and scheduling.

Linear programming problems are expressed in terms of a single linear *objective function* that specifies the benefit or cost associated with each *decision variable*. For example, if the profit (Z) from decision variable X_1 (chairs) is \$20 and from X_2 (tables) is \$70, the linear objective may be to maximize $Z = \$20X_1 + \$70X_2$. *Constraints* express the resource limitations or needs to produce the end products and may be stated as less than or equal to ($\leq$), equal to ($=$), or greater than or equal to ($\geq$) a specified amount. Thus if each chair (X_1) required 10 minutes of assembly time, and each table (X_2) required 20 minutes, the number of chairs and tables that could be assembled would be limited by the total assembly time available, say 420 minutes. The linear equation for the assembly time constraint would then be $10X_1 + 20X_2 \leq 420$. Other constraints (as many as apply) would be formulated in a similar manner. Taken together, the constraints define a *feasible region*, an area within which all possible solution combinations lie. The *optimal solution* (or mix of variables) depends upon the criteria (e.g., profit or cost) expressed in the objective function, but will always be at some intersection of constraints (a *corner*) of the feasible region.

One of the easiest methods of solving two-variable (two-product) problems is the graphic method. Table 6-4 lists the steps of solution.

Table 6-4   Graphic Method of Solving Linear Programming Problems

1. Formulate the problem in terms of a linear objective function and linear constraints.
2. Set up a graph with one decision variable on each axis, and plot the constraints. They define the feasible region.
3. Determine the slope of the objective function, and indicate the slope in the feasible region on the graph.
4. Move the objective function parallel to itself in an optimizing direction until it is constrained.
5. Read off the solution values of the decision variable from the respective axes.

Example 6.2   A chemical firm produces automobile cleaner X and polisher Y and realizes \$10 profit on each batch of X and \$30 on Y. Both products require processing through the same machines, A and B, but X requires 4 hours in A and 8 in B, whereas Y requires 6 hours in A and 4 in B. During the forthcoming week machines A and B have 12 and 16 hours of available capacity, respectively. Assuming that demand exists for both products, how many batches of each should be produced to realize the optimal profit Z? (*Hint*: Follow the steps outlined in Table 6-4.)

   1. The objective function is:

$$\text{Max } Z = \$10X + \$30Y$$

The constraints are:
$$\text{A: } \quad 4X + 6Y \leq 12$$
$$\text{B: } \quad 8X + 4Y \leq 16$$
$$\text{Also: } \quad X \geq 0, \ Y \geq 0$$

2. The variables are X and Y. The constraints are plotted as equalities. To graph:

$$\text{A:} \quad \text{If } X = 0, Y = 2$$
$$\text{If } Y = 0, X = 3$$
$$\text{B:} \quad \text{If } X = 0, Y = 4$$
$$\text{If } Y = 0, X = 2$$

Note that the graph (Fig. 6-4) establishes a feasible region bounded by the explicit capacity constraints of A and B and the implicit constraints that production of $X \geqslant 0$ and production of $Y \geqslant 0$.

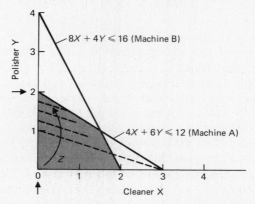

Fig. 6-4   Graphic linear programming solution

3. The slope of the objective function is:

$$Z = 10X + 30Y$$

The standard slope-intercept form of a linear equation is

$$Y = mX + b \tag{6.2}$$

where m is the slope of the line (that is, change in Y per unit change in X) and b is the Y intercept.
   Expressing our objective in this form, we have:

$$30Y = -10X + Z \qquad\qquad Y = -\tfrac{1}{3}X + \frac{Z}{30}$$

The slope $= -1/3$; that is, the line decreases one unit in Y for every three positive units of X. This is plotted at any convenient spot within the feasible region (and shown as dashed lines in Fig. 6-4). The dashed line from $Y = 1$ to $X = 3$ illustrates this.
   4. The slope of the objective function is moved away from the origin until restrained by the furthermost intersection of constraint A and the implicit constraint $X \geqslant 0$. The optimal solution will always be at a corner in the feasible region.
   5. The arrows point to the solution, which is determined by the X and Y coordinates at the corner. In this example, $X = 0$ and $Y = 2$, so the firm should produce no cleaner and two batches of polisher for a profit of:

$$Z = \$10(0) + \$30(2) = \$60$$

As can be seen from the graph, the constraint imposed by machine B (that is, that $8X + 4Y \leqslant 16$) has no effect, for it is the 12 hours of machine A (denoted by $4X + 6Y \leqslant 12$) that are constraining production of the more profitable polisher. The graph also reveals that profit would continue to increase if more hours could be made available on machine A up to the point of doubling output (to $X = 0$ and $Y = 4$). At this point, the time available from machine B would become constraining.

Example 6.2 assumed that the profit contribution was known and that the constraint amounts, processing time, and available machine time were known with certainty. Problem 6.5 contains two decision variables and three constraint equations, and additional comments are made with respect to the sensitivity of the solution to changes in the constraints. Problem 6.6 extends the graphic method to the solution of minimization problems.

LINEAR PROGRAMMING (SIMPLEX METHOD)

Realistic linear programming problems often have several decision variables and many constraint equations. Such problems cannot be solved graphically, so algorithms such as the simplex procedure are used. The *simplex method* is an iterative procedure that progressively approaches and ultimately reaches an optimal solution to linear programming problems. Numerous computer programs are available for both mainframe and personal computers. Although the simplex method is especially useful for large-scale problems (solved with a computer), it will be illustrated below for the same problem that was solved graphically in Example 6.2. Additional examples in the problem section extend its application to three and more decision variables. Table 6-5 outlines a general simplex procedure.

Table 6-5　Simplex Procedure

1. *Set up initial simplex table.* Formulate the objective function and constraints, and enter the decision variables, variables in solution, solution (RHS) values, C (contribution from the variable), Z (cost of introducing the variable), and $C - Z$ (net contribution of the variable).

2. *Select the pivot column.* It is the column with the largest positive number in the bottom $(C - Z)$ row. It becomes the new variable in solution.

3. *Select the pivot row.* It is the row with the smallest ratio of RHS value divided by pivot column value. Use only positive numbers. This identifies the variable leaving the solution.

4. *Circle the pivot.* It is at the intersection of the pivot row and pivot column.

5. *Convert the pivot into a 1.* Do this by dividing each value in the pivot row by the pivot value. Enter this new row in a new table.

6. *Generate other rows for the next table with zeros in the pivot column.* This is done by multiplying the new row (from step 5) by the negative of the element in the pivot column that is to be converted and adding the result to the old row. Enter the revised row in the new table, and continue this procedure for each row in the center section of the table.

7. *Test for optimality.* Compute the values of Z and $C - Z$. Z values for each column are Σ(column elements)(C). If all $C - Z$ values are ≤ 0, the solution is optimal. Read the values for the variables in solution from the RHS column and the value of the objective function from row Z in the RHS column. If the solution is not optimal, return to step 2.

Slack Variables. The simplex method begins with a statement of the objective function and constraint equations. Computerized linear programming (LP) routines will automatically arrange these inputs, but for manual solutions we must construct our own simplex table. This necessitates that the constraints be stated as equalities rather than as inequalities. In maximization problems we accomplish this by adding a *slack variable* (S) to each constraint. The slack represents an unused amount, or the difference between what *is* being used and the limit of what *could be* used. For example, by adding slack variables to the inequality constraints of Example 6.2 we get new equations as shown in Table 6-6. Note that S_1 relates to the machine A constraint and S_2 to machine B.

Table 6-6

Constraint	Inequality	Equation with Slack
Machine A hr	$4X + 6Y \leq 12$	$4X + 6Y + S_1 = 12$
Machine B hr	$8X + 4Y \leq 16$	$8X + 4Y + S_2 = 16$

The machine A constraint now says 4 hours times the number of units of X produced plus 6 hours times the number of units of Y produced plus slack hours = 12 hours. Thus, if one unit of X and one of Y are produced, we have 2 hours of slack time S on machine A, since $4(1) + 6(1) + 2 = 12$. If no X or Y is produced, we "produce" all slack, and $S_1 = 12$.

Initial Solution. The simplex method always begins with a feasible solution wherein only slack is produced. This corresponds to the origin of the graphic solution, where both X and Y equal zero.

Each simplex table is a solution that graphically corresponds to a corner of the feasible region. We begin with a poor, but feasible solution that corresponds to the origin, where only slack is produced, that is, zero profit. Thus the slack variables (for example, S_1 and S_2) are *in the solution*, and the other decision variables (X and Y) are not in the solution (that is, have values of zero).

Example 6.3 Arrange the objective and constraint equations from Example 6.2 into an initial simplex table (Table 6-7).

Objective function: $\text{Max } Z = \$10X + \$30Y$

Constraints: Machine A hr: $4X + 6Y \leqslant 12$

Machine B hr: $8X + 4Y \leqslant 16$

Table 6-7   Simplex Format

C →		10	30	0	0	Solution
↓	Variables		Decision Variables			Values
	in Solution	X	Y	S_1	S_2	(RHS)
0	S_1	4	6	1	0	12
0	S_2	8	4	0	1	16
	Z	0	0	0	0	0
	$C - Z$	10	30	0	0	0

Elements of the Simplex Table. The *central portion* of the simplex table consists of the coefficients of the constraint equations from:

$$4X + 6Y + 1S_1 + 0S_2 = 12$$
$$8X + 4Y + 0S_1 + 1S_2 = 16$$

Note that a one (1) has been assigned to the slack variable associated with its own constraint, and a zero (0) has been assigned to the other slack variable.

The variables-in-solution column tells what variables are in solution (in this case, only slack), and the solution-values column gives the amount in solution. The numbers come from the right-hand side (RHS) of the constraint equations (in this case, 12 hours of slack for machine A, and 16 hours of slack for machine B).

The C in the upper left corner is both a row heading and a column heading. It specifies the amount of contribution to the objective function from each unit of the variables it refers to. Thus, each unit of X (cleaner) contributes \$10 to profits, and each unit of Y (polisher) contributes \$30 to profits, but the slack time from machines A and B yields \$0 contribution for both S_1 and S_2.

The Z row in the table shows the opportunity cost, or the amount of contribution that must be given up to introduce (or produce) one unit (or one more unit) of the variable in each column. It is computed for each column by multiplying the elements of the column by the contribution in the C column and then adding. For example, the Z value for column X is $(4 \times 0) + (8 \times 0) = 0$. This means that to introduce one unit of X (cleaner) into solution, we must give up 4 hours of slack time on machine A at a cost of \$0 and 8 hours of slack time on machine B, also at a cost of \$0. The Z value for the RHS column represents the total contribution from variables currently in solution. Because this (initial) solution is to "produce" 12 hours of slack on machine A (at \$0 contribution) and 16 hours of slack on machine B (at \$0 contribution), our total profit from this initial solution is zero. The Z row in the initial solution always has zeros, but it changes as the solution progresses.

The values in the bottom $(C - Z)$ row represent the *net contribution* from introducing one unit of the column variable into solution. In the initial table, they are simply the coefficients of the objective function followed by zeros for the slack variable columns. Thus, we would increase the value of the objective function by a full \$10 for each unit of X produced and by \$30 for each unit of Y produced, because nothing but worthless slack must be given up to introduce X or Y at this stage. Producing more slack would obviously not improve profits.

Computational Methodology. The solution methodology for maximization problems involves selecting a pivot column and row and revising the table values until all quantities in the bottom row are less than or equal to zero.

Example 6.4 Use the simplex method to solve the linear programming problem of Example 6.3.

We will follow the steps of the simplex procedure listed in Table 6-3.

(1) The objective and constraints are:

$$\text{Max } Z = \$10X + 30Y$$

Subject to:
$$4X + 6Y + 1S_1 + 0S_2 = 15$$
$$8X + 4Y + 0S_1 + 1S_2 = 16$$

This yields the simplex table (Table 6-8) developed in Example 6.3.

Table 6-8

$C \rightarrow$		10	30	0	0	Solution	
$\downarrow$	Variables in Solution		Decision Variables			Values	
		X	Y	S_1	S_2	(RHS)	
0	S_1	4	⑥	1	0	12	$\frac{12}{6} = 2$ (minimum)
0	S_2	8	4	0	1	16	$\frac{16}{4} = 4$
	Z	0	0	0	0	0	
	$C - Z$	10	30	0	0		
			↑				

(2) The *pivot column* has the largest positive number (30) in the bottom row.

(3) The *pivot row* has the smallest ratio:

$$\frac{12}{6} = 2 \qquad \frac{16}{4} = 4$$

Therefore row 1 is the pivot row.

(4) The pivot is *circled*.

(5) Divide each value in the pivot row by the pivot (6), and enter the values in a new table (Table 6-9).

Table 6-9

	X	Y	S_1	S_2	RHS
Y	$\frac{2}{3}$	1	$\frac{1}{6}$	0	2

(6) Generate other rows for the next table such that all elements in the pivot column equal zero.
We begin with the S_2 row, which has a 4 in the Y column. Multiply the new row (from step 5 above) by the negative of the value we wish to convert (-4), and add it to the old S_2 row. Multiply the new row by -4. The result is shown in Table 6-10.

Table 6-10

	X	Y	S_1	S_2	RHS
	$-4(\frac{2}{3})$	$-4(1)$	$-4(\frac{1}{6})$	$-4(0)$	$-4(2)$
to get result	$-\frac{8}{3}$	-4	$-\frac{2}{3}$	0	-8
Add to old row	8	4	0	1	16
to get new row	$\frac{16}{3}$	0	$-\frac{2}{3}$	1	8

And enter into new table (Table 6-11):

Table 6-11

$C \rightarrow$		10	30	0	0	
$\downarrow$	Variables in Solution	X	Y	S_1	S_2	RHS
30	Y	$\frac{2}{3}$	1	$\frac{1}{6}$	0	2
0	S_2	$\frac{16}{3}$	0	$-\frac{2}{3}$	1	8
	Z					

If there were more rows to convert, we would repeat this step for the next row. Since there are no more, we go on to compute Z and $C - Z$.

(7) Values in the Z row are Σ (column elements)(C). For example:

for X: $\qquad Z = (\frac{2}{3})(30) + (\frac{16}{3})(0) = 20$

for Y: $\qquad Z = 1(30) + 0(0) = 30$

for S_1: $\qquad Z = \frac{1}{6}(30) - \frac{2}{3}(0) = 5$

for S_2: $\qquad Z = 0(30) + 1(0) = 0$

for RHS: $\qquad 2(30) + 8(0) = 60$

After entering these and the $C - Z$ values in the next matrix (Table 6-12) we have:

Table 6-12

$C \rightarrow$		10	30	0	0	Solution
$\downarrow$	Variables in Solution		Decision Variables			Values
		X	Y	S_1	S_2	(RHS)
30	Y	$\frac{2}{3}$	1	$\frac{1}{6}$	0	2
0	S_2	$\frac{16}{3}$	0	$-\frac{2}{3}$	1	8
	Z	20	30	5	0	60
	$C - Z$	-10	0	-5	0	

Repeat steps 2 through 7 until all values in the bottom row are ≤ 0. Since all values are ≤ 0, the optimal solution is already reached. Variables in solution are identified by columns in the central portion of the table that have one entry of 1 and remaining values of zero. The solution values are given in the right-hand column as seen in Table 6-13.

Table 6-13

	X	Y	S_1	S_2	RHS
	—	1	—	0	2
	—	0	—	1	8
Z	—	—	—	—	60

Therefore, X = not in solution

                                                        Y = 2 units

                                                        Z = $60

Note that the slack variable associated with constraint 2 also has a 1 and zeros, which signifies that we have slack in solution and that the constraint is not binding. Thus we have only one (nonslack) decision variable in the solution (Y) and one binding constraint (number 1). This agrees with the fundamental theorem of linear programming, which states that the number of (nonslack) decision variables in solution always equals the number of constraints that are binding.

This solution is the same as that given for Example 6.2, so you may want to review that example for further interpretation of the output.

Optimal Solution.   Referring back to the initial solution (step 1 of Example 6.4), note the configuration of 1s and 0s in the two rows directly below the slack variable symbols. They form what is called an *identity matrix*. It is a square array of numbers with 1s on the diagonal and 0s elsewhere. A problem with three constraints would have three rows consisting of 1   0   0 and 0   1   0 and 0   0   1.

In a simplex table, a decision variable column that has a (positive) 1 with zeros elsewhere in that column identifies a variable in solution. In our initial table the 1 and 0 below the slack variables indicated that both S_1 and S_2 were in solution (that is, being produced). The value, or amount, of the variable in solution is given in the RHS column. (The RHS values for variables not in solution are automatically equal to zero.) Thus our initial table (6-8) had 12 hours of machine A slack time and 16 hours of machine B slack time in solution, and no cleaner or polisher was produced (that is, neither X nor Y was in the initial solution, so $X = 0$ and $Y = 0$).

Example 6.5 presents and interprets the optimal solution to the problem posed in Example 6.4. The graphic solution is repeated to aid in understanding the corresponding elements of the simplex solution.

Example 6.5   Interpret the optimal solution to the cleaner-polisher problem in Example 6.4.

The solution shown in Table 6-14 is optimal because all values in the $C - Z$ row are less than or equal to zero.

Table 6-14   Simplex Solution

| $C \rightarrow$ | | 10 | 30 | 0 | 0 | Solution |
| $\downarrow$ | Variables | | Decision Variables | | | Values |
	in Solution	X	Y	S_1	S_2	RHS
30	Y	2/3	1	1/6	0	2
0	S_2	16/3	0	−2/3	1	8
	Z	20	30	5	0	60
	$C - Z$	−10	0	−5	0	(Profit)

Variables in solution

Two columns have 1s and 0s.

Y is in the solution with a (RHS) value of 2.

S_2 is in the solution with a (RHS) value of 8.

The value of $Y = 2$ can be read from the RHS column in the table (and agrees with the graph, Fig. 6-5).

Recall that each unit requires 4 hours of machine B time, so 2 units of Y use 8 hours of the 16 hours available. This leaves 8 hours of machine B slack, as indicated by the RHS value of 8 for S_2, which is also in solution.

Value of the objective function

$Z = $60 profit, as shown in the RHS column. This comes from producing two units of Y at $30 each plus eight units of slack at $0.

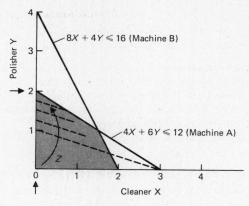

Fig. 6-5

Values in the C − Z row

The figures in the bottom row of Table 6-14 (−10, 0, −5, 0) reveal the following:

(1) (*−10*) To produce one can of X (cleaner) would reduce profits by \$10 because it would take machine A time away from the production of Y.

> *Note:* The \$10 amount is explained by the X column. Introducing one unit of "out variable" X would:

	X	
Y	$\frac{2}{3}$	←reduce Y by $\frac{2}{3}$ unit @ \$30/unit = \$20 reduction
S_2	$\frac{16}{3}$	←reduce S_2 by $\frac{16}{3}$ units @ \$0/unit = \$0 reduction
Z	20	←for a total amount of \$20 − \$0 = \$20 cost
$C − Z$	−10	←which is offset by \$10 profit from each unit of X

The result is a net (loss) contribution of $C − Z = \$10 − \$20 = −\$10$.

(2) (*0*) The first zero indicates that Y is in solution (being produced).

(3) (*−5 and 0*) These two values are referred to as *shadow prices. Shadow prices go with constraints* and show the amount of change in the objective function that would result from each unit of change in the constraint. Thus they show the net effect of increasing (or decreasing) the slack or idle time of machines A and B by one unit.

(4) (*−5*) Since machine A is fully utilized, to take 1 hour out of production and acquire 1 hour of idle time would reduce profit by \$5. (Profit from Y is \$30 for each 6 hours of work on A, that is, a rate of \$5 per hour.) Conversely, if another hour could be made available, say by shifting a current job from A, the time on A could be profitably utilized at a profit rate of \$5 per hour.

(5) (*0*) The zero corresponding to the constraint of machine B signifies that machine B already has slack time (see Fig. 6-5). Increasing B's available time (or decreasing it) by one unit would have no effect on profits.

SENSITIVITY ANALYSIS

Sensitivity (or postoptimality) analysis is concerned with the effect of changes in the parameters of the problem on a linear programming solution. While our concern here will be limited to the effect of changes in constraints, analysis can also be made to determine the effect of changes in the objective function, and the addition of new variables and new constraints.

Refer to the graphic solution (Fig. 6-5) of Example 6.2. If the time availability for machine A were increased, the profits would increase (at \$5 per additional hour) until they were ultimately constrained by machine B. Sensitivity analysis enables one to determine the ranges over which shadow prices hold. For $\leq$ constraints, the range can be determined by dividing the RHS value of the final simplex matrix by the negative of the values in the columns with shadow prices. The *smallest positive quotient* then tells how much the constraint can be changed until another constraint becomes binding.

Example 6.6   Determine the effect of changes in the binding constraint shown in the optimal solution of Example 6.5.

Machine A is the only active (explicit) constraint. The sensitivity ratios for this constraint are:

For Y:
$$\frac{\text{RHS}}{-S_1} = \frac{2}{-1/6} = -12$$

For S_2:
$$\frac{\text{RHS}}{-S_1} = \frac{8}{2/3} = \frac{24}{2} = 12$$

The smallest positive ratio is the 12 associated with S_2. This suggests that constraint A may be relaxed by 12 hours (to 24 hours) before the machine B constraint begins to limit the solution.

A glance at the graphic solution shows that as constraint A is relaxed (i.e., as more hours are added), the machine B constraint takes effect at $Y = 4$. At that point, the profit would be $Z = \$10X + \$30Y = \$10(0) + \$30(4) = \$120$. Also, at $Y = 4$, both machines would be fully utilized, as can be shown by substituting values for X and Y into the constraint equations.

	Old Constraint	Revised Limit	at $X = 0$, $Y = 4$
Machine A:	$4X + 6Y \leq 12$	$4X + 6Y \leq 24$	$4(0) + 6(4) = 24$
Machine B:	$8X + 4Y \leq 16$	no change	$8(0) + 4(4) = 16$

MINIMIZATION AND OTHER FORMS OF CONSTRAINTS

The simplex procedure can also be used to solve cost minimization problems which have objective functions of the form Min $Z = AX_1 + BX_2 + \cdots + MX_n$. Constraints in minimization problems are often of a $\geq$ type rather than the $\leq$ type we just encountered. In these types of constraints we must subtract a *surplus* variable (instead of adding a slack variable). To handle both $=$ and $\geq$ types of constraints, artificial variables are also used (in addition to the S variables). The artificial variables serve only to state the equations in a form suitable for the simplex table and have no other meaning. They are typically assigned very large coefficients (M's), which will quickly drive them out of solution. Problem 6.6 illustrates a graphic solution to a minimization problem, and Prob. 6.10 illustrates the simplex formulation for a different minimization problem.

Solved Problems

RESEARCH AND DEVELOPMENT (EVPI)

6.1   A product-line manager has identified three possible courses of action with expected values (\$000) of $E(A) = 10$, $E(B) = 20$, and $E(C) = 30$. If the EPC = 40, what is the EVPI?

$$\text{EVPI} = \text{EPC} - \text{EMV}^* = 40 - 30 = 10, \text{ or } \$10,000$$

6.2   A petrochemical company's R&D department has received corporate authorization to commence work on any or all of three potential pollution control products. Top management has agreed to allocate \$20,000 each to all projects undertaken. If research efforts are not successful, the product will be scrapped after a year, but the patent rights on any successful development can be sold to a plastics firm for \$50,000, yielding a \$30,000 profit on each.

(a) Set up a payoff table.

(b) Determine how many projects should be undertaken to (1) maximize the maximum possible payoff and (2) to maximize the minimum possible payoff.

(c) If the probabilities for success of 0, 1, 2, or 3 projects are .10, .30, .50, and .10, respectively, how many projects should be undertaken under an EMV criteria?

(d) What is the expected value of perfect information with respect to the success or failure of the project?

(a) The payoff (in $000) from each successful project is $30, whereas each unsuccessful project costs the firm $20. Payoff values are shown in Table 6-15.

Table 6-15

Number Projects Undertaken	(Potential State) Number of Successes			
	0	1	2	3
0	0*	0	0	0
1	−20	30*	30	30
2	−40	10	60*	60
3	−60	−10	40	90*

(b) Maximax = undertake 3 projects in hopes of 3 successes.
Maximin = undertake 0 projects and limit monetary losses to zero.

(c)
$$E(0) = 0$$
$$E(1) = -20(.1) + 30(.3) + 30(.5) + 30(.1) = 25$$
$$E(2) = -40(.1) + 10(.3) + 60(.5) + 60(.1) = 35 \leftarrow EMV^*$$
$$E(3) = -60(.1) - 10(.3) + 40(.5) + 90(.1) = 20$$

Undertake 2 projects for EMV = $35,000.

(d)
$$EVPI = EPC - EMV^*$$

where payoff values for computing EPC are starred in Table 6-15.

$$EPC = 0(.1) + 30(.3) + 60(.5) + 90(.1) = 48$$
$$EVPI = 48 - 35 = 13 \quad \text{or} \quad \$13,000$$

LINEAR PROGRAMMING (GRAPHIC)

6.3 What is the slope for the objective function Max $Z = 10X + 15Y$?

The slope form is $Y = mX + b$, where m = slope.

Rearranging:
$$15Y = -10X + Z$$
$$Y = -\frac{10}{15}X + \frac{Z}{15}$$

Therefore, slope is −10/15, or −2/3.

6.4 Business Services Co. produces two pocket communicators, X and Y, in a facility that has limited production time available. Price, cost, and production times are shown in Table 6-16. A linear programming problem is to be formulated that will maximize the profit contribution of the two lines. Find (a) the objective function, and (b) its slope.

Table 6-16

	Line X	Line Y
Selling price per unit	$187	$100
Variable costs (production and marketing)	32	38
Production hours per unit	3	2

(a)   Contribution for X: $P - \text{VC} = \$187 - 32 = \$155$

   Contribution for Y: $P - \text{VC} = \$100 - 38 = \$62$

$$\text{Max } Z = 155X + 62Y$$

(b) $Z = 155X + 62Y$

$$62Y = -155X + Z$$

$$Y = -\frac{155X}{62} + \frac{Z}{62} = -\frac{5}{2}X + \frac{Z}{62}$$

Therefore, $\text{Slope} = -5/2$

6.5   An electronic-goods manufacturer has distributors who will accept shipments of either transistor radios or electronic calculators to stock for Christmas inventory. Whereas the radios contribute $10 per unit and the calculators $15 per unit to profits, both products use some of the same components. Each radio requires 4 diodes and 4 resistors, while each calculator requires 10 diodes and 2 resistors. The radios take 12.0 minutes and the calculators take 9.6 minutes of time on the company's electronic testing machine, and the production manager estimates that 160 hours of test time are available. The firm has 8,000 diodes and 3,000 resistors in inventory. What product or mix of products should be selected to obtain the highest profit?

The decision variables are radios R and calculators C and we must determine how many of each should be produced to maximize profit Z.

(1)   The objective function is:

$$\text{Max } Z = \$10R + \$15C$$

The constraints are:

Diodes (8,000 available): Radios require 4 each, and calculators 10 each.

$$4R + 10C \leq 8,000$$

Resistors (3,000 available): Radios require 4 each, and calculators require 2 each.

$$4R + 2C \leq 3,000$$

Testing (9,600 minutes available): Radios require 12.0 minutes, and calculators require 9.6 minutes.

$$12.0R + 9.6C \leq 9,600$$

(2)   To graph the variables and constraints see Fig. 6-6:

Diodes: $4R + 10C \leq 8,000$

Plotting this as an equality, we have:

If $R = 0$, then $C = 800$

If $C = 0$, then $R = 2,000$

Resistors: $4R + 2C \leq 3,000$

If $R = 0$, then $C = 1,500$

If $C = 0$, then $R = 750$

Testing: $12.0R + 9.6C \leq 9,600$

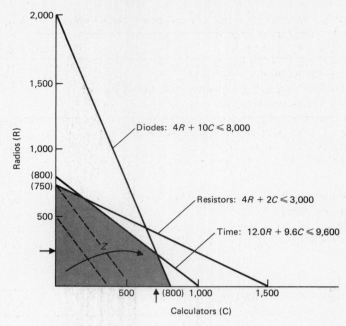

Fig. 6-6

Note that the resulting graph (Fig. 6-6) establishes a feasible region bounded by the time, diode, and resistor constraints and the implicit constraints that $R \geqslant 0$ and $C \geqslant 0$.

(3) Find the slope of the objective function. We can express our objective function in slope-intercept form, where the Y axis corresponds to R and the X axis to C.

$$Z = 10R + 15C$$

or

$$10R = -15C + Z$$

Thus,

$$R = -\frac{15}{10}C + \frac{Z}{10} = -\frac{3}{2}C + \frac{Z}{10}$$

therefore, the slope $= -\frac{3}{2}$, which means that for every 3-unit decrease in Y there is a 2-unit increase in X. This slope is plotted as a dashed line on the graph by marking off 3 units (negative) in R for each 2 units (positive) in C.

(4) Move the objective function to optimize. The slope of the objective function (iso-objective line) is moved away from the origin until constrained. In this case the binding constraints are the diode inventory supply and testing machine time availability.

(5) Read the solution values. The arrows point to the approximate R and C coordinates of the constraining intersection.

$$\text{Number of radios} \cong 240$$
$$\text{Number of calculators} \cong 700$$

Note that the simultaneous solution of the two binding constraint equations would lend more accuracy to the answer:

$$4R + 10C = 8,000 \rightarrow \text{times } (-3) = -12R - 30C = -24,000$$
$$\text{add:} \quad \underline{12R + 9.6C = \quad 9,600}$$
$$-20.4C = -14,400$$
$$C = 705 \text{ calculators}$$

Substituting to solve for R:

$$4R + 10(705) = 8,000$$

Therefore,

$$R = \frac{8,000 - 7,050}{4} = 237 \text{ radios}$$

Comment: We had two decision variables (that is, products) to choose from and established a profit function Z and constraints and optimized the function by moving it away from the origin. The graph of this example (Fig. 6-6) showed that the resistor supply was not constraining, so only two constraints (diodes and test time) were binding. Similarly, there were two decision variables in the solution, that is, we ended up producing both radios and calculators. The number of variables in solution will always equal the number of explicit constraints that are binding.

The graphic linear programming solution gives an indication of the sensitivity of the solution to changes in the constraints. If, for example, additional diodes could be purchased from an outside supplier with no increase in cost, profit would be maximized by extending the iso-objective line to the next corner and producing 1,000 calculators and no radios. In this case we would have one explicit constraint (time) binding and only one decision variable (calculators) in the final solution.

6.6   A textile mill has received an order for fabric specified to contain at least 45 kilograms of wool and 25 kilograms of nylon. The fabric can be woven out of any suitable mix of two yarns (A and B). Material A costs \$2 per kilogram, and B costs \$3 per kilogram. They contain the proportions of wool, nylon, and cotton (by weight) shown in Table 6-17.

Table 6-17

	Wool (%)	Nylon(%)	Cotton (%)
A	60	10	30
B	30	50	20

What quantities (kilograms) of A and B yarns should be used to minimize the cost of this order?

(1)   Objective function is:

$$\text{Min } C = \$2A + \$3B$$

The constraints are:

$$.60A + .30B \geq 45 \text{ kg}$$
$$.10A + .50B \geq 25 \text{ kg}$$

(2)   To graph, see Fig. 6-7.

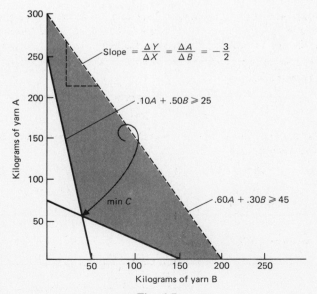

Fig. 6-7

(3)   The slope of the objective is:

$$2A = -3B + C$$

$$A = -\frac{3}{2}B + \frac{C}{2}$$

Therefore, $\text{Slope} = -\frac{3}{2}$

(4 and 5)   From Fig. 6-7, it appears that to optimize, we have:

$$A = 55\,\text{kg} \qquad B = 40\,\text{kg}$$

Simultaneous solution of the two constraint equations reveals that

$$A = 55\,\text{kg} \qquad B = 39\,\text{kg}$$

LINEAR PROGRAMMING (SIMPLEX)

6.7   The Simplex Calculator Company makes a profit of \$5 on each Model X and \$20 on each Model Y. Each calculator requires the following time (in minutes) on the cleaning and testing machines as shown in Table 6-18.

Table 6-18

	X Requirements	Y Requirements	Time Available
Cleaning	2	4	10
Testing	6	3	12

(a)   State the objective function and constraints. (b) Arrange the equations in a simplex format.

(a)   Objective function: $\text{Max } Z = 5X + 20Y$

Constraints:

Cleaning $2X + 4Y \leqslant 10$

Testing $6X + 3Y \leqslant 12$

(b)   See Table 6-19.

Table 6-19

$C \rightarrow$		5	20	0	0	
$\downarrow$	Variables in Solution	X	Y	S_1	S_2	RHS
0	S_1	2	4	1	0	10
0	S_2	6	3	0	1	12
	Z	0	0	0	0	0
	$C - Z$	5	20	0	0	

Table 6-20

$C \rightarrow$		4	8	6	0	0	0	
$\downarrow$	Variables in Solution							RHS
		5	9	0	1	0	0	36
		0	8	5	0	1	0	24
		2	0	5	0	0	1	7
		0	0	0	0	0	0	0
		4	8	6	0	0	0	

6.8 The initial matrix of a maximization linear programming problem was as shown in Table 6-20, where the decision variables are designated A, B, etc. (*a*) State the original constraint equations. (*b*) How many decision variables are there? (*c*) State the objective function. (*d*) What is the value of the first pivot?

(*a*) $5A + 9B \leq 36$, $8B + 5C \leq 24$, and $2A + 5C \leq 7$

(*b*) Three

(*c*) Max $Z = 4A + 8B + 6C$

(*d*) Ratios are $36/9 = 4$ and $24/8 = 3$. Therefore, pivot is the 8.

6.9 A commercial fertilizer manufacturer produces three grades, W, X, and Y, which net the firm $40, $50, and $60 in profits per ton, respectively. The products require the labor and materials per batch that are shown in Table 6-21.

Table 6-21

	W	X	Y	Total Available
Labor hours	4	4	5	80 hr
Raw material A (lb)	200	300	300	6,000 lb
Raw material B (lb)	600	400	500	5,000 lb

What mix of products would yield maximum profits?

The objective function is:

$$\text{Max } Z = 40W + 50X + 60Y$$

The constraints are:

Labor	$4W + 4X + 5Y \leq 80$
Material A	$200W + 300X + 300Y \leq 6,000$
Material B	$600W + 400X + 500Y \leq 5,000$

(1) Using the simplex method, we set up Table 6-22 as follows:

Table 6-22

$C \rightarrow$ $\downarrow$	Variables in Solution	40 W	50 X	60 Decision Variables Y	0 S_1	0 S_2	0 S_3	Solution Values (RHS)
0	S_1	4	4	5	1	0	0	80
0	S_2	200	300	300	0	1	0	6,000
0	S_3	600	400	(500)	0	0	1	5,000
	Z	0	0	0	0	0	0	0
	$C - Z$	40	50	60 $\uparrow$	0	0	0	

(2) The pivot column has the largest positive number (60) in the bottom row—column Y. (Therefore, introduce Y into solution.) *Note*: This is because Y contributes the most ($60) to profits.

(3) The pivot row has the smallest result of:

$$\frac{80}{5} = 16 \qquad \frac{6,000}{300} = 20 \qquad \frac{5,000}{500} = 10$$

Therefore row 3 is the pivot row, and S_3 should be removed from the solution.

Note: S_3 is removed because raw material B is the most restrictive constraint on Y. As computed above, the 80 labor hours divided by 5 hours per unit of Y will permit production of 16 units of Y, and raw material A will permit 6,000 lb $\div$ 300 lb per unit = 20 units of Y, but there is only enough raw material B for $5,000 \div 500 = 10$ units.

(4)   The pivot is circled.

(5)   By dividing values in the pivot row by 500, we obtain the new row (Table 6-23), which we will now refer to as the Y row.

Table 6-23

	W	X	Y	S_1	S_2	S_3	RHS
Y	$\frac{6}{5}$	$\frac{4}{5}$	1	0	0	$\frac{1}{500}$	10

(6)   Convert other values in the pivot column to zero. For S_1 (row 1), multiply new Y row by -5 and add to old S_1 row. For S_2 (row 2), multiply new Y row by -300 and add to old S_2 row.

(7)   Compute Z and $C - Z$ values (Table 6-24) and check for optimality.

Table 6-24

$C \rightarrow$ $\downarrow$	Variables in Solution	40	50	60 Decision Variables	0	0	0	Solution Values (RHS)
		W	X	Y	S_1	S_2	S_3	
0	S_1	-2	0	0	1	0	$-\frac{1}{100}$	30
0	S_2	-160	60	0	0	1	$-\frac{3}{5}$	3,000
60	Y	$\frac{6}{5}$	$\left(\frac{4}{5}\right)$	1	0	0	$\frac{1}{500}$	10
	Z	72	48	60	0	0	$\frac{3}{25}$	600
	$C - Z$	-32	2	0	0	0	$-\frac{3}{25}$	
			$\uparrow$					

(8)   Since the X column has a positive value in the bottom row, repeat.

(9)   The pivot column is column X; therefore, introduce X into solution.

(10) Pivot row:

$$\frac{30}{0} = \infty \qquad \frac{3,000}{60} = 50 \qquad \frac{10}{\frac{4}{5}} = 12.5$$

Therefore, remove Y from solution, and introduce X.

(11) By dividing values in the pivot row by $\frac{4}{5}$, we get a new pivot row (Table 6-25), which is now the X row.

Table 6-25

	W	X	Y	S_1	S_2	S_3	RHS
X	$\frac{3}{2}$	1	$\frac{5}{4}$	0	0	$\frac{1}{400}$	$\frac{25}{2}$

(12) By converting other values in the pivot column into zero, we get new values:
S_1 (row 1): The column value is already zero. Leave as is.
S_2 (row 2): Multiply the new X row by -60 and add to the old S_2 row.

(13) Compute the Z and $C - Z$ values (Table 6-26), and check for optimality.

(14) Since no values are >0 in the bottom row, the solution is complete. The only variable in solution is X, and $\frac{25}{2} = 12.5$ units are produced. The profit is \$625.

Table 6-26

| C → | | 40 | 50 | 60 | 0 | 0 | 0 | Solution |
↓	Variables in Solution	W	X	Y Decision Variables	S_1	S_2	S_3	Values (RHS)
0	S_1	-2	0	0	1	0	$-\frac{1}{100}$	30
0	S_2	-250	0	-75	0	1	$-\frac{9}{20}$	2,250
50	X	$\frac{3}{2}$	1	$\frac{5}{4}$	0	0	$\frac{1}{400}$	$\frac{25}{2}$
	Z	75	50	$\frac{125}{2}$	0	0	$\frac{1}{8}$	625
	C − Z	-35	0	$-\frac{5}{2}$	0	0	$-\frac{1}{8}$	

Comment: The initial matrix (Table 6-22) was a feasible solution at the W, X, Y origin, where no product was produced and the profit was zero. The \$60 in the bottom row indicated that for each unit of Y introduced, the objective function would be increased by \$60. The next matrix (Table 6-24) called for production of 10 units of Y (only) for a profit coefficient of \$600. However, the positive 2 in the bottom row under the X variable column indicated that for every unit of X introduced the objective function would be increased by \$2. The final solution (Table 6-26) called for 12.5 units of X, which raised the profit an additional \$25 to a total of \$625. This is the best that can be obtained given the existing constraints.

MINIMIZATION

6.10 A food supplement for livestock is to be mixed in such a way as to contain exactly 25 pounds of vitamin A, at least 15 pounds of vitamin B, and at least 40 pounds of vitamin C. The supplement is to be made from two commercial feeds. Each pound of feed #1 contains 2 ounces of A, 6 ounces of B, and 4 ounces of C, and costs \$5. A pound of feed #2 contains 4 ounces of A, 1 ounce of B, and 3 ounces of C, and costs \$3. Let X_1 be the pounds of feed #1 and X_2 be the pounds of feed #2. (*a*) Formulate the objective functions and constraints for a linear programming problem that will minimize the cost of the food supplement while satisfying the vitamin content requirements. (*b*) Arrange the problem in an initial simplex format.

(*a*)
$$\text{Min } Z = 5X_1 + 3X_2$$

Vitamin A: $2X_1 + 4X_2 = 400$(i.e., 25 lb @ 16 oz/lb = 400 oz)

Vitamin B: $6X_1 + 1X_2 \geqslant 240$

Vitamin C: $4X_1 + 3X_2 \geqslant 640$

(*b*) The initial simplex table (Table 6-27) is shown below. Note that the = constraint (vitamin A requirements) requires one artificial variable (A_1) to ensure its equality. The two ≥ constraints each require a slack variable and an artificial variable. The slack variables in ≥ constraints represent

Table 6-27

| C → | | 5 | 3 | M | 0 | M | 0 | M | Solution |
↓	Variables in Solution	X_1	X_2	A_1 Decision Variables	S_2	A_2	S_3	A_3	Values RHS
M	A_1	2	4	1	0	0	0	0	320
M	A_2	6	1	0	-1	1	0	0	240
M	A_3	4	3	0	0	0	-1	1	640
	Z	12M	8M	M	$-M$	M	$-M$	M	1,200M
	C − Z	$5-12M$	$3-8M$	0	M	0	M	0	

amounts that must be subtracted from the constraint value; hence, they must have a negative sign. All artificial variables are assigned an extremely large cost M to ensure that they are driven out of solution by the simplex iterative procedure.

The solution procedure is the same as in maximization problems except that the variable with the most *negative* value in the bottom $(C - Z)$ row is always the one introduced. Problems such as this, or others that involve more than two or three variables or constraints, are most easily solved on a computer. The solution to this problem is to produce 136 units of X_1 and 32 units of X_2 for a minimum total cost of $776.

Supplementary Problems

6.11   If an analyst evaluating 4 courses of action (A, B, C, D) has determined that the expected value of perfect information is $1,360 and the expected monetary value is $4,560, what is the expected profit under certainty?   *Ans.* $5,920

6.12   Given the payoff matrix, Table 6-28, with the probability values shown, find (*a*) EMV*, (*b*) EPC, (*c*) EVPI.   *Ans.* (*a*) $54,000 (*b*) $64,000 (*c*) $10,000

Table 6-28

	Profit ($000) if demand is		
	Low ($p = .2$)	Medium ($p = .6$)	High ($p = .2$)
A	30	60	60
B	40	50	20
C	80	40	−20

6.13   The research department of an automobile firm has developed a new type of bicycle gear mechanism which could be very profitable if accepted nationally by teenagers. The firm must decide whether to go into production of the product themselves, enter into a lease agreement with a New England manufacturer, or sell the patent rights to the Swish Bicycle Company. It estimates its present-value payoffs under the alternative actions as shown in Table 6-29.

Table 6-29

	Market Condition (values in $000)		
	Poor	Good	Excellent
Produce gears themselves	(80)	40	200
Lease production rights	20	50	100
Sell patent rights	50	50	50

The research department has also made a study of the market and feels it will most likely be either excellent ($p = .4$) or poor ($p = .4$) with only a 20 percent chance it can be classified as good. (*a*) What course of action should be followed under a criterion of (1) maximax, (2) maximin, (3) maximum probability?   (*b*) For which course of action is the expected value highest and what is the EMV*?   (*c*) What is the expected profit under certainty (EPC)?   (*d*) What is the EVPI?
Ans.   (*a*) (1) produce, (2) sell, (3) either produce or sell (*b*) lease, EMV* = $58,000 (*c*) $110,000 (*d*) $52,000

6.14   Southern Oak Furniture Association (SOFA) must select one model of a chair to produce from their current line, but they have no firm orders from distributors and are uncertain about demand. They have estimated the likelihood of demand and associated profits per day as shown in Table 6-30.

Table 6-30

	Profit ($) if demand is		
	Low $(p = .3)$	Medium $(p = .5)$	High $(p = .2)$
Contemporary	2,500	6,000	10,000
Danish	500	5,000	15,000
Early American	−4,000	4,000	25,000

(a) What is the optimal choice and the EMV*?   (b) Suppose the firm could send representatives around to all its distributors and establish with certainty what the actual demand would be. How much could the firm justify paying per day for this type of information?
Ans.   (a) Early American with EMV* = 5,800 (b) $2,950

6.15   A mining operations manager must decide whether to extend existing tunnels at a mine or sink a new shaft. Present-value payoff amounts (in millions) are as shown in Table 6-31 with probabilities for the various states of nature as indicated in parenthesis. What is the best alternative on the basis of (a) maximax, (b) maximin, (c) maximum expected value?
Ans.   (a) new shaft (b) extend tunnel (c) new shaft

Table 6-31

	Profit if ore grade is:		
	Low $(p = .2)$	Medium $(p = .4)$	High $(p = .4)$
Extend tunnels	80	150	200
New shaft	5	30	380

6.16   Suppose some exploratory drilling could reduce the uncertainty associated with the ore grade in Prob. 6.15. What is the maximum cost that would be justified to obtain perfect information?
Ans. $63 million

6.17   The objective function for a linear programming problem concerned with product mix is Max $Z = 25X + 5Y$. What is the slope of this objective?   *Ans.*   −5

6.18   Use the graphic method of linear programming to solve Prob. 6.7.
Ans.   Slope of objective = −1/4, $X = 0$, $Y = 2\frac{1}{2}$, $Z = 50$.

6.19   Sunstroke Paint Co. makes a profit of $5 per gallon on its oil-based paint and $7 per gallon on its latex paint. Both paints contain two ingredients, A and B. The oil-based paint contains 80 percent A and 20 percent B, whereas the latex paint contains 40 percent A and 60 percent B. Sunstroke currently has 20,000 gallons of A and 8,000 gallons of B in inventory and cannot obtain more at this time. The company wishes to use linear programming to determine the appropriate mix of oil-based and latex paint to produce to maximize its total profit. (a) Let A be X_1 and B be X_2. State the objective function and constraints. (b) What is the slope of the objective function?
Ans.   (a) Max $5X_1 + 7X_2$, $.8X_1 + .4X_2 \leqslant 20,000$, $.2X_1 + .6X_2 \leqslant 8,000$ (b) −5/7 or −7/5 (depending upon choice of variables)

6.20 A production analyst has formulated the matrix shown in Table 6-32 for a maximization problem. Using the simplex method, complete the next two iterations and determine the resultant value of the objective function.   *Ans.* 4

Table 6-32

$C \rightarrow$		1	1	0	0	
$\downarrow$	Variables in Solution	X_1	X_2	S_1	S_2	RHS
0	S_1	1	11/2	1	0	12
0	S_2	2	1	0	1	4
	Z	0	0	0	0	0
	$C-Z$	1	1	0	0	

6.21 A data processing manager wishes to formulate a linear programming model to help him decide how to use his personnel as programmers (X_1) or systems analysts (X_2) in such a way as to maximize revenues (Z). Each programmer earns \$40 per hour, and each systems analyst earns \$50 per hour. Programming work during the coming week is limited to 50 hours, maximum. The production scheduler has also specified that the total programming time plus two times the systems analysis time be limited to 80 hours or less. State the objective function and constraints.
Ans. Max $Z = 40X_1 + 50X_2$, $X_1 \le 50$, $X_1 + 2X_2 \le 80$

6.22 Solve Prob. 6.21 via the graphic method, using X_1 for the horizontal axis and X_2 for the vertical axis.
Ans. $X_1 = 50$, $X_2 = 15$, $Z = \$2,750$

6.23 Set up the initial simplex table (Table 6-33) for Prob. 6.21.
Ans.

Table 6-33

$C \rightarrow$		40	50	0	0	
	Variables in Solution		Decision Variables			
		X_1	X_2	S_1	S_2	RHS
0	S_1	1	0	1	0	50
0	S_2	1	2	0	1	80
	Z	0	0	0	0	0
	$C-Z$	40	50	0	0	

6.24 Solve Prob. 6.21 via the simplex method.   *Ans.* $X_1 = 50$, $X_2 = 15$, $Z = \$2,750$

6.25 A manufacturer makes \$5 profit on each unit of X and \$10 on each unit of Y. Each product requires different amounts of time on each of two machines as shown (in hours) in Table 6-34. Use (a) the graphic, and (b) the simplex methods to determine what quantity of X and Y should be produced to maximize profits.
Ans. $X = 0$, $Y = 4$, $Z = 40$ (*Note*: Slope of objective = slope of one of the constraints, so multiple solutions are possible down to $X = 4/5$, $Y = 18/5$.)

Table 6-34

Machine	Requirements for X	Y	Total Available
A	2	4	16 hr
B	6	2	12 hr

6.26   Max $Z = 6X + 9Y$ subject to $2X + 6Y \leqslant 30$, $4X + 3Y \leqslant 36$.   *Ans.* $X = 7$, $Y = 8/3$, $Z = 66$

6.27   Precast Co. can produce grade A material, which yields a profit of $1 per unit, and grade B material, which yields a profit of $2 per unit. Each unit of A requires 2 hours of machining and 1 hour of finishing. Each unit of B requires 1 hour of machining and 3 hours of finishing. If 200 hours of machining capacity and 300 hours of finishing capacity are available, (*a*) what amounts of A and B should be produced to maximize profits, and (*b*) what is the profit?   *Ans.*   (*a*) $A = 60$, $B = 80$ (*b*) $220

6.28   A company producing a standard and a deluxe line of electric clothes dryers has the time requirements (in minutes) shown in Table 6-35 in departments where either model can be processed:

Table 6-35

	Standard	Deluxe
Metal frame stamping	3	6
Electric motor installation	10	10
Wiring	10	15

The standard models contribute $30 each and the deluxe $50 each to profits. The motor installation production line has a full 60 minutes available each hour, but the stamping machine is available only 30 minutes per hour. There are two lines for wiring, so the time availability is 120 minutes per hour. What is the optimal combination of output in units per hour? (Solve graphically.)
Ans.   standard = 2, deluxe = 4

6.29   Solve Prob. 6.28 via the simplex method.   *Ans.*   standard = 2, deluxe = 4

6.30   Southern Oak Furniture Association (SOFA) has a plant in Arkansas which produces three models of chairs. The profit contributions per chair are as follows:

$$C = \text{Contemporary} = \$10$$
$$D = \text{Danish} = 15$$
$$E = \text{Early American} = 25$$

The firm's dry-kiln capacity for green lumber limits the total production of any mix of chairs to 1,000 per day. If all production went into contemporary chairs and the dry kilns did not limit production, the firm could produce 1,500 chairs, but the Danish models take 1.5 times as long, and the Early American models take twice as long as the contemporary models. Also, the Danish models require special inlaid backs, which come from a single supplier who cannot supply more than 500 per day. Assuming that the firm's retailers would accept any mix of models, use the simplex method to determine the optimal selection to maximize profits.
Ans.   Produce 750 Early American chairs for a profit of $18,750.

Chapter 7

Process Planning and Analysis

Simulation

PROCESS-PLANNING ACTIVITIES

Process planning consists of designing and implementing a work system to produce the desired products in the required quantities at the appropriate times within acceptable costs. This transformation of resources into higher-valued goods and services is the technological heart of a production operation. It merges input from the market environment (shown on the left side of Fig. 7-1) and the organization's own technological base (on the right) into an economically efficient

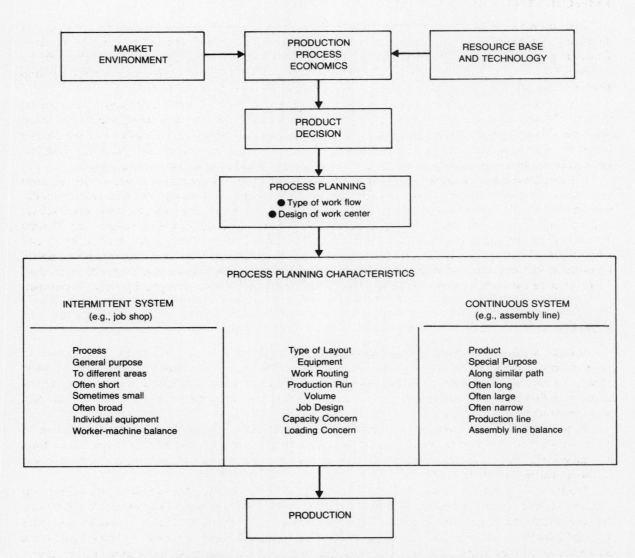

Fig. 7-1 Process planning considerations in intermittent and continuous systems

124

productive activity. The actual transformation processes range from mechanical assembly, electrical, and chemical process (largely for goods) to medical, educational, and informational processes (for services).

Computer-aided process planning involves the use of computers to help plan routings and schedules. Preparing schedules for group-technology work centers is less complicated than for individual machines because of reduced number of items and number of routings. Computer simulation is also an effective way of planning an efficient process flow.

As illustrated in Fig. 7-1, process-planning activities are concerned with (1) the type of work flow, and (2) the design of work centers. Work flow is a function of the type of layout (process or product) and whether it is designed for intermittent or continuous processing activities. In intermittent systems, planning efforts are focused on individual equipment capacities and worker-machine balance, whereas in continuous systems, the concerns are with line capacity and assembly line balancing. (See Chap. 5 problems.)

INTERMITTENT AND CONTINUOUS PRODUCTION SYSTEMS

Intermittent systems are used to produce small quantities (or batches) of many different items on relatively general-purpose equipment. Over 50 percent of all manufacturing is done in batches. Processing equipment and personnel are located according to function, and products flow through the facilities on irregular paths. Jobs are individually routed, scheduled, and controlled on a job or shop *order-control* system. The goods or services are often customized or *made to order*.

Continuous systems are used to produce large volumes of a single item (or relatively few items) on specialized equipment following a fixed path. Items follow a similar production sequence, which can be anything from a pipeline (for oil) to an assembly line (for computers). Routing and scheduling focus on *flow controls* that govern the rate of flow of raw materials and finished products. High-volume, line-assembled products are often of standardized design and *made for stock*.

Flexible production systems are a computer-enhanced form of continuous systems and are used to produce large volumes of customized products on highly automated equipment that is individually responsive to logic commands. Flexible systems rely heavily on microprocessors to store, manipulate, and transmit information for production activities. By using computer-aided manufacturing (CAM) systems, firms are able to combine the benefits of intermittent (process) layouts with the speed advantages of continuous (product-line) layouts. Flexible production systems require more capital investment, but operate with reduced labor cost. Machine utilization may increase from 25 percent to 70 percent or even 80 percent. In some plants, processing times have dropped by over 50 percent.

ROBOTS

Robots are computerized manipulators that can perform a variety of tasks in response to programmed commands or sensory input (e.g., from vision, sound, or touch systems). The simplest robots do manual manipulations or fixed-sequence activities. More intelligent robots have microprocessors that can store, manipulate, and react to information concerning materials, times, locations, and manufacturing activities.

Robots are a vital element in most flexible production systems because they can handle information, and do physical work. And the quality of the work is typically more consistent than human efforts. They don't miss welds, and they also save on the amount of welding rod used because of the uniformity of their welds.

Traditional "hard automation" is designed to accomplish specific tasks that produce identical outputs. Robots are more flexible; they can perform a variety of functions. Programmable robots can be reprogrammed simply by changing their software, or instructions. "Smart" robots can even respond (almost instantaneously) to online needs. They can (with a camera-sensitive lens) locate parts on a moving conveyor, retrieve, assemble, inspect, sort, and relocate those parts as necessary. Some robots can even recognize voice commands and respond to questions by way of a speech synthesizer.

Most robot applications are found in industrial plants in Japan, Europe, and the United States. Firms like Ford and General Motors employ thousands of robots in such diverse tasks as materials-handling, welding, painting, assembly, inspection, and testing activities. A robot's cost ($50,000 to $150,000) is often recovered in two to three years. Savings stem from higher machine utilization, improved quality, and reduced space requirements, plus reductions in material and labor costs. Labor savings are often dramatic; for example, requiring 100 workers instead of 500 or gaining a doubling of output without any increase in the number of workers. And with robots there are no collective bargaining agreements to negotiate or retirement costs to fund.

Robots do replace workers, so the threat of putting individuals out of work is real. However, the collapse of whole industries that do not automate with robots may be worse. Thus one challenge to industry is to retrain the work force for new and upgraded positions in programming, control, and maintenance of high technology equipment. A second challenge is to consciously direct human efforts away from tasks that can be done by robots and other machines toward more people-oriented functions. This may follow the realization that full employment is unattainable and that leisure time can be spent productively and rewardingly in activities that serve humanity.

ASSEMBLY AND FLOW-PROCESS CHARTS

Assembly and flow-process charts are useful aids for planning and managing transformation processes. *Assembly charts* show the material requirements and assembly sequence of components that make up a mechanical assembly. They use standard symbols of ○ for operations and □ for inspections. When the chart also provides complete instructions on how to produce an item, including specifications for the component parts plus operating and inspection times, it is referred to as an *operations-process chart*.

Example 7.1 An electric heater assembly consists of the following parts, as shown in Fig. 7-2:

(1)	Body	(4)	Switch	(7)	Resistor wire	(10)	End plates
(2)	Bracket	(5)	Internal wiring	(8)	Porcelain rod	(11)	Plastic end caps
(3)	Insulator	(6)	Cord	(9)	Copper end caps	(12)	Screen

Parts 2 and 3 are subassembled, as are 7 and 8 plus 7, 8, and 9. A test follows the heater element installation (i.e., after 7, 8 and 9), and a final inspection terminates the assembly. Draw an assembly chart.

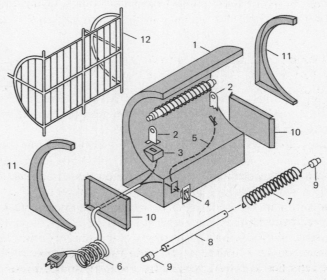

Fig. 7-2

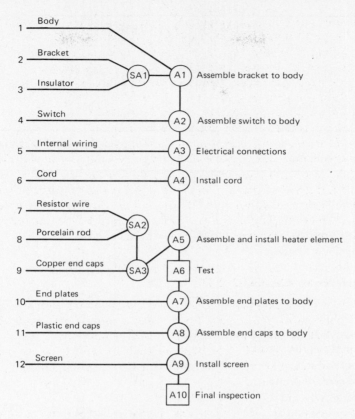

Fig. 7-3 Assembly chart for electric heater

Flow-process charts use symbols similar to assembly charts, except that the nonproductive activities of transport (⇒), delay (D), and storage (▽) are also included. They also have room for time, distance moved, and other relevant information.

Example 7.2 Construct a simplified flow-process chart (that is, a chart with no analysis or action entries) for the activity of counting one inventory item, entering the count on a computerized inventory record file, and obtaining a printout of the record. Make whatever time and distance assumptions are appropriate. See Fig. 7-4 for solution.

Most flow-process charts are also designed to facilitate analysis by questioning why each activity is done, and whether that activity can be improved upon by eliminating a task, combining tasks, changing the sequence of operations, or simplifying tasks or operations in any way. Problem 7-2 illustrates one such chart.

WORKER-MACHINE AND ACTIVITY CHARTS

Worker-machine charts are graphic devices for modeling the simultaneous activities of a worker and the equipment he or she operates. They help identify idle time and costs of both workers and machines. Process planners can then analyze alternative worker-machine combinations and determine the most efficient arrangement.

Worker-machine charts show the time required to complete tasks that make up a work cycle. A *cycle* is the length of time required to progress through one complete combination of work activities. Many worker-machine activities are characterized by a load-run-unload sequence. The chart must be continued long enough past the start-up time to reach an equilibrium cycle time.

<table>
<tr><td colspan="5" align="center">FLOW PROCESS CHART
(Simplified Version)</td></tr>
<tr><td colspan="2">Job Inventory Count
☒ Existing method
☐ Proposed method</td><td colspan="3">Date July 6th
Charted by B. Roe
Chart No. 231</td></tr>
</table>

Details of Method	Activity	Time (min)	Distance (ft)	Notes and Analysis
1. Walk to storage location	○⇨□D▽	1.25	110	
2. Visually locate item	●⇨□D▽	.30		
3. Inspect and confirm stock number	○⇨■D▽	.10		
4. Count number in stock	●⇨□D▽	Varies		
5. Return to computer station	○⇨□D▽	1.25	110	
6. Insert inventory record disk	●⇨□D▽	.20		
7. Wait for computer to "boot up"	○⇨□D▽	.25		
8. Type in inventory count	●⇨□D▽	2.20		
9. Save new count on disk	●⇨□D▽	.50		
10. Call for computer print routine	●⇨□D▽	.10		
11. Wait for printer to print record	○⇨□D▽	1.50		
12. Inspect record for accuracy	○⇨■D▽	.30		
13. File inventory record printout	○⇨□D▽	.50		
14. Remove inventory record disk	●⇨□D▽	.10		
15. File inventory record disk	○⇨□D▽	.45		
16. _____	○⇨□D▽			
17. _____	○⇨□D▽			

Fig. 7-4

Example 7.3 An operator at Goodtire Rubber Co. is expected to take 2 minutes to load and 1 minute to unload a molding machine. There are several machines of this type, all doing the same thing, and the automatic run time on each is 4 minutes. Respective costs are $8 per hour for the operator and $20 per hour for each machine.

(a) Construct a worker-machine chart for the most efficient one-worker, two-machine situation.

(b) What is the cycle time?

(c) What is the worker's idle time per cycle?

(d) What is the total idle time per cycle for both machines?

(e) What is the total cost per hour?

(f) What is the total cost per cycle?

(g) What is the idle time cost per hour?

(a) If the operator begins by loading machine 1, the cycle does not reach an efficient steady state until the ninth minute, as shown in Fig. 7-5.

(b) CT = 7 minutes

(c) The worker is idle 1 minute per cycle.

(d) The machines are not idle (at steady-state operation).

(e) Cost = worker cost + 2 (cost for each machine) = $8 + 2($20) = $48/hr = $48 per 60 min

(f) $$\text{Cost/cycle} = \frac{\$48}{60 \text{ min}} \left(\frac{7 \text{ min}}{\text{cycle}}\right) = \$5.60/\text{cycle}$$

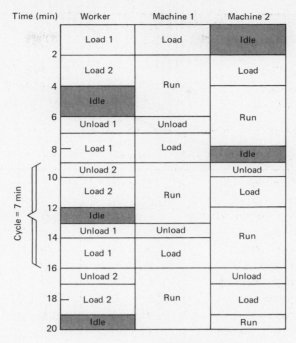

Fig. 7-5 Worker-machine chart

(g) $$\text{Idle time cost/hr} = \frac{1\text{ min}}{\text{cycle}}\left(\frac{60\text{ min/hr}}{7\text{ min/cycle}}\right)\frac{\$8}{60\text{ min}} = \$1.14/\text{hr}$$

Activity charts are similar to worker-machine charts, except all components represent machines (or workers). Problem 7.3 illustrates an activity chart for a mining operation.

EQUIPMENT SELECTION (MACHINE BREAKPOINTS)

Process-planning decisions often concern the selection of equipment capacities required to produce a specified level of output. When the processing costs of alternative ways of doing a job can be allocated into their fixed- and variable-cost components, the most economical alternative is the one with the lowest costs at the expected volume. A graph of the respective costs will reveal the machine breakpoints.

Example 7.4 Brackets for an electric generator can be processed on any of three machines with costs as shown in Table 7-1.

Table 7-1

	Machine X	Machine Y	Machine Z
Fixed cost per setup	$100	$200	$600
Variable cost per unit	3	2	1

Which machines should be used for production runs of up to 500 units?

At 500 units:

$$\text{TC} = \text{FC} + \text{VC}(Q)$$
$$\text{TC}_X = 100 + 3(500) = \$1600$$
$$\text{TC}_Y = 200 + 2(500) = \quad 1200$$
$$\text{TC}_Z = 600 + 1(500) = \quad 1100$$

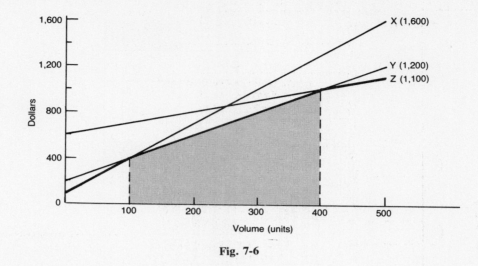

Fig. 7-6

For each machine, graph the FC at zero volume and the TC at 500 units as a linear function as shown in Fig. 7-6. For $0 \leqslant 100$ units use X, for 100 to 400 units use Y, and for over 400 units use Z.

SIMULATION MODELING OF OPERATIONS

Some problems are too complex to solve with pure mathematics, or they involve random elements or risk situations that defy a practical mathematical solution. In such situations, analysts sometimes construct a model of the real-world problem and use a trial-and-error approach to arrive at a reasonable solution to the problem.

Simulation is a means of modeling the essence of an activity or system so that experiments can be conducted to evaluate the system's behavior or response over time. It is not an optimizing technique (like linear programming), but it does permit the decision maker to attack problems that are too complex or unsuitable for ordinary mathematics. Simulations may be done manually or physically, but most realistic business problems are done on computer. No attempt is made to duplicate reality in all respects—only the relevant variables of the problem under study are included.

Table 7-2 lists the advantages and disadvantages of using simulation, and Fig. 7-7 describes the steps in a simulation.

Table 7-2   Advantages and Disadvantages of Using Simulation

Advantages	Disadvantages
1. Facilitates understanding of complex systems.	1. Does not suggest a solution methodology.
2. Applies to problems that defy mathematical solution.	2. Does not apply to deterministic problems.
3. Avoids risk or disruptive experimentation with actual system.	3. Does not necessarily yield an optimal solution.
4. Compresses time to reveal long-range effects.	4. Requires expertise to construct sophisticated models.
5. Less costly than real-world experimentation.	5. Uses expensive labor and computer time.

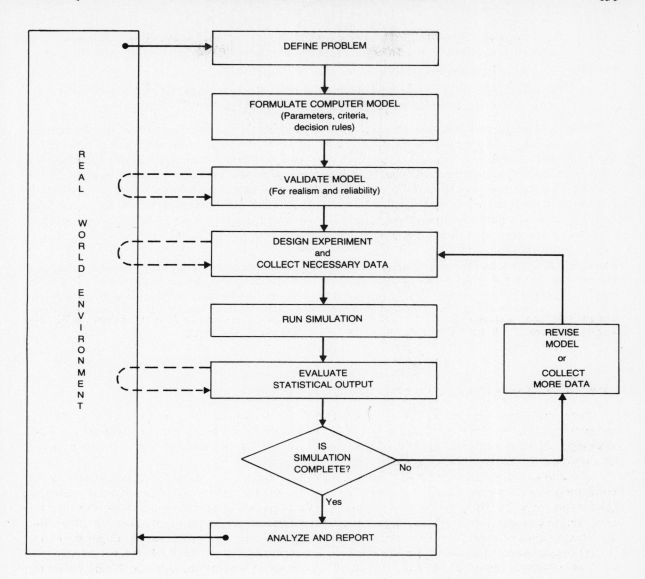

Fig. 7-7　Flowchart showing steps in the simulation process

MONTE CARLO SIMULATION USING EMPIRICAL DATA

Numerous production activities, such as process planning, scheduling, and maintenance efforts, are influenced by uncertainties, such as variable work times, unknown demand, and breakdowns. Simulations of uncertain activities that involve a stochastic sampling process are frequently referred to as Monte Carlo methods. *Monte Carlo simulations* use random observations from a probability distribution to duplicate the variability pattern in the system under study. For example, the following steps would simulate an assembly activity.

(1)　Collect actual (empirical) data on the distribution of assembly times (or estimate them from a pilot activity).

(2)　Develop a probability distribution and a cumulative probability distribution.

(3) Assign an interval of random numbers to each class of the distribution. (Optionally, the cumulative distribution may be plotted, showing relative frequency on the vertical axis.)

(4) Using random numbers (RN's), derive simulated assembly times.

(5) Interpret the results (e.g., determine the proportion of actual times that exceed estimated times or the effect of one work station on the next).

The random-number assignment (step 3) is arranged so that the probability of obtaining a random number in the specified interval corresponds exactly with the empirical frequency reflected in the probability distribution (step 2). Thus, if 10 observations (from 100 total) lie in the first class, the random-number range assigned to that class would be 00 to 09. This represents 10 percent of the possible two-digit numbers from 00 to 99. (*Note*: The upper end of each interval will always be one less than the cumulative probability value.) The actual random numbers used (step 4) can come from either a random number table such as Appendix A (which is useful for small, hand calculations) or from computer-generated random numbers (for large studies).

Example 7.5 A process planner is working on plans for producing a new detergent. She wishes to simulate a raw-material demand in order to plan for adequate materials-handling and storage facilities. On the basis of usage for a similar product introduced previously, she has developed a frequency distribution of demand in tons per day for a two-month period. Use this data (shown in Table 7-3) to simulate the raw material usage requirements for 7 periods (days).

Table 7-3

Demand (X) (tons/day)	Frequency (no. days)
10	6
11	18
12	15
13	12
14	6
15	3
	60

(1) Data are given in frequencies. (2) To formulate a probability distribution, divide each frequency by the total (60); for example, $6 \div 60 = .10$, and $18 \div 60 = .30$. Then formulate a cumulative-probability distribution by successively summing the probability values (Table 7-4).

Table 7-4

Demand (tons/day)	Frequency (no. days)	Probability P(X)	Cumulative Probability
10	6	.10	.10
11	18	.30	.40
12	15	.25	.65
13	12	.20	.85
14	6	.10	.95
15	3	.05	1.00
	60		

(3) Next, assign random-number intervals so that the number of values available to each class corresponds with the probability (Table 7-5). Using 100 two-digit numbers (00–99) we assign 10 percent (00–09) to the first class, 30 percent (10–39) to the second class, and so on.

Table 7-5

Demand (tons/day)	Probability $P(X)$	Corresponding Random Numbers
10	.10	00–09
11	.30	10–39
12	.25	40–64
13	.20	65–84
14	.10	85–94
15	.05	95–99
	1.00	RN = 27

(4) We obtain random numbers (RN) from column 1 of Appendix A (for convenience), so the first seven numbers are:

$$27 \qquad 13 \qquad 80 \qquad 10 \qquad 54 \qquad 60 \qquad 49$$

The first RN, 27, falls into the second class of the distribution and corresponds to a demand of 11 tons per day.

Table 7-6

Random number	27	13	80	10	54	60	49
Simulated demand	11	11	13	11	12	12	12

(5) This extremely small simulation yields a mean of $\bar{X} = 11.7$ tons (Table 7-6) and a standard deviation of $s = .76$ ton. The expected value from the empirical probability distribution is $E(X) = \Sigma[XP(X)] = 12.05$ tons, suggesting that the small sample size of only 7 periods has resulted in some error. A much larger sample should be simulated before the simulation results are used for making decisions.

Note that in Example 7.5 the width of the random number "target" in each class corresponds *exactly* with the relative frequency of the class. This helps to ensure that the simulated results have the same type of distribution as the original data. This is more apparent in the graphic method (see Prob. 7.4), where the vertical distances on the graph correspond to the relative frequencies of the respective classes.

SIMULATIONS USING KNOWN STATISTICAL DISTRIBUTIONS

When values to be used in a simulation follow a known statistical distribution, the computations can be simplified. For example, simulated values can be obtained from uniform and normal distributions as follows:

Uniform Distribution

$$\text{Simulated value} = a + (b - a)(\text{RN}_\%) \tag{7.1}$$

where a = minimum value

b = maximum value

$\text{RN}_\%$ = random number (as a percent) from a table of uniformly distributed random numbers (See Appendix H.)

Normal Distribution

$$\text{Simulated value} = \mu + \sigma(\text{RN}_{\text{ND}}) \tag{7.2}$$

where μ = mean of database being simulated

             σ = standard deviation of database being simulated

     RN_{ND} = random number (as a Z score) from a table of normally
                 distributed random numbers (See Appendix I.)

Poisson Distribution

        Simulated value = value of c that corresponds to the cumulative $P(\leqslant c|\lambda)$

where c = cumulative number of occurrences of an event (and the upper limit of the class)

       λ = average number of occurrences (and mean of the Poisson distribution)

The simulated class (and value of c) is determined probabilistically by expressing a random number RN_{ND} as a decimal and assigning it to the appropriate class. (See Prob. 7.7 for example.)

Example 7.6 (*Uniform Distribution*)   The diameters of trees arriving at a lumber mill vary uniformly from 2 feet to 3 feet. The time required to saw a 2-foot log is 5 seconds and to saw a 3-foot log is 8 seconds; within that range it varies directly with the diameter. Simulate the time required to saw five logs selected at random in the 2–3 foot range.

$$\text{Simulated value} = a + (b - a)(RN_{\%})$$

where $a = 5$ seconds, $b = 8$ seconds, and $b - a = 3$ seconds. $RN_{\%}$ will be taken from the first five values of three-digit numbers from column 2 of the Random Number Table (Appendix A). See Table 7-7.

Table 7-7

RN	$a + (b - a)(RN_{\%})$	=	Simulated Value
435	$5 + 3(.435)$	=	6.31 sec
143	$5 + 3(.143)$	=	5.43 sec
362	$5 + 3(.362)$	=	6.09 sec
620	$5 + 3(.620)$	=	6.86 sec
573	$5 + 3(.573)$	=	6.72 sec

Example 7.7 (*Normal Distributions*)   A patient-care service in a hospital has normally distributed times with a mean of 15 minutes and standard deviation of 2 minutes. Simulate four values of the times required to perform this service, using the table of normally distributed random numbers.

$$\text{Simulated value} = \mu + \sigma(RN_{ND})$$

where $\mu = 15$, $\sigma = 2$, and RN_{ND} are from column 1 of Appendix H. See Table 7-8.

Table 7-8

RN_{ND}	$\mu + \sigma(RN_{ND})$	=	Simulated Value
.34	$15 + 2(.34)$	=	15.68 min
-1.09	$15 + 2(-1.09)$	=	12.82 min
-1.87	$15 + 2(-1.87)$	=	11.26 min
1.57	$15 + 2(1.57)$	=	18.14 min

Solved Problems

ASSEMBLY AND FLOW-PROCESS CHARTS

7.1 A production analyst estimated the times for activities associated with a new casting process and came up with the information in Table 7-9. Show the activities in the form of a flow-process chart (Fig. 7-8).

Table 7-9

Number	Classification	Time
1	Perform casting operation	12 min
2	Inspect casting	2 min
3	Wait for lift truck	13 min
4	Transport to warehouse	4 min
5	Store: await shipment	3 days

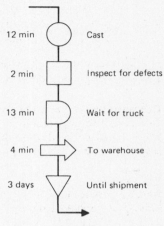

Fig. 7-8

7.2 A flow-process chart is to be constructed for the activity of installing a zirconium control rod (C/R) in a pressurized water reactor during a shutdown. The C/R is to be transferred from a water pit, to a cask, to the reactor, and installed. Make whatever assumptions are required to construct the flow-process chart.

See Fig. 7-9.

FLOW PROCESS CHART

Job _C/R installation_

[X] Existing method

[ ] Proposed method

Date _July 18_
Charted by _L.J. Smith_
Chart no. _1F423_

Details of method	Activity	Time	Distance (ft)	What?	Where?	When?	Who?	How?	Notes	Eliminate	Combine	Change sequence	Simplify	Other
In pit	○⇨□ D ▼	8:10	—											
Inform supervisor	●⇨□ D ▽	8:33	—					X	Eliminate signature — use intercom	X		X		
Wait for approval	○⇨□ ● ▽	8:45	—											
Lift C/R into cask	●⇨□ D ▽	9:16	20											
To reactor	○➡□ D ▽	9:19	130											
Clear area	●⇨□ D ▽	9:40	—		X				Need advance warning			X		
Quality inspection	○⇨■ D ▽	9:47	—											
Install C/R	●⇨□ D ▽	10:03	12											
In reactor	○⇨□ D ▼	10:15	—											

Fig. 7-9

WORKER-MACHINE AND ACTIVITY CHARTS

7.3 The accompanying portion of an activity chart (Fig. 7-10) is for an automatic-loader mining operation. The loader, in the mine, requires 8 minutes to load a skip car. There are three skips, and they take 9 minutes to travel loaded to the ore dump, 2 minutes to dump, and 7 minutes to return empty. The operating cost of each skip is $200 per hour, and the automatic-loader cost (including worker and machine) is estimated at $350 per hour.

(*a*) What is the length of the cycle?

(*b*) What is the idle-time cost per hour?

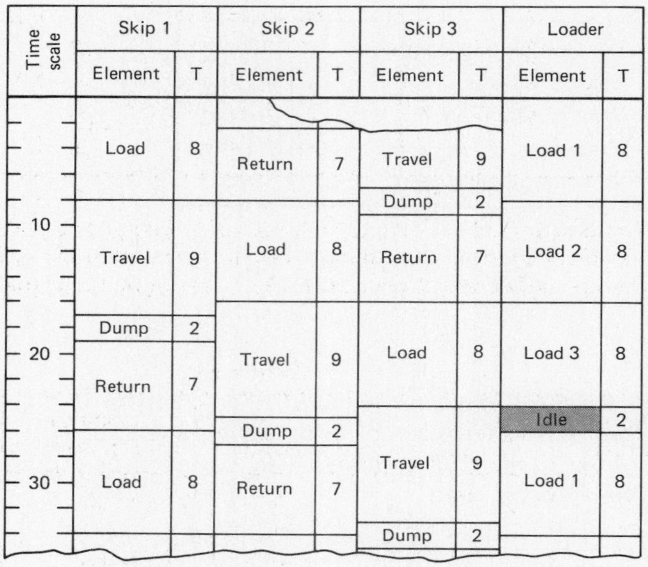

Fig. 7-10

(*a*) *Cycle length*: The system is in a similar state at times 8 and 34. Therefore,

$$\text{Cycle length} = 34 - 8 = 26 \text{ min}$$

(*b*) *Idle-time cost*: The loader is idle 2 minutes per cycle = 2/26 = 1/13 of each hour. Therefore,

$$\text{Cost/hr} = 1/13(\$350) = \$26.92/\text{hr}$$

MONTE CARLO SIMULATION USING EMPIRICAL DATA

7.4 Generator Service Co. (GSCO) has ongoing contracts with several electric utilities wherein GSCO agrees to provide technicians whenever a customer has a generator shutdown and needs technical assistance. The GSCO operations manager is concerned with maintaining enough technicians to give the needed service while staying within a limited budget for personnel. He has collected data on the number of service requests per day over a 200-day period as shown in Table 7-10. (*a*) Simulate the service requests for a 1-week (7-day) period by using random numbers applied to a cumulative distribution. (*b*) Compare the simulated values with the historical average.

Table 7-10

Number of service requests	0	1	2	3	4	5	6
Frequency	30	40	60	44	20	6	0

(a) Data are given in frequencies. Develop a relative cumulative probability distribution (Table 7-11) by first converting the frequencies into probabilities (i.e., divide each by the total frequency) and then successively summing the probabilities.

Table 7-11

Number of Service Requests	Frequency	Probability	Cumulative Probability
0	30	30/200 = .15	.15
1	40	40/200 = .20	.15 + .20 = .35
2	60	.30	.35 + .30 = .65
3	44	.22	.87
4	20	.10	.97
5	6	.03	1.00
	200	1.00	

Now assign two-digit random number intervals to the cumulative probabilities so they correspond with the probability intervals. For example, assign 15 percent of the random numbers (00–14) to the first class (zero requests), and 20 percent (15–34) to the second class (one request) as shown in Table 7-12.

Table 7-12

Request Class	Frequency	Probability	Cumulative Probability	Random No. Assigned
0	30	.15	.15	00–14
1	40	.20	.35	15–34
2	60	.30	.65	35–64
3	44	.22	.87	65–86
4	20	.10	.97	87–96
5	6	.03	1.00	97–99

Finally, select 7 two-digit random numbers from a random-number table, determine which request class they fall into, and record the corresponding number of service requests as shown in Table 7-13.

Table 7-13

Day	1	2	3	4	5	6	7	
Random number	85	68	99	21	17	56	12	Total
Corresponding number of service requests	3	3	5	1	1	2	0	15

(b) Note that the mean number of requests from the 7-day simulation is 15/7 = 2.14 service requests. This compares with the mean of the historical data of

$$\mu = 0(.15) + 1(.20) + 2(.30) + 3(.22) + 4(.10) + 5(.03) = 2.01$$

7.5 Empirical data collected on the time required to weld a transformer bracket were recorded to the nearest quarter minute, as shown in Table 7-14

Table 7-14

Weld Time (min)	Number of Observations
< .25	0
.25 < .75	24
.75 < 1.25	42
1.25 < 1.75	72
1.75 < 2.25	38
2.25 < 2.75	14
2.75 < 3.25	10

(*a*)   Formulate a cumulative distribution in percentage terms.

(*b*)   Graph the frequency and cumulative distributions.

(*c*)   A simulation is to be conducted using random numbers. What simulated weld times (to the nearest .25 minute) would result from the random numbers 25, 90, and 59?

(*d*)   What proportion of the times exceed 2.0 minutes?

(*a*)   Cumulative distributions are usually formulated on a scale where the cumulative percentage is more than or less than a corresponding *x* axis amount. We shall use a "less than" percentage and so will need to identify the upper-class boundaries (UCB) as the *Y* coordinates for the cumulative distribution (Table 7-15).

(*b*)   The frequency distribution is constructed by extending vertical lines from the class boundaries to the appropriate frequency level for the class. For the cumulative distribution, values of the cumulative percentage of time <UCB are plotted at weld times corresponding to the UCB. For example, the frequency (12 percent) is plotted at UCB = .75 (as illustrated in Fig. 7-11).

(*c*)   The simulated time for random number (RN) 25 is determined by entering the cumulative graph at 25 (as shown by the arrow) and proceeding horizontally to the curve and then down to the weld time. The result is a reading of 1.0 minute (rounded to the nearest .25 minute). Times for random numbers 90 and 59 are 2.5 and 1.5 minutes, respectively. (A larger graph would lend more accuracy.)

(*d*)   From the cumulative distribution, about 12 percent of the times exceed 2.0 minutes.

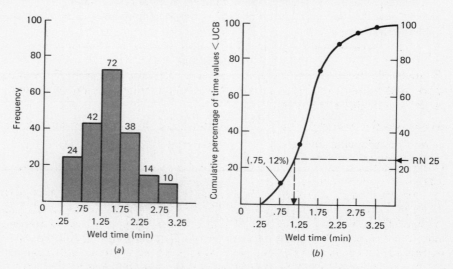

Fig. 7-11   Frequency and cumulative distributions

Table 7-15

Weld Time (min)	Frequency in Numbers	Upper-Class Boundary (UCB)	Cumulative Number of Times <UCB	Cumulative Percentage of Times <UCB
< .25	0	.25	0	0
.25 < .75	24	.75	24	12
.75 < 1.25	42	1.25	66	33
1.25 < 1.75	72	1.75	138	69
1.75 < 2.25	38	2.25	176	88
2.25 < 2.75	14	2.75	190	95
2.75 < 3.25	10	3.25	200	100

7.6 In an aircraft assembly operation, activity A precedes activity B, and inventory may accumulate between the two activities. With the use of random numbers, a simulated sample of performance times yielded the values shown (minutes) in Table 7-16.

Table 7-16

Activity A		Activity B	
Random Number	Time (min)	Random Number	Time (min)
07	.3	63	.5
90	.8	44	.4
02	.2	30	.4
50	.5	98	.9
76	.6	30	.4
47	.5	72	.6
13	.3	58	.5
06	.3	96	.9
79	.7	37	.4

(a) Simulate the assembly of six parts, showing idle time in activity B, waiting time of each part, and number of parts waiting. *Note*: Omit the first random number of A so that activity B begins at time zero.

(b) What was the average length of the waiting line ahead of B (in number of units)?

(c) What was the average output per hour of the assembly line?

(a) Our interest lies in activity B, so we can set up Table 7-17 to show when parts arrive at B, how long it takes B to work on them, and the resultant idle and waiting times:

Activity B begins at 0, and it takes .5 minute to complete the first part. B is then idle for .3 minute until part 2 arrives from A at .8 minute. Part 2 takes .4 minute, so the ending time is .8 + .4 = 1.2 minutes. By this time part 3 has been waiting .2 minute because it became available at .8 + .2 = 1.0 minute, but work could not be begun on it until 1.2 minutes. However, before activity B is finished on part 3 at 1.6 minutes, part 4 has arrived (at 1.0 + .5 = 1.5 minutes), and so one part is waiting. We continue systematically in this manner through part 6, noting that when it is finished at time 3.5 minutes, there are two parts waiting, for their availability times were 2.9 minutes and 3.2 minutes, respectively.

Table 7-17

Part Number	Part Available for Activity B at Time	Activity B Beginning Time	Activity B Ending Time	Activity B Idle Time	Waiting Time of Part	Number Parts Waiting at B End Time
1	—	0	.5	0	0	0
2	.8	.8	1.2	.3	0	1
3	1.0	1.2	1.6	0	.2	1
4	1.5	1.6	2.5	0	.1	1
5	2.1	2.5	2.9	0	.4	2
6	2.6	2.9	3.5*	0	.3	2
7	2.9				1.0†	
8	3.2					

*Total run time.
†Total waiting time.

(*b*) The average length of the waiting line (that is, average inventory) ahead of B can be expressed in equation form as follows:

$$\text{Average inventory} = \frac{\text{total waiting time}}{\text{total run time}} \qquad (7.3)$$

$$= \frac{1.0 \text{ assembly minute}}{3.5 \text{ minutes}} = .29 \text{ assembly}$$

(*c*) Average output per hour:

$$\text{Units/hr} = \frac{6 \text{ units}}{3.5 \text{ min}} \left(\frac{60 \text{ min}}{\text{hr}} \right) = 102.9 \text{ units/hr}$$

SIMULATIONS USING KNOWN STATISTICAL DISTRIBUTIONS

7.7   *Simulated Poisson Arrivals.* The pattern of arrivals of patients to the emergency room of a large metropolitan hospital can be described by a Poisson distribution with a mean of four per hour. Simulate the number of patient arrivals for an 8-hour shift. (*Note*: For random numbers, use the first three digits of column 3 of the Random Number Table, Appendix A.)

First, obtain the cumulative probability distribution from the Poisson Distribution Values, Appendix D. For a mean of $\lambda = 4$, the cumulative probabilities can be taken directly from the table as $P(X \leq c | \lambda)$. Thus $P(X \leq 0 | \lambda = 4) = .018$ and $P(X \leq 1 | \lambda = 4) = .092$, etc., as seen in Table 7-18.

Table 7-18

No. patients c	0	1	2	3	4	5	6	7	8	9	10	11	12
Cumulative $P(c)$	.018	.092	.238	.433	.629	.785	.889	.949	.979	.992	.997	.999	1.000

Next, obtain eight random numbers (one to represent the number of patients arriving during each hour of the shift).

     853   540   985   903   266   373   920   164

Next, convert each random number to a number of patients per hour by assigning each to the appropriate cumulative probability class. For example, the first RN 853 falls within the .785 to .889 class (in Table 7-18), which belongs to the interval classified as 6 patients (or anything between 5 and 6) as shown in Table 7-19. Note also that because we are using only three random digits in our random number scale of 000–999, we must advance any random numbers that happen to lie on the upper

Table 7-19   Simulated Number of Patient Arrivals

RN	853	540	985	903	260	373	920	164
No. arrivals	6	4	9	7	3	3	7	2

boundary into the next larger class. Thus, the first class should represent 18/1000 of the numbers, and this is satisfied by the digits 000–017. So, a random number exactly 018 would be interpreted as one patient arrival rather than as zero.

Supplementary Problems

7.8   A toy car is to be assembled in the following order:

(1)   Start with base frame   (5)   Assemble wheels onto axles

(2)   Add upper body   (6)   Snap on wheel and axle assembly

(3)   Install motor   (7)   Snap on bumper

(4)   Snap on hood   (8)   Inspect

Draw an assembly chart.   *Ans.*   See Example 7.1 and Fig. 7-3 for a comparable chart.

7.9   Drexron Furniture Co. maintains a constant stock of chair backs for a standard line of dining room chairs. The activities and associated times for producing one lot are as shown in Table 7-20. Illustrate the activities in the form of a simplified flow-process chart.

Ans.   See Prob. 7.1 for comparable chart. Symbols, in sequence, are $\bigcirc$, $\Rightarrow$, $\bigcirc$, $\square$, D, $\Rightarrow$, $\bigcirc$, D, $\Rightarrow$, $\triangledown$

Table 7-20

Number	Activity	Time
1	Rough cut—saw shop	20 min
2	Move to lathe shop	10 min
3	Turn in lathes	60 min
4	Inspect for flaws	5 min
5	Wait for lift truck	15 min
6	Move to gluing area	10 min
7	Glue rods to backplate	30 min
8	Wait for glue to dry	180 min
9	Move to warehouse	10 min
10	Store for later use	

7.10   The operations shown in Table 7-21 must be performed on a housing which is part of a motor-mounting bracket. The housings are then inspected before going on to the next assembly operation. This takes 6 seconds for each.

(*a*)   Construct an operations process chart showing the activities, appropriate symbols, and times in minutes.

(*b*)   How many of each type of machine would be required for a production rate of 300 parts per hour, assuming 80 percent utilization of the X-100 shear machine and 100 percent utilization of the others?

   Ans.   (*a*) shear = .75 min/part, form = .15 min/part, clean = .40 min/part, inspect = .10 min/part (*b*) shear = 5 machines, form = 1 machine, clean = 2 machines

Table 7-21

Operation	Machine	Output, parts/hr
Shear	Shear X-100	80
Form	Main press	400
Clean	Ultrasonic tank	150

7.11 Rework Prob. 7.3, except with load times of 8 minutes, travel times of 6 minutes and return times of 4 minutes. Assume 2-minute dump times. Find the (a) length of the cycle, and (b) the idle time cost per hour.   *Ans.*   (a) 24 minutes (b) $100 per hour

7.12 A construction firm uses dump trucks to haul asphalt to a distant location, where a paving machine applys a four-inch layer to a new roadway. Trucks require 3 minutes for loading at the asphalt plant, 7 minutes to travel loaded to the new roadway, 10 minutes to dump the asphalt into the paving machine, and 5 minutes to return empty. The firm has only one paving machine, and it paves only while it is being fed (and pulled) by a truck during its dumping activity. (a) How many trucks are required to pave the roadway as quickly as possible?   (b) Construct an activity chart for a two-truck, one-paving-machine arrangement.   (c) If the paving machine cost is $80 per hour, and the truck cost is $34 per hour, how many trucks should be used to minimize the idle equipment cost?
Ans.   (a) 2.5 trucks are required, so use 3 trucks. (b) The cycle time is 25 min. (c) With 2 trucks, idle machine cost = $16 per hour, and with 3 trucks, idle truck time cost = $17 per hour, so use 2 trucks.

7.13 A production analyst is planning for the manufacture of valve fittings. Each fitting must be milled on any one of three milling machines, X, Y, or Z. The set-up and operating costs for each are as shown in Table 7-22.

Table 7-22

	Setup	Operating
X	$10	$.30/unit
Y	30	.10/unit
Z	40	.05/unit

(a) Graph the cost structure for the three alternatives for volumes up to 250 units. (b) For what *range* of outputs should the analyst specify the use of machine Y?
Ans.   (a) Graph should show $ on Y axis, units on X. (b) $0 \leqslant 100$ use X, $100 \leqslant 200$ use Y, >200 use Z

7.14 A large grocery distribution center in Denver is computerizing its order service department. Orders from customers in Colorado (and adjacent states) will go via phone line directly into the company's main computer, which will generate "pick lists" with standard times to fill each order. To assist in planning for the proper number of delivery trucks, planners have collected the data shown in Table 7-23 from the past year (300 days).

Table 7-23

No. trucks required, X	20	21	22	23	24	25	26	27	28	29	30	31	32
No. days, frequency	0	4	18	25	28	41	68	56	31	22	5	2	0

(a) Simulate the demand for trucks over a 10-day period. (*Note*: Use the first three digits from column 6, Appendix A for your random numbers.) Compute (b) the mean and (c) the standard deviation of your simulated sample.   *Ans.*   (a) See Table 7-24. (b) $\bar{X} = 26.2$ trucks (c) $s = 2.0$ trucks

Table 7-24

RN	697	667	248	063	887	432	732	970	449	425
No. trucks	27	27	24	22	28	26	27	29	26	26

7.15 Data were collected on the assembly times for 1,000 water valves (size 2 inches, 150 pounds) at the Drain Company, as shown in Table 7-25.

Table 7-25

Time		Number of Valves
LCB	UCB	
1.0	Under 1.5 min	0
1.5	Under 2.0 min	20
2.0	Under 2.5 min	120
2.5	Under 3.0 min	280
3.0	Under 3.5 min	430
3.5	Under 4.0 min	120
4.0	Under 4.5 min	30
4.5	Under 5.0 min	0
		1,000

(*a*) Graph the data as a cumulative distribution.   (*b*) What percentage of the assembly times exceed 4.0 minutes?   (*c*) What would be the simulated assembly time for a random number of 44? (Estimate to the nearest half minute.)

Ans.   (*a*) Graph should show assembly times (in minutes) on *X* axis and cumulative percentages on *Y* axis (*b*) 3 percent (*c*) approximately 3 minutes

7.16 Operation B follows operation A. In a simulated operating time of 440 minutes, operator B was idle 15.2 minutes, and the total waiting time of assemblies before B was 1,980 minutes. If B completed 92 parts during the production run, what was the average inventory of parts waiting for B in terms of number of assemblies?   *Ans.*   4.5 assemblies

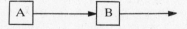

Table 7-26   Operator A

Unit	1	2	3	4	5	6	7	8	9	10
Random no.	76	60	07	22	14	94	87	11	37	88
Time (sec)	8	6	2	4	4	11	10	3	5	10

Table 7-27   Operator B

Unit	1	2	3	4	5	6	7	8	9	10
Random no.	69	46	17	13	38	12	42	29	36	44
Time (sec)	7	6	4	4	5	3	6	5	5	6

7.17 An assembly operation has been simulated using random numbers with the results as shown in Tables 7-26 and 7-27. Operator B started at time zero.

A simulation of the assembly of 10 units has been begun in Table 7-28. Complete the remaining portion of the table and utilize the data from the first 8 units to determine the average length of the waiting line ahead of B.

Table 7-28

Unit No.	Unit Available for B at Time	Activity B Data			Unit Data	
		Beginning Time	Ending Time	Idle Time	Waiting Time	Number Waiting
1	0	0	7	0	0	1
2	6	7	13	0	1	2
3	8	13	17	0	5	2
4	12	17	21	0	5	1
5						
6						
7						
8						
9						
10						

Ans.   For 8 parts: B ending time = 48, total waiting time = 19 seconds, average length of line = .40 units

7.18 In the meal preparation kitchens of New York International Airlines, dinners are prepared on an assembly line where there is limited space for an inventory of partially filled plates. A simulation of two adjacent workers (where Y is dependent upon X) developed the random numbers and times shown (in seconds) in Table 7-29.

Table 7-29

Activity X		Activity Y	
Random Number	Time	Random Number	Time
72	22	84	32
18	10	26	12
77	23	13	8
84	27	60	24
5	7	53	22
20	11	22	12
46	27	90	36

(*a*) Simulate the preparation of five meals, and determine the idle time for activity Y, the waiting time of each meal, and the number of meals waiting (omitting the first random number of X).   (*b*) What was the average length of the waiting line upstream from Y?   (*c*) What was the average output per minute of the production line?

Ans.   (*a*) Follow tabular format for simulation (*b*) .47 meal (*c*) 2.83 meals per minute

7.19 A promotional campaign is being planned where winners have an equal (uniform) chance of winning either 1, 2, 3 . . . up to 10 hours of professional instruction in small computer operations. Simulate the amount of time the firm will have to provide for the first five winners of the contest. Use the first two-digit random numbers from column 7, Appendix A, and round your simulated times to the nearest whole hour.   *Ans.*   9, 8, 7, 2, 3, for an average of 5.8 hours per winner

7.20 The time required to service a customer at the Pacific Airlines Counter is normally distributed with a mean of 2 minutes and standard deviation of .5 minute. Simulate the service times for three customers using a table of normally distributed random numbers. (Assume the numbers selected from the table at random are: $-.48$, 1.54, and $-.22$.)   *Ans.*   1.76, 2.77, and 1.89

7.21 A process planner must plan for maintenance facilities capable of repairing an average of three motors per day. Breakdowns are assumed to follow a Poisson distribution. Using the first 3 digits of column 4 of the Random Number Table, Appendix A, simulate the number of motor breakdowns over a 10-day period.   *Ans.*   5, 1, 2, 3, 1, 3, 7, 6, 0, 7

7.22 A governmental agency must plan for the staffing of a social services office. Service times for one worker can be described by a Poisson distribution with a mean of 2.6 people per hour. Using the first 3 digits of column 5 of the Random Number Table, Appendix A, simulate the number of people served per hour by one social worker over an 8-hour day.   *Ans.*   2, 2, 1, 3, 1, 2, 4, 2

Chapter 8

Job Design and
Work Measurement

Statistical Sample Size

OVERVIEW

Employees are the most valuable asset of an organization. They have an intrinsic value that no equipment can match, and a diversity of skills, emotions, and levels of performance that cannot be found in any machine.

Jobs are the activities performed by workers to meet organizational goals. As depicted in Fig. 8-1, job designs dictate work methods, which in turn require some form of measurement and yield some degree of job satisfaction. Much of the managerial effort devoted to human resource management concerns these four areas: (1) job design, (2) job satisfaction, (3) work methods, and (4) work measurement.

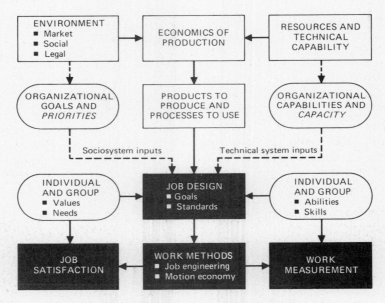

Fig. 8-1 Elements of job design and work methods

Work is the actual activity employees undertake to complete the job and obtain the extrinsic rewards. Umstat suggests that work goals should be (1) clear and specific, (2) moderately difficult, and (3) accepted.

POLICY FOUNDATIONS

All workers share a common *human essence*, which is the basis for civil rights and fair employment practices. In addition, Maslow suggests that workers have a *hierarchy of needs* including

146

(1) self-preservation, (2) safety, (3) belonging, (4) respect, and (5) self-actualization. The highest (self-actualization) includes the use of knowledge, values, and skills in decision-making activities. Recognizing this, a sound human resource management policy rests upon two cornerstones:

(1)   Treat all employees with equal, human respect.

(2)   Where possible, design jobs to foster satisfaction of higher-level needs.

APPROACHES TO JOB DESIGN

Job design is the conscious structuring of the content and methods of work effort. The design may specify *what* task is to be done, *how* to do it, and if necessary, *when* and *where* to do it. Job designs should be consistent with organizational objectives, and agreed on by both employee and employer.

Past approaches to job design have emphasized the objective efficiency of getting the job done, or the behavioral satisfactions of the employees, or both. See Table 8-1. The *efficiency approach* stems from Taylor's scientific-management concepts and has given us quantitative measures such as time studies, work sampling, and methods-improvement studies. The *behavioral* emphasis has developed from the Hawthorn studies, plus the work of Herzberg, Hackman and Oldham, and others, and has been exemplified by some Japanese management systems. The behavioral approach has laid claim to productivity and quality improvements as a result of having more broadly trained and highly motivated employees. Many firms have successfully blended appropriate elements of both systems.

Table 8-1   A Comparison of Some Job Design Characteristics

Highly Objective ◄——— Job Design ———► Highly Behavioral		
On *job* to be done	Emphasis	On *individual* hired
Written in detail	Job description	*Unwritten*
Highly *specialized*	Job assignments	Widely *diversified*
Specific—and *limited*	Job training	General—and *continuous*
Highly *specified*—no discretion	Job methods	Highly *unspecified*—much freedom
Immediate objective measure	Performance	Measured over *long run* only

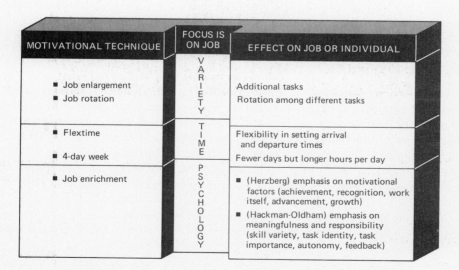

Fig. 8-2   Motivational techniques used in job design

JOB SATISFACTION

The specialization of labor, coupled with the use of highly automated assembly lines, has resulted in many monotonous jobs. The *sociotechnical systems approach* is concerned with effectively blending the sociological concerns of the workers with modern technology of robots and computer-controlled machines. It emphasizes the need for individual and group autonomy to do well-defined and responsible tasks. Jobs that require skill or knowledge generate respect within the worker's own work group. A variety of tasks, arranged into a meaningful work cycle that evidences a contribution to the end product or service, is also motivating to workers.

Figure 8-2 identifies some motivational techniques used in job design. *Job enlargement* involves increasing the horizontal scope of a job by adding different tasks of the same skill and responsibility level. *Job enrichment* involves increasing the vertical scope of a job by requiring additional skills or responsibility. The *Hackman-Oldham* approach to job enrichment emphasizes the need for (1) meaningful work, (2) responsibility for outcomes, and (3) knowledge of actual results.

WORK METHODS AND MOTION ECONOMY

Work methods are ways of doing work. Both new and existing jobs can be analyzed by the relatively standardized approach described in Table 8-2.

Table 8-2   Steps in a Methods-Improvement Study

1. *Select* the job to be studied.
2. Document and *analyze* the present method.
3. *Develop* an improved method.
4. *Implement* the improved method.
5. *Maintain* and follow up on the new method.

Jobs that have a high labor content and are done frequently, or are unsafe or tiring offer the most potential for improvement. Analysis of the present job method makes use of flow-process and worker-machine charts (see Chap. 7) plus a questioning technique which asks of every activity: (*a*) what is its purpose, and (*b*) why is it necessary? In addition, standardized lists of *Principles of Motion Economy* is useful for studying work methods.[1] Micromotion studies using high-speed cameras are also used in job improvement. The improved method of doing a job typically flows from the earlier analysis and must be convincingly applied and monitored.

WORKER SAFETY AND PRODUCTIVITY

Worker safety and productivity are basic concerns in job design. Accidents result from both facility hazards and employee (or management) negligence. Roughly 5 percent of employees incur a work-related injury or illness each year. In addition to untold grief, the resulting absenteeism exacts a staggering effect upon productivity. The Occupational Saftey and Health Act (OSHA) has forced a widespread upgrading of industrial safety standards in the United States since the 1970s.

Accidents are regarded as chance occurrences. The probability of their happening can be analyzed on a statistical basis by using the standard rules of probability (see Chap. 2).

Example 8.1 Company safety records show that 40 percent of all accidents occur when new employees (those with less than one year's service) are operating equipment, and 60 percent occur when experienced employees

---

[1]R.M. Barnes, *Motion and Time Study Design and Measurement of Work*, 6th ed., John Wiley, New York, 1968, p. 220.

are operating it. The firm averages six accidents over a 300-workday year. What is the chance that on any given day during the year an accident will happen to (a) a new employee, (b) an experienced employee?

$$P(\text{new}|\text{accident}) = P(N|A) \quad = .40$$
$$P(\text{old}|\text{accident}) = P(O|A) \quad = .60$$
$$P(\text{accident}) = P(A) = 6/300 = .02$$

(a) $$P(A \text{ and } N) = P(A)P(N|A) = (.02)(.40) = .008$$
(b) $$P(A \text{ and } O) = P(A)P(O|A) = (.02)(.60) = .012$$

In addition to a motivating and safe environment, productivity is also influenced by the wages paid to employees and by the amount of capital investment per employee. Wage levels depend largely upon the industry, the locality, and the classification system used by the firm. Collective bargaining agreements have, in the past, tended to push up union wages faster than corresponding increases in output, which has had a detrimental effect on productivity. High interest rates (and inflation) that discourage investment in labor-saving equipment also stifle productivity.

WORK-MEASUREMENT OBJECTIVES

Labor standards are declarations of the amount of time that should reasonably be used to perform a specified activity at a sustainable rate, using established methods under normal working conditions. Standards satisfy the needs of the worker, provide a measure of performance for the organization, and facilitate scheduling and costing of operations. Methods used to set standards include (1) historical (estimates from experience), (2) time study, (3) predetermined time standards, and (4) work sampling.

TIME-STUDY EQUATIONS

Time-study methods were originally developed by Taylor and are still the most widely used technique for work measurement of short, repetitive tasks. The task is broken down into basic elemental motions, and each element is timed with a stopwatch. Then the average time over several cycles is computed and adjusted for the speed and skill, or performance rating (PR), of the worker studied. Finally, an allowance factor (AF) is applied for personal needs, unavoidable delays, and fatigue. Table 8-3 summarizes the calculations; symbols are explained in the examples that follow.

Table 8-3   Steps in Conducting a Time Study

1. Select the job, inform the worker, and define the best method.
2. Time an appropriate number of cycles n. Use a sample size chart or graph to determine n, or

    If s is known: $$n = \left(\frac{Zs}{e}\right)^2 \qquad (8.1)$$

    If s is unknown: $$n = \frac{Z^2[n'\Sigma X^2 - (\Sigma X)^2]}{e^2(\Sigma X)^2} \qquad (8.2)$$

3. Compute the *cycle time* $$\text{CT} = \frac{\Sigma \text{ times}}{n \text{ cycles}} \qquad (8.3)$$

4. Compute the *normal time* $$\text{NT} = \text{CT} \times \text{PR} \qquad (8.4)$$

5. Compute the *standard time* $$\text{ST} = \text{NT} \times \text{AF} \qquad (8.5)$$

    If allowances are a percentage of the total (workday) time: / If allowances are a percentage of the working time:

    $$\text{AF} = \frac{1}{1 - \% A_{\text{total}}} \qquad\qquad \text{AF} = 1 + \% A_{\text{work}} \qquad (8.6)$$

STATISTICAL SAMPLE SIZE

The required sample size n can be determined from numerous charts, graphs, or equations, as illustrated in Table 8-4 and Fig. 8-3. The chart in Fig. 8-3 is for ± 5 percent accuracy for various coefficient-of-variation values, V.

Table 8-4   Number of Cycles for a Time Study*

When time per cycle is $\geq$ (minutes):	Minimum number of cycles to be timed if annual activity is:		
	<1,000	1,000–10,000	>10,000
480	1	1	2
120	1	2	4
60	2	3	5
30	3	4	8
12	5	6	12
7.2	6	8	15
4.8	8	10	20
3.0	10	12	25
1.2	15	20	40
.72	20	25	50
.48	25	30	60
.30	30	40	80
.18	40	50	100
.12	50	60	120
<.12	60	80	140

*Benjamin W. Niebel, *Motion and Time Study*, 7th ed., Richard D. Irwin, Inc., Homewood, IL, 1982, p. 337.

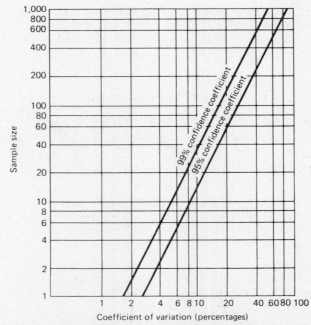

Fig. 8-3   Time-study sample size chart (for $\pm 5\%$ accuracy). (From A. Abruzzi, *Work Measurement*, Columbia University Press, New York, 1952.)

Table 8-4 gives a suggested minimum number of observations to be included as a function of the cycle time and its annual frequency. It is representative of the simplified tables used widely in industry. Figure 8-3 permits us to read the sample size directly from a chart, once a value for the coefficient of variation V has been estimated from a preliminary or partial sample. The coefficient of variation tells how much variability exists in the data relative to the value of the mean.

$$V = \frac{s}{\bar{X}} \qquad (8.7)$$

Example 8.2 A packaging firm has an order for 8,000 plastic inserts which have a .50-minute assembly time. How large a sample should be taken to set a time standard for the assembly activity?

From Table 8-4, for cycle times between .48 to .72 minute, use $n = 30$ cycles.

Example 8.3 A preliminary sample showed a mean of 1.25 minutes and a standard deviation of 15 seconds. How many cycles should be timed in order to be 95 percent confident that the resultant standard time is accurate within plus or minus 5 percent of the population value?

$$V = \frac{s}{\bar{X}}$$

where
$$s = \frac{15}{60} = .25 \text{ min}$$

$$V = \frac{.25}{1.25} = .20 = 20\%$$

Therefore, from Fig. 8-3, use $n = 60$ cycles.

Whereas tables and graphs always assume some values for the confidence level desired Z and the precision or maximum error e, these values can be individually specified if one uses an equation to calculate the sample size. Then, for example, if one wished to have 92 percent confidence that the error is held to within plus or minus .25 minute, the Z value (from the normal distribution) would be 1.75 and e would be .25. If the standard deviation is known, Eq. 8.1 may be used to find n. Otherwise, data from a preliminary sample of n' is needed and Eq. 8.2 is used.

Example 8.4 How large a sample size is needed to be 92 percent confident that a time-study result is accurate within plus or minus .12 minute, if the standard deviation is $s = .45$ minute?

$$n = \left(\frac{Zs}{e}\right)^2 = \left(\frac{1.75 \times .45}{.12}\right)^2 = 43$$

ADJUSTMENTS, ALLOWANCES, AND STANDARD TIMES

The performance rating (PR), done by an experienced analyst, adjusts the standard so that it is not geared to the skill or effort level of the particular worker being observed. Thus, if the worker under study has a high PR, for instance 120 percent, the cycle time will be multiplied by 1.20, resulting in a longer normal time, which will serve as a fair standard for an average worker.

Allowances take account of unavoidable delays, rest breaks, and personal time. Two methods are in common use to compute an allowance factor. Either method can be used so long as one follows a consistent calculation of the allowance factor, AF, so it is *very important* to distinguish whether the allowance percentage ($\%A$) applies to the total time (including allowable time) or to the working time only.

Example 8.5 A job being time studied has allowances of 20 minutes per 8-hour day for rest breaks and 28 minutes per day for unavoidable delays. Compute the allowance factor if allowances are computed as a percentage of (a) total available time, and (b) working time only.

(a) Allowances as a percentage of total time:

$$\%A_{\text{total}} = \frac{20 + 28}{(8 \text{ hr})(60 \text{ min/hr})} = \frac{48}{480} = .10 = 10\% \qquad \text{AF} = \frac{1}{1 - \%A_{\text{total}}} = \frac{1}{1 - .10} = 1.11$$

(b) Allowances as a percentage of working time:

$$\%\,A_{\text{work}} = \frac{20 + 28}{480 - (20 + 28)} = \frac{48}{432} = .111 = 11.1\%$$

$$AF = 1 + \%\,A_{\text{work}} = 1 + .11 = 1.11$$

Unless otherwise stated, we will assume allowances are computed as a percentage of total time.

Example 8.6 A time study of a food service activity yielded a cycle time of 3.4 minutes and a performance rating of 85 percent. Using the 48-minute allowance per 8-hour day (from Example 8.5), compute the standard time.

$$NT = CT \times PR = 3.4 \times .85 = 2.89 \text{ min}$$
$$ST = NT \times AF$$

where
$$AF = \frac{1}{1 - .10} = 1.11$$

Therefore,
$$ST = (2.89)(1.11) = 3.21 \text{ min}$$

Example 8.7 A time study of a shop worker revealed the actual times shown in Table 8-5. The standard deviation of the sample (with the 10.20-minute cycle omitted) was $s = .21$ minute. The analyst rated the worker at 90 percent PR, and the company allows the following per 8-hour day:

Personal time   20 min
Delay time   30 min

Table 8-5

Time (min/cycle)		
Worker	Machine	Total
2.30	.80	3.1
1.80	.80	2.6
2.00	.80	2.8
2.20	.80	3.0
1.90	.80	2.7
10.20*	.80	11.0
2.20	.80	3.0
1.80	.80	2.6

*Unusual, nonrecurring situation.

(a) Find the standard time.

(b) Determine whether the sample was of adequate size for the analyst to be 99 percent confident that the resultant standard time is within 5 percent of the true value. If it was not, how many cycles should have been time-studied to gain this level of confidence?

(a) Cycle time should omit the unusual situation of taking 10.20 minutes.

$$\text{Worker CT} = \frac{\Sigma \text{ times}}{n \text{ cycles}}$$

$$= \frac{2.30 + 1.80 + 2.00 + 2.20 + 1.90 + 2.20 + 1.80}{7} = 2.03 \text{ min}$$

$$\text{Machine CT} = .80 \text{ min}$$

$$NT = CT \times PR = \underset{\text{(worker time)}}{2.03(.90)} + \underset{\text{(machine time)}}{.80(1.00)} = 2.63 \text{ min}$$

$$ST = NT \times AF$$

where

$$\%A_{total} = 50 \text{ min as } \% \text{ of } 480 = \frac{50}{480} = 10.42\%$$

Therefore,

$$AF = \frac{1}{1 - \%A_{total}} = \frac{1}{1 - .1042} = 1.116$$

$$ST = (2.63)(1.116) = 2.94 \text{ min/cycle}$$

(b) Coefficient of variation:

$$V = \frac{s}{\bar{x}} = \frac{.21}{2.03} = 10.34\%$$

Using Fig. 8-3, $n \cong 40$ cycles would have been required. The 7 cycles were not adequate for 99 percent confidence.

Although time-study methods are widely used, an increasing number of firms with exceptionally good labor relations hesitate to institute them because they fear that definitive standards would damage an already cooperative work environment. Firms that emphasize group activities and participative decision-making are less likely to rely upon published standards to measure or motivate their employees. Also, when the labor cost constitutes a small proportion of the end-product cost (e.g., less than 15 percent) the benefits of enforcing rigid production standards may not outweigh the costs.

PREDETERMINED TIME STANDARDS

Predetermined time standards are job times that are established by defining a job in terms of very small basic elements, using published tables to find the time for each element, and adding the element times to determine a total time for the job. Three measurement systems are *methods time measurement* (MTM), *basic motion time* (BMT), and *work factor*. Advantages of these methods are (1) the standard can be determined from universally available data, (2) the standard can be completed before a job is done, (3) no performance rating is required, (4) there is no disruption of normal activities, and (5) the methods are widely accepted as fair systems of determining standards.

The MTM system uses times for basic motions ("therbligs") consisting of activities such as search, select, grasp, and transport loaded. Times are measured in time-measurement units (TMUs) where one TMU equals .0006 minute.

WORK SAMPLING

Work sampling is a work-measurement technique that consists of taking random observations of workers to determine the proportion of time they spend doing various activities. It is particularly useful for analyzing group activities and long-cycle activities. Data is recorded in the form of counts of times working or idle rather than as stopwatch times. However, once collected, the data can be used for standards purposes, as well as for methods or cost analysis. See Table 8-6.

SAMPLE SIZE FOR WORK SAMPLING

Sample size is based upon the same statistical theory as used for time study, except we are dealing with a distribution of proportions rather than a distribution of means. (See Chap. 2, Discrete and Continuous Data.)

Example 8.8 A data processing manager estimates that a computer operator is idle 20 percent of the time and would like to do a work-sampling study that would be accurate within ±4 percentage points. The manager wishes to have 95 percent confidence in the resulting study. How many observations should be made?

Table 8-6 Steps in Conducting a Work-Sampling Study

1. Select the job (or group) to be studied and inform the workers.
2. Delineate the operations and prepare lists of worker activities.
3. Estimate the number of observations required, n.

$$n = \frac{Z^2 pq}{e^2} \tag{8.8}$$

   where Z = standard normal deviate for desired confidence level
   p = estimated proportion of time of activity of interest
       (use past experience; otherwise let $p = .5$)
   $q = 1 - p$
   e = maximum error for precision level

4. Prepare a schedule of random observation times.
5. Observe, rate, and record worker activities per schedule.
   (*Note*: Sample size is often recomputed as study data becomes available.)
6. Record starting time, stopping time, and number of acceptable units completed during the period.
7. Compute the *normal time*.

$$NT = \frac{(\text{total time})(\%\ \text{working})(PR)}{\text{number units completed}} \tag{8.9}$$

8. Compute the *standard time*.

$$ST = NT \times AF \tag{8.5}$$

   where $$AF = \frac{1}{1 - \%\,A_{\text{total}}} \quad \text{or} \quad AF = 1 + \%\,A_{\text{work}} \tag{8.6}$$

$$n = \frac{Z^2 pq}{e^2}$$

where $Z = 1.96$ for 95% confidence
   p = idle time estimate = .20
   $q = 1 - p = 1 - .20 = .80$
   e = maximum error = .04

$$n = \frac{Z^2 pq}{e^2} = \frac{(1.96)^2(.20)(.80)}{(.04)^2} = 384 \text{ observations}$$

Note that we have used the estimate of idle time (20 percent) to calculate n. If early study results indicate that p will be outside the range of 20 percent ±4 percent, then the number of observations may have to be adjusted as the study progresses.

Making Random Observations.   A random number table (Appendix A) may be used to ensure that observations are made at random intervals.

Example 8.9   The manager in Example 8.8 would like to set up a random schedule for the 384 observations over a one-week period of five 8-hour workdays. (*a*) Illustrate the process by using a random number table to select 8 of the 384 observation times. (*b*) Show how a tally of 100 observations might be recorded if the operator were idle on 14 occasions and on another filing assignment during 20 of the observations.

(*a*)   Minutes available = 60 min/hr × 8 hr/day = 480 min/day = 2,400 min/week (Thus day 1 includes minutes 1–480, day 2 includes 481–960, etc.). This requires a four-digit column of random numbers between 0001 and 2400 (eliminate numbers >2400). From the first column of Appendix A, the first number is 2776 and is discarded because it is >2400. The next number is 1302, which is the 1302 − 0960, or the 342d minute of day 3. See Table 8-7. For an 8:00 a.m. to 5:00 p.m. workday, this is 1:42 p.m. After the 384 times are obtained, they would be chronologically arranged.

Table 8-7

Day 1	Day 2	Day 3	Day 4	Day 5
0001–0480	0481–0960	0961–1440	1441–1920	1921–2400
	0810	1302 (1:42 p.m.) 1087 1212	1771 1547	2230 2130

(*b*) See Table 8-8.

Table 8-8

	Tally of All Observations (Total Time)		Working and Idle Time Only	
	Tally	Number	Number	Percent
Working	THL THL THL THL THL THL THL THL THL THL THL THL THL I	66	66	82.5
Idle	THL THL IIII	14	14	17.5
Other assignment	THL THL THL THL	20		
Total		100	80	100

Work-sampling studies can be done by part-time observers and need not disturb the workers. A quick glance can identify a worker's activity, which is subsequently recorded on the tally sheet. Some analysts also rate the worker's performance (PR); otherwise a 100 percent PR is assumed. Being done over a relatively long time period, work-sampling studies are reliable, yet less costly than time studies. However, they are not as useful for short, repetitive tasks because they do not focus on the job details or work methods employed.

Example 8.10 A work-sampling study of customer service representatives in a telephone company office showed that a receptionist was working 80 percent of the time at 100 percent PR. This receptionist handled 200 customers during the 8-hour study period. Company policy is to give allowances of 10 percent of total on-the-job time. Find the normal time and the standard time per customer.

$$\text{NT} = \frac{(\text{total time})(\% \text{ working})(\text{PR})}{\text{number units completed}} = \frac{(480 \text{ min})(.80)(1.00)}{200} = 1.92 \text{ min/customer}$$

$$\text{ST} = (\text{NT})(\text{AF})$$

where $\text{AF} = 1/(1 - .10) = 1.11$.

$$\text{ST} = (1.92)(1.11) = 2.13 \text{ min/customer}$$

Solved Problems

WORKER SAFETY AND PRODUCTIVITY

8.1   Let θ represent the probability of defective wiring and A represent an accidental fire. In a large, old factory spot-checks have established that $P(\theta) = .20$. Given that a plant has defective wiring, the probability of a fire occurring at some time during the year is .7 (that is, $P(A|\theta) = .7$), and if the wiring is not defective, the chance of a fire is reduced to .1 (that is, $P(A|\bar{\theta}) = .1$). A recent fire burned one employee severely and caused \$90,000 damage. Although evidence is destroyed, the operations manager has been asked by an insurance company to estimate the likelihood that the fire was due to defective wiring.

$$P(\theta) = .2 \qquad \text{thus} \quad P(\bar{\theta}) = 1 - .2 = .8$$
$$P(A|\theta) = .7 \qquad \text{thus} \quad P(\bar{A}|\theta) = 1 - .7 = .3$$
$$P(A|\bar{\theta}) = .1 \qquad \text{thus} \quad P(\bar{A}|\bar{\theta}) = 1 - .1 = .9$$

We wish to find the probability of defective wiring θ given the occurrence of the recent fire A.

$$P(\theta|A) = \frac{P(\theta)P(A|\theta)}{P(\theta)P(A|\theta) + P(\bar{\theta})P(A|\bar{\theta})} = \frac{(.2)(.7)}{(.2)(.7) + (.8)(.1)} = .64$$

Thus, there is a 64 percent chance of defective wiring.

STATISTICAL SAMPLE SIZE

8.2   An analyst wants to obtain a cycle time estimate that is within ±5 percent of the true value. A preliminary run of 20 cycles took 40 minutes to complete and had a calculated standard deviation of .3 minute. What is the value of the coefficient of variation to be used for computing the sample size for the forthcoming time study?

$$V = \frac{s}{\bar{X}}$$

where s = standard deviation of sample = .3 min/cycle

$$\bar{X} = \text{mean of sample} = \frac{\Sigma X}{n} = \frac{40 \text{ min}}{20 \text{ cycles}} = 2 \text{ min/cycle}$$

$$V = \frac{.3}{2} = .15$$

8.3   How large a sample should be taken to provide 99 percent confidence that a sample value is within ±5 percent of the true value if the coefficient of variation is estimated to be 15 percent?

From Fig. 8-3, for $V = 15$ percent, $n \cong 80$.

8.4   Past records of a certain work activity show that it has a mean time of 60 seconds and a standard deviation of 9 seconds. How many time-study observations should be made to be 95 percent confident that the sample mean is within 3 seconds (±3) of the true population value?

$$V = \frac{s}{\bar{X}}$$

where $s = 9 \text{ sec}$
$\bar{X} = 60 \text{ sec}$

$$V = \frac{9}{60} = .15$$

Figure 8-3 can be used because the 3-second accuracy required corresponds to $3/60 = 5$-percent accuracy. Therefore, $n = 35$ observations.

8.5 Suppose we make a preliminary estimate that the standard deviation of an activity is 9 seconds. How many time-study observations should be made to be 95-percent confident that the sample mean is within 3 seconds (± 3) of the true population value?

Note the similarity between this and the previous problem. In this case we have no mean value available to estimate the coefficient of variation, so we must calculate the sample size instead of using Fig. 8-3. Our method is similar to that followed for the work sampling in Example 8.8, except in this case we are dealing with means ($\bar{x}$'s) rather than sample proportions (p's). Both situations rely on the fact that the sample means and proportions are normally distributed (Fig. 8-4) about the population parameters (that is, μ and π, respectively) if the sample size is sufficiently large (say 30 or more for means and 100 or more for proportions). In solving this problem we wish to set one-half the accuracy interval width ($Zs_{\bar{x}}$) equal to 3 seconds.

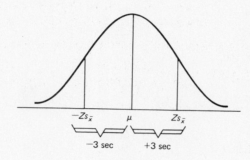

Fig. 8-4

$$e = Zs_{\bar{x}} = Z\frac{s}{\sqrt{n}}$$

Thus,

$$n = \left(\frac{Zs}{e}\right)^2$$

where $e = 3$
       $Z = 1.96$
       $s = 9$

Therefore,

$$n = \left[\frac{(1.96)(9)}{3}\right]^2 \cong 35 \text{ observations}$$

Note that the chart method (previous problem) and the calculation method (this problem) are essentially equivalent, but the chart is perhaps a little easier to use if V can be estimated.

8.6 A time-study analyst wishes to estimate the cycle time for an assembly operation within $\pm.03$ minute at a confidence level of 95.5 percent. If the cycle time standard deviation, σ, is known to be .08 minute, how many observations are required?

$$n = \left(\frac{Z\sigma}{e}\right)^2 \qquad \text{(Since } \sigma \text{ is known, we use it instead of } s.\text{)}$$

where $e = .03$
       $Z = 2$
       $\sigma = .08$

Thus,

$$n = \left[\frac{2(.08)}{.03}\right]^2 = 28.4, \text{ use 29 observations}$$

Note that as the sample size gets below 30, the t is a more appropriate distribution than the normal. However, the normal approximation should be adequate in this case.

8.7   An assembly activity in an ammunition factory, is to be analyzed by a time study. A preliminary sample of $n' = 30$ cycles reveals the following:

$$\Sigma X = 670 \text{ sec} \qquad \Sigma X^2 = 16{,}400 \qquad s = 6.6 \text{ sec}$$

The firm wishes to be 95 percent confident that the resultant time is accurate within ± 5 percent. Find the required sample size (a) by use of the coefficient of variation using Fig. 8-3, and (b) by use of Equation 8.2.

(a)
$$V = \frac{s}{\bar{X}}$$

where
$$\bar{X} = \frac{\Sigma X}{n} = \frac{670}{30} = 22.3 \text{ sec}$$

$$V = \frac{6.6}{22.3} = .30 = 30\%$$

From Fig. 8-3, $n \cong 150$.

(b)
$$n = \frac{Z^2[n' \Sigma X^2 - (\Sigma X)^2]}{e^2(\Sigma X)^2} = \frac{(1.96)^2[30(16{,}400) - (670)^2]}{(.05)^2(670)^2} = 147$$

ADJUSTMENTS, ALLOWANCES, AND STANDARD TIMES

8.8   A time study of a nursing-home activity yielded a cycle time of 4.00 minutes, and the nurse was rated at PR = 95 percent. The nursing home uses a 20 percent per day allowance factor. Find the standard time.

$$NT = CT \times PR = (4.00)(.95) = 3.80 \text{ min}$$
$$ST = NT \times AF$$

where
$$AF = \frac{1}{1 - \% A_{total}} = \frac{1}{1 - .20} = 1.25$$

Thus
$$ST = (3.80)(1.25) = 4.75 \text{ min}$$

8.9   An operator in a fruit-packing plant was clocked by a stopwatch with results as shown in Table 8-9. The allowance for this type of work is 15 percent. Find (a) the normal time per cycle and (b) the standard time per cycle.

Table 8-9

Element	Time for Cycle (min)					Performance Rating
	1	2	3	4	5	
1. Obtain 2 boxes	.82	—	.80	—	.85	130
2. Pack 4 items/box	.44	.42	.46	.40	.41	110
3. Set box aside	.71	.67	.69	.71	.68	115

(a)
$$NT = CT \times PR$$

For element 1, each box suffices for 2 cycles.

$$NT = \frac{.82 + .80 + .85}{6}(1.30) = .535$$

For element 2:

$$NT = \frac{.44 + .42 + .46 + .40 + .41}{5}(1.10) = .469$$

For element 3:

$$NT = \frac{.71 + .67 + .69 + .71 + .68}{5}(1.15) = \underline{.796}$$

$$Total = 1.800$$

Thus, $NT = 1.80$ min/cycle.

(b)
$$ST = NT \times AF$$

where
$$AF = \frac{1}{1 - .15} = 1.18$$

$$ST = (1.80)(1.18) = 2.12 \text{ min/cycle}$$

WORK SAMPLING

8.10 The State of Oreida Mental Health Division has a health-care activity that has a normal time of 8 minutes, but the activity seems to have been prolonged recently by an increasing number of unavoidable delays. D. R. Mix, a management analyst called in to determine a new standard, conducted a work-sampling study and obtained the results shown in Table 8-10.

Table 8-10

Activity	Number of Observations	Percentage of Observations
Working	585	78
Unavoidable delay	90	12
Personal time	75	10
Total	750	100

The Mental Health Division grants its workers a personal-time allowance of 8 percent of total time, and Mr. Mix wishes to retain that allowance in the new standard.

(a) Incorporate the unavoidable-delay time, and determine a standard time for this activity.

(b) Determine how precise the estimate is of unavoidable time, assuming the analyst wishes to have 95 percent confidence in the estimate.

(c) State whether the same precision applies to the estimate of personal time.

(a) Allowances should now consist of:

$$\begin{array}{ll}\text{Personal time} & \text{8 percent} \\ \text{Unavoidable delay} & \underline{12} \text{ percent} \\ \text{Total} & 20 \text{ percent}\end{array}$$

$$ST = NT \times AF = (8 \text{ min})\left(\frac{1}{1 - .2}\right) = 10 \text{ min}$$

(b) For 95 percent confidence interval, $Z = 1.96$. Half the interval width h is

$$h = e = Zs_p$$

where

$$s_p = \sqrt{\frac{pq}{n}} = \sqrt{\frac{(.12)(.88)}{750}} = .011$$

$$h = 1.96(.011) = .023$$

The interval is ± 2.3 percent—that is, the analyst could be 95 percent confident that the true unavoidable delay time is from 9.7 percent to 14.3 percent of total time.

(c) The precision interval for the personal-time estimate would be slightly smaller (better) due to the use of 10 percent instead of 12 percent for the value of p. In general, for a given level of precision, the sample size required for various activities is governed by the activities with p values closest to .5.

Supplementary Problems

8.11 In a chemical plant, the probability of any given employee being injured from a fall is $P(F) = .005$ and from chemical inhalation is $P(C) = .020$. If a worker falls, the probability of injury from chemical inhalation increases to $P(C|F) = .100$. What is the probability that an employee will be injured (a) by both a fall and chemical inhalation, (b) by either a fall or chemical inhalation? *Ans.* (a) .0005 (b) .0245

8.12 Data collected by a safety committee show that over 80 percent of the accidents in a plant are caused by 10 percent of the 400 employees, whom they classify as accident prone AP. The firm has 120 employees over 50 years of age and 6 of them are included in the AP classification.

An employee is selected at random for a potentially hazardous task. What is the probability that the employee is (a) an AP employee, (b) either AP or over 50? (c) If selection is restricted to those 50 years old or younger, what is the probability of selecting an AP employee?   *Ans.* (a) .10 (b) .385 (c) .12

8.13 Due to a purchasing error, 30 percent of the half-inch-diameter bolts in a stockroom bin are low-tensile steel (that is, $P(L) = .30$). Before any bolts are used in construction, they are supposed to be examined by an inspector to ensure that only high-tensile bolts are used. The bolts look very much alike and there is a .2 probability that the inspector will incorrectly identify any bolt. A bolt is withdrawn from stock, routinely inspected, and installed at a critical point in a guardrail five stories above ground. What is the probability that it was a low-tensile bolt? (*Hint*: Let $I =$ incorrect identification and $\bar{I} =$ correct identification. The probability we seek is $P(\bar{L}|\bar{I})$.)   *Ans.* .30

8.14 A customer-service activity in a bank takes an estimated 3 minutes and must be performed 25 times per day and 200 days per year. Estimate the sample size required to set a time standard for this activity.   *Ans.* From Table 8-3, $n = 12$

8.15 A textile workers' union in New York City has requested that a new time study be made of a skirt-sewing activity. Previous data indicate the activity has a mean time of $\bar{X} = 1.80$ minutes and a standard deviation of .40 minute. What is the best preliminary estimate of the sample size required in order to have 95 percent confidence in the result. (*Hint*: Use Fig. 8-3, and assume an accuracy of ± 5 percent.)   *Ans.* From Fig. 8-3, $n \cong 65$

8.16 Sixty samples of an electronic-assembly operation revealed an average time of 3.20 minutes per unit. The performance rating was estimated at 105 percent, and allowances are set at 20 percent of the total time available. What is the standard time in minutes per piece?   *Ans.* 4.20 minutes

8.17 A time study of an Iowa City grain-elevator loading activity revealed a cycle time of 8.57 minutes for a worker rated at 107 percent. The allowances are as follows: personal time = 25 minutes per day, fatigue = 84 minutes per day, delay = 35 minutes per day. Determine the standard time for an 8-hour-per-day operation.   *Ans.* 13.10 minutes

8.18 An activity has a cycle time of 2.20 minutes per cycle and a calculated normal time of 2.64 minutes per cycle. Allowances are 10 percent. What was (*a*) the performance rating factor of the worker studied and (*b*) the resultant standard time?   *Ans.*   (*a*) 120 percent (*b*) 2.93 minutes per cycle

8.19 A time study of 40 cycles of a worker-machine operation revealed an operator time of .60 minute per cycle and a machine time of 1.40 minutes per cycle. The worker was rated at 115 percent, and allowances for the operation, based on an 8-hour workday, are as follows: personal = 30 minutes per day, fatigue = 20 minutes per day, delay = 30 minutes per day. Calculate the standard time per cycle for the (combined) worker-machine operation.   *Ans.*   2.51 minutes per cycle

8.20 Time-study data taken for a bulk-filling activity in a cannery in Baltimore were recorded on a *continuous* basis, as shown in Table 8-11 (that is, the times given are cumulative amounts).

Table 8-11

	Cycle Time (sec)					
	1	2	3	4	5	RF
Grasp bag	4	37	74	105	338	120
Locate for fill	16	51	84	117	352	120
Machine-fill	26	61	94	127	362	
Set on conveyor	34	68	102	334*	369	110

*Bag broke open due to presence of a foreign object on the conveyor.

The firm's labor contract requires a 15 percent allowance for all workers on the bulk-filling line. Compute the standard time for this activity.   *Ans.*   44.62 ($\cong$45) seconds per cycle

8.21 A work-sampling study is to be made of an airline ticket counter in a major airport. The operations manager feels the ticket agents are idle 30 percent of the time and wishes to have 95.5 percent confidence that the accuracy is within 4 percentage points. How many observations should be made?   *Ans.*   525

8.22 An analyst wishes to develop a labor-cost standard for a manual computer-card-sorting activity. The elements consist of (1) collecting the cards, (2) sorting them, and (3) filing the sorted deck. For element 2, the standard deviation is estimated to be $\sigma = 2.25$. To determine the sorting time to an accuracy of within ±.5 minute with 95.5 percent confidence, how large a sample should be taken?   *Ans.*   81

8.23 A work-sampling study is to be made of food-service activities in a major hotel chain. Analysts have defined the activities as shown in Table 8-12. They wish to be 95.5 percent confident that the true proportions of time of the various elements are accurate within ±3 percent. How many samples should be taken to be sure the 95.5 percent confidence level holds for all elements?   *Ans.*   1,100

Table 8-12

Element	Estimated Time (%)
Taking orders	20
Filling and serving orders	45
Table set-up	10
Billing	10
Delays	15
Total	100

8.24 A work-sampling study was made of a cargo-loading operation for the purpose of developing a standard time. During the total 120 minutes of observation the employee was working 80 percent of the time and loaded 60 pieces of cargo. The analyst rated the performance at 90 percent. If the firm wishes to incorporate a 10 percent allowance factor for fatigue, delays, and personal time, what is the standard time for this operation in minutes per piece?   *Ans.*   1.60 minutes per piece

Chapter 9

Forecasting

Statistical Methods

PRODUCTION AND INVENTORY CONTROL OVERVIEW

Production and inventory control (P&IC) guides the flow of products from the initial forecasting of demand to the final delivery of finished goods and services. Production-control personnel specify and control which *goods and services* are produced, in *what quantities*, and at *what time*. These control activities have been significantly enhanced by the use of analytical techniques, computers, and professionally trained people.

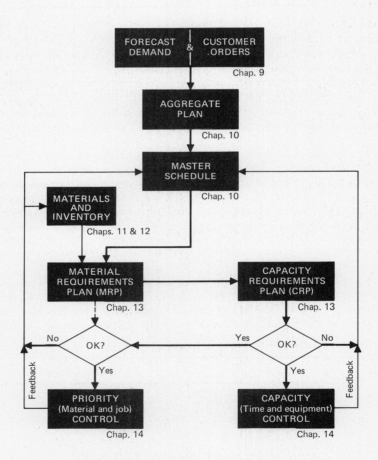

Fig. 9-1 Production and inventory control flowchart

Figure 9-1 identifies the major P&IC activities. Forecasts (Chap. 9) give the organization vital estimates of demand from the market environment. Production quantities are then planned and scheduled on an overall or master level (Chap. 10). Existing inventory levels and safety stock policies are also assessed (Chaps. 11 and 12). Plans to satisfy the additional material and capacity requirements are then formulated and evaluated (Chap. 13). If materials can be scheduled to arrive when needed, and sufficient capacity exists in the work centers, orders are released and production activities are carried out (Chap. 14).

PRIORITY AND CAPACITY CONCEPTS

We must now attach increased meaning to the terms *priority* and *capacity* introduced in Fig. 8-1. *Priorities* stem from the market environment and relate to the importance-ranking assigned to *materials*. As the production process adds value in the form of assembled materials and labor, the priorities of materials (under MRP) become translated into priorities of jobs (on the shop floor). *Capacities* stem from the technical and capital facilities of the organization. Capacities relate to the labor and equipment *time* available to process the scheduled jobs. Effective planning and control of priorities and capacities is the key to a successful production system.

FORECASTING OBJECTIVES AND USES

Forecasts are estimates of the occurrence, timing, or magnitude of uncertain future events. The purpose of forecasting is to use the best available information to guide future activities toward organizational goals. Our concern is primarily with forecasts of demand, but firms also forecast such things as raw-material prices, labor costs, interest rates, and revenues. Good forecasts enable managers to plan for appropriate levels of personnel, raw materials, capital, inventory, and a host of other variables. This planning results in better use of capacity, improved employee relations, and improved service to customers.

COSTS OF FORECASTING

The optimal level of forecasting is one where the cost of implementing a forecasting method just offsets the cost of operating with a poor or inadequate forecast. As forecasting activity increases, the costs for collecting and analyzing data increase, as do system control costs. On the other hand, poor forecasts can result in unplanned labor, materials, or capital costs, as well as expediting costs and lost revenues.

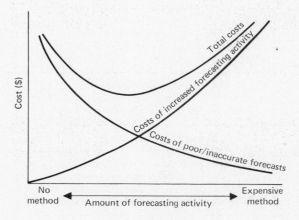

Fig. 9-2   Costs of forecasting

Example 9.1   A consultant estimates that an improved forecasting system would enable a transformer manufacturer to reduce its average finished-goods inventory by 300 units (without affecting customer service).

Table 9-1   Summary of Forecasting Methods

Method	Description	Time Horizon	Relative Cost
Opinion and judgment (qualitative)			
Sales force composites	Estimates from field salespeople are aggregated	SR–MR	L–M
Executive opinion	Marketing, finance, and production managers jointly prepare forecast	SR–LR	L–M
Field sales and product-line management	Independent estimates from regional salespeople are reconciled with national projections from head-quarters product-line managers	MR	M
Historical analogy	Forecast from comparison with similar product previously introduced	SR–LR	L–M
Delphi	Experts answer a series of questions (anonymously), receive feedback, and revise estimates	LR	M–H
Market surveys	Questionnaires and panels are used for data to anticipate consumer behavior	MR–LR	H
Time series (quantitative)			
Naive	Use simple rule that forecast equals latest value or latest plus or minus some percentage	SR	L
Moving average	Forecast is simply average of n most recent periods	SR	L
Trend projection	Forecast is linear, exponential, or other projection of past trend	MR–LR	L
Decomposition	Time series is divided into trend, seasonal, cyclical, and random components	SR–LR	L
Exponential smoothing	Forecast is an exponentially weighted moving average, where latest values carry most weight	SR	L
Box-Jenkins	A time-series–regression model is proposed, statistically tested, modified, and retested until satisfactory	MR–LR	M–H
Associative (quantitative)			
Regression and correlation	Use one or more associate variables to forecast via a least-squares equation (regression) or via a close association (correlation) with an explanatory variable	SR–MR	M–H
Econometric	Use simultaneous solution of multiple-regression equations that relate to broad range of economic activity	SR–LR	H

Key: L = low, M = medium, H = high, SR = short range, MR = medium range, LR = long range.

How much increased forecasting activity would this justify? Assume a product cost of \$4,000 and use a 20-percent-per-year cost for carrying the finished goods.

$$\text{Cost savings} = (\text{interest rate}) (\text{unit value}) (\text{number of units})$$
$$= (.20) (\$4,000) (300) = \$240,000/\text{yr}$$

FORECASTING DECISION VARIABLES AND METHODOLOGY

Forecasting activities are a function of (1) the type of forecast (e.g., demand, technological), (2) the time horizon (short, medium, or long range), (3) the database available, and (4) the methodology employed (qualitative or quantitative). Forecasts of *demand* are based primarily on nonrandom trends and relationships, with an allowance for random components. Forecasts for groups of products tend to be more accurate than those for single products and short-term forecasts are more accurate than long-term forecasts (greater than five years). Quantification also enhances the objectivity and precision of a forecast. Table 9-1 summarizes some of the more commonly used forecasting methods.

OPINION AND JUDGMENTAL METHODS

Some opinion and judgment forecasts are largely intuitive, whereas others integrate data and perhaps even mathematical or statistical techniques into the method. Judgmental forecasts often consist of (1) forecasts by individual sales representatives, (2) forecasts by division or product-line level management, and (3) combined estimates of salespeople and product-line managers. Historical analogy relies on comparisons, Delphi relies on expert opinions, and market surveys rely on consumer response—which is not always reliable. All these methods can incorporate experiences and personal insights into the forecast. However, they may differ from one individual to the next and are not all amenable to analysis. Because they are often unobjective, there may be little basis for improvement over time.

TIME SERIES METHODS

A *time series* is a set of observations of a variable over time. It is usually tabulated or graphed to show the nature of the time dependence. The components of a time series are generally classified as trend T, cyclical C, seasonal S, and random or irregular R. The forecast (Y_c) is a function of these components.

$$Y_c = T \cdot C \cdot S \cdot R \tag{9.1}$$

The *trend* is a gradual long-term directional movement in the data (growth or decline). *Cyclical* factors are long-term swings around the trend line, and are often associated with business cycles. *Seasonal* effects are similar variations occurring during corresponding periods. Thus we have monthly, weekly, and even daily seasonals. *Random* components are sporadic (and unpredictable) effects due to chance and unusual occurrences. They are the residual after the trend, cyclical, and seasonal variations are removed.

Three methods of describing a trend are (1) freehand curve, (2) moving average, and (3) least squares. A *freehand curve* is simple, but highly subjective. A *moving average* is obtained by repetitively summing and averaging the values from a given number of periods, each time deleting the oldest value and adding the latest value.

$$MA = \frac{\Sigma X}{\text{number of periods}} \tag{9.2}$$

Each time the moving average is updated, the newly calculated value becomes the forecast for the next period.

**Table 9-2   Forecasting Procedure for
Using Time Series**

1. Plot historical data to confirm
   type of relationship (e.g.,
   linear, quadratic).
2. Develop trend equation.
3. Develop seasonal index.
4. Project trend into future.
5. Multiply monthly trend value
   by seasonal index.
6. Modify projected values for
   cyclical or irregular effects.

Example 9.2   The annual shipments (in tons) of welded tube by an aluminum producer to machinery manufacturers are as shown in Table 9-3. (*a*) Estimate the shipments for year 12 by a freehand curve. (*b*) Compute a 3-year moving average, then use it to forecast shipments in year 12.

Table 9-3

Year	Shipments (tons)
1	2
2	3
3	6
4	10
5	8
6	7
7	12
8	14
9	14
10	18
11	19

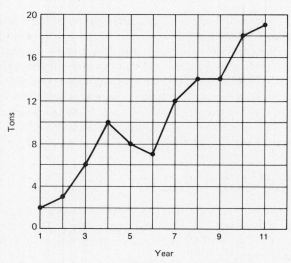

Fig. 9-3

(*a*)   A straight line connecting years 1 and 11 (Fig. 9-3) seems to be a fairly good freehand representation of the data. Extending this trend to year 12 we obtain about 21 tons.

(*b*)   See Table 9-4. The moving average forecast for year 12 would be 17.0 tons.

Moving averages smooth out fluctuations, while preserving the general pattern of the data (longer averages result in more smoothing). They can be applied to any data, but they neither generate values for the ends of the data series, nor yield a forecasting equation.

The *weighted moving average* allows the most recent values to be emphasized by varying the weights assigned to each component of the average.

$$MA_{wt} = \frac{\Sigma\,(wt)\,X}{\Sigma\,wt} \tag{9.3}$$

Weights can be either percentages or any real number. In Example 9.2, if a weight of 3 is assigned to year 11, 2 to year 10, and 1 to year 9, the weighted moving average is 17.8 tons.

Table 9-4

Year	Shipments (tons)	Three-Year Moving Total		Three-Year Moving Average
1	2	—		—
2	3	- - - - - - - 11 - - - → ÷ 3 =		3.7
3	6	19 ÷ 3 =		6.3
4	10	24		8.0
5	8	25		8.3
6	7	27		9.0
7	12	33		11.0
8	14	40		13.3
9	14	46		15.3
10	18	- - - - - - 51 - - - → ÷ 3 =		17.0
11	19	—		—

Least squares is a mathematical technique of fitting a trend to data points. The resulting *line of best fit* has the following properties: (1) the summation of all vertical deviations about it is zero, (2) the summation of all vertical deviations squared is a minimum, and (3) the line goes through the means $\bar{X}$ and $\bar{Y}$. For linear equations, the line of best fit is found by the simultaneous solution for a and b of the following two *normal equations*:

$$\Sigma\, Y = na + b\, \Sigma\, X$$

$$\Sigma\, XY = a\, \Sigma\, X + b\, \Sigma\, X^2 \tag{9.4}$$

Where the data can be coded so that $\Sigma\, X = 0$, two terms in the above expressions drop out, and we have:

$$\Sigma\, Y = na$$

$$\Sigma\, XY = b\, \Sigma\, X^2 \tag{9.5}$$

Coding is easily accomplished with time-series data, for we simply designate the center of the time period as $X = 0$ and have an equal number of plus and minus periods on each side, which sum to zero.

Example 9.3 Use the least-squares method to develop a linear-trend equation for the data of Example 9.2. State the equation complete with signature, and forecast a trend value for year 16.

See Table 9-5 for the data. Rearranging Equation 9.5, we have:

$$a = \frac{\Sigma\, Y}{n} = \frac{113}{11} = 10.3$$

$$b = \frac{\Sigma\, XY}{\Sigma\, X^2} = \frac{181}{110} = 1.6$$

The forecasting equation is of the form $Y = a + bX$.

$$Y = 10.3 + 1.6X \qquad (\text{yr } 6 = 0,\ X = \text{years},\ Y = \text{tons})$$

Table 9-5

Year	X Year Coded	Y Shipments (tons)	XY	X^2
1	-5	2	-10	25
2	-4	3	-12	16
3	-3	6	-18	9
4	-2	10	-20	4
5	-1	8	-8	1
6	0	7	0	0
7	1	12	12	1
8	2	14	28	4
9	3	14	42	9
10	4	18	72	16
11	5	19	95	25
	0	113	181	110

Since year 16 is 10 years distant from the origin (year 6), we have

$$Y = 10.3 + 1.6(10) = 26.3 \text{ tons}$$

Seasonal Indexes.   A *seasonal index* (SI) is a ratio that relates a recurring seasonal variation to the corresponding trend value at the given time. Analysts often use a *ratio-to-moving-average* method to tabulate data in monthly (or quarterly) terms, and to compute a 12-month (or 4-quarter) moving average to dampen all seasonal fluctuations. Actual monthly (or quarterly) values are then compared to the moving average, centered on the actual month. The ratios obtained for the same months (or quarters) are then averaged and applied to forecasted trend values to obtain seasonalized forecast values.

$$\text{Seasonalized forecast} = \text{seasonal index (trend forecast)}$$
$$Y_{sz} = (\text{SI})Y_c \qquad\qquad (9.6)$$

EXPONENTIAL SMOOTHING

Exponential smoothing is a moving-average forecasting technique that weights past data exponentially so that the most recent data carry more weight in the moving average. With simple exponential smoothing, the forecast F_t is made up of the last period forecast F_{t-1} plus a portion α of the difference between the last period actual demand A_{t-1} and the last period forecast F_{t-1}.

$$F_t = F_{t-1} + \alpha(A_{t-1} - F_{t-1}) \qquad\qquad (9.7)$$

The smoothing constant α is a number between 0 and 1 which enters multiplicatively into each forecast, but whose influence declines exponentially as the data becomes older. A low α gives more weight to past data. An α of 1 would reflect a total adjustment to recent demand, and the forecast would be last period's actual demand.

Example 9.4   A firm uses simple exponential smoothing with $\alpha = .1$ to forecast demand. The forecast for the week of February 1 was 500 units, whereas actual demand turned out to be 450 units.

(a)   Forecast the demand for the week of February 8.

(b)   Assume that the actual demand during the week of February 8 turned out to be 505 units. Forecast the demand for the week of February 15. Continue forecasting through March 15, assuming that subsequent demands were actually 516, 488, 467, 554, and 510 units.

(a)
$$F_t = F_{t-1} + \alpha(A_{t-1} - F_{t-1})$$
$$= 500 + .1(450 - 500) = 495 \text{ units}$$

(b)   Arranging the procedure in tabular form, we have Table 9-6.

Table 9-6

Week	Actual Demand A_{t-1}	Old Forecast F_{t-1}	Forecast Error $A_{t-1} - F_{t-1}$	Correction $\alpha(A_{t-1} - F_{t-1})$	New Forecast (F_t) $F_{t-1} + \alpha(A_{t-1} - F_{t-1})$
Feb. 1	450	500	−50	−5	(495)
8	505	495	10	1	496
15	516	496	20	2	498
22	488	498	−10	−1	497
Mar. 1	467	497	−30	−3	494
8	554	494	60	6	500
15	510	500	10	1	501

The *selection of* α depends upon the characteristics of demand. High values of α are more responsive to fluctuations in demand. Low values of α are appropriate for relatively stable demand (no trend or cyclical demand) but with a high amount of random variation.

Simple exponential smoothing is only a smoothed average centered on the current period. It does not extrapolate for trend effects, so no α value will fully compensate for a trend in the data. Typical α values range from .01 to .40. Low α values effectively dampen random variation (noise). High values are more responsive to changes in demand (new product introductions, promotional campaigns). A satisfactory α can generally be determined by trial-and-error testing to see which value minimizes forecast error. This can be done quite easily by modeling the forecast on a computer program such as VisiCalc and trying different values of α. An α value that yields an approximately equivalent degree of smoothing as a moving average of n periods is:

$$\alpha = \frac{2}{n+1} \tag{9.8}$$

ADJUSTED EXPONENTIAL SMOOTHING

Adjusted exponential-smoothing models have all the features of simple exponential-smoothing models, plus they project into the future (for example, to time period $t + 1$) by adding a trend correction increment, T_t, to the current period smoothed average, $\hat{F}_t$.

$$\hat{F}_{t+1} = \hat{F}_t + T_t \tag{9.9}$$

Figure 9-4 depicts the components of a trend-adjusted forecast that utilizes a second smoothing coefficient β. The β value determines the extent to which the trend adjustment relies on the latest difference in forecast amounts ($\hat{F}_t - \hat{F}_{t-1}$) versus the previous trend T_{t-1}. Thus:

$$\hat{F}_t = \alpha A_{t-1} + (1 - \alpha)(\hat{F}_{t-1} + T_{t-1}) \tag{9.10}$$

$$T_t = \beta(\hat{F}_t - \hat{F}_{t-1}) + (1 - \beta)T_{t-1} \tag{9.11}$$

A low β gives more smoothing of the trend and may be useful if the trend is not well established. A high β will emphasize the latest trend and be more responsive to recent changes in trend. The initial trend adjustment T_{t-1} is sometimes assumed to be zero.

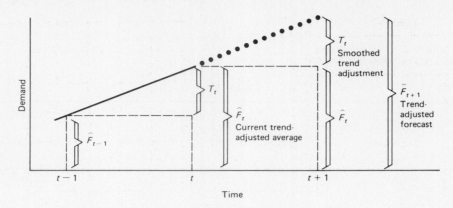

Fig. 9-4   Components of a trend-adjusted forecast

Self-Adaptive Models.   Self-adjusting computer models that change the values of the smoothing coefficients (α's and β's) in an adaptive fashion have been developed; these models help to minimize the amount of forecast error.

REGRESSION AND CORRELATION METHODS

Regression and correlation techniques quantify the statistical association between two or more variables. *Simple regression* expresses the relationship between a dependent variable Y and one independent variable X in terms of the slope and intercept of a line of best fit relating the two variables. *Simple correlation* expresses the degree or closeness of the relationship between two variables in terms of a correlation coefficient which provides an indirect measure of the variability of points from the line of best fit. Neither regression nor correlation gives proof of a cause-effect relationship.

Multiple regression and correlation analysis (involving more than two variables) and nonlinear models are also useful, but are beyond our scope here.

Regression.   The simple linear regression model takes the form $Y_c = a + bX$, where Y_c is the dependent variable and X the independent variable. Values for the slope b and intercept a are obtained by using the *normal equations* written in the convenient form:

$$b = \frac{\Sigma XY - n\bar{X}\bar{Y}}{\Sigma X^2 - n\bar{X}^2} \qquad (9.12)$$

$$a = \bar{Y} - b\bar{X} \qquad (9.13)$$

In Eqs. 9.12 and 9.13, $\bar{X} = (\Sigma X)/n$ and $\bar{Y} = (\Sigma Y)/n$ are the means of the independent and dependent variables respectively, and n is the number of pairs of observations made.

Example 9.5   The general manager of a building materials production plant feels the demand for plasterboard shipments may be related to the number of construction permits issued in the county during the previous quarter. The manager has collected the data shown in Table 9-7.

(*a*)   Review the scatter diagram (Fig. 9-5) to see whether the data can be satisfactorily described by a linear equation.

(*b*)   Compute values for the slope b and intercept a.

(*c*)   Determine a point estimate for plasterboard shipments when the number of construction permits is 30.

(*a*)   The scatter diagram (Fig. 9-5) shows that the data are not perfectly linear, but do approach linearity over this short range.

Table 9-7

Construction Permits (X)	Plasterboard Shipments (Y)
15	6
9	4
40	16
20	6
25	13
25	9
15	10
35	16

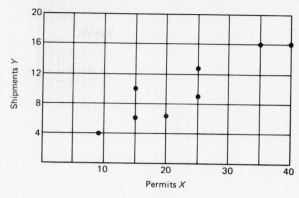

Fig. 9-5

(*b*) See Table 9-8 and the accompanying calculations.

Table 9-8

X	Y	XY	X^2	Y^2
15	6	90	225	36
9	4	36	81	16
40	16	640	1,600	256
20	6	120	400	36
25	13	325	625	169
25	9	225	625	81
15	10	150	225	100
35	16	560	1,225	256
184	80	2,146	5,006	950

$$n = 8 \text{ pairs of observations}$$

$$\bar{X} = \frac{184}{8} = 23$$

$$\bar{Y} = \frac{80}{8} = 10$$

$$b = \frac{\Sigma XY - n\overline{XY}}{\Sigma X^2 - n\bar{X}^2} = \frac{2{,}146 - 8(23)(10)}{5{,}006 - 8(23)(23)} = .395$$

$$a = \bar{Y} - b\bar{X} = 10 - .395(23) = .91$$

(*c*) The regression equation is

$$Y_c = .91 + .395X \qquad (X = \text{permits, } Y = \text{shipments})$$

Then, letting $X = 30$,

$$Y_c = .91 + .395(30) = 12.76 \cong 13 \text{ shipments}$$

Standard Deviation of Regression. A regression line describes the relationship between a given value of the independent variable X and the mean $\mu_{Y \cdot X}$ of the corresponding probability distribution of the dependent variable Y. The point estimate, or forecast, is the mean of that distribution for any given value of X.

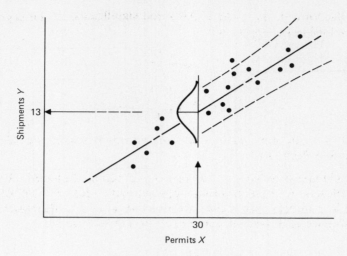

Fig. 9-6   Regression line

The *standard deviation* of *regression* $S_{Y \cdot X}$ is a measure of the dispersion of data points around the regression line (Fig. 9-6).

$$S_{Y \cdot X} = \sqrt{\frac{\Sigma\, Y^2 - a\, \Sigma\, Y - b\, \Sigma\, XY}{n - 2}} \qquad\qquad (9.14)$$

Example 9.6   Given the data on permits and shipments in the previous example, compute the standard deviation of regression ($S_{Y \cdot X}$).

$$S_{Y \cdot X} = \sqrt{\frac{\Sigma\, Y^2 - a\, \Sigma\, Y - b\, \Sigma\, XY}{n - 2}} = \sqrt{\frac{950 - (.91)(80) - (.396)(2{,}146)}{8 - 2}} = 2.2 \text{ shipments}$$

Interval Estimate.   A prediction interval can be established for an *individual* forecast value of Y_c by using the expression:

$$\text{Prediction interval} = Y_c \pm t S_{\text{IND}} \qquad\qquad (9.15)$$

where t = value from t–distribution table for specified confidence level, and

$$S_{\text{IND}} = S_{Y \cdot X} \sqrt{1 + \frac{1}{n} + \frac{(X - \bar{X})^2}{\Sigma\,(X - \bar{X})^2}} \qquad\qquad (9.16)$$

Example 9.7   Using the data from Examples 9.5 and 9.6, develop a 95 percent prediction interval estimate for the specific number of shipments to be made when 30 construction permits were issued during the previous quarter. *Note*: $\bar{X} = 23$ for the $n = 8$ observations, and $\Sigma\,(X - \bar{X})^2 = 774$. Also, from Example 9.5, $Y_c = 13$ shipments, where $X = 30$, and, from Example 9.6, $S_{Y \cdot X} = 2.2$ shipments.

$$\text{Prediction interval} = Y_c \pm t S_{\text{IND}}$$

where the t-value (from statistical table) for $n - 2 = 8 - 2 = 6$ degrees of freedom = 2.447 and where

$$S_{\text{IND}} = S_{Y \cdot X} \sqrt{1 + \frac{1}{n} + \frac{(X - \bar{X})^2}{\Sigma\,(X - \bar{X})^2}} = 2.2 \sqrt{1 + \frac{1}{8} + \frac{(30 - 23)^2}{774}} = 2.40$$

$$\text{Prediction interval} = 13 \pm 2.447(2.40) = 7.1 \text{ to } 18.9 \qquad (\text{use } 7 \text{ to } 19 \text{ shipments})$$

For large samples ($n \geq 100$), Eq. 9.15 can be approximated by using the normal (Z) distribution rather than the t, in the form of $Y_c \pm ZS_{Y \cdot X}$. Also, the significance of the regression-line slope (b) coefficient can be tested using the expression:

$$t_{\text{calc}} = \frac{b}{S_b} \tag{9.17}$$

where

$$S_b = S_{Y \cdot X} \sqrt{\frac{1}{\Sigma (X - \bar{X})^2}} \tag{9.18}$$

If the value of $t_{\text{calc}} > t_{\text{df}}$ from the t-table, the relationship between the X and Y variables is statistically significant. See Prob. 9.10.

Correlation.   The simple linear *correlation coefficient r* is a number between -1 and $+1$ that tells how well a linear equation describes the relationship between two variables. As illustrated in Fig. 9-7, r is designated as positive if Y increases as X increases, and negative if Y decreases as X increases. An r of zero indicates an absence of any relationship between the two variables.

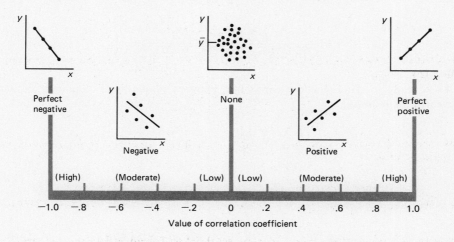

Fig. 9-7   Interpretation of correlation coefficient

The deviation of all points (Y) from the regression line (Y_c) consists of deviation accounted for by the regression line (explained) and random deviation (unexplained). See Fig. 9-8.

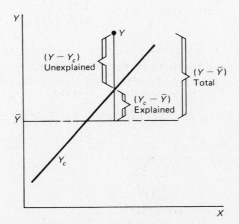

Fig. 9-8   Deviation of dependent variable

$$\text{Total variation} = \text{explained} + \text{unexplained}$$

$$\Sigma\,(Y - \bar{Y})^2 = \Sigma\,(Y_c - \bar{Y})^2 + \Sigma\,(Y - Y_c)^2$$

The *coefficient of determination* r^2 is the ratio of explained to total variation:

$$r^2 = \frac{\Sigma\,(Y_c - \bar{Y})^2}{\Sigma\,(Y - \bar{Y})^2} \tag{9.19}$$

The *coefficient of correlation* r is the square root of the coefficient of determination:

$$r = \sqrt{\frac{\Sigma\,(Y_c - \bar{Y})^2}{\Sigma\,(Y - \bar{Y})^2}} \tag{9.20}$$

When the sample size is sufficiently large (e.g., greater than 50), the value of r can be computed more directly from:

$$r = \frac{n\,\Sigma\,XY - \Sigma\,X\,\Sigma\,Y}{\sqrt{[n\,\Sigma\,X^2 - (\Sigma\,X)^2][n\,\Sigma\,Y^2 - (\Sigma\,Y)^2]}} \tag{9.21}$$

Example 9.8 A study to determine the correlation between plasterboard shipments X and construction permits Y revealed the following:

$$\Sigma\,X = 184 \qquad \Sigma\,X^2 = 5{,}006$$
$$\Sigma\,Y = 80 \qquad \Sigma\,Y^2 = 950$$
$$\Sigma\,XY = 2{,}146 \qquad n = 8$$

Compute the correlation coefficient.

$$r = \frac{n\,\Sigma\,XY - \Sigma\,X\,\Sigma\,Y}{\sqrt{[n\,\Sigma\,X^2 - (\Sigma\,X)^2][n\,\Sigma\,Y^2 - (\Sigma\,Y)^2]}} = \frac{8(2{,}146) - (184)(80)}{\sqrt{[8(5{,}006) - (184)^2][8(950) - (80)^2]}} = \frac{2{,}448}{\sqrt{7{,}430{,}400}} = .90$$

The significance of any value of r can be statistically tested under a hypothesis to show that there is no correlation. To test, the computed value of r is compared with a tabled value for a given sample size and significance level.

FORECAST CONTROLS

A simple measure of forecast error is to compute the deviation of the actual from the forecast values. Deviations will vary from plus to minus, but they should tend to average out near zero if the forecast is on target.

$$\text{Forecast error} = \text{actual demand} - \text{forecast demand} \tag{9.22}$$

The individual forecast errors are usually summarized in a statistic such as average error, mean squared error, or mean absolute deviation (MAD).

$$\text{MAD} = \frac{\Sigma\,|\text{Error}|}{n} \tag{9.23}$$

The estimate of the MAD can be continually updated by using an exponential smoothing technique.

Thus the current MAD_t is:

$$MAD_t = \alpha(\text{actual} - \text{forecast}) + (1 - \alpha)\,MAD_{t-1} \qquad (9.24)$$

where α is a smoothing constant. Higher values of α will make the current MAD_t more responsive to current forecast errors.

When the average deviation (MAD) is divided into the cumulative deviation [Σ (actual $-$ forecast)], the result is a *tracking signal*:

$$\text{Tracking signal} = \frac{\Sigma\,(\text{actual} - \text{forecast})}{\text{MAD}} \qquad (9.25)$$

Tracking signals are one way of monitoring how well a forecast is predicting actual values. They express the cumulative deviation (also called the running sum of forecast error, RSFE) in terms of the number of average deviations (MAD's). Action limits for tracking signals commonly range from three to eight. When the signal goes beyond this range, corrective action may be required.

Example 9.10   A high-valued item has a tracking-signal-action limit of 4 and has been forecast as shown in Table 9-9. Compute the tracking signal and indicate whether some corrective action is appropriate.

Table 9-9

Period	Actual	Forecast	Error (A − F)	|Error|	(Error)² (A − F)²
1	80	78	2	2	4
2	92	79	13	13	169
3	71	83	−12	12	144
4	83	79	4	4	16
5	90	80	10	10	100
6	102	83	19	19	361
		Totals	36	60	794

$$\text{MAD} = \frac{\Sigma\,|\text{Error}|}{n} = \frac{60}{6} = 10$$

$$\text{Tracking signal} = \frac{\Sigma\,(\text{actual} - \text{forecast})}{\text{MAD}} = \frac{36}{10} = 3.6$$

Action limit of 4 is not exceeded. Therefore, no action is necessary.

Control charts are a second way of monitoring forecast error. Variations of actual from forecast (or average) values are quantified in terms of the estimated standard deviation of forecast S_F.

$$S_F = \sqrt{\frac{\Sigma\,(\text{actual} - \text{forecast})^2}{n - 1}} \qquad (9.26)$$

Control limits are then set, perhaps at two or three standard deviations away from the forecast average $\bar{X}$, or the $2S_F$ or $3S_F$ limits are used as maximum acceptable limits for forecast error. Note that the limits are based on individual forecast values, so you assume that the errors are normally distributed around the forecast average. See Fig. 9-9.

Example 9.11   (a) Compute the $2S_F$ control limits for the data given in Example 9.10. (b) Are all forecast errors within these limits?

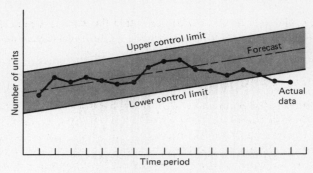

Fig. 9-9   Control limits for forecasts

(*a*)   Control limits for error $= \pm 2S_F$

$$S_F = \sqrt{\frac{\Sigma\,(\text{actual} - \text{forecast})^2}{n - 1}} = \sqrt{\frac{794}{6 - 2}} = 14$$

Thus, Control limits for error $= \pm 2(14) = \pm 28$.

    Note: Control limits about the mean would be

$$\text{CL} = \bar{X} \pm 2S_F$$

where $$\bar{X} = \frac{78 + 79 + 83 + 79 + 80 + 83}{6} = 80$$

Therefore $$\text{CL} = 80 \pm 2(14) = 52 \text{ to } 108 \quad (\text{rounded to integer values})$$

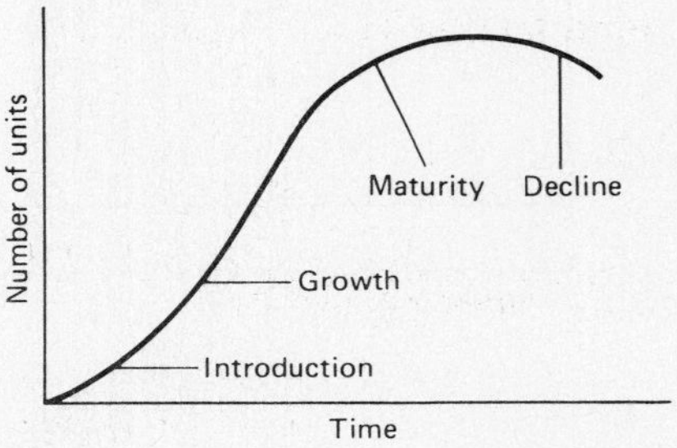

Introduction
- Data: No data available;
  rely on qualitative methods.
- Time: Need long horizon.
- Methods: Judgment, Delphi, and
  historical analogy are useful.
  Market surveys important.

Growth
- Data: Some data available for analysis.
- Time: Still need long horizon; trends and cause-effect relationships important.
- Methods: Market surveys and historical comparison still useful. Regression and
  computer simulation models justified. Tracking product history now
  important.

Maturity
- Data: Considerable data available on demand, inventory levels, etc.
- Time: More uses of short-term forecasts; still need long-term projections, but trends
  change only gradually.
- Methods: Statistical and quantitative methods more useful. Time series helpful for trend,
  seasonal. Regression and correlation use associations and leading indicators.
  Exponential smoothing very useful. Econometric methods feasible.

Decline
- Data: Abundant data (but not necessarily on decline).
- Time: Shorter horizon.
- Methods: Continue use of maturity methods as applicable. Judgment, historical analogies,
  and market surveys may signal changes.

Fig. 9-10   Life cycle effects upon forecasting methodology

(b) All forecast errors (as calculated in Example 9.10) are within the ±28 error limit. *Note*: Since *n* is less than 30, this distribution of forecast errors does not wholly satisfy the normality assumption. See Prob. 9.11.

FORECAST APPLICATION

Forecasts should be sufficiently accurate and flexible to plan for future activities. Low-accuracy methods may suffice; higher accuracy usually costs more to design and implement. *Long-term forecasts*—used for location, capacity, and new-product decisions—require techniques with long-term horizons. *Short-term forecasts*—such as those for production-and-inventory control, labor levels, and cost controls—can rely more on recent history. Figure 9-10 relates the method to the product life cycle.

Solved Problems

TIME SERIES METHODS

9.1 A food processing company uses a moving average to forecast next month's demand. Past actual demand (in units) is as shown in Table 9-10.

(a) Compute a simple 5-month moving average to forecast demand for month 52.

(b) Compute a weighted 3-month moving average, where the weights are highest for the latest months and descend in order of 3, 2, 1.

Table 9-10

Month	Actual Demand
43	105
44	106
45	110
46	110
47	114
48	121
49	130
50	128
51	137
52	

(a) $$MA = \frac{\Sigma X}{\text{number of periods}} = \frac{114 + 121 + 130 + 128 + 137}{5} = 126 \text{ units}$$

(b) $$MA_{wt} = \frac{\Sigma (wt)(X)}{\Sigma wt}$$

where

wt × value	= total
3 × 137	= 411
2 × 128	= 256
1 × 130	= 130

and the totals are $\overline{6}$ $\overline{797}$

Thus, $$MA_{wt} = \frac{797}{6} = 133 \text{ units}$$

9.2 The following forecasting equation has been derived by a least-squares method to describe the shipments of welded aluminum tube.

$$Y_c = 10.27 + 1.65X \qquad (1985 = 0, \ X = \text{years}, \ Y = \text{tons/yr})$$

Rewrite the equation by (a) shifting the origin to 1990; (b) expressing X units in months, retaining Y in tons per year; (c) expressing X units in months, and Y in tons per month.

(a) $$Y_c = 10.27 + 1.65(X + 5)$$
$$= 18.52 + 1.65X \qquad (1990 = 0, \ X = \text{years}, \ Y = \text{tons per year})$$

(b) $$Y_c = 10.27 + \frac{1.65X}{12}$$

$$= 10.27 + .14X \qquad \text{(July 1, 1985 = 0, } X = \text{months, } Y = \text{tons per year)}$$

(c) $$Y_c = \frac{10.27 + .14X}{12}$$

$$= .86 + .01X \qquad \text{(July 1, 1985 = 0, } X = \text{months, } Y = \text{tons per month)}$$

SEASONAL INDEX

9.3   A sportswear manufacturer wishes to use data from a 5-year period to develop seasonal indexes. Trend values and ratios of actual A to trend T for most months have already been computed as shown in Table 9-11.

Table 9-11

Month	Jan.	Feb.	Mar.	April	May	June	July	Aug.	Sept.	Oct.	Nov.	Dec.
Ratio A/T	.72	.58	.85			1.43	1.21	1.05	.98	.92	.88	1.12

Compute the seasonal relatives for April and May, correct the total to equal 12.00, and determine the resulting seasonal indexes. See Tables 9-12 and 9-13.

Table 9-12

Year	1	2	3	4	5
April actual	382	401	458	480	533
April trend	400	436	472	508	544

April A/T .96   .92   .97   .94   .98
April total = 4.77
April average = $4.77 \div 5 = .95$

Table 9-13

Year	1	2	3	4	5
May actual	485	530	560	592	656
May trend	403	439	475	511	547

May A/T 1.20   1.21   1.18   1.16   1.20
May total = 5.95
May average = $5.95 \div 5 = 1.19$

Table 9-14

Month	Jan.	Feb.	Mar.	April	May	June	July	Aug.	Sept.	Oct.	Nov.	Dec.	12 mo.
Ratio A/T	.72	.58	.85	.95	1.19	1.43	1.21	1.05	.98	.92	.88	1.12	11.88

$$\text{Correction factor} = \frac{12}{11.88} = 1.01$$

Multiplying each month's ratio by the 1.01 correction factor we have Table 9-15.

Table 9-15

Month	Jan.	Feb.	Mar.	April	May	June	July	Aug.	Sept.	Oct.	Nov.	Dec.	12 mo.
SI	.73	.59	.86	.96	1.20	1.44	1.22	1.06	.99	.93	.89	1.13	12.00

9.4   The production manager of the sportswear firm in the previous problem has projected trend values for next summer (June, July, August) of 586, 589, and 592. Using the seasonal indexes given (1.44, 1.22, 1.60), what actual seasonalized production should the manager plan for?

June: $Y_{sz} = \text{SI}(Y_c) = (1.44)(586) = 844$

July: $Y_{sz} = \qquad (1.22)(589) = 719$

August: $Y_{sz} = \qquad (1.06)(592) = 628$

EXPONENTIAL SMOOTHING

9.5   Lakeside Hospital has used a 9-month, moving-average forecasting method to predict drug and surgical dressing inventory requirements. The actual demand for one item is as shown in Table 9-16. Using the previous moving-average data, convert to an exponential smoothing forecast for month 33.

Table 9-16

Month	24	25	26	27	28	29	30	31	32
Demand	78	65	90	71	80	101	84	60	73

$$MA = \frac{\Sigma X}{\text{no. periods}} = \frac{78 + 65 + \cdots + 73}{9} = 78$$

Thus, assume the previous forecast was $F_{t-1} = 78$.

Then estimate α as

$$\alpha = \frac{2}{n+1} = \frac{2}{9+1} = .2$$

so

$$F_t = F_{t-1} + \alpha(A_{t-1} - F_{t-1}) = 78 + .2(73 - 78) = 77 \text{ units}$$

9.6   A shoe manufacturer, using exponential smoothing with $\alpha = .1$, has developed a January trend forecast of 400 units for a ladies' shoe. This brand has seasonal indexes of .80, .90, and 1.20, respectively, for the first three months of the year. Assuming that actual sales were 344 units in January and 414 units in February, what would be the seasonalized (adjusted) March forecast?

(a)   Deseasonalize actual January demand.

$$\text{Demand} = \frac{344}{.80} = 430 \text{ units}$$

(b)   Compute the deseasonalized forecast.

$$F_t = F_{t-1} + \alpha(A_{t-1} - F_{t-1})$$
$$= 400 + .1(430 - 400) = 403$$

(c)   Seasonalized (adjusted) February forecast would be

$$F_{t(sz)} = 403(.90) = 363$$

Repeating for February, we have:

(a)
$$\text{Demand} = \frac{414}{.90} = 460 \text{ units}$$

(b)
$$F_t = 403 + .1(460 - 403) = 409$$

(c)
$$F_{t(sz)} = 409(1.20) = 491$$

9.7   Develop an adjusted exponential forecast for the week of 5/14 for a firm with the demand shown in Table 9-17. Let $\alpha = .1$ and $\beta = .2$. Begin with a previous average of $\hat{F}_{t-1} = 650$, and let the initial trend adjustment, $T_{t-1}, = 0$.

Table 9-17

Week	3/19	3/26	4/2	4/9	4/16	4/23	4/30	5/7
Demand	700	685	648	717	713	728	754	762

Using Eqs. 9.9, 9.10, and 9.11, we have:

Week 3/19:
$$\hat{F}_t = \alpha A_{t-1} + (1 - \alpha)(\hat{F}_{t-1} + T_{t-1})$$
$$= .1(700) + .9(650 + 0) = 655.00$$
$$T_t = \beta(\hat{F}_t - \hat{F}_{t-1}) + (1 - \beta)T_{t-1}$$
$$= .2(655 - 650) + .8(0) = 1.0 + 0 = 1.00$$
$$\hat{F}_{t+1} = \hat{F}_t + T_t = 655 + 1 = 656.00$$

The 656.00 is the adjusted forecast for week 3/26.

Week 3/26:
$$\hat{F}_t = .1(685) + .9(655 + 1.0) = 658.90$$
$$T_t = .2(658.9 - 655) + .8(1.0) = 1.58$$
$$\hat{F}_{t+1} = 658.9 + 1.58 = 660.48$$

The remainder of the calculations are in Table 9-18. The trend-adjusted forecast for the week of 5/14 is $711.89 \cong 712$ units.

Table 9-18

(1) Week	(2) Previous Average $\hat{F}_{t-1}$	(3) Actual Demand A_{t-1}	(4) Smoothed Average $\hat{F}_t$	(5) Smoothed Trend T_t	(6) Next- Period Projection $\hat{F}_{t+1}$
Mar. 19	650.00	700	655.00	1.00	656.00
26	655.00	685	658.90	1.58	660.48
Apr. 2	658.90	648	659.23	1.33	660.56
9	659.23	717	666.20	2.46	669.06
16	660.20	713	673.09	3.35	676.44
23	673.09	728	681.60	4.39	685.99
30	681.60	754	691.79	5.74	698.53
May 7	692.79	762	704.88	7.01	711.89
14		770			

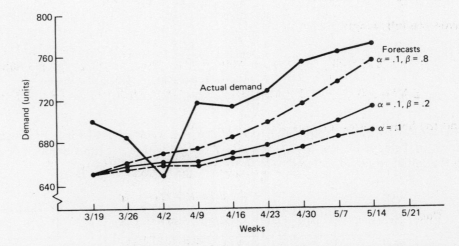

Fig. 9-11 Forecast results using simple and trend-adjusted exponential smoothing

9.8   Using the demand data from Prob. 9.7 and a value of 770 for the week of May 14,

   (a)   Compute the mean absolute deviation (MAD) forecast error for the following: (1) simple
         exponential smoothing ($\alpha = .1$), (2) adjusted exponential smoothing ($\alpha = .1$ and $\beta = .2$),
         (3) adjusted exponential smoothing ($\alpha = .1$ and $\beta = .8$).

   (b)   Compare the actual demand and the three forecasts on a graph.

         Computations of the forecast values for adjusted exponential smoothing ($\alpha = .1$; $\beta = .2$) are given in
   the previous example; computations for simple exponential smoothing and for $\alpha = .1$ and $\beta = .8$ are not
   shown, but the results are given in Table 9-19. The forecast error = actual demand − forecast, and is
   computed as shown. The best fit of these models is $\alpha = .1$ and $\beta = .8$ for a MAD of 31.6. The graph (Fig. 9-11)
   confirms that for these data, which have a strong trend, the higher value of β yields better results.

Table 9-19

Week	Actual Demand	Simple: $\alpha = .1$		Adjusted: $\alpha = .1$; $\beta = .2$		Adjusted: $\alpha = .1$; $\beta = .8$	
		Forecast	Error	Forecast	Error	Forecast	Error
3/19	700	650	50	650	50	650	50
3/26	685	655	30	656	29	659	26
4/2	648	658	−10	660	−12	668	−20
4/9	717	657	60	661	56	671	46
4/16	713	663	50	669	44	684	29
4/23	728	668	60	676	52	697	31
4/30	754	674	80	686	68	714	40
5/7	762	682	80	699	63	734	28
5/14	770	690	80	712	58	756	14
Σ |error|			500		432		284
$\text{MAD} = \dfrac{\Sigma \|error\|}{9}$			55.6		48.0		31.6

REGRESSION AND CORRELATION

9.9   Given the following:

$$\Sigma X = 80 \qquad \Sigma Y = 1{,}200 \qquad n = 20 \qquad \Sigma (Y - Y_c)^2 = 800$$

$$\Sigma X^2 = 340 \qquad \Sigma Y^2 = 74{,}800 \qquad \Sigma XY = 5{,}000 \qquad \Sigma (Y - \bar{Y})^2 = 2{,}800$$

Find (a) linear regression equation, (b) $S_{Y \cdot X}$, (c) r.

(a)
$$b = \frac{\Sigma XY - n\bar{X}\bar{Y}}{\Sigma X^2 - n\bar{X}^2} = \frac{5{,}000 - (20)(4)(60)}{340 - (20)(4)(4)} = 10$$

$$a = \bar{Y} - b\bar{X} = 60 - 10(4) = 20$$

Thus,
$$Y_c = 20 + 10X$$

(b)
$$S_{Y \cdot X} = \sqrt{\frac{\Sigma (Y - Y_c)^2}{n - 2}} = \sqrt{\frac{800}{20 - 2}} = 6.67$$

(c) Because the explained variation is equal to the total minus the unexplained variation, the correlation coefficient is sometimes expressed in the form

$$r = \sqrt{1 - \frac{\text{unexplained variation}}{\text{total variation}}} = \sqrt{1 - \frac{\Sigma (Y - Y_c)^2}{\Sigma (Y - \bar{Y})^2}} \qquad (9.27)$$

Thus, $$r = \sqrt{1 - \frac{800}{2,800}} = .85$$

9.10 Test whether the regression line slope of $b = .395$ developed in Example 9.5 is significant at the 5-percent level. [*Given*: $S_{Y \cdot X} = 2.2$; $\Sigma (X - \bar{X})^2 = 774$.]

Note: This test requires use of the t statistical distribution.

$$t_{\text{calc}} = \frac{b}{S_b}$$

where $$S_b = S_{Y \cdot X} \sqrt{\frac{1}{\Sigma (X - \bar{X})^2}} = 2.2 \sqrt{\frac{1}{774}} = .079$$

Thus, $$t_{\text{calc}} = \frac{.395}{.079} = 5.00$$

Test: slope is significant if $t_{\text{calc}} > t_{.05, 6df}$. In this case, $t_{.05, 6df} = 2.447$. Thus, slope is significant since $5.00 > 2.447$.

FORECAST CONTROLS

9.11 Use the Lakeside Hospital data of Prob. 9-5 to compute (a) a 3-month moving average (MA) and (b) the 90-percent control limits that could be expected for individual demand values (assuming a normal distribution)

(a) See Table 9-20.

Table 9-20

Month	Actual Demand	3-Month MA	Forecast Demand	Deviation	(Deviation)²
24	78				
25	65	77.7			
26	90	75.3			
27	71	80.3	78	−7	49
28	80	84.0	75	5	25
29	101	88.3	80	21	441
30	84	81.7	84	0	0
31	60	72.3	88	−28	784
32	73		82	−9	81
					1,380

(b) $$S_F = \sqrt{\frac{\Sigma (\text{actual} - \text{forecast})^2}{n - 1}} = \sqrt{\frac{1,380}{6 - 1}} = 16.6$$

Since n is less than 30, we should use the t distribution rather than the Z for the control limits. Referring to any standard statistics text, we find that for $n - 1 = 5$ degrees of freedom at the 90 percent level, $t = 2.015$. The mean forecast value is:

$$\bar{X} = \frac{78 + 75 + 80 + 84 + 88 + 82}{6} = 81.2$$

Control limits $= \bar{X} \pm tS_F = 81.2 \pm 2.015(16.6) = 47.8$ to 114.6

Note. The control limits explicitly recognize the variability in this data and, in turn, the uncertainty associated with trying to forecast it. A larger sample would yield tighter limits.

9.12 The moving-average forecast and the actual demand for a hospital drug are as shown in Table 9-21. Compute the tracking signal, and comment on the forecast accuracy.

Table 9-21

Month	Actual Demand	Forecast Demand	Error $(A - F)$	|Error|
27	71	78	−7	7
28	80	75	5	5
29	101	83	18	18
30	84	84	0	0
31	60	88	−28	28
32	73	85	−12	12
			−24	70

The deviation and cumulative deviation have already been computed above:

$$\text{MAD} = \frac{\Sigma\,|\text{actual} - \text{forecast}|}{n} = \frac{70}{6} = 11.7$$

$$\text{Tracking signal} = \frac{\Sigma\,(\text{actual} - \text{forecast})}{\text{MAD}} = \frac{-24}{11.7} = -2.05 = |2.05|$$

The demand exhibits substantial variation, but a tracking signal as low as 2.05 (that is, ≤ 4) would not suggest any action at this time.

Supplementary Problems

9.13 The demand over the past 9 months for a new breakfast cereal is shown in Table 9-22. Develop a forecast for November using a 5-period moving average where the weights are (from earliest to latest) 1, 1, 2, 2, and 4.

Table 9-22

Month	Feb.	Mar.	Apr.	May	June	July	Aug.	Sept.	Oct.
Units	70	76	75	80	92	87	93	114	105

Ans. 101 units

9.14 A sugar beet processing cooperative is committed to accepting beets from local producers and has experienced the following supply pattern (in thousands of tons per year and rounded) shown in Table 9-23.

Table 9-23

Year	Tons	Year	Tons
4	100	9	400
5	100	10	400
6	200	11	600
7	600	12	800
8	500	13	800

The operations manager would like to project a trend to determine what facility additions will be required by year 18. (a) Graph the data, and connect the points by straight line segments. (b) Sketch in a freehand curve, and extend it to year 18. What would be your year-18 forecast on the basis of the curve? (c) Compute a 3-year moving average, and plot it as a dotted line on your graph.
Ans.   (a) Graph should show time on X axis, tons on Y. (b) Curves will differ, but forecasts will $\cong 1{,}200$ (thousand) tons. (c) Averages are 133, 300, 433, 500, 433, 466, 600, 733.

9.15   Use the data of Prob. 9-14 to develop a least-squares line of best fit. Omit year 4. (a) State the equation, complete with signature, when the origin is year 9. (b) Use your equation to estimate the trend value for year 18.   Ans.   (a) $Y = 489 + 75X$ (year 9 = 0, X = years, Y = tons) (b) 1,164,000 tons

9.16   A trend equation describing passenger tickets sold was found to be:

$$Y_c = 25{,}480 + 8{,}370X \qquad (1985 = 0,\ X = \text{years},\ Y = \text{tickets})$$

Convert the equation to a 1992 base.
Ans. $Y_c = 84{,}070 + 8{,}370X$ (1992 = 0, X = years, Y = tickets)

9.17   A forecasting equation is of the form:

$$Y_c = 720 + 144X \qquad (1990 = 0,\ X\ \text{unit} = 1\ \text{year},\ Y = \text{annual sales})$$

(a) Forecast the annual sales rate for 1990 and also for 1 year later. (b) Change the time (X) scale to months, and forecast the annual sales rate at July 1, 1990, and also at 1 year later. (c) Change the sales (Y) scale to monthly, and forecast the monthly sales rate at July 1, 1990, and also at 1 year later.
Ans.   (a) 720 units, 864 units (b) $Y_c = 720 + 12X$ (July 1, 1990 = 0, X units = 1 month, Y = annual sales rate in units); 720 units per year; 864 units per year (c) $Y_c = 60 + 1X$ (July 1, 1990 = 0, X units = 1 month, Y = monthly sales rate in units); 60 units per month; 72 units per month

9.18   Data collected on the monthly demand for a housewares items were as shown in Table 9-24. (a) Plot the data as a 1-month moving average. (b) Plot a 5-month moving average as a dotted line. (c) What conclusion can you draw with respect to length of moving average versus smoothing effect? (d) Assume

Table 9-24

January	100
February	90
March	80
April	150
May	240
June	320
July	300
August	280
September	220

that the 12-month moving average centered on July was 231. What is the value of the ratio to moving average that would be used in computing a seasonal index?

Ans. (*a*) Graph should show time on *X* axis, units on *Y* axis. (*b*) First moving average value will be 132 centered on March. (*c*) Longer average yields more smoothing. (*d*) 1.3

9.19 The data shown in Table 9-25 and Fig. 9-12 include the number of lost-time accidents for the Cascade Lumber Co. over the past seven years. (*Note:* The number of employees is shown for reference only. You will not need it to solve this problem.)

Table 9-25

Year	Number of Employees (000)	Number Accidents
1	15	5
2	12	20
3	20	15
4	26	18
5	35	17
6	30	30
7	37	35
		140

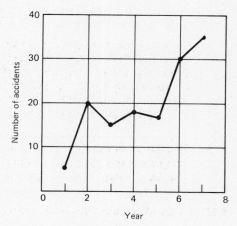

Fig. 9-12

(*a*) Use the normal equations to develop a linear time-series equation for forecasting the number of accidents. State the equation complete with signature. (*b*) Use your equation to forecast the number of accidents in year 10.

Ans. (*a*) $Y_c = 20 + 4X$ (year 4 = 0, X = years, Y = number of accidents) (*b*) 44

9.20 Forecast demand for March was 950 units, but actual demand turned out to be only 820. If the firm is using a simple exponential smoothing technique with $\alpha = .2$, what is the forecast for April? *Ans.* 924 units

9.21 Using the results from Prob. 9.20, assume the April demand was actually 980 units. Now what is the forecast for May?   *Ans.* 935 units

9.22 A forecaster is using an exponential smoothing model with $\alpha = .4$ and wishes to convert to a moving average. What length of moving average is approximately equivalent?   *Ans.* 4 period

Table 9-26

Year	Quarter	Actual Enrollment (000)	Old Forecast (000)	Forecast Error (000)	Correction (000)	New Forecast (000)
1	1st	20.50	20.00	.5	.20	20.20
	2d	21.00				
	3d	19.12				
2	1st	20.06				
	2d	22.00				
	3d					

9.23 A university registrar has adopted a simple exponential smoothing model ($\alpha = .4$) to forecast enrollments during the three regular terms (excluding summer). The results are shown in Table 9-26. (a) Use the data to develop an enrollment forecast for the third quarter of year 2. (b) What would be the effect of increasing the smoothing constant to 1.0?

Ans. (a) 20,800 (b) Forecast would reflect the total amount of variation of previous demand from previous forecast—therefore, no smoothing.

9.24 In Example 9.4, assume that the actual demand for the next three weeks in the sequence is March 22 = 561, March 29 = 587, April 5 = 615. (a) Extend the simple exponential forecast to cover these periods. (b) Using a value of $\beta = .6$, compute the adjusted exponential forecast for the week of April 12th.   *Ans.* (a) 525 (b) 554

9.25 A firm producing photochemicals has a weekly demand pattern as shown in Table 9-27. Using a smoothing constant of $\alpha = .5$ for both original data and trend, and beginning with week 1, (a) compute the simple exponentially smoothed forecast, and (b) compute the trend-adjusted exponentially smoothed forecast for the first five periods.

Table 9-27

Week	1	2	3	4	5	6	7	8	9	10	11	12	13	14	15
Demand	30	34	22	16	10	10	14	20	30	36	30	10	12	20	30

Ans. (a) 24 (b) 10

9.26 Find the regression equation resulting from the values $\Sigma X = 70$, $\Sigma Y = 90$, $\Sigma XY = 660$, $\Sigma X^2 = 514$, $n = 10$.   *Ans.* $Y_c = .25 + 1.25X$

9.27 Use the data from Prob. 9.19 to develop a linear-regression equation for forecasting the number of accidents on the basis of the number of employees. Use the equation to forecast the number of accidents when the number of employees is 22(000).   *Ans.* 18 accidents, from equation $Y_c = 4.3 + .63X$

9.28 A producer of roofing materials has collected data relating interest rates to sales of asphalt shingles and found that the unexplained variation = 680, and explained variation = 2840. (a) Find the correlation coefficient. (b) Explain its meaning.

Ans. (a) $r = .90$ (b) 81 percent of the variation in shingle sales is associated with interest-rate levels

9.29 The Carpet Cleaner Co. is attempting to do a better job of inventory management by predicting the number of vacuums the company will sell per week on the basis of the number of customers who respond to magazine advertisement in an earlier week. On the basis of a sample of $n = 102$ weeks, the following data were obtained.

$$a = 25 \qquad \Sigma (Y - Y_c)^2 = 22,500$$

$$b = .10 \qquad \Sigma (Y - \bar{Y})^2 = 45,000$$

(a) Provide a point estimate of the number of vacuums sold per week when 80 inquiries were received in the earlier week. (b) Estimate (at the 95.5 percent level) the number of vacuums sold per week when 80 inquiries were received the week earlier. (c) State the value of the coefficient of determination. (d) Explain the meaning of your r^2 value.

Ans. (a) 33 (b) Using the large-sample approximation, the interval is 3 to 63 because $S_{Y \cdot X} = 15$ (c) .5 (d) 50 percent of the variation in number of vacuums sold is explained by the magazine advertisements.

9.30 A recreation operations planner has had data collected on automobile traffic at a selected location on an interstate highway in hopes that the information can be used to predict weekday demand for state-operated campsites 200 miles away. Random samples of 32 weekdays during the camping season resulted in data from which the following expression was developed:

$$Y_c = 18 + .02X$$

where X is the number of automobiles passing the location and Y is the number of campsites demanded that day. In addition, the unexplained variation is $\Sigma (Y - Y_c)^2 = 1,470$, and the total variation is $\Sigma (Y - \bar{Y})^2 = 4,080$. (a) What is the value of the coefficient of determination? (b) Explain, in words, the meaning of the coefficient of determination. (c) What is the value of the coefficient of correlation?

Ans. (a) .64 (b) It tells the percentage of variation in campsites demanded that is associated with automobile traffic at the selected site. (c) .80

9.31 Allan's Underground Systems installs septic systems for new houses constructed outside the city limits. To help forecast his demand, Mr. Allan has collected the data shown in Table 9-28 on the number of county building permits issued per month, along with the corresponding number of bid requests he has received over a 15-month period.

Table 9-28

Month	1	2	3	4	5	6	7	8	9	10	11	12	13	14	15
No. building permits	8	20	48	60	55	58	50	45	34	38	10	5	12	29	50
No. bid requests	20	7	8	4	18	40	48	54	47	42	30	22	20	4	3

(a) Compute the simple correlation coefficient r between the number of building permits issued and the number of bid requests received in that month. Use all 15 periods of data. (b) Use the first 12 months of data for building permits and compute r between the number of building permits issued in a month and the number of bid requests received 2 months later (i.e., a 2-month lag). (c) Repeat (b), but use a 3-month lag. (d) Which type of regression model would be best to forecast bid requests: a same-month model, a 2-month lag model, or a 3-month lag model?

Ans. (a) .08 (b) .84 (c) .96 (d) A 3-month lag model is best. It permits Allan to explain 93 percent of the variation in number of bid requests.

9.32 Two experienced managers have resisted the introduction of a computerized exponential smoothing system, claiming that their judgmental forecasts are "much better than any impersonal computer could do." Their past record of prediction is as shown in Table 9-29.

Table 9-29

Week	Actual Demand	Forecast Demand
1	4,000	4,500
2	4,200	5,000
3	4,200	4,000
4	3,000	3,800
5	3,800	3,600
6	5,000	4,000
7	5,600	5,000
8	4,400	4,800
9	5,000	4,000
10	4,800	5,000

(a) Compute the MAD. (b) Compute the tracking signal. (c) On the basis of your calculations, is the judgmental system performing satisfactorily?   Ans. (a) 570 (b) .53 (c) yes

Chapter 10

Aggregate Planning and Master Scheduling

PLANNING OBJECTIVES

Aggregate planning is the process of planning the quantity and timing the output over the intermediate range (often three months to a year) by adjusting the production rate, employment, inventory, and other controllable variables. The objective of aggregate planning is to respond to irregular market demands by effectively utilizing the organization's resources. Of course, demands cannot always be met, and planners must balance the variability of demand against the more stable availability of capacity.

Figure 10-1 illustrates how aggregate planning links long-range and short-range planning activities. It is "aggregate" in the sense that it does not focus on individual goods or services, but lumps them into homogeneous categories (families or pseudoproducts) such as customers served, number of motors, or tons of metal.

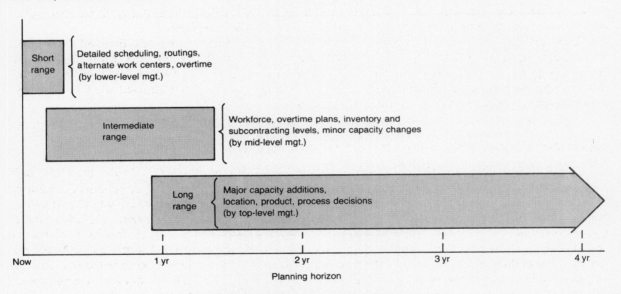

Fig. 10-1 Planning levels and activities

Master scheduling follows aggregate planning and expresses the overall plan in terms of specific end items, which can be assigned priorities. It makes use of information from both forecasts and orders on hand, and is the major control over production activities. Figure 10-2 illustrates a simplified aggregate plan and master schedule.

Aggregate planning strategies are the courses of action available to planners. They include the use of both single (pure strategies) and combinations (mixed strategies) of decision variables. The major pure strategies used in manufacturing activities are:

(1) Varying work-force size   (4) Accepting back orders

(2) Overtime and idle time   (5) Subcontracting

(3) Varying inventory levels   (6) Capacity utilization

Aggregate Plan

Month	J	F	M	A	M	J	J	A	S
Number of motors	40	25	50	30	30	50	30	40	40

Master Schedule

Month	J	F	M	A	M	J	J	A	S
AC motors:									
5 hp	15	—	30	—	—	30	—	—	10
25 hp	20	25	20	15	15	15	20	20	20
DC motors:									
20 hp	—	—	—	—	—	—	10	10	—
WR motors:									
10 hp	5	—	—	15	15	5	—	10	10

Fig. 10-2 Aggregate plan and master schedule for electric motors

Nonmanufacturing activities rely more upon shifting or managing demand (by fixed schedules, appointments, etc.) because the inventory strategy is not available to them.

Each strategy gives the firm a different flexibility in responding to uncertain demand. However, the benefits must be matched against countervailing costs such as training and layoff costs, wage premiums (for overtime), carrying costs, and reduced customer service. Accepting back orders (to delay filling orders) can result in stockout costs of lost customers. Subcontracted work is typically more expensive, as is the use of overloaded facilities.

PLANNING GUIDELINES: ADJUSTMENT TO THE FORECAST

Planning and control activities range from top-level business planning of new products and earnings per share (eps) down to plant monitoring and control. The aggregate, or production, plan is a high-level "negotiated decision" that coordinates the activities of marketing, finance, and other functions. Inputs typically include (1) profit objectives, (2) forecasts and orders, (3) sales plans, (4) inventory objectives, (5) capital-budgeting plans, (6) labor availability, and (7) facility availability.

Aggregate, or production, planning guidelines (Table 10-1) emphasize the need for a well-defined policy to meet fluctuations in demand, for the importance of a good forecast, and for the advisability of planning in units (or cost of goods sold) rather than in sales dollars. The strategy of responding to demand in a controlled manner is summarized in Magee's *Modified Response Model* depicted in Fig. 10-3. The model matches inventory (on hand and on order) against demand to determine how much additional production seems warranted. However, in order to limit excessive fluctuations, only a fraction K of the resultant discrepancy is added to (or subtracted from) the forecasted (or budgeted) production level. The fraction K is a control number $(0 \le K \le 1)$ which limits the amount of adjustment to current demand conditions. Letting Δ represent the difference between planned and actual values, the production level is:

$$\text{Production level} = \text{planned or forecasted production} + K(\Delta \text{ demand} + \Delta \text{ inventory} + \Delta \text{ deliveries})$$
$$(10.1)$$

Example 10.1 An industrial chemicals producer has developed the forecast shown in Table 10-2. The firm uses a modified response model (with a control number of $K = .8$) to set actual production levels. Since it takes almost 30 days of lead time to adjust production, the incremental response is effective after an intervening month. If the actual demand (which includes inventory and delivery changes) is 11,500 units in April, what modified production quantity should be scheduled for June?

Table 10-1   Aggregate Planning Guidelines

1. Determine corporate policy regarding controllable variables.
2. Use a good forecast as a basis for planning.
3. Plan for appropriate units of capacity.
4. Maintain as stable a work force as is practical.
5. Maintain needed control over inventories.
6. Maintain flexibility to change.
7. Respond to demand in a controlled manner.
8. Evaluate planning on a regular basis.

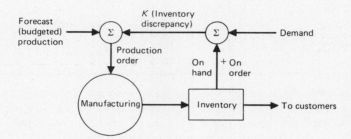

Fig. 10-3 Modified response model

Table 10-2

Month	Forecast	Actual
April	12,000	11,500
May	16,000	
June	14,000	
July	10,000	

In this situation, Magee's Model can be reduced to:

$$\text{Production level} = \text{forecast} + K(\Delta D) \qquad (10.2)$$

where $\Delta D = \text{actual} - \text{planned} = 11{,}500 - 12{,}000 = -500$.

Thus,
$$\text{Production level} = 14{,}000 + .8(-500)$$
$$= 14{,}000 - 400 = 13{,}600 \text{ units}$$

GRAPHING AND CHARTING METHODS

Graphing and charting techniques work with a few variables at a time on a trial-and-error basis to meet the forecasted demand, or to deliver a modified response to demand. Production requirements charts and cumulative workload projections convey an initial understanding of the aggregate planning problem.

Example 10.2 A firm has developed the following forecast in units (Table 10-3) for an item which has a demand influenced by seasonal factors.

Table 10-3

Jan.	220	Apr.	396	July	378	Oct.	115
Feb.	90	May	616	Aug.	220	Nov.	95
Mar.	210	June	700	Sept.	200	Dec.	260

(*a*) Prepare a chart showing the daily demand requirements. (*Note*: Available workdays per month are given below.) (*b*) Plot the demand as a histogram and as a cumulative requirement over time. (*c*) Determine the production rate required to meet average demand, and plot this as a dotted line on the graphs.

(*a*)   See Table 10-4.

Table 10-4   Chart of Production Requirements

	(1)	(2)	(3)	(4)	(5)
				Cumulative	
Month	Forecast Demand	Production Days	Demand/Day (1) ÷ (2)	Production Days	Cumulative Demand
January	220	22	10	22	220
February	90	18	5	40	310
March	210	21	10	61	520
April	396	22	18	83	916
May	616	22	28	105	1,532
June	700	20	35	125	2,332
July	378	21	18	146	2,610
August	220	22	10	168	2,830
September	200	20	10	188	3,030
October	115	23	5	211	3,145
November	95	19	5	230	3,240
December	260	20	13	250	3,500
	3,500	250			

(*b*)   See Figs. 10-4 and 10-5.

(*c*) $$\text{Average requirement} = \frac{\text{total demand}}{\text{total production days}} = \frac{3,500}{250} = 14 \text{ units/day}$$

The histogram (Fig. 10-4) and the cumulative graph (Fig. 10-5) show how the forecast (or modified response) deviates from average requirements. One pure strategy to meet demand might consist of varying the size of the work force by hiring and laying off as required. The production rate would then exactly follow the forecast requirement, as shown by the solid line in the histogram (Fig. 10-4). An inventory-adjustment strategy would result in a steady rate of production, as shown by the dashed line. A third plan might be to produce at some low, steady rate, and subcontract all excess demand to other firms.

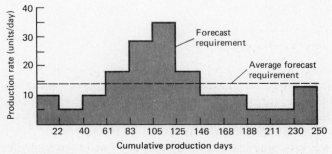

Fig. 10-4 Histogram of forecast and average requirement

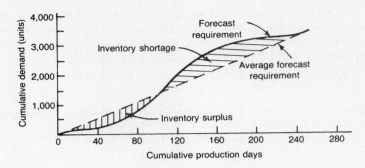

Fig. 10-5 Cumulative graph of forecast and average requirement

Example 10.3 Use the data from Example 10-2 to determine the monthly inventory balances required to follow a plan of letting the inventory absorb all fluctuations in demand. In this case we have a constant work force, no idle time or overtime, no back orders, no use of subcontractors, and no capacity adjustment. Assume that the firm does not use safety stock or cushion inventory to meet the demand.

The firm can satisfy demand by producing at an average requirement (14 units per day) and accumulating inventory during periods of slack demand (periods below the dashed line in Fig. 10-5) and depleting it during periods of strong demand. Disregarding any safety stock, the inventory balance is:

$$\text{Inventory balance} = \Sigma \, (\text{production} - \text{demand}) \qquad (10.3)$$

See Table 10-5 for the solution. The pattern of demand is such that column 4 reveals a maximum negative balance of 566 units at the *end* of July, so 566 additional units must be carried in stock initially if demand is to be met. Column 5 shows the resulting inventory balances required.

Table 10-5

Month	(1) Production at 14 Units/Day	(2) Forecast Demand	(3) Inventory Change	(4) Ending Inventory Balance	(5) Ending Balance with 566 on Jan. 1
January	308	220	+88	88	654
February	252	90	+162	250	816
March	294	210	+84	334	900
April	308	396	−88	246	812
May	308	616	−308	−62	504
June	280	700	−420	−482	84
July	294	378	−84	−566	0
August	308	220	+88	−478	88
September	280	200	+80	−398	168
October	322	115	+207	−191	375
November	266	95	+171	−20	546
December	280	260	+20	0	566
		3,500			

Cost Computation. Once the inventory requirements are known (i.e., peak and average amounts), the carrying costs can be weighed against the costs of alternative plans. Carrying costs are typically based upon average inventory amounts, and storage costs are based upon the maximum number of units needing storage at any one time.

Example 10.4   Given the data of Example 10.2, the firm has determined that to follow a plan of meeting demand by varying the size of the work force (strategy 1) would result in hiring and layoff costs estimated at $12,000. If the units cost $100 each to produce, the carrying costs per year are 20 percent of the average inventory value, and the storage costs (based on maximum inventory) are $.90 per unit, which plan results in the lower cost: varying inventory, or varying employment?

From Example 10.3,

$$\text{Maximum inventory requiring storage} = 900 \text{ units (from Table 10-5, column 5)}$$

$$\text{Average inventory balance} \cong \frac{654 + 816 + 900 + \cdots + 566}{12} \cong 460 \text{ units}$$

Plan 1 (varying inventory):

$$\text{Inventory cost} = \text{carrying cost} + \text{storage cost}$$
$$= (.20)(460)(\$100) + (\$.90)(900) = \$10,010$$

Plan 2 (varying employment): $12,000
Therefore, varying inventory is the strategy with the lower cost.

MIXED STRATEGIES

Alternative plans that make use of overtime, subcontract work, back orders, etc. can be compared. A mixed strategy may yield the best solution. Although numerous combinations of strategies exist, the realities of the situation will limit the number of practical solutions.

Example 10.5   Given the data from Examples 10.2, 10.3, and 10.4, suppose the firm wishes to investigate two other alternatives. A third plan is to produce at a rate of 10 units per day and subcontract the additional requirements at a delivered cost of $107 per unit. Any accumulated inventory is carried forward at a 20 percent carrying cost (no extra storage cost).

The fourth plan is to produce at a steady rate of 10 units per day and use overtime to meet the additional requirements at a premium of $10 per unit. Accumulated inventory is, again, carried forward at a 20 percent cost.

Plan 3 (produce at 10 units per day, carry inventory, and subcontract):

Referring to Example 10.2, a production rate of 10 units per day exceeds demand during only three months (February, October, and November). The inventory accumulated during these periods must be carried at a cost of 20 percent($100) ÷ 12 months = $1.67 per unit-month. Units are carried until they can be used to help meet demand in a subsequent month as shown in Table 10-6. Assume an equilibrium condition where the excess production from October and November (150 units) is on hand January 1.

Table 10-6

Month	Demand	Production at 10 Units/Day	Inventory to Carry	Inventory Carried Until	Number Months	Cost at $1.67 per Unit-Month
Initial			150	150 units to April	3	$ 750
Feb.	90	180	90	26 units to April	2	87
				64 units to May	3	320
Oct.	115	230	115	60 units to Dec.	2	200
				55 units to year end	3	275
Nov.	95	190	95	95 units to year end	2	317
						$1,949

Inventory cost (from Table 10-6) is $1,949. Add the marginal cost of subcontracting:

$$\text{Number of units} = \text{demand} - \text{production}$$
$$= 3,500 - 10(250) = 1,000 \text{ units}$$
$$\text{Cost/unit} = \$107 - 100 = \$7/\text{unit}$$
$$\text{Marginal cost} = 1,000 \text{ units } (\$7/\text{unit}) = \$7,000$$

The total cost of plan 3 (inventory cost + marginal cost) is $8,949 ($1,949 + $7,000).

Plan 4:

This plan differs from plan 3 only in the marginal cost, which is now due to overtime rather than subcontracting.

$$
\begin{array}{ll}
\text{Inventory cost (same as plan 3)} & \$\ 1,949 \\
\text{Add marginal cost of overtime:} & \\
\quad \text{1,000 units @ \$10/unit} & \underline{10,000} \\
\text{Total cost of plan 4} & \overline{\$11,949}
\end{array}
$$

Compare the four plans (Table 10-7).

Table 10-7   Comparisons of Plans

Plan		Strategy	Cost
1	(pure)	Vary inventory	$10,010
2	(pure)	Vary employment	12,000
3	(mixed)	Subcontract and carry inventory	8,949
4	(mixed)	Overtime and carry inventory	11,949

On the basis of this limited comparison, plan 3 has the least cost.

MATHEMATICAL PLANNING MODELS

Mathematical models attempt to refine or improve upon the trial-and-error approaches. Table 10-8 summarizes the major mathematical approaches.

Table 10-8   A Summary of Some Mathematical Aggregate Planning Models

Approach	Linear Programming	Linear Decision Rule (LDR)	Management Coefficients	Computer Search Models
Application	Minimizes costs of employment, overtime, and inventories subject to meeting demand	Uses quadratic cost functions to derive rules for work-force size and number of units	Develops regression model that incorporates managers' past decisions to predict capacity needs	Computer routine searches numerous combinations of capacity and selects the one of least cost
Strengths	■ Understandable ■ Yields optimal plan ■ Powerful and inclusive ■ Flexible	■ Permits nonlinear cost functions ■ Yields optimal plan ■ Theoretical value	■ No limitations on form of costs or constraints ■ Incorporates past experience	■ Accepts wide range of cost functions ■ Flexible ■ Easily changed
Limitations	■ Requires linear cost functions ■ Outputs require interpretation	■ Complex—not easily understood ■ Requires quadratic cost functions ■ Outputs not always realistic (variables unconstrained)	■ Nonoptimal, but reasonably close ■ Relies on expertise of individual manager ■ Model not directly transferable to others	■ Nonoptimal, but does well compared with other rules ■ Doesn't always locate global minimum

A useful version of the linear-programming model (the transportation algorithm) views the aggregate planning problem as one of allocating capacity (supply) to meet forecast requirements (demand) where supply consists of the inventory on hand and units that can be produced using regular time (RT), overtime (OT), and subcontracting (SC). Demand consists of individual-period requirements plus any desired ending inventory. Costs associated with producing units in the given period or producing them and carrying them in inventory until a later period are entered in the small boxes inside the cells in the matrix, as is done in the standard transportation linear-programming format.

Example 10.6 Given the accompanying supply, demand, cost, and inventory data (Tables 10-9, 10-10, and 10-11) for a firm that has a constant work force and wishes to meet all demand (that is, with no back orders), allocate production capacity to satisfy demand at minimum cost.

Table 10-9　Supply Capacity (Units)

Period	Regular Time	Overtime	Subcontract
1	60	18	1,000
2	50	15	1,000
3	60	18	1,000
4	65	20	1,000

Table 10-10　Demand Forecast

Period	Units
1	100
2	50
3	70
4	80

Table 10-11　Additional Data

Inventory	Cost Data
Initial=20 Final=25	Regular time cost/unit=$100 　(labor=50 percent of the cost) Overtime cost/unit=$125 Subcontracting cost/unit=$130 Carrying cost/unit-period=$2

The initial linear programming matrix in units of capacity is shown in Fig. 10-6, with entries determined as explained below. Because total capacity exceeds demand, a *slack* demand of unused capacity is added to achieve the required balance in supply versus demand.

Initial inventory. There are 20 units available at no additional cost if used in period 1. Carrying cost is $2 per unit per period if units are retained until period 2, $4 per unit until period 3, and so on. If the units are unused during any of the four periods, the result is a $6-per-unit cost, plus $2 per unit to carry it forward to the next planning horizon, for $8 total if unused.

Regular time. Cost per unit-month is $100 if units are used in the month produced; otherwise, a carrying cost of $2 per unit-month is added on for each month the units are retained. Unused regular time costs the firm 50 percent of $100=$50.

Overtime. Cost per unit is $125 if the units are used in the month produced; otherwise, a carrying cost of $2 per unit-month is incurred, as in the regular-time situation. Unused overtime has zero cost.

Subcontracting. Cost per unit is $130 plus any costs for units carried forward. This latter situation is unlikely, however, because any reasonable demand can be obtained when needed, as indicated by the arbitrarily high number (1,000) assigned to subcontracting capacity. There is no cost for unused capacity here.

Note: If the initial allocations are made so as to use regular time as fully as possible, the solution procedure is often simplified. Overtime and subcontracting amounts can also be allocated on a minimum-cost basis.

Final inventory. The final-inventory requirement (25 units) must be available at the end of period 4 and has been added to the period 4 demand of 80 units to obtain a total of 105 units.

Since no back orders are permitted, production in subsequent months to fill demand in a current month is not allowed. These unavailable cells, along with the cells associated with carrying forward any subcontracted units, may therefore be blanked out, since they are infeasible. The final solution, following normal methods of distribution linear programming, is shown in Fig. 10-7. This result flows from a least-cost allocation.

The optimal solution values can be taken directly from the cells. Thus in period 2, for example, the planners will schedule the full 50 units to be produced on regular time plus 12 units on overtime to be carried forward to period 4. This leaves 3 units of unused overtime capacity and no subcontracting during that period. Due to the similar carrying cost for units produced on regular time or overtime, it does not matter which physical units are carried forward, once overtime production is required. Thus, different optimal solutions (but with identical costs) may be obtained.

Supply, units from		Demand, units for					Total Capacity Available
		Period 1	Period 2	Period 3	Period 4 and Final	Unused Capacity	
Initial inventory		0	2	4	6	8	20
1	Regular	100	102	104	106	50	60
	Overtime	125	127	129	131	0	18
	Subcontract	130				0	1,000
2	Regular		100	102	104	50	50
	Overtime		125	127	129	0	15
	Subcontract		130			0	1,000
3	Regular			100	102	50	60
	Overtime			125	127	0	18
	Subcontract			130		0	1,000
4	Regular				100	50	65
	Overtime				125	0	20
	Subcontract				130	0	1,000
Demand		100	50	70	105	4,001	4,326

Fig. 10-6   Linear programming format for scheduling

MASTER-SCHEDULING OBJECTIVES

The master production schedule (MPS) formalizes the production plan and converts it into specific material and capacity requirements. Labor, material, and equipment needs for each job must then be assessed. Thus the MPS drives the entire production and inventory system by setting specific production goals and responding to feedback from all downstream operations. Some key functions of a master schedule are listed in Table 10-12.

Supply, units from		Demand, units for				Unused Capacity	Total Capacity Available
		Period 1	Period 2	Period 3	Period 4 and Final		
Initial inventory		0 / 20	2	4	6	8	20
1	Regular	100 / 60	102	104	106	50	60
	Overtime	125 / 18	127	129	131	0	18
	Subcontract	130 / 2	▨	▨	▨	0 / 998	1,000
2	Regular	▨	100 / 50	102	104	50	50
	Overtime		125	127	129 / 12	0 / 3	15
	Subcontract		130			0 / 1,000	1,000
3	Regular	▨	▨	100 / 60	102	50	60
	Overtime			125 / 10	127 / 8	0	18
	Subcontract			130		0 / 1,000	1,000
4	Regular	▨	▨	▨	100 / 65	50	65
	Overtime				125 / 20	0	20
	Subcontract				130 / 0	0 / 1,000	1,000
Demand		100	50	70	105	4,001	4,326

Fig. 10-7　Matrix for planning decision

Table 10-12　Master Schedule Functions

1. Translate aggregate plans into specific end items
2. Evaluate alternative schedules
3. Generate material requirements
4. Generate capacity requirements
5. Facilitate information processing
6. Maintain valid priorities
7. Effectively utilize capacity

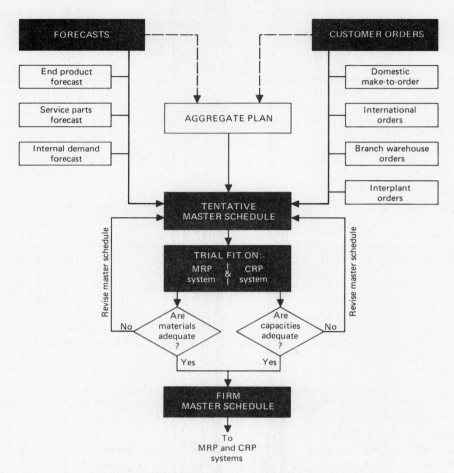

Fig. 10-8 Market influences on the master schedule

Computerized P&IC systems often have *simulation capabilities* that enable planners to "trial fit" alternative master schedules. See Fig. 10-8. Specific material and capacity requirements (e.g., hours needed at key work centers) are then generated and evaluated for adequacy. Once the MPS is implemented, any delays and changes should be reflected in an updated master schedule, so that valid priorities are maintained for all jobs.

DISCRETE-ASSEMBLY VERSUS PROCESS-INDUSTRY SCHEDULING

Discrete-assembly manufacturing typically begins with many raw materials and other components that are combined into one or a few end items (for example, many components go into one typewriter). As illustrated in Fig. 10-9a, master scheduling (MPS) starts with the end items and works backward to determine raw material and component needs. Most computerized MRP scheduling systems are designed to accommodate this traditional type of scheduling. Material availability is a major concern in this kind of manufacturing. Firms that produce large volumes of few items often produce for stock.

Process-industry manufacturing is almost the reverse of assembly manufacturing. It usually begins with only a few types of raw materials that are sorted, milled, or somehow processed into multiple end items and by-products. For example, many petroleum products come from crude oil, and numerous cuts of meat come from steers. Fig. 10-9c illustrates the forward scheduling concept needed to accommodate processing activities. Master scheduling begins at the raw-material (input)

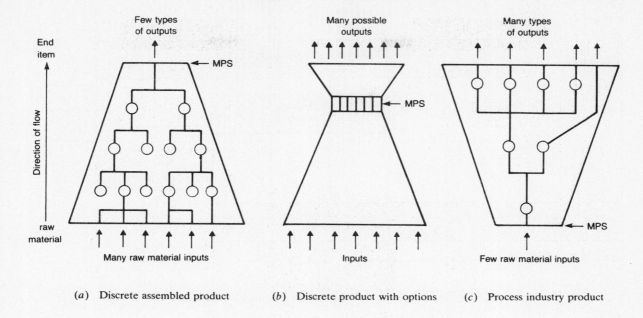

Fig. 10-9 Master scheduling in discrete assembly versus process industry

level rather than at the end-item level. But the natural variability of the raw materials results in uncertain yields in the various categories of output. This makes scheduling, cost estimating, and control over work-in-process and finished goods inventory difficult. Capacity to handle the variable levels of materials is a major concern in process industries.

Firms *assembling* a high volume of *products to-order* usually do not produce all of the options available. The many options may number in the thousands. As depicted in Fig. 10-9*b*, assemble-to-order firms often begin their master schedule at a major subassembly level. They plan using historical need patterns or forecast proportions of the options and leave the end-item specification to an assembly sheet. For example, an auto manufacturer may plan (master schedule) for 30 percent of a production run to have four-wheel drive, but not specify precisely which cars are to have four-wheel drive until the specific car build-sheet is released.

MPS INPUTS, PLANNING HORIZON, AND POLICY GUIDELINES

Two *major inputs* to the MPS are from (1) forecasts (end item, service parts, and internal demand), and (2) customer orders (in addition to warehouse and interplant orders). Forecasts of demand are the major input for make-to-stock items. Customers' orders can reduce uncertainty in make-to-order companies. However, to be competitive, many make-to-order firms must anticipate orders by using forecasts for long time-horizon periods, and matching those forecasts with customer orders as they become available.

The *time horizon* covered by the MPS depends upon the type of product, volume of production, and component lead times. It can be in weeks, months, or some combination, but the schedule must extend far enough in advance so that the lead times for all purchased and assembled components are adequately encompassed. Figure 10-10 illustrates a 10-week lead time for an item assembled from three component parts.

Master schedules often have both firm and flexible (or tentative) portions. The near-term firm portion encompasses the minimum lead time necessary and is not open to change. Table 10-13 illustrates.

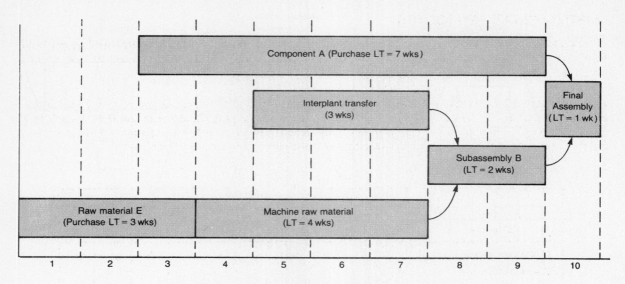

Fig. 10-10   Assembly with 10-week cumulative lead time

Table 10-13   Master Schedule for a Furniture Company

	Week																	
	← Firm → (emergency changes only)					← Flexible → (capacity firm and material ordered)								← Open → (additions and changes OK)				
Item	1	2	3	4	5	6	7	8	9	10	11	12	13	14	15	16	17	18
R28 Table	50		50	50		40			40	40		40	40			40		
R30 Table		80		20	60		80	80			60				80			
L7 Lamp	20		20		10	20			20	20	10	20	20	20				

Table 10-14 lists some *master scheduling guidelines* that have wide applicability. The scheduling process generally consists of consolidating the gross requirements, subtracting the on-hand inventory, and grouping the net requirements into planned orders of appropriate lot sizes. The orders are then converted into load reports on key work centers, and the entire material and capacity requirements are reviewed for feasibility.

Table 10-14   Master Scheduling Guidelines

1. Work from an aggregate production plan
2. Schedule common modules whenever possible
3. Load facilities realistically
4. Release orders on a timely basis
5. Monitor inventory levels closely
6. Reschedule as required

MASTER-SCHEDULING METHOD

Example 10.7 illustrates a master-scheduling method that incorporates demand from both forecasts and orders. Note that the number of units to be produced during each production cycle is specified as an economic run length (ERL—see Chap. 11).

Example 10.7 Shown below in Tables 10-15 and 10-16 are the expected demands for X and Y, which have beginning inventories of 60 and 40 units, respectively. The economic production run length (ERL) for X is 90 units, and for Y is 50 units. Item Y has an uncertain demand, so the firm tries to maintain 30 units of extra (safety) stock to ensure good service. Develop the tentative master schedule for X and Y.

Table 10-15   Item X

Initial inventory = 60 ERL = 90	Week									
	1	2	3	4	5	6	7	8	9	10
Customer forecast		5	30	40	50	40	50	50	50	50
Interplant forecast			5			5			5	
Customer orders	40	40	30	10	10	5				
Warehouse orders	15	10		5						

Table 10-16   Item Y

Initial inventory = 40 ERL = 50	Week									
	1	2	3	4	5	6	7	8	9	10
Customer forecast			5	10	5	5	10	10	15	10
Service forecast			5		10			10		
Domestic orders	10	15	10	10						
International orders		5	5			5				

Service-level requirements necessitate that Y's ending inventory is not permitted to go below 30 units. *Consolidated requirements* are determined by summing the forecast and order data.

For X: Week 1 = 40 + 15 = 55
                             Week 2 = 5 + 40 + 10 = 55

Required production is determined by

$$\text{Production} = \text{beginning inventory} - \text{consolidated requirements}$$

See Table 10-17.

Table 10-17   Item X

Initial inventory = 60 ERL = 90	Week									
	1	2	3	4	5	6	7	8	9	10
Requirements	55	55	65	55	60	50	50	50	55	50
Beginning inventory	60	5	40	65	10	40	80	30	70	15
Production required		90	90		90	90		90		90
Ending inventory	(5)	40	65	10	40	80	30	70	15	55

For X: Week $1 = 60 - 55 = 5$ (No new production is needed.)

                    Week $2 = 5 - 55 = (-50)$ (Schedule an ERL amount.)

Ending inventory is determined by

$$\text{Ending inventory} = \text{beginning inventory} + \text{production} - \text{requirements}$$
$$\text{Week } 2 = 5 + 90 - 55 = 40$$

See Table 10-18 for Y.

Table 10-18   Item Y

Initial inventory = 40 ERL = 50, SS = 30	Week									
	1	2	3	4	5	6	7	8	9	10
Requirements	10	20	25	20	15	10	10	20	15	10
Beginning inventory	40	30	60	35	65	50	40	30	60	45
Production required		50		50				50		
Ending inventory	30	60	35	65	50	40	30	60	45	35

The production-required rows show the tentative master schedule amounts (Table 10-19).

Table 10-19   Master Production Schedule

Week Number	1	2	3	4	5	6	7	8	9	10
Product X	—	90	90	—	90	90	—	90	—	90
Product Y	—	50	—	50	—	—	—	50	—	—

Solved Problems

GRAPHING AND CHARTING METHODS

10.1 High Point Furniture Co. maintains a constant work force (no overtime, back orders, or subcontracting) which can produce 3,000 tables per quarter. The annual demand is 12,000 units and is distributed seasonally in accordance with the quarterly indexes: $Q_1 = .8$, $Q_2 = 1.40$,

Table 10-20

Quarter	(1) Production at 3,000/Q	(2) Seasonal Demand (SI)$Y_c = Y_{sz}$	(3) Inventory Change	(4) Inventory Balance	(5) Balance with 600 on Jan. 1
1st	3,000	(.8)(3,000) = 2,400	600	600	1,200
2d	3,000	(1.4)(3,000) = 4,200	−1,200	−600	0
3d	3,000	(1.0)(3,000) = 3,000	0	−600	0
4th	3,000	(.8)(3,000) = 2,400	600	0	600

$Q_3 = 1.00$, $Q_4 = .80$. Inventories are accumulated when demand is less than capacity and are used up during periods of strong demand. To supply the total annual demand: (*a*) How many tables must be accumulated during each quarter? (*b*) What inventory must be on hand at the beginning of the first quarter?

See Table 10-20. (*a*) The inventory accumulation is given in column 3. (*b*) From column 4, the largest negative inventory is 600 units; therefore, 600 must be on hand on January 1. Column 5 shows the resulting balance at the end of each quarter.

10.2 Use the data from Example 10.2. Suppose the firm wishes to produce at either 10 units per day or, by adding a second shift, at 20 units per day. Each time a shift is added or laid off, it costs the firm an estimated $3,500. Any accumulated inventory is carried forward. Determine the cost of this plan.

At a shift-change cost of $3,500 this plan will permit a maximum of two changes ($7,000), for with any additional changes the cost of plan 1 ($10,010) will automatically be exceeded. From a long-range planning standpoint, since each year represents a cycle, we can assume the firm will want to enter the next year at the same respective level as the present, so two changes would also be a minimum.

Referring to the forecast of Table 10-4, we must construct a new chart to reflect an increased production of 20 units per day for a continuous number of days N where

$$\text{Total production} = N \text{ days @ } 20/\text{day} + (250 - N) \text{ days @ } 10/\text{day}$$
$$3,500 = N(20) + (250 - N)(10)$$
$$N = 100 \text{ days}$$

Allocating this increased rate to the block of months with the largest demand places it in the April-to-July period. Since the June demand rate markedly exceeds the 20-unit-per-day production rate, we should begin production at this faster rate in March in order to build up inventory for the June peak. (A more precise placement of the 100-day period could be determined by formulating and minimizing an expression for carrying costs.) See Table 10-21.

Table 10-21

Month	(1) Production	(2) Forecast Demand	(3) Inventory Change	(4) Ending Inventory Balance	(5) Ending Balance with 150 on Jan. 1
January	220*	220	0	0	150
February	180*	90	+90	90	240
March	420†	210	+210	300	450
April	440†	396	+44	344	494
May	440†	616	−176	168	318
June	400†	700	−300	−132	18
July {15 days @ 6 days @}	300†} 60*}	378	−18	−150	0
August	220*	220	0	−150	0
September	200*	200	0	−150	0
October	230*	115	+115	−35	115
November	190*	95	+95	60	210
December	200*	260	−60	0	150

*At 10 per day.
†At 20 per day.

$$\text{Maximum inventory} = 494 \text{ units (from Table 10-21, column 5)}$$

$$\text{Average inventory balance} \cong \frac{150 + 240 + \cdots + 150}{12}$$

$$\cong 179 \text{ (from Table 10-21, column 5)}$$

$$\text{Inventory cost} = \text{carrying cost} + \text{storage cost}$$

$$= (.20)(179)(\$100) + (\$.90)(494) = \$\ 4{,}025$$

$$\text{Shift-change cost} = (\$3{,}500)(2) = \qquad\qquad \underline{7{,}000}$$

$$\text{Total cost of plan} = \qquad\qquad\qquad \$11{,}025$$

10.3 Michigan Manufacturing produces a product which has a 6-month demand cycle, as shown in Table 10-22 and Fig. 10-11. Each unit requires 10 worker-hours to produce, at a labor cost of $6 per hour regular rate (or $9 per hour overtime). The total cost per unit is estimated at $200, but units can be subcontracted at a cost of $208 per unit. There are currently 20 workers employed in the subject department, and hiring and training costs for additional workers are $300 per person, whereas layoff costs are $400 per person. Company policy is to retain a safety stock equal to 20 percent of the monthly forecast, and each month's safety stock becomes the beginning inventory for the next month. There are currently 50 units in stock carried at a cost of $2 per unit-month. Unit shortage, or stockouts, have been assigned a cost of $20 per unit-month.

Table 10-22

	January	February	March	April	May	June
Forecast demand	300	500	400	100	200	300
Work days	22	19	21	21	22	20
Work hrs at 8/day	176	152	168	168	176	160

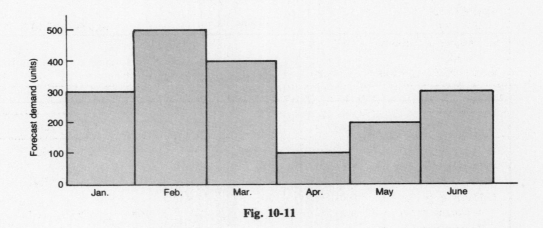

Fig. 10-11

Three aggregate plans are proposed.

Plan 1: Vary work-force size to accommodate demand.

Plan 2: Maintain constant work force of 20 and use overtime and idle time to meet demand.

Plan 3: Maintain constant work force of 20 and build inventory or incur stockout cost. The firm must begin January with the 50-unit inventory on hand.

Compare the costs of the three plans in table form.

We must first determine what the production requirements are, as adjusted to include a safety stock of 20 percent of next month's forecast. Beginning with a January inventory of 50, each subsequent month's inventory reflects the difference between the forecast demand and the production requirement of the previous month. See Table 10-23. The costs of the three plans are shown in Tables 10-24, 10-25, and 10-26.

Table 10-23

	Forecast Demand	Cumulative Demand	Safety Stock at 20 Percent Forecast	Beginning Inventory	Production Requirement (fcst. + SS − beg. inv.)
January	300	300	60	50	$300 + 60 - 50 = 310$
February	500	800	100	60	$500 + 100 - 60 = 540$
March	400	1,200	80	100	$400 + 80 - 100 = 380$
April	100	1,300	20	80	$100 + 20 - 80 = 40$
May	200	1,500	40	20	$200 + 40 - 20 = 220$
June	300	1,800	60	40	$300 + 60 - 40 = 320$

Table 10-24   Plan 1 (Vary Work-Force Size)

	January	February	March	April	May	June	Total
1. Production required	310	540	380	40	220	320	
2. Production hours required (1×10)	3,100	5,400	3,800	400	2,200	3,200	
3. Hours available per worker at 8/day	176	152	168	168	176	160	
4. Number of workers required ($2 \div 3$)	18	36	23	3	13	20	
5. Number of workers hired		18			10	7	
6. Hiring cost ($5 \times \$300$)		$5,400			$3,000	$2,100	$10,500
7. Number of workers laid off	2		13	20			
8. Layoff cost ($7 \times \$400$)	$800		$5,200	$8,000			$14,000

Table 10-25   Plan 2 (Use Overtime and Idle Time)

	January	February	March	April	May	June	Total
1. Production required	310	540	380	40	220	320	
2. Production hours required (1×10)	3,100	5,400	3,800	400	2,200	3,200	
3. Hours available per worker at 8/day	176	152	168	168	176	160	
4. Total hours available (3×20)	3,520	3,040	3,360	3,360	3,520	3,200	
5. Number of OT hours required ($2 - 4$)		2,360	440			0	
6. OT prem.* ($5 \times \$3$)		$7,080	$1,320			0	$8,400
7. Number IT hours ($4 - 2$)	420			2,960	1,320		
8. IT cost ($7 \times \$6$)	$2,520			$17,760	$7,920		$28,200

*Incremental cost of OT = overtime cost − regular time cost = $9 − $6 = $3.

Table 10-26   Plan 3 (Use Inventory and Stockout Based on Constant 20-Worker Force)

	January	February	March	April	May	June	Total
1. Production required	310	540	380	40	220	320	
2. Cumulative production required	310	850	1,230	1,270	1,490	1,810	
3. Total hours available at 20 workers	3,520	3,040	3,360	3,360	3,520	3,200	
4. Units produced (3 ÷ 10)	352	304	336	336	352	320	
5. Cumulative production	352	656	992	1,328	1,680	2,000	
6. Units short (2 − 5)		194	238				
7. Shortage cost (6 × $20)		$3,880	$4,760				$8,640
8. Excess units (5 − 2)	42			58	190	190	
9. Inventory cost (8 × $2)	$84			$116	$380	$380	$960

Note that plan 3 assumes that a stockout cost is incurred if safety stock is not maintained at prescribed levels of 20 percent of forecast. The firm is in effect managing the safety-stock level to yield a specific degree of protection by absorbing the cost of carrying the safety stock as a policy decision.

Summary:

> Plan 1: $10,500 hiring + $14,000 layoff = $24,500
>
> Plan 2: $8,400 overtime + $28,200 idle time = $36,600
>
> Plan 3: $8,640 stockout + $960 inventory = $9,600

Plan 3 is the preferred plan.

MATHEMATICAL PLANNING MODELS

10.4 Idaho Instrument Co. produces calculators in its Lewiston plant and has forecast demand over the next 12 periods, as shown in Table 10-27. Each period is 20 working days (approximately one month). The company maintains a constant work force of 40 employees, and there are no subcontractors available who can meet its quality standards. The company can, however, go on overtime if necessary, and encourage customers to back order calculators. Production and cost data follow.

Production capacity:

> Initial inventory: 100 units (final included in period 12 demand)
>
> RT hours: (40 employees)(20 days/period)(8 hr/day) = 6,400 hr/period
>
> OT hours: (40 employees)(20 days/period)(4 hr/day) = 3,200 hr/period
>
> Standard labor hours per unit: 10 hr

Costs:

> Labor: RT = $6/hr   OT = $9/hr
>
> Material and overhead: $100/unit produced
>
> Back-order costs: apportioned at $5/unit-period (and increasing in reverse)
>
> Inventory carrying cost: $2/unit-period

Option A. Assume five periods constitute a full demand cycle and use the transportation linear programming approach to develop an aggregate plan based on the first five periods only. (*Note*: A planning length of five periods is useful for purposes of methodology, but in reality the planning horizon should cover a complete cycle, or else the plan should make inventory, personnel, and other such allowances for the whole cycle.)

Table 10-27

Period	Units	Period	Units	Period	Units
1	800	5	400	9	1,000
2	500	6	300	10	700
3	700	7	400	11	900
4	900	8	600	12	1,200

Supply, units for		Demand, units for						Total Capacity available
		Period 1	Period 2	Period 3	Period 4	Period 5	Unused Capacity	
Initial inventory		0 / 100	2	4	6	8	10	100
1	RT	160 / 640	162	164	166	168	60	640
	OT	190	192	194	196	198	0 / 320	320
2	RT	165 / 60	160 / 500	162 / 60	164 / 20	166	60	640
	OT	195	190	192	194	196	0 / 320	320
3	RT	170	165	160 / 640	162	164	60	640
	OT	200	195	190	192	194	0 / 320	320
4	RT	175	170	165	160 / 640	162	60	640
	OT	205	200	195	190	192	0 / 320	320
5	RT	180	175	170	165 / 240	160 / 400	60	640
	OT	210	205	200	195	190	0 / 320	320
Demand		800	500	700	900	400	1,600	4,900

Fig. 10-12

Option B. Determine the optimal production plan for the 12-period cycle using a transportation linear-programming format. (*Note*: This more realistic option involves a substantial amount of calculation and should be done on a computer, using a transportation LP code. Several are available for microcomputer.)

Option A

$$RT \text{ cap, avail./period} = 6{,}400 \text{ hr} \div 10 \text{ hr/unit} = 640 \text{ units}$$
$$OT \text{ cap. avail./period} = 3{,}200 \text{ hr} \div 10 \text{ hr/unit} = 320 \text{ units}$$
$$RT \text{ cost} = (10 \text{ hr/unit})(\$6/\text{hr}) + \$100 \text{ mat'l. and OH} = \$160/\text{unit}$$
$$OT \text{ cost} = (10 \text{ hr/unit})(\$9/\text{hr}) + \$100 \text{ mat'l. and OH} = \$190/\text{unit}$$

See Fig. 10-12. Note that the back orders are shown in the lower left portion of the matrix.

The solution of *Option B* is left as an exercise. See Prob. 10.13.

10.5 The High Point Furniture Co. (of Prob. 10.1) has decided to make a modified next-period response to demand fluctuations that deviate from the seasonalized forecast values, using a control number of $K = .4$. Actual demand during the four quarters turns out to be 2,800, 3,800, 3,500, and 2,200 units, respectively. The firm begins the year with 600 units on hand, excess inventory is carried forward, but unfilled demand is lost.

(*a*) By how much does actual total demand differ from the forecast?

(*b*) Show the respective inventory balances at the end of each quarter and indicate how many unit sales are actually lost via stockout under this plan.

(*c*) Would the cost of such a plan be justified?

See Table 10-28.

(*a*) Actual − forecast = 12,300 − 12,000 = 300 units.

(*b*) Balances shown in row 8. The 500 units represent lost sales. Note that the adjustments take one quarter to implement so the first adjustment (160) occurs in the second quarter.

(*c*) More information is needed to determine the full economic value of the plan. Average inventory on hand is 490 units, and more units have been produced than forecasted (12,200 versus 12,000). The costs of changing production levels, carrying inventory, stockouts, and the benefits of any additional profit should be compared with what would have occurred without modifying the response given the same actual demand.

Table 10-28

	Quarter				
	1st	2d	3d	4th	Total
1. Actual demand	2,800	3,800	3,500	2,200	12,300
2. Forecast demand	2,400	4,200	3,000	2,400	12,000
3. Difference ΔD	400	−400	500	−200	
4. $K(\Delta D)$, where $K = .4$	160	−160	200	−80	
5. Production adjustment	0	160	−160	200	
6. Actual production (3,000 + row 5)	3,000	3,160	2,840	3,200	12,200
7. Difference (row 6 − row 1)	200	−640	−660	1,000	
8. Balance with 600 January 1	800	160	−500*	1,000	

*No backlog allowed, thus these 500 units are lost sales.

MASTER-SCHEDULING METHOD

10.6 Clear Lake Foundry produces three types of castings (A, B, C) to customer order. The standard hours per unit and proposed delivery schedule over the next five periods are as shown in Table 10-29.

Table 10-29

Product	Standard Hours/Unit	Demand in Units/Period				
		1	2	3	4	5
A	10	8	10	10	8	10
B	60	4	8	2	—	2
C	30	10	6	—	30	20

Plant capacity is set at 620 standard hours per period, based on single-shift operation. (*a*) Arrange the data into a tentative master schedule. (*b*) What changes would you recommend in order to better utilize the plant capacity?

(*a*)　See Table 10-30.

Table 10-30　Master Schedule for Castings

Product	Period and Units/Period					Standard Hours/Unit
	1	2	3	4	5	
A	8	10	10	8	10	10
B	4	8	2	—	2	60
C	10	6	—	30	20	30
Standard hrs of load	620	760	220	980	820	Cumulative: 3,400
Standard hrs of capacity @ 620 hr/period	620	620	620	620	620	Cumulative: 3,100

(*b*)　See if the sales force can get some of the customers who were scheduled for shipments in period 2 to accept delay until period 3, and reschedule work from periods 2, 4, and 5 into period 3. In total the plant is approximately 10 percent overloaded, so you may want to plan on some overtime in periods 2, 4, or 5. In any event, the master schedule should be revised to reflect a better balance of load versus capacity.

Supplementary Problems

10.7　A relay manufacturer uses a modified response method to plan production for the upcoming months and has found that a control number of .2 is satisfactory. Given the forecast shown in Table 10-31, if actual demands in January and February were 5,600 and 4,300 units respectively, what modified production quantity should be scheduled for March? *Note*: Adjustments can be made almost instantaneously.

Table 10-31

Forecast Demand	
January	5,000 units
February	5,200 units
March	5,800 units

Ans.   5,620 units

10.8   Rainwear Manufacturing, Inc., produces outdoor apparel which has a demand projected to be as shown in Table 10-32. The plant has a 2-week vacation shutdown in July, so the available production days per month are 22, 19, 21, 21, 22, 20, 12, 22, 20, 23, 19, and 21, respectively.

Table 10-32

January	4,400	April	6,300	July	1,200	October	9,200
February	4,750	May	4,400	August	3,300	November	7,600
March	6,300	June	2,000	September	5,000	December	7,350

(*a*) Prepare a chart showing the daily production requirements. (*b*) Plot the demand as a histogram and as a cumulative requirement over time. (*c*) Determine the production rate required to meet average demand, and plot this as a dotted line on your graph.
Ans.   (*a*) Chart should show January through December daily demands of 200, 250, 300, 300, 200, 100, 100, 150, 250, 400, 400, 350. (*b*) Histogram should show cumulative production days on *x* axis, production rate (units per day) on *y* axis. Cumulative requirement should show cumulative production days on *x* axis and cumulative demand (units) on *y* axis. (*c*) 255.4 units

10.9   The Speedee Bicycle Co. makes 10-speed bikes that sell for $100 each. This year's demand forecast is shown in Table 10-33. Units not sold are carried in stock at a cost of 20 percent of the average inventory value per year, and storage costs are $2 per bike per year, based upon maximum inventory.

Table 10-33

Bike Demand Forecast	
Quarter	Units
First	30
Second	120
Third	60
Fourth	70

(*a*) Plot the demand as a histogram on a quarterly basis and show the average requirement as a dotted line on your graph. (*b*) Assume Speedee wishes to maintain a steady work force and to produce at a uniform rate (that is, with no overtime, back orders, subcontracting, or capacity changes) by letting inventories absorb all fluctuations. How many bikes must they have on hand on January 1 in order to meet the forecast demand throughout the year? (*c*) For an incremental amount of $400 in labor costs (total), Speedee can vary its work-force size so as to produce exactly to demand. Compare the costs of producing at a uniform versus variable rate, indicate which plan is less costly, and show the net difference in cost.
Ans.   (*a*) Histogram should show quarters on *x* axis and production rate (units per quarter) on *y* axis. (*b*) 10 (*c*) Variable rate is $50 per year less costly.

10.10 An aggregate planner at Duotronix has estimated the demand requirements (Table 10-34) for forthcoming work periods, which represent one complete demand cycle for them. The company is a "going concern" and expects the next demand cycle to be similar to this one. Five plans are being considered.

Table 10-34

Period	Forecast	Period	Forecast
1	400	6	1,200
2	400	7	600
3	600	8	200
4	800	9	200
5	1,200	10	400

Plan 1: Vary the labor force from an initial capability of 400 units to whatever is required to meet demand. See Table 10-35.

Table 10-35

Amount of Change	Incremental Cost to Change Labor Force	
	Increase	Decrease
200 units	$ 9,000	$ 9,000
400 units	15,000	18,000
600 units	18,000	30,000

Plan 2: Maintain a stable work force capable of producing 600 units per period and meet demand by overtime at a premium of $40 per unit. Idle-time costs are equivalent to $60 per unit.

Plan 3: Vary inventory levels, but maintain a stable work force producing at an average requirement rate with no overtime or idle time. The carrying cost per unit per period is $20. (The company can arrange to have whatever inventory level is required before period 1 at no additional cost.)

Plan 4: Produce at a steady rate of 400 units per period and accept a limited number of back orders during periods when demand exceeds 400 units. The stockout cost (profit, goodwill, and so on) of lost sales is $110 per unit.

Plan 5: Produce at a steady rate of 200 units per period and subcontract for excess requirements at a marginal cost of $40 per unit.

Graph the forecast in the form of a histogram and analyze the relevant costs of the various plans. You may assume the initial (period 1) work force can be set at a desired level without incurring additional cost. Summarize your answer in the form of a table showing the comparative costs of each plan.

Ans.   Graph shows period on x axis and demand level on y axis. Plan costs are: plan 1 = $90,000, plan 2 = $140,000, plan 3 = $160,000, plan 4 = $220,000, plan 5 = $160,000.

10.11 Two mixed-strategy plans have been proposed for the Duotronix situation in Prob. 10.10. Assume that the pattern inherent in the demand cycle given will be repeated in the next demand cycle.

Plan 6 (back orders and limited inventory): Produce at a steady rate of 500 units per period, and carry inventory at $20 per unit-period. Assume that the 700 units of excess demand can be satisfied by back orders placed in period 5 and filled in periods 8, 9, and 10. No inventory is available at the beginning of period 1, and none should be available at the beginning of the next cycle.

Plan 7 (subcontracting and limited inventory): Produce at a steady rate of 300 units per period, and subcontract for excess requirements at a marginal cost of $40 per unit. A 200-unit inventory is available at the beginning of period 1 and should also be available at the beginning of the next cycle. Carry inventory at $20 per unit-period.

Determine the comparative costs of the two plans.

Ans.   Plan 6: carrying cost = \$8,000, back-order cost = \$110,000, total = \$118,000. Plan 7: carrying cost = \$8,000, subcontract cost = \$120,000, total = \$128,000.

10.12   Sun Valley Ski Co., producers of the famous *Sun-Ski*, has a production cost of \$60 per pair during regular time and \$70 per pair on overtime. The firm's production capacity and forecast quarterly demands are shown in Table 10-36. Beginning inventory is 200 pairs, and stock is carried at a cost of \$5 per pair-quarter. Demand is to be met without any hiring, layoff, subcontracting, or back orders. Unused regular time has a \$20-per-pair cost.

(*a*)   Develop the preferred plan and present it in the form of a solved matrix.

(*b*)   What is the minimum total cost of the plan?

Table 10-36

Supply, Units from		Demand, Units for					Total Capacity Available
		First Quarter	Second Quarter	Third Quarter	Fourth Quarter and Final	Unused Capacity	
Initial inventory							200
1	Regular						700
	Overtime						300
2	Regular						700
	Overtime						300
3	Regular						700
	Overtime						300
4	Regular						700
	Overtime						300
Forecast demand		900	500	200	1,900	700	4,200

Ans.   (*a*) One optimal solution is:

Initial inventory: use in 1st Q
1   RT: use in 1st Q
2   RT: use 500 in 2nd Q, 200 in 4th Q
3   RT: use 200 in 3rd Q, 500 in 4th Q

3   OT: use 200 in 4th Q
4   RT: use 700 in 4th Q
4   OT: use 300 in 4th Q

(*b*)   \$208,500

10.13   Complete option (*b*) of Prob. 10.4.

Ans.   The solution should have the following entries in the row-column (r, c) matrix locations: (Initial inventory, 1) = 100, (1 RT, 1) = 640, (2 RT, 1) = 60, (2 RT, 2) = 500, (2 RT, 3) = 60, (2 RT, 4) = 20, (3 RT, 3) = 640, (4 RT, 4) = 640, (5 RT, 4) = 240, (5 RT, 5) = 400, (6 RT, 6) = 300, (6 RT, 9) = 80, (6 RT, 10) = 60, (6 RT, 11) = 200, (7 RT, 7) = 400, (7 RT, 9) = 240, (8 RT, 8) = 600, (8 RT, 9) = 40, (9 RT, 9) = 640, (10 RT, 10) = 640, (11 RT, 11) = 640, (11 OT, 11) = 60, (11 OT, 12) = 240, (12 RT, 12) = 640, (12 OT, 12) = 320.

10.14   Shown in Table 10-37 is the expected demand for an end item *X*, which has a beginning inventory of 30 units. The production lot size is 70 units, and the firm maintains a safety stock of 10 units.

Table 10-37

	Week number							
	1	2	3	4	5	6	7	8
Customer forecast	5	5	5	10	5	5	10	5
Service forecast	—	—	20	—	—	20	—	—
International orders	—	—	—	30	—	25	—	40
Warehouse orders	—	5	—	10	20	—	30	—

Complete a tentative master schedule by determining the requirements, beginning inventory, production required, and ending inventory for each period. Then summarize your results in a master schedule.   *Ans.*   See Table 10-38.

Table 10-38

Week number	1	2	3	4	5	6	7	8
MPS amount	—	—	70	—	70	70	—	70

10.15   Medical Instruments Co. markets two ultrasonic cardiograms to an international market: ECHO 27 and VUE 5. The anticipated demand over the next six periods is shown in Table 10-39.

Table 10-39

	Expected Demand during Period					
	1	2	3	4	5	6
Domestic orders						
ECHO 27	20	20	15	10	5	5
VUE 5	35	30	20	20	10	—
International orders						
ECHO 27	8	6	4	—	—	2
VUE 5	12	5	7	5	—	—
Forecast						
ECHO 27	5	3	10	20	30	30
VUE 5	—	5	5	10	10	30

Additional data (Table 10-40):

Table 10-40

	Beginning Inventory	Lot Size	Safety Stock
ECHO 27	64	40	10
VUE 5	50	60	20

Develop a tentative master schedule based upon the data given.

   Ans.   The solution should show requirements, beginning inventory, production required, and ending inventory for ECHO 27 and VUE 5. Then the master schedule will be as shown in Table 10-41.

Table 10-41

Period	1	2	3	4	5	6
ECHO 27	—	40	—	40	40	40
VUE. 5	60	—	60	60	—	—

10.16 The master schedule for two items, X and Y, to be produced in Work Center #7M is shown in Table 10-42. The standard hours required are 4 hours for X and 2 hours for Y. Work Center #7M has a total of 80 hours available per week.

Table 10-42

	Master Schedule for Week Number						Std. Hours per Unit
	12	13	14	15	16	17	
Item X	15	—	20	10	—	5	4
Item Y	12	40	—	15	45	30	2

(a) Compute the ratio of 6-week load to 6-week capacity. (b) Should any changes be made to improve the schedule? If so, what?

Ans.   (a) Ratio = 484/480 = 101 percent (b) Schedule is in relatively good overall balance, but could be better. Shift 5 units of Y from week 16 to week 15.

Chapter 11

Materials Management:
Purchasing and Inventory Acquisition
Calculus

SCOPE OF MATERIALS MANAGEMENT

Materials are the raw materials, components, subassemblies, and supplies used to produce a good or service. Most materials are transformed into finished products, but supplies are consumed in daily operations. Materials become direct costs whereas supplies are often classified as overhead.

Materials management is the planning, organizing, and controlling of the flow of materials; from their initial purchase, through internal operations, to the distribution of finished goods. Figure 11-1 identifies the major concerns of materials management as (1) purchasing, (2) transportation (incoming and outgoing), (3) control through production-and-inventory management (includes receiving, storage, shipping, materials handling, and inventory counting), and (4) warehousing and distribution.

PURCHASING PROCESS

Purchasing is the acquisition of goods or services in exchange for funds. Figure 11-2 illustrates the process, which differs depending on the type of item. High-volume items are often supplied under a *blanket purchase order*, which establishes a firm price, but enables the buyer to use extended delivery dates. High-value items (for example, turbine generators) may require engineering consultants, whereas low-value items (for example, stationery) are often supplied under *open purchase orders*, with little day-to-day involvement of the purchasing department.

Purchasing is done by professional buyers who have specialized knowledge about selected product lines and are familiar with engineering specifications, contract law, shipping regulations, and a myriad of related factors. Table 11-1 outlines the major responsibilities of purchasing department personnel.

Table 11-1   Purchasing Department Responsibilities

> 1. Identify and develop sources of supply.
> 2. Select suppliers and negotiate contracts.
> 3. Maintain working relations and control vendor performance.
> 4. Evaluate supply-demand economics, and initiate cost and make-vs-buy studies.
> 5. Maintain supply system database.

United States firms often use more suppliers than their foreign competitors. For example, General Motors has approximately 3,500 suppliers, compared to Toyota's 250. Alternative sources of supply sometimes force more competitive prices and reduce the risk of materials shortages. However, close relations with a few (certified) suppliers can give the firm more consistent, high-

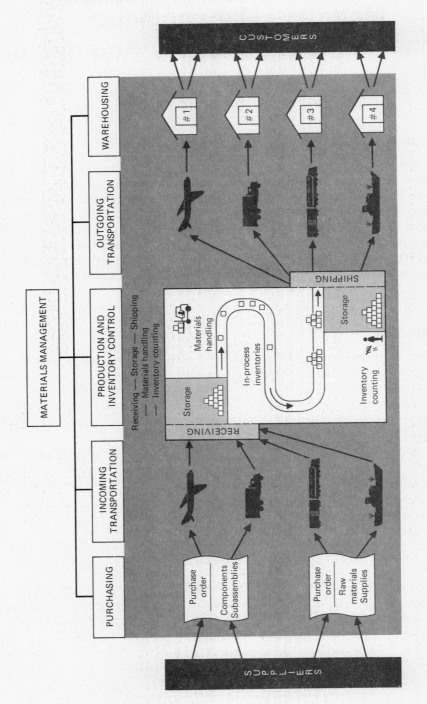

Fig. 11-1 Major elements of materials management systems

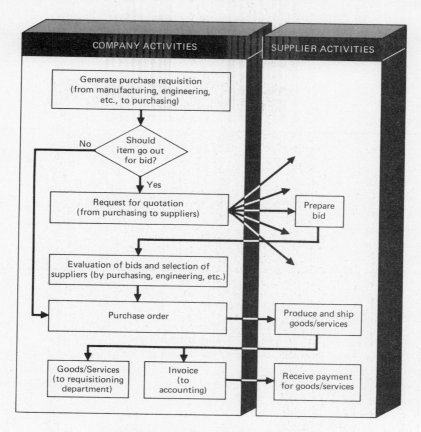

Fig. 11-2 The purchasing process

quality supplies, and better coordination of deliveries. The result is fewer rejects and lower inventory levels. Firms need very reliable suppliers if they are to enjoy the benefits of low on-hand inventories ("stockless" production).

Important variables to consider in selecting suppliers include: (1) price, (2) delivery, (3) quantity, (4) quality, (5) service, (6) maintenance, (7) technical support, (8) financial stability, and (9) terms of purchase. Trade discounts (based upon whether the buyer is a manufacturer, distributor, or user), cash discounts (for prompt payment), and shipping terms (for instance, F.O.B. shipping point) all affect cost. In some cases, suppliers are ranked on the basis of several criteria, which are assigned importance ratings of 1 to 10.

$$\text{Expected score} = \Sigma (\text{importance rating} \times \text{criteria value}) \qquad (11.1)$$

Example 11.1 A municipal utility in Texas has four suppliers for watt-hour meters. The company's computer has recognized a low-stock situation and must issue a purchase recommendation to the buyer on the basis of the criteria shown in Table 11-2. What rank will the computer give to the respective vendors?

The computer will sum the weighted scores for each potential vendor and print out a list of ranks, with "1" being the highest and "4" being the lowest.

$$\text{Supplier A} = 6(.4) + 3(.7) + 4(.8) + 1(.5) + 8(.6) + 2(.5) + 3(.5) = 15.50$$
$$\text{Supplier B} = 6(.4) + 3(.7) + 4(.9) + 1(.3) + 8(.4) + 2(.6) + 3(.4) = 14.00$$
$$\text{Supplier C} = 6(.6) + 3(.3) + 4(.2) + 1(.2) + 8(.3) + 2(.0) + 3(.3) = \ 8.80$$
$$\text{Supplier D} = 6(.7) + 3(.2) + 4(.3) + 1(.2) + 8(.3) + 2(.9) + 3(.3) = 11.30$$

Ranks are 1 = supplier A, 2 = supplier B, 3 = supplier D, 4 = supplier C.

Table 11-2

Criteria	Importance Rating (1–10)	Vendor			
		(A) Western Supply House	(B) General Selectric	(C) Roundy Corp.	(D) Ohio Meters
1. Price	6	.4	.4	.6	.7
2. Field service	3	.7	.7	.3	.2
3. Delivery reliability	4	.8	.9	.2	.3
4. Delivery time	1	.5	.3	.2	.2
5. Ease of maintenance	8	.6	.4	.3	.3
6. Adaptability to automatic computer readout	2	.5	.6	.0	.9
7. Product life	3	.5	.4	.3	.3

MAKE VERSUS BUY DECISIONS

Decisions concerning whether to make or buy components involve both economic and non-economic considerations. Economically, an item is a candidate for in-house production if the firm has sufficient capacity and if the component's value is high enough to cover all the variable costs of production plus make some contribution to fixed costs. Low volumes of usage favor buying, which takes little or no fixed costs. Figure 11-3 illustrates.

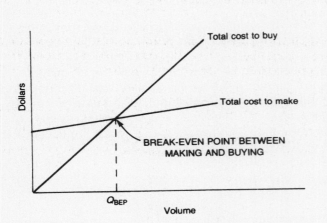

Less Economic Factors

Inputs
- Availability of funds and skilled personnel
- Availability and volume of supply from others
- Desire for alternative sources of supply

Processing
- Employee preferences and stability concerns
- Desire to develop R&D facilities
- Need to control trade secrets
- Desire to expand into new product line
- Need to control delivery lead times
- Impact upon production flexibility

Outputs
- Need to control quality or reliability
- Goodwill and reciprocity impact on customers

Fig. 11-3 Economic and less economic factors influencing make versus buy decisions

Example 11.2 Auburn Machine Co. produces parts that are shipped nationwide. It has an opportunity to produce plastic packaging cases, which are currently purchased at \$.70 each. Annual demand depends largely on economic conditions, but long-run estimates are as shown in Table 11-3.

If the company produces the cases itself, it must renovate an existing work area and purchase a molding machine, which will result in annual fixed costs of \$8,000. Variable costs for labor, materials, and overhead are estimated at \$.50 per case. (*a*) Should Auburn Machine make or buy the cases? (*b*) At what volume of production is it more profitable to produce in-house rather than purchase from an outside supplier?

Table 11-3

Demand	Chance, %
20,000	10
30,000	30
40,000	40
50,000	15
60,000	5

(*a*) First, determine the expected volume by treating the percentage of chance as an empirical probability. Thus, $E(D) = 37,500$ units as seen in Table 11-4.

Table 11-4

Demand D	Chance $P(D)$	$D \cdot P(D)$
20,000	.10	2,000
30,000	.30	9,000
40,000	.40	16,000
50,000	.15	7,500
60,000	.05	3,000
		37,500

Next, Auburn Machine should produce the cases if the expected cost to produce is less than the expected cost to purchase.

Expected cost to produce:

$$TC = FC + VC(V) = \$8,000 + (\$.50/\text{unit})(37,500 \text{ units}) = \$26,750$$

Expected cost to purchase:

$$TC = (\text{price})(V) = (\$.70/\text{unit})(37,500 \text{ units}) = \$26,250$$

Conclusion: Continue to purchase the cases.

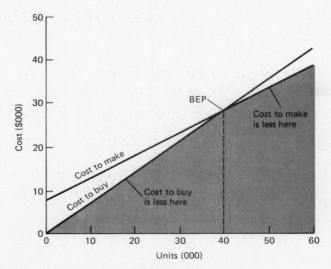

Fig. 11-4

(b) The break-even point (Fig. 11-4) is the volume of production where the total costs to make equal the total costs to buy:

$$\text{TC to make} = \text{TC to buy}$$
$$\text{FC} + \text{VC}(V) = P(V)$$
$$\$8,000 + (\$.50)V = (\$.70)V$$
$$\$.20V = \$8,000$$
$$V = 40,000 \text{ units}$$

For volumes above 40,000 units, it is more economical to make the cases in-house.

PURCHASE-QUANTITY DECISIONS: SINGLE-PERIOD MODEL

In an economic (theoretical) sense, firms should purchase and hold materials until the marginal revenue from acquiring and holding them equals the marginal cost (MR = MC). But the incremental marginal revenue (MR) from each item during a single period is a function of the likelihood, or probability, that the items will be demanded $P(D)$ during that period. Thus we have:

$$(\text{MR})P(D) = \text{MC}$$

Solving for $P(D)$ yields a measure of the likelihood of sale, where the incremental gain from selling an item just offsets the incremental cost of acquiring and holding the item for sale. Recognizing that the marginal revenue includes both marginal cost (MC) and marginal profit (MP), we have, for a single period:

$$P(D) = \frac{\text{MC}}{\text{MR}} = \frac{\text{MC}}{\text{MC} + \text{MP}} \tag{11.2}$$

where $P(D)$ represents the cumulative probability of needing the *next* unit.

Example 11.3 An item costs $6 to produce, sells for $10, and has an estimated cumulative probability distribution of demand during the next period as shown in Table 11-5.

Table 11-5

Unit number	1	2	3	4	5	6	7	8
$P(\text{selling} \geq \text{this unit})$	1.00	.92	.82	.75	.62	.40	.15	.10

How many units should be ordered?

$$P(D) = \frac{\text{MC}}{\text{MC} + \text{MP}}$$

where MC $= \$6$
MP $= \$10 - \$6 = \$4$

$$P(D) = \frac{\$6}{\$6 + \$4} = .60$$

Therefore, order 5 units when $P(\text{selling} \geq 5 \text{ units})$ of .62 is just greater than the equating probability of .60. It seems intuitively correct that since the cost ($6) represents 60 percent of the value of the item, the likelihood of sale, $P(D)$ should also equal 60 percent. If the cost were a higher proportion (for example, 82 percent), then fewer units would be justified (3 units) because the marginal cost is higher.

Marginal, or incremental, analysis can be applied to single-period inventories in an attempt to balance the costs of carrying excess stock (C_{os} = overstocking) against the opportunity costs of having too little stock (C_{us} = understocking). The *single-period model* applies to situations where unused items are not normally carried forward from one period to the next, or a penalty exists for doing so. The assumptions for this model are that (1) demand can be estimated, (2) purchase quantity is limited and may not be increased beyond the initial amount, and (3) costs exist for overstocking and understocking. The (optimal) balance point is that where the expected cost of understocking $C_{us}P(D)$ equals the expected cost of overstocking $C_{os}[1 - P(D)]$. In this expression, $P(D)$ is the cumulative probability that the level of demand will be a given level of units ordered d.

$$C_{us}P(D) = C_{os}[1 - P(D)]$$

$$\text{Single-period } P(D) = \frac{C_{os}}{C_{os} + C_{us}} \tag{11.3}$$

Purchase quantities appropriate for multiple-period situations involve consideration of stockout costs and reorder frequency. They are discussed in Chap. 12.

Example 11.4 An operations manager of Nationwide Car Rentals must decide on the number of vehicles of a certain model to allocate to his agency in the Nashville area. The cars are obtained from an auto leasing firm at a cost of $20 per day. Nationwide rents the cars to its customers for $30 per day. If a car is not used, the auto leasing firm gives Nationwide an $8 rebate.

Records of past demand have yielded the empirical probability distribution shown in Table 11-6. How many units of this model should Nationwide stock if it seeks to balance the costs of overstocking and understocking?

Table 11-6

Demand d (no. of cars)	Probability of Demand $P(d)$	Cumulative Probability $P(D \geq d)$
6 (or less)	0	1.00
7	.03	1.00
8	.07	.97
9	.15	.90
10	.20	.75
11	.23	.55
12	.15	.32
13	.12	.17
14	.05	.05
15 (or more)	0	0

The cumulative probability $P(D)$ that demand will be at least the amount d is shown in the column on the right. It is computed by recognizing that 100 percent of the time demand was greater than or equal to 7 cars (therefore $P(D) = 1.0$). Because the $P(d = 7 \text{ cars}) = .03$, the cumulative $P(D) \geq 8$ cars is $1.00 - .03 = .97$. Other values follow by subtraction in the same manner. The equating probability is:

$$P(D) = \frac{C_{os}}{C_{os} + C_{us}}$$

where $C_{os} = \$20 - \$8 = \$12$

$C_{us} = \$30 - \$20 = \$10$

Thus,

$$P(D) = \frac{\$12}{\$12 + \$10} = .545$$

Stock 11 cars, the amount closest to the $P(D \geq d)$ value. See Fig. 11-5. *Note*: For computed values midway between the cumulative values, stock less rather than more because the cost of overstocking ($12) is greater than the cost of understocking ($10).

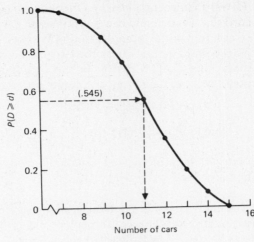

Fig. 11-5

MATERIALS HANDLING, STORAGE, AND RETRIEVAL

Materials handling is the movement of materials from receiving, through operations, to final shipment. It often represents a significant part of the cost-of-goods-sold, but adds no tangible value to the product. Conventional systems use workers, assisted by trucks, fork lifts, cranes and hoists, conveyors, pipelines, and other equipment. Automated systems use robots and computer-guided vehicles. About one-third of all robots are used for materials handling. Some of the automatically guided vehicle systems are directed by software commands emitted from wires buried in the shop floor.

Table 11-7 lists some guidelines for conventional systems.

Table 11-7   Materials Handling Guidelines

1. Plan handling as a complete system.
2. Minimize handling volume and frequency.
3. Optimize load size and weight.
4. Use direct, rapid, steady flows.
5. Minimize idle time of equipment and operators.
6. Allow for breakdowns, changes, and maintenance.

Automated storage and retrieval systems (AS/AR) are computer-controlled materials handling systems which receive, store, and deliver inventory to high, cube-storage locations in quantities specified by the computer. Highly automated systems are integrated with production so that material requirements are automatically identified from the bill-of-material database. Items are selected by part-retrieval robots; computer-controlled stackers and conveyors move them to appropriate kitting locations or work stations. In addition, inventory, work-in-process, and material-requirements-planning (MRP) records are automatically updated.

PURPOSE OF INVENTORIES

Inventories are idle resources that possess economic value. Firms often classify their inventories as (1) raw materials, (2) work in process, or (3) finished goods. All inventories represent an investment designed to facilitate production activities and serve customers. However, carrying inventories consumes working capital, which may not be earning any return on investment and may be urgently needed elsewhere. Hence the problem of inventory management is to maintain adequate, but not excessive, levels of inventories. Table 11-8 summarizes some of the major reasons for holding inventories.

Table 11-8 Major Reasons for Carrying Inventories

1. *Service customers* with variable (immediate and seasonal) demands.
2. *Protect against* supply errors, shortages, and stockouts.
3. *Help level production activities*, stabilize employment, and improve labor relations.
4. *Decouple successive stages* in operations so breakdowns do not stop the entire system.
5. *Facilitate the production of different products* on the same facilities.
6. Provide a means of obtaining and handling materials in economic lot sizes and of *gaining quantity discounts.*
7. Provide a means of *hedging against future price and delivery uncertainties*, such as strikes, price increases and inflation.

DEPENDENT AND INDEPENDENT DEMAND

Dependent demand inventory consists of the raw materials, components, and subassemblies that are used in the production of parent or end items. For example, the demand for computer keyboards depends on the demand for the parent item, computers. *Manufacturing inventory* is largely dependent and predictable. The requirements for all components vis-à-vis other components are fixed by design and production quantities are dictated by the firm's master schedule.

Independent demand inventory consists of the finished products, service parts, and other items whose demand arises more directly from the uncertain market environment. Thus, distribution inventories often have an independent and highly uncertain demand. Dependent demands can usually be calculated, whereas independent demands usually require some kind of forecasting.

INVENTORY COSTS AND THE EOQ EQUATION

The major costs associated with procuring and holding inventories are as follows:

(1) *Ordering and setup costs* for placing orders, expediting, inspection, and changing or setting up facilities to produce in house

(2) *Carrying costs* on invested capital, handling, storage, insurance, taxes, obsolescence, spoilage, and data-processing costs

(3) *Purchase costs* including the price paid, or the labor, material, and overhead charges necessary to produce the item

The total cost (TC) of stocking inventory is the sum of the cost of ordering, plus the cost of carrying, plus the purchase cost. If D equals demand in units on an annual basis, C_o equals cost to prepare or set up for an order, C_c equals cost to carry a unit in stock for a given time period, P equals purchase cost, Q equals lot size, and $Q/2$ equals average inventory, then the relationship can be expressed mathematically:

$$\text{Total cost} = \text{ordering cost} + \text{carrying cost} + \text{purchase cost}$$

where Ordering cost $= \left(\dfrac{C_o \, \$}{\text{order}}\right)\left(\dfrac{\text{order}}{Q \text{ units}}\right)\left(\dfrac{D \text{ units}}{\text{yr}}\right)$

Carrying cost $= \left(\dfrac{C_c \, \$}{\text{unit-yr}}\right)\left(\dfrac{Q \text{ units}}{2}\right)$

Purchase cost $= \left(\dfrac{P \, \$}{\text{unit}}\right)\left(\dfrac{D \text{ units}}{\text{yr}}\right)$

Thus,
$$\text{TC} = C_o \frac{D}{Q} + C_c \frac{Q}{2} + PD \tag{11.4}$$

Differentiating with respect to the order quantity Q yields the slope of the TC curve. (Refer to Prob. 11.5 for an explanation of differentiation.)

$$\frac{d\text{TC}}{dQ} = -C_o D Q^{-2} + \frac{C_c Q^o}{2} + 0$$

Setting this first derivative equal to zero identifies the point where the TC is a minimum.

$$0 = -\frac{C_o D}{Q^2} + \frac{C_c Q^o}{2} + 0$$

Thus,
$$Q = \text{EOQ} = \sqrt{\frac{2 C_o D}{C_c}} \tag{11.5}$$

Equation (11.5) is the economic order quantity (EOQ) or economic lot size (ELS) equation. It yields the order quantity that will satisfy estimated demand at the lowest total cost. Four assumptions underlying the basic EOQ model are the following:

(1) Demand and lead time are known and constant.

(2) Replenishment is instantaneous at the expiration of the lead time.

(3) Purchase costs do not vary with the quantity ordered.

(4) Ordering and carrying-cost expressions include all relevant costs, and these costs are constant.

Figure 11-6 describes the relationship between the relevant ordering and carrying costs.

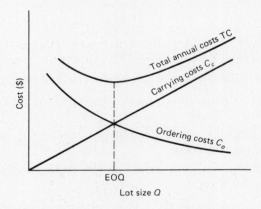

Fig. 11-6   Economic order quantity (EOQ)

Example 11.5   Overland Motors uses 25,000 gear assemblies each year and purchases them at \$3.40 each. It costs \$50 to process and receive an order, and inventory can be carried at a cost of \$.78 per unit-year. (*a*) How many assemblies should be ordered at a time? (*b*) How many orders per year should be placed?

(*a*)
$$\text{EOQ} = \sqrt{\frac{2 C_o D}{C_c}} = \sqrt{\frac{2(50)(25,000)}{.78}} = 1,790 \text{ assemblies}$$

(*b*)
$$\text{Orders/yr} = \frac{D}{Q} = \frac{25,000}{1,790} = 14 \text{ orders/yr}$$

ECONOMIC RUN LENGTHS (ERL)

The EOQ equation assumes instantaneous replenishment. When a firm takes time to produce its own inventory and uses some of it as it is produced, only a portion of the production goes into inventory. If the proportion used is represented by the ratio of demand rate d over production rate p the proportion going into inventory is $[1 - (d/p)]$. The economic production run length is thus:

$$ERL = \sqrt{\frac{2C_oD}{C_c[1 - (d/p)]}} \qquad (11.6)$$

where C_o = setup cost in $/setup

   D = annual demand in units/yr

   C_c = carrying cost in $/unit-yr

   d = demand rate in units/period

   p = production rate in units/period

Example 11.6   A plastics molding firm produces and uses 24,000 teflon bearing inserts annually. The cost of setting up for production is $85 and the weekly production rate is 1,000 units. If the production cost is 2.50 per unit and the annual storage and carrying cost is $.50 per unit, how many units should the firm produce during each production run?

The demand and production rates must be in the same units, so we arbitrarily put both into annual terms, assuming a 52-week year.

$$ERL = \sqrt{\frac{2C_oD}{C_c[1 - (d/p)]}} = \sqrt{\frac{2(85)(24,000)}{.50[1 - (24,000/52,000)]}} = 3,893 \text{ inserts}$$

At a production rate of 1,000 units per week, each production run will last about one month, so the firm will be producing inserts about every other month.

QUANTITY DISCOUNTS

Quantity discounts are lower unit prices offered to buyers who purchase in large volumes. They make price P a function of lot quantity Q with a resulting discontinuous total-cost function (Fig. 11-7).

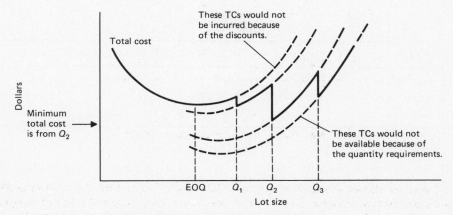

Fig. 11-7   Quantity discount situation

The most expedient approach to finding an optimal order quantity in a discount situation is to follow these steps:

(1)   Determine the EOQ on the basis of the nondiscounted base price.

(2) Compare the total cost at this EOQ point with that for price breakpoints at higher volumes.

(3) If the EOQ happens to fall in a quantity discount range, recalculate it using the quantity discount price and recheck to see if the revised EOQ or a price breakpoint (to the right) has the lower total cost.

Example 11.7 A producer of photo equipment buys lenses from a supplier at $100 each. The producer requires 125 lenses per year, and the ordering cost is $18 per order. Carrying costs per unit-year (based on average inventory) are estimated to be $20 each. The supplier offers a 6 percent discount for purchases of 50 lenses and an 8 percent discount for purchases of 100 or more lenses at one time. What is the most economical amount to order at a time?

Disregarding quantity discounts, the EOQ amount would be:

$$\text{EOQ} = \sqrt{\frac{2C_oD}{C_c}} = \sqrt{\frac{2(18)(125)}{20}} = 15 \text{ lenses}$$

And the total annual cost associated with this EOQ is:

$$\text{TC} = \text{ordering} + \text{carrying} + \text{purchase}$$

$$= C_o\frac{D}{Q} + C_c\frac{Q}{2} + D(P)$$

$$= 18\left(\frac{125}{15}\right) + 20\left(\frac{15}{2}\right) + 125(100) = \$12,800$$

For a 50-unit order, the purchase cost is reduced by 6 percent of $100, or $6. Assuming that the ordering and carrying costs remain constant, the total annual cost associated with a 50-unit order is:

$$\text{TC} = 18\left(\frac{125}{50}\right) + 20\left(\frac{50}{2}\right) + 125(100-6) = \$12,295$$

Similarly, the total annual cost associated with a 100-unit order is:

$$\text{TC} = 18\left(\frac{125}{100}\right) + 20\left(\frac{100}{2}\right) + 125(100-8) = \$12,522$$

The 50-unit lot size results in the lowest total annual cost. Although the purchase price per unit is less with the 100-unit order, the carrying costs begin to outweigh such savings. The costs and direction of change up ($\uparrow$) or down ($\downarrow$) are shown in Table 11-9.

Table 11-9

Order Quantity	Ordering Cost + Carrying Cost + Purchase Cost = Total			
15-unit order	$150	$ 150	$12,500	$12,800
50-unit order	45 $\downarrow$	500 $\uparrow$	11,750 $\downarrow$	12,295 $\downarrow$
100-unit order	22 $\downarrow$	1,000 $\uparrow$	11,500 $\downarrow$	12,522

Example 11.7 assumed a constant carrying cost of $20. If the carrying cost is given as a percentage of the price ($\%P$), it will also be reduced by a small but proportionate amount as larger quantity discounts come into effect.

ABC CLASSIFICATION AND BAR CODING

The ABC classification system is a widely used method of categorizing inventories according to quantity and value. Table 11.10 summarizes the key characteristics of this system.

Table 11-10   Characteristics of ABC Classification System

Groups	Quantity (% of items)	Value (% of $)	Degree of Control	Types of Records	Safety Stock	Ordering Procedures
A items	10–20%	70–80%	Tight	Complete, accurate	Low	Careful, accurate; frequent reviews
B items	30–40%	15–20%	Normal	Complete, accurate	Moderate	Normal ordering; some expediting
C items	40–50%	5–10%	Simple	Simplified	Large	Order periodically: 1- to 2-year supply

Bar codes are alternating vertical dark and light spaces that label inventory items with digitally encoded information. They are read with optical scanners (light pens) linked to microprocessors. The encodation form of alpha and numeric data was largely standardized by the adoption of MIL-STD-1189 in 1982. Bar codes are now an inexpensive, versatile, and easy method of automating data input that identifies an inventory item, its cost, its location, and other necessary inventory information. They are also useful for conveying production information such as the source of an item, what work was done on the item, and who did it.

INVENTORY COUNTING

Inventory records must be highly accurate (98–99 + percent) to facilitate automated production systems. Two methods of auditing inventory records are by (1) periodic physical counting (e.g., once a year) and (2) cycle counting. *Cycle counting* is a continuous physical counting of inventory so that all items are counted at a specified frequency, and inventory records are periodically reconciled with actual data. A *cycle* is the time required to count all items in inventory at least once.

Example 11.8   Empire Building Supply has 6,400 items in stock; 400 are class A items, 1,000 are B items, and 5,000 are C items. The company operates 250 days per year and wishes to count A, B, and C items with a relative frequency of 5, 2, and 1 times a year. How many items should the company count per day, on the average?

Item Type	Number	Count Frequency	Total Counts
A	400	5	2,000
B	1,000	2	2,000
C	5,000	1	5,000
			9,000

$$\text{Number of items counted/day} = \frac{\Sigma \text{ total counts}}{\text{number of days}} = \frac{9,000 \text{ counts}}{250 \text{ days}} = 36 \text{ items counted/day}$$

Note: In a well-disciplined inventory management system, a cycle counter may be able to count and reconcile as many as 40 items per day, so this *may* be within the capacity of one cycle counter at Empire Building Supply.

WAREHOUSING

Warehousing is concerned with receiving and storing finished goods, and distributing them to customers. Major decisions relate to (1) the location and size of warehouses, (2) ordering and handling materials, and (3) record keeping. To provide the same level of protection against running out of stock, a smaller amount of safety stock is needed for one location than when several locations are used. Assuming that statistical variations are independent across warehouses, the combined (standard deviation) effect of safety stocks in several locations is the square root of the sum of the individual effects.

$$\text{Combined effect (SD)} = \sqrt{\Sigma \, (\text{SD})^2} \qquad\qquad (11.7)$$

Example 11.9   Figure 11-8 depicts the safety stock amounts in four warehouses in Ohio. Show that one central warehouse or back-up supply at the factory could provide the same service with less stock.

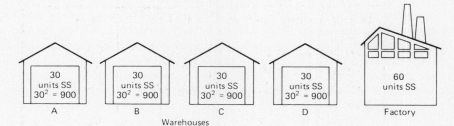

A   B   C   D   Factory

Warehouses

Fig. 11-8

$$\text{Combined effect (SD)} = \sqrt{\Sigma \, (\text{SD})^2} = \sqrt{900 + 900 + 900 + 900} = \sqrt{3,600} = 60 \text{ units}$$

The equivalent effect at the central warehouse can be obtained by stocking 60 units.

The assumption here is, of course, that the same stock can be shipped just as quickly from the central warehouse without any adverse time loss due to transportation.

Solved Problems

MAKE VERSUS BUY DECISIONS

11.1   The Evergreen Garden Tractor Co. has extra capacity that can be used to produce gears that the company is now buying for $10 each. If Evergreen makes the gears, it will incur materials costs of $3 per unit, labor costs of $4 per unit, and variable overhead costs of $1 per unit. The annual fixed cost associated with the unused capacity is $8,000. Demand over the next year is estimated at 4,000 units. Would it be profitable for the company to make the gears?

We assume that the unused capacity has no alternative use.

Cost to make:

$$\text{VC/unit} = \text{materials} + \text{labor} + \text{overhead}$$
$$= \$3 + \$4 + \$1 = \$8/\text{unit}$$
$$\text{TVC} = (4,000 \text{ units})(\$8/\text{unit}) = \$32,000$$
$$Add: \text{FC} \qquad\qquad\qquad +8,000$$
$$\text{Total costs} \qquad\qquad\quad \overline{\$40,000}$$

Cost to buy:

$$\text{Purchase cost} = (4,000 \text{ units})(\$10/\text{unit}) = \$40,000$$
$$Add: \text{FC} \qquad\qquad\qquad +8,000$$
$$\text{Total costs} \qquad\qquad\quad \overline{\$48,000}$$

Making the gears is advantageous because it can be done for $32,000 in variable costs versus the $40,000 cost of purchasing the gears. The $40,000 total cost to make the gears covers both fixed and variable costs, whereas the $40,000 purchase cost does not help cover any fixed cost, yet the fixed cost must be covered.

11.2 A telephone equipment company manager must decide whether to make or buy a relay and a switch. Capacity is available, and no other uses of the capacity are apparent. See Table 11-11.

Table 11-11

	Relay	Switch
Quantity required (units/yr)	30,000	18,000
If make:		
Material cost/unit	$.085	$.025
Direct labor hours	400	220
Overhead (variable)	$12/labor hr	$12/labor hr
If buy:		
Purchase price/unit	$.48	$.22

The direct labor cost is $16 per hour, and the variable portion of overhead is $12 per labor hour. The fixed overhead of the available capacity is estimated at $2,600 per year.

See Table 11-12.

Table 11-12

	Relay Only	Switch Only	Relay and Switch
Cost to make:			
Materials cost [units × cost/unit]	$ 2,550	$ 450	$ 3,000
Direct labor [labor hr × $16/hr]	6,400	3,520	9,920
Overhead (variable) [labor hr × $12/hr]	4,800	2,640	7,440
Total variable cost	$13,750	$6,610	$20,360
Add: Fixed cost	2,600	2,600	2,600
Total cost to make	$16,350	$9,210	$22,960
Cost to buy:			
Purchase price [price/unit]	$ .48	$ .22	
Total purchase price [units × price/unit]	$14,400	$3,960	$18,360
Add: Unavoidable fixed cost	2,600	2,600	2,600
Total cost to buy	$17,000	$6,560	$20,960
Summary:			
Purchase price [price/unit]	$ .48	$ .22	
Variable cost [Total VC ÷ units]	$.4583	$.3672	
Cost to make	$16,350	$9,210	$22,960
Cost to buy (including FC)	17,000	6,560	20,960
Advantage	$ 650	$2,650	$ 2,000
	(make)	(buy)	(buy)

Note that the fixed cost of $2,600 must be paid regardless of whether the company makes the relay only, the switch only, or both. The total cost to buy both ($20,960) is equal to the cost to make ($22,960), so on first glance it may appear advantageous to buy both. However, on closer examination we see that making the relay is profitable, but making the switch is not. The variable cost of the relay ($.4583) is less than the purchase price ($.48), so there will be enough contribution to cover the fixed cost of $2,600, plus a profit of $650. (This is not highly profitable, however, so if something better comes along, it should be investigated.)

The variable cost of producing the switch ($.3672) exceeds the purchase price ($.22), so the firm would be losing money on every switch it produced, with no contribution to the fixed overhead. The switch should be bought.

11.3   Northwest Products Co. has received an order for 800 portable heating cells from a military agency. The heaters have a special casing that must be molded to such close tolerances that some of them don't fit and must be reworked. The percentages of defectives, along with the probabilities of occurrence are as shown in Table 11-13.

Table 11-13

% Defective D	Probability $P(D)$
0	.60
1	.20
2	.10
3	.05
4	.03
5	.02

The casings cost $60 to make and $50 each to rework. A buyer in the purchasing department has located a potential supplier who will agree to supply 100 percent acceptable casings at a cost of $62 per casing. We must now determine whether the company should purchase the casings or produce them.

(a)   What is the break-even point in the proportion of defectives such that the cost of making the casings would be equal to the cost of buying them?

(b)   What proportion of defectives can be expected if the firm produces its own casings?

(c)   On the basis of this data, should Northwest make or buy the casings?

(a)   Let P = the proportion of defectives where cost to make equals cost to buy. Then

$$\text{Production cost to make} = \text{purchase cost to buy}$$
$$\text{Initial cost} + \text{rework cost} = (\text{price})(\text{volume})$$

$$(\$60/\text{unit})(800 \text{ units}) + P(\$50/\text{unit})(800 \text{ units}) = (\$62/\text{unit})(800 \text{ units})$$
$$\$48,000 + \$40,000 \, P = \$49,600$$

Therefore,
$$P = \frac{\$1,600}{\$40,000} = .04 = 4\%$$

(b)   The expected proportion of defectives is found as follows:

$$E(D) = \Sigma[D \cdot P(D)]$$
$$= 0(.60) + .01(.20) + .02(.10) + .03(.05) + .04(.03) + .05(.02)$$
$$= 0 + .002 + .002 + .0015 + .0012 + .001$$
$$= .0077 = .77\% \quad \text{(that is, less than 1\% defective)}$$

(c) The company should make the casings because it produces less than 1 percent defective casings on the average, and it is more profitable to make them until the defect rate is greater than or equal to 4 percent.

MATERIALS HANDLING, STORAGE, AND RETRIEVAL

11.4 Lakeview Lumber uses forklift trucks to transport lumber from the mill to a storage warehouse .3 mile away. The lift trucks can move three loaded pallets per trip and travel at an average speed of 6 miles per hour (allowing for loading, delays, and travel). If 420 pallet loads must be moved during each 8-hour shift, how many lift trucks are required?

$$\text{Distance/trip} = .3(\text{over}) + .3(\text{return}) = .6 \text{ mile}$$
$$\text{Time/trip} = .6 \text{ mile} \div 6 \text{ miles/hr} = .1 \text{ hr}$$
$$\text{Capacity/trip} = 3 \text{ pallets}$$
$$\text{Capacity/shift} = \left(\frac{3 \text{ pallets}}{.1 \text{ hr}}\right)\left(\frac{8 \text{ hr}}{\text{shift}}\right) = 240 \text{ pallets/shift/lift truck}$$
$$\text{Number of lift trucks} = \frac{420 \text{ pallets/shift}}{240 \text{ pallets/shift/lift truck}} = 1.75 \text{ lift trucks (use 2 lift trucks)}$$

INVENTORY COSTS AND THE EOQ EQUATION

11.5 *Calculus Explanation and Derivation.* If carrying costs consist of two components—(1) C_i = interest cost per unit-year on the average inventory investment and (2) C_s = storage space cost per unit-year to accommodate Q units—set up an equation for total costs, and derive an expression for the EOQ which includes both these terms.

$$\text{TC} = \text{ordering} + \text{interest} + \text{storage} + \text{purchase}$$
$$= C_o\left(\frac{1}{Q}\right)D + C_i\frac{Q}{2} + C_sQ + PD$$

The TC equation can be differentiated by standard calculus methods, where the differential of $Y = X^n$ is

$$\frac{dY}{dX} = nX^{n-1}$$

and when a constant a is included, the differential of Y with respect to X is

$$Y = aX^n$$
$$\frac{dY}{dX} = naX^{n-1}$$

The differential of a constant (by itself) is, of course, equal to zero; so, for example, if $Y = 4 + 5X^3$,

$$\frac{dY}{dX} = 0 + 15X^2$$

The differential of TC with respect to Q can be obtained most easily if we first move the Q's into the numerator (by adjusting to a negative exponent) so that

$$\text{TC} = C_oDQ^{-1} + \frac{C_iQ}{2} + C_sQ + PD$$

Upon differentiating, the purchase cost is a constant and drops out:

$$\frac{d\text{TC}}{dQ} = -C_oDQ^{-2} + \frac{C_iQ^o}{2} + C_sQ^o + 0$$

Letting $Q^o = 1$ and setting the first derivative equal to zero, the order quantity is now

$$0 = -\frac{C_o D}{Q^2} + \frac{C_i}{2} + C_s$$

$$\frac{C_o D}{Q^2} = \frac{C_i + 2C_s}{2}$$

$$Q = \sqrt{\frac{2C_o D}{C_i + 2C_s}} \qquad (11.8)$$

11.6 An inventory manager is reviewing some annual ordering data for three years ago, when the firm used only 2,000 cases and had carrying charges of only 6 percent of the $20 per case purchase price. At that time, it cost the firm only $10 to write up an order. The manager has come across the following equation:

$$Q = \sqrt{\frac{2(10)(2,000)}{1.20}} = \sqrt{\frac{2()10()2,000()}{1.2()}}$$

Identify the units associated with the numbers used in the equation, and show what units Q results in.

$$Q = \sqrt{\frac{2\left(\genfrac{}{}{0pt}{}{\text{pure}}{\text{number}}\right)10(\$)2,000\,(\text{cases/yr})}{1.20(\$/\text{case-yr})}} = 183 \text{ cases}$$

Note that the $ and yr units cancel, leaving cases², so the answer is in cases.

11.7 A San Antonio stockyard uses about 200 bales of hay per month, and pays a broker $80 per order to locate a supplier who handles the ordering and delivery arrangements. Its own storage and handling costs are estimated at 30 percent per year. If each bale costs $3, what is the most economical order quantity?

The purchase price is relevant for computing carrying charges (only), and they must be in the same units as demand. We will (arbitrarily) use months.

$$\text{EOQ} = \sqrt{\frac{2C_o D}{C_c}}$$

where $C_c = \%$

$P = (.30/\text{yr})(\$3/\text{unit}) = \$.90/\text{unit-yr} = \$.90/12 = \$.075/\text{unit-mo.}$

$$\text{EOQ} = \sqrt{\frac{2(\$80)(200)}{\$.075}} = 653 \text{ bales}$$

11.8 Far West Freeze Dry purchases 1,200 tins of tea annually in economic order quantity lots of 100 tins and pays $9.85 per tin. If processing costs for each order are $10, what are the implied carrying costs of this policy?

$$Q = \sqrt{\frac{2C_o D}{C_c}}$$

Solving for C_c we have:

$$C_c = \frac{2C_o D}{Q^2} = \frac{2(10)(1,200)}{(100)^2} = \$2.40/\text{tin-yr}$$

11.9 A manufacturer requires 600 printed circuit boards per year and estimates an ordering cost of $20 per order. Inventory is financed by short-term loans at approximately 10 percent, which work out to a carrying charge of $.10 per unit-year based upon the average inventory. Storage costs, based on adequate space for maximum inventory, are $.025 per unit-year, and the purchase price is $1 per unit. Find (a) the most economical order quantity, (b) the total annual cost of the inventory, and (c) the number of orders placed per year.

(*a*) The EOQ can be determined from the total-cost expression:

$$TC = \text{ordering} + \text{interest} + \text{storage} + \text{purchase}$$

$$= \frac{\$20(600)}{Q} + \frac{\$.10}{\text{unit-yr}}\left(\frac{Q}{2}\right)\text{units} + \frac{\$.025Q}{\text{unit-yr}} + \$1.00(600)$$

$$= \frac{12,000}{Q} + .05Q + .025Q + 600 = \frac{12,000}{Q} + .075Q + 600$$

Differentiating, we have:

$$\frac{d\text{TC}}{dQ} = \frac{-12,000}{Q^2} + .075$$

Setting the first derivative $= 0$,

$$Q = \sqrt{\frac{12,000}{.075}} = 400 \text{ units/order}$$

Alternatively, we could use Eq. 11.8:

$$Q = \sqrt{\frac{2C_o D}{C_i + 2C_s}} = \sqrt{\frac{2(20)(600)}{.10 + 2(.025)}} = 400 \text{ units/order}$$

(*b*) Substituting $Q = 400$ into the TC expression, we have:

$$TC = \frac{12,000}{400} + .075(400) + 600 = \$660$$

(*c*)

$$\text{Orders/yr} = \frac{D}{Q} = \frac{600}{400} = 1.5 \text{ orders/yr} = 3 \text{ orders every 2 yr}$$

ECONOMIC RUN LENGTHS (ERL)

11.10 The Finish Creamery Co. produces ice cream bars for vending machines and has an annual demand for 72,000 bars. The company has the capacity to produce 400 bars per day. It takes only a few minutes to adjust the production setup (cost estimated at \$7.50 per setup) for the bars, and the firm is reluctant to produce too many at one time because the storage cost (refrigeration) is relatively high at \$1.50 per bar-year. The firm supplies vending machines with its "Fin-Barrs" on 360 days of the year. (*a*) What is the most economical number of bars to produce during any one production run? (*b*) What is the optimal length of the production run in days?

(*a*)

$$\text{ERL} = \sqrt{\frac{2C_o D}{C_c[1 - (d/p)]}}$$

where C_o = setup cost = \$7.50

D = annual demand = 72,000 bars/yr

C_c = carrying cost = \$1.50/bar-yr

d = daily demand rate = $\dfrac{72,000}{360}$ = 200 bars/day

p = daily production rate = 400 bars/day

$$\text{ERL} = \sqrt{\frac{2(7.50)(72,000)}{1.50[1 - (200/400)]}}$$

$$= 1,200 \text{ bars/run}$$

(*b*) Optimal number of days of the run is

$$\text{Number of days} = \frac{1,200 \text{ bars}}{400 \text{ bars/day}} = 3 \text{ days}$$

11.11 A firm has a yearly demand for 52,000 units of a product which it produces. The cost of setting up for production is \$80, and the weekly production rate is 1,000 units. The carrying cost is \$3.50 per unit-year. How many units should the firm produce on each production run?

$$Q = \sqrt{\frac{2C_oD}{C_c[1-(d/p)]}} = \sqrt{\frac{2(80)(52,000)}{3.50[1-(1,000/1,000)]}} = \sqrt{\infty} = \infty$$

Note that the demand and production rates in this problem are equal and the equation (rightly) suggests they should have an infinite (continuous) run.

Supplementary Problems

11.12 The Madison headquarters of Fred's Fast Foods must select a national grocery chain to supply its fast-food chains with fresh vegetables on a nationwide basis. It has developed the following criteria and scores for prospective vendors (Table 11-14). Which supplier has the highest expected score, and what is its value?

Table 11-14

	Rating (1–10)	Potential Suppliers of Vegetables		
		Food Fair	A & R	SaleWay
Price	8	.7	.3	.5
Quality	3	.2	.8	.5
Delivery	5	.5	.4	.4
Location	2	.1	.7	.6

Ans.   Food Fair, 8.9

11.13 Banktel, Inc., produces an automatic cash machine in leased facilities in an industrial park. The product uses special-purpose punch keys which the firm currently purchases at \$4.20 each. It is considering leasing additional space and producing the keys itself. The long-term lease would result in annual costs of \$4,800. The labor, materials, and variable overheads are estimated at \$2.80 per key, and fixed overhead would be an additional \$1,080 per year. Demand is estimated as shown in Table 11-15.

Table 11-15

Demand D	Probability P(D)
2,000	.05
3,000	.10
4,000	.30
5,000	.40
6,000	.15

(a) Should Banktel produce the keys? (b) What is the break-even volume where it becomes profitable to produce them rather than buy from a supplier?   *Ans.*   (a) Cost to produce is \$420 less. (b) 4,200 units

11.14 New England Grocery Supply Co. has collected the historical data shown in Table 11-16 of weekly demand for a line of breakfast cereals. An operations analyst estimates that it costs the company $1.50 per case per week to be overstocked because of spoilage and carrying costs. Being understocked results in lost profits of $2.40 per case.

Table 11-16

Weekly Demand (no. of cases)	Probability of Demand $P(d)$
500	.10
600	.20
700	.30
800	.30
900	.05
1,000	.05

(a) Compute the cumulative probability of demand that equates the cost of understocking with the cost of overstocking. (b) Assuming that the company must purchase lots of 100, how many lots should it stock?   *Ans.*   (a) .385 (b) 800 cases

11.15 (*Requires use of discount tables*) Yakima Packing Co. is considering the purchase of a conveyor system if the savings in labor costs justify it. The conveyor would cost $80,000 and would be expected to last 10 years, after which the salvage value would be $8,000. Operation and maintenance costs would be $6,000 per year. (a) Assuming that the firm uses an 18 percent cost of capital, compute the equivalent annual cost of the conveyor. (b) The conveyor is expected to reduce the existing $120,000-per-year labor cost by 25 percent. Does that savings justify the purchase of the conveyor system?
Ans.   (a) $23,461 (b) Yes, purchase advantage is $6,539 per year.

11.16 The hospital operations manager at Mercy General has asked the stores department to begin ordering inventory on an economic-lot-size basis. The hospital uses 500 electrocardiogram tape rolls per year, has an ordering cost of $10 per order, and estimates carrying costs at $.25 per unit-year. How many tapes should be ordered each time?   *Ans.*   200

11.17 Factory Built Homes, Inc., (FBH) purchases paneling components from a nearby western New York mill for $5 per unit. It expects to use about 4,000 units during the coming year. FBH estimates that it costs $30 to place an order and $1.50 per unit-year for carrying and storage costs. The mill can provide FBH with immediate delivery of any reasonable quantity. (a) What is the most economical quantity for FBH to order? (b) How many orders per year should be placed? (c) What is the total yearly cost associated with ordering, carrying, and purchasing the EOQ amount?
Ans.   (a) 400 units per order (b) 10 (c) $20,600

11.18 In the ERL model, if the demand rate is 40 units per month, and the production rate is 200 units per month, what percentage of the production goes into inventory?   *Ans.*   80 percent

11.19 Spokane Public Power Co. purchases transformers at a cost of $330 and uses an ordering cost of $45 per order. Inventory is carried at a cost of 10 percent of the per-unit price (based on average inventory). Storage costs, based upon adequate space for maximum inventory, are $6 per transformer. Annual demand is 800 units. (a) Compute the total yearly cost if the firm orders in EOQ amounts. (b) The supplier has offered the power company a 10 percent discount for purchasing in quantities of 200. Assuming this affects all costs except ordering and per-unit storage costs, compute the total yearly cost for this quantity discount situation.
Ans.   (a) TC = $900 + $660 + $240 + $264,000 = $265,800 (b) $241,950

11.20 Golden Valley Cannery uses 64,000 size 7X cans annually and can purchase any quantity up to 10,000 cans at $.040 per can. At 10,000 cans the unit cost drops to $.032 per can, and for purchases of 30,000 it is $.030 per can. The costs of ordering are $24 per order, and interest costs are 20 percent of the price per can and apply to the average inventory. Storage costs are $.02 per can-year and are based upon maximum inventory. (Disregard safety stock costs.) (a) What is the EOQ, disregarding the quantity discounts? (b) What is the most economical order quantity, considering the quantity discounts?
       Ans.   (a) 8,000 cans (b) TC for 10,000 unit purchase is least at $2,433.

11.21 A governmental supply warehouse is implementing a cycle counting system whereby class A items are counted monthly, B items quarterly, and C items annually. Of the 6,300 items in inventory, 900 are in class A, 2,100 are in class B, and the remainder are in class C. Assuming that there are 250 workdays per year, how many items should be counted per day?   *Ans.*   90 items per day

11.22 Midwest Computer Stores has five retail locations that each carry a reserve supply of 8 Orange III computers. Assuming shipments from a centralized warehouse would provide satisfactory service, how many units would have to be maintained at the centralized location to provide an equivalent level of service?   *Ans.*   18

Chapter 12

Inventory Control:
Safety Stocks, Order Points,
and Service Levels

Statistical Methods

INVENTORY CONTROL SYSTEMS

Inventory control systems are the monitoring and ordering techniques used to control the quantity and timing of inventory transactions. The traditional inventory control systems are classified as either periodic, or perpetual (continuous). However, other inventory control measures are used (e.g., inventory "turns") and numerous combinations exist (e.g., base stock system). In addition, broad-based scheduling systems, such as MRP systems, often incorporate inventory control activities as an integral part of the larger systems.

The periodic and continuous monitoring systems, by themselves, are essentially order launching techniques. They look at historical average use as a basis for releasing new orders. This is often satisfactory for *distribution* inventories. MRP systems (Chap. 13) plan ahead to a forecast (or calculation) of projected material requirements that are then scheduled to arrive according to a specific time-phased sequence. Time-phased systems are most useful in *manufacturing* environments.

Periodic systems rely upon a count of inventory at periodic intervals such as weekly or monthly. A variable quantity of inventory is then ordered on this regular *fixed interval* basis. The order quantity Q is the amount needed to bring the inventory on hand and on order to a specified level, which may be adjusted to reflect expected changes in demand. Periodic systems offer the advantage of processing orders for several items at the same time, so they work well for relatively consistent demands. However, extra inventory (safety stock) must be carried to protect against shortages between review periods.

Perpetual systems are *continuous* in that they maintain a current record of the inventory level of each item on an ongoing basis. When the amount on hand drops to a predetermined level (the order point), a *fixed quantity Q* is ordered. This can be an EOQ amount. (See Chap. 11.) Some continuous systems use a *batch* processing mode to accumulate the inventory additions and the withdrawal requirements over a short period and update the master records regularly (often daily), whereas others are totally *online*, recording transactions on a computer as they occur. Because they constantly monitor demand, continuous systems are often used for inventories that have large, unexpected fluctuations in demand, such as end-item inventories. They require less safety stock to provide the same level of customer service as periodic systems.

Inventory control systems monitor both demand and *lead time*, i.e., the time from placing an order to receiving delivery. If both demand D and lead time LT are known and constant, required inventory levels and associated costs can be easily computed.

Example 12.1 (Constant Demand, Constant Lead Time.) Columbia Packing Co. has contracted to pack 3,000 boxes of fruit per month at a constant rate during June, July, and August. Boxes are ordered in quantities of $Q = 3,000$/order from a supplier who always delivers them in 10 days. (*a*) What is the maximum (I_{max}) and average (I_{ave}) amount of inventory on hand? (*b*) What carrying cost is incurred if the boxes cost \$2 each and the carrying cost is 30 percent per year?

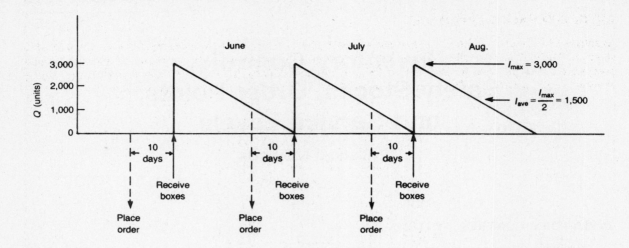

Fig. 12-1

(*a*)   See Fig. 12-1.

(*b*)

$$\text{Carrying cost} = (\%\ \text{rate})(\text{time})(\text{unit cost})(I_{\text{ave}})$$
$$= (.30/\text{yr})(\tfrac{3}{12}\,\text{yr})(\$2/\text{box})(1{,}500\,\text{boxes}) = \$225/\text{yr}$$

METHODS OF HANDLING INVENTORY UNCERTAINTIES

The major uncertainties associated with managing inventories are variability of demand and variability of lead time. Most of the approaches to handling these uncertainties make use of *safety stock* (*SS*), which is an amount of inventory held in excess of regular usage quantities to provide specified levels of protection against stockout. Some methods of handling uncertainties are summarized in Table 12-1.

Table 12-1   Methods of Protecting against Shortages and Stockouts

Method	Description
Informal decision rules	1. *Ratios*: Order on basis of ratio (e.g., on-hand inventory/expected usage during LT) 2. *Ultra conservative*: Allow for largest daily usage × longest LT 3. *Safety stock percentage*: Let $SS = D_{\text{ave}}$ plus a 25–40 percent safety factor 4. *Square root of LT*: Let $SS = D_{\text{ave}}$ during LT
Expected-value approach	Construct payoff and expected-value tables where alternatives are amounts of inventory to stock and uncontrollable variable is D or LT (especially suitable for handling perishable inventories).
Incremental approach	Add inventory to point where incremental cost = incremental gain × P(gain).
Safety stock (statistical)	1. *Empirical*: Use empirical data to formulate a probability distribution of D or LT and compute required SS for specified service level. 2. *Known distribution*: Use known (or assumed) statistical distribution of D or LT and compute required SS for specified service level.

EXPECTED-VALUE APPROACH

Example 12.2 Idaho Potato Co. believes that next period's demand can be approximated from the past data shown in Table 12-2. The selling price is $100 per thousand pounds, cost is $60 per thousand pounds, and any potatoes not sold are used for hog feed at $10 per thousand pounds. (a) Develop a payoff matrix, and (b) an expected profit matrix. (c) What level of potatoes should be stocked to maximize expected profits?

Table 12-2

Demand X (lb)	Frequency $f(X)$ (no. periods)
20,000	10
25,000	20
40,000	50
60,000	20

All solution values are in 000 lbs.

(a) The payoff matrix shows the *state of nature* (demand) on the horizontal scale and *action* of stocking various amounts of inventory (supply) on the vertical. Each cell's payoff value is systematically computed recognizing that the profit (on units sold) and loss (on unsold units) are

$$\text{Profit} = \text{sales revenue} - \text{cost} = \$100 - \$60 = \$40$$
$$\text{Loss} = \text{cost} - \text{revenue from hog feed} = \$60 - \$10 = \$50$$

Thus for (Table 12-3) the cell of:

$$\text{Stock 20, demand 20: profit} = 20(\$40) = \$800$$
$$\text{Stock 20, demand 25: profit} = 20(\$40) = \$800$$
$$\text{Stock 25, demand 20: profit} = 20(\$40) - 5(\$50) = \$550$$
$$\text{Stock 40, demand 20: profit} = 20(\$40) - 20(\$50) = -\$200 \text{ (loss)}$$

Table 12-3   Payoff Matrix

		State of Nature (demand)			
		20	25	40	60
Action (supply)	20	800	800	800	800
	25	550	1,000	1,000	1,000
	40	(200)	250	1,600	1,600
	60	(1,200)	(750)	600	2,400

Table 12-4   Expected Profit Matrix

		State of Nature (demand)				
		(.1) 20	(.2) 25	(.5) 40	(.2) 60	Expected Profit
Action (supply)	20	80	160	400	160	800
	25	55	200	500	200	955
	40	(20)	50	800	320	1,150
	60	(120)	(150)	300	480	510

(*b*) Expected values are computed by multiplying the payoff value X by its probability of occurrence $P(X)$. Thus for Table 12-4 the cell:

$$\text{Stock 20, demand 20: } E(X) = 800(.1) = 80$$
$$\text{Stock 20, demand 25: } E(X) = 800(.2) = 160$$

The expected value for each course of action is the summation of the cell row expected values, or $\Sigma\, XP(X)$. Thus for the course of action:

$$\text{Stock 20: } \Sigma\,[XP(X)] = 800(.1) + 800(.2) + 800(.5) + 800(.2) = 800$$

$$\text{Stock 25: } \Sigma\,[XP(X)] = 550(.1) + 1{,}000(.2) + 1{,}000(.5) + 1{,}000(.2)$$

$$= 55 + 200 + 500 + 200 = 955$$

(*c*) The maximum expected value is from stocking 40 (thousand) pounds for $1,150.

SAFETY STOCKS, ORDER POINTS, AND SERVICE LEVELS

Figure 12-2 identifies the interdependent variables of order quantity, lead time, order point, and safety stock in an inventory-control system. Safety stocks (SS) are the primary means of allowing for random variations in demand and lead time. The *order point* (OP) is the inventory level at which a replenishment order Q is placed. It should include a sufficient quantity to handle demand during the lead time (D_{LT}) plus a designated margin of safety stock.

$$\text{OP} = D_{LT} + \text{SS} \qquad\qquad (12.1)$$

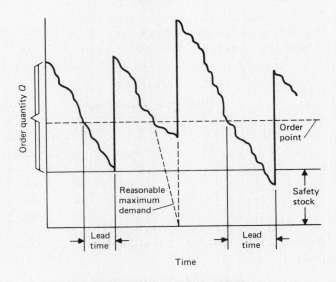

Fig. 12-2 Inventory variables

Example 12.3 A nationwide trucking firm has an average demand of 10 new tires per week and receives deliveries from a Dayton, Ohio, tire company about 20 business days (5 days per week) after placing an order. If the firm seeks to maintain a safety stock of 15 tires, what is the order point?

$$\text{OP} = D_{LT} + \text{SS} = (10 \text{ tires/week})(4 \text{ weeks}) + 15 \text{ tires} = 55 \text{ tires}$$

Stockouts. If no safety stock were carried, and reorders were placed so that inventory was scheduled to arrive (on the average) when the previous inventory was used up, the organization would run out of stock on about half of the order cycles. Costs of being out of stock include shutdown and idle-time costs (at the manufacturing level), and lost sales and goodwill (at the distribution level). Firms often try to carry sufficient safety stock to meet any reasonable maximum demand during the lead time. (See Fig. 12-2.) However, that quantity should be more precisely defined on the basis of knowledge of the probability distributions of demand and lead time.

Stockout costs increase the order quantity so as to decrease the frequency of exposure to risk of stockout. Letting C_e be the cost of exposure to a stockout, the EOQ equation takes the form:

$$Q = \sqrt{\frac{2D(C_o + C_e)}{C_c}} \tag{12.2}$$

An implied cost of C_e can be estimated by dividing the total annual carrying cost per year by the number of orders per year that would be placed, as determined from a preliminary calculation of the EOQ (without including C_e).

Example 12.4   A container manufacturer produces corrugated bales of pressboard on a multipurpose production line at a rate of 50 bales per week. The cost to set up for production of bales is \$3,000. The bales are used in another part of the plant at a rate of 20 bales per week (1,000 per year), and the firm uses a cost of \$9,000 for being out of stock. If carrying costs are \$140 per bale per year, what is the most economic production run length?

This problem necessitates that we modify Eq. 12.2, adjusting it for a noninstantaneous (ELS) supply:

$$\text{ELS}_m = \sqrt{\frac{2D(C_o + C_e)}{C_c(1 - d/e)}} \tag{12.3}$$

$$= \sqrt{\frac{2(1,000)(\$3,000 + \$9,000)}{\$140[1 - (20/50)]}} = 535 \text{ bales}$$

The *service level* (SL) of an inventory is a number that represents the percentage of order cycles in which all demand requests can be supplied from stock. The converse of SL is a percentage figure representing the stockout risk (SOR).

$$\text{SL} = 100\% - \text{SOR} \tag{12.4}$$

Service levels range from 50 percent (with no safety stock) to 100 percent, but values in the 95 to 99.7 percent level are common.

Because of the difficulty of identifying the numerous costs of being out of stock, analysts sometimes approach the problem by asking, "What would you be willing to pay *not* to be out of stock on 90 or 95 percent of the order cycles?" This amount corresponds to the carrying cost of the safety stock.

INCREMENTAL APPROACH: MULTIPLE-PERIOD MODEL WITH INDIVIDUAL-UNIT STOCKOUT COSTS

The *single-period model* described in Eq. 11.3, shown below, focused upon the costs of overstocking C_{os} and understocking C_{us} to meet a one-time demand.

$$\text{Single-period } P(D) = \frac{C_{os}}{C_{os} + C_{us}} \tag{11.3}$$

The model is, however, also useful for identifying an optimum stocking level under conditions where demand can be approximated by continuous or discrete probability distributions. A major requirement remains that costs of excess units (overstocking) and costs of shortages (understocking) can be estimated.

Insofar as $P(D)$ is the cumulative probability that demand will be exceeded, it also represents the stockout risk (SOR). Thus:

$$\text{(Single period) SOR} = \frac{C_{os}}{C_{os} + C_{us}} \tag{12.5}$$

and since the SOR is the complement of the service level, we have:

$$\text{SL} = 100\% - \text{SOR}\% = \frac{C_{us}}{C_{os} + C_{us}} \tag{12.6}$$

Problems 12.2, 12.3, and 12.4 illustrate the use of the single-period model applied to uniform-, normal-, and Poisson-distributed demand, respectively.

Multiple-period models apply to the bulk of continuous production operations, which have recurring demand. Purchase quantities may be influenced by the type of inventory (dependent vs. independent), the type of inventory classification (A, B, or C), the associated costs of ordering, carrying, and purchasing, etc., and the type of inventory control system used. The overstocking and understocking costs of the single-period model are replaced by per unit carrying costs C_c and per unit stockout costs C_{so}. In addition, carrying costs per unit are known (not probabilistic), and stockout costs per unit must be multiplied by the number of opportunities for stockout, or order cycles D/Q. The multiple period SOR is thus:

$$\overbrace{\left(\begin{matrix}\text{Expected stockout}\\ \text{cost/unit}\end{matrix}\right) \left(\begin{matrix}\text{number of order}\\ \text{cycles this occurs}\end{matrix}\right)} = \left(\begin{matrix}\text{carrying cost}\\ \text{of the unit}\end{matrix}\right)$$

$$\overbrace{\left(\begin{matrix}\text{Probability of}\\ \text{stockout}\end{matrix}\right) \left(\begin{matrix}\text{stockout}\\ \text{cost/unit}\end{matrix}\right) \left(\frac{D \text{ units/yr}}{Q \text{ units/order}}\right)} = \left(\begin{matrix}\text{carrying cost}\\ \text{per unit-yr}\end{matrix}\right)$$

$$(\text{SOR}) C_{so}\left(\frac{D}{Q}\right) = C_c$$

Therefore,
$$\text{(Multiple period) SOR} = \frac{C_c}{C_{so}}\left(\frac{Q}{D}\right) \tag{12.7}$$

Note that Eq. 12.7 applies to situations where individual stockout costs per unit are known (or estimated). This is in contrast to the stockout cost per order cycle of Eq. 12.2.

Example 12.5 A construction equipment dealer experiences an annual demand of about 300 electric generators and orders in quantities of 50 units per order. Carrying costs are \$900 per unit-year, and stockout costs are estimated at \$2,000 per unit. What optimum probability of stockout should be used to determine the appropriate inventory-stocking level?

$$\text{SOR} = \frac{C_c}{C_{so}}\left(\frac{Q}{D}\right) = \left(\frac{\$900/\text{unit-yr}}{\$2,000/\text{unit-order}}\right)\left(\frac{50 \text{ units/order}}{300 \text{ units/yr}}\right) = .075$$

The stock should be enough that demand is exceeded only 7.5 percent of the time.

USE OF EMPIRICAL DATA TO SET SAFETY-STOCK LEVELS

Empirical data describing past demand, and lead-time variations, may be used to establish safety-stock levels if the service level and carrying cost of inventory is specified. First, assume that demand is variable and that lead times are constant. Once the stockout risk is established, and data collected on past demand, a cumulative distribution of demand can be formulated, and the maximum demand for a given stockout risk (D_{SOR}) can be obtained directly from the cumulative distribution. The required safety stock is then the difference between this maximum demand (D_{SOR}) and the average demand (D_{ave}).

$$\text{SS} = D_{SOR} - D_{ave} \tag{12.8}$$

In the example that follows (Example 12.6), the service level (SL) represents the percentage of order cycles that demand is met from stock on hand.

Example 12.6   (Variable Demand, Constant Lead Time)   The data shown in Table 12-5 represent weekly demand on a $250 item which has a constant lead time of 1 week. The firm has a 20 percent per year cost for carrying inventory. Determine the safety-stock level and carrying cost for providing a service level of (*a*) 90 percent and (*b*) 95 percent.

Table 12-5

Weekly Demand (number of units)	Frequency (number of weeks this demand occurred)	Cumulative Frequency (number of weeks demand exceeded lower-class boundary)	Cumulative Percentage (percentage of weeks demand exceeded lower-class boundary)
< 50	1	104	100.0
50 < 100	7	103	99.0
100 < 150	11	96	92.3
150 < 200	16	85	81.7
200 < 250	19	69	66.3
250 < 300	20	50	48.1
300 < 350	14	30	28.8
350 < 400	9	16	15.4
400 < 450	5	7	6.7
450 < 500	2	2	1.9
	$\overline{104}$		

The 90 percent and 95 percent service levels represent stockout risks of 10 percent and 5 percent, respectively (per Eq. 12.4). We can formulate a frequency distribution (histogram) and cumulative distribution (ogive) of demand as shown in Figs. 12-3 and 12-4.

Because it is readily available and sufficiently representative of the central tendency of the data, we use the median (the fiftieth percentile value) of the cumulative distribution as our estimate of average demand.

$$D_{\text{ave}} = \text{average demand} \cong 240 \text{ units}$$

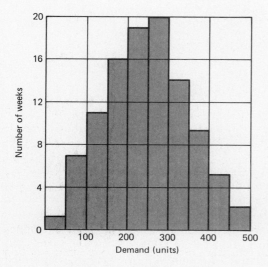

Fig. 12-3   Frequency of demand

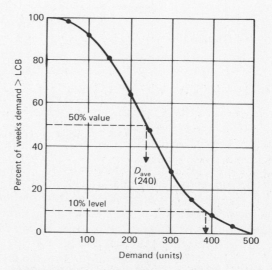

Fig. 12-4   Cumulative distribution of demand

(*a*)   90 percent service level (10 percent SOR):

$$D_{\text{SOR}} = \text{demand level corresponding to 10 percent risk of stockout}$$

$$\cong 385 \text{ units (from graph)}$$

$$SS = \text{safety stock level} = D_{\text{SOR}} - D_{\text{ave}} = 385 - 240 = 145 \text{ units}$$

$$SS \text{ cost} = \left(\frac{\$250}{\text{unit}}\right)\left(\frac{20\%}{\text{yr}}\right)(145 \text{ units}) = \$7{,}250/\text{yr}$$

(*b*)   95 percent SL (5 percent SOR):

$$D_{\text{SOR}} = \text{demand level corresponding to 5 percent risk of stockout}$$

$$\cong 430 \text{ units (from graph)}$$

$$SS = D_{\text{SOR}} - D_{\text{ave}} = 430 - 240 = 190 \text{ units}$$

$$SS \text{ cost} = \left(\frac{\$250}{\text{unit}}\right)\left(\frac{20\%}{\text{yr}}\right)(190 \text{ units}) = \$9{,}500/\text{yr}$$

Variations in lead time are the second major cause of uncertainty in inventory management, although lead times are generally more controllable than demand. Lead time uncertainty can also be handled by developing cumulative probability distributions of lead times for the given inventory item. The safety-stock level (as in weeks of usage) required to guard against this uncertainty can be determined by referring to the cumulative distribution. This is done by using the cumulative distribution to find the lead time required to limit the stockout risk to a given level (LT_{ave}), and subtracting the average lead time (LT_{ave}) from LT_{SOR}.

$$SS = LT_{\text{SOR}} - LT_{\text{ave}} \tag{12.9}$$

USE OF STATISTICAL DISTRIBUTIONS TO SET SAFETY-STOCK LEVELS

If the distribution of demand during lead time D_{LT} is symmetrical and unimodal, the normal distribution may satisfactorily describe it. See Fig. 12-5. An average demand (D_{ave}) would just use up the cycle (nonsafety stock) inventory during the lead time.

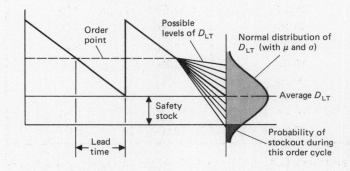

Fig. 12-5   Normal distribution of demand during lead time

Both the standard deviation (σ) and mean absolute deviation (MAD) are useful measures of dispersion of individual demand values from the mean value ($\sigma \cong 1.25 \text{ MAD}$). If the service level (SL) is expressed as a percentage of the area under the normal curve above the stockout line, the required safety stock can be calculated in terms of deviations from the mean. Conversely, if the number of units of safety stock is specified, we can determine how much protection against stockout (i.e., the percent of SL) the safety stock provides. Table 12-6 gives the safety-stock-level factors (SF) for normally distributed variables. The factors are simply the number of standard (and mean absolute) deviations required to include the specified percentage of area under the normal curve cumulated in the positive direction.

Table 12-6 Safety-Stock-Level Factors for Normally Distributed Variables*

$SS = SF_\sigma(\sigma)$ or $SS = SF_{MAD}(MAD)$ $OP = D_{LT} + SS$		
	Safety Factor Using:	
Service Level (percent of order cycles without stockout)	Standard Deviation SF_σ	Mean Absolute Deviation SF_{MAD}
50.00	0.00	0.00
75.00	0.67	0.84
80.00	0.84	1.05
84.13	1.00	1.25
85.00	1.04	1.30
89.44	1.25	1.56
90.00	1.28	1.60
93.32	1.50	1.88
94.00	1.56	1.95
94.52	1.60	2.00
95.00	1.65	2.06
96.00	1.75	2.19
97.00	1.88	2.35
97.72	2.00	2.50
98.00	2.05	2.56
98.61	2.20	2.75
99.00	2.33	2.91
99.18	2.40	3.00
99.38	2.50	3.13
99.50	2.57	3.20
99.60	2.65	3.31
99.70	2.75	3.44
99.80	2.88	3.60
99.86	3.00	3.75
99.90	3.09	3.85
99.93	3.20	4.00
99.99	4.00	5.00

* Adapted from G.W. Plossl and O.W. Wight, *Production and Inventory Control: Principles and Techniques*, 1967, p. 108. Reprinted by permission of Prentice-Hall, Inc., Englewood Cliffs, N.J.

Example 12.7 (Computation of SL) The demand for a product during its lead time is normally distributed with mean $\mu = 1,000$ units and standard deviation $\sigma = 40$ units. What percent service can a firm expect to offer if (a) it provides for average demand only, (b) it carries 60 units of safety stock?

(a) Average demand (1,000 units) would include no safety stock. Thus, service = 50 percent.
(b) With 60 units of SS:

$$SF_\sigma = \frac{SS}{\sigma} = \frac{60}{40} = 1.5$$

Thus, from Table 12-6, the service level = 93.32 percent.

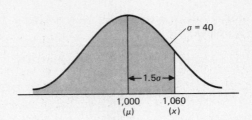

Note that the same result would be obtained from using any table of the normal distribution where:

$$Z = \frac{x - \mu}{\sigma} = \frac{1,060 - 1,000}{40} = 1.5$$

The Z value of 1.5 yields a probability value of .4332 which, when added to .5000, results in an SL of 93.32 percent.

Examples 12.8 and 12.9 illustrate the computation of SS amounts necessary to satisfy specified service levels.

Example 12.8 (Computation of SS Using σ) A firm has a normal distribution of demand during a (constant) lead time, with $\sigma = 250$ units. The firm wants to provide 98 percent service. (a) How much safety stock should be carried? (b) If the demand during the lead time averages 1,200 units, what is the appropriate order point?

(a) $$SS = SF_\sigma(\sigma) = (2.05)(250) = 512 \text{ units}$$

(b) $$OP = D_{LT} + SS = 1,200 + 512 = 1,712 \text{ units}$$

If the number of stockouts allowed per time period is designated, estimate the total number of reorder cycles. The service level is the number of cycles the stock is adequate as a percentage of the total number of cycles.

Example 12.9   (Computation of SS Using MAD) A firm has a normally distributed forecast of demand, with MAD = 60 units during the fixed lead time of 1 week. It desires a service level which limits stockouts to one order cycle per year. (a) How much safety stock should be carried? (b) If D_{LT} averages 500 units, what is the appropriate order point?

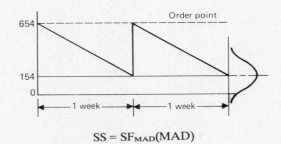

(a) $$SS = SF_{MAD}(MAD)$$

where SF_{MAD} depends upon the service level:

$$1 \text{ week's supply/order} = 52 \text{ orders/yr}$$

$$1 \text{ stockout in } 52 = \frac{51}{52} \text{ in stock} = 98\% \text{ service}$$

Thus, $$SF_{MAD} = 2.56 \text{ (from Table 12-6)}$$

$$SS = 2.56(60) = 154 \text{ units}$$

(b) $$OP = D_{LT} + SS = 500 + 154 = 654 \text{ units}$$

If lead times are shorter than the order cycle, the uncertainty is confined to the later part of the demand cycle. The safety stock remains a direct function of MAD (or σ) and is computed in the same manner as above. However, if the lead time is longer than the order cycle, each of the individual order cycles within the span of the lead time adds some of its own demand uncertainty to the ending distribution. For constant LT's longer than order cycles, if the demand in each period is independent, the estimated standard deviation of demand during lead time (σ_K) is:

$$\sigma_k = \sqrt{n\sigma_{oc}^2}$$

(12.10)

where n = number of periods or order cycles in the lead time

σ_{oc}^2 = variance of an order cycle (i.e., a representative independent variance)

OTHER DEMAND AND LEAD-TIME DISTRIBUTIONS

Previous examples have assumed a constant lead time and variable demand. If demand were constant and lead time varied, the same theory would hold. However if both demand and lead time vary simultaneously, the combined distribution is likely to be of some nondeterminant form, and computer simulation may be the most effective way of estimating an appropriate level of safety stock. One conservative approach is to use the longest normal lead time.

Many demands have a normal distribution at the production-plant level and a Poisson distribution at the retail level. The Poisson distribution also has some applicability in estimating lead time.

Solved Problems

METHODS OF HANDLING INVENTORY UNCERTAINTIES

12.1   *Informal Decision Rules.* Trident Value Co. has experienced the demand pattern shown in Fig. 12-6. Lead times for reorders vary from 2 to 8 days. What amount of safety stock would be carried under a decision rule of (*a*) largest daily usage × longest lead time, (*b*) average demand plus 30 percent safety factor, and (*c*) square root of average demand during lead time.

(*a*) $\text{SS} = (D_{max})(LT_{max}) = (40 \text{ units/day})(8 \text{ days}) = 320$ units

(*b*) $\text{SS} = D_{ave} + 30\%$

where $D_{ave} = \dfrac{30 + 15 + \cdots + 20}{20} = 21$ units

$$\text{SS} = 21 + .30(21) = 27.3$$

Use 28 units.

(*c*) $\text{SS} = \sqrt{D_{ave}} \text{ during LT}$

where $LT_{ave} = \dfrac{2 + 8}{2} = 5$ days

$$D_{ave} = \left(21 \frac{\text{units}}{\text{day}}\right)(5 \text{ days}) = 105 \text{ units}$$

$$\text{SS} = \sqrt{105} = 10.25$$

Use 11 units.

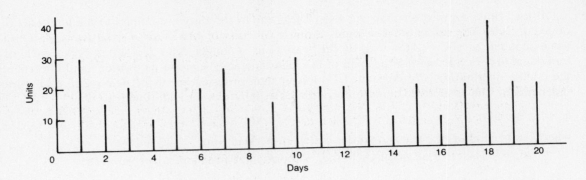

Fig. 12-6

12.2 *Incremental Approach*: *Uniformly Distributed, Single-Period Demand.* The *City Chronicle* has a daily newspaper demand that varies uniformly between 20,000 and 24,000 copies per day. The paper costs 8 cents per issue to produce and generates a revenue of 20 cents per issue. Unsold papers have no value. (*a*) What is the optimal level of papers to stock, and (*b*) what service level would that optimal level correspond with?

(*a*)   This is a problem of balancing the cost of understocking inventory C_{us} with that of overstocking C_{os}. From Eq. 11.3, the balance point is where the cumulative probability of demand $P(D)$ establishes the equality of

$$C_{us}P(D) = C_{os}[1 - P(D)]$$

Thus
$$P(D) = \frac{C_{os}}{C_{os} + C_{us}}$$

where C_{os} = cost/unit − salvage value = \$.08 − 0 = \$.08
C_{us} = revenue/unit − cost/unit = \$.20 − \$.08 = \$.12

Therefore,
$$P(D) = \frac{.08}{.08 + .12} = .40$$

Because demand is uniform, we can depict it with a straight (linear) line from the minimum demand (20,000) to the maximum demand (24,000). Going into the curve (Fig. 12-7) from .4 and down to the horizontal axis yields an optimal value of 22,400.

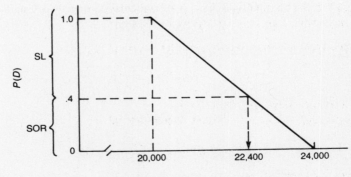

Fig. 12-7

(*b*)   The .40 means that the probability demand will be exceeded, and represents a stockout risk established on the basis of the costs given. Thus the corresponding service level is:

$$SL = 1 - SOR = 1 - .4 = .6$$

Note: Algebraically, the point representing a 60 percent service level is an inventory of:

$$I_{OPT} = D_{min} + \%SL(\Delta \text{ inventory}) = 20,000 + .60(24,000 - 20,000) = 22,400 \text{ units}$$

12.3 *Incremental Approach*: *Normally Distributed Demand.* Demand for a chemical product is normally distributed with μ equals 80 gallons per week and σ equals 5 gallons per week. If C_{os} is \$.15 per gallon and C_{us} is \$.50 per gallon, what is the optimal level to stock?

$$P(D) = \frac{C_{os}}{C_{os} + C_{us}} = \frac{.15}{.15 + .50} = .231$$

$$I_{OPT} = \mu + Z\sigma$$

where Z is for a probability area of $.500 - .231 = .269$. Therefore $Z = .73$.

$$I_{OPT} = 80 + .73(S) = 83.65 \text{ gal}$$

See Fig. 12-8.

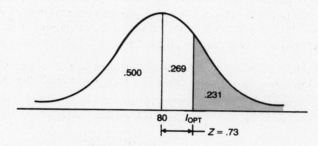

Fig. 12-8

Note: The solution above corresponds to an SL of $1 - SOR = 1.00 - .231 = .769 = 76.9$ percent. Some analysts compute the SL percentage directly by reversing the equation for $P(D)$ to:

$$SL\% = \frac{C_{us}}{C_{os} + C_{us}} = \frac{.50}{.15 + .50} = .769$$

12.4 *Incremental Approach*: *Poisson Demand.* A large city hospital has determined that the demand for ambulances can be approximated by a Poisson distribution with a mean of 6 per day. The cost for having an ambulance available is \$460 per day, and its life-support value, when used, is placed at \$2,000 per day. If unused, of course, its service value is zero. What is the optimum number of ambulances to maintain?

The two expected costs are equal for the cumulative probability:

$$P(D) = \frac{C_{os}}{C_{os} + C_{us}}$$

where $C_{os} = \text{cost/unit} - \text{salvage} = \$460 - 0 = \$460$

$C_{us} = \text{value/unit} - \text{cost/unit} = \$2,000 - \$460 = \$1,540$

$$P(D) = \frac{\$460}{\$460 + \$1540} = .23$$

Thus, $SL = 1.00 - .23 = .77$.

Cumulative probabilities for a Poisson distribution with a mean of 6.0 are then obtained from Appendix D (Table 12-7).

Table 12-7

Demand (ambulances per day)	0	1	2	3	4	5	6	7	8	9
Cumulative probability	.002	.017	.062	.151	.285	.446	.606	.744	.847	. . .

Seven ambulances would closely approximate the service level which balances the expected costs and benefits (i.e., 77 percent), but eight would be required to equal or exceed the 77 percent.

SAFETY STOCKS, ORDER POINTS, AND SERVICE LEVELS

12.5 A producer of SUN-STOP suntan lotion uses 400 gallons per week of a chemical which is ordered in EOQ quantities of 5,000 gallons at a quantity discount cost of \$3.75 per gallon. Procurement lead time is two weeks, and a safety stock of 200 gallons is maintained. Storage cost is \$.01 per gallon-week. Find (a) the maximum inventory on hand (on the average), (b) the average inventory maintained, and (c) the order point (in units).

(a) Maximum inventory: I_{max} = safety stock + EOQ = 200 + 5,000 = 5,200 gal

(b) Average inventory: $I_{ave} = \dfrac{I_{max} + I_{min}}{2} = \dfrac{5,200 + 200}{2} = 2,700$ gal

(c) Order point: OP = D_{LT} + SS = (400)(2) + 200 = 1,000 units

12.6 A firm has an annual demand of 1,000 units, ordering costs of \$10 per order, and carrying costs of \$10 per unit-yr. Stockout costs are estimated to be about \$40 each time the firm has an exposure to stockout. How much safety stock is justified by the carrying costs?

$$Q = \sqrt{\frac{2D(C_o + C_e)}{C_c}} = \sqrt{\frac{2(1,000)(10 + 40)}{10}} = 100 \text{ units}$$

Therefore, $\text{Orders/yr} = \dfrac{D}{Q} = \dfrac{1,000 \text{ units/yr}}{100 \text{ units/order}} = 10 \text{ orders/yr}$

Stockout costs are (\$40/trial)(10 trials/yr) = \$400/yr. At carrying costs of \$10/unit-yr, the \$400 will fund:

$$\frac{\$400/yr}{\$10/unit\text{-}yr} = 40 \text{ units of safety stock}$$

Note that, given a cumulative distribution of demand, this SS could be used to find the corresponding level of service provided.

INCREMENTAL APPROACH: MULTIPLE-PERIOD MODEL WITH INDIVIDUAL-UNIT STOCKOUT COSTS

12.7 Supermarket Supply Co. distributes grocery products to customers in Arizona, New Mexico, Texas, and Oklahoma. Demand for canned corn averages 280 cases per month. Lead time to obtain a shipment is about a month, and demand during the lead time is normally distributed with a standard deviation of 60 cases. The company estimates their ordering cost at \$8.00 per order, carrying cost at \$2.40 per case-year and stockout cost at \$2.00 per case. Find (a) the EOQ disregarding stockout costs, (b) the number of orders per year if the EOQ is used, (c) the optimum level of SOR, and (d) the reorder point.

(a) $\text{EOQ} = \sqrt{\dfrac{2C_o D}{C_c}} = \sqrt{\dfrac{2(8)(280 \times 12)}{2.40}} = 150 \text{ cases/order}$

(b) $\dfrac{\text{Orders}}{\text{Year}} = \dfrac{D}{Q} = \dfrac{(280 \times 12) \text{ cases/yr}}{150 \text{ cases/order}} = 22.4 \text{ orders/yr}$

(c)
$$\text{SOR} = \frac{C_c}{C_{so}}\left(\frac{Q}{D}\right) = \left(\frac{\$2.40/\text{case-yr}}{2.00/\text{case-order}}\right)\left(\frac{150 \text{ cases/order}}{3,360 \text{ cases/yr}}\right) = .054, \text{ or } 5.4\% \text{ risk of stockout}$$

Thus, $\text{SL} = 1.00 - .054 = .946 = 94.6$ percent.

(d)
$$\text{RP} = D_{\text{LT}} + \text{SS}$$

where $\quad \text{SS} = \text{SF}_\sigma(\sigma) = 1.56(60) = 94$ cases

$$\text{RP} = (280 \text{ cases/month})(1 \text{ month LT}) + 94 \text{ cases} = 374 \text{ cases}$$

USE OF EMPIRICAL DATA TO SET SAFETY-STOCK LEVELS

12.8 Given the data from Example 12.6, suppose the manager is willing to allocate only $3,000 per year to the carrying of safety stock for the $250 item. For what percentage of order cycles can he or she expect to run out of stock?

We can compute how much safety stock the $3,000 would fund by dividing the $3,000 by the carrying cost per unit-year.

$$\text{SS} = \frac{\$3,000 \text{ allocated/yr}}{\$250/\text{unit } (20\%/\text{yr})} = 60 \text{ units}$$

The stockout risk corresponding to $\text{SS} = 60$ units is:

$$\text{SS} = D_{\text{SOR}} - D_{\text{ave}}$$
$$D_{\text{SOR}} = \text{SS} + D_{\text{ave}}$$

where $D_{\text{ave}} = 240$ units (from Fig. 12-4).

$$D_{\text{SOR}} = 60 + 240 = 300 \text{ units}$$

From the cumulative distribution (Fig. 12-4) a demand of 300 units corresponds to a percentage value of approximately 29 percent. Therefore the manager may expect to run out of stock on approximately 29 percent of the order cycles. That is, if the firm places an order each week, it may run out of stock on $(.29)(52) \cong 15$ occasions. Knowing this, the manager may want to reconsider the $3,000 allocation.

USE OF STATISTICAL DISTRIBUTIONS TO SET SAFETY-STOCK LEVELS

12.9 *LT Less than Order Cycle.* A firm has a normally distributed demand, with $D_{\text{LT}} = 500$ units, and $\text{MAD} = 60$ units, during the fixed lead time of one week, and it orders a 5-week supply. It wishes to limit stockouts to one order cycle per year. (a) How much safety stock should be carried, and (b) what is the appropriate order point?

This problem differs from previous ones in that the lead time (1 week) is less than the order cycle (5 weeks). Because the uncertainty is confined to the latter phase of a single demand cycle, no special adjustments are required.

(a) A 5-week supply results in $52/5 = 10.4$ orders per year. Being out of stock one time results in $9.4/10.4 = 90$ percent SL. From Table 12-6, $\text{SF}_{\text{MAD}} = 1.60$. Therefore,

$$\text{SS} = \text{SF}_{\text{MAD}}(\text{MAD}) = 1.60(60) = 96 \text{ units}$$

(b)
$$\text{OP} = D_{\text{LT}} + \text{SS} = 500 + 96 = 596 \text{ units}$$

See Fig. 12-9.

12.10 *LT Equals Order Cycle.* Hospital Supply Co. obtains surgical masks from a factory in Chicago and sells them to hospitals on a year-round basis. Demand during the 1-month lead time is normally distributed with a mean of 30 cases per month and MAD equal to 6 cases.

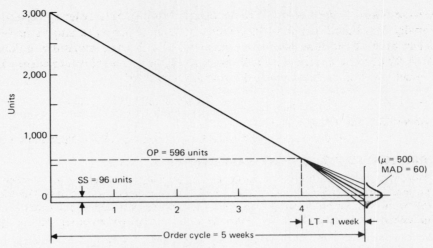

Fig. 12-9 Product with 5-week order cycle and 1-week lead time (90% SL)

(*a*) How much safety stock should Hospital Supply Co. carry to ensure that demand is met on 90 percent of the order cycles? (*b*) What should be the reorder point for the service level used in (*a*)? (*c*) Suppose the masks cost $100 per case, and the carrying cost is 20 percent per year. What level of service would result from allocating $400 per year to carry safety stock?

(*a*) $$SS = SF_{MAD}(MAD) = 1.60(6) = 9.6, \text{ say 10 cases}$$

(*b*) $$RP = D_{LT} + SS = 30 + 10 = 40 \text{ cases}$$

(*c*) $$\text{Carrying cost/unit} = (.20)(\$100/\text{unit}) = \$20/\text{unit-yr}$$

Therefore, $400 would fund an SS of

$$\frac{\$400/\text{yr}}{\$20/\text{unit/yr}} = 20 \text{ units}$$

From $$SS = SF_{MAD}(MAD)$$

we have $$SF_{MAD} = SS/MAD = 20/6 = 3.33$$

From Table 12-6 of safety-stock-level factors for normally distributed variables, the service level is

$$SL = 99.6\%$$

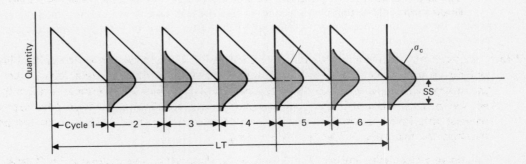

Fig. 12-10 Lead time containing 6 order cycles

12.11 *LT Greater Than Order Cycle.* A tire distributor has a weekly order cycle, and has experienced a normally distributed demand with a mean of 40 units per week and a standard deviation of 5 units per week. Lead time is constant at 6 weeks, and each demand is independent. See Fig. 12-10. A 90 percent service level is desired. (*a*) How much safety stock should be carried? (*b*) How much stock is on hand when the reorder is placed?

(*a*)
$$SS = SF_\sigma(\sigma)$$

where SF_σ for 90% = 1.28

$\sigma = \sigma_k$ of demand during 6-week LT $= \sqrt{n\sigma_{oc}^2} = \sqrt{(6)5^2} = 12.25$ units

Thus, $SS = (1.28)(12.25) = 15.68$, use 16 units.

(*b*) The safety stock of 16 units is designed to protect the distributor over 6 order cycles of demand uncertainty (and it is assumed that the lead time of 6 weeks is constant). Therefore the distributor can work with an order plan based upon the amount used during one order cycle D_{oc}. The actual (physical) inventory on hand I_{OH} when the distributor places an order will be:

$$I_{OH} = D_{oc} + SS = 40 + 16 = 56 \text{ tires}$$

Note, however, that in terms of units on hand *and on order* the (book value) order point would be substantially higher, for it would be triggered by 6 weeks of demand at 40 units per week plus the 16 units of safety stock, or $OP = 6(40) + 16 = 256$ units.

12.12 Robotic Devices Ltd. produces a microprocessor which has an average demand of 600 units per work day, with $\sigma = 40$. The production rate is 2,000 per day, and each run costs \$325 to set up and requires a four-day scheduling and set-up time. The company works 250 days a year, and carrying costs for the microprocessor are \$8.00 per unit-yr.

(*a*) Find the optimal production quantity.

(*b*) What reorder point will give the firm a 95 percent chance of meeting any customer demand that occurs during the four-day lead time? Assume that demand during the set-up time is normally distributed and independent from one day to the next.

(*a*)
$$ERL = \sqrt{\frac{2C_oD}{C_c(1 - d/p)}} = \sqrt{\frac{2(\$325)(600 \times 250)}{\$8[1 - (600/2,000)]}} = 4,173 \text{ units}$$

(*b*)
$$OP = D_{LT} + SS$$

where $SS = SF_\sigma(\sigma)$. In this case $\sigma = \sigma_k = \sqrt{n\sigma_{oc}^2} = \sqrt{4(40)^2} = 80$ and $SF_\sigma =$ for 96% SL = 1.75 (Table 12-6).

Thus,
$$SS = (1.75)(80) = 140 \text{ units}$$

$$OP = (600)(4) + 140 = 2,540 \text{ units}$$

The firm should begin preparations for a production run of 4,173 units whenever existing inventory levels drop to 2,540 units.

12.13 An inventory control analyst has determined that the lead time for a certain item is distributed as Poisson with a mean μ equal to 1.8 weeks. Each week the firm uses 200 of these items, and the analyst wishes to establish a safety-stock level that gives 99 percent assurance that the item will be in stock when it is needed. How many units of safety stock should be kept on hand to provide this level of service? (Round any fractional weeks of lead time to the next highest number, for example, >7 weeks = 8 weeks.)

Using a cumulative Poisson distribution, we need to find a numerical value for X such that

$$P(X \geq ? \mid \mu = 1.8) = .01$$

where .01 is the SOR and 1.8 is the mean, μ.

From the Poisson distribution table, Appendix D, we find

$$P(X > 5 | \mu = 1.8) = .01$$

Thus, maximum value (that is, >5) = 6. The lead time that will be exceeded only 1 percent of the time is 6 weeks.

$$SS = L_{SOR} - L_{ave} = 6.0 - 1.8 = 4.2 \text{ weeks}$$

$$\text{Number of items} = (4.2 \text{ weeks}) \left(\frac{200 \text{ items}}{\text{week}}\right) = 840 \text{ items of SS}$$

Supplementary Problems

12.14 A firm with a steady demand orders a raw material in quantities of 5 tons per order from a supplier who always delivers in 30 days. The price is $250 per ton, and the carrying and storage cost is 35 percent per year. Find (a) I_{max}, (b) I_{ave}, and (c) the annual carrying and storage cost.
Ans. (a) 5 tons (b) 2.5 tons (c) $219/year

12.15 Demand during lead time varies uniformly between 8,000 units and 12,000 units. Each unit costs $3.00, sells for $4.00, and has a salvage value of $1.20 if not sold. Use the single-period model to find the optimal level of inventory to stock. *Ans.* 9,428 units

12.16 A raw material has a normally distributed demand during lead time with $\mu = 200$ lbs/week, $\sigma = 10$ lbs/week, $C_{os} = \$.80$/lb, and $C_{us} = \$3.20$/lb. Find the optimal level to stock, assuming the single-period model applies. *Ans.* 208.4 lbs

12.17 A Poisson-distributed demand with a mean of 8 per week has an acquisition cost of $80, an unused salvage value of $10, and a sale price (benefit value) of $640. How many units of the product should be stocked to balance the expected costs and benefits of overstocking and understocking?
Ans. 11 units

12.18 Evergreen Nursery Co. has established the demand pattern shown in Table 12-8 for a product that costs $40 each, sells for $90 each, and (if not sold immediately) has a salvage value of $10. Use a payoff and an expected-value matrix to determine what amount of the product should be stocked to maximize expected profits. *Ans.* Stock 20 for an expected value of $760.

Table 12-8

Demand X (units)	Frequency $f(X)$ (no. periods)
10	30
20	60
30	10

12.19 A lumber distributor orders plywood sheets in economic lot sizes of 2,000 sheets per order, and it takes 10 days before the mill delivers the plywood. The distributor sells roughly 40 sheets per day (12,000 per year) and maintains a safety stock of 300 sheets. (a) What is lead time? (b) What is the appropriate order point? (c) If it costs the firm $30 to place an order, what is the implied holding (including storage) cost?
Ans. (a) 10 days (b) 700 sheets (c) $.18 per sheet

12.20 Maintenance Supply Co. has an annual demand of 400 motors, which cost them $1,020 each. Ordering costs are $38 per order, and carrying costs are $200 per motor-year. Stockout costs are approximately $90 per exposure to stockout. How much safety stock is justified by the carrying costs?   *Ans.* 8 motors

12.21 The Browne and Chocolate Candy Co. supplies customers in the Nashville area with 60,000 boxes of "Brunchie" candy per yr at a rate of 200 per day. The plant can produce 400 per day, but management hesitates to build up too large an inventory, because the spoilage, storage, and carrying costs run to $1.50 per box-yr. The changeover cost to produce "Brunchies" is only $25 per setup, and management feels a cost of $75 is incurred in loss of goodwill each time the company runs out of stock and must tell customers they have to wait for their candy. What is the most economical number of boxes to produce during any one production run?   *Ans.*   4,000 boxes

12.22 Multiple-Period Model with Individual Unit Stockout Costs. Muffler Installations, Inc., has an annual demand of about 7,500 mufflers per year. Demand during the 2-week lead time is normally distributed with a mean of 300 and standard deviation of 50. The firm estimates its ordering cost at $20 per order, holding cost at $10 per unit-year, and stockout cost at $15 for each lost muffler sale. The operations manager would like to establish a fixed-quantity inventory system that would carry an optimal amount of safety stock, i.e., where the cost of adding one more unit of stock just equals the expected gain from adding that unit. (*a*) How many mufflers should be ordered at one time? (*b*) How much safety stock should be carried? (*c*) What reorder point should the company use?
Ans.   (*a*) 173 units (*b*) SOR = .0154, SS = 108 (*c*) 408 units

12.23 A Kansas City feedlot operator supplies beef to several meat-packing plants. The steers have an average value of $450, and the operator finances them through a local bank, paying 10 percent interest on the borrowed funds. The data given in Table 12-9 represents the weekly demand over the past 100 weeks.

Table 12-9

Weekly Demand (no. steers)	Frequency (no. weeks)
0 < 100	10
100 < 200	35
200 < 300	40
300 < 400	10
400 < 500	5
	100

(*a*) Prepare a histogram of the frequency distribution of demand. (*b*) Graph the cumulative distribution of demand. The feedlot operator wishes to keep enough stock in the lot to supply weekly demand 90 percent of the time. Feed costs to maintain a steer at a prescribed weight are $5 per week. (*c*) What level of safety stock (that is, how many steers) should the operator carry to provide the 90 percent service level? (*d*) What is the annual cost of carrying this safety stock?
Ans.   (*a*) and (*b*) should be of sufficient size and accuracy to yield reasonably accurate values for the 50 percent and 10 percent demand levels. Values may vary, but should be around 130 to 150 steers for (*c*), and from $39,650 to $45,750 for (*d*).

12.24 Data on the distribution of lead times for a pump component were collected as shown in Table 12-10. Management would like to set safety-stock levels that will limit the stockout risk to 10 percent. (*a*) Graph the cumulative distribution. (*b*) How many weeks of safety stock are required to provide the desired service level?
Ans.   (*a*) Graph should have weeks on *x* axis and the percentage of time the lower boundary is exceeded on the *y* axis (*b*) 3

Table 12-10

Lead Time (weeks)	Frequency of Occurrence
0 < 1	10
1 < 2	20
2 < 3	70
3 < 4	40
4 < 5	30
5 < 6	10
6 < 7	10
7 < 8	10
	200

12.25 A manufacturer of water filters purchases components in EOQs of 850 units per order. The total need (demand) averages 12,000 components per year, and MAD = 32 units during the lead time. If the manufacturer carries a safety stock of 80 units, what service level does this give the firm? Assume a normal distribution of D_{LT}.   *Ans.*   97.72 percent

12.26 An aluminum firm purchases coke from a foreign supplier who takes 4 weeks to deliver it. The company uses 800 tons of coke per week and places an order every 4 weeks. Demand during the 4-week lead time is normally distributed with a mean absolute deviation of MAD = 600 tons. The company wishes to carry enough safety stock to limit their stockouts to one order cycle over a two-year period (104 weeks). What order point should they use?   *Ans.*   4,520 tons (from 4,514 to 4,532, depending upon rounding)

12.27 The Hotel-Restaurant Supply Co. orders potatoes in units of 500 bags per order and receives them 10 days later. Its deliveries and usage average 20 bags per day, and it maintains an extra rotating stock of 40 bags to be sure it does not run out of stock. Assume that the demand is normally distributed during the lead time, with $\sigma = 16$ bags. (a) What is the lead time? (b) What is the order point? (c) What service level does the safety stock provide? (d) Suppose the firm's management felt that running out of stock during two order cycles of the year were acceptable. By how much could the safety stock be reduced? Assume that there are 250 working days per year.
Ans.   (a) 10 days (b) 240 bags (c) 99.38 percent (d) 26 or 27 bags

Chapter 13

Material-Requirements Planning: MRP and CRP

MRP AND CRP OBJECTIVES

Material-requirements planning (MRP) is a technique for determining the quantity and timing for the acquisition of dependent demand items needed to satisfy master schedule requirements. By identifying precisely *what*, *how many*, and *when* components are needed, MRP systems are able to (1) reduce inventory costs, (2) improve scheduling effectiveness, and (3) respond quickly to market changes.

Capacity-requirements planning (CRP) is a technique for determining what personnel and equipment capacities are needed to meet the production objectives embodied in the master schedule and the material requirements plan. Whereas MRP focuses upon the priorities of *materials*, CRP is concerned primarily with *time*. Nevertheless, both the material and time requirements must be integrated within one system, and CRP activities are often assumed to be included within the concept of an MRP system. Computerized MRP systems can effectively manage the flow of thousands of components throughout a manufacturing facility.

Figure 13-1 describes MRP and CRP activities in schematic form. Forecasts and orders are combined in the production plan, which is formalized in the master production schedule (MPS). The MPS, along with a bill-of-material (BOM) file and inventory status information, is used to formulate

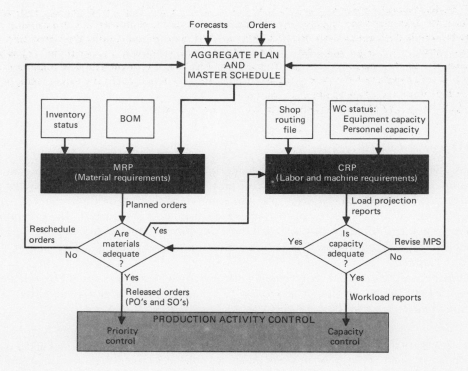

Fig. 13-1 Material and capacity planning flowchart

257

Table 13-1   MRP Terminology

MRP. A technique for determining the quantity and timing of dependent-demand items.

Parent and component items. A *parent* is an assembly made up of basic parts, or *components*. The parent of one subgroup may be a component of a higher-level parent.

Dependent demand. Demand for components that is derived from the demand for other items.

Lot size. The quantity of items required for an order. The order may be either purchased from a vendor or produced in-house. Lot sizing is the process of specifying the order size.

Time phasing. Scheduling to produce or receive an appropriate amount (lot) of material so it will be available in the time periods when needed—not before or after.

Time bucket. The time period used for planning purposes in MRP—usually a week.

Requirements. Projected needs for raw materials, components, subassemblies, or finished goods. Gross requirements are total needs from all sources, whereas net requirements are "net" after using available inventory.

Requirements explosion. The breaking down (exploding) of parent items into component parts that can be individually planned and scheduled.

Bill of materials. A listing of all components (subassemblies and materials) that go into an assembled item. It frequently includes the part numbers and quantity required per assembly.

Scheduled receipt. Materials *already on order* from a vendor or in-house shop. The MRP shows both the quantity and projected time of receipt.

Planned receipt. Materials that *will be ordered* from a vendor or in-house shop. Otherwise it is similar to a scheduled receipt. (*Note*: Many MRP formats do not distinguish between scheduled receipts and planned receipts.)

Lead-time offset. The supply time, or number of time buckets between releasing an order and receiving the materials.

Planned order release. The plan (that is, quantity and date) to initiate the purchase or manufacture of materials so that they will be received on schedule after the lead-time offset.

the material-requirements plan. The MRP determines what components are needed and when they should be ordered from an outside vendor or produced in-house. The CRP function translates the MRP decisions into hours of capacity (time) needed. If materials, equipment, and personnel are adequate, orders are released, and the workload is assigned to the various work centers. See Table 13-1 for definitions of common MRP terminology.

TIME-PHASING CONCEPTS

End items, such as TV sets, have an *independent demand* that is closely linked to the ongoing needs of consumers. It is random but relatively constant. *Dependent* demand is linked more closely to the production process itself. Many firms use the same facilities to produce different end items because it is economical to produce large lots once the set-up cost is incurred. The components that go into a TV set, such as 24-inch picture tubes, have a dependent demand that is governed by the lot size and model of TV set that happen to be in production at any one time. Dependent demand is predictable, but "lumpy."

MRP systems compute material requirements and specify when orders should be released so that materials arrive exactly when needed. The process of scheduling the receipt of inventory as needed over time is *time phasing*.

Example 13.1   (*a*) Use a sketch to illustrate the difference between on-hand inventory levels under independent and under dependent demand. (*b*) Suppose the use of traditional order point techniques for a component resulted in an average inventory of 80 units. How much carrying cost would be saved by time phasing if the average inventory dropped to 15 units? Assume an item value of $20 and a carrying charge of 30 percent per year. (*c*) What would be the impact of extending this same savings to 2,000 components?

(*a*)   See Fig. 13-2.

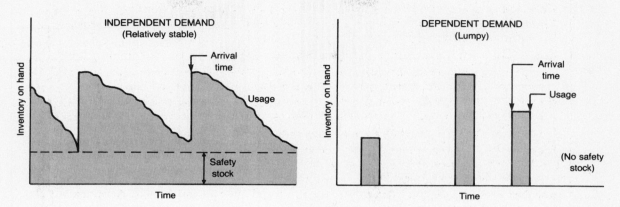

Fig. 13-2

(*b*)   First carrying cost = I_{ave}(Item value)(%)   Second carrying cost = I_{ave}(Item value)(%)

  = 80 units($20/unit)(.30/yr)   = 15 units($20/unit)(.30/yr)

  = $480/yr   = $90/yr

Thus, savings = $480 − $90 = $390/yr

(*c*)

Savings = 2,000 items($390/item-yr)

= $780,000/yr

MRP INPUTS AND OUTPUTS

As indicated in Fig. 13-1, MRP inputs and outputs are:

Inputs

- MPS of end items required.
- Inventory status file of on-hand and on-order items, lot sizes, lead times, etc.
- Product structure (BOM) file of what components and subassemblies go into each end product.

Outputs

- Order release data to CRP for load profiles.
- Orders to purchasing and in-house production shops.
- Rescheduling data to MPS.
- Management reports and inventory updates.

BILL OF MATERIALS

A *bill of materials* (BOM) is a listing of all the materials, components, and subassemblies needed to assemble one unit of an end item. Two common methods of describing a BOM are a product structure tree, and an indented BOM. Both depict the *parent-component* relationships on a hierarchical basis, which reveals what components are needed for each higher-level parent assembly.

Figure 13-3 illustrates the dependency structure of BOM's and includes *level coding* information. Level 0 is the highest (e.g., the end-item code) and level 3 the lowest for this BOM. Note that the 4 clamps (C20) constitute a subassembly that is combined with base (A10) and two springs (B11) to complete the end-item bracket (Z100). However, the same clamp (C20) is also a component of the base (A10). In order to facilitate the calculation of net requirements, the product tree has been

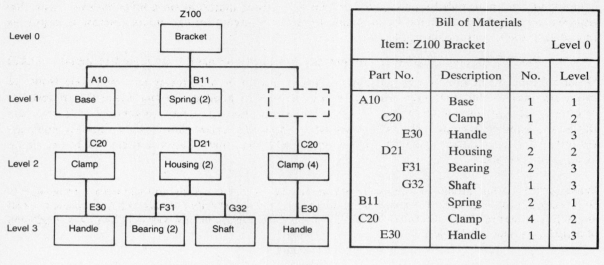

(a) Product structure tree   (b) Indented bill of materials

Fig. 13-3 Bill of materials for Z100 bracket

restructured from where the clamp components might have been (shown dashed) to the lower level consistent with the other (identical) clamp. This *low-level coding* enables the computer to scan the product structure *level by level*, starting at the top, and obtain an accurate and complete count of all components needed at that level.

Example 13.2 Determine the quantities of A10, B11, C20, D21, E30, F31, and G32 needed to complete 50 of the Z100 brackets depicted in Fig. 13-3. (For simplicity use A, B, . . . , E as part numbers.)

First determine the requirements for one bracket as shown in Table 13-2, and then multiply by 50. Note that parts C and E are used in two different subassemblies, so their separate amounts must be summed. For 50 brackets, each of the requirements column amounts must be multiplied by 50 to obtain the gross requirements.

Table 13-2

Component	Dependency Effect	Requirements
A (Base)	1A per Z	1
B (Spring)	2B's per Z	2
C (Clamp)	$(1C \text{ per } A) \cdot (1A \text{ per } Z) + (4C\text{'s per } Z)$	5
D (Housing)	$(2D\text{'s per } A) \cdot (1A \text{ per } Z)$	2
E (Handle)	$(1E \text{ per } C) \cdot (1C \text{ per } A) \cdot (1A \text{ per } Z) + (1E \text{ per } C) \cdot (4C\text{'s per } Z)$	5
F (Bearing)	$(2F\text{'s per } D) \cdot (2D\text{'s per } A) \cdot (1A \text{ per } Z)$	4
G (Shaft)	$(1G \text{ per } D) \cdot (2D\text{'s per } A) \cdot (1A \text{ per } Z)$	2

MRP LOGIC

The master production schedule dictates *gross or projected requirements* for end items to the MRP system. Gross requirements do not take account of any inventory on hand or on order. The MRP computer program then "explodes" the end-item demands into requirements for subassemblies, components and materials by processing all relevant bills of materials on a level-by-level basis. *Net requirements* are then calculated by adjusting for existing inventory and items already on order, as recorded in the inventory status file.

$$\text{Net requirements} = \text{gross requirements} - (\text{inventory on hand} + \text{scheduled receipts}) \qquad (13.1)$$

Order releases are planned for components in a time-phased manner (using lead-time data from the inventory file) so that materials will arrive precisely when needed. At this stage the material is referred to as a *planned order receipt*. When the orders are actually issued to vendors or to in-house shops, the planned receipt technically becomes a *scheduled receipt*. Some MRP formats maintain separate lines for planned and scheduled receipts, whereas others combine them under the single heading of receipts.

Example 13.3   A firm producing wheelbarrows is expected to deliver 40 wheelbarrows in week 1, 60 in week 4, 60 in week 6, and 50 in week 8. Among the requirements for each wheelbarrow are two handlebars, a wheel assembly, and one tire for the wheel assembly. Order quantities, lead times, and inventories on hand at the beginning of period 1 are shown in Table 13-3.

Table 13-3

Part	Order Quantity	Lead Times	Inventory on Hand
Handlebars	300	2 wk	100
Wheel Assemblies*	200	3 wk	220
Tires	400	1 wk	50

*90 wheel assemblies are also needed in period 5 for a garden tractor shipment

A shipment of 300 handlebars is already scheduled to be received at the beginning of week 2. Complete the material-requirements plan for the handlebars, wheel assemblies, and tires and show *what quantities* of orders must be released and *when* they must be released in order to satisfy the MPS.

Figure 13-4 depicts the master schedule and component part schedules. We shall assume that the customer completes the final assembly, so no time allowance is required there. Note that because each wheelbarrow requires two handlebars, the projected material requirements for handlebars are double the number of end products. The projected requirements of 80 handlebars in period 1 are adequately satisfied by the 100 units on hand at the beginning of period 1, leaving 20 on hand at the end of period 1.

$$\text{On hand at end of period} = \text{on hand at end of previous period} + \text{receipts} - \text{projected requirements} \qquad (13.2)$$

With the receipt of 300 handlebars in period 2, the on-hand inventory will be adequate until week 8, which at first glance will be 20 units short. To overcome this, a planned order release for the standard order quantity (300) has been scheduled for week 6, because handlebars have a two-week lead time. The planned receipt of 300 in week 8 will thus result in an end-of-period inventory of 280 units.

Moving on to the wheel assemblies, note that each end item requires one wheel assembly, so the projected requirements coincide with end-product demand. In addition, the 90 wheel assemblies needed for the garden tractor in week 5 are automatically incorporated into the projected requirements. The on-hand stock is adequate until week 6, when quantities will drop to −30 unless a planned order is released in week 3.

The bottom chart of Fig. 13-4 illustrates the MRP for tires, which are a subcomponent of the wheel assemblies. Note that the planned order release of 200 units from the above wheel assemblies plan shows up as a projected requirement for 200 tires in the same week (week 3) on the subcomponent plan. Since on-hand inventory is inadequate to supply this need, a planned order release is scheduled for week 2. It should ensure that an order of 400 tires will be available by the beginning of week 3.

Key features of MRP systems are (1) the generation of lower-level requirements, (2) time phasing of those requirements, and (3) the planned order releases that flow from them. Note particularly that planned order releases of parent items (such as the wheel assemblies in Example 13.3) generate

End-Item Master Schedule: Wheelbarrows

Week no.	1	2	3	4	5	6	7	8
Requirements	40			60		60		50

Component Materials Plan: Handlebars

Order quantity=300 Lead time=2 weeks		1	2	3	4	5	6	7	8
Projected requirements		80			120		120		100
Receipts			300						300
On hand at end of period	100	20	320	320	200	200	80	80	280 −20
Planned order release							(300)		

negative amount
so place order
in week 6

Component Materials Plan: Wheel Assemblies

Order quantity=200 Lead time=3 weeks		1	2	3	4	5	6	7	8
Projected requirements		40			60	90*	60	50	
Receipts							200		
On hand at end of period	220	180	180	180	120	30	170 −30	170	120
Planned order release				(200)					

*Requirements from another product (garden tractor) which uses the same wheel assembly.

Subcomponent Materials Plan: Tire for Wheel Assembly

Order quantity=400 Lead time=1 week		1	2	3	4	5	6	7	8
Projected requirements				200					
Receipts				400					
On hand at end of period	50	50	50	250 −150	250	250	250	250	250
Planned order release			(400)						

Fig. 13-4 MRP master schedule and component plans

projected requirements at the component level (e.g., tires). In Example 13.3, if two tires had been required for each wheel assembly (instead of one) the projected requirement for tires would have been $200 \times 2 = 400$ in week 3 instead of 200.

LOT-SIZING METHODS

In Example 13-3, the order quantities were all specified. Numerous *lot-sizing* methods are in use, including (1) fixed order quantity amounts, e.g., 300 handlebars, (2) EOQ or ERL amounts, (3) lot for lot, which is ordering the exact amount of the net requirements for each period, (4) fixed period requirements, e.g., a two-month supply, and (5) various least-cost approaches, e.g. least unit cost, least total cost. The part-period algorithm is a method that uses a ratio of ordering costs to carrying costs per period, which yields a part-period number. Then requirements for current and future periods are cumulated until the cumulative holding cost (in part-period terms) is as close as possible to this number.

SYSTEM REFINEMENTS

Additional capabilities of MRP systems stem from the use of planning BOM's, firm planned orders, pegging capability, and rescheduling capability. *Planning BOM's* are phantom or artificial BOM's created to facilitate planning. They give planners last-minute scheduling flexibility by allowing them to work with common modules and options. *Firm planned order* capability enables planners to instruct the computer to accept and hold firm to certain requirements, even though normal MRP logic would automatically delay or reschedule such orders. *Pegging* refers to the ability to work backward from components to identify the parent item, or the items that generated the component requirements. This is useful for identifying which end items might be affected by late or defective components. *Rescheduling capability* enables firms to maintain valid priorities, which are essential for the credibility of the MRP system. If proposed master-schedule requirements cannot be met, the MRP program can be rerun (again and again) until a suitable plan is derived.

MRP II is an extension of MRP concepts to include product cost information that will yield financial, as well as material and capacity, reports. *Closed-loop* MRP includes feedback from both internal production operations and vendor orders.

Regenerative MRP systems use batch processing to replan the whole system (full explosion of all items) on a regular basis (e.g., weekly). *Net change* MRP systems are online and react continuously to changes from the master schedule, inventory file, and other transactions.

CRP INPUTS AND OUTPUTS

Capacity is a measure of the productive capability of a facility per unit of time. In terms of the relevant time horizon, capacity management decisions are concerned with the following:

(1) *Long range*—resource planning of capital facilities, equipment, and human resources

(2) *Medium range*—requirements planning of labor and equipment to meet MPS needs

(3) *Short range*—control of the flow (input-output) and sequencing of operations

Capacity-requirements planning (CRP) applies primarily to medium-range activities. As depicted in Fig. 13-5, the CRP system receives planned and released orders from the material-requirements planning system, and attempts to develop loads for the firm's work centers that are in good balance with the work-center capacities. Like MRP, CRP is an iterative process which involves planning, revision of capacity (or revision of the master schedule), and replanning until a reasonably good load profile is developed.

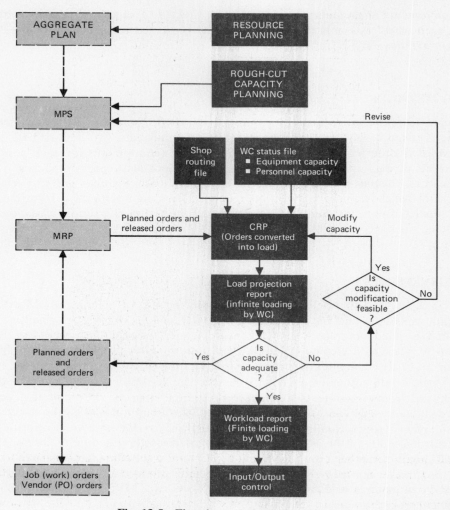

Fig. 13-5 Flowchart of the CRP process

As indicated in Fig. 13-5, CRP inputs and outputs are:

Inputs	Outputs
• Planned and released orders from the MRP system	• Load reports of planned and released orders on key work centers
• Loading capacities from the work center status file	• Verification reports to the MRP system
• Routing data from the routing file	• Capacity modification data
• Changes which modify capacity, give alternative routings, or alter planned orders	• Rescheduling data to the MPS

CRP ACTIVITIES: INFINITE AND FINITE LOADING

Planned order releases (in the MRP system) are converted to standard hours of load on key work centers in the CRP system. Figure 13-6 illustrates this transition for a planned order release of 300 handlebars in period 6 (from Fig. 13-4) to 6.2 standard hours of work in work center (WC) 4. These

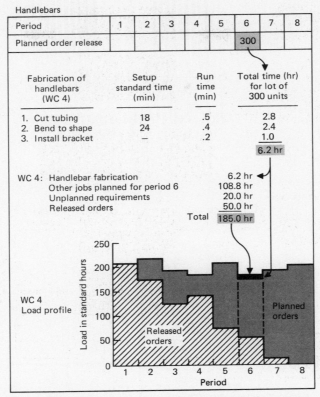

Handlebars

Period	1	2	3	4	5	6	7	8
Planned order release						300		

Fabrication of handlebars (WC 4)	Setup standard time (min)	Run time (min)	Total time (hr) for lot of 300 units
1. Cut tubing	18	.5	2.8
2. Bend to shape	24	.4	2.4
3. Install bracket	—	.2	1.0
			6.2 hr

WC 4: Handlebar fabrication   6.2 hr
        Other jobs planned for period 6   108.8 hr
        Unplanned requirements   20.0 hr
        Released orders   50.0 hr
                    Total 185.0 hr

Fig. 13-6 Transition of planned order release from MRP to load in CRP system

hours and the hours for other jobs planned for WC 4 during period 6, plus the hours for orders already released, make up the total expected load of 185 standard hours. Note that 20 hours have been allowed for unplanned or emergency jobs.

Infinite loading is the practice of loading work centers with all loads when they are required, without regard to the actual capacity of the work centers. CRP often uses infinite loading on an initial load profile to evaluate, or "size up", the proposed load from the MPS, and help planners make decisions regarding the use of overtime, alternate routings, etc. *Finite loading* limits the load assigned to a work center to the maximum capacity of the work center. Finite loading is most useful when making the final assignment of work to work centers, after the major adjustments have been made by using infinite loading procedures.

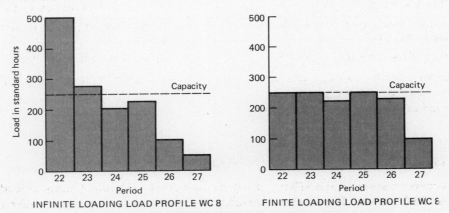

INFINITE LOADING LOAD PROFILE WC 8   FINITE LOADING LOAD PROFILE WC 8

Fig. 13-7 Infinite and finite loading profiles

Example 13.4 Use charts to illustrate the difference between infinite and finite loading.

See Fig. 13-7.

Solved Problems

BILL OF MATERIALS

13.1 Given the product structure tree shown in Fig. 13-8 for wheelbarrow W099, develop an indented bill of materials.

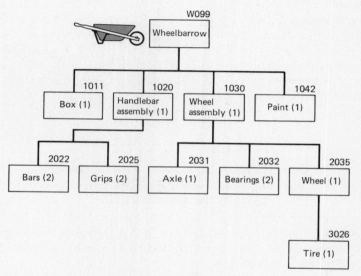

Fig. 13-8

See Table 13-4.

Table 13-4

Bill of Materials Part No. W099: Wheelbarrow				Level 0
Part No.	Description	Quantity/Assembly	Units	Level
1011	Box: deep size, aluminum	1	each	1
1020	Handlebar assembly	1	each	1
2022	Aluminum bars	2	each	2
2025	Grips: neoprene	2	each	2
1030	Wheel assembly	1	each	1
2031	Axle	1	each	2
2032	Bearing: normal-duty	2	each	2
2035	Wheel	1	each	2
3026	Tire: size A	1	each	3
1042	Paint: blue	1	pint	1

13.2 For the wheelbarrow of Prob. 13.1, there are 5 types of boxes available, 3 handlebar options, 2 choices of bearings, 3 sizes of tires, and 5 possible colors of paint. (*a*) If every option were considered a master schedule item, how many items would the master schedule have to accommodate for this product (wheelbarrows) alone? (*b*) What would be the effect of offering the choice of a white stripe on the front?

(*a*) There are $5 \times 3 \times 2 \times 3 \times 5 = 450$ combinations.

(*b*) Offering a stripe would mean each wheelbarrow could come either with or without a stripe, so the potential number of end items would double to 900. *Note*: To simplify the master scheduling, planners would most likely develop schedules of the level-1 items (rather than the finished product, level zero) and specify the specific end item on a final assembly bill of materials.

13.3 A flashlight is assembled from three major subassemblies: a head assembly, two batteries, and a body assembly. The head assembly consists of a plastic head, a lens, a bulb subassembly (comprising a bulb and bulb holder), and a reflector. The body assembly consists of a coil spring and a shell assembly, which in turn is made up of an on-off switch, two connector bars, and a plastic shell. The on-off switch is assembled from a knob and two small metal slides. The plastic head is made from one unit of orange plastic powder, and the plastic shell is made from three units of orange plastic powder. Develop a product structure tree of the flashlight, and include the level coding for each component.

See Fig. 13-9.

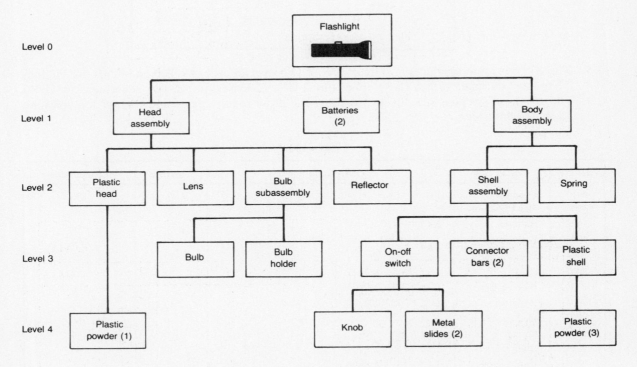

Fig. 13-9

13.4 Design an indented bill of materials for the flashlight in Prob. 13.3. (*Note*: Assign appropriate four-digit part numbers to the components.)

See Table 13.5.

Table 13-5

Bill of Materials Item: 0010 Flashlight			Level: 0
Part No.	Description	No.	Level
1001	Head assembly	1	1
2001	Plastic head	1	2
4001	Plastic powder	1	4
2002	Lens	1	2
2003	Bulb assembly	1	2
3001	Bulb	1	3
3002	Bulb holder	1	3
2004	Reflector	1	2
1002	Batteries	2	1
1003	Body assembly	1	1
2005	Shell assembly	1	2
3003	On-off switch	1	3
4002	Knob	1	4
4003	Metal slides	2	4
3004	Connector bars	2	3
3005	Plastic shell	1	3
4001	Plastic powder	3	4
2006	Spring	1	2

13.5 The company that produces flashlights (Prob. 13.3) has an order for 200 end items (flashlights). They have on hand 10 head assemblies (no. 1001), 12 lenses (no. 2002), 50 springs (no. 2006), and 15 on-off switches (no. 3003). Compute the gross requirements and the net requirements to satisfy the order.

Table 13-6

Part No.	Description	Gross Requirements	On Hand	Net Requirements
0010	Flashlight	200	0	200
1001	Head assembly	$1 \times 200 = 200$	10	190
1002	Batteries	$2 \times 200 = 400$	0	400
1003	Body assembly	$1 \times 200 = 200$	0	200
2001	Plastic head	$1 \times 1 \times 200 = 200$	10	190
2002	Lens	$1 \times 1 \times 200 = 200$	22	178
2003	Bulb assembly	$1 \times 1 \times 200 = 200$	10	190
2004	Reflector	$1 \times 1 \times 200 = 200$	10	190
2005	Shell assembly	$1 \times 1 \times 200 = 200$	0	200
2006	Spring	$1 \times 1 \times 200 = 200$	50	150
3001	Bulb	$1 \times 1 \times 1 \times 200 = 200$	10	190
3002	Bulb holder	$1 \times 1 \times 1 \times 200 = 200$	10	190
3003	On-off switch	$1 \times 1 \times 1 \times 200 = 200$	15	185
3004	Connector bars	$2 \times 1 \times 1 \times 200 = 400$	0	400
3005	Plastic shell	$1 \times 1 \times 1 \times 200 = 200$	0	200
4001	Plastic powder	$(1 \times 1 \times 1 \times 200) + (3 \times 1 \times 1 \times 1 \times 200) - 10 = 790$	0	790
4002	Knob	$1 \times 1 \times 1 \times 1 \times 200 = 200$	15	185
4003	Metal slides	$2 \times 1 \times 1 \times 1 \times 200 = 400$	30	370

Gross requirements are the total quantities needed to produce the 200 flashlights, whereas *net* requirements are the quantities needed in addition to existing inventory levels (or scheduled receipts). The net requirements must therefore take into account the components already assembled (or hidden) in completed assemblies.

We shall first determine the gross requirements by taking account of all dependencies. For example, the gross requirements of connector bars (no. 3004) are (2 connector bars per shell assembly) times (1 shell assembly per body assembly) times (1 body assembly per flashlight) times (200 flashlights), or $2 \times 1 \times 1 \times 200 = 400$. See Table 13-6.

Then we compute the on-hand inventory by totaling both the individual stock items on hand plus any units of the same item that are already in subassemblies or assemblies. For example, the on-hand inventory of lenses consists of 12 lenses in stock plus 10 lenses already installed in the head assemblies. Requirements will be computed on a level-by-level basis so that components used in more than one subassembly (such as the plastic powder, no. 4001) can be combined.

13.6 The product structure tree for X is as shown in Fig. 13-10, with the number of units required shown in parentheses. What quantities of E, J, and K are required to complete 500 units of X?

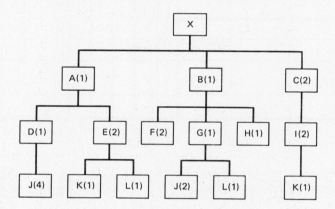

Fig. 13-10

Working from the top (highest level) down, we have:

A: (1)(number of X's) = 1(500) = 500

B: (1)(number of X's) = 1(500) = 500

C: (2)(number of X's) = 2(500) = 1,000

D: (1)(number of A's) = 1(500) = 500

E: (2)(number of A's) = 2(500) = 1,000

F: (2)(number of B's) = 2(500) = 1,000

G: (1)(number of B's) = 1(500) = 500

H: (1)(number of B's) = 1(500) = 500

I: (2)(number of C's) = 2(1,000) = 2,000

J: (4)(number of D's) + (2)(number of G's) = 4(500) + 2(500) = 3,000

K: (1)(number of E's) + (1)(number of I's) = 1(1,000) + 1(2,000) = 3,000

L: (1)(number of E's) + (1)(number of G's) = 1(1,000) + 1(500) = 1,500

Quantities for E, J, and K are 1,000, 3,000, and 3,000, respectively.

MRP LOGIC

13.7 Complete the material-requirements plan for item X shown in Fig. 13-11. Note that this item has an independent demand that necessitates that a safety stock of 40 units be maintained.

Order quantity = 70
Lead time = 4 weeks
Safety stock = 40

		Week											
		1	2	3	4	5	6	7	8	9	10	11	12
Projected requirements		20	20	25	20	20	25	20	20	30	25	25	25
Receipts			70										
On hand at end of period	65												
Planned order release													

Fig. 13-11

The material-requirements plan for end item X is shown in Fig. 13-12.

Order quantity = 70
Lead time = 4 weeks
Safety stock = 40

		Week											
		1	2	3	4	5	6	7	8	9	10	11	12
Projected requirements		20	20	25	20	20	25	20	20	30	25	25	25
Receipts			70			70			70			70	
On hand at end of period	65	45	95	70	50	100 / 30	75	55	105 / 25	75	50	95 / 25	70
Planned order release		70			70			70					

Fig. 13-12

13.8 Clemson Industries produces products X and Y, which have demand, safety stock, and product structure levels as shown in Fig. 13-13. The on-hand inventories are as follows: X = 100, Y = 30, A = 70, B = 0, C = 200, and D = 800. The lot size for A is 250, and the lot size for D is 1,000 (or multiples of these amounts); all the other items are specified on a lot-for-lot (LFL) basis (that is, the quantities are the same as the net requirements). The only scheduled receipts are 250 units of X due in period 2. Determine the order quantities and order release dates for all requirements using an MRP format.

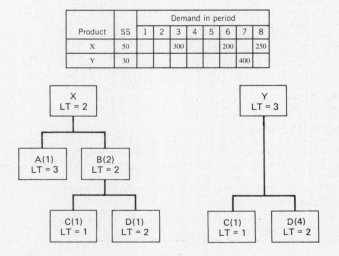

		Demand in period							
Product	SS	1	2	3	4	5	6	7	8
X	50			300			200		250
Y	30							400	

X
LT = 2

A(1)
LT = 3

B(2)
LT = 2

C(1)
LT = 1

D(1)
LT = 2

Y
LT = 3

C(1)
LT = 1

D(4)
LT = 2

Fig. 13-13

	1	2	3	4	5	6	7	8

X: OQ = LFL, LT = 2, SS = 50

		1	2	3	4	5	6	7	8
Projected requirements				300			200		250
Receipts			250				200	250	
On hand at end of period	100	100	350	50	50	50	50 / −150	50	50 / −200
Planned order release					200		250		

Y: OQ = LFL, LT = 3, SS = 30

		1	2	3	4	5	6	7	8
Projected requirements								400	
Receipts								400	
On hand at end of period	30	30	30	30	30	30	30	30	30
Planned order release					(400)				

A: OQ = 250, LT = 3

		1	2	3	4	5	6	7	8
Projected requirements					200		250		
Receipts					250		250		
On hand at end of period	70	70	70	70	120 / −130	120	120	120	120
Planned order release			250		250				

B: OQ = LFL, LT = 2

		1	2	3	4	5	6	7	8
Projected requirements					400		500		
Receipts					400		500		
On hand at end of period	0	0	0	0	0 / −400	0	0 / −500	0	0
Planned order release			(400)		(500)				

C: OQ = LFL, LT = 1

		1	2	3	4	5	6	7	8
Projected requirements				400		900			
Receipts				200		900			
On hand at end of period	200	200	0 / −200	0	0 / −900	0	0	0	0
Planned order release			200		900				

D: OQ = 1,000, LT = 2

		1	2	3	4	5	6	7	8
Projected requirements				400		2,100			
Receipts						2,000			
On hand at end of period	800	800	400	400	300 / −1,700	300	300	300	300
Planned order release			2,000						

Fig. 13-14

First, establish the codes (lowest level) applicable to each product as shown in Table 13-7. Items C and D appear both at level 1 in product Y and at level 2 in product X, so they are assigned to level 2. Thus their requirements are not netted out until all level 0 and 1 requirements have been netted out.

Table 13-7

Item	Low-level Code
X	0
Y	0
A	1
B	1
C	2
D	2

Next, set up an MRP format for all items (see Fig. 13-14), and enter the end-item gross requirements for X and Y. They both have low-level codes of 0 and so can be netted out using order quantities that match their requirements (preserving safety stocks, of course). This results in planned order releases of 200 and 250 units for X (periods 4 and 6) and 400 units of Y (period 4).

Next, explode the planned order releases for X and Y (that is, multiply them by the quantities required of the level-1 items, A and B). (Note that C and D are not level-1 items.) Projected requirements for A (200 and 250 units) are direct results of the planned order releases for X. Two units of B are required for each X, so item B's projected requirements in periods 4 and 6 are 400 and 500, respectively. Items A and B are then netted, and the order release dates and amounts are set.

Next, explode the level-2, planned-order releases to the level 3 items. The arrows in Fig. 13-14 show that requirements for C and D come from planned-order releases for both B and Y. End item Y requires 4 units of D, so the projected requirements in period 4 are 2,100 units, with 1,600 from Y (that is, 4×400) and 500 from B. Together, they generate a planned-order release for 2,000 units of D in period 2.

LOT SIZING: PART-PERIOD ALGORITHM (PPA)

13.9 The ordering cost to order an item is \$225 and carrying cost is \$.75 per period. Net requirements per month are as shown in Table 13-8. Use the part-period algorithm to determine the size and timing of orders.

Table 13-8

Month	1	2	3	4	5	6	7	8	9
Requirement	250	150	300	150	100	400	250	200	300

First, express the *ordering cost* in terms of an equivalent number of part-periods of carrying cost by dividing the order cost, C_O, by the carrying cost, C_C.

$$\text{PPA order cost} = \text{PPA } C_O = \frac{C_O}{C_C} = \frac{\$225}{\$.75} = 300 \text{ part-periods}$$

Next, express the *carrying cost* in terms of part periods by assigning one part-period cost for each time period a unit is held in stock (i.e., weight each unit by the number of periods it is carried).

$$\text{PPA carrying cost} = \text{PPA } C_C = 0/\text{unit if units used during period they arrive}$$
$$= 1/\text{unit for units carried forward 1 period}$$
$$= 2/\text{unit for units carried forward 2 periods, etc.}$$

Next, cumulate requirements until the part-period carrying cost PPA C_C is as close as possible to the part-period ordering cost PPA C_O. Do not divide a period's requirements. Begin with an order to be received in period 1 for the period-1 requirements. Multiply the number of units required times PPA C_O of zero, and add other periods (appropriately weighted).

Cumulate requirements until Σ PPA C_C is closest to 300.

	Month 1	Month 2	Month 3
No. required $\times$ PPA C_c	$250 \times 0 = 0$	$150 \times 1 = 150$	$300 \times 2 = 600$
Cumulative total	0	150	750

The value nearest 300 is 150 (see Month 2). The first order will include requirements for months 1 and 2 only (400 units).

Next, continue by reassigning the next (unfilled) order a PPA C_C of zero, and repeat the previous step until the allocation is complete. For convenience we can arrange the results of this procedure in table form, where each additional row identifies another order. See Table 13-9.

Table 13-9

Order No.	Month No. req'd.	1 250	2 150	3 300	4 150	5 100	6 400	7 250	8 200	9 300
1	No. $\times$ PPA C_C Cum. Total	250×0 0	150×1 150	300×2 750						
2	No. $\times$ PPA C_C Cum. Total			300×0 0	150×1 150	100×2 350				
3	No. $\times$ PPA C_C Cum. Total						400×0 0	250×1 250	200×2 650	
4	No. $\times$ PPA C_C cum. Total								200×0 0	300×1 300
Order size		400		550			650		500	

Conclusion: Order 400 units in period 1, 550 in period 3, 650 in period 6, and 500 in period 8.

CRP ACTIVITIES: INFINITE AND FINITE LOADING

13.10 A work center operates 6 days per week on a two-shift-per day basis (8 hours per shift) and has four machines with the same capability. If the machines are utilized 75 percent of the time at a system efficiency of 90 percent, what is the rated output in standard hours per week?

$$\text{Rated capacity} = \begin{pmatrix} \text{number of} \\ \text{machines} \end{pmatrix} \begin{pmatrix} \text{machine} \\ \text{hours} \end{pmatrix} \begin{pmatrix} \text{percentage of} \\ \text{utilization} \end{pmatrix} \begin{pmatrix} \text{system} \\ \text{efficiency} \end{pmatrix} \qquad (13.3)$$

$$= (4)(8 \times 6 \times 2)(.75)(.90) = 259 \text{ standard hr/week}$$

13.11 The Metric Instrument Company Ltd. uses an MRP system and plans to adjust capacity when the cumulative deviation exceeds one-half of the forecasted average per week. They have calculated capacity requirements per week for their testing laboratory over the next 8 weeks as shown in Table 13-10.

(a) Formulate a capacity-requirements plan showing the average requirement as a dotted line.

(b) Assume actual requirements for the first 5 weeks were 390, 460, 280, 510, and 550, and compute the cumulative deviation of (actual − planned) hours.

Table 13-10

Week	Hours	Week	Hours
1	400	5	420
2	380	6	410
3	210	7	500
4	530	8	350

(c)   Would these types of actual requirements necessitate any adjustments?

(a)   See Fig. 13-15. Average Requirement = 400 hr/wk.

Capacity-Requirements Plan

(Testing Lab in Standard Labor Hours)

Week	Hours	Week	Hours
1	400	5	420
2	380	6	410
3	210	7	500
4	530	8	350

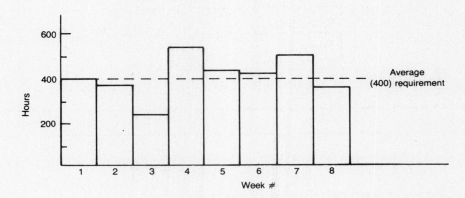

Fig. 13-15

(b)   See Fig. 13-16.

Report of Cumulative Deviation

Week number	1	2	3	4	5	6	7	8
Planned hours	400	400	400	400	400	400	400	400
Actual hours	390	460	280	510	550			
Cumulative deviation	−10	50	−70	40	190			

Fig. 13-16

(c)   No, the cumulative deviation would have to reach $400 \div 2 = 200$ hours, but is only 190 hours by the end of the 5th week.

Supplementary Problems

13.12 By using a time-phased plan for component inventories, a firm can reduce average inventory levels from 105 units to 42.5 units. If the average component value is $12 and the reduction applies to 4,000 components, how much of a savings would result? Use inventory carrying costs of 30 percent per year.   *Ans.* $900,000 per year

13.13 Determine the net requirements for the three items shown in Table 13-11.

Table 13-11

	Switches	Microprocessors	Keyboards
Projected (gross) requirements	55	14	28
On-hand inventory	18	2	7
Inventory on order (scheduled receipts)	12	12	10

Ans. 25 switches, 0 microprocessors, 11 keyboards

13.14 Given the product structure tree shown in Fig. 13-17 and the inventory shown in Table 13-12, compute the net requirements for A, B, C, D, and E to produce 50 units of X.

Table 13-12

Component	A	B	C	D	E
Inventory on hand and on order	20	10	15	30	100

Ans.   A = 30, B = 40, C = 45, D = 0, E = 60

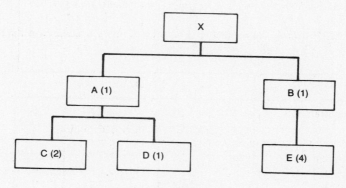

Fig. 13-17

13.15 Given the product structure tree shown in Fig. 13-18, compute the net requirements to produce 100 units of subassembly A. No stock is on hand or on order.
Ans.   400 C's, 200 D's, 400 G's, 400 J's, 800 H's

13.16 Given the product structure tree shown in Fig. 13-18 of Prob. 13.15, what net amounts of C are required to produce 200 units of X? The only on-hand inventory is 50 units of subassembly B and 30 units of subassembly F.   *Ans.* 4,880

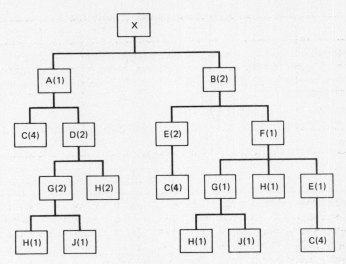

Fig. 13-18

13.17 End item X is assembled from three major assemblies, A, B, and C. Subassembly A consists of two units of D, two units of E, and one F. To make B, component G and three units of H are needed. Subassembly C requires two units of J and one F. Component D requires two units of J and one unit of K. Construct a product structure tree for X and determine what quantities of A, B, C, D, E, F, G, H, J, and K are required to produce 100 units of X?

   Ans. Requires 100 units each of A, B, C, and G; 200 units of D, E, F, and K; 300 units of H; and 600 units of J.

13.18 A skateboard consists of one baseplate and two wheel assemblies. Each wheel assembly comprises 1 mounting bracket, 1 axle, and 2 wheels. Each wheel has 1 bearing and 1 steel shell. (*a*) Draw the product structure tree showing the BOM levels. (*b*) Assume the firm has an order for 300 skateboards and has 200 completed skateboards on hand, plus 40 wheel assemblies and 50 bearings. How many *more* bearings (net requirements) are needed?

   Ans. (*a*) Skateboard = level 0; baseplate(1) and wheel assembly(2) = level 1; mounting bracket(1), axle(1), and wheels(2) = level 2; bearing(1) and shell(1) = level 3 (*b*) 270 bearings

13.19 Complete the MRP format shown in Fig. 13-19. How many units are on hand at the end of period 8? OQ = 200 and LT = 3 weeks.   *Ans.*   85 units

Week		1	2	3	4	5	6	7	8
Projected requirements		40	85	10	60	130	110	50	170
Receipts									
On hand at end of period	140								
Planned order release									

Fig. 13-19

13.20 Given the forecast requirements for end item Y shown in Fig. 13-20, complete the material-requirements plan. Note that a scheduled receipt of 60 units is due in period 2 and a safety stock of 25 is to be maintained. LT = 25 weeks and OQ = 60 units.

   Ans. Planned order releases of 60 units in periods 2, 5, and 8

Week		1	2	3	4	5	6	7	8	9	10
Projected requirements		20	20	20	30	20	20	20	25	20	35
Receipts			60								
On hand at end of period	50										
Planned order release											

Fig. 13-20

13.21 A master scheduler would like to determine whether an order for 200 units of product A can be supplied in period 8. See Fig. 13-21. No stock of any components is on hand or on order, and all order sizes are lot-for-lot. Determine the amount and date of the planned order releases for all components.

Ans. 400 B in period 5, 1,600 C in period 4 and 400 in period 6, 400 D in period 1, 1,600 E in period 2 and 400 in period 4, 1,600 F in period 3 and 400 in period 5

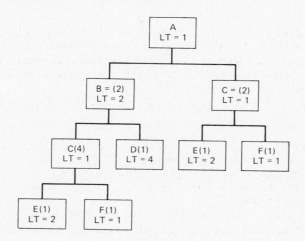

Fig. 13-21

13.22 Industrial Supply Co. produces a maintenance and repair parts cart (MRP cart) for use in warehouses. The cart design and product structure are shown in Fig. 13-22. The firm has 2 axles (number 2005) and 1 wheel assembly (number 2006) in stock. They have an order for 3 carts in period 10. Use an MRP format with lot-for-lot ordering (i.e., order the exact number of units required), and determine the order size and order release period for all components.   *Ans.*   See Table 13-13.

Table 13-13

Item	Quantity	Release Date	Item	Quantity	Release Date
Cart (C099)	3	wk 8	Support (2004)	6	wk 5
Bed (1001)	3	wk 7	Axle (2005)	4	wk 5
Frame (1002)	3	wk 6	Wheel assembly (2006)	11	wk 3
W&A assembly (1003)	6	wk 6	Tire (3001)	11	wk 1
Ring (2001)	3	wk 5	Wheel (3002)	11	wk 1
Handle (2002)	3	wk 5	Bearing (3003)	11	wk 1
Grip (2003)	6	wk 4	Cap (3004)	11	wk 1

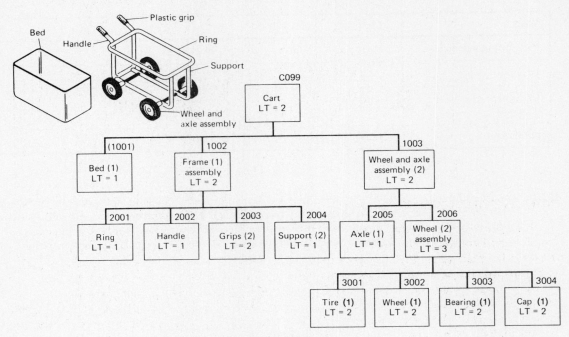

Fig. 13-22

13.23 The cost for placing an item on order is $90, and the carrying charge is $.45 per month. Net requirements per month are as shown in Table 13-14. Use the part-period algorithm to determine the size and timing of orders.

Table 13-14

Month	1	2	3	4	5	6	7	8
Requirement	180	150	250	450	125	50	200	210

Ans.   Order 330 units in period 1, 250 in period 3, 625 in period 4, and 410 in period 7

13.24 An office furniture manufacturer has a work center with 3 metal presses which are each operated $7\frac{1}{2}$ hours per shift on a 3-shift-per-day, 6-day-per-week basis. The presses are allocated to furniture production 80 percent of the time, with the remainder reserved for special-order jobs. If the machine efficiency is 95 percent, what is the rated output for furniture production in standard hours per week?
Ans.   308 hours

Chapter 14

Production Activity Scheduling and Control

Assignment Linear Programming, Dynamic Programming

PRIORITY AND CAPACITY CONTROL

Production-activity controls (PAC) are the priority and capacity management techniques used to schedule and control production operations. *Priority control* ensures that production activities follow the priority plan (e.g., the material-requirements plan) by controlling the orders to vendors and in-house production shops. *Capacity control* helps by monitoring work centers to ensure they are providing the amount of labor and equipment time that is necessary (and was planned) to do the scheduled work. Although the material in this chapter applies most directly to manufacturing facilities, many of the concepts apply equally well to service systems. Services are consumed as they are produced, so no inventories can accumulate. Nevertheless, the concepts of priority (e.g., of medical care in hospitals) and capacity control (e.g., in the utilization of operating rooms) still apply.

Figure 14-1 identifies the major PAC functions. The *priority-control system* is concerned with the relative status and the sequencing of jobs in work centers; activities include *order release*, *dispatching* (or scheduling work), and *status control*. As orders, due dates, and quantities change, the priority-control system should constantly reflect valid priorities—whether higher or lower than previously planned.

The *capacity-control system* is concerned with the load (standard hours) on production facilities. Capacity-control activities include *lead-time control*, *balance* of workload, and *input-output control*. By controlling the load on individual work centers, manufacturing lead times can be controlled and capacities can be better utilized. See Table 14-1 for definitions of PAC terms.

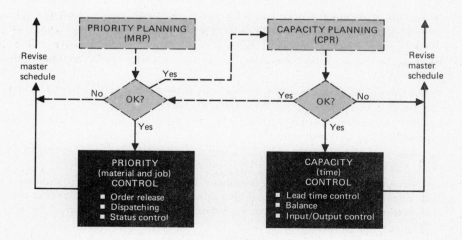

Fig. 14-1 Priority- and capacity-control activities

279

Table 14-1 Production Activity Control Terms*

1. *Control* (as related to the type of system):

   Flow. Control of *continuous operations* by setting common production rates for all items, feeding work into the system at a specified rate, and monitoring the rate.

   Order. Control of *intermittent operations* by monitoring the progress of each individual order through successive operations in its production cycle.

2. *Control* (as related to jobs and time):

   Priority. Control over the status of jobs and work activities by specifying the order in which materials or jobs are assigned to work centers.

   Capacity. Control over the labor and machine *time* used for jobs and work activities by planning and monitoring the time requirements of key work centers.

3. *Critical ratio.* A dynamic scheduling technique. Priority index numbers are calculated for ranking jobs according to which are in most urgent need of work time so that orders can be shipped on schedule.

4. *Dispatching.* Selecting and sequencing jobs to be run at individual work centers and actually authorizing or assigning the work to be done. The dispatch list is the primary means of priority control.

5. *Expediting.* Finding discrepancies between planned and actual work output, and correcting them by attempting to speed up the processing in less than the normal lead time.

6. *Input control.* Control over the work being sent to a supplying facility, whether this is the shop itself or an outside vendor.

7. *Lead time.* The period between the decision to release an order and the completion of the first units. Includes wait, move, setup, queue, and run time.

8. *Line of balance.* A charting technique that uses lead times and assembly sequencing to compare planned component completions with actual component completions.

9. *Loading.* Assigning hours of work to work centers in accordance with the available capacity of the work centers.

   Finite capacity. Rescheduling work into other periods if insufficient capacity exists in the required time period.

   Infinite capacity. Assigning work to the given time period whether or not sufficient capacity exists.

10. *Output control.* Dispatching, expediting, and any other follow-up necessary to get scheduled work from a work center or vendor.

11. *Priority decision rules.* Rules used by a dispatcher to determine the sequence in which jobs will be done.

12. *Routing.* Determining which machines or work centers will be used to manufacture a particular item. Routing is specified on a route sheet; the route sheet identifies operations to perform, sequence, and possibly materials, tolerances, tools, and time allowances.

13. *Scheduling.* Setting operation start dates for jobs so that they will be completed by their due date.

    Forward scheduling. Starting with a known start date and proceeding from the first operation to the last to determine the completion date.

    Backward scheduling. Starting with a given due date and working backward to determine the required start date.

14. *Setup time.* The time required to adjust a machine and attach the proper tooling to make a particular product.

15. *Shop order* (*manufacturing order*). A document conveying the authority to produce a specific quantity of a given item. It may also show the materials and machines to use, the sequence of operations, and the due dates that have been assigned by the scheduler.

16. *Work center.* An area or work station where a particular type of work is performed.

*The definitions are taken largely from the *American Production and Inventory Control Society* (*APICS*) *Dictionary*, 5th ed., 1984 (modified and/or condensed).

PAC OBJECTIVES AND DATA REQUIREMENTS

The PAC system should provide accurate information on (1) the current status of jobs (e.g., what orders are in process and where), (2) upcoming jobs, (3) the adequacy of materials and capacities, (4) equipment and labor utilization, and (5) job progress and efficiency. The use of a PAC system requires realistic, understandable, and timely information. Table 14-2 summarizes some of the data requirements for a PAC system. In addition, *routing files* are used to specify what is to be done (operation), where it is to be done (work center), and how long it should take (standard time). Online computer systems give planners the added flexibility of easily and quickly replanning and making last-minute schedule modifications, which enable them to work with actual order information (if available) rather than forecast data.

Table 14-2   Planning and Control Data for PAC

	Priority Data	Capacity Data
Planning information	Item number and description Lot size and manufacturing lead time Quantity on hand, allocated, and on order	Work center (WC) number and capacity Alternative WC's Efficiency, utilization, and queue times
Control information	Shop order number Priority and due date Order quantity and balance due Quantity completed, scrapped, and disbursed	Operation number Set-up and run time Quantity done and scrapped Date due and lead time remaining

SCHEDULING STRATEGY AND GUIDELINES

Although scheduling actually begins with the aggregate plan and master production schedule, the priority-control activities of releasing orders and assigning work to be done (dispatching) are also often referred to as scheduling. The type and level of detail in scheduling depends largely on the type of production system, as summarized in Table 14-3. *Continuous systems* produce a limited class of products at fixed rates on assembly lines that usually follow fixed paths of manufacturing. The problems of order release, dispatching, and monitoring the work status are less complex than in intermittent systems.

Intermittent and *job-shop systems* typically produce batches or a wide variety of products on the same facilities. Each order may be individually routed to its unique combination of work centers. The variable work-flow paths and processing times generate queues and work-in-process inventories which require significantly greater production-activity controls.

Scheduling strategies differ widely among firms and range from very detailed scheduling to no scheduling at all. Detailed schedules of specific jobs on specific equipment at specified times far in the future are usually impractical. A cumulative scheduling of total workload is useful for long-range planning of approximate capacity needs. For continuous systems, production rates can be firmed up as the master schedule is implemented. In some cases, specific end items (or options) need only be designated on the assembly bill of materials a few hours before production takes place. Some flexible production systems can even respond almost online to individual requirements.

For intermittent systems, schedules may be planned on the basis of the estimated total labor and equipment (standard hours) requirements per week at key work centers. If detailed scheduling is desirable, capacity may then be allocated to specific jobs as late as a week, or a few days, before the actual work is to be performed. However, detailed scheduling is not always necessary.

In addition to the *cumulative* and *cumulative-detailed combination* methods, a third strategy involves the use of *priority decision rules*. Priority decision rules are heuristic guidelines, such as *first*

Table 14-3 Characteristics of Scheduling Systems

	High Volume	Intermediate Volume		Low Volume
Type of production system	Continuous (flow operations)	Intermittent (flow and batch operations)	Job Shop (batch or single jobs)	Project (single jobs)
Key characteristics	• Specialized equipment • Same sequence of operations unless guided by microprocessors and/or "smart" robots	• Mixture of equipment • Similar sequence for each batch	• General purpose equipment • Unique sequence for each job	• Mixture of equipment • Unique sequence and location for each job
Design concerns	• Line balancing • Changeover time and cost	• Line and worker-machine balance • Changeover time and cost	• Worker-machine balance • Capacity utilization	• Allocating resources to minimize time and cost
Operational concerns	• Material shortages • Equipment breakdowns • Quality problems • Product mix and volume	• Material and equipment problems • Set-up costs and run lengths • Inventory accumulations (run-out times)	• Job sequencing • Work center loading • Work flow and work in process	• Meeting time schedule • Meeting budgeted costs • Resource utilization

come, first served, which are alternatives to more detailed capacity planning. However, priority rules are also used in conjunction with cumulative and detailed scheduling methods.

Table 14-4 lists some general guidelines for scheduling jobs and loading facilities. Releasing all available jobs (number 4) as they are received is a common cause of increased manufacturing lead times and excess work in process. Good scheduling systems will release work at a reasonable rate that will keep unnecessary backlogs from the production floor and minimize customer waiting time. In service systems, the release of jobs can be more difficult because the incoming flow of orders (customers) and the service times often have more variability than in goods manufacturing.

Table 14-4 Scheduling and Loading Guidelines

1. Provide a realistic schedule.
2. Allow adequate time *for* operations.
3. Allow adequate time *before*, *between*, and *after* operations.
4. Don't release all available jobs to the shop.
5. Don't schedule all available capacity in the shop.
6. Load only selected work centers.
7. Make orderly changes when necessary.
8. Gear shop responsibility to the schedule.

FORWARD VERSUS BACKWARD SCHEDULING

Forward scheduling is akin to releasing all available jobs to the shop in that it begins as soon as requirements are known. This immediate release can result in early completion of a job at a possible cost of more work in process, and in higher inventory carrying costs than necessary. Backward (or *set back*) scheduling uses the same lead-time offset logic as MRP. Components are delivered "when needed" rather than "as soon as possible."

Example 14.1 A job due at the end of period 12 requires a 2-period lead time for material acquisition, 1 period of run time for operation 1, 2 periods for operation 2, and 1 period for final assembly. Allow 1 period of transit time prior to each operation. Illustrate the completion schedule under (*a*) forward and (*b*) backward scheduling approaches.

Forward scheduling (*a*) is shown above the time period line, and backward scheduling (*b*) below the line in Fig. 14-2.

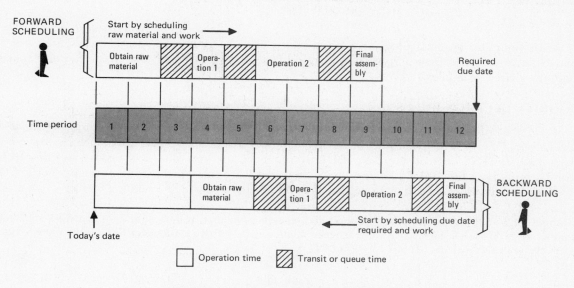

Fig. 14-2 Forward and backward scheduling

Three general classes of scheduling methodologies are (1) charts and graphs, (2) priority decision rules, and (3) mathematical programming methods.

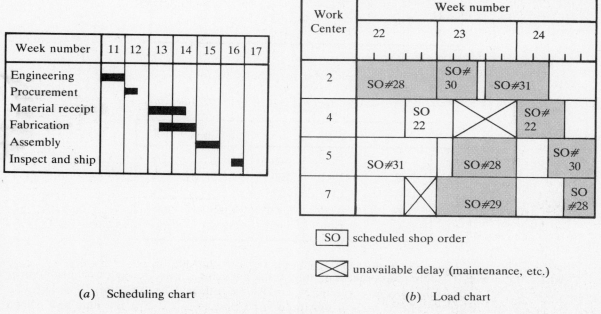

(*a*) Scheduling chart   (*b*) Load chart

Fig. 14-3

SCHEDULING CHARTS AND GRAPHS

Gantt charts are bar charts that depict the schedule of work or load on facilities over a time horizon. *Scheduling* (or *progress*) *charts* depict the sequential work activities necessary to complete a job. *Load charts* show the work-hours assigned to a group of workers or machines.

Example 14.2   Illustrate (*a*) a scheduling chart and (*b*) a load chart.

See Fig. 14-3.

With computer graphics programs, Gantt charts can vividly portray the plans and status of all jobs in process. If the firm's information system is adequately designed, the charts can also readily generate revised schedules.

PRIORITY DECISION RULES

Priority decision rules are simplified guidelines (heuristics) for determining the sequence in which jobs will be done. The simplest rules assign jobs on the basis of a single criterion such as: first come, first served (FCFS), earliest due date (EDD), least slack (or time due, less processing) time (LS), shortest processing time (SPT), longest processing time (LPT), and preferred customer order (PCO). Most single-criterion rules are static in that they do not incorporate an updating feature.

Example 14.3   Shown in Table 14-5 are the time remaining (number of days until due) and work remaining (number of days) for five jobs which were assigned a letter as they arrived. Sequence the jobs by priority rules: (*a*) FCFS, (*b*) EDD, (*c*) LS, (*d*) SPT, and (*e*) LPT.

Table 14-5

Job	Number of Days until Due	Number of Days of Work Remaining
A	8	7
B	3	4
C	7	5
D	9	2
E	6	6

See Table 14-6. The numerical amounts included in parentheses are for reference only.

Table 14-6

	FCFS	EDD	LS	SPT	LPT
1st	A	B(3)	B(-1)	D(2)	A(7)
2d	B	E(6)	E(0)	B(4)	E(6)
3d	C	C(7)	A(1)	C(5)	C(5)
4th	D	A(8)	C(2)	E(6)	B(4)
5th	E	D(9)	D(7)	A(7)	D(2)

Johnson's rule yields a minimum processing time for sequencing *n* jobs through two machines or work centers where the same processing sequence must be followed by all jobs. Jobs with the shortest processing times are placed early if that processing time is on the first machine and placed late if that processing time is on the second machine. This procedure maximizes the concurrent operating time of both work centers.

Example 14.4 Wonderloaf Bakery has orders for five specialty jobs (A, B, C, D, and E) that must be processed sequentially through two work centers (baking and decoration). The amount of time (in hours) required for the jobs is shown in the table below. Determine the schedule sequence that minimizes the total elapsed time for the five jobs, and present it in the form of a Gantt chart.

Work Centers	Time Required for Job (hours)				
	A	B	C	D	E
1 (Baking)	5	4	8	7	6
2 (Decoration)	3	9	2	4	10

Johnson's rule says to identify the shortest processing time. If it is at the first work center, place the (entire) job as early as possible. If it is at the second work center, place the job as late as possible. Eliminate that job from further consideration, and apply the decision rule to the remaining jobs. Break any ties between jobs by sequencing the job on the first work center earliest and that on the second work center latest. Jobs having the same time at both work centers can be assigned at either end of the available sequence. See Fig. 14-4.

(a) The shortest time is for job C in work center 2 (2 hours). Place job C as late as possible.

				C

(b) The next shortest time is for job A in work center 2. Place job A as late as possible.

			A	C

(c) The next shortest time is a tie between jobs B and D. Sequence the job on the first work center (job B) as early as possible.

B			A	C

(d) The next shortest time is for job D in work center 2. Place the job as late as possible.

B		D	A	C

(e) Place job E in the remaining opening.

B	E	D	A	C

The sequential times are as follows:

Work Center 1	4	6	7	5	8
Work Center 2	9	10	4	3	2

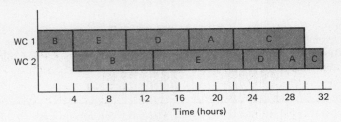

Fig. 14-4

Critical ratio (CR) is a dynamic dispatching rule that yields a priority index number that expresses the time remaining/work remaining ratio. It can be constantly updated (often daily) with a computer to provide close control. If the CR is less than 1.0, the job is behind schedule; if the CR = 1.0, the job is on schedule; and if the CR is larger than 1.0, the job has some slack.

$$CR = \frac{\text{time remaining}}{\text{work remaining}} = \frac{TR}{WR} \qquad (14.1)$$

where   TR = date due − date now = DD − DN

   WR = lead (work) time remaining = LTR

Example 14.5   Today is day 22 on the production-control calendar, and four jobs are on order as shown. Determine the critical ratio for each job, and assign priority ranks.

Job	Date Due	Workdays Remaining
A	28	8
B	26	2
C	24	2
D	30	12

See Table 14-7.

Table 14-7

Job	Time Remaining (DD − DN)	Work Remaining (LTR)	$CR = \dfrac{DD - DN}{LTR}$	Priority
A	28 − 22 = 6	8	.75	2
B	26 − 22 = 4	2	2.00	4
C	24 − 22 = 2	2	1.00	3
D	30 − 22 = 8	12	.67	1

With the critical ratio, jobs would be assigned in the order of D, A, C, and B. Job B is the only one with some slack. Jobs A and D have critical ratios of less than 1, meaning that the orders will not be shipped on time unless they are expedited. Job C, with an index of 1, is the only job on schedule.

MATHEMATICAL PROGRAMMING METHODS

Scheduling can be viewed as a complex resource allocation problem wherein firms seek to optimize a production or service objective, subject to materials, labor, and capacity constraints. The interdependencies, cost uncertainties, and necessary assumptions often make a mathematical solution difficult or tenuous. However, scheduling and production control is a very fertile area for the use of standard simplex and distribution linear programming, assignment linear programming, and dynamic programming methods. Chapter 6 described the graphic and simplex methods, which apply equally well to scheduling problems. Problems 14.6, 14.7, and 14.8 illustrate some applications of assignment linear programming and dynamic programming to scheduling problems.

PRIORITY CONTROL

The major priority-control activities, as per Fig. 14-1, are *order release, dispatching*, and *status control. Order release* converts a need from a planned order status to a real order in the shop or with a vendor by assigning it either a shop order or purchase order number.

Figure 14-5 illustrates how a planned-order release (from an MRP system) becomes an order, with a specific priority, on a dispatch list.

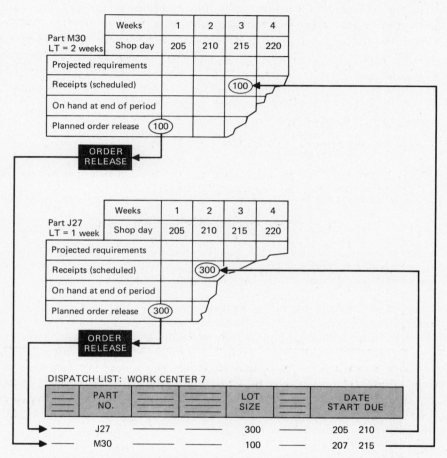

Fig. 14-5   Relationship between planned order releases and dispatch list

Scheduling is implemented via the dispatch list. It lists all jobs available to a work center and ranks them by a relative priority (for example, by due date or critical ratio). In continuous systems where all items are the same, one order release can suffice for a large production run so the scheduling function is greatly simplified. Service systems such as doctors' offices, airlines, and hotels often rely on appointment or reservation systems to set priorities.

Status control reports measure the progress of orders and show problems and changes such as internal slippages, defects, lot size errors, and anticipated delays. Bar codes on materials can simplify tracking them through a shop and speed the preparation of status reports. With high-speed data transmittal, adjustments in the master schedule and MRP system can be based on valid priorities.

CAPACITY CONTROL

The major capacity-control functions, shown in Fig. 14-1, are *lead-time control, balance*, and *input-output control*. Total *lead time* consists of the time that orders wait in unreleased backlog, plus the manufacturing lead time (the interval between when an order is released to production and when it is available for shipment). Of the manufacturing lead time, only about 10 percent (or less) is usually working, or run, time; the bulk of it is waiting, or queue, time.

For most work centers, the capacity (possible *rate* of work flow) is relatively fixed, much like flow through a funnel. If work is released to the facility at a rate faster than its output rate, both the manufacturing lead times and the work in process will increase. But output will not increase. The only result is a mounting inventory, a worsening shortage of space, lost orders, unnecessary expediting, and increased inventory carrying costs. Furthermore, priority techniques, such as red (urgent) tags, and expediting do not solve capacity problems.

Example 14.6 A farm machinery manufacturer has an output rate of 320 hours per week and has measured the load on his shop as follows:

Unreleased shop orders	640 hr
Work in process:	
Current requirements	960
Long-term orders	320
Total	1,920 hr

(*a*) Find the manufacturing lead time and (*b*) comment on the inclusion of long-term orders in the lead time.

(*a*)
$$\text{Lead time} = \frac{\text{work in process}}{\text{rate of output}} = \frac{960 \text{ hr} + 320 \text{ hr}}{320 \text{ hr/week}} = 4 \text{ weeks}$$

(*b*) Once the long-term orders are released to the shop, they become part of the work in process, and so they are included as "released backlog." If they contain only deferred requirements and are not required to keep the shop loaded, they should not have been released to the shop.

A second function of capacity control is to maintain an effective *balance* of workload against work-center capacity. Balance can often be improved by shifting work from one period to another. If the total load is off balance, additional equipment, alternate routings, or labor adjustments may be necessary.

Input-output controls are one of the most effective capacity-control devices for intermittent production systems. Output reports compare the actual hours of work delivered by a work center with the planned hours. If the cumulative deviation of actual minus planned hours exceeds some preset standard (such as 1 week's average), corrective action in the form of overtime, subcontracting, or revision of the master schedule may be called for.

Example 14.7 Shop 42 has an average capacity capability of 200 hours per week of work. Actual (standard) hours delivered during weeks 9, 10, 11, and 12 were 180, 210, 170, and 160 respectively. (*a*) Formulate an output control report showing the cumulative deviation. (*b*) The maximum allowable cumulative deviation limit is one week's average. Is corrective action called for?

(*a*) See Table 14-8.

Table 14-8 Output Control Report: Shop 42

Hours	Week Number				
	9	10	11	12	13
Actual hours	180	210	170	160	
Planned hours	200	200	200	200	200
Cumulative deviation	−20	−10	−40	−80	

(b) By the end of week 12, the cumulative deviation (−80) does not exceed the planned average (200), so no corrective action is yet required.

Output control alone does little to control lead times, however. The input to a facility must be equal to or less than the output. Thus combination input-output control reports are a more effective control device. (See Prob. 14.8.) They are structured in different ways, but the result can be interpreted as follows: If the actual minus the planned value is negative, it signifies that there was less input (or output) than planned: if it is positive, it signifies that there was more input (or output) than planned.

In service industries, such as restaurants and universities, the input-output control focuses upon the hours and customers served at the facility rather than the units produced at the work center.

Solved Problems

SCHEDULING STRATEGY AND GUIDELINES

14.1 A firm that produces athletic supplies on an intermittent production system has the production and inventory characteristics shown in Table 14-9 as of June 30th. Rank the items in terms of the urgency of scheduling replenishment inventories.

Table 14-9

Item	Inventory on Hand	Released Orders (and WIP)	Demand Rate
A (soccer balls)	20 cases	30 cases	12 cases/wk
B (volleyballs)	110 cases	—	32 cases/wk
C (basketballs)	70 cases	30 cases	40 cases/wk

One method of scheduling the production of produce-to-stock inventory is to assign the highest priority to items with the lowest *runout time*.

$$\text{Runout time} = \frac{\text{inventory on hand} + \text{orders in process}}{\text{demand rate}} \qquad (14.2)$$

$$A = \frac{20 + 30}{12} = 4.2 \text{ weeks} \qquad B = \frac{110}{32} = 3.4 \text{ weeks} \qquad C = \frac{70 + 30}{40} = 2.5 \text{ weeks}$$

The scheduling sequence should be basketballs first, then volleyballs, then soccer balls.

Table 14-10

Activity	Scheduled Start Date	Scheduled End Date	Actual End Date	Notes
Cast rod	June 28	July 5	July 6	Maintenance scheduled for July 1 took extra day
Form wires	June 29	July 7	Open	Is one-half day behind schedule
Fabricate end caps	July 5	July 7	Open	Started on July 7th
Assemble heater	July 11	July 13	Open	Assembly area unavailable on July 8th

SCHEDULING CHARTS AND GRAPHS

14.2   A foundary producing rod castings experienced the work progress shown in Table 14-10 as of July 7th. Using standard symbols, formulate a Gantt chart depicting the progress on this job.

See Fig. 14-6.

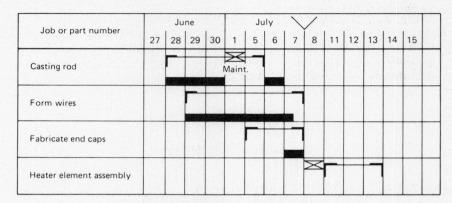

Fig. 14-6   Progress chart

14.3   The hours shown in Table 14-11 are required to complete six jobs which are routed through four work centers. The hours available at the work centers are 40 hours at number 4, 32 at number 5, 36 at number 8, and 30 at number 12. Develop a load chart for assigning the jobs to the work centers.

Table 14-11

	Hours Required at Work Center			
Job Number	4	5	8	12
A21	4	2	7	4
A22	7	—	—	8
A23	4	10	12	3
B14	—	5	6	5
B15	2	4	5	—
B16	8	1	6	7

Begin with the total time available at each work center, and subtract the time for each job to obtain a cumulative total of unused time. For example $40 - 4 = 36$, $36 - 7 = 29$, etc. See Table 14-12 and Fig. 14-7.

Table 14-12

Job Number	Work Center 4 hours		Work Center 5 hours		Work Center 8 hours		Work Center 12 hours	
	Required	Available	Required	Available	Required	Available	Required	Available
A21	4	40	2	32	7	36	4	30
A22	7	36	—	30	—	29	8	26
A23	4	29	10	30	12	29	3	18
B14	—	25	5	20	6	17	5	15
B15	2	25	4	15	5	11	—	10
B16	8	23	1	11	6	6	7	10
Unused:		15		10		0		3

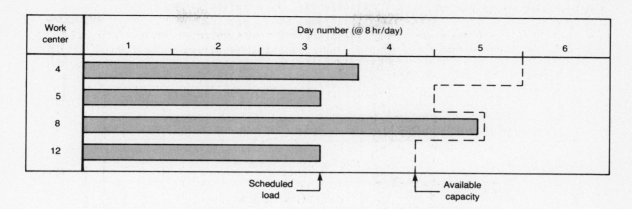

Fig. 14-7

14.4 A manufacturing coordinator has the shop orders shown in Table 14-13 due to be shipped a week (5 working days) from now. Sequence the jobs according to priority as established by (*a*) least slack and (*b*) critical ratio.

Table 14-13

Shop Order Number	427	430	432	433	435	436
Number of days of work remaining	2	4	7	6	5	3

(*a*)   The least-slack sequence is 432, 433, 435, 430, 436, 427.

(*b*) $$\text{Critical ratio} = \frac{\text{time remaining}}{\text{work remaining}} = \frac{5 \text{ days}}{\text{work remaining}} \text{ (shown in Table 14-14)}$$

Table 14-14

SO Number	427	430	432	433	435	436
CR	$\frac{5}{2} = 2.50$	$\frac{5}{4} = 1.25$	$\frac{5}{7} = .71$	$\frac{5}{6} = .83$	$\frac{5}{5} = 1.00$	$\frac{5}{3} = 1.67$

The CR sequence is 432, 433, 435, 430, 436, 427.

Note: When the time remaining is constant across all jobs, the least slack and critical ratio result in the same priority.

14.5 A job shop has 8 shop orders that must be processed sequentially through three work centers. Each job must be finished in the same sequence in which it was started. Times (in hours) required at the various work centers are as shown in Table 14-15. Use Johnson's rule to develop the job sequence that will minimize the completion time over all shop orders.

This is a special (3 WC) case of Johnson's rule, which may be used if the largest of the times at the middle work station (WC #2) is less than or equal to the smallest time required at one or both of the other two WC's. The (modified) procedure is to add the job times of WC #1 + WC #2 and of WC #2 + WC #3. Then use these combined times to solve the problem in the standard two-station approach as seen in Table 14-16.

Table 14-15

Job No.	A	B	C	D	E	F	G	H
WC #1 time	4	8	5	9	3	4	9	6
WC #2 time	6	4	7	1	4	2	5	2
WC #3 time	8	7	9	7	9	8	9	7

Table 14-16

Job No.	A	B	C	D	E	F	G	H
WC #1 + WC #2	10	12	12	10	7	6	14	8
WC #2 + WC #3	14	11	16	8	13	10	14	9

Now, the times are scanned, and the lowest value (6) is with the first combination (WC #1 + WC #2), so we place job F as early as possible. The next lowest (7) is also with the first combination, so job E goes second. Jobs D and H are tied for next, with D going as late as possible (last), and H going third. Continuing on, we have (Table 14-17):

Table 14-17

1st	2nd	3rd	4th	5th	6th	7th	8th
F	E	H	A	C	G	B	D

MATHEMATICAL PROGRAMMING METHODS

14.6 *Assignment Linear Programming.* A scheduler has four jobs that can be done on any of four machines with respective times (minutes) as shown in Table 14-18. Determine the allocation of jobs to machines that will result in minimum time.

Table 14-18

Job	Machine			
	1	2	3	4
A	5	6	8	7
B	10	12	11	7
C	10	8	13	6
D	8	7	4	3

The solution method involves five steps.

Step 1. Subtract the smallest number in each row from all others in the row, and enter the results in the form of a new matrix.

Step 2. Using the new matrix, subtract the smallest number in each column from all others in the column, again forming a new matrix.

Step 3. Check to see if there is a zero for each row and column, and draw the minimum number of lines necessary to cover all zeros in the matrix.

Step 4. If the number of lines required is less than the number of rows, modify the matrix again by adding the smallest uncovered number to all values at line intersections and subtracting it from each uncovered number, including itself. Leave the other (lined-out) numbers unchanged.

Step 5. Check the matrix again via zero-covering lines, and continue with the modification (step 3) until the optimal assignment is obtained.

The five steps result in the following (Fig. 14-8):

1. *Row subtraction*

	1	2	3	4
A	0	1	3	2
B	3	5	4	0
C	4	2	7	0
D	5	4	1	0

2. *Column subtraction*

	1	2	3	4
A	0	0	2	2
B	3	4	3	0
C	4	1	6	0
D	5	3	0	0

3. *Cover all zeros*

	1	2	3	4
A	0	0	2	2
B	3	4	3	0
C	4	1	6	0
D	5	3	0	0

4. *Modify matrix*

	1	2	3	4
A	0	0	2	3
B	2	3	2	0
C	3	0	5	0
D	5	3	0	1

5. *Cover zeros again*

	1	2	3	4
A	[0]	0	2	3
B	2	3	2	[0]
C	3	[0]	5	0
D	5	3	[0]	1

Optimum assignments

Job A to machine 1 at 5 min
Job B to machine 4 at 7 min
Job C to machine 2 at 8 min
Job D to machine 3 at 4 min

Fig. 14-8

Note that the final allocation (square boxes in step 5 above) should begin with those jobs that are limited to one machine (B and D), for once they are assigned, this may constrain the assignment of the remaining jobs (A and C).

14.7 A bank operations manager has five tellers (T) whom he must assign to customer services of checking accounts (C), foreign exchange (F), notes (N), and savings (S) accounts. Three tellers are not yet qualified for foreign exchange, and one teller cannot handle notes. Work-sampling studies have shown that, working under constant queues, the tellers can handle the number of customers per hour shown in Table 14-19. Assuming the manager wishes to serve as many customers as possible, what assignments should be made? The extra teller will be assigned a data processing task.

Table 14-19

	Customers Served per Hour			
	Checking	Foreign	Notes	Savings
T1	60	X	30	50
T2	70	60	40	50
T3	30	X	10	30
T4	40	X	X	60
T5	40	70	50	80

The number of workers does not balance the number of assignments, so we must add an extra column (call it D = data processing) and assign it a low priority (zero service) so that it will absorb the poorest teller. See Table 14-20.

Table 14-20

	C	F	N	S	D
T1	60	X	30	50	0
T2	70	60	40	50	0
T3	30	X	10	30	0
T4	40	X	X	60	0
T5	40	70	50	80	0

Since this is a maximization problem, we must first convert the matrix values to relative costs by subtracting all values from the largest number, 80, as shown in Table 14-21.

Table 14-21

	C	F	N	S	D
1	20	X	50	30	80
2	10	20	40	30	80
3	50	X	70	50	80
4	40	X	X	20	80
5	40	10	30	0	80

We then follow the same steps as we did in solving Prob. 14.6. See Fig. 14-9.

1. *Row subtraction*

	C	F	N	S	D
1	0	X	30	10	60
2	0	10	30	20	70
3	0	X	20	0	30
4	20	X	X	0	60
5	40	10	30	0	80

2. *Column subtraction*

	C	F	N	S	D
1	0	X	10	10	30
2	0	0	10	20	40
3	0	X	0	0	0
4	20	X	X	0	30
5	40	0	10	0	50

3. *Cover zeros*

	C	F	N	S	D
1	0	X	10	10	30
2	0	0	10	20	40
3	0	X	0	0	0
4	20	X	X	0	30
5	40	0	10	0	50

4. *Modify matrix*

	C	F	N	S	D
1	0	X	0	10	20
2	0	0	0	20	30
3	10	X	0	10	0
4	20	X	X	0	20
5	40	0	0	0	40

5. *Cover zeros again*

	C	F	N	S	D
1	0	X	0	10	20
2	0	0	0	20	30
3	10	X	0	10	0
4	20	X	X	0	20
5	40	0	0	0	40

Fig. 14-9

Step 5 requires five lines to cover all zeros, so a solution has been reached. Note that the maximum number of lines will never exceed the number of rows. Assigning tellers and tasks that have only one choice first, we assign T4 to S and T3 to D. We can then assign T1 to C, T2 to F, and T5 to N. See Table 14-22.

Alternatively, we could assign T2 to C, T5 to F, and T1 to N and have an equally optimal assignment as revealed by the total number of customers served per hour. See Table 14-23.

Table 14-22		Table 14-23	

Solution	
T1 at checking	= 60
T2 at foreign	= 60
T3 at data processing	= 0
T4 at savings	= 60
T5 at notes	= 50
Cust/hr	230

Alternative Solution	
T1 at notes	= 30
T2 at checking	= 70
T3 at data processing	= 0
T4 at savings	= 60
T5 at foreign	= 70
Cust/hr	230

DYNAMIC PROGRAMMING

14.8 Precision Castings has 11 orders for custom castings to be supplied during the next four weeks. Their furnaces and casting facilities are normally used for regular production of standard castings, but they can also be scheduled for use on up to four custom orders per week. Operating costs vary somewhat, depending on the number of custom jobs the firm attempts to produce each week. This is because the mold preparation, furnace heats required, inventory, and overtime requirements tend to vary. If no custom work is performed, however, the facilities are assigned an idle-time cost. Considering the various costs, as well as income from custom units, the accompanying profit matrix of Table 14-24 has been derived. Use a dynamic programming approach to schedule the production of the 11 units over the four periods in such a way as to maximize profits.

Table 14-24

Number of Units N Produced in Time Period	Profit ($00) from Producing N Units in Time Period (Week)			
	A	B	C	D
0	−4	−4	−4	−4
1	4	9	8	3
2	12	10	15	11
3	20	22	20	20
4	18	16	24	18

We will first determine the optimal production plan for period D and then work backward, following the principle that once an optimal plan has been achieved in a later period, the plan will remain optimal regardless of the schedule preceding the period. The alternatives available for period D are taken from the profit matrix above (Table 14-24, column D) and arranged diagonally in Table 14-25. Other cells in the matrix are blocked out as infeasible, for in this last period we can (and must) accumulate only the number of units produced during the period. The asterisks indicate that any one of the production amounts is a potential optimum at this point.

Table 14-25

Number of Units Produced in Period P	Cumulative Units from Period D				
	0	1	2	3	4
0	−4*				
1		3*			
2			11*		
3				20*	
4					18*

Regressing back to include the previous period C, it is possible to accumulate up to 8 units in the two periods (by producing 4 in each). The feasible accumulations are only those combinations resulting from the two periods. Thus, for example, if only 1 unit were produced in period C, it would not be possible to accumulate 6 units from periods C and D together, for D can contribute only up to 4 units. See Table 14-26.

Table 14-26

Number of Units Produced in Period C	Cumulative Units from Periods C and D								
	0	1	2	3	4	5	6	7	8
0				16	14				
1				19*	28*	26			
2				18	26	35*	33		
3				26	23	31	40*	38	
4					20	27	35	44*	42*

Similarly, a minimum of 3 units must be accumulated in periods C and D, for the total requirement is 11, and the maximum capability is of 4 each (or 8 total) from periods A and B. Thus, the cumulative cells representing quantities less than 3 are also blocked out as infeasible.

The resultant profits are computed individually for each feasible combination. For example, consider the alternative ways shown in Table 14-27 in which 3 units may be accumulated, and the profit possibilities that result. The optimum value(s) is marked with an asterisk, and thereafter it is the only profit value (and way of accumulating 3 units) that is carried forward. The computations for accumulations of 4 through 8 are performed in similar manner with resultant profits as shown.

Table 14-27

Three Units of Production		Resultant Profit		
Period C	Period D	From C	From D	Total
0	3	−4	20	16
1	2	8	11	19*
2	1	15	3	18
3	0	20	−4	16

The continued regression back to periods B and A follows a similar pattern, using optimal values from the preceding matrixes. See Table 14-28. At least $11 - 4 = 7$ units must be accumulated during the last three periods. If zero units are produced in period B, the optimal profit from accumulating the 7 units in periods C and D of 44* (from the previous C and D table) is now combined with the profit of producing zero in period $B(-4)$ given in the initial profit matrix, for a result of 40, which is entered in the new period B table (Table 14-29). Other values are similarly computed. For example, for 7 units, see Table 14-29.

Table 14-28

Number of Units Produced in Period B	Cumulative Units from Periods B, C, and D				
	7	8	9	10	11
0	40	38			
1	49	53	51		
2	45	50	54	52	
3	50*	57*	62*	66*	64*
4	35	44	51	56	60

Table 14-29

Seven Units of Production		Resultant Profit		
Period B	Periods C and D	From B	From C and D	Total
0	7	−4	44	40
1	6	9	40	49
2	5	10	35	45
3	4	22	28	50*
4	3	16	19	35

Finally, we continue until production during period A is included and derive the final table (Table 14-30) with an optimal profit of 77.

Table 14-30

Number of Units Produced in Period A	Profit from Cumulative Units from Periods A, B, C, and D
	11
0	60
1	70
2	74
3	77*
4	68

We can determine the schedule by going progressively from A to D. The optimum production in A is 3 units, leaving $11 - 3 = 8$ units for B, C, and D. Carrying the 8-unit requirement forward to period B, the optimum (57*) also happens to be 3 units. This leaves 5 units to be accumulated in stages C and D. The optimal period-C production for 5 cumulative units is 2, leaving 3 units for period D. The resulting profit can be verified from the initial profit matrix shown in Table 14-31.

Table 14-31

Period	Production	Profit
A	3	20
B	3	22
C	2	15
D	3	20
		77

Note that in some applications two or more cells may each exhibit a maximum (optimal) value. In these cases two or more paths, or production schedules, may yield the same optimal result.

CAPACITY CONTROL

14.9 Work center 4 has an average capacity of 260 hours a week, had a released backlog of 160 hours, and an unreleased backlog of 180 hours as of the beginning of week 21. The planner scheduled to work off the backlog over the next 5 weeks by scheduling a 10 percent reduction in planned input, along with 6 hours of overtime each week. Actual input and output hours for the 5 weeks were as shown in Table 14-32. Depict this situation in an input-output report for WC4, and determine the released backlog at the end of week 25.

Table 14-32

Week Number	21	22	23	24	25	26
Actual input	230	240	235	250	220	
Actual output	265	260	270	280	280	

Planned reductions were to come from:

    (1)   Reduced input: 5 wks @26 hr/wk = 130 hr

    (2)   Increased output: 5 wks @6 hr/wk =   30 hr

                                         160 hr

Table 14-33 Input-Output Report WC4

	Week Number	21	22	23	24	25	26
Input	Actual hours	230	240	235	250	220	
	Planned hours	234	234	234	234	234	260
	Cumulative deviation (actual − planned)	−4	+2	+3	+19	+5	
Output	Actual hours	265	260	270	280	280	
	Planned hours	266	266	266	266	266	260
	Cumulative deviation (actual − planned)	−1	−7	−3	+11	+25	

The initial released backlog (as of week 20) was 160 hours. Actual reductions came from (see Table 14-33):

$$
\begin{array}{ll}
(1) & \text{Reduced input:} \quad 130 - 5 = 125 \\
(2) & \text{Increased output:} \ 30 + 25 = \underline{\ 55\ } \\
& \qquad\qquad\text{Total reductions} = 180
\end{array}
$$

Net effect as of the end of week 25 was

$$160\ \text{hr} - 180\ \text{hr} = -20\ \text{hr}$$

(*Analysis*: Five more hours than planned of input were released to the shop, so the input reduction was only 125 hours, but 30 more hours than planned of output were delivered. Therefore, all the released backlog is removed. In addition, 20 hours of the original 180 hours of unreleased backlog has been worked off.)

Supplementary Problems

14.10 A piece of mining equipment requires the manufacturing times shown in Table 14-34. Each of the activities must be done sequentially, except that the steel fabrication can begin 2 weeks after purchasing begins, and the hydraulics and electrical activities can be done concurrently. Construct a Gantt scheduling chart for this job.

Table 14-34

Activity	Weeks	Activity	Weeks
1. Engineering	3	5. Electrical	4
2. Purchasing	3	6. Control	1
3. Steel fabrication	1	7. Field test	2
4. Hydraulics	2	8. Packaging	1

   Ans.   Chart should show the following activities occurring during the weeks noted: engineering (1–3), purchasing (4–6), steel fabrication (6), hydraulics (7–8), electrical (7–10), control (11), field test (12–13), package (14).

14.11 A wood pattern shop has five shop orders that must be processed through six work centers during the coming week. The capacities of the work centers (in hours) are number 9 = 40, number 10 = 20, number 11 = 20, number 12 = 20, number 13 = 20, number 14 = 30. See Table 14-35. (*a*) Is the shop capacity sufficient to complete all jobs?   (*b*) Assume that the scheduling guidelines require 4 hours of move time *between* work centers (not included above). Rank the shop orders according to the longest processing (and transit) time.

Table 14-35

Shop Order	Hours Required at Work Center					
	9	10	11	12	13	14
A	4	3	—	—	7	5
B	6	9	13	—	3	4
C	12	—	7	10	5	7
D	6	4	—	—	—	8
E	11	2	—	9	8	4

Ans. (*a*) Total shop load is 147 hours versus a capacity of 150 hours. However, work center 13 is overloaded, so it may restrict shop capacity. The balance is reasonably close, however. (*b*) With 4 hours of move time, the processing time per order is A = 31, B = 51, C = 57, D = 26, and E = 50. Therefore, the rank according to LPT is C, B, E, A, D.

14.12 The orders shown in Table 14-36 were received in a jobshop where scheduling is done by priority decision rules.

Table 14-36

Job Number	Shop Calendar Date		Production Days Required
	Received	Due	
870	317	368	20
871	319	374	30
872	320	354	10
873	326	373	25
874	333	346	15

In what sequence would the jobs be ranked according to the following decision rules: (*a*) earliest due date, (*b*) shortest processing time, (*c*) least slack, (*d*) first come, first served?
Ans. (*a*) 874, 872, 870, 873, 871 (*b*) 872, 874, 870, 873, 871 (*c*) 874, 873, 872, 871, 870 (*d*) 870, 871, 872, 873, 874

14.13 A market research firm has seven customer orders that must be processed sequentially through two activities: (1) data compilation, and (2) analysis. Estimated times (in hours) are as shown in Table 14-37.

Table 14-37

	A	B	C	D	E	F	G
(1) Data compilation	5	7	2	1	8	3	16
(2) Analysis	4	9	7	2	2	9	5

(*a*) Use Johnson's rule to develop a schedule that will permit all work to be completed in the minimum amount of time. (*b*) What is the total time required to process the seven jobs?
Ans. (*a*) Sequence is: D, C, F, B, G, A, E (*b*) 44 hours

14.14 Use Johnson's rule to determine the sequence that results in the minimum flow time for the seven jobs listed below. All jobs must follow the same sequence of machine first, and then polish. Times are in minutes.

	Time Required to Do Job						
	A	B	C	D	E	F	G
Machine	10	6	5	4	6	9	7
Polish	2	3	12	5	9	11	6

(*a*) What is the optimal sequence of jobs?   (*b*) What is the minimum time flow to finish these seven jobs?   *Ans.* (*a*) Sequence is D, C, E, F, G, B, A; (*b*) 52 minutes

14.15 A defense contractor in Chicago has six different jobs in process with delivery requirements as shown in Table 14-38. Today is day 60, and the contractor uses a critical-ratio scheduling technique. Rank the jobs according to priority, with the first being the highest.

Table 14-38

	A	B	C	D	E	F
Promised (date due)	60	72	67	72	65	70
Days of work remaining	2	2	5	4	5	6

Ans.   Priority 1st = A, 2nd = E, 3rd = C, 4th = F, 5th = D, 6th = B

14.16   Collins Heating Co. has four central-heating installations to design within an 8-week period (40 hours per week). They also have four capable designers, each of whom has been asked to estimate how long it would take to do each job. The work operations scheduler has compiled the estimates shown in Table 14-39. (*a*) Use assignment linear programming methods to determine how the jobs should be assigned so as to minimize the work time.   (*b*) Assuming that the estimates are correct, can the jobs be completed within the 8-week period without planning for overtime?   (*c*) Assuming one designer per job and no overtime, could the work be completed in 5 weeks?   (*d*) In 3 weeks?

Table 14-39

Designers	Hours to Complete Job			
	1	2	3	4
A	100	140	280	70
B	130	160	200	60
C	80	130	300	90
D	150	110	250	50

Ans.   (*a*) Assign A to 4 at 70, B to 3 at 200, C to 1 at 80, and D to 2 at 110 for 460 hours total. (*b*) Time available = (40)(4)(48) = 1,280 hours, so the jobs can be done without overtime. (*c*) Yes, no individual job requires more than 5 weeks. (*d*) No, although the total time available is (40)(4)(3) = 480 hours, there is not sufficient time (200 hours) for drafter B to complete his job in 3 weeks (i.e., $3 \times 40 = 120$ hours available).

14.17   *Dynamic Programming.* Surfside Swimming Pools has orders for six units to be produced on an overtime basis during the next 3 weeks. They must schedule at least one unit per week and can go up to three units per week. Considering their normal load, overtime costs, selling prices, and so forth, they would gain the profit shown in Table 14-40 at the various production levels. Use dynamic programming to schedule production of the six units over the 3-week period in such a way as to maximize profit from the order.

Table 14-40

No. Units Produced	Profit ($000) from Producing N Units		
	Week 1	Week 2	Week 3
1	4	3	5
2	7	10	6
3	12	12	9

Ans.   The optimum schedule is to produce: in week 1, three units for $12(000) profit; week 2, two units for $10(000) profit; week 3, one unit for $5(000) profit for a total of $27(000).

14.18   Indiana Equipment Co. has a small shop with an output capacity of 280 hours per week. The production controller has been asked to provide a delivery estimate for a sales representative in Tampa. He generally allows 3 weeks for order release to obtain materials and tooling. The current lead-time situation is as shown in Table 14-41.

Table 14-41

Unreleased backlog	1,400 hours
Active orders (except current)	540 hours
Current orders	300 hours

Assuming the controller follows a first-come, first-served policy, what is the best delivery time (in weeks) he can offer?

Ans.   During the ninth week. (*Note*: There are already 8 weeks of work (total), and the order release can be accomplished while the job is in unreleased backlog.)

14.19   The Automated Billing Equipment Co. produces electric meter reading equipment which automatically transmits meter readings to a billing center at preset times. Production controllers in the factory have estimated the standard hours of capacity requirements at an assembly work station over the next quarter as shown in Table 14-42. The company uses an MRP system with output controls designed to signal corrective action when the cumulative deviation exceeds one-half the weekly average as computed from the forecast.

Table 14-42

Week number	1	2	3	4	5	6	7	8	9	10	11	12
Estimated hours	370	340	290	350	360	410	320	350	330	340	380	360

Suppose the company plans to produce at a steady rate equal to the average estimated requirement. (*a*) Formulate an estimated-requirements graph showing the average requirement as a dotted line. (*b*) Assume that actual standard hours delivered over the first 8 weeks are 360, 310, 340, 280, 360, 300, 270, 370. Construct an output-control chart, and determine the cumulative deviation. (*c*) Is corrective action warranted? If so, when?

Ans.   (*a*) Average requirement = 350 hours (*b*) cumulative deviation at end of week 8 = −210 hours (*c*) Yes, during (or at end of) week 7, when the cumulative deviation exceeds |175| for the first time.

14.20   The following input-output report describes the status of jobs at work center 7. The unreleased backlog at the end of period 10 is 120 hours. (*a*) Compute the cumulative deviations for the charts above. (*b*) Has the backlog been worked off (eliminated) by the end of week 16? Explain. (*c*) Is the output less than or greater than planned? Why?

	Period Number	11	12	13	14	15	16
Input	Actual hours	245	220	310	280	300	285
	Planned hours	240	240	300	300	300	300
	Cumulative deviation						
Output	Actual hours	295	295	310	270	305	285
	Planned hours	300	300	300	300	300	300
	Cumulative deviation						

Ans.   (*a*) Cumulative deviation of input in period 16 is −40 and for output is also −40. (*b*) Yes, 1,640 hours were input and 1,760 hours were output, so 120 hours of backlog were worked off. (*c*) Output was 40 hours less than planned, because input was 40 hours less than planned. It appears that work center 7 did not have enough work to do.

Chapter 15

Operations Analysis of Manufacturing and Service Activities

Calculus, Learning Curves, Queuing, and Simulation

OPERATIONS ANALYSIS AND CONTROL

Operations analysis is the use of analytical and quantitative methods to systematically study data relating to the productivity of operations over time. Key elements of this definition are the (1) analytical methods, (2) data, (3) productivity, and (4) time.

(1) *Analytical methods.* The analytical methods used in operations analysis range from mathematically deterministic techniques such as calculus to highly stochastic approaches, such as Monte Carlo simulations. Many examples are described in other chapters. This chapter is limited to a brief application of four techniques: calculus, learning curves, queuing, and simulation.

(2) *Importance of data.* Any systematic analysis of operations implies an underlying body of knowledge and an availability or relevant data. The principles of economics, organizational management, and operations form the knowledge base that gives direction to the analysis of operations. The database in organizations is often part of a computerized management information system (MIS) or decision support system (DSS).

(3) *Productivity.* As a ratio of the value of outputs to the cost of inputs, productivity is a relative measure of the effectiveness of a transformation process. Although benefits and costs are commonly measured in economic values (such as dollars), other measures of productivity are useful, such as units shipped per number of employees, scheduled production compared to actual production, or units inspected per hour of employee time. Productivity measures must be both meaningful and measurable.

(4) *Focus on time.* A unifying concept underlying the analysis of ongoing operations is the focus on time. *Time* is a consistent, measured period in which availability of resources differs. When it is used effectively, we view time as profitable, but when it is used unwisely, it represents an opportunity cost. The techniques reviewed in this chapter are ways of expressing an interface of operations with time. *Calculus* is a means of describing the rate of change of activities in time. *Learning curves* depict the improvement in output over time. *Queuing theory* enables us to analyze waiting lines and service times. Finally, *simulation* is a technique for moving a system through time in an accelerated or isolated manner so that time-dependent characteristics can be studied in isolation.

Operations analysis involves abstracting a problem from the overall (macro) environment, then breaking it down into its component (micro) parts. The problem's solution must then be synthesized and implemented to complete the *macro-micro-macro* cycle. *Operations control* follows to ensure that the redesigned system (or solution) conforms to the organizational goals. Control involves measurement, feedback, comparison with a standard, and correction when necessary.

ANALYSIS OF GOODS VERSUS SERVICES SYSTEMS

Although physical goods are the tangible result of production, services generate a significant portion of the GNP in many nations (about 70 percent in the United States). *Services* are generally intangible products that convey value directly to consumers as they are produced. Production and consumption usually occur simultaneously, and no inventory accrues. Service locations tend to be decentralized to meet a highly variable demand with an output that is often customized, (e.g., restaurants and hospitals). *Equipment-based services* (e.g., electric utilities, phone companies, and mass transit systems) tend to be the most predictable and measurable—and the most subject to control. *People-based services* (e.g., entertainment, legal, and investment advisory services) are more dependent on the individual skill or knowledge levels of the provider, and have more variability in the quality of output. They are generally less measurable, less standardized, and less subject to control.

Just as some products add little or no value to the assets of a nation, so too with services. Many services are "paper" transactions that simply redistribute wealth rather than create it. For example, many real estate transactions just change ownership of goods, and lawyers use lawsuits to help settle disputes over ownership. On the other hand, a real estate transaction that facilitated the location of a new plant or a legal contract that facilitated its construction would be adding value.

Table 15-1 identifies some distinctions relevant to the analysis of goods versus services systems. Goods-producing facilities are concerned primarily with tangible *materials*, and with the quantities and qualities of the physical output. Services focus on the flows and attention given to customers, so *timing* of delivery, procedures, and environmental conditions assumes more importance. With services, customers often become an integral part of the productive environment, such as in a hospital. Exceptions exist, however, such as with auto repair and legal representation.

Table 15-1 Operations Analysis and Control in Goods versus Services Systems

Goods	Primary Area of Concern	Services
• Influenced largely by *raw materials*, *labor* supply, and *inventory* considerations	Location and layout	• Influenced strongly by location and convenience of *customers*
• Interface *with machines* • May require technical skill • Motivation is important	Human resource inputs	• Interface *with customers* • Requires more interpersonal skills • Training is important
• Number of *units*	Forecasting	• Number of *customers*
• Availability and timing of *materials* that are built into the product	Inventory management	• Availability and timing of *supplies consumed* by customer
• Gross quantities and types of *products* produced • Specific *end items* to be produced	Aggregate planning and master scheduling	• Gross quantities and types of *customers* served • Specific *types* of customers to be served
• Flow of *materials* and scheduling of *facility* time	Material and capacity planning	• Flow of *customers* and scheduling of *personnel* time
• Priority rules applied to *materials* and *jobs* • Input-output control of *hours* (and *units*) *produced*	Production activity control	• Priority rules applied to *customers* • Input-output control of *hours* (and *customers*) *served*
• Quality inherent in stored product	Quality control	• Quality in the service and process (e.g., time, environment)
• Preventive and repair activities on equipment and product	Maintenance	• Care and attention to individual performing the service

APPLICATIONS OF CALCULUS

Analysis of operations often necessitates that data be expressed and evaluated using equations or summary statistics. *Elementary mathematics* may be sufficient to describe production volumes, costs, and revenues that are constant or linearly related. For example, if output is constant at 8 units per hour, the volume y resulting from x hours of production would be $y = 8x$. A graph of volume y versus time x would be a line segment with a slope of 8, where the slope tells the change in one variable (Δy) resulting from a change in another variable (Δx). The slope value of 8 signifies that the output y increases by 8 units for each additional hour x used. If $x = 40$, then $y = 8(40) = 320$ units.

But not all business computations are that simple. For example, the production rate may improve slightly with every unit produced, so that output is not a linear function of time, but rather an exponential function of the number of units already produced (i.e., there is a learning or improvement effect). In this case, the output volume is a curvilinear function of the time to produce the first unit, and the slope of the relationship is not constant, but variable.

Calculus is a useful deterministic technique for finding the slope or length of curved functions and volumes resulting from nonlinear relationships among the variables. With nonlinear functions, the slope of the curve, or rate of change, in y relative to x varies from one point to another, depending upon the value of x. At any given point x it is equal to the slope of the line tangent to the curve at that point.

Example 15.1   Total costs for product A are linear at $\$10 + \$5x$ and are curvilinear for product B at $\$10 + \$2x^2$, where x is the number of units produced. How would you determine the rate of change in costs as volume increases from 2 units to 4 units for (*a*) product A, and (*b*) product B?

(*a*)   The rate of change in costs is measured by the slope of the cost function shown in Fig. 15-1. Because product A has a straight-line (linear) cost function, its slope ($\Delta y / \Delta x$) is constant.

$$\text{Slope} = \frac{\text{change in } y}{\text{change in } x} = \frac{\Delta y}{\Delta x} = \frac{y_2 - y_1}{x_2 - y_1} = \frac{\$30 - \$20}{4 - 2} = \frac{\$10}{2} = \$5/\text{unit}$$

(*b*)   Product B has a second-order cost function (i.e., has an x^2 value), and its slope is not constant, but depends upon the value assigned to x. The rate of change is equal to the slope of the line tangent to the curve at the corresponding value of x as seen in Fig. 15-1*b*.

The slope of a function at any point may be determined by finding the first *derivative* of the function. The *derivative* is the calculus expression of the rate at which the function is changing, and is

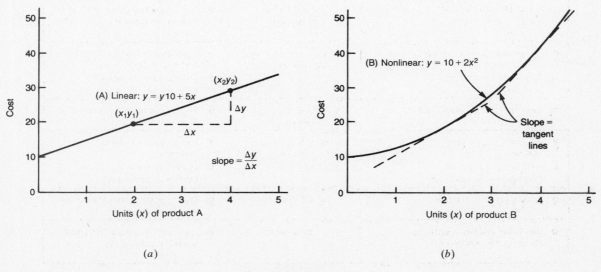

(*a*)   (*b*)

Fig. 15-1

the slope of the tangent to the curve at some point whose abscissa is the given value of x. It is also referred to as the instantaneous rate of change of the curve at that tangent. The function must, of course, be continuous (no breaks) and smooth (no sudden change in direction), but many production functions satisfy these conditions.

Insofar as points of zero slope often identify maximum or minimum values of a function, differential calculus is an important optimizing technique. (See Fig. 15-2.) The local maximum (or minimum) values can be determined by (1) finding the first derivative, (2) setting it equal to zero, (3) solving for the value of x that satisfies the zero derivative equation, and (4) substituting this volume of x back into the original equation.

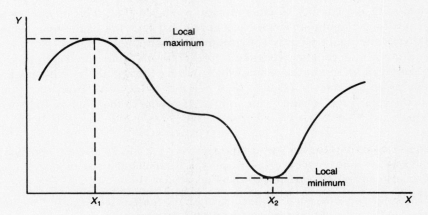

Fig. 15-2   Maximum and minimum points

RULES FOR DIFFERENTIATION

Think of finding the derivative of a function (differentiating) as the problem of finding the rate of change in the vertical dimension (Δy) relative to the change in the horizontal dimension (Δx) at a given point. The standard symbol used to denote the derivative of y with respect to x is dy/dx [or y' or $f'(x)$]. If we let c and n represent constants, we can express the derivatives of various functions as follows:

1. If $y = cx^n$, then the first derivative of y with respect to x is:

$$\frac{dy}{dx} = ncx^{n-1} \qquad (15.1)$$

Example 15.2

(a) $y = 9x^2 \qquad \dfrac{dy}{dx} = (2)(9)x^1 = 18x$

(b) $y = 5x^{-3} \qquad \dfrac{dy}{dx} = (-3)(5)x^{-4} = -15x^{-4} = \dfrac{-15}{x^4}$

(c) $y = -6x^{1/3} \qquad \dfrac{dy}{dx} = \left(\dfrac{1}{3}\right)(-6)x^{-2/3} = -2x^{-2/3} = \dfrac{-2}{x^{2/3}}$

(d) $y = \dfrac{1}{4}x^5 \qquad \dfrac{dy}{dx} = (5)\left(\dfrac{1}{4}\right)x^4 = \dfrac{5x^4}{4}$

2. The derivative of a constant is zero, and the derivative of a constant times a variable is the constant.

Example 15.3

(a)
$$y = 20 \qquad \frac{dy}{dx} = 0$$

(b)
$$y = 7x \qquad \frac{dy}{dx} = 7$$

3.   The derivative of the sum or difference of two functions is the sum or difference of the individual derivatives. If we let $g(x)$ be one function, and $h(x)$ another, then if $y = g(x) + h(x)$

$$\frac{dy}{dx} = g'(x) + h'(x) \tag{15.2}$$

Example 15.4

$$y = 3x^4 + 5x^{-2} \qquad \frac{dy}{dx} = 12x^3 - 10x^{-3}$$

$$y = 2x - 3x^2 \qquad \frac{dy}{dx} = 2 - 6x$$

$$y = 7x^3 - 2x^2 + 3x + 4 \qquad \frac{dy}{dx} = 21x^2 - 4x + 3$$

4.   The derivative of a composite function $y = [f(x)]^n$ is:

$$\frac{dy}{dx} = n[f(x)]^{n-1}f'(x) \tag{15.3}$$

Example 15.5

$$y = (x^2 + 1)^2 \qquad \frac{dy}{dx} = 2(x^2 + 1)(2x)$$

$$= 4x(x^2 + 1) = 4x^3 + 4x$$

$$y = (7 - 4x)^3 \qquad \frac{dy}{dx} = 3(7 - 4x)^2(-4)$$

$$= (-12)(7 - 4x)^2 = -192x^2 + 672x - 588$$

5.   The derivative of a product of two functions is the first times the derivative of the second, plus the second times the derivative of the first. If $y = [g(x)][h(x)]$, then

$$\frac{dy}{dx} = g(x)h'(x) + g'(x)h(x) \tag{15.4}$$

Example 15.6

$$y = (x^3 + 4x)(2x - 3) \qquad \frac{dy}{dx} = (x^3 + 4x)(2) + (2x - 3)(3x^2 + 4)$$

$$= 2x^3 + 8x + 6x^3 + 8x - 9x^2 - 12$$

$$= 8x^3 - 9x^2 + 16x - 12$$

Derivatives of additional functions, such as the quotient of two functions and the natural logarithm of a function, can be found in any good calculus text.

FINDING MAXIMUM AND MINIMUM VALUES

As suggested in Fig. 15-2, the point of zero slope on a function may be either a local maximum or local minimum. (*Note*: The point of zero slope is not necessarily a "global" optimum unless all points on the function are known to lie within these extremes.) Once the point of interest is identified, the type of optimum (i.e., whether a maximum or minimum) can be determined by finding the second derivative of the function at the point in question. The second derivative d^2y/dx^2, or y'', or $f''(x)$ is simply the derivative of the first derivative, and represents the rate of change in the slope of the tangent line.

If the value of the second derivative is negative, the point is a local maximum. If the value of the second derivative is positive, the point is a local minimum. In the event that the second derivative is zero, evaluate y' at points close to $x = 0$. If the sign of the first derivative changes from positive on the left of the point to negative on the right, then the point is a maximum; otherwise, it is a minimum.

Example 15.7 A cost curve is defined by the function $y = x^2 - 10x + 30$ where $y =$ cost in dollars, and $x =$ hours of labor. Find the point of zero slope, and indicate whether it is a maximum or minimum.

See Fig. 15-3.

$$\frac{dy}{dx} = 2x - 10$$

The point of zero slope is where

$$2x - 10 = 0$$
$$2x = 10$$
$$x = 5$$
$$\frac{d^2y}{dx^2} = 2 \text{ (a positive value)}$$

Thus, $x = 5$ is a minimum cost point.

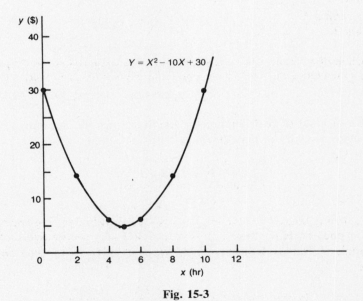

Fig. 15-3

LEARNING-CURVE EFFECTS

Learning- or *improvement-curve effects* are the reductions in time per unit to perform specified activities. As the number of repetitions of doing a task increase, improvement results from the development of individual skills, plus other factors such as better organization of work, improved methods, and enhanced work environment. Learning-curve information is useful for planning and scheduling work, budgeting costs, negotiating price and delivery of purchased items, and pricing the firm's own products.

The degree of improvement depends upon the task being performed, but is normally expressed in terms of the percentage of time it takes to complete the unit which represents a *doubling* of output. For example, if an activity followed an 80 percent learning curve and required 100 hours for the first unit, the second would take 80 hours, the fourth 64 hours, and the eighth 51.2 hours. See Fig. 15-4.

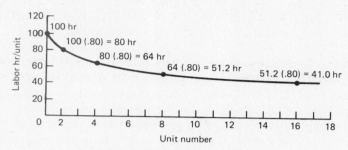

Fig. 15-4   80 percent learning curve

Mathematically, the number of direct labor hours required to produce the *N*th unit of a product Y_N, is exponentially related to the time to produce the first unit, Y_1, by the expression

$$Y_N = Y_1 N^X \qquad (15.5)$$

where Y_N = time to produce *N*th unit

Y_1 = time to produce first unit

N = unit number

$X = \dfrac{\log \text{ of learning \%}}{\log 2}$

Example 15.8   Production of a certain type of television series program follows an 80 percent learning curve and requires 100 hours to complete the first unit. Estimate the time required for the fourth unit of the series.

$$Y_N = Y_1 N^X$$

where $Y_1 = 100$

$N = 4$

$X = \dfrac{\log .80}{\log 2} = -.322$

$$Y_4 = 100(4)^{-.322} = \frac{100}{(4)^{.322}} = 64 \text{ hr}$$

The exponential learning curve function appears as a straight line on log-log paper, but has been tabled for easier use. Appendix H contains coefficients of learning percentages in the common range of 70–98 percent. To use the tables, first express the desired unit number as a percentage of a base unit with known time:

$$\text{Percentage of base} = \frac{\text{desired unit number}}{\text{known base number}} \qquad (15.6)$$

Then enter the table row corresponding to the percentage of base, go over to the column relevant to the specified learning percentage, and read off the learning coefficient *L*. The time to produce the desired unit Y_N is then

$$Y_N = Y_B(L) \qquad (15.7)$$

where Y_B = base unit time

L = learning coefficient

Example 15-9 The labor component of a ship construction activity required 12,000 worker days for the first project, and the firm has now received an order for two additional ships. Assuming that a 90 percent learning curve applies, how many worker days are expected for the third unit?

Express the unknown unit as a percentage of the base unit:

$$\text{Percentage of base} = \frac{\text{desired unit number}}{\text{known base number}} = \frac{\text{unit 3}}{\text{unit 1}} = \frac{3}{1} = 3.00 = 300\%$$

Determine the appropriate coefficient from Appendix H, and multiply it by the base unit time.

$$Y_N = Y_B(L) = (12,000)(.8492) = 10,190 \text{ worker days}$$

The learning curve is applicable primarily in labor-intensive industries, for instance, those with assembly work. Continued improvement often extends over a long period of time (perhaps years), although the curve may level off in some cases. For example, highly routine activities may eventually be converted to robotic operations, which tend to operate at a constant pace.

When substantial changes are introduced to the routine work pattern, they may cause changes in the curve and temporarily increase the time (and costs). The expectation is that the changes will generate long-term savings that outweigh the temporary learning cost. (See Prob. 15.25.)

QUEUING MODELS

Queuing theory is a quantitative (mathematical) approach to the analysis of systems that involve waiting lines, or queues. Examples range from supermarket checkout counters to banking activities and manufacturing jobs awaiting processing. The waiting lines may form even though the system (facility) has enough capacity, *on the average*, to handle the demand. This is because the arrival times and service times for the customers (jobs) are random and variable.

The *objective of queuing analysis* is to evaluate the service and the costs of a facility so as to maximize its usefulness. This often results in minimizing the total costs associated with the idle time of facilities or services versus the waiting time costs of employees or customers. Numerous computer software programs are available for queuing analysis. Calculations typically seek to estimate:

(1) System utilization ($\%U$) or average usage rate of capacity

(2) Mean number of customers in the queue N_q or in the system N_s

(3) Mean time customers spend in the queue T_q or in the system T_s

(4) Related idle facility and waiting time costs

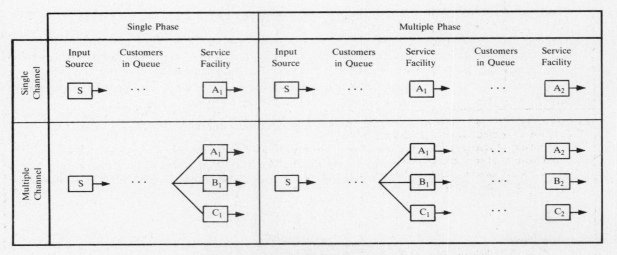

Fig. 15-5 Types of queuing systems

Figure 15-5 illustrates the structure of four variations of queuing systems. The simplest of these is a single-channel, single-phase system. Multiple-channel, single-phase systems, such as those found at banks and toll-road pay stations, have more than one service facility. Multiple-phase systems incorporate two or more service activities and are more difficult to analyze mathematically. Simulation is often the most feasible technique for analysis of multiple-phase systems.

As depicted in Fig. 15-5, the most relevant characteristics of queuing systems are:

(1) *Input source.* This may be finite or infinite, and it generates customer arrivals, which are assumed to follow a Poisson distribution rate (λ units per period) unless specified otherwise.

Table 15-2   Equations for Queuing Model Computations

	Model 1	Model 2	Model 3	Model 4
Channel: Phase: Arrival rate: Service rate: Queue length: Designation:	Single Single Poisson Poisson Unlimited M/M/1	Single Single Poisson Constant Unlimited M/D/1	Single Single Poisson Poisson Limited M/M/1/Q	Multiple Single Poisson Poisson Unlimited M/M/C
T_s = mean time in system	$\dfrac{1}{\mu-\lambda}$	$T_q+\dfrac{1}{\mu}$	$T_q+\dfrac{1}{\mu}$	$T_q+\dfrac{1}{\mu}$
N_s = mean number in system	$\dfrac{\lambda}{\mu-\lambda}$	$N_q+\dfrac{\lambda}{\mu}$	$\dfrac{\lambda}{\mu}\left\{\dfrac{1-(Q+1)\left(\frac{\lambda}{\mu}\right)^Q + Q\left(\frac{\lambda}{\mu}\right)^{Q+1}}{\left(1-\frac{\lambda}{\mu}\right)\left[1-\left(\frac{\lambda}{\mu}\right)^{Q+1}\right]}\right\}$	$N_q+\dfrac{\lambda}{\mu}$
T_q = mean waiting time in queue	$\dfrac{\lambda}{\mu(\mu-\lambda)}$	$\dfrac{\lambda}{2\mu(\mu-\lambda)}$	$\dfrac{N_q}{\lambda(1-P_Q)}$	$P_0\left[\dfrac{1}{\mu C(C!)\left(1-\frac{\lambda}{\mu C}\right)^2}\left(\dfrac{\lambda}{\mu}\right)^C\right]=\dfrac{N_q}{\lambda}$
N_q = mean number in queue	$\dfrac{\lambda^2}{\mu(\mu-\lambda)}$	$\dfrac{\lambda^2}{2\mu(\mu-\lambda)}$	$\left(\dfrac{\lambda}{\mu}\right)^2\left\{\dfrac{1-Q\left(\frac{\lambda}{\mu}\right)^{Q-1}+(Q-1)\left(\frac{\lambda}{\mu}\right)^Q}{\left(1-\frac{\lambda}{\mu}\right)\left[1-\left(\frac{\lambda}{\mu}\right)^Q\right]}\right\}$	$P_0\left[\dfrac{\lambda\mu\left(\frac{\lambda}{\mu}\right)^C}{(C-1)!(C\mu-\lambda)^2}\right]$
P_n = probability of n units in system	$\left(1-\dfrac{\lambda}{\mu}\right)\left(\dfrac{\lambda}{\mu}\right)^n$ where $n=0,1,\ldots$ $\lambda<\mu$	Not available	$\left[\dfrac{1-\frac{\lambda}{\mu}}{1-\left(\frac{\lambda}{\mu}\right)^{Q+1}}\right]\left(\dfrac{\lambda}{\mu}\right)^n$ where $n=0,1,\ldots Q$	$P_0\dfrac{\left(\frac{\lambda}{\mu}\right)^n}{n!}$ for $0\le n\le C$ $P_0\dfrac{\left(\frac{\lambda}{\mu}\right)^n}{C!C^{n-C}}$ for $n\ge C$ where $P_0=\dfrac{1}{\displaystyle\sum_{n=0}^{C-1}\dfrac{\left(\frac{\lambda}{\mu}\right)^n}{n!}+\dfrac{\left(\frac{\lambda}{\mu}\right)^C}{C!}\left[1-\dfrac{\lambda}{\mu(C)}\right]^{-1}}$ where $\lambda<C\mu$

λ = arrival rate μ = service rate n = number customers in system (waiting and being served)
C = number of channels in multiple channel system
P_0 = probability of zero units P_Q = probability of the maximum number in the system
Q = maximum number of arrivals that can be in system, both waiting and being served
Note: For single-channel, single-phase systems with Poisson arrivals and general (nonspecified) service times, the number in the waiting line is

$$N_q = \frac{(\lambda\sigma)^2+\left(\frac{\lambda}{\mu}\right)^2}{2\left(1-\frac{\lambda}{\mu}\right)}$$

where σ = standard deviation of the service time distribution

(2) *Customers.* They form in a queue length that can theoretically vary from zero to infinity, unless the model used assumes a limited queue length. Customers are allocated to service facilities according to a dispatching rule called the *queue discipline.* A first-in, first-out discipline is assumed unless otherwise stated.

(3) *Service rate.* The service rate (μ) must be greater than the arrival rate (λ) or the queue can become infinite. *Service rate* (units serviced per period) is also Poisson distributed, but analysis often concerns the reciprocal of service rate, which is service time (time per unit). Poisson service rates have negative exponential service times, which offer a strong probability of short service times, but allow for an occasional task that far exceeds the average time. Thus, a Poisson service rate of 5 units per hour has a negative exponential distribution time of 60 minutes per 5 units, or 12 minutes per unit.

Table 15-2 lists some equations useful for selected queuing problems. Consult a reference text for additional models (e.g., Kostas and Dervitsiotis, *Operations Management,* McGraw Hill, 1981, pp. 244–245 or Allen, *Probability, Statistics, and Queuing Theory,* Academic Press, 1978).

SINGLE-CHANNEL, SINGLE-PHASE SYSTEMS

Computations for single-channel, single-phase queuing models are relatively straightforward. The problem in Example 15.10 assumes an infinite number of customers, unlimited waiting-line length, Poisson arrivals, and negative exponential service times. The queue discipline is first-in, first-out, with no defections or balking from the waiting line.

Example 15.10   An equipment service facility has Poisson arrival and service rates and operates on a first-come, first-served queue discipline. Requests for service average λ = three per day. The facility can service an average of μ = six machines per day. Find the:

(a) Utilization factor (% U) of the service facility

(b) Mean time T_s in the system

(c) Mean number N_s in the system

(d) Mean waiting time T_q in the queue

(e) Probability P of finding $n = 2$ machines in the system

(f) Expected number N_q in the queue

(g) Percentage of time the service facility is idle (percentage I)

(a) Utilization factor:

$$\% U = \frac{\text{mean arrival rate}}{\text{mean service rate}} = \frac{\lambda}{\mu} \tag{15.8}$$

$$= \frac{3}{6} = 50\%$$

(b) Mean time in the system:

$$T_s = \frac{1}{\text{mean service rate} - \text{mean arrival rate}} = \frac{1}{\mu - \lambda} \tag{15.9}$$

$$= \frac{1}{6-3} = \frac{1}{3} \text{ day}$$

(c) Mean number in the system:

$$N_s = (\text{mean time in system})(\text{mean arrival rate}) \tag{15.10}$$

$$= \left(\frac{1}{\mu - \lambda}\right)\lambda = \frac{\lambda}{\mu - \lambda}$$

$$= \frac{3}{6-3} = 1 \text{ machine}$$

(d) Mean waiting time:

$$T_q = \text{mean time in system} - \text{service time} \qquad (15.11)$$

$$= \frac{1}{\mu - \lambda} - \frac{1}{\mu} = \frac{\lambda}{\mu(\mu - \lambda)}$$

$$= \frac{1}{6-3} - \frac{1}{6} = \frac{1}{6} \text{ day}$$

(e) Probability of $n = 2$ machines in the system:

$$P_n = (\text{probability of no others})(\text{probability of two}) \qquad (15.12)$$

$$= \left(1 - \frac{\lambda}{\mu}\right)\left(\frac{\lambda}{\mu}\right)^n$$

$$= \left(1 - \frac{3}{6}\right)\left(\frac{3}{6}\right)^2 = .125$$

(f) Mean number in the queue:

$$N_q = (\text{mean number in system}) - (\text{mean number being served}) \qquad (15.13)$$

$$= \frac{\lambda}{\mu - \lambda} - \frac{\lambda}{\mu} = \frac{\lambda^2}{\mu(\mu - \lambda)}$$

$$= \frac{3^2}{6(6-3)} = \frac{1}{2} \text{ machine}$$

(g) Percentage of idle time:

$$\%I = \text{total} - \text{percentage utilization} = 100 - \%U \qquad (15.14)$$

$$= 100\% - 50\% = 50\%$$

When service rates are constant, as in machine-paced systems, the mean waiting time $T_{q(c)}$ and number in the queue $N_{q(c)}$ are reduced by half. (See model 2 in Table 15-2.)

Example 15.11 Metropolitan Collection Co. (MCC) garbage trucks currently wait an average of 6 minutes each trip before being able to dump their load. MCC is considering hauling to a different collection center at an extra cost of \$8 per trip for each truck. The new center can process the loads at a constant rate of 30 units per hour. Arrivals at the new center will be Poisson-distributed, with an average rate of 24 loads per hour. The system is a single-channel, single-phase system with unlimited queue length. If waiting time for the trucks is valued at \$200 per hour, how much of a savings per hour would result?

The mean waiting time at the new center is estimated as:

$$T_{q(c)} = \frac{\lambda}{2\mu(\mu - \lambda)} = \frac{24}{2(30)(30 - 24)} = \frac{1}{15} \text{ hr}$$

Current waiting cost/trip:

$$\left(\frac{6 \text{ min}}{\text{trip}}\right)\left(\frac{\text{hr}}{60 \text{ min}}\right)\left(\frac{\$200}{\text{hr}}\right) = \$20.00$$

Less: New waiting cost/trip:

$$\left(\frac{1}{15}\frac{\text{hr}}{\text{trip}}\right)\left(\frac{\$200}{\text{hr}}\right) = -13.33$$

$$\text{Savings} = \$6.67/\text{trip}$$

The extra cost of \$8/trip exceeds the savings of \$6.67/trip in waiting time; the change is not worthwhile.

MULTIPLE-CHANNEL, SINGLE-PHASE SYSTEMS

Multiple-channel, single-phase systems (model 4 of Table 15-2) are commonly encountered in banks, post offices, and numerous retail activities where a single line of customers may be served at any one of two or more work stations. In addition to the assumptions of Poisson arrivals, Poisson service rates (i.e., negative exponential service times), and unlimited queue length, we also assume that the servers work independently of each other but at the same average service rate μ.

For multiple-channel, single-phase systems, where $C = $ number of channels or servers, the average utilization of capacity is $\lambda/C\mu$. The calculations (model 4) can be simplified by use of Table 15-3, which gives average queue lengths N_q for various ratios of r, the ratio of the arrival rate to the service rate:

Table 15-3*

Average Queue Lengths (N_q) for $C = 1$ to 11 Channels for Common Ratios of $r = \lambda/\mu$
All values assume Poisson arrivals, negative exponential service times

$r = \frac{\lambda}{\mu}$	1	2	3	4	5	6	7
.10	.0111						
.20	.0500	.0020					
.30	.1285	.0069					
.40	.2666	.0166					
.50	.5000	.0333	.0030				
.60	.9000	.0593	.0061				
.70	1.6333	.0976	.0112				
.80	3.2000	.1523	.0189				
.90	8.1000	.2285	.0300	.0041			
1.0		.3333	.0454	.0067			
1.2		.6748	.0904	.0158			
1.4		1.3449	.1778	.0324	.0059		
1.6		2.8444	.3128	.0604	.0121		
1.8		7.6734	.5320	.1051	.0227	.0047	
2.0			.8888	.1739	.0398	.0090	
2.2			1.4907	.2770	.0659	.0158	
2.4			2.1261	.4305	.1047	.0266	.0065
2.6			4.9322	.6581	.1609	.0426	.0110
2.8			12.2724	1.0000	.2411	.0659	.0180
3.0				1.5282	.3541	.0991	.0282
3.2				2.3856	.5128	.1452	.0427
3.4				3.9060	.7365	.2085	.0631
3.6				7.0893	1.0550	.2947	.0912
3.8				16.9366	1.5184	.4114	.1292
4.0					2.2164	.5694	.1801
4.2					3.3269	.7837	.2475
4.4					5.2675	1.0777	.3364
4.6					9.2885	1.4867	.4532
4.8					21.6384	2.0708	.6071

$r = \frac{\lambda}{\mu}$	6	7	8	9	10	11
3.0	.0991	.0282	.0077			
3.2	.1452	.0427	.0122			
3.4	.2085	.0631	.0189			
3.6	.2947	.0912	.0283	.0084		
3.8	.4114	.1292	.0412	.0127		
4.0	.5694	.1801	.0590	.0189		
4.2	.7837	.2475	.0827	.0273	.0087	
4.4	1.0777	.3364	.1142	.0389	.0128	
4.6	1.4867	.4532	.1555	.0541	.0184	
4.8	2.0708	.6071	.2092	.0742	.0260	
5.0	2.9375	.8102	.2786	.1006	.0361	.0125
5.2	4.3004	1.0804	.3680	.1345	.0492	.0175
5.4	6.6609	1.4441	.5871	.1779	.0663	.0243
5.6	11.5178	1.9436	.6313	.2330	.0883	.0330
5.8	26.3726	2.6481	.8225	.3032	.1164	.0443
6.0		3.6828	1.0707	.3918	.1518	.0590
6.2		5.2979	1.3967	.5037	.1964	.0775
6.4		8.0768	1.8040	.6454	.2524	.1008
6.6		13.7692	2.4198	.8247	.3222	.1302
6.8		31.1270	3.2441	1.0533	.4090	.1666
7.0			4.4471	1.3471	.5172	.2119
7.2			6.3135	1.7288	.6521	.2677
7.4			9.5102	2.2324	.8203	.3364
7.6			16.0379	2.9113	1.0310	.4211
7.8			35.8956	3.8558	1.2972	.5250
8.0				5.2264	1.6364	.6530
8.2				7.3441	2.0736	.8109
8.4				10.9592	2.6470	1.0060
8.6				18.3223	3.4160	1.2484
8.8				40.6824	4.4806	1.5524

*Elwood S. Buffa, *Modern Production/Operations Management*, 6th ed. John Wiley & Sons, New York, 1980, pp. 644–45. Reprinted by permission of John Wiley & Sons, Inc.

$$r = \frac{\lambda}{\mu} \tag{15.15}$$

Once r is computed, and the number of channels C specified, N_q can be taken from the table, and other values (T_q, T_s, N_s, etc.) computed more easily.

Example 15.12 A new post office is being designed with six service counters. During peak hours, customers are expected to arrive at a (Poisson-distributed) rate averaging 4 per minute. Service time is negative exponential, with some customers taking only a few seconds and others taking several minutes; the mean is 1 minute and 12 seconds. If all six service counters are staffed (a) what is the average utilization of capacity, (b) how many customers, on average, will be in the waiting line, (c) what is their average waiting time, and (d) what is their average time in the post office?

(a)

$$C = 6 \text{ counters (service channels)}$$

$$\lambda = 4 \text{ cust/min}$$

$$\mu = \frac{60 \text{ sec/min}}{72 \text{ sec/cust}} = .833 \text{ cust/min}$$

$$\% \text{ Utilization} = \frac{\lambda}{C\mu} = \frac{4}{(6)(.833)} = 80\%$$

(b) N_q can be taken from Table 15-3 where $r = \dfrac{\lambda}{\mu} = \dfrac{4}{.833} = 4.80$

Thus, $N_q = 2.07$ customers.

(c)

$$T_q = \frac{N_q}{\lambda} = \frac{2.07 \text{ cust}}{4 \text{ cust/min}} = .518 \text{ min} = 31 \text{ sec}$$

(d)

$$T_s = T_q + \frac{1}{\mu} = \frac{.518 \text{ min}}{\text{cust}} + \frac{1}{.833 \text{ cust/min}} = 1.72 \text{ min}$$

SIMULATION

Simulation techniques (see Chap. 7) are useful for analyzing complex problems that defy mathematical solution. Although they do not yield optimal results, they are relatively easy to use and offer a feasible approach to a wide range of problems. In addition, numerous computer simulation languages (e.g., GPSS, MODEL) and software packages are available.

Most computer simulations accommodate uncertainties by incorporating probability distributions into the simulation model. The distributions may be of a known statistical type if appropriate (e.g., normal, uniform, Poisson) or they may be derived from actual (empirical) data. Once the variable patterns of activity are structured into the model, random numbers are used to simulate activities and times. Then the system behavior is analyzed—much like the queue lengths and waiting times computed earlier. By utilizing computer simulations, analysts can compress years of hypothetical operations into minutes. This enables them to experiment with numerous decision alternatives at little or no risk.

Solved Problems

RULES FOR DIFFERENTIATION

15.1 Find the first derivative of the functions:

$$(a) \quad y = 10x^4 \qquad (b) \quad M = 3Q^2 + 2Q \qquad (c) \quad P = -\frac{8}{x^{1/2}}.$$

(a)
$$\frac{dy}{dx} = 40x^3$$

(b)
$$\frac{dM}{dQ} = 6Q + 2$$

(c) Rewrite equation to: $P = -8x^{-1/2}$

$$\frac{dP}{dx} = \left(-\frac{1}{2}\right)(-8)x^{-1/2 - 2/2} = 4x^{-3/2} = \frac{4}{x^{3/2}} = \frac{4}{\sqrt{x^3}}$$

15.2 Find the first derivative of the functions:

$$(a) \quad y = x^4 - 3x^2 + 7x + 12 \qquad (b) \quad y = (3 + 4x)^3 \qquad (c) \quad y = (4x + 7)(x^2 - 1)$$

(a)
$$\frac{dy}{dx} = 4x^3 - 6x + 7$$

(b)
$$\frac{dy}{dx} = 3(3 + 4x)^2(0 + 4) = 12(3 + 4x)^2$$

(c)
$$\frac{dy}{dx} = (4x + 7)(2x) + (x^2 - 1)(4) = 12x^2 + 14x - 4$$

15.3   A cost curve is defined by the function $y = x^3/3 - 2x^2 + 3x$ where y = cost (in dollars) and x = pounds of a specified raw material. (a) Graph the function. (b) Find the point of zero slope. (c) Indicate whether the zero slope points are local maximums or minimums.

(a)   See Fig. 15-6.

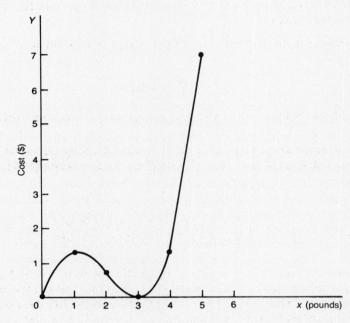

Fig. 15-6

(b)   This is a cubic equation.

$$\frac{dy}{dx} = x^2 - 4x + 3$$

Therefore, the points of zero slope are where

$$x^2 - 4x + 3 = 0$$

Factoring we have

$$(x - 1)(x - 3) = 0$$

Setting each of these terms equal to zero we have

$$x - 1 = 0 \qquad x - 3 = 0$$

The equation has two zero derivative points (roots) which are at $x = 1$ and $x = 3$ where the y values are 4/3 and 0, respectively.

(c)   The second derivative is:

$$\frac{d^2y}{dx^2} = 2x - 4$$

We can substitute the x values of 1 and 3 into the second derivative equation to determine its sign.

At $x = 1$, $\dfrac{d^2y}{dx^2} = 2(1) - 4 = 2 - 4 = -2$

A negative sign means the point $y = 4/3$ is a maximum.

At $x = 3$, $\dfrac{d^2y}{dx^2} = 2(3) - 4 = 6 - 4 = 2$

A positive sign means the point $y = 0$ is a minimum.

15.4   A firm makes $8 revenue on each unit sold, so the total revenue function is $R(x) = 8x$. Find and explain the marginal revenue.

   Marginal revenue is the instantaneous rate of change in total revenue, or derivative of the total revenue function.

$$\frac{dR}{dx} = R'(x) = 8$$

Thus the slope of the total revenue function, or average rate of change (marginal revenue) is $8.

15.5   A firm makes $8 revenue on each unit sold, but offers quantity discounts which result in a total revenue function of $R(x) = 8x - .01x^2$. Find the marginal revenue (MR) at sale volumes of 100 and 200 units.

$$R'(x) = 8 - .02x$$
At $x = 100$, $\text{MR} = R'(100) = 8 - .02(100) = \$6/\text{unit}$
At $x = 200$, $\text{MR} = R'(200) = 8 - .02(200) = \$4/\text{unit}$

15.6   A firm that produces small toys has a revenue function of $R(x) = 8x - .01x^2$. It has fixed rental costs of $300 per month, and variable costs of $2 per unit. Find (*a*) the marginal revenue, and (*b*) the marginal cost. Also find (*c*) the total profit function, (*d*) the marginal profit function, and (*e*) the marginal profit when 100 and 200 units are sold to a given customer.

(*a*) $\text{MR} = R'(x) = 8 - .02x$

(*b*)   Costs are FC + VC(x): $C(x) = 300 + 2x$
       so the marginal cost is $C'(x) = 2$

   [$C'(x) = 2$ is the instantaneous rate of change in the total cost function and means that an increase of one unit of production will increase total costs by $2.]

(*c*)   Total profit = total revenue − total cost = $R(x) - C(x)$
$$P(x) = (8x - .01x^2) - (300 + 2x) = -.01x^2 + 6x - 300$$

(*d*)   Marginal profit is the first derivative of the total profit function and the difference between the derivative of the total cost function and the derivative of the total revenue function.

$$P'(x) = -.02x + 6$$

   This represents the *rate* of change in total profit (slope of the total profit function) and indicates that the average profit decreases (due to a quantity discount offered on the sale accounts).

(*e*)   At 100 units, $P'(100) = -.02(100) + 6 = \$4/\text{unit}$
       At 200 units, $P'(200) = -.02(200) + 6 = \$2/\text{unit}$

15.7   The graph (Fig. 15-7) depicts the annual demand function for a firm producing short-wave radios. Annual production costs include relatively fixed costs of $800,000 and variable costs of

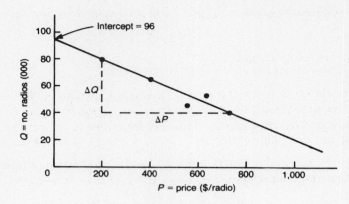

Fig. 15-7

$100 per radio. (*a*) Express the total revenues and total costs as linear functions of the price *P*. (*b*) At what price per radio is the profit maximized? (*c*) What is the optimal number of radios to produce? (*d*) At the optimum rate, what is the break-even price?

(*a*)   Revenues $= P \cdot Q$, so we must express the demand Q as a function of price in the form of $y = a + bx$, or, for this problem, $Q = a - bP$, where $a =$ intercept $= 96,000$, and $b =$ slope $= \Delta Q / \Delta P = 40,000/500 = 80$. Therefore, the demand function is

$$Q = 96,000 - 80P$$
$$\text{TR} = P \cdot Q = P(96,000 - 80P) = 96,000P - 80P^2$$
$$\text{TC} = \text{FC} + (\text{VC})Q = \$800,000 + 100Q = \$800,000 + 100(96,000 - 80P) = \$10,400,000 - 8,000P$$

(*b*)   Optimum profit is when MR = MC.

$$\text{MR} = \frac{d\text{TR}}{dP} = 96,000 - 160P \qquad \text{MC} = \frac{d\text{TC}}{dP} = -8,000$$
$$96,000 - 160P = -8,000$$
$$P = \$650/\text{radio}$$

(*c*)   Optimum number of radios is at the optimum price ($650).

$$Q = 96,000 - 80(650) = 44,000 \text{ radios}$$

(*d*)   The break-even price, at a rate of 44,000 is where TR = TC.

$$PQ = \text{FC} + (\text{VC})Q$$
$$P(44,000) = 800,000 + 100(44,000)$$
$$P = \frac{5,200,000}{44,000} = \$118.18$$

LEARNING-CURVE EFFECTS

15.8   The operations manager of International Resort Hotels is preparing a budget for the labor cost required to handle several major conventions of the same type during the coming year. She estimates that the first one will take 300 labor hours at $12 per hour. Assuming that the work follows a 78 percent learning curve, what is the firm's estimated labor cost for the eighth convention?

$$\text{Percentage of base} = \frac{\text{desired unit number}}{\text{known base number}} = \frac{\text{8th}}{\text{1st}} = 800\%$$

Using the 78 percent column for 800 percent of base in Appendix H,

$$Y_n = Y_B(L) = 300(.4746) = 142.4 \text{ hr}$$

The estimated cost = (142.4 hr)($12/hr) = $1,708.

15.9 Emerald Electric has a new plant for producing home freezers. The firm has gone through a preliminary manufacturing period and believes it is experiencing an 88 percent learning curve. The 200th unit has required 1.40 labor hours for an assembly activity. Estimate the comparable time for (*a*) the 100th unit, (*b*) the 500th unit, (*c*) the 1,000th unit, and (*d*) the 5,000th unit.

(*a*) The 100th unit has already been completed, but we can estimate its time as a percentage of the base 200 as

$$\text{Percentage base of} = \frac{\text{desired unit number}}{\text{known base number}} = \frac{100\text{th}}{200\text{th}} = \frac{100}{200} = 50\%$$

$$Y_N = Y_B(L) = 1.40(1.1364) = 1.5910 \text{ hr}$$

(*b*) $$\text{Percentage of base} = \frac{500\text{th}}{200\text{th}} = 250\%$$

$$Y_N = 1.40(.8445) = 1.1823 \text{ hr}$$

(*c*) $$\text{Percentage of base} = \frac{1,000\text{th}}{200\text{th}} = 500\%$$

$$Y_N = 1.40(.7432) = 1.0405 \text{ hr}$$

(*d*) $$\text{Percentage base of} = \frac{5,000\text{th}}{200\text{th}} = 2,500\%$$

Note that our table of learning coefficients does not go to this high of a percentage of the base, so we must establish a new (higher) base to operate from. The time for the 1,000th unit, developed in (*c*), will work satisfactorily, so we can designate 1.0405 hours for the 1,000th unit as the new base (100 percent) point.

$$\text{Percentage base of} = \frac{5,000\text{th}}{1,000\text{th}} = 500\%$$

$$Y_N = 1.0405(.7432) = .7733 \text{ hr}$$

QUEUING MODELS

15.10 Patients arrive at a medical clinic with an arrival rate that is Poisson distributed with a mean of 6 per hour. Treatment (service) time averages 8 minutes and can be approximated by the negative exponential distribution. Find (*a*) the mean waiting time, (*b*) the mean number in the queue, and (*c*) the percentage of idle time.

$$\lambda = \text{arrival rate} = 6/\text{hr}$$

$$\mu = \text{service rate} = \left(\frac{\text{unit}}{8 \text{ min}}\right)\left(\frac{60 \text{ min}}{\text{hr}}\right) = 7.5/\text{hr}$$

(*a*) $$T_q = \frac{\lambda}{\mu(\mu - \lambda)} = \frac{6}{7.5(7.5 - 6)} = .53 \text{ hr} = 32 \text{ min}$$

(*b*) $$N_q = \frac{\lambda^2}{\mu(\mu - \lambda)} = \frac{6^2}{7.5(7.5 - 6)} = 3.20 \text{ units}$$

(*c*) $$\%I = 100 - \%U = 100 - \frac{\lambda}{\mu} = 100 - \frac{6}{7.5} = 20\%$$

15.11 Rent-A-Dent Ltd. receives an average of 15 requests per day for older-model cars. It can fill 20 such requests per day. However, if fewer than 3 cars are rented, the company loses money as follows: If only 2 cars are rented the loss equals $220 per day, if only 1 car is rented the loss equals $260 per day, if no cars are rented the loss equals $290 per day. The losses are, of course, offset by gains from renting 3 or more cars. Considering the *losses only*, what is the expected value of the loss per day? Assume that there are Poisson arrivals and service rates, and that there is unlimited line length with no defects from the queue.

$$P(n = 2) = \left(1 - \frac{\lambda}{\mu}\right)\left(\frac{\lambda}{\mu}\right)^2 = \left(1 - \frac{15}{20}\right)\left(\frac{15}{20}\right)^2 = .141$$

$$P(n = 1) = \left(1 - \frac{15}{20}\right)(.75)^1 = \qquad\qquad .188$$

$$P(n = 0) = \left(1 - \frac{15}{20}\right)(.75)^0 = (.25)(1) = \qquad \underline{.250}$$
$$.579$$

Expected loss $= \Sigma[XP(X)] = \$220(.141) + \$260(.188) + \$290(.250) = \$152.40/\text{day}$

15.12 A service desk at an office of charity in a large city is staffed by one social worker who receives an average of three people (customers) an hour seeking some kind of aid (food, housing, etc.). The social worker talks with them and assists them directly or guides them to other facilities in the city. This takes an average of 15 minutes. Assume that arrivals are Poisson distributed, that service time has an exponential distribution, and that the queue discipline is first-come first-served. Find (*a*) the probability of zero customers, (*b*) the probability of two customers in the office at one time, (*c*) the average number of customers in the system, (*d*) the average time a customer spends in the system, including service time, and (*e*) the average number of customers waiting to be served.

Remember that λ = arrival rate = 3 per hour and μ = service rate = (60 min/15 min per cust.) = 4 per hour.

(*a*)
$$P_0 = 1 - \frac{\lambda}{\mu} = 1 - \frac{3}{4} = .25$$

(*b*)
$$P_2 = \left(1 - \frac{\lambda}{\mu}\right)\left(\frac{\lambda}{\mu}\right)^n = \left(1 - \frac{3}{4}\right)\left(\frac{3}{4}\right)^2 = .14$$

(*c*)
$$N_s = \frac{\lambda}{\mu - \lambda} = \frac{3}{4 - 3} = 3 \text{ customers}$$

(*d*)
$$T_s = \frac{1}{\mu - \lambda} = \frac{1}{4 - 3} = 1 \text{ hr}$$

(*e*)
$$N_q = \frac{\lambda^2}{\mu(\mu - \lambda)} = \frac{3^2}{4(4 - 3)} = \frac{9}{4} = 2.25 \text{ customers}$$

15.13 Use the data from Prob. 15.12 to find the number of people waiting for service if the service time is normally distributed with a mean of 15 minutes and a standard deviation of .025 minutes.

From Table 15-2 for nonspecified service times:

$$N_q = \frac{(\lambda\sigma)^2 + \left(\frac{\lambda}{\mu}\right)^2}{2\left(1 - \frac{\lambda}{\mu}\right)} = \frac{(3 \times .025)^2 + \left(\frac{3}{4}\right)^2}{2\left(1 - \frac{3}{4}\right)} = 1.14 \text{ customers}$$

Note that the assumption of the normal distribution substantially increases the queue length.

15.14 Use the data from Prob. 15.12, except assume that the number of persons in the system is limited to five (model 3 of Table 15.2). Find (a) the probability of two customers in the office at one time, (b) the probability of five customers in the office at one time, (c) the average number of people in the system, (d) the average number in the queue, (e) the average waiting time, and (f) the average time in the system.

(a)
$$P_2 = \left[\frac{1-\frac{\lambda}{\mu}}{1-\left(\frac{\lambda}{\mu}\right)^{Q+1}}\right]\left(\frac{\lambda}{\mu}\right)^n = \left[\frac{1-\frac{3}{4}}{1-\left(\frac{3}{4}\right)^{5+1}}\right]\left(\frac{3}{4}\right)^2 = .17$$

(b)
$$P_5 = \left[\frac{1-\frac{3}{4}}{1-\left(\frac{3}{4}\right)^{5+1}}\right]\left(\frac{3}{4}\right)^5 = .072$$

(c)
$$N_s = \frac{\lambda}{\mu}\left\{\frac{1-(Q+1)\left(\frac{\lambda}{\mu}\right)^Q + Q\left(\frac{\lambda}{\mu}\right)^{Q+1}}{\left(1-\frac{\lambda}{\mu}\right)\left[1-\left(\frac{\lambda}{\mu}\right)^{Q+1}\right]}\right\} = \left(\frac{3}{4}\right)\left\{\frac{1-(5+1)\left(\frac{3}{4}\right)^5 + 5\left(\frac{3}{4}\right)^{5+1}}{\left(1-\frac{3}{4}\right)\left[1-\left(\frac{3}{4}\right)^{5+1}\right]}\right\} = 1.68 \text{ persons}$$

(d)
$$N_q = \left(\frac{\lambda}{\mu}\right)^2\left\{\frac{1-Q\left(\frac{\lambda}{\mu}\right)^{Q-1} + (Q-1)\left(\frac{\lambda}{\mu}\right)^Q}{\left(1-\frac{\lambda}{\mu}\right)\left[1-\left(\frac{\lambda}{\mu}\right)^Q\right]}\right\} = \left(\frac{3}{4}\right)^2\left\{\frac{1-5\left(\frac{3}{4}\right)^{5-1} + (5-1)\left(\frac{3}{4}\right)^5}{\left(1-\frac{3}{4}\right)\left[1-\left(\frac{3}{4}\right)^5\right]}\right\} = 1.08 \text{ persons}$$

(e)
$$T_q = \frac{N_q}{\lambda[1-P_O]} = \frac{1.08}{3[1-.072]} = .388 \text{ hr} = 23.3 \text{ min}$$

(f)
$$T_s = T_q + \frac{1}{\mu} = .388 + \left(\frac{1}{4}\right) = .638 \text{ hr} = 38.3 \text{ min}$$

Supplementary Problems

15.15 Find the first derivative of the functions (a) $y = 4x^3$ (b) $y = x^3 - 10x^2$ (c) $y = x^2 - 120x + 80$ (d) $y = 50x$ *Ans.* (a) $12x^2$ (b) $3x^2 - 20x$ (c) $2x - 120$ (d) 50

15.16 Find the first derivative of the functions (a) $y = (x-2)^2$ (b) $y = 5x(x^3 - 4)$ (c) $y = 5/x^2$ *Ans.* (a) $2x - 4$ (b) $20x^3 - 20$ (c) $-10/x^3$

15.17 At what value of Q does the total cost function $TC = 4Q^2 - 240Q + 75$ have a slope of zero? *Ans.* Solving for first derivative and setting it = 0 gives $Q = 30$

15.18 Find the points of zero slope for the function $y = 4x + 16/x$ and indicate whether they are maximums or minimums.
    Ans. At $x = 2$, the y value of 16 is a minimum. At $x = -2$, the y value of -16 is a maximum. (Curve is asymptotic to y axis.)

15.19 Find the points of zero slope for the function $y = x - 4/x^2$, graph it, and indicate whether they are maximums or minimums.   *Ans.* At $x = -2$ is a maximum ($y = -3$)

15.20 A firm's revenue function is $R(x) = 8x - .002x^2$, and its cost function is $C(x) = 85 + .20x$. Find (a) the marginal revenue, (b) the marginal cost.   *Ans.* (a) $8 - .004x$ (b) $.20$

15.21 Given the following cost and revenue functions: $C(x) = 2x^3 - 20x^2 + 10x + 50$, $R(x) = 200x - 2x^2$. Find the (a) profit function (b) the marginal profit function, (c) the profit at 1, 4, and 10 units of production, and (d) the marginal profit at 1, 4, and 10 units.

Ans. (a) $P(x) = -2x^3 + 18x^2 + 190x - 50$ (b) $P'(x) = -6x^2 + 36x + 190$ (c) 156, 870, 1,650 (d) 220, 238, -50

15.22 The maintenance cost for a shop is defined by a fixed component of $12,000 per month, plus a variable component of $5x^2 - $300x$, where x is the number of hours of preventive maintenance per month. (a) What is the maintenance cost when 20 hours of preventive maintenance are used? (b) What is that cost when 35 hours of preventive maintenance are used? (c) What amount of preventive maintenance will minimize the total monthly cost?   Ans. (a) $8,000 (b) $7,625 (c) 30 hours for a cost of $7,500

15.23 A firm that produces small electric heaters has experienced the demand pattern shown in Fig. 15-8, where the least-squares line has an intercept of 5,500 units. The annual production costs include fixed costs of $40,000, and variable costs of $10 per unit. (a) Express the demand function as a linear equation. (b) Express the total revenues and total costs as a function of price P. (c) At what price per heater is the profit maximized? (d) What is the optimal number of heaters to produce? (e) At the optimum production rate (from (d) above) what is the break-even price (i.e., to what point can the price be lowered before the firm starts to lose money)?

Ans. (a) $Q = 5,500 - 75 P$ (b) $TR = 5,500 P - 75 P^2$ and $TC = 95,000 - 750 P$ (c) $41.67 (d) 2,375 units (e) $26.84

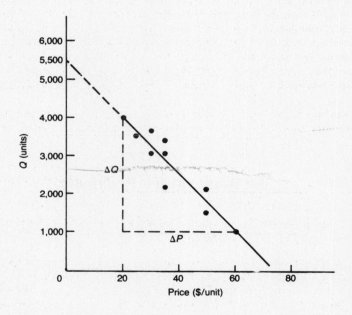

Fig. 15-8

15.24 A manufacturer of radar assemblies has received a contract for 32 units and has produced the first one in 100 hours. If the activity follows a 90 percent learning curve, how long will it take to produce (a) the second unit, (b) the fourth unit, (c) the last unit?   Ans. (a) 90 hours (b) 81 hours (c) 59 hours

15.25 Cranston Manufacturing Co. must determine whether to purchase new equipment for $18,500 to assist on a contract operation that has been following a 90 percent learning curve. The company has just completed the fourth unit, which took 30 days at a direct labor cost of $950 per day, and the contract calls for a total of eight units. The new equipment is expected to increase the time of the fifth unit to 31 days, but would generate other improvements that would put the operation on a 70 percent learning curve. Is the new installation economically justified?

Ans.   Yes, savings of $24,945 do outweigh the $18,500 cost.

15.26   Rocket Control Inc., a Long Beach firm, does control-panel wiring for solid-fueled rocket engines. The firm is currently preparing delivery estimates for a government contract for 80 panels. The first unit is expected to take 200 worker-hours, and the firm usually experiences an 84 percent learning curve for this type of work. (*a*) What average time per unit can be expected for the first three units?   (*b*) How many worker-hours should be scheduled for the 40th unit?   *Ans.*   (*a*) 173 hours per unit (*b*) 79.1 hr

15.27   Airframe International engineers have developed a new design for a wing section. Assembling the first unit required 5,000 direct labor hours at $30 per hour. This type of work follows a 90 percent learning curve, and the firm has orders for 50 such wing sections. (*a*) How many direct labor hours can be expected for the tenth unit?   (*b*) Estimate the direct labor cost (to the nearest $100) for the third unit.   *Ans.*   (*a*) 3,524 hours (*b*) $127,000.

15.28   Given Poisson arrivals of 15 per hour, a Poisson service rate of 18 per hour, and a single-channel, single-phase queue with unlimited line, find (*a*) T_s (*b*) N_s (*c*) T_q (*d*) N_q.   *Ans.*   (*a*) .33 hour (*b*) 5 units (*c*) .28 hour (*d*) 4.17 units

15.29   An automatic car wash uses a chain drive that requires a constant time of 5 minutes per car to wash and clean a car. The demand for service follows a Poisson distribution with a mean of $\lambda =$ four per hour. (*a*) Express the service time as a service rate. (*b*) What is the mean waiting time (in minutes) for service?   *Ans.*   (*a*) .20 car per minute (*b*) 1.26 minutes

15.30   A large television service firm has Poisson arrival rates and negative exponential service times, and serves customers 24 hours per day on a first-come, first-served basis. If the firm receives service orders at a mean rate of 30 per day and has the personnel and facilities to handle up to 35 per day, (*a*) how many sets, on the average, will it have in its shop at any one time; (*b*) how many hours, on the average, will a customer have to wait *before the service firm starts work* on his or her set; (*c*) how many hours, on the average, would the customer have to wait before the firm started work on his or her set if the firm had a *constant* service rate of 35 per day?   *Ans.*   (*a*) 6 sets (*b*) 4.11 hours (*c*) 2.06 hours

15.31   A customer service system that is capable of handling requests *arriving* at a rate of 800 per hour is to be installed at a major brokerage house. Two alternatives are being considered (see Table 15-4):

Table 15-4

	Mean Service Rate	Operating Cost
System X	$\mu = 860$ calls/hr	$400/hr
System Y	$\mu = 840$ calls/hr	$250/hr

Analysts use a waiting-time (or lost-business) penalty cost of $1 per minute ($60 per hour) for each request that must wait before being served. Both proposals are for single-channel, single-phase systems with service on a first-come first-served basis. If call arrivals are Poisson distributed and service times are exponential, (*a*) what are the respective waiting times for X and Y, and (*b*) what are the respective total costs for X and Y?   *Ans.*   (*a*) 1.0 minute and 1.43 minutes (*b*) $1,200 per hour and $1,400 per hour

15.32   Use the data from Prob. 15.12, except assume that two social workers are on duty (model 4). Otherwise: $\lambda = 3$ per hour, $\mu = 4$ per hour, FCFS. Find (*a*) P_0, (*b*) P_2, (*c*) N_q, (*d*) N_s, (*e*) T_q, (*f*) T_s.   *Ans.*   (*a*) .455 (*b*) .128 (*c*) .123 customer (*d*) .873 customer (*e*) 2.46 minutes (*f*) 17.46 minutes. *Note*: These values are considerably smaller than the single-channel values of Prob. 15.12

15.33   Given a multiple-channel, single-phase queuing problem that satisfies the conditions of model 4 (Table 15-2), where $C = 6$, $\lambda = 4$ customers per minute, and $\mu = 45$ seconds per customer. (*a*) Use the equations of model 4 to compute the average queue length N_q, and (*b*) compute N_q using the r ratio and Table 15-3.   *Ans.*   Both answers should be the same except for rounding: $N_q \cong .10$

Chapter 16

Project Management

CPM and PERT

Project management involves the three phases: planning, scheduling, and control, as illustrated in Fig. 16-1. This chapter summarizes these three activities, with major emphasis on two network techniques, CPM and PERT.

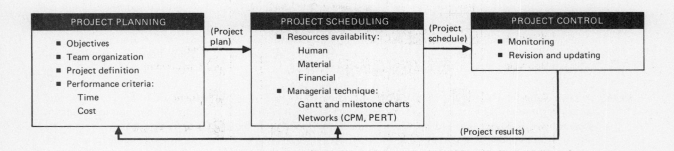

Fig. 16-1 Project management flowchart

PROJECT PLANNING

A *project* is a set of unique activities that must be completed within a specified time by utilizing appropriate resources, usually at a job site. Examples are the design of a space vehicle, construction of a hydroelectric dam, marketing of a new product, and merging of two firms. Planning begins with *well-defined objectives*. The *project team* is typically drawn from several organizational departments and may include personnel from areas such as engineering, production, marketing, and accounting. *Project definition* involves identifying the controllable and uncontrollable variables involved, and establishing project boundaries. *Performance criteria* should relate to the project objectives and are often evaluated in terms of time and cost.

PROJECT SCHEDULING

Project scheduling involves charting the resource requirements or anticipated progress in completing component activities over the project's time horizon. Resource requirements are best managed by giving individual attention to the personnel, material, and financial needs of the project, as illustrated in Fig. 16-2. Each of the charts offers some means of comparing actual levels with planned levels. Computer graphics can provide these types of data on a real-time basis, at almost any level of detail that project managers deem appropriate.

Techniques for scheduling projects include traditional Gantt (load and progress) charts and network techniques. Gantt charts are easily understood and easily updated (if on computer) but they do not reflect the interrelationships among resources or the precedence relationships among project

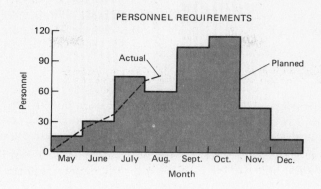

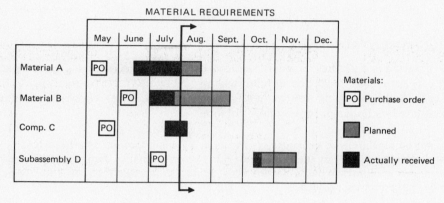

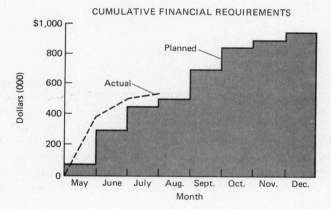

Fig. 16-2　Project resource requirements scheduling

Table 16-1　Network Scheduling Advantages

1. *Coordinates total project* and all interrelated activities. Shows relationship of each activity to whole project.
2. *Forces logical planning* of all activities. Facilitates work organization and assignment.
3. *Identifies precedence relationships* and activity sequences that are especially critical.
4. *Provides completion time (and/or cost) estimates* and a standard for comparing with actual values.
5. *Facilitates better use of resources* by identifying areas where human, material, or financial resources can be shifted.

activities. Network techniques such as CPM and PERT, though more complicated, show precedence relationships and yield valuable tradeoff information for improved use of resources. See Table 16-1.

PROJECT CONTROL

Project controls are activities designed to measure the status of component activities, transmit that data to a control center where it is compared with the plan (i.e., the standard), and initiate corrective action when required. Computerized reporting systems often accumulate data online. Control reports can then be developed on a management-by-exception principle, which minimizes unnecessary paperwork. Managerial attention is then focused on critical or near-critical activities that are potentially troublesome.

NETWORK FUNDAMENTALS

A *network* diagram is a mathematical model that uses small circles (nodes) connected by links or branches (arcs) to represent precedence relationships. Networks are frequently used to describe inventory or cash flows, shipping routes, and communication links. Network problems are also sometimes formulated as linear-programming problems.

Example 16.1   An oil pipeline is to be constructed from a Wyoming location (A) through some mountainous terrain to a distribution center (F) at the least cost (Fig. 16-3). Alternative routes and construction costs (in millions of dollars) are as shown. What is the least-cost route? (*Note*: See Prob. 16.1 for formulation of this example as a linear-programming problem.)

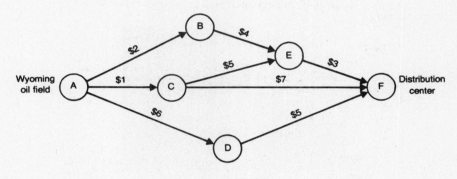

Fig. 16-3

The alternative paths and respective costs are:

$$\text{Path A-B-E-F} = \$2 + 4 + 3 = \$9 \text{ (million)}$$
$$\text{A-C-E-F} = \$1 + 5 + 3 = \$9 \text{ (million)}$$
$$\text{A-C-F} \quad = \$1 + 7 \quad = \$8 \text{ (million)} \leftarrow \text{least cost path}$$
$$\text{A-D-F} \quad = \$6 + 5 \quad = \$11 \text{ (million)}$$

The *critical-path method* (CPM) and *program evaluation and review technique* (PERT) are network techniques for analyzing a system in terms of activities and events that must be completed in a specified sequence in order to achieve a goal. Some activities can be done concurrently, whereas others have precedence requirements. Although some formulations of CPM differ with this nomenclature, we shall consider *activities* as component tasks that take time and are designated by arrows

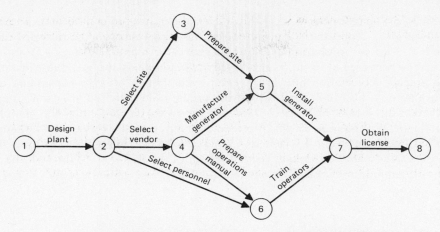

Fig. 16-4   Network diagram for power plant construction

($\rightarrow$).[1] *Events* are points in time and indicate that some activities have been completed and others may begin. They are the *nodes* and are designated by circles ($\bigcirc$). The network diagram consists of the activities and events in their proper relationship, as illustrated in Fig. 16-4.

Figure 16-4 shows, in a network diagram, the work activities necessary to construct an electrical power plant (the objective). Precedence relationships are indicated by the arrows and circles. For example, the plant design (activity 1-2) must be completed before anything else can take place. Then the selection of the site, vendor, and personnel can take place concurrently. The generator

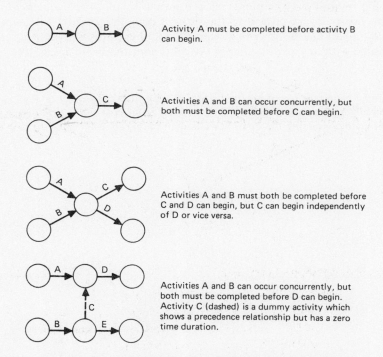

Fig. 16-5   Commonly used network diagram symbols

---

[1]We use the activity-on-arrow (AOA) convention here. The activity-on-node (AON) approach uses circles (or rectangles) to represent project activities, and arrows to show the required sequence. The AON method avoids the need for "dummy" activities. Well-developed computer programs are commercially available for both methods.

installation (activity 5-7) cannot begin until the site has been prepared (3-5) and the generator has been manufactured (4-5). Note that there are really four paths through the network diagram from event 1 to event 8. The site preparation (3-5) and generator manufacturing (4-5) are on different paths, but since they converge at event 5, either activity could delay the generator installation.

Sometimes precedence relationships are needed even though no time-consuming activities are involved. For example, in Fig. 16-4, suppose the site preparation activity (3-5) cannot begin until the vendor is notified. This means that the vendor selection activity (2-4) must be completed before activity 3–5 can begin. We can indicate this preference requirement by means of a "dummy activity," drawn as a dotted line from event 4 to event 3 which would be assigned a zero time. This dummy activity would then create another unique sequential path (1–2–4–3–5–7–8) through the network.

A summary of common network diagram sequences and arrangements is shown in Fig. 16-5.

CRITICAL-PATH METHOD (CPM)

The steps involved in implementing CPM are:

(1) Define the project in terms of activities and events.

(2) Construct a network diagram showing the precedence relationships.

(3) Develop a point estimate of each activity time.

(4) Compute the time requirement for each path in the network.

(5) Shift resources as warranted to optimize attainment of objectives.

The path with the longest time sequence as computed in step 4 is the *critical path*; the activity times of all items on this path are critical to the project completion date. The sum of these activity times is the expected mean time of the critical path (T_E). Other paths will have excess (or slack) time, and the slack associated with any path is simply the difference between T_E and the time for the given path.

Example 16.2 The time estimates for completing the plant construction project of Fig. 16-4 are as shown (in months) on the accompanying network diagram (Fig. 16-6). (*a*) Determine the critical path. (*b*) How much slack time is available in the path containing the operations-manual preparation?

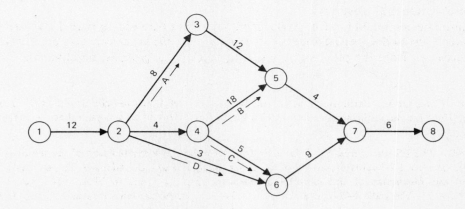

Fig. 16-6

See Table 16-2.

(*a*) Path B is critical, with a time requirement of 44 months.

Table 16-2

	Path	Times
A:	1–2–3–5–7–8	$12 + 8 + 12 + 4 + 6 = 42$
B:	1–2–4–5–7–8	$12 + 4 + 18 + 4 + 6 = 44$
C:	1–2–4–6–7–8	$12 + 4 + 5 + 9 + 6 = 36$
D:	1–2–6–7–8	$12 + 3 + 9 + 6 = 30$

(*b*) The manual preparation is on path C:

$$\text{Slack} = \text{critical path B} - \text{path C}$$
$$= 44 - 36 = 8 \text{ months}$$

The slack in path C suggests that, other things remaining the same, the manual writing (activity 4–6) could fall behind by 8 months before it would jeopardize the scheduled finish date for the project.

EARLIEST AND LATEST ACTIVITY TIMES

In managing the activities of a project, it is sometimes useful to know how soon or how late an individual activity can be started or finished without affecting the scheduled completion date of the total project. Four symbols are commonly used to designate the earliest and latest activity times.

(1) ES: the earliest start time for an activity. The assumption is that all predecessor activities are started at their earliest start time.

(2) EF: the earliest finish time for an activity. The assumption is that the activity starts on its ES and takes its expected time, t. Therefore, $EF = ES + t$.

(3) LF: the latest finish time for an activity without delaying the project. The assumption is that successive activities take their expected time.

(4) LS: the latest start time for an activity without delaying the project. $LS = LF - t$.

ES and EF are calculated in a left-to-right sequence (sometimes called a *forward pass*). The ES of an activity is the sum of the times of all preceding activities on that path. Where two paths converge at a node, the longest time path governs.

Latest times are computed in reverse. Begin with the critical or ending time T_E and subtract each preceding activity up to the specified activity. If two or more paths converge on one event en route, the figure developed from the path with the shortest total time governs, because that path has the least slack.

Example 16.3 Compute the earliest-start (ES) and latest-start (LS) times for the activities in the network of Example 16.2. What are the earliest and latest times for the completion of event 6 such that the schedule will not be delayed?

See Fig. 16-7. The ES time (in months) for each activity is shown on the left side of the tee at the beginning of the activity. Activity 1-2 begins at zero, and the other activity times are summed. For example, the ES for activity 6-7 is the maximum of the cumulative times leading to event 6. Thus: via path 1–2–4–6, the time $= 12 + 4 + 5 = 21$. Via path 1–2–6, the time $= 12 + 3 = 15$. Therefore, ES = month 21 because the longest path governs.

The LS time for each activity is on the right side of the tee, and we begin with T_E and work backward. Thus the LS for activity 6-7 is

$$T_E - \text{preceding activity times} = 44 - 6 - 9 = 29$$

Other ES and LS times are shown in Table 16-3, along with slack times. Note that the ES and LS for all activities on the critical path are equal. For activities off the critical path the LS turns out to be the ES plus the

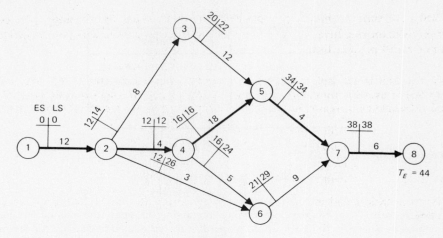

Fig. 16-7

Table 16-3

Activity	Time	ES	LS	EF	LF	Slack
1-2	12	0	0	12	12	0
2-3	8	12	14	20	22	2
2-4	4	12	12	16	16	0
2-6	3	12	26	15	29	14
3-5	12	20	22	32	34	2
4-5	18	16	16	34	34	0
4-6	5	16	24	21	29	8
5-7	4	34	34	38	38	0
6-7	9	21	29	30	38	8
7-8	6	38	38	44	44	0

amount of slack in the path (which seems like an easier way to compute it). The table also includes EF and LF times. They are also easily computed, for the EF is simply the ES plus the activity time, and LF is the LS plus the activity time.

Example 16.4 Compute the slack associated with each activity in Example 16.3.

The slack is shown in the far right column in Table 16-3. The total slack for an activity is the difference between LS and ES (or between LF and EF). Although we associate slack with each activity, it really belongs to the path because once any activity uses up the slack in its path, all activities along that path become critical. Activities along the critical path will always have zero slack if the target date (or planned completion date) for the project is the same as the earliest finish of the last activity.

Free slack is the amount of time an activity can be delayed without delaying the earliest start time of any succeeding activity.

Example 16.5 Determine the free slack time associated with activities 2-6 and 4-6 in Example 16.2.

The ES of the succeeding activity (6-7) is month 21, so the starting date for activity 2-6 could be delayed 6 months (until month 18) without affecting activity 6-7's ES date. However, if activity 4-6 is delayed any time at all, it will delay the ES of activity 6-7. Thus, activity 2-6 has 6 months of free slack, and activity 4-6 has zero free slack. However, both activities have some total slack because neither is on the critical path.

Activity and path time estimates give project planners a basis for shifting resources to achieve the project objectives more efficiently. For example, shifting more resources to critical-path activities may reduce the overall project time.

Example 16.6 The firm in Example 16.2 has determined that by shifting three engineers from writing the manual (activity 4-6) to assisting with manufacturing (activity 4-5), activity 4-5 could be reduced to 15 months, whereas activity 4-6 would be increased to 10 months. What would be the net effect on the schedule?

> Path A remains the same, at 42 months
> Path B = 12 + 4 + 15 + 4 + 6 = 41 months
> Path C = 12 + 4 + 10 + 9 + 6 = 41 months
> Path D remains the same, at 30 months

Path A would become critical, and the new estimated completion time would be 42 months, a 2-month saving over the initial time.

PERT

PERT, like CPM, is also a time-oriented planning and control device. However, PERT analysis yields both a central measure of completion time for a project *and* a measure of dispersion (a standard deviation). Given the mean and standard deviation of the completion time distribution for a project, probabilities of finishing the project in less time or more time than the mean time can be readily determined. There are other subtle differences between CPM and PERT, such as CPM's emphasis on cost, but the basic difference is the incorporation of statistical probabilities into the network.

PERT incorporates uncertainty (and probability) by including three time estimates for each activity rather than only one. These estimates are designated as

a: *optimistic time.* This is the best time that could be expected if everything went exceptionally well, and it would be achieved only about 1 percent of the time.

m: *most likely time.* This is the best estimate, or mode expectation.

b: *pessimistic time.* This is the worst time that could reasonably be expected if everything went wrong, and it would occur only about 1 percent of the time.

The expected mean time (t_e) and variance (σ^2) of each activity are determined as:

$$t_e = \frac{a + 4m + b}{6} \tag{16.1}$$

$$\sigma^2 = \left(\frac{b - a}{6}\right)^2 \tag{16.2}$$

where a = optimistic time estimate

     m = most likely time estimate

     b = pessimistic time estimate

Individual activity times are then summed over the respective paths, and the path with the longest time is the critical path. Variances of component activity times along the critical path may also be summed. The ending time distribution is approximately normal with completion time T_E and standard deviation σ

$$T_E = \sum t_e \tag{16.3}$$

$$\sigma = \sqrt{\sum \sigma_{\text{cp}}^2} \tag{16.4}$$

where σ_{cp}^2 is the variance of an individual activity on the critical path.

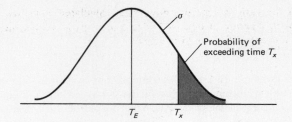

Fig. 16-8   Ending time distribution

Given the mean and standard deviation of the ending distribution, the probabilities of various completion times may be calculated using the normal distribution. For example, to determine the probability that a project would exceed time T_x in Fig. 16-8, we would compute

$$Z = \frac{T_x - T_E}{\sigma}$$

then find the probability associated with that Z value from the normal distribution values in Appendix B (or a hand calculator) and subtract it from .5000. The result would represent the shaded area under the curve in Fig. 16-8.

Example 16.7   Project planners have sought the judgment of various knowledgeable engineers, foremen, and vendors and have developed the time estimates shown in Table 16-4 for the plant construction project depicted in Fig. 16-4. (a) Determine the critical path.   (b) What is the probability the project will be finished within four years?   (c) What is the probability that it will take more than 55 months?

Table 16-4

Activity		Time Estimates		
Description	Number	a	m	b
Design plant	1–2	10	12	16
Select site	2–3	2	8	36
Select vendor	2–4	1	4	5
Select personnel	2–6	2	3	4
Prepare site	3–5	8	12	20
Manufacture generator	4–5	15	18	30
Prepare manual	4–6	3	5	8
Install generator	5–7	2	4	8
Train operators	6–7	6	9	12
License plant	7–8	4	6	14

Table 16-5

t_e $\dfrac{a + 4m + b}{6}$	σ^2 $\left(\dfrac{b - a}{6}\right)^2$
12.33	1.00
11.67	32.11
3.67	.44
3.00	.11
12.67	4.00
19.50	6.25
5.17	.69
4.33	1.00
9.00	1.00
7.00	2.78

Table 16-6

Path	Times
A 1–2–3–5–7–8	$12.33 + 11.67 + 12.67 + 4.33 + 7.00 = 48.00^*$
B: 1–2–4–5–7–8	$12.33 + 3.67 + 19.50 + 4.33 + 7.00 = 46.83$
C: 1–2–4–6–7–8	$12.33 + 3.67 + 5.17 + 9.00 + 7.00 = 37.17$
D: 1–2–6–7–8	$12.33 + 3.00 + 9.00 + 7.00 = 31.33$

*Critical path.

(a) Values for t_e and σ^2 for the various activities have been calculated as shown in Table 16-5. The t_e values are entered on the network diagram in Fig. 16-9. The critical path, as determined in Table 16-6, is now A and has been shown by a heavy solid line in the figure.

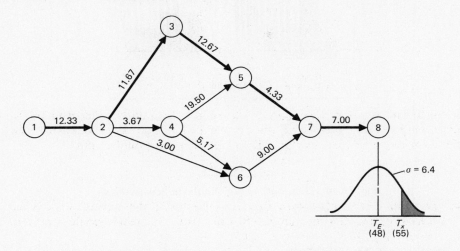

Fig. 16-9 Network diagram showing critical path and ending time distribution

(b) The best estimate of completion time is $T_E = 48.0$ months, so there is a 50 percent chance that the project will be finished within the 4-year time period.

(c) To determine any other completion time probabilities, we must calculate the standard deviation of the distribution of completion times *along the critical path*.

$$\sigma = \sqrt{\sum \sigma_{cp}^2} = \sqrt{1.00 + 32.11 + 4.00 + 1.00 + 2.78} = 6.4 \text{ months}$$

$$Z = \frac{T_x - T_E}{\sigma} = \frac{55.0 - 48.0}{6.4} = 1.09$$

$$P(X > T_x) = .5000 - .3621 = .1379$$

Therefore, probability $\cong .14$

Example 16.8 Although the CPM problem (Example 16.2) and the PERT problem (Example 16.7) had the same mean times for each activity, their critical paths (and critical path times) differed. Explain why.

The critical paths differed because PERT incorporates a measure of uncertainty, whereas CPM does not. For example, the site selection activity (2-3) has a most likely time estimate of 8 months, but a pessimistic time estimate of 36 months, resulting in $t_e = 11.67$ months, in contrast to the 8-month figure used in the CPM calculations.

PERT-SIMULATION

PERT simulation (PERT-SIM) is an extension of basic PERT, and it takes account of near critical paths in a network. A comprehensive probability distribution can be used (in a computer) for each activity. See Fig. 16-10. Random numbers are used to obtain a sample time for each activity; the resultant times occur in proportion to the probabilities expressed in the respective probability distributions. After hundreds of trials are run through the computer, a distribution of simulated completion times is developed as an output. The output reflects the probability of different completion times (i.e., different critical paths). Computer output can also show a critical index of the percentage of time that each activity in the network is likely to be on the critical path.

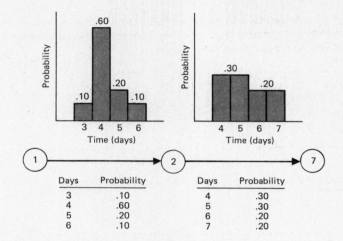

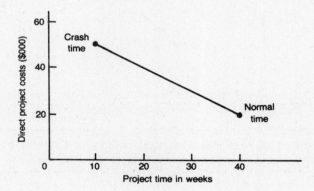

Fig. 16-10   Distributions for simulated activity times

CRASHING: TIME-COST TRADEOFFS

An extension of CPM and PERT referred to as *crashing* a project focuses attention on the tradeoff between time and cost objectives. The *normal* estimate of the time required for each activity (and its associated cost) has already been discussed. The *crash time* estimate is the shortest time that could be achieved if all effort (at any reasonable cost) were made to reduce the activity time. The use of more workers, better equipment, overtime, etc. would generate higher direct costs for individual activities as illustrated in Fig. 16-11. However, shortening the overall time of the project would also reduce certain fixed and overhead expenses of supervision, as well as indirect costs that vary with the length of the project.

Fig. 16-11   Crash time and crash cost

Time-cost models search for the optimum reductions in time. We seek to shorten the length of a project to the point where the savings in indirect project costs is offset by the increased direct expenses incurred in the individual activities.

Example 16.9   A network has four activities with expected times as shown in Fig. 16-12. The minimum feasible times and cost per day to gain reductions in the activity times are shown in Table 16-7. If fixed project costs are $90 per day, what is the lowest cost time schedule?

Table 16-7

Activity	Minimum Time	Direct Costs of Time Reduction ($)
1–2	2	40 (each day)
1–3	2	35 (first day), 80 (second day)
2–4	4	None possible
3–4	3	45 (first day), 110 (other days)

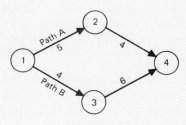

Fig. 16-12

First we must determine the critical path (*) and critical path time cost (Table 16-8).

Table 16-8

	Path Times	Total Project Cost
Path A	5 + 4 = 9	
Path B	4 + 6 = 10*	10 days × $90/day = $900

Next, we must select the activity that can reduce critical path time at the least cost. Select activity 1-3 at $35 per day, which is less than the $90 per day fixed cost. Reduce activity 1-3 to 3 days as shown in Fig. 16-13. Revise the critical path time cost (Table 16-9).

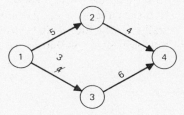

Fig. 16-13

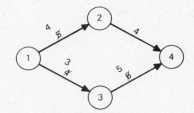

Fig. 16-14

Table 16-9

Revised Path Times	Total Fixed Cost	Savings over Previous Schedule
A: 5 + 4 = 9 B: 3 + 6 = 9	9 × $90 = $810	$900 − ($810 + $35) = $55

Both paths are now critical, so we must select an activity on each path. Select activity 1-2 at $40 per day and 3-4 at $45 per day, where $40 + $45 is less than $90. Reduce activity 1-2 to 4 days and 3-4 to 5 days as shown in Fig. 16-14. Revise the critical path time and cost (Table 16-10).

Table 16-10

Revised Path Times	Total Fixed Cost	Savings over Previous Schedule
A: 4 + 4 = 8 B: 3 + 5 = 8	8 × $90 = $720	$810 − ($720 + $40 + $45) = $5

Again we must reduce the time of both paths. Activity 1-2 is a good candidate on path A, for it is still at 4 days and can go to 3 for a $40 cost. But when this cost is combined with the $80 cost for reducing activity 1-3 another day, the sum is greater than $90, so further reduction is not economically justified. The lowest-cost schedule is as shown in Table 16-10.

The final step in time-cost analysis is to compare the *crash times* and the costs associated with them (*crash costs*). A sufficient number of intermediate schedules are computed such that the total of the direct and indirect (fixed) project costs can be plotted.

Example 16.10 Graph the total relevant costs for the previous example, and indicate the optimal time-cost tradeoff value.

See Table 16-11 and Fig. 16-15.

Table 16-11

Project Length (days)	Indirect Cost	Activity Reduced	Relevant Direct Cost	Relevant Total Cost
10	$900	None	$ 0	$900
9	810	1-3	$ 0 + $ 35 = 35	845
8	720	1-2 and 3-4	35 + 85 = 120	840
7	630	1-2 and 1-3	120 + 120 = 240	870
6	540	1-2 and 3-4	240 + 150 = 390	930

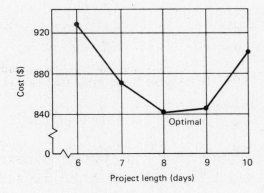

Fig. 16-15

Figure 16-15 is the crash-time diagram for completing the project in 6 to 10 days. The lowest total cost is to complete the project in 8 days at a cost of $840. However, extending it to 9 days adds only $5 to this cost.

Solved Problems

NETWORK FUNDAMENTALS

16.1   Formulate Example 16.1 (Fig. 16-16) as a linear-programming problem.

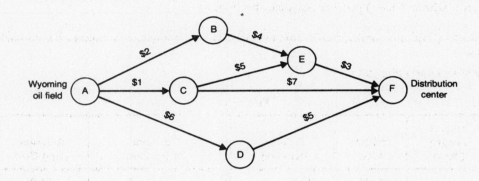

Fig. 16-16

To formulate Fig. 16-16 as a linear-programming problem, we would set up an objective function to minimize the cost of the various links subject to origin, destination, conservation of flow, and non-negativity constraints. Letting X_{AB} represent the inclusion of a link from A to B we have an objective function of

$$\text{Min } Z = 2X_{AB} + 4X_{BE} + 3X_{EF} + X_{AC} + 5X_{CE} + 7X_{CF} + 6X_{AD} + 5X_{DF}$$

Constraints: Use a zero-one formulation where X_{ij} is any link.

$$\text{Let } X_{ij} = \begin{cases} 1 \text{ if the link is part of the least-cost path} \\ 0 \text{ if the link is not part of the least-cost path} \end{cases}$$

Thus, if path A-B-E-F is the least-cost path, then

$$X_{AB} = X_{BE} = X_{EF} = 1 \qquad \text{and} \qquad X_{AC} = X_{CE} = X_{CF} = X_{AD} = X_{DF} = 0$$

Note: A zero-one formulation means that for any given route, the objective function will have ones(1) for the variables representing links on that path and zeros (0) for other links.

The *origin constraint* states that the solution is restricted to exactly one path leaving the origin.

$$X_{AB} + X_{AC} + X_{AD} = 1$$

The *destination constraint* states that the solution is restricted to exactly one path arriving at the destination.

$$X_{EF} + X_{CF} + X_{DF} = 1$$

The *conservation of flow constraints* state that the flows entering a node are equal to those leaving.

for B: $X_{AB} = X_{BC}$	for D: $X_{AD} = X_{DF}$
for C: $X_{AC} = X_{CE} + X_{CF}$	for E: $X_{BE} + X_{CE} = X_{EF}$

The *non-negativity constraints* are as follows:

$$X_{AB} \geq 0 \qquad X_{AC} \geq 0 \qquad X_{AD} \geq 0 \qquad X_{BE} \geq 0$$
$$X_{CE} \geq 0 \qquad X_{CF} \geq 0 \qquad X_{DF} \geq 0 \qquad X_{EF} \geq 0$$

The solution (via computer) would be to use path A-C-F.

CPM and PERT

16.2 A small manufacturing firm has developed the following list of activities (Table 16-12) necessary to release a contract for a new plant. Draw the appropriate network diagram.

Table 16-12

Activity Description	Preceding Activity	Activity Time in Weeks		
		Optimistic	Most Likely	Pessimistic
A-B Feasibility study	none	4	6	10
B-C Acquire site	A-B	2	8	24
B-D Prepare plans	A-B	10	12	16
B-F Marketing strategy	A-B	4	5	10
C-D Soil test	B-C	1	2	3
D-E Legal approvals	C-D and B-D	6	8	30
D-F Loan application	C-D and B-D	2	3	4
E-F Evidence approval	D-E	0	0	0
E-G Obtain bids	D-E	6	6	6
F-G Secure financing	D-F and B-F	2	6	12
G-H Release contract	E-G and F-G	2	2	3

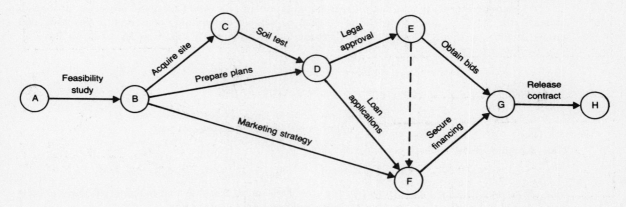

Fig. 16-17

See Fig. 16-17. Note that activity E-F (evidencing legal approval) takes no time and is a dummy activity.

16.3 Compute the expected activity time (t_e) and activity variance (σ^2) for activities A-B and B-C of Prob. 16.2.

A-B:
$$t_e = \frac{a + 4m + B}{6} = \frac{4 + 4(6) + 10}{6} = 6.33 \text{ weeks}$$

$$\sigma^2 = \left(\frac{b-a}{6}\right)^2 = \left(\frac{10-4}{6}\right)^2 = \left(\frac{6}{6}\right)^2 = 1.00 \text{ week}$$

B-C:
$$t_e = \frac{a + 4m + b}{6} = \frac{2 + 4(8) + 24}{6} = 9.67 \text{ weeks}$$

$$\sigma^2 = \left(\frac{b-a}{6}\right)^2 = \left(\frac{24-2}{6}\right)^2 = \left(\frac{22}{6}\right)^2 = 13.44 \text{ weeks}$$

16.4   Given the data shown in Table 16-13 for a PERT network:

(a)   Draw the network diagram and find the critical path.

(b)   What are the parameters of the ending time distribution?

(c)   Which activity has the most precise time estimate?

(d)   Determine the earliest start, latest start, and slack time for all events in the system.

(e)   Each day the project can be shortened is worth $5,000. Should the firm pay $12,500 to reduce activity 3–5 to 2 days?

(a)   See Tables 16-14 and 16-15, and Fig. 16-18.

Table 16-13

Preceding Event	Event	Activity Time		
		a	*m*	*b*
1	2	5	6	13
1	3	2	7	12
2	4	1.5	2	2.5
2	5	1	3	5
3	5	4	5	6
3	6	1	1	1
4	7	2	3	10
5	7	4	5	6
6	7	3	5	7

Table 16-14

Activity	$\dfrac{a + 4m + b}{6}$	$\left(\dfrac{b - a}{6}\right)^2$
1–2	7	1.78
1–3	7	2.77
2–4	2	.02
2–5	3	.44
3–5	5	.11
3–6	1	.00
4–7	4	1.78
5–7	5	.11
6–7	5	.44

Table 16-15

Path	Times
A: 1–2–4–7	7 + 2 + 4 = 13
B: 1–2–5–7	7 + 3 + 5 = 15
C: 1–3–5–7	7 + 5 + 5 = 17*
D: 1–3–6–7	7 + 1 + 5 = 13

*Critical path.

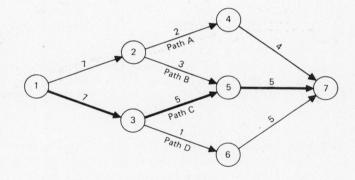

Fig. 16-18

(b)
$$T_E = 17$$

$$\sigma_{cp} = \sqrt{\sum \sigma_{cp}^2} = \sqrt{2.77 + .11 + .11} = 1.73$$

(c)   The most precise time is for activity 3-6, with a variance of zero.

(d)   The ES and LS times for activities on the critical path (path C) are both the same and are simply cumulative totals of the activity times. They are dominating values, for they are maximums in terms of computing ES times (in the forward direction) and minimums in terms of computing LS times (in the reverse direction). See Fig. 16-19. Values for all activities in the network are shown in Table 16-16.

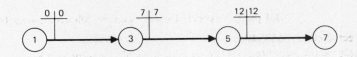

Fig. 16-19

Table 16-16

Activity	Time	ES	LS	Slack
1-2	7	0	2	2
1-3	7	0	0	0
2-4	2	7	11	4
2-5	3	7	9	2
3-5	5	7	7	0
3-6	1	7	11	4
4-7	4	9	13	4
5-7	5	12	12	0
6-7	5	8	12	4

For example, the ES for activity 5-7 is the maximum of

$$\text{Via path B} = 7 + 3 = 10$$
$$\text{Via path C} = 7 + 5 = 12$$

Therefore ES = day 12.

For example, the LS for activity 1-2 is the minimum of

$$\text{Via path A} = 17 - 4 - 2 - 7 = 4$$
$$\text{Via path B} = 17 - 5 - 3 - 7 = 2$$

Therefore LS = day 2.

(e)   Activity 3-5 is on the critical path, and the reduction from 5 to 2 days would reduce the path C time to $17 - 3 = 14$ days. However, path B would become critical at 15 days, so the net reduction would be 2 days at $5,000 per day = $10,000 savings versus the $12,500 cost. The firm should not pay the $12,500.

16.5   Worldwide Constructors, Inc., uses PERT and expected-value techniques to prepare bids and manage construction jobs. Its bid price is set to give it a 30 percent gross profit over expected costs. In calculating the PERT network for a bridge construction job, T_E was found to be equal to 60 days, and total variance along the critical path was $\sigma_{cp}^2 = 36$. See Fig. 16-20. Total expenses for the project are estimated at $335,000, but if the bridge is not completed within 70 days, there is a penalty of $50,000. Determine the appropriate bid price.

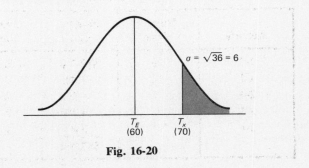

Fig. 16-20

$$\text{Bid price} = \text{expected costs} + \text{penalty allowance} + \text{profit}$$

where   expected costs = \$335,000

penalty allowance = (amount of penalty)(probability of penalty)

$$Z = \frac{T_x - T_E}{\sigma} = \frac{70 - 60}{6} = 1.67$$

$$P(Z) = .4525$$

$$P(X > T_x) = .5000 - .4525 = .0475$$

Penalty allowance = (\$50,000)(.0475) = \$2,375

Profit = .30(\$335,000 + \$2,375) = \$101,212

Bid price = \$335,000 + \$2,375 + \$101,212 = \$438,587

16.6   An electrical firm has developed a PERT plan for the electrical wiring activity of power plant control panels. It expects that assembly operations will follow a 90 percent learning curve. The project team, composed of workers, electricians, and supervisors, feels the first assembly will most likely be completed in 14 days but could take as long as 24 days, or if everything went exceptionally well, it would be finished in 10 days. What is the expected assembly time of the fourth unit?

$$t_e = \frac{a + 4m + b}{6} = \frac{10 + 4(14) + 24}{6} = 15$$

$$\text{Fourth unit \% base} = \frac{4}{1} = 400\%$$

Then, from Appendix H we have

$$Y_N = Y_B(L) = 15(.81) = 12.15 \text{ days}$$

CRASHING: TIME-COST TRADEOFFS

16.6   The network diagram shown in Fig. 16-21 has the time and direct costs given in Table 16-17. The time-cost tradeoffs are cumulative amounts; that is, you can reduce activity 1-2 by 2 weeks, for a total of \$16,000 − \$12,000 = \$4,000, or \$2,000 a week.

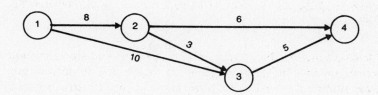

Fig. 16-21

Table 16-17

Activity	Normal Time	Normal Cost	Crash Time	Crash Cost
1-2	8	\$12,000	6	\$13,600
1-3	10	6,000	7	10,500
2-4	6	8,000	4	10,000
2-3	3	14,000	2	17,000
3-4	5	7,000	2	9,700
		\$47,000		

(a) Compute the total direct costs for completing the project in 16, 15, 14, 13, 12, or 11 weeks.

(b) The indirect project costs are shown in Table 16-18. Graph the total project cost (direct and indirect), and determine the least cost project completion time.

Table 16-18

Project duration (weeks)	16	15	14	13	12	11
Indirect costs (dollars)	23,000	19,100	17,200	14,400	13,700	13,200

(a) For convenience, set up a table (Table 16-19) to show the incremental cost of reducing each activity, the maximum reduction possible, and a far right column for keeping a tally of the reductions used.

Table 16-19

Activity	Normal		Crash		Incremental Cost of Reduction	Reduction	
	Time	Cost	Time	Cost		Max	Used
1-2	8	$12,000	6	$13,600	$ 800/wk	2	✓✓
1-3	10	6,000	7	10,500	1,500/wk	3	✓
2-4	6	8,000	4	10,000	1,000/wk	2	✓
2-3	3	14,000	2	17,000	3,000/wk	1	
3-4	5	7,000	2	9,700	900/wk	3	✓✓✓

Next, compute the times for each path (A = 14, B = 16, C = 15) and identify the critical path (shown dashed in Fig. 16-22). Begin the time-cost analysis by reducing the time for the activity on the critical path (or paths) which has the smallest total of all incremental costs, (i.e., activity 1-2). Draw a new network diagram and compute a revised direction cost for each reduced time.

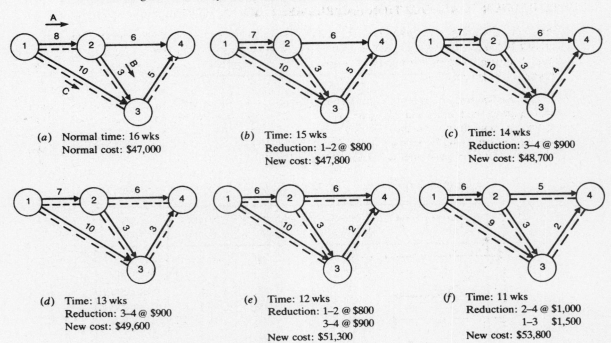

(a) Normal time: 16 wks
Normal cost: $47,000

(b) Time: 15 wks
Reduction: 1–2 @ $800
New cost: $47,800

(c) Time: 14 wks
Reduction: 3–4 @ $900
New cost: $48,700

(d) Time: 13 wks
Reduction: 3–4 @ $900
New cost: $49,600

(e) Time: 12 wks
Reduction: 1–2 @ $800
          3–4 @ $900
New cost: $51,300

(f) Time: 11 wks
Reduction: 2–4 @ $1,000
          1–3 $1,500
New cost: $53,800

Fig. 16-22 Crash times and costs

(b) See Table 16-20 and Fig. 16-23.

Table 16-20

Time (wk)	11	12	13	14	15	16
Direct costs	$53,800	$51,300	$49,600	$48,700	$47,800	$47,000
Indirect costs	13,200	13,700	14,400	17,200	19,100	23,000
Total costs	$67,000	$65,000	$64,000	$65,900	$66,900	$70,000

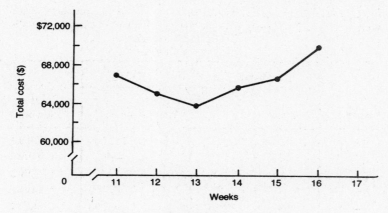

Fig. 16-23

The least cost project completion time is 13 weeks.

LIMITED RESOURCE ALLOCATION (SUPPLEMENTARY MATERIAL)

16.8   The accompanying schedule-time graph (top two charts of Fig. 16-24) depicts a project with activity times (a through g) as shown on the horizontal axis and a critical path (a, b, e, g) of 7 days. Numbers above the activities represent personnel requirements. Develop an improved personnel balance.

The dashed lines represent slack time and potential relocation zones for activities on the respective paths. Locate maximum and minimum resource requirements, and try to shift activities into slack positions to smooth the demand. The solution is shown in the bottom half of Fig. 16-24 with the revised network and personnel balance as shown. The solution consists simply of shifting activities c and f, which reduces the range of personnel requirements from $20 - 6 = 14$ to $16 - 12 = 4$.

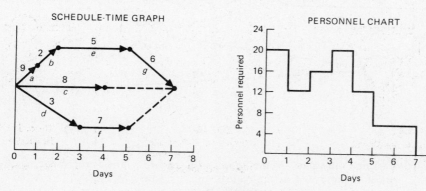

Fig. 16-24

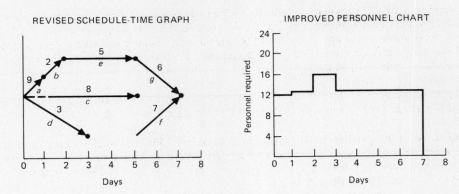

Fig. 16-24   *(cont.)*

Supplementary Problems

16.9   A large power transformer is to be transported from a factory (A) to a destination (H). Alternative routes and associated costs ($) are as shown in Fig. 16-25. What is the least cost route?
Ans.   A-D-E-G-H for a cost of $570

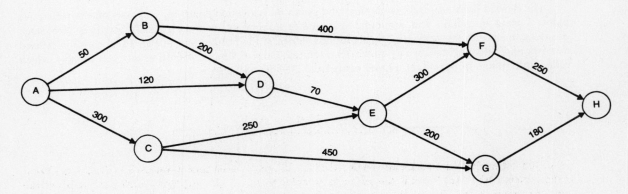

Fig. 16-25

16.10   In Prob. 16.9, assume the values on the network diagram (Fig. 16-25) represent activity times (days) to complete a project. What would be the critical path?   *Ans.*   A-C-E-F-H for 1,100 days

16.11 In developing a PERT network for a bridge construction project, the construction foreman felt the optimistic estimate of a concrete pouring activity was 30 days. The project quality control inspector, citing all the possible delays and rework, said (pessimistically) that it could take as long as 180 days. Both agreed the most likely time was 45 days. Estimate (a) the expected activity time t_e and (b) the activity variance σ^2.   *Ans.*   (a) 65 days (b) 625

16.12 The expected completion time of a PERT project is $T_E = 15$ days, and $\sigma^2_{cp} = 4$ days. What is the probability that the project will take 18 or more days to complete?   *Ans.*   .07

16.13 A PERT network has expected times (t_e) in days as shown in Fig. 16-26. The time estimates for activity 6-7 are $a = 1$, $m = 4$, and $b = 7$. For the network, what is the (a) expected completion time T_E?   (b) completion time standard deviation σ_{cp}?   (c) probability the project will take more than 20.5 days to complete?   *Ans.*   (a) 18 days (b) 3 (c) .20

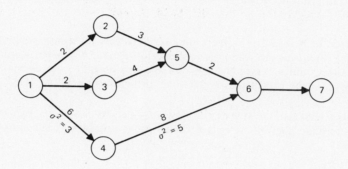

Fig. 16-26

16.14 A microwave relay station construction project is being planned on a PERT basis with the data shown in Table 16-21 given in days.

Table 16-21

Activity	a	m	b
1-2	2	3	10
1-3	8	12	20
1-4	10	14	16
2-5	6	10	12
3-5	14	20	26
3-7	3	5	7
4-6	8	12	20
5-7	1	1	1
6-8	6	10	12
7-8	1	3	7

(a) Construct a PERT network diagram showing the expected mean time t_e for each activity.   (b) What is the critical path?   (c) What is the expected completion time T_E?   (d) How much slack exists in the path containing event 2?   (e) What is the latest day event 2 can be completed without delaying the project?   (f) Find σ_{cp}.   (g) What is the probability the project will take longer than 41 days to complete?

Ans.   (a) The network diagram should show activities as arrows and events as circles, beginning with event 1 and ending with 8 (b) 1-3-5-7-8 (c) 37 days (d) 19 days (e) day 23 (f) 3 days (g) .0918

16.15 Given the data in the previous problem, assume that each day of improvement in the completion schedule results in a $3,000 savings (or bonus). For a cost of $2,000 the firm could do any *one* of the following: (*a*) reduce the t_e of activity 3-7 by 3 days; (*b*) reduce the t_e of activity 1-3 by 2 days, or (*c*) reduce the t_e of activities 3-5, 6-8, and 7-8 by 1 day each. Evaluate the alternative choices and indicate which, if any, is preferable.   *Ans.*   (*c*) for a $4,000 savings

16.16 A building contractor company has bid on a job for a water reservoir that must be completed within 34 days ($T_L = 34$), or else the company must pay a $2,000 penalty. If the project is finished within 28 days, the company will get a $1,000 bonus. Expenses associated with the project are estimated to be $30,000. The company has developed a PERT chart of the project and found that $T_E = 31$ days. The variance estimates of the five activities along the critical path are 1.3, 2.2, 2.1, .9, and 2.5 days, respectively. (*a*) What is the probability of obtaining the bonus (accurate to two digits)?   (*b*) Assuming that the company wishes to adjust its bid price to allow for the expected bonus or penalty and come out with only a long-run expected profit of $5,000, for what contract price should it be willing to accept the job? *Ans.*   (*a*) .1587 (*b*) $35,160

16.17 A PERT chart is to be used to estimate the assembly time for a new component which is later to be manufactured. Subsequent production is expected to follow a 70 percent learning curve. The optimistic, most likely, and pessimistic assembly times for the first assembly are estimated at 2, 4, and 12 hours, respectively. What is the expected assembly time of the fourth unit?   *Ans.*   2.45 hours

16.18 The earliest start (ES) and latest start (LS) times for activity 6-7 of a network diagram are as shown in Fig. 16-27. Determine appropriate values for all other activities of the network, and show them in a similar manner.

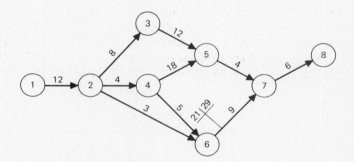

Fig. 16-27

Ans.   The chart should show the times found in Table 16-22.

Table 16-22

Activity	1-2	2-3	2-4	2-6	3-5	4-5	4-6	5-7	6-7	7-8
ES	0	12	12	12	20	16	16	34	21	38
LS	0	14	12	26	22	16	24	34	29	38

16.19 *PERT Cost.* A network has time (in weeks) and direct costs (in dollars) as shown in Fig. 16-28 and Table 16-23. Crash costs are cumulative totals; i.e., the incremental amount above normal costs can be apportioned equally among the time intervals. (*a*) Compute the total direct costs for finishing the project in 9, 10, 11, 12 or 13 weeks. (*b*) The indirect project costs are shown in Table 16-24. Graph the total project costs (direct and indirect) and determine the least cost project completion time.

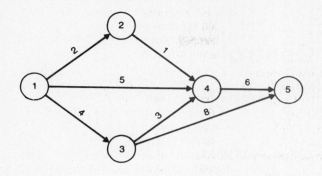

Fig. 16-28

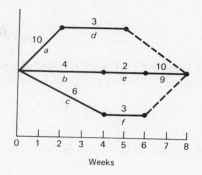

Fig. 16-29

Table 16-23

Activity	Normal Time	Normal Cost	Crash Time	Crash Cost
1-2	2	$ 500	1	$ 800
1-4	5	900	3	1,300
1-3	4	800	3	1,000
2-4	1	400	1	400
3-4	3	1,200	2	1,800
4-5	6	700	4	900
3-5	8	600	4	1,200
		$5,100		

Table 16-24

Project duration	9	10	11	12	13
Indirect costs	$6,000	$6,150	$6,200	$6,500	$7,100

Ans. (*a*) Direct costs for completion times are as shown in Table 16-25. (*b*) The least cost project completion time is 11 weeks, at a cost of $5,400 direct +$6,200 indirect = $11,600 total.

Table 16-25

Project duration	9	10	11	12	13
Direct costs	$6,400	$5,650	$5,400	$5,200	$5,100

16.20 *Limited Resource Allocation.* A government naval shipyard has received orders to proceed with a ship construction project and is using CPM. It has developed a schedule-time graph (Fig. 16-29) to show employment requirements over a portion of the project. The numbers above the activities indicate the number of shipfitters required for the respective activities. Develop an improved personnel balance that minimizes the range of the number of shipfitters required.

Ans. Use 14 shipfitters during periods 1 and 2, 10 during 3, 13 during 4, 11 during 5 and 6, and 13 during 7 and 8; and so the range is $14 - 10 = 4$.

Chapter 17

Quality Control

Statistical Methods

DEFINITION OF QUALITY

Quality is a measure of how closely a good or service conforms to specified standards. The standards may relate to time, materials, performance, reliability, or any quantifiable (objective and measurable) characteristic.

When quantifiable standards are absent, quality becomes a matter of opinion and is not controllable from a scientific standpoint. Assessments that depend on subjective feelings or substitute measures, such as the name of an artist or performer, belong more in the realm of art than science. Industrial quality is not dictated by who made the product, the price paid for it, or the preferences of the individual who owns or uses it. Thus, expensive products with extra features are not necessarily *high* quality, and inexpensive goods or services are not necessarily *low* quality.

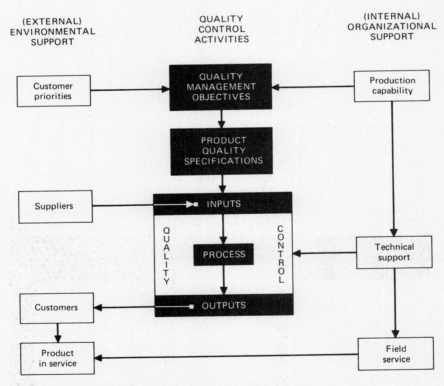

Fig. 17-1 Elements of quality-assurance system

QUALITY ASSURANCE AND QC CIRCLES

Quality assurance is the system of policies, procedures, and guidelines that establishes and maintains the specified standards of product quality. Figure 17-1 identifies the major elements of a quality-assurance system. Responsibility for controlling quality rests with everyone who is in a position to affect quality. Firms that install automatic controls or use robotic operations often experience an improvement in the quality of their products (e.g., welds from robots are more consistent).

Quality control (QC) *circles* are small groups of employees who meet voluntarily on a regular basis to share ideas in an attempt to identify, analyze, and solve quality or job-related problems. The groups are often made up of 8 to 10 individuals who perform similar jobs. In many companies, their recommendations have resulted in a reduced number of defects, reduced absenteeism, and a general improvement in job satisfaction and productivity.

QUALITY-CONTROL COSTS

Quality costs are classified into *inspection and control* costs, and *defective product* costs. See Fig. 17-2. The optimal level of expenditure on quality-control activities occurs where the total costs are minimized.

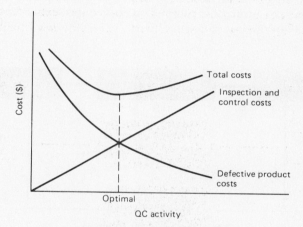

Fig. 17-2   Quality costs

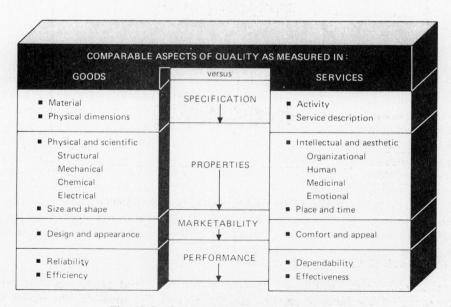

Fig. 17-3   Quality in goods versus services

QUALITY MEASURES IN GOODS AND SERVICES

Quality control involves *measurement* of the quality characteristic, *feedback* of the data, *comparison* with specified standards, and *correction* when necessary. Quality control in the production of goods rests heavily upon the measurement of material characteristics. Physical properties, design, and product reliability are key elements. Services often convey intellectual or aesthetic values whose quality is more difficult to measure. Surrogate measures such as service environment or service times are often used to evaluate the quality of services. A comparison of the characteristics of quality in goods and services is found in Fig. 17-3.

STATISTICAL METHODS OF CONTROLLING QUALITY

The two major approaches to controlling quality are *acceptance sampling* of incoming or outgoing products, and *process control* of the actual transformation activities. See Fig. 17-4. Both methods involve statistical sampling techniques. However, acceptance sampling methods rely upon estimating the levels of defective items before or after a process has been completed. Process control is more useful during a process to ensure that production is not outside of acceptable limits. The primary means of process control is via the use of control charts.

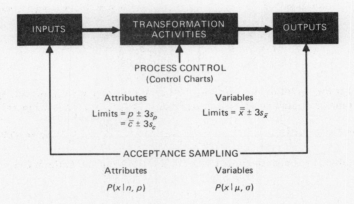

Fig. 17-4 Statistical techniques for controlling quality

The quality characteristic being observed is classified as either an attributes or variables characteristic. *Attributes characteristics* are either present or not, such as defective or nondefective, or passing a test or failing it. There is no measure of the degree of conformance. For attributes data, a discrete distribution, such as the binomial or Poisson, is used to make inferences about the population characteristic being controlled. *Variables characteristics* are present in varying degrees and are measurable. Examples are dimensions, weights, and times. For variables data, continuous distributions such as the normal are used.

Figure 17-5 describes the significant characteristics of some of the most common statistical distributions used in quality assessment. If the variable of interest in a population is known to follow a normal, Poisson, or other statistical distribution, the probabilities of obtaining specific outcomes from that population can be determined by *deductive logic*, using probability theory. Other applications call for an inference about the quality level of the population on the basis of limited sample evidence. Making this inference is an *inductive* process.

Example 17.1 (Binomial Distribution) Fifteen percent of the accounts audited by a CPA firm turn out to have errors that necessitate the payment of additional taxes. What is the chance that exactly 2 accounts taken from a random sample of 10 will owe additional taxes?

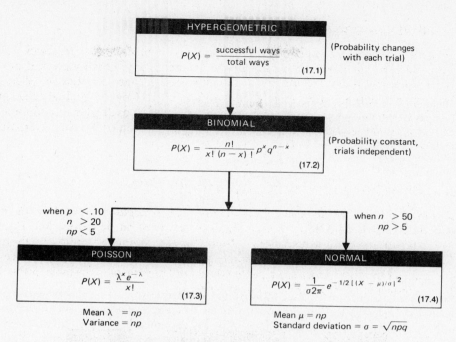

Fig. 17-5   Probability distributions useful in quality control

This problem calls for the use of deductive logic. The error rate is given as a percentage and can be taken as constant. If we can assume that each account is independent of others, then the binomial distribution applies.

$$P(X = 2 \mid n = 10, p = .15) = \frac{n!}{x!(n-x)!} p^x q^{n-x} = \frac{10!}{2!8!}(.15)^2(.85)^8 = .2759$$

Note that the solution value could also be obtained more directly from the table of binomial probabilities given in Appendix C.

Example 17.2   (Normal Distribution)   Cans of corn at the Cresent Valley Cannery are filled by a machine which can be set for any desired average weight. The fill is normally distributed with a standard deviation of .4 ounce. If quality standards specify that 98 percent of the cans should contain 16 ounces or more, where should the quality-control supervisor recommend the machine be set on the ounce scale?

The machine average μ must be set high enough so that 48 percent of the cans containing less than the mean still contain 16.0 ounces. Knowing that the fill is normally distributed (Fig. 17-6), we can use the expression for the standard normal deviate.

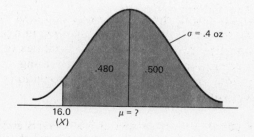

Fig. 17-6

$$Z = \frac{X - \mu}{\sigma}$$

where X = specified fill = 16.0 oz
        μ = unknown mean setting
        σ = .4 oz
        Z = number of standard deviations from μ to X (*Note*: This corresponds to an area of 48%. We must enter the body of the normal distribution table—Appendix B—as close as possible to the value of .48 and read off the number of standard deviations from the margin.)

For $P(X) = .480$, $Z = -2.05$.

Therefore $\mu = X + Z\sigma = 16.0 + 2.05(.4) = 16.8$ oz

ACCEPTANCE SAMPLING PLANS

Quality control inspections are frequently upon receipt of raw materials or upon completion of the product. A general *guideline* is to *inspect whenever the cost of inspection at a given stage is less than the probable loss from not inspecting.*

When 100 percent inspection is uneconomical or infeasible (e.g., if it destroys the product), the decision to accept or reject a lot is made on the basis of sample evidence. But every sample is not necessarily representative of the population. Thus acceptance sampling involves some risk of rejecting good lots and accepting bad lots. The amount of risk can be specified and statistically controlled in terms of a sampling plan.

A *sampling plan* is a decision rule that specifies how large a sample n should be taken and the allowable measurement, number, or percentage c of defectives in the sample. Sampling plans for *attributes* are based upon a qualitative (countable) classification of the item (e.g., percent good or bad), and the probabilities of defectives in the parent population are estimated from discrete distributions such as the binomial and Poisson. Sampling plans for *variables* are based on a quantitative (measurable) characteristic and typically use the normal distribution. We shall let c represent the specified acceptable limit, and X the hypothetical, or actual percent or number, of defectives.

Example 17.3   Illustrate a sampling plan for (*a*) attributes and (*b*) variables.

(*a*)   *Attributes plan*: Select a random sample of size $n = 40$, and count the number of defectives X. If $X \leq 3$, accept the lot; otherwise, reject it.

(*b*)   *Variables Plan*: Select a random sample of size $n = 40$, and measure the mean tensile strength, $\bar{X}$. If $X \geq 12,000$ psi, accept the lot; otherwise, reject it.

OPERATING CHARACTERISTIC CURVES

An *operating characteristic curve* is a graphic description of a specific sampling plan (n, c combination), which shows the probability that the plan will accept lots of various (possible) quality levels. Figure 17-7a illustrates the operating characteristic (OC) curves for an attributes measurement where there is 100 percent inspection of a shipment of $N = 100$ items. If $\leq 2\frac{1}{2}$ percent are defective, the shipment is accepted, and if $> 2\frac{1}{2}$ are defective, it is rejected. Assuming accurate inspection, there is no risk of error. If the lot contains either 0, 1, 2 defectives, the probability of acceptance is 1.0, whereas with 3 or more defectives the $P(\text{accept}) = 0$.

In Fig. 17-7b the shipment is much larger ($N = 1,000$), and the producer and consumer must adopt a sampling plan to reduce inspection costs. Two risks result:

(1)   *Producer's risk* is the risk of getting a sample which has a higher proportion of defectives than the lot as a whole, and rejecting a good lot. It is designated as the alpha (α) risk. Producers hope to keep this risk low, between 1–5 percent. If a good lot is rejected, we refer to this as a type I error.

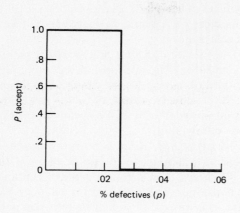

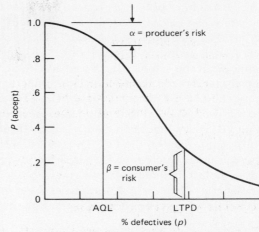

(a) OC curve for 100 percent inspection   (b) OC curve for less than 100 percent inspection

Fig. 17-7 Operating characteristic curves

(2) *Consumer's risk* is the risk of getting a sample which has a lower proportion of defectives than the lot as a whole, and accepting a bad lot. It is designated as the beta (β) risk. Consumers want to keep this risk low. If a bad lot is accepted, we refer to this as a type II error.

To derive a sampling plan, the producer and consumer must not only specify the level of the α and β risk, but also the lot quality level to which these risks pertain. Thus we must further define *good lot* and *bad lot* in terms of the percent defective in the population.

The *acceptable quality level* (AQL) is the quality level of a good lot. It is the percent defective that can be considered satisfactory as a process average, and represents a level of quality which the producer wants accepted with a high probability of acceptance.

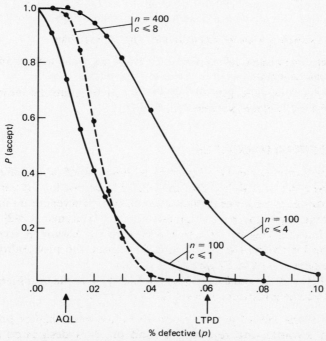

Fig. 17-8 Effect on the OC curve of changing the sample size and the acceptance number

The *lot tolerance percent defective* (LTPD) is the quality level of a bad lot. It represents a level of quality which the consumer wants accepted with a low probability of acceptance. Lots which have a quality level between the AQL and LTPD are in an indifferent zone.

The α risk at the AQL level and β risk at the LTPD level establish two points which largely determine what the sample size n and acceptance number c must be. The appropriate sampling plan (n, c combination) can be found by consulting *tables of* standard plans such as the Dodge and Romig tables, or the U.S. Military Standard MIL-STD-105 tables. Alternatively, a *trial and error* procedure can be followed wherein different values of n and c are tried in order to find the combination that yields an OC curve that most closely passes through the two points.

For a small sample, the OC curve is relatively flat, resulting in high risks to both the producer and the consumer. Increasing n makes the OC curve more discriminating, to the point where a 100 percent sample eliminates all risk (Fig. 17-7a). Figure 17-8 shows how increasing the acceptance number from $c \leq 1$ to $c \leq 4$ shifts the risk from producer to consumer. The sampling plan depicted by the dashed line shows the effect of increasing the sample size; it is more discriminating between good (AQL) and bad (LTPD) lots.

SAMPLING PLANS FOR ATTRIBUTES

Once the α and β risks are set (at the AQL and LTPD points, respectively) a sampling plan (n, c values) can be determined. If the data is expressed in terms of proportions (e.g., percent defective) then the binomial, Poisson, or even normal-approximation distribution is used to calculate the probabilities of acceptance for the attributes sampling plan.

Example 17-4 A shipment of 1,000 semiconductors is to be inspected on a sampling basis. The producer and consumer have agreed to adopt a plan whereby the α risk is limited to 5 percent at AQL = 1 percent defective, and the β risk is limited to 10 percent at LTPD = 5 percent defective. Construct the OC curve for the sampling plan $n = 100$ and $c \leq 2$, and indicate whether this plan satisfies the requirements.

To construct the OC curve we must determine the probabilities of acceptance of the shipment for various possible values of the true percentage of defectives in the population. Since the shipment is accepted when there are ≤ 2 defectives in the sample, the probabilities we seek are $P(x \leq 2)$, given the alternative values of the population. If we were working with a binomial distribution, we could write this probability as

$$P(X \leq 2 | n, p)$$

and obtain the values from a calculator or Appendix C. However, from Fig. 17-5 note that the binomial probabilities of defectives can be approximated by a Poisson distribution here because the sample size (100) is >20. We appear to be working with a small percent defective of $p < .10$, and np looks to be in the neighborhood of 5. Using Appendix D we can obtain the Poisson probabilities as

$$P(X \leq 2 | \lambda)$$

where X = number of defectives in sample

λ = mean of Poisson distribution = np

p = (alternative) percentage of defectives in population

Thus, for the AQL percentage of $p = .01$, we can find the probability of acceptance of the lot as

$$P(X \leq 2 | \lambda)$$

where $\lambda = np = (100)(.01) = 1$. Therefore

$$P(X \leq 2 | \lambda = 1) = .92$$

(from Appendix D).

Probabilities for other possible values of the true mean are given in Fig. 17-9a, and these values are plotted as an OC curve in Figure 17-9b.

Note that this plan ($n = 100$, $c \leq 2$) yields an α risk of .08 and a β risk of .12. Both exceed the respective limits of .05 and .10. Since both risks are exceeded, a larger sample size will be required, and the calculations will have to be repeated.

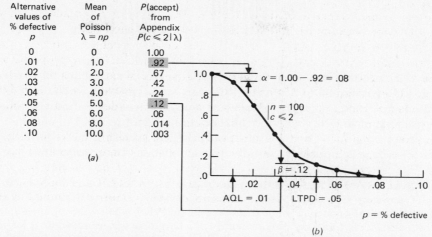

Alternative values of % defective p	Mean of Poisson $\lambda = np$	P(accept) from Appendix $P(c \leq 2 | \lambda)$
0	0	1.00
.01	1.0	.92
.02	2.0	.67
.03	3.0	.42
.04	4.0	.24
.05	5.0	.12
.06	6.0	.06
.08	8.0	.014
.10	10.0	.003

(a)

(b)

Fig. 17-9   OC curve values and operating characteristic curve for sampling plan $n = 100$, with $c \leq 2$

SAMPLING PLANS FOR VARIABLES

Sampling plans for variables require measurements of the characteristic being controlled. Because measurements yield more information than counts (i.e., they yield a measure of dispersion) the n and c values of sampling plans can be calculated more directly. They capitalize on the fact that means of sufficiently large samples are normally distributed in a sampling distribution which has a mean $= \mu$ and standard error $\sigma_{\bar{x}} = \sigma/\sqrt{n}$.

The first sampling plan example (Example 17.5) assumes that the sample size is predetermined, and that only one risk is to be controlled (i.e., either α or β). Simply use the normal distribution and solve for the critical limit c. If c is given, solve for n.

Example 17.5   (Given α Risk Only: Solving for c)   A metals firm produces titanium castings whose weights are normally distributed with a standard deviation of $\sigma = 8$ pounds. Casting shipments averaging less than 200 pounds are considered poor quality, and the firm would like to minimize such shipments. Design a sampling plan for a sample of $n = 25$ that will limit the risk of rejecting lots that average 200 pounds to 5 percent.

The problem situation is described schematically in Fig. 17-10. We assume that the distribution of sample means is approximately normal, with mean $\mu = 200$ and standard error:

$$\sigma_{\bar{x}} = \frac{\sigma}{\sqrt{n}} = \frac{8}{\sqrt{25}} = 1.6 \text{ lb}$$

The limit c is then:

$$c = \mu - Z\sigma_{\bar{x}}$$

where Z = value corresponding to area of .450 = 1.64 (from Appendix B).

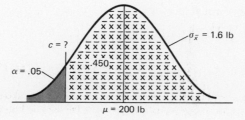

Fig. 17-10

Thus, $c = 200 - 1.64(1.6) = 197.4 \text{ lb}$

Plan: Take a random sample of $n = 25$ ingots and determine the mean weight. If $\bar{x} > 197.4 \text{ lb}$ accept the shipment; otherwise reject it.

In Example 17.5, with the limit set at 197.4 pounds, the risk of rejecting a lot that really averages 200 pounds (a good lot) is limited to 5 percent. The plan was established wholly on the basis of the α risk and a given sample size. A larger sample size would, of course, be more discriminating. For example, with a sample of $n = 100$ the reject limit could be raised to 198.7 pounds.

If both the producers (α) risk and consumers (β) risk are specified, the required sample size (n) and reject limit (c) can be computed by setting up two equations for c rather than one.

Example 17.6 (Given α and β Risks: Solving for n and c) A metals firm produces titanium castings whose weights are normally distributed, with a standard deviation of $\sigma = 8.0$ pounds. Casting shipments averaging 200 pounds are of good quality, and those averaging 196 pounds are of poor quality. Design a sampling plan that satisfies the following requirements: (*a*) The probability of rejecting a lot with an average weight of 200 pounds is .05. (*b*) The probability of accepting a lot with an average weight of 196 pounds is .10.

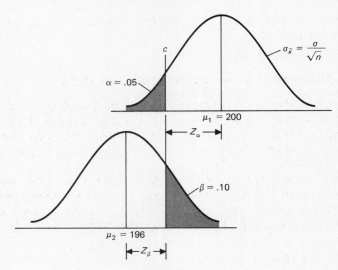

Fig. 17-11

The problem situation is described schematically in Fig. 17-11. The solution procedure is to first set up simultaneous equations defining the reject limit c in terms of Z standard errors. Then solve for n and substitute it back into either one of the equations to find c. The two equations locating c are

(*a*)   From above: $c = \mu_1 - Z_\alpha \dfrac{\sigma}{\sqrt{n}} = 200 - 1.645 \dfrac{(8)}{\sqrt{n}}$

(*b*)   From below: $c = \mu_2 + Z_\beta \dfrac{\sigma}{\sqrt{n}} = 196 + 1.28 \dfrac{(8)}{\sqrt{n}}$

Setting the two equations for c equal to each other:

$$200 - 1.645 \frac{(8)}{\sqrt{n}} = 196 + 1.28 \frac{(8)}{\sqrt{n}}$$

$$n = \left(\frac{23.40}{4}\right)^2 = 34$$

Therefore, $c = 200 - 1.645 \dfrac{(8)}{\sqrt{34}} = 197.7 \text{ lb}$

Plan: Take a random sample of $n = 34$ ingots, and determine the mean weight. If $\bar{x} > 197.7$ pounds, accept the shipment; otherwise, reject it.

AVERAGE OUTGOING QUALITY LEVELS

An *average outgoing quality* (AOQ) curve shows the average expected quality in all outgoing lots after the rejected lots from the sample have been 100 percent inspected and all defects removed. Incoming lots with a small percentage of defects will be passed with a resultant high outgoing quality. Those with a slightly larger proportion of defectives will result in the worst outgoing quality, because lots that have a large proportion of defects will end up undergoing 100 percent inspection, with only the acceptable items being passed. The AOQ curve has the true percentage of defectives in lots undergoing inspection on the x axis and the percentage of defectives (P_D) in lots of size N after inspection on the y axis.

$$\text{AOQ} = \frac{P_D P_A (N - n)}{N} \qquad (17.5)$$

where P_A is the probability of accepting the lot for various values of the percent defective (from the OC curve), and n is the sample size.

PROCESS CONTROL FOR VARIABLES VIA CONTROL CHARTS

Control charts are graphic devices used to monitor selected quality characteristics of a production process over time. *Variables control charts*, such as mean $\bar{X}$ and range $\bar{R}$ charts, are used to monitor continuous (measurable) data (e.g., the weight or dimensions of a product). *Attributes control charts*, such as proportion p and number c charts are used to monitor discrete (countable) data (e.g., the percentage or number of defects in a product).

Many processes have broad natural tolerance limits within which most individual observations lie. However, as the central limit theorem states, sample means and sample proportions exhibit much less variation than individual values. See Fig. 17-12 where T_{UN} and T_{LN} are the upper and lower natural tolerance limits and UCL and LCL are the upper and lower control limits.

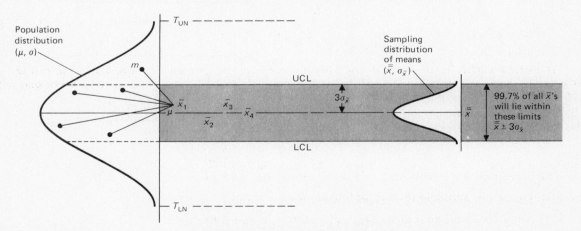

Fig. 17-12   Control limits for sample means

Control limits are the boundaries within which sample statistics can be expected to vary due simply to the randomness of the sample used. They are computed from the relatively tight sampling distributions and are typically set at 3 (or possibly 2) standard errors away from the process average.

When a process is "in control," 99.7 percent of the sample averages should be within ± 3 standard errors of the chart centerline. If sample averages fall outside the control limits, some assignable cause is probably responsible and corrective action should be taken.

Example 17.7 A control chart is established, with limits of ± 2 standard errors, for use in monitoring samples of size $n = 20$. Assume the process is in control. (a) Would you expect many *individual values* to lie outside these limits? (b) How likely would a *sample mean* fall outside the control limits? (c) What kind of error would be committed in erroneously concluding that the process is out of control?

(a) Yes, the limits are set to control mean values, not individual values. (b) Assuming normality, 95.5 percent of the sample means are within ± 2 standard errors, so about 4.5 percent of the means would lie outside. (c) Type I. This is concluding the process is out of control when it is not.

Figure 17-13 illustrates and lists some expressions for computing control limits for variables. A control chart of means ($\bar{X}$ chart) reveals variation *among* sample means and is used to signal a shift in the process mean. The range ($\bar{R}$) chart monitors variability *within* samples and is used to signal a change in the spread or dispersion of the data. The range is a common measure of dispersion, and the standard expressions for means (Eqs. 17.6 and 17.7) have been adapted to the use of ranges (Eqs. 17.8 and 17.9) by using standardized conversion factors as given in Table 17-1. These factors also facilitate calculation of range control limits (Eqs. 17.10 and 17.11).

Means ($\bar{X}$-charts)

$$\text{UCL}_{\bar{X}} = \bar{\bar{X}} + Z\sigma_{\bar{X}} \qquad (17.6)$$
$$\text{LCL}_{\bar{X}} = \bar{\bar{X}} - Z\sigma_{\bar{X}} \qquad (17.7)$$

Stating the equations in terms of ranges we have

$$\text{UCL}_{\bar{X}} = \bar{\bar{X}} + A\bar{R} \qquad (17.8)$$
$$\text{LCL}_{\bar{X}} = \bar{\bar{X}} - A\bar{R} \qquad (17.9)$$

Range ($\bar{R}$-charts)

$$\text{UCL}_R = B\bar{R} \qquad (17.10)$$
$$\text{LCL}_R = C\bar{R} \qquad (17.11)$$

where $\bar{\bar{X}}$ is mean of sample $\bar{X}$'s, $\bar{R}$ is mean of sample R's, and B and C are control factors from Table 17-1.

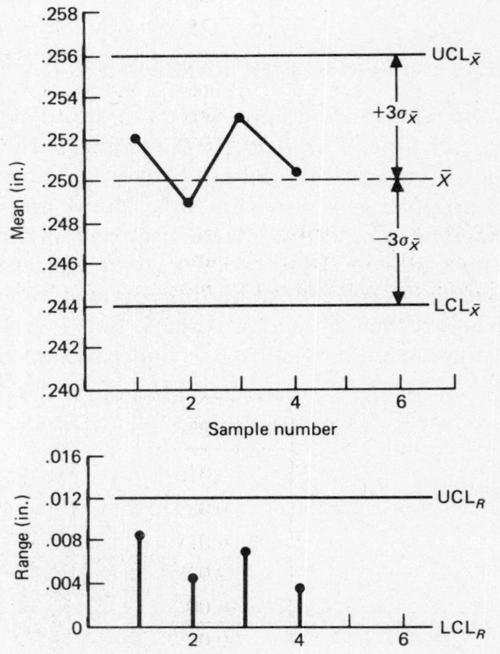

Fig. 17-13 Control chart limits for variables

The procedure for establishing and using control limits is:

(1) Select job and quality characteristic to be monitored.

(2) Take 20–25 samples of size n, and compute $\bar{X}$ and R for each.

(3) Establish and graph the control limits.

(4) Plot $\bar{X}$ and R points, and look for causes of any points outside limits.

(5) Discard points outside limits with assignable causes, and recalculate the control limits.

(6) Use revised limits, and begin regular sampling activities (assuming the sampling is economically justified).

Table 17-1   Factors for Computing Control Limits*

Sample Size n	Mean Factor A	Upper Range B	Lower Range C
2	1.880	3.268	0
3	1.023	2.574	0
4	.729	2.282	0
5	.577	2.114	0
6	.483	2.004	0
7	.419	1.924	.076
8	.373	1.864	.136
9	.337	1.816	.184
10	.308	1.777	.223
12	.266	1.716	.284
14	.235	1.671	.329
16	.212	1.636	.364
18	.194	1.608	.392
20	.180	1.586	.414
25	.153	1.541	.459

*Adapted from and used with permission of "Quality Control of Materials," *Special Technical Publication 15-C*, American Society for Testing Materials, Philadelphia, 1951, pp. 63, 72.

Example 17.8 (Variables Chart) A precision casting process is designed to produce blades having a diameter of $10.000 \pm .025$ centimeters. To establish control limits, 20 samples of $n = 5$ blades are randomly selected from the first 500 blades produced as follows (Table 17-2):

Table 17-2

Sample 1	Sample 2	$\cdots$	Sample 20
10.010	10.018		10.004
9.989	9.992		9.988
10.019	9.996		9.990
9.978	10.014		10.019
10.008	10.005		9.983
50.004	50.025		49.984
$\bar{X} = 10.0008$	10.0050	$\cdots$	9.9968
$R = \ \ .041$	.026	$\cdots$	.0036

The grand mean, $\bar{\bar{X}}$, of the sample means and the mean of the sample ranges, $\bar{R}$, were found to be

$$\bar{\bar{X}} = \frac{\Sigma \bar{X}\text{'s}}{\text{no. samples}} = \frac{10.0008 + 10.0050 + \cdots + 9.9968}{20} = 10.002 \text{ cm}$$

$$\bar{R} = \frac{\Sigma R\text{'s}}{\text{no. samples}} = \frac{.041 + .026 + \cdots + .036}{20} = .032 \text{ cm}$$

(a) Find the control limits for the sample means and (b) find the control limits for the sample ranges.

(a) Mean:
$$\text{UCL}_{\bar{x}} = \bar{\bar{X}} + A\bar{R} = 10.002 + .577(.032) = 10.020 \text{ cm}$$
$$\text{Center} = \bar{\bar{X}} \qquad\qquad\qquad\qquad = 10.002 \text{ cm}$$
$$\text{LCL}_{\bar{x}} = \bar{\bar{X}} - A\bar{R} = 10.002 - .577(.032) = 9.984 \text{ cm}$$

(b) Range:
$$\text{UCL}_R = B\bar{R} = (2.114)(.032) = .068 \text{ cm}$$
$$\text{Center} = \bar{R} \qquad\qquad\qquad = .032 \text{ cm}$$
$$\text{LCL}_R = C\bar{R} = (.000)(.032) = .000 \text{ cm}$$

PROCESS CONTROL FOR ATTRIBUTES VIA CONTROL CHARTS

Figure 17-14 lists some expressions for computing control limits for attributes. A control chart for proportions (p chart) is based on the binomial distribution (or normal approximation) and is sensitive to a change in the proportion of defectives in a process. The numbers (c chart) is based upon the Poisson distribution, which assumes a small (rare event) probability of a defect occurring. It is especially useful for controlling the defect rate when the number of nondefectives is unavailable, because it uses only the average number of defects.

Proportions (p charts)	Numbers (c charts)
$\text{UCL}_p = p + 3s_p$ $\qquad\qquad$ (17.12) $\text{LCL}_p = p - 3s_p$ $\qquad\qquad$ (17.13) where p = proportion of defectives in sample $\quad = \dfrac{\text{number of defectives}}{\text{total number of items}}$ $s_p = \sqrt{\dfrac{pq}{n}}$ where n = sample size to be used for monitoring	$\text{UCL}_c = \bar{c} + 3s_c$ $\qquad\qquad$ (17.14) $\text{LCL}_c = \bar{c} - 3s_c$ $\qquad\qquad$ (17.15) where $\bar{c}$ = average number of defects per unit $\quad = \dfrac{\Sigma c}{N} = \dfrac{\text{total no. of defects/unit in samples}}{\text{no. of samples}}$ $s_c = \sqrt{\bar{c}}$ $\qquad\qquad$ (17.16)

Fig. 17-14 Control limits for attributes data

Example 17.9 (Attributes p Chart) A sportswear firm has set up for automated production of a line of sweaters. Twenty samples of size $n = 50$ are to be withdrawn randomly during the first week of production in order to establish control limits for the process. Defects remain in the shipment but bring less revenue, for they eventually sell as "seconds." The defectives detected in the 20 samples are shown in Table 17-3. Compute the control limits for this process.

$$\text{UCL}_p = p + 3s_p$$

where
$$p = \frac{\text{number of defectives}}{\text{total number of items}} = \frac{40}{50 \times 20} = .040$$
$$s_p = \sqrt{\frac{pq}{n}} = \sqrt{\frac{(.040)(.960)}{50}} = .028$$
$$\text{UCL}_p = .040 + 3(.028) = .124$$
$$\text{LCL}_p = p - 3s_p = .040 - 3(.028) = .000$$

By use of these limits, a preliminary chart is constructed (Fig. 17-15) and the data points plotted.

Note that the fraction defective in sample 17 is outside the upper control limit. Suppose the reason for this is investigated, and the cause is found to be that a new machine was phased in at that point before receiving final adjustments from a mechanic. This data point is then discarded and a new value for p and new control limits are calculated.

$$p = \frac{33}{50 \times 19} = .0347 \qquad\qquad s_p = \sqrt{\frac{(.0347)(.9653)}{50}} = .0259$$
$$\text{UCL}_p = .0347 + 3(.0259) = .112 \qquad\qquad \text{LCL}_p = .0347 - 3(.0259) = .000$$

Table 17-3 Defective Items in 20 Samples of
$n = 50$ Sweaters

Sample Number	Number Defectives	Percent Defective
1	2	.04
2	3	.06
3	4	.08
4	1	.02
5	0	.00
6	2	.04
7	4	.08
8	1	.02
9	1	.02
10	3	.06
11	0	.00
12	1	.02
13	2	.04
14	1	.02
15	0	.00
16	3	.06
17	7	.14
18	2	.04
19	1	.02
20	2	.04
	40	

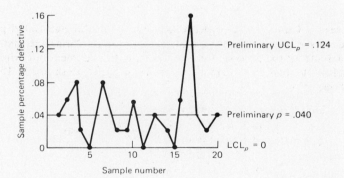

Fig. 17-15

None of the remaining sample values fall outside the new limits, so these limits become the standard for controlling the process in the future.

Example 17.10 (Attributes c Chart) The Metropolitan Transit System uses the number of written passenger complaints per day as a measure of its service quality. For 10 days, the number of complaints received was as shown in Table 17-4. Compute the $3s_c$ control limits.

  We seek limits for the number of defects per unit, where defects are written customer complaints and the unit is 1 day. Thus the Poisson distribution applies:

Table 17-4

Day (sample) no.	1	2	3	4	5	6	7	8	9	10	Total
No. of complaints/day	4	8	2	0	3	9	10	0	6	4	46

$$\bar{c} = \text{average number of defects per unit} = \frac{46 \text{ complaints}}{10 \text{ days}} = 4.6 \text{ complaints/day}$$

$$s_c = \sqrt{\bar{c}} = \sqrt{4.6} = 2.14$$

$$\text{UCL}_c = \bar{c} + 3s_c = 4.6 + 3(2.14) = 11.0$$

$$\text{LCL}_c = \bar{c} - 3s_c = 4.6 - 3(2.14) = 0 \quad \text{(negative values are assigned zero)}$$

The (process) average is 4.6 complaints per day, and control limits are from zero to 11 complaints per day.

Solved Problems

QUALITY-CONTROL COSTS

17.1 The marketing manager of Roller Bearings International (RBI) estimates that "defective bearings that get into the hands of industrial users cost RBI an average of $20 each" in replacement costs and lost business. The production manager counters that "the bearings are only about 2 percent defective now, and the best a sampling plan could do would be to reduce that to 1 percent defective—but not much better (unless we go to 100 percent inspection)." Should RBI adopt a sampling plan if it costs (a) $.10 per bearing? (b) $.25 per bearing? (c) How much per bearing can RBI afford to spend on inspection costs before it begins to lose money on inspections?

For purposes of illustration, assume that all comparisons are based upon a lot of 100 bearings.

(a) Without inspection:

$$\text{Defect cost} = 100(.02)(\$20/\text{bearing}) = \qquad \$40$$

With inspection:

$$\text{Inspection cost} = 100(\$.10/\text{bearing}) = \$10$$
$$\text{Defect cost} = 100(.01)(\$20/\text{bearing}) = \underline{\$20}$$
$$\$30 \longrightarrow \underline{30}$$
$$\text{Advantage from inspection:} \qquad \$10 \text{ (or \$.10/bearing)}$$

(b) Without inspection:

$$\text{Defect cost} = \qquad \$40$$

With inspection:

$$\text{Inspection cost} = 100(\$.25/\text{bearing}) = \$25$$
$$\text{Defect cost} = \underline{\$20}$$
$$\$45 \longrightarrow \underline{45}$$
$$\text{Disadvantage from inspection:} \qquad \$5 \text{ (or \$.05/bearing)}$$

(c) Let X = the inspection cost per bearing. Then the minimum cost is where

$$\text{Defect cost without inspect} = \text{inspect cost} + \text{defect cost with inspect}$$
$$100(.02)(\$20/\text{bearing}) = X(100) + (100)(.01)(\$20/\text{bearing})$$
$$X = \frac{40 - 20}{100} = \$.20/\text{bearing}$$

STATISTICAL METHODS OF CONTROLLING QUALITY

17.2 Xistor Radio Co. wishes to make performance tests on some finished radios. The quality control inspector has randomly selected five radios. In how many ways can radios be selected for three tests if:

(a) Any radio can be used for any or all of the tests, so both duplication and different order of selection count as a different way (*multiple choices*)?

(b) No radio can be used for more than one test, but the order of selection makes a difference (*permutations*)?

(c) No radio can be used for more than one test, and the order of selection of the radios does not count (*combinations*)?

Let $x = 3$ radios chosen from $n = 5$ radios.

(a) Multiple choices

$$N^x = 5^3 = 5 \cdot 5 \cdot 5 = 125 \text{ ways}$$

(b) Permutations

$$P_x^n = \frac{n!}{(n-x)!} = \frac{5!}{(5-3)!} = \frac{5 \cdot 4 \cdot 3 \cdot 2 \cdot 1}{2 \cdot 1} = 60 \text{ ways}$$

(c) Combinations

$$C_x^n = \frac{n!}{x!(n-x)!} = \frac{5!}{3!(5-3)!} = \frac{5 \cdot 4 \cdot 3 \cdot 2 \cdot 1}{3 \cdot 2 \cdot 1 \cdot 2 \cdot 1} = 10 \text{ ways}$$

17.3 A quality control sample of $n = 100$ items is taken, and the standard deviation is calculated to be .250 inch.

(a) Estimate the standard error of the mean.

(b) What would be the standard error if the sample size were 1,000 instead of 100?

(a)
$$s_{\bar{x}} = \frac{s}{\sqrt{n}} = \frac{.250}{\sqrt{100}} = .025 \text{ inch}$$

(b)
$$s_{\bar{x}} = \frac{.250}{\sqrt{1,000}} = .008 \text{ inch}$$

17.4 Which probability distribution will yield an appropriate answer in a reasonable amount of time if we wish to know the probability of getting 10 or fewer defects in a sample of 400 from a population that is 1 percent defective?

(a) hypergeometric   (c) normal   (e) Student t

(b) binomial   (d) Poisson

$$n = 400 = >20$$
$$np = (400)(0.01) = 4 = <5$$
$$p = .01 = <.10$$

Poisson distribution is appropriate

$$P(X \leq 10 | \lambda = 4) = .997 \text{ (from Appendix D)}$$

17.5 In an industrial plant, the mean weight of a certain packaged chemical is $\mu = 82.0$ kg and standard deviation is $\sigma = 4.0$ kg. If a sample of $n = 64$ packages is drawn from the population for inspection, find the probability that

(a) An *individual package* in the sample will exceed 82.5 kg. (Assume that the population is normally distributed for this part.)

(b)   The *sample mean* will exceed 82.5 kg.

(a)
$$Z = \frac{x - \mu}{\sigma} = \frac{82.5 - 82.0}{4} = .125$$

$$P(Z) = .050 \quad \text{(Appendix B)}$$

$$P(X > 82.5) = .500 - .050 = .450 \qquad \text{(See Fig. 17-16)}$$

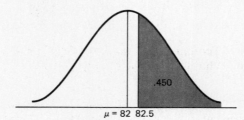

.450

$\mu = 82$ 82.5

Fig. 17-16

(b)
$$Z = \frac{\bar{x} - \mu}{\sigma_{\bar{x}}}$$

where $\sigma_{\bar{x}} = \dfrac{\sigma}{\sqrt{n}} = \dfrac{4}{\sqrt{64}} = .5$

$$Z = \frac{82.5 - 82.0}{.5} = 1.0$$

$$P(Z) = .34 \quad \text{(Appendix B)}$$

$$P(\bar{x} > 82.5) = .50 - .34 = .16$$

17.6   *Hypergeometric Distribution.* A shipment of 20 transistors received six weeks ago was delivered to an assembly area without inspection upon receipt of delivery. Four of the transistors were installed in a space vehicle, and the remainder were mixed with existing inventory. The supplier has just notified the firm that five of the transistors were defective.

(*a*)   What is the probability that all four transistors installed in the vehicle were good?

(*b*)   What is the probability that there was one defective in the lot of four?

(*a*)
$$P(X = 4 \text{ good}) = \frac{\text{successful ways}}{\text{total ways}}$$

The successful and total number of ways of selecting 4 transistors from 20 must be computed recognizing that no transistor can be used more than once and that a different order of selection of the same 4 would not change anything. In this case we are concerned with *combinations* of x items chosen from $n = 20$:

$$C_x^n = \frac{n!}{x!(n - x)!}$$

(See Prob. 17.2 for additional distinction between multiple choices, permutations, and combinations.) Note that the lot is known to have contained

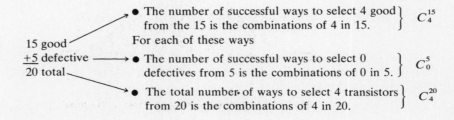

Thus,
$$P(X = 4) = \frac{C_4^{15} \cdot C_0^5}{C_4^{20}} = \frac{\dfrac{15!}{4!11!} \cdot \dfrac{5!}{0!5!}}{\dfrac{20!}{4!16!}} = .28$$

(b)
$$P(X = 3) = \frac{C_3^{15} \cdot C_1^5}{C_4^{20}} = \frac{\dfrac{15!}{3!12!} \cdot \dfrac{5!}{1!4!}}{\dfrac{20!}{4!16!}} = .47$$

17.7 *Binomial Distribution.*   Ten percent of the fire bricks baked in an obsolete oven turn out to be defective in some way. What is the chance that exactly 2 will be defective in a random sample of 10?

   The defective rate is given as a percentage and can be taken as constant. If we can assume each brick produced is independent of the previous brick, then the binomial distribution applies.

$$P(X = 2 \mid n = 10,\ p = .10) = \frac{n!}{x!(n-x)!}\, p^x q^{n-x} = \frac{10!}{2!8!}\, (.10)^2 (.90)^8 = .1937$$

Note that the solution value could also be obtained more directly from the table of binomial probabilities given in Appendix C.

17.8 *Poisson Approximation.* A very large shipment of textbooks comes from a publisher who usually supplies about 1 percent with imperfect bindings. What is the probability that among 400 textbooks taken from this shipment, exactly 3 will have imperfect bindings?

   This problem could be solved by using the binomial expression for $P(X = 3 \mid n = 400,\ p = .01)$. However, unless one has a calculator that handles exponents, the solution would be tedious. It can be closely approximated by the Poisson distribution since $p < .10$, $n > 20$, and $np < 5$.

$$P(X) = \frac{\lambda^x e^{-\lambda}}{x!}$$

where $\lambda = np = 400(.01) = 4.0$
   $x = 3$
   $e = 2.718 \text{(constant)}$

$$P(X = 3 \mid \lambda = 4.0) = \frac{\lambda^x e^{-\lambda}}{x!} = \frac{4^3 e^{-4}}{3!} = \frac{(64)(.018)}{3 \cdot 2} = .195$$

   The solution could also be obtained more directly from the table of summed Poisson probabilities given in Appendix D. Go down the λ column to $\lambda = 4$ and then right to the columns where the events are designated as $\leq c$ (rather than $\leq x$). Since we need $c = 3$, we must find the difference between $c \leq 3$ and $c \leq 2$, which is $.433 - .238 = .195$.

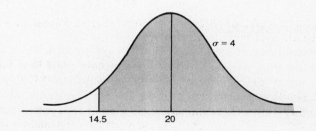

Fig. 17-17 Normal approximation to binomial

17.9 *Normal Approximation.* In a precious metals manufacturing process, 20 percent of the ingots contain impurities and must be remelted after inspection. If 100 ingots are selected for shipment without inspection, what is the probability 15 or more ingots will contain impurities?

This binomial problem $P(X \geq 15 | n = 100, \ p = .20)$ may be solved by using the normal approximation to the binomial, since $n > 50$ and $np = 100(.20) > 5$. (See Fig. 17-17.)

$$\mu = np = 100(.20) = 20$$
$$\sigma = \sqrt{npq} = \sqrt{20(.8)} = 4$$

Since we are using a continuous distribution to estimate discrete probabilities, the appropriate continuous value for ≥ 15 becomes 14.5

$$Z = \frac{X - \mu}{\sigma} = \frac{14.5 - 20}{4} = -1.375$$
$$P(Z) = .415 \text{ (from Appendix B)}$$
$$P(X > 14.5) = .415 + .500 = .915$$

The normal distribution is, of course, useful in its own right for continuous variables, aside from its use as an approximation to the binomial probabilities.

SAMPLING PLANS FOR ATTRIBUTES

17.10 An orange grower (producer) and packing plant (consumer) have agreed on a sampling plan that calls for a sample of 150 oranges from a shipment, and acceptance if 3 or less are spoiled. (*a*) Does this plan meet the specifications of limiting the grower's risk of rejecting lots that are as good as 2 percent spoiled to less than or equal to 20 percent, and does it limit the packing plant's risk of accepting shipments that are as bad as 4 percent spoiled to less than or equal to 25 percent?   (*b*) What would be the effect of changing the acceptance value to $c \leq 4$?

(*a*) This is an attributes plan calling for $\alpha \leq .20$ at AQL $= .02$ and $\beta \leq .25$ at LTPD $= .04$. Though we could construct an entire OC curve, it is necessary to check only two points: AQL and LTPD.

p	$\lambda = np$	$P(x \leq 3 | \lambda)$		Risk
.02	$(150)(.02) = 3.0$	$P(x \leq 3 | \lambda = 3.0) = .647$	so	$\alpha = 1.000 - .647 = .353$
.04	$(150)(.04) = 6.0$	$P(x \leq 3 | \lambda = 6.0) = .151$	so	$\beta = .151$

The grower's risk (α) of .35 is larger than .20 and so is unsatisfactory (too high). The packing plant's risk (β) of .15 is less than .25 and so is satisfactory.

(*b*) With $c \leq 4$: $P(x \leq 4 | \lambda = 3.0) = .815$, so $\alpha = 1.000 - .815 = .185$
$$P(x \leq 4 | \lambda = 6.0) = .285, \text{ so } \beta = .285$$

The grower's risk (α) is less than .20 and is satisfactory, but the packing plant's risk (β) is greater than .25 and so is unsatisfactory.

SAMPLING PLANS FOR VARIABLES

17.11 A videogame manufacturer purchases a 4-inch plastic disk from a supplier, where $\sigma = .30$ inch. The manufacturer wishes to design a sampling plan that limits the risk of accepting shipments with an average diameter of ≤ 3.900 inches to .01 and also limits the chance of accepting disks of ≥ 4.100 inches to .01. The sample size should also be large enough to limit the risk of rejecting a lot that really averages 4.000 inches to .10.

(*a*) Find the appropriate sampling plan (i.e., n and c values).
(*b*) Construct the OC curve for this sampling plan. What is the probability of accepting a lot that averages (1) 3.920 inches, (2) 3.959 inches, (3) 4.000 inches, (4) 4.041 inches?

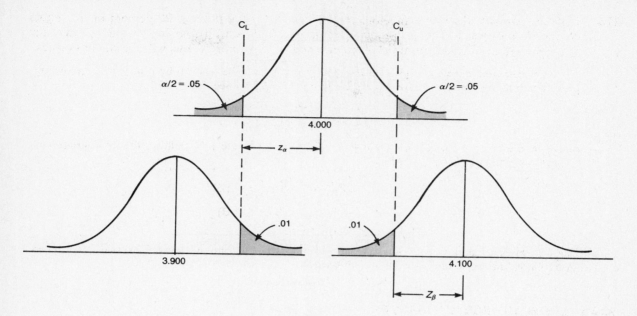

Fig. 17-18

(a) See Fig. 17-18. For normal distribution area of .450,

$$Z_\alpha = 1.645$$

and for .490

$$Z_\beta = 2.33$$

Establishing equations for the limit C_L we have from below:

$$C_L = 3.900 + Z_\beta \frac{\sigma}{\sqrt{n}} = 3.900 + 2.33 \frac{(.2)}{\sqrt{n}}$$

and from above:

$$C_L = 4.000 - Z_\alpha \left(\frac{\sigma}{\sqrt{n}} \right) = 4.000 - 1.645 \frac{(.2)}{\sqrt{n}}$$

Setting the two equations equal we have

$$3.900 + \frac{.466}{\sqrt{n}} = 4.000 - \frac{.329}{\sqrt{n}}$$

$$\frac{.795}{\sqrt{n}} = .100$$

Thus,

$$n = 63.2$$

$$C_L = 3.900 + \frac{2.33(.2)}{\sqrt{63.2}} = 3.959 \text{ inches}$$

Using similar procedures, the upper limit is 4.041 inches.

The sampling plan is: Take a random sample of $n = 63$ disks and measure the diameter. If $\bar{x}$ is from 3.959 inches to 4.041 inches accept the shipment; otherwise, reject it.

(b) For the OC curve (Fig. 17-19), use the normal distribution to compute P(accept), which is the area between C_L and C_u for selected values of μ. For example, at $\mu = 3.920$

$$Z = \frac{X - \mu}{\sigma_{\bar{x}}} = \frac{3.959 - 3.920}{.2/\sqrt{63}} = \frac{.0390}{.0252} = 1.5478$$

Thus,

$$P(Z) = .4392$$

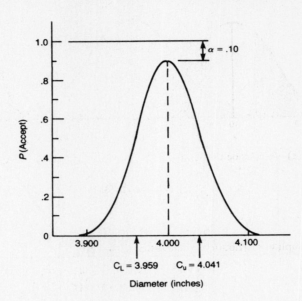

Fig. 17-19

and

$$P(\text{accept}) = .5000 - .4392 = .0608$$

(1) at $\mu = 3.920$, $P(\text{accept}) = .061$

(2) at $\mu = 3.959$, $P(\text{accept}) = .500$

at $\mu = 3.980$, $P(\text{accept}) = .785$

(3) at $\mu = 4.000$, $P(\text{accept}) = .900$

(4) at $\mu = 4.041$, $P(\text{accept}) = .500$

AVERAGE OUTGOING QUALITY LEVELS

17.12 An OC curve reveals that lots with a true percentage of defectives of 2 percent have a probability of being accepted of $P_A = .67$. If the sampling plan for lots of $N = 1,000$ called for samples of size $n = 100$, what would be the average outgoing quality (AOQ) level?

$$\text{AOQ} = \frac{P_D P_A (N - n)}{N} = \frac{(.02)(.67)(1,000 - 100)}{1,000} = .012 = 1.2\%$$

In the above example, since the sample size is $n = 100$ and 2 percent of the items in the sample are defective (on the average), then the 2 defective items would be removed from the sample and replaced before the lot was allowed to continue on its way. For lots of $N = 1,000$ items, the number of defects would then be reduced to 2 percent of the 900 uninspected items. This amounts to 18 in 1,000, or 1.8 percent of the items. Since the probability of acceptance of a lot of 2 percent defectives is (from the OC curve) only .67, then the expected value or average outgoing quality level for lots (of 2 percent defectives) is (.67)(1.8 percent) or 1.2 percent defective.

CONTROL CHARTS FOR VARIABLES

17.13 A control chart is established for a normally distributed variable which has $\mu = 10$, and $\sigma = 1$. If control limits for samples of size $n = 16$ are set at ± 3 standard errors, what percent of the individual values in the population would lie outside the control limits?

See Fig. 17-20.

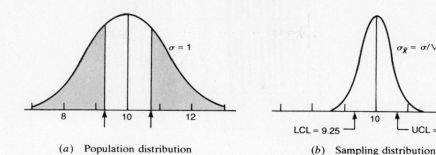

(a)   Population distribution   (b)   Sampling distribution

Fig. 17-20

From the sampling distribution, the control limits are:

$$UCL = \bar{\bar{x}} + Z\sigma_{\bar{x}} = 10 + 3(\tfrac{1}{4}) = 10\tfrac{3}{4}$$
$$LCL = \bar{\bar{x}} - Z\sigma_{\bar{x}} = 10 - 3(\tfrac{1}{4}) = 9\tfrac{1}{4}$$

When superimposed on the population distribution (shown by the arrows), the percentage of area included would be:

Within UCL: $Z = \dfrac{x - \mu}{\sigma} = \dfrac{10.75 - 10.0}{1} = .75$ therefore $P(Z) = .273$

Within LCL: $Z = \dfrac{x - \mu}{\sigma} = \dfrac{9.25 - 10.0}{1} = .75$ therefore $P(Z) = \underline{.273}$
                                                                           Total   .546

The area outside control limits is $1.000 - .546 = .454$, so approximately 45 percent of the individual observations would lie outside the control limits!

7.14   Nuclear Fuel Co. manufactures uranium pellets to a specified diameter of $.500 \pm .005$ centimeter. In 25 random samples of 9 pellets each, the overall mean of the means $(\bar{\bar{X}})$ and the range $(\bar{R})$ were found to be .501 centimeter and .003 centimeter, respectively. Construct an $\bar{X}$ and R chart which includes the specified tolerances.

   See Fig. 17-21.

$$UCL_{\bar{x}} = \bar{\bar{X}} + A\bar{R} = .501 + (.337)(.003) = .502$$
$$LCL_{\bar{x}} = \bar{\bar{X}} - A\bar{R} = .501 - (.337)(.003) = .500$$
$$UCL_R = B\bar{R} = (1.816)(.003) = .0054$$
$$LCL_R = C\bar{R} = (.184)(.003) = .0006$$

CONTROL CHARTS FOR ATTRIBUTES

7.15   A daily sample of 30 items was taken over a period of 14 days in order to establish attributes control limits. If 21 defectives were found, what should be the LCL_p and UCL_p?

$$p = \frac{\text{no. of defectives}}{\text{total observations}} = \frac{21}{420} = .05$$
$$s_p = \sqrt{\frac{pq}{n}} = \sqrt{\frac{(.05)(.95)}{30}} = .04$$
$$UCL_p = p + 3s_p = .05 + 3(.04) = .17$$
$$LCL_p = p - 3s_p = .05 - 3(.04) = 0$$

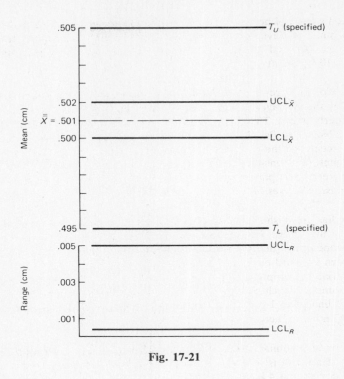

Fig. 17-21

Supplementary Problems

17.16 A control chart is to be established with ±2 standard error limits for use in monitoring samples of size $n = 25$ from a process having a standard deviation of $\sigma = 5$ ounces. Assuming the process output is normally distributed and is "in control" what proportion of the individual values lie outside the control limits?   *Ans.*   69 percent

17.17 A cosmetics producer has established QC activity levels in units of equivalent worker-hours of inspection and control effort devoted to a product per day. Each equivalent worker-hour unit currently costs $20. The firm estimates that with zero equivalent worker-hour units, the defective product costs are $400, and each additional unit reduces them by $30. What is the optimal level of QC activity in terms of equivalent worker-hours?
Ans.   Since each hour of inspection and control costs only $20 and reduces defective products costs by $30/hr, use as many hours as needed to eliminate the $400 cost, or $400 ÷ $30/hr = 13.3 hr.

17.18 A random sample of 400 items is drawn from a production process in order to test the hypothesis that the process has 10 percent defectives. Eighty defectives are found. (*a*) What is the theoretical (hypothesized) standard error of proportion (σ_p)? (*b*) What is the estimated standard error of proportion based upon the sample evidence only (s_p)?   *Ans.*   (*a*) .015 (*b*) .02

17.19 The operations department of a city-owned gas company has a quality service performance standard of no more than four complaints per hour. If the company averages four complaints per hour, what is the probability of 30 minutes passing with no complaints?   *Ans.*   .135

17.20 If defective components are coming off an assembly line at an average rate of 3.5 per minute, what is the probability that more than 5 defects will arrive in 1 minute?   *Ans.*   .142

17.21 The manufactured weight of boxes of laundry soap is known to be normally distributed with a mean of 20 pounds and a standard deviation of .4 pound. Approximately what percent of the boxes in a carload shipment could be expected to weigh less than 19.5 pounds if an incoming receipt inspection is made?   *Ans.*   10.6 percent

17.22 Northeast Paper Co. packages a large volume of tissue under a brand name for a national chain food store. Occasionally the packages are defective because they are from end cuts, the color is bleached, or they are not properly sealed. The paper company and food chain have agreed to adopt a sampling plan so that the risk to Northeast Paper Co. of rejecting lots that are as good as .5 percent defective ($p = .005$) is limited to 2 percent and the risk of the food chain accepting lots as bad as 4 percent defective is no more than 5 percent. (*a*) Construct an OC curve for the sampling plan ($n = 200, c \leq 3$).   (*b*) Does this plan satisfy the agreed-upon paper company risk?   (*c*) Does this plan satisfy the food chain risk?   *Ans.*   (*a*) Use Poisson (*b*) yes (*c*) yes

17.23 A national bank has established quality standards for its branch banks and allocates a portion of its salary budget on this basis. One measure of service level is the time required to complete all arrangements for opening a checking account. A time of more than 12 min is considered *poor service* and times have a known standard deviation of 4.2 min.

Design a variables sampling plan, for a sample of $n = 36$ observations, that will allow the headquarters to sample branch banks so that the risk of rejecting a branch's claim (that it averages 12 minutes or less) is limited to 1 percent (when the true mean time is really 12 minutes).   *Ans.*   If $\bar{x} \leq 13.63$ minutes, accept.

17.24 The QC supervisor at National Bakery has been asked to direct the receipt inspection of a carload shipment of flour. Each bag is supposed to weigh at least 50 kilograms, and the Chicago Mill has said that the standard deviation is 4 kilograms. Management wishes to limit the risk of rejecting a good lot to 2 percent. On the other hand, if the true mean weight of the bags is only 48 kilograms, management wants to limit the chance of accepting the shipment to 5 percent. (*a*) Diagram the situation in terms of a sampling distribution showing the α and β risks.   (*b*) How large a sample size is required?   (*c*) What is the critical value c of the sample mean that will satisfy the given conditions?   *Ans.*   (*a*) $\alpha = .02$ when $\mu_1 = 50$ $\beta = .05$ when $\mu_2 = 48$ (*b*) 55 bags (*c*) 48.88 kg

17.25 In an effort to set up a control chart of a process, samples of size $n = 25$ are taken, and it is determined that $\bar{\bar{X}} = .98$ centimeter and the standard deviation (s) = .020 centimeter. Find the control limits for the process.   *Ans.*   UCL = .992 cm, LCL = .968 cm

17.26 The U.S. Department of Testing (USDT) requires that the 100-pound-bag shipments of the Prarie Seed Co. do in fact average 100 pounds or over. Sample data (Table 17-5) from $N = 10$ samples of $n = 6$ bags each showed the following weight deviations from 100 pounds (over, +, and under, −).

Table 17-5

Sample Number	1	2	3	4	5	6	7	8	9	10
	2	3	4	1	6	0	2	−1	1	5
	−1	0	5	2	4	−2	3	−1	2	4
	4	3	6	2	3	2	2	2	0	5
	1	1	2	0	4	−1	2	0	0	2
	0	2	4	4	1	3	4	1	4	3
	2	1	2	2	4	0	6	−1	3	0
Σ	8	10	23	11	22	2	19	0	10	19
Mean ($\bar{X}$)	1.33	1.67	3.83	1.83	3.67	.33	3.17	0	1.67	3.17
Range (R)	5	3	4	4	5	5	4	3	4	5

(a) What are the center line ($\bar{\bar{X}}$) and the upper and lower control limits for $\bar{X}$?   (b) What are the upper and lower control limits for the range? (Round your calculations to two significant digits beyond the decimal.)

Ans.   (a) Initial calculations yield $\bar{X}$ = 102.07 and limits of 104.10 pounds and 100.04 pounds, but the mean from sample 8 is outside the limits. Removing sample 8, we have $\bar{X}$ = 102.30 pounds, and limits of 104.39 and 100.21. (b) Using the revised mean of 102.30, the range limits are 8.68 pounds and 0 pounds.

17.27   A quality control policy requires setting up control limits on the basis of data from random samples of $n = 100$ per day taken from a 10-day pilot run of a plastics molding activity. A total of 200 defectives were found. (a) What are the UCL_p and LCL_p for the process (in percentage of defectives)?   (b) If samples of $n = 100$ continue to be taken, what would be the control limits in numbers of defectives (rather than in percentage)?   (*Hint:* This is not *c*. $\mu = np$ and $\sigma = \sqrt{npq}$.)

Ans.   (a) UCL = .32, LCL = .08 (b) 32 and 8

Chapter 18

Maintenance

Statistical, Simulation, and Queuing Methods

MAINTENANCE OBJECTIVES

Maintenance is any activity designed to keep equipment or other assets in the condition that will best support organizational goals. This sometimes reduces to an objective of minimizing long-run maintenance costs. However, concerns of safety, reliability, employment stability, and even economic survival suggest that maintenance activities must be responsive to a broad range of objectives. Maintenance decisions should reflect the long-run viability of the entire system.

PREVENTIVE AND BREAKDOWN MAINTENANCE COSTS

Maintenance activities are of two general types. *Preventive maintenance* (PM) is the routine inspection and service activities designed to detect potential failure conditions and make minor adjustments or repairs that will help prevent major operating problems. *Breakdown maintenance* is the repair, often of an emergency nature and at a cost premium, of facilities and equipment that have been used until they fail to operate.

An effective preventive maintenance program necessitates a records system, trained personnel, regular inspections, and service. These costs increase with increasing maintenance activity, as shown in Fig. 18-1. On the other hand, when equipment breaks down, workers and machines are idle, resulting in lost production time, delayed schedules, and expensive emergency repairs. These downtime costs decrease as crew sizes become larger and with increased maintenance activity. Breakdown costs usually exceed preventive maintenance costs up to a point M as shown in Fig. 18-1. Beyond M, additional preventive maintenance is not economically justified (although safety or other objectives may warrant it).

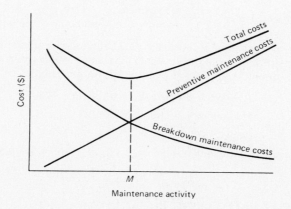

Fig. 18-1 Maintenance costs

373

EXPECTED-VALUE MODEL FOR ESTIMATING BREAKDOWN COST

Expected-value and simulation techniques are useful for estimating breakdown costs. The expected-value model requires data on the frequency and cost of past breakdowns.

Example 18.1   Worldwide Travel Services (WTS) has experienced the number of breakdowns per month in its automated reservations processing system over the past 2 years shown in Table 18-1.

Table 18-1

Number of breakdowns	0	1	2	3	4
Number of months this occurred	2	8	10	3	1

Each breakdown costs the firm an average of $280. For a cost of $150 per month, WTS could have engaged a data-processing firm to perform preventive maintenance, which is guaranteed to limit the breakdowns to an *average* of one per month. (If the breakdowns exceed this limit, the firm will process WTS data free of charge.) Which maintenance arrangement is preferable from a cost standpoint, the current breakdown policy or a preventive maintenance contract arrangement?

By converting the frequencies into a probability distribution and determining the expected cost per month of breakdowns, we have the information shown in Table 18-2

Table 18-2

Number of Breakdowns X	Frequency in Months $f(X)$	Frequency in Percentages $P(X)$	Expected Value $X \cdot P(X)$
0	2	.083	.0
1	8	.333	.333
2	10	.417	.834
3	3	.125	.375
4	1	.042	.168
	24		1.710

Breakdown cost per month:

$$\text{Expected cost} = \left(\frac{1.71 \text{ breakdowns}}{\text{month}}\right)\left(\frac{\$280}{\text{breakdown}}\right) = \frac{\$479}{\text{month}}$$

Preventive maintenance cost per month: Since the data processing firm guarantees to limit the cost to an "average" of one breakdown per month and the expected number (1.710) is greater than 1, we may assume that WTS will, in the long run, always incur the cost of one breakdown per month.

Average cost of breakdown/month	$280
Maintenance contract cost/month	150
Total	$430

Preventive maintenance advantage = $479 − $430 = $49/month

SIMULATION MODEL FOR ESTIMATING BREAKDOWN COST

Simulated breakdown and repair time values can also be used to estimate breakdown costs and help reach decisions on the appropriate crew size.

Example 18.2 A management analyst is attempting to study the total cost of the present maintenance policy for machinery in a decentralized section of a shoe manufacturing plant in Boston. The analyst has collected historical data and simulated breakdowns of machinery over a 16-hour period as shown in Table 18-3.

Table 18-3

Request for Repair (arrival time)	Total Repair Time Required (worker-hours)
0100	1.0
0730	3.0
0800	.5
1150	2.0
1220	.5
	7.0

The firm has two maintenance technicians and charges their time (working or idle) at $34 per hour each. The downtime cost of the machines, from lost production, is estimated at $360 per hour. (a) Determine the simulated service maintenance cost. (b) Determine the simulated breakdown maintenance cost. (c) Determine the simulated total maintenance cost. (d) Would another technician be justified?

(a)   Simulated service maintenance cost:

$$\text{Service cost} = (2 \text{ technicians})(\$34/\text{hr})(16 \text{ hr}) = \$1,088$$

(b)   Simulated breakdown maintenance cost (note that we assume that two technicians are twice as effective as one and reduce the downtime accordingly):

Table 18-4

(1) Request Arrival Time	(2) Repair time Required (2 Technicians)		(3) Repair Time Begins	(4) Repair Time Ends	(5) Machine Downtime(hr) (2 Technicians)	(6) Machine Downtime(hr) (3 Technicians)
	Hr	Min				
0100	.50	30	0100	0130	.50	.33
0730	1.50	90	0730	0900	1.50	1.00
0800	.25	15	0900	0915	1.25	.67
1150	1.00	60	1150	1250	1.00	.67
1220	.25	15	1250	1350	.75	.33
	3.50				5.00	3.00

The machine downtime is shown in Table 18-4, in hours, in column 5, as the decimal difference between the request arrival time (1) and the ending repair time (4). Note that on the 0800 breakdown the technicians were not available until 0900, when they finished the earlier job.

$$\text{Breakdown cost} = (\$360/\text{hr})(5 \text{ hr}) = \$1,800$$

(c)   Simulated total maintenance cost:

$$\text{Total cost} = \text{service} + \text{breakdown} = \$1,088 + \$1,800 = \$2,888/\text{period}$$

(d)   The machine downtime hours for three technicians would have to be calculated in the same way as was done for two. The calculations are not included, but the final result is shown in column 6.

Service maintenance cost	$= (3)(\$34)(16) = \$1,632$
Breakdown maintenance cost	$= (\$360)(3\,\text{hr}) = \underline{1,080}$
Total	$\$2,712$

There appears to be an advantage to adding a third technician.

PROBABILITY MODEL FOR SELECTING PREVENTIVE MAINTENANCE POLICY

Probability models are especially useful for analysis of (1) whether a breakdown or a preventive maintenance (PM) policy should be followed, and (2) if a PM policy is followed, how often service should be performed. Data are collected on (1) the preventive maintenance servicing cost, (2) the breakdown cost, and (3) the probability of breakdown. The probability of breakdown reflects the fact that breakdowns occur even if preventive maintenance is performed, but the chance of a breakdown usually increases with time after a maintenance activity.

The cumulative expected number of breakdowns B in M months is:

$$B_n = N \sum_1^n P_n + B_{n-1}P_1 + B_{n-2}P_2 + \cdots + B_1P_{n-1} \qquad (18.1)$$

where N = number of units

P = probability of breakdown during a given month after maintenance

n = maintenance period

Example 18.3 A computer service center has established the following probabilities of failure after maintenance (Table 18-5) for a line of printers that have been in service for several years.

Table 18-5

Years after maintenance	1	2	3	4	5
Probability of breakdown	.2	.4	.2	.1	.1

If they have 75 such printers, what is the expected number of breakdowns in the second year?

$$B_n = N \sum_1^n P_n + B_{n-1}P_1 = N(P_1 + P_2) + B_{2-1}P_1 = N(P_1 + P_2) + B_1P_1$$

where $N = 75$ units

$P_1 = .2$

$P_2 = .4$

$B_1 = N(P_1) = 75(.2) = 15$

$$B_2 = 75(.2 + .4) + 15(.2) = 45 + 3 = 48 \text{ printers}$$

QUEUING MODELS FOR ANALYZING MAINTENANCE SERVICE FACILITIES

Maintenance is a service activity that involves many characteristics of standard queuing systems (see Chap. 15). Attention must be given to the rates of arrival of service requests, the service times required, and other considerations, such as the length of the waiting line.

Example 18.4 Breakdowns of conveyor belt drives in a canning plant occur according to a Poisson distribution on an average of $\lambda = 2$ per day. Repair service times follow a negative exponential distribution with a mean time of one third of a day. All breakdowns are handled on a first-come, first-served basis by the one available maintenance crew.

(a) What is the average number of conveyors down at any time?   (b) What is the average waiting time before the maintenance crew can begin service?

First compute the service *rate*, which is

$$\mu = \left(\frac{\text{conveyor}}{.33 \text{ day}}\right) = 3 \text{ conveyors/day}$$

(*a*) The mean number in the system (both in breakdown awaiting service and in repair) is:

$$N_s = (\text{mean time in maintenance system})(\text{mean arrival rate})$$

$$N_s = \frac{\lambda}{\mu - \lambda} \qquad\qquad\qquad\qquad (15.10)$$

$$= \frac{2}{3-2} = 2 \text{ conveyors}$$

(*b*) The mean waiting time is:

$$T_q = \text{total time in system} - \text{service time}$$

$$T_q = \frac{\lambda}{\mu(\mu - \lambda)} \qquad\qquad\qquad\qquad (15.11)$$

$$= \frac{2}{3(3-2)} = \frac{2}{3} \text{ day}$$

FAILURE RATES

A *failure* is an event that changes a product from operational to nonoperational. The failure rate (FR) can be expressed as either a percentage of failures among the total number of products tested or in service, or as a number of failures per given operating time.

$$FR_\% = \frac{\text{number of failures}}{\text{number tested}} \qquad\qquad\qquad (18.2)$$

$$FR_n = \frac{\text{number of failures}}{\text{operating time}} = \frac{F}{TT - NOT} \qquad\qquad\qquad (18.3)$$

where F = number of failures
        TT = total time
        NOT = nonoperating time

Example 18.5 Fifty artificial heart valves were tested for 10,000 hours at a medical research center, and 3 valves failed during the test. What was the failure rate in terms of (*a*) percentage of failures? (*b*) number of failures per unit-year? (*c*) On the basis of these data, how many failures could be expected during a year from the installation of these valves in 100 patients?

(*a*) $$FR_\% = \frac{\text{number of failures}}{\text{number tested}} = \frac{3}{50} = 6.0\%$$

(*b*) $$FR_n = \frac{\text{number of failures during period}}{\text{operating time}} = \frac{F}{TT - NOT}$$

Note that the operating time is reduced by those units that failed. In the absence of actual data, we assume that failures are averaged throughout the test period. Therefore,

Total time = (10,000 hr)(50 units)	= 500,000 unit-hr
Less: Nonoperating time of 3 failed units for	
average of $\dfrac{10,000}{2}$ hr	− 15,000 unit-hr
Operating time	= 485,000 unit-hr

$$FR_n = \frac{3 \text{ failures}}{485,000 \text{ unit-hr}} = .0000062 \text{ failure/unit-hr}$$

or in terms of years, $$FR_n = (.0000062)\left(\frac{24 \text{ hr}}{\text{day}}\right)\left(\frac{365 \text{ days}}{\text{yr}}\right) = .0542 \text{ failure/unit-yr}$$

(c) From 100 units,

$$\left(\frac{.0542 \text{ failure}}{\text{unit-yr}}\right)(100 \text{ units}) = 5.42 \text{ failures/yr}$$

The mean time between failure (MTBF) is another useful term in maintenance and reliability analysis. The MTBF is the reciprocal of FR_n:

$$\text{MTBF} = \frac{\text{operating time}}{\text{number of failures}} = \frac{\text{TT} - \text{NOT}}{F} \qquad (18.4)$$

Example 18.6 Find the MTBF for the heart valves described in Example 18.5.

$$\text{MTBF} = \frac{\text{TT} - \text{NOT}}{F} = \frac{500,000 - 15,000}{3} = 161,666.67 \text{ unit-hr/failure}$$

$$\frac{161,666.67}{(24)(365)} = 18.46 \text{ unit-yr/failure}$$

The 18.46 unit-year per failure figure represents the mean service time between failures that might be expected from a group of units during their several years of service. It is not necessarily indicative of the expected life of an individual unit.

RELIABILITY AGAINST FAILURE

Product reliability is the mathematical probability of a product performing a specific function in a given environment for a specific length of time or number of cycles. As suggested in Fig. 18-2, early failures (perhaps due to improper assembly or damage in shipment) may tend to follow a negative exponential pattern. During the typical operating lifetime, failures occur on a *rare-event* basis, often described by a Poisson distribution. As components wear out and fail, the products may follow a pattern described by a normal distribution.

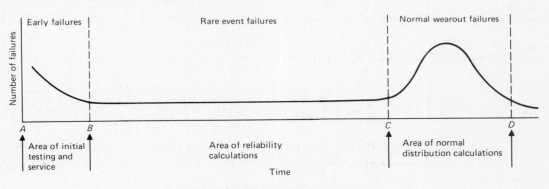

Fig. 18-2 Product failure rates

Example 18.7 The manufacturing area in the plant of a New Jersey drug manufacturer requires 5,000 fluorescent light tubes. The lights have a normally distributed lifetime, with a mean of 4,000 hours and a standard deviation of 120 hours. The plant manager has found that after 10 percent of the lights burn out, the quality of items and the productivity of workers in the plant are affected. He would like to schedule maintenance activities so that all lights are replaced when 10 percent fail. After how many hours of operation should the replacement activities be scheduled?

At the mean lifetime μ, 50 percent of the lights are still operating. We wish to find the earlier time X such that 40 percent more (or 90 percent total) are operating. Since the distribution is normal, we know (from Appendix B) that the number of standard deviations required to include an area of .40 is $Z = 1.28$. See Fig. 18-3.

$$-Z = \frac{X - \mu}{\sigma}$$

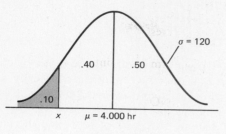

Fig. 18-3

- Improve the design of components.
- Simplify the design of the system.
- Improve production techniques.
- Improve quality control.
- Test components and the system.
- Install parallel systems.
- Perform periodic preventive maintenance.
- Derate components and/or the system.

Fig. 18-4 Ways to improve reliability

then

$$X = \mu - Z\sigma = 4{,}000 - 1.28(120) = 3{,}846 \text{ hr}$$

Figure 18-4 describes ways to improve product or system reliability. The use of parallel systems is a standard design procedure in many hazardous and capital-intensive applications. The reliability of components in series R_s is:

$$\text{(Series) } R_s = R_1 \cdot R_2 \cdots R_n \tag{18.5}$$

For parallel circuits the reliability R_p of the system is determined by

$$\text{(Parallel) } R_p = 1 - (1 - R_{s1})(1 - R_{s2}) \tag{18.6}$$

Example 18.8 An acid control system has three components in series with individual reliabilities (R_1, R_2, and R_3) as shown in Fig. 18-5.

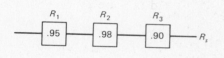

Fig. 18-5

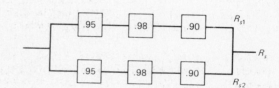

Fig. 18-6

(*a*) Find the reliability of the system.

(*b*) What would be the reliability of the system if a parallel circuit were added?

(*a*)
$$\text{Series } R_s = R_1 \cdot R_2 \cdot R_3 = (.95)(.98)(.90) = .84$$

(*b*) The parallel system design would be as shown in Fig. 18-6, where R_{s1} and R_{s2} are the computed reliabilities of the respective series circuits.

$$\text{Parallel } R_p = 1 - (1 - R_{s1})(1 - R_{s2}) = 1 - (1 - .84)(1 - .84) = .97$$

The MTBF can be used to express the reliability of a component or a system if the failure rate is constant. If we again let R represent the system reliability, and t the time period in question, then

$$R = e^{-(t/\text{MTBF})} \tag{18.7}$$

where e = the base of the natural logarithms, 2.7183.

Example 18.9 Safety valves used in an oil refinery have a constant failure rate with a MTBF of 16 years. What is the probability that a newly installed valve will function without failure for the next 8 years?

$$R = e^{-(t/\text{MTBF})} = e^{-(8/16)} = e^{-1/2} = \frac{1}{e^{1/2}} = \frac{1}{\sqrt{e}} = \frac{1}{\sqrt{2.7183}} = \frac{1}{1.6478} = .6065$$

Solved Problems

PREVENTIVE AND BREAKDOWN MAINTENANCE COSTS

18.1 *Replacement Decision Where Operating Life Is Known and Constant.* An automatic machine at an underground mine in Wyoming has two clutches that must be replaced periodically. Clutch A costs $40, can be installed for $50, and will operate satisfactorily for 300 hours. Clutch B costs only $30, can be installed for $35, and will operate for 400 hours. See Fig. 18-7. Both parts can be installed on one shutdown for $45. Compare the costs of replacing the clutches individually and replacing them together (use a cycle time of 3,600 hours).

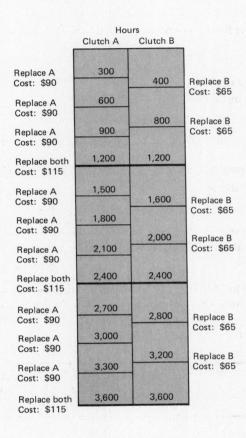

Fig. 18-7

Individual replacement:

A: 9 times at $90 = $810
B: 6 times at 65 = 390
A + B: 3 times at 115 = 345
Total $1,545

All joint replacement (every 300 hr):

A + B: 12 times at $115 = $1,380

Conclusion: Costs of individual replacement are $1,545 − 1,380 = $165 more per 3,600 hours.

EXPECTED-VALUE AND PROBABILITY MODELS

18.2   The housewares plant of a chemical company has 15 identical molding machines which produce a variety of molded products that generate a profit of $100 per machine per day. The machines fail according to a Poisson distribution with an average of 2.2 machines down each day.

(*a*)   What is the chance of having exactly three machines down on a given day?

(*b*)   What is the expected amount of lost profit per day due to this Poisson failure rate of 2.2 per day?

(*c*)   If backup machines could be maintained for a cost of $40 per machine per day, how many would be justified?

(*a*)   Since failures follow the Poisson distribution, the probability of X machines failing on any given day is:

$$P(X) = \frac{\lambda^x e^{-\lambda}}{x!}$$

where X = number of machines broken down = 3
  λ = mean failure rate = 2.2/day
  e = 2.718

$$P(X = 3) = \frac{(2.2)^3 e^{-2.2}}{3!} = .1966 = 20 \text{ percent chance}$$

(Note that the values may be calculated or taken from Appendix D.)

(*b*)   The expected loss per day is:

$$E(X) = X \cdot P(X)$$

where x = amount of loss = $100/machine-day
  $P(X)$ = mean value of distribution = 2.2 machines/day

Therefore, $E(X) = 100(2.2) = \$220/\text{day}$

Note that the expected loss could also be obtained by computing the sum of the loss amounts times the (Poisson) probability with which they occur as shown in Table 18-6. Probability values are from Appendix D.

Table 18-6

Number Failed	Poisson $P(X)$	Amount of Lost Profit X	Expected Loss of Profit $X \cdot P(X)$
0	.1108	0	$ 0
1	.2438	100	24
2	.2681	200	54
3	.1966	300	59
4	.1082	400	43
5	.0476	500	24
6	.0174	600	10
7	.0055	700	4
8	.0019	800	2
9	.0005	900	0
10	.0001	1,000	0
			$220

(c) With no backup machines, the lost profit is as indicated in (b) above. By having one backup machine, there is no lost profit with either zero or one breakdown. With two breakdowns, the loss is only $100, and it occurs with a probability of .2681 so the expected loss is ($100)(.2681) = $27. Similarly, with three breakdowns, the expected loss is ($200)(.1966) = $39. As we go to two backup machines, there is no loss until three machines have failed and the expected loss in ($100) × (1.966) = $20. Remaining values are shown in Table 18-7. *Conclusion*: Two backup machines minimize the loss of expected profit.

Table 18-7   Expected Loss of Profit

Number of Machines Broken Down	Number of Backup Machines				
	0	1	2	3	4
0	0	0	0	0	0
1	24	0	0	0	0
2	54	(100)(.2681) = 27	0	0	0
3	59	(200)(.1966) = 39	20	0	0
4	43	(300)(.1082) = 32	22	11	0
5	24	(400)(.0476) = 19	14	10	5
6	10	(500)(.0174) = 9	7	5	3
7	4	(600)(.0055) = 3	3	2	2
8	2	(700)(.0019) = 1	1	1	1
9	0	(800)(.0005) = 0	0	0	0
10	0	(900)(.0001) = 0	0	0	0
Total expected loss	$ 220	$ 130	$ 67	$ 29	$ 11
Add cost of backup machines at $40 ea.	+ 0	+ 40	+ 80	+120	+160
Total	$ 220	$ 170	$ 147	$ 149	$ 171

18.3 *Probability Model.* A copper refinery in Arizona has 40 flotation cells which can be serviced on a preventive maintenance schedule at $100 each. If the cells break down, it costs $500 to get them back into service (including unscheduled clean-out time and all breakdown costs). Records show that the probabilities of breakdown after maintenance are as shown in Table 18-8.

Table 18-8

Months after Maintenance	Probability of Breakdown
1	.2
2	.1
3	.3
4	.4

Should a preventive maintenance (PM) policy be followed? If so, how often should the cells be serviced?

Determine the costs of the alternative preventive maintenance policies, and compare them with the cost of a breakdown policy.

(a) *Preventive maintenance every month*

$$\text{Cost} = \text{servicing cost} + \text{breakdown cost}$$

$$= \begin{pmatrix} \text{number of} \\ \text{units} \\ \text{serviced} \end{pmatrix}\begin{pmatrix} \text{service} \\ \text{cost/} \\ \text{unit} \end{pmatrix} + \begin{pmatrix} \text{expected number} \\ \text{of breakdowns} \\ \text{between services} \end{pmatrix}\begin{pmatrix} \text{breakdown} \\ \text{cost/} \\ \text{unit} \end{pmatrix}$$

$$= (40 \text{ cells})(\$100/\text{cell}) + (40 \text{ cells} \times .2)(\$500/\text{cell})$$

$$= \$4,000 + 8(\$500) = \$8,000$$

(b) *Preventive maintenance every second month*

Note that a bimonthly policy involves a ($4,000) servicing cost plus the cost of individual breakdowns in *both* the first month and the second month. During the first month $40 \times .2 = 8$ machines are expected to break down. During the second month $40 \times .1 = 4$ machines are expected to break down. In addition, some of the machines (20 percent) that broke down in the first month (and were repaired on a breakdown basis) are expected to break down *again* in the second month (before the scheduled maintenance takes place).

$$\text{Cost} = \begin{pmatrix} \text{servicing} \\ \text{cost} \end{pmatrix} + \left[\begin{pmatrix} \text{during} \\ \text{month} \\ 1 \end{pmatrix} + \begin{pmatrix} \text{during} \\ \text{month} \\ 2 \end{pmatrix} + \text{(repeats)} \right] \begin{pmatrix} \text{breakdown} \\ \text{cost/unit} \end{pmatrix}$$

$$= \$4,000 + (40 \times .2 + 40 \times .1 + 8 \times .2)\$500$$

$$= \$4,000 + (8 + 4 + 1.6)\$500 = \$4,000 + \$6,800 = \$10,800$$

$$\text{Cost/month} = \$10,800 \div 2 = \$5,400$$

(c) *Preventive maintenance every third month*

Beyond a 2-month period it becomes more expedient to set up these calculations in a tabular format so that the expected number of breakdowns can be systematically determined before multiplying those values by the breakdown cost ($500). As shown in Table 18-9, a pattern for

Table 18-9

Type of PM Policy	Determination of Expected Number of Breakdowns during Period				Cumulative Expected Number of Breakdowns during PM Period
	1	2	3	4	
1-month PM policy	(40)(.2) = 8.0	Same as period 1	Same as period 1	Same as period 1	8.0
2-month PM policy	(40)(.2)=8.0	(40)(.1)=4.0 (8)(.2)=<u>1.6</u> 5.6	Same as period 1	Same as period 2	8.0 <u>5.6</u> 13.6
3-month PM policy	(40)(.2) = 8.0	(40)(.1) = 4.0 (8)(.2) = <u>1.6</u> 5.6	(40)(.3) = 12.0 (8)(.1) = .8 (5.6)(.2) = <u>1.12</u> 13.92	Same as period 1	8.0 5.6 <u>13.92</u> 27.52
4-month PM policy	(40)(.2) = 8.0	(40)(.1) = 4.0 (8)(.2) = <u>1.6</u> 5.6	(40)(.3) = 12.0 (8)(.1) = .8 (5.6)(.2) = <u>1.12</u> 13.92	(40)(.4) = 16.0 (8)(.3) = 2.4 (5.6)(.1) = .56 (13.92)(.2) = <u>2.78</u> 21.74	8.0 5.6 13.92 <u>21.74</u> 49.26

computing the expected number of breakdowns emerges wherein the 40 cells are assigned the respective probabilities of failure for 1, 2, 3, or 4 months after maintenance as given in the original data. Note that each probability applies to the whole (40-cell) population and not just to the remaining units, thus preserving the full chance for all 40 units to fail anywhere throughout the 4-month period. In addition, each time some cells fail in an earlier month, they are repaired and restored to a renewed status, and there, they regain their original probability (.2) of failing again in the next period. Thus under the 3-month PM policy, the eight units expected to breakdown in period 1 gain a renewed probability of .2 of breakdown in period 2 because period 2 then becomes their first month after maintenance. Adding their expected value of breakdown (1.6) to the original period 2 value (4.0) gives an expected breakdown total of 5.6 cells, which in turn is renewed and carried forward to period 3, resulting in a 1.12 expected value. Note that period 3 also contains an original allocation of breakdowns (12.0) plus the second-period probability, of failure (.1) associated with that portion of the (eight) cells which were renewed in period 1 and did not fail in period 2.

The cumulative expected number of breakdowns B in M months may also be expressed by means of the equation

$$B_n = N \sum_1^n P_n + B_{n-1}P_1 + B_{n-2}P_2 + \cdots + B_1 P_{n-1} \qquad (18.1)$$

where N = number of cells

P = probability of breakdown during a given month after maintenance

n = maintenance period

Thus:
$$B_1 = N(p_1) = (40)(.2) = 8.0$$
$$B_2 = N(p_1 + p_2) + B_1 p_1 = 40(.2 + .1) + 8(.2) = 13.6$$
$$B_3 = N(p_1 + p_2 + p_3) + B_2 p_1 + B_1 p_2$$
$$\quad = 40(.2 + .1 + .3) + 13.6(.2) + 8(.1) = 27.52$$
$$B_4 = N(p_1 + p_2 + p_3 + p_4) + B_3 p_1 + B_2 p_2 + B_1 p_3$$
$$\quad = 40(1.0) + 27.52(.2) + 13.6(.1) + 8(.3) = 49.26$$

The differences between the monthly cumulative totals then represent the individual period breakdowns. Thus the expected number of breakdowns during period 2 is $13.6 - 8.0 = 5.6$, which agrees with Table 18-9. Table 18-10, preventive maintenance cost analysis, carries forward the cost analysis to the determination of an expected total cost for the various preventive maintenance policies.

Table 18-10   Preventive Maintenance Cost Analysis—PM Policy

	1 Month	2 Months	3 Months	4 Months
Cumulative breakdowns during PM period	8.00	13.60	27.52	49.26
Cost at $500 each	$ 4,000	$ 6,800	$ 13,760	$ 24,630
Add: PM cost at $100/ cell	+4,000	+4,000	+4,000	+4,000
Total cost for M-month PM policy	$ 8,000 (1M)	$ 10,800 (2M)	$ 17,760 (3M)	$ 28,630 (4M)
Monthly cost	$ 8,000	$ 5,400	$ 5,920	$ 7,158

The cost of following any PM policy (for example, $5,400 for a 2-month policy) must then be compared with the cost of a breakdown policy. The expected cost of following a breakdown policy C_p is simply the cost C_r of repairing the cells N divided by the expected number of periods between breakdowns $\Sigma T_n(p_n)$:

$$C_p = \frac{NC_r}{\Sigma T_n(p_n)} \qquad (18.8)$$

where T_n = number of time periods after repair

p_n = probability of breakdown during given time period, n

Thus:
$$\Sigma\, T_n(p_n) = 1(.2) + 2(.1) + 3(.3) + 4(.4)$$

$$= 2.9 \text{ months between breakdowns}$$

$$C_p = \frac{NC_r}{\Sigma\, T_n(p_n)} = \frac{(40 \text{ cells})(\$500/\text{breakdown-cell})}{2.9 \text{ months/breakdown}} = \$6,897/\text{month}$$

Conclusion: Both the 2-month and 3-month preventive maintenance policies (at expected costs of \$5,400 and \$5,920, respectively) are preferred to the breakdown policy (\$6,897), with the 2-month policy being most preferable.

SIMULATION MODEL FOR ESTIMATING BREAKDOWN COST

18.4 *Replacement Decision Where Operating Life Is Variable.* Anodized Aluminum, Inc. has three heavily used circuit breakers which control electrolytic processing equipment in a large mill. The failure of any breaker stops operations with resulting downtime costs of \$300 per hour. The breakers cost \$150 each and installation time is 30 minutes for replacing one, 45 minutes for two, and one hour for all three. Installation labor cost is \$90 per hour. Historical data on breaker life have been collected and simulated to help determine which maintenance policy to adopt:

(*a*) Replace each breaker after it fails.

(*b*) Replace all three breakers after any one fails. (Simulated service times until failure are as shown in Table 18-11.)

(*c*) Replace each breaker after it fails, plus any other breakers with 30 days or more operating time.

Table 18-11

Days until Failure		
Breaker A	Breaker B	Breaker C
18	3	28
2	30	11
46	24	33
13	42	20
42	21	38
25	22	13
2	21	29
16	14	45
12	20	20
27	31	35
15	12	20
20	22	19
32	38	32
9	31	15

For purposes of illustration we shall assume a cumulative operating time of 200 days is adequate for comparison of the policies. Thus we cumulate times until 200 days is reached.

(a) *Replace each breaker after it fails* (See Table 18-12):

Table 18-12

Replacement Period Number	Days until Failure					
	Breaker A		Breaker B		Breaker C	
	Ind.	Cumul.	Ind.	Cumul.	Ind.	Cumul.
1	18	18	3	3	28	28
2	2	20	30	33	11	39
3	46	66	24	57	33	72
4	13	79	42	99	20	92
5	42	121	21	120	38	130
6	25	146	22	142	13	143
7	2	148	21	163	29	172
8	16	164	14	177	45	217
9	12	176	20	197	20	237
10	27	203	31	228	35	272
11	15	218	12	240	20	292
12	20	238	22	262	19	311
13	32	270	38	300	32	343
14	9	279	31	331	15	358
Number of replacements by 200th day		9		9		7 (25 total)

Table 18-13

Downtime Number	Next Failure Time (days)	
	Incremental	Cumulative
1	3	3
2	2	5
3	24	29
4	13	42
5	21	63
6	13	76
7	2	78
8	14	92
9	12	104
10	27	131
11	12	143
12	19	162
13	32	194
14	9	203

$$\underset{\text{(breakers)}}{\text{Material cost}} = \binom{\text{number}}{\text{replaced}}\left(\frac{\text{cost}}{\text{breaker}}\right) = (25)(\$150) = \$3,750$$

$$\text{Labor cost} = \binom{\text{number}}{\text{replaced}}\binom{\text{number}}{\text{of hr}}\left(\frac{\text{cost}}{\text{hr}}\right)$$

$$= (25 \text{ breakers})\left(\frac{.5 \text{ hr}}{\text{breakdown}}\right)\left(\frac{\$90}{\text{hr}}\right) = 1,125$$

$$\text{Downtime cost\dag} = \binom{\text{number}}{\text{replaced}}\binom{\text{number}}{\text{of hr}}\left(\frac{\text{cost}}{\text{hr}}\right)$$

$$= (25)(.5)(\$300) \qquad\qquad = \underline{\quad 3,750\quad}$$

$$\text{Total cost} \quad \$8,625$$

(b)   *Replace all three breakers after any one breaker fails.* With this policy, the first failure is breaker B at three days so A and C are also replaced at that time. The next failure is A at two days later so it, plus B and C, are replaced then. Continuing on we can determine the number of breakdowns for 200 hours of operation by always cumulating the shortest time of the three breakers as shown in Table 18-13. (We reach 200 hours after breakdown number 13.)

$$\text{Material cost} = \binom{\text{number of}}{\text{downtimes}}\left(\frac{\text{breakers}}{\text{downtime}}\right)\left(\frac{\text{cost}}{\text{breaker}}\right)$$

$$= (13)(3)(\$150) \qquad\qquad = \$\,5,850$$

$$\text{Labor cost} = \binom{\text{number of}}{\text{downtimes}}\left(\frac{\text{number of hr}}{\text{breakdown}}\right)\left(\frac{\text{cost}}{\text{hr}}\right)$$

$$= (13 \text{ breakdowns})\left(\frac{1 \text{ hr}}{\text{breakdown}}\right)\left(\frac{\$90}{\text{hr}}\right) = 1,170$$

$$\text{Downtime cost} = \binom{\text{number of}}{\text{downtimes}}\binom{\text{number of hr}}{\text{broke down}}\left(\frac{\text{cost}}{\text{hr}}\right)$$

$$= (13)(1)(\$300) \qquad\qquad = \underline{\quad 3,900\quad}$$

$$\text{Total cost} \quad \$10,920$$

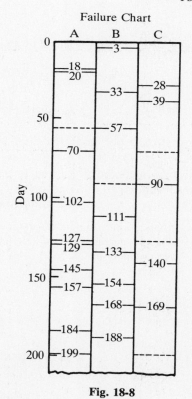

Failure Chart

Fig. 18-8

†No two breakers failed at the same time.

(c) *Replace each breaker after it fails, plus any other breakers with 30 days or more operating time.* The accompanying chart (Fig. 18-8) identifies additional replacements with dotted lines. The first joint replacement occurs on the seventh failure when B fails after 24 days of operation. By that time (day 57) breaker A has operated for $57 - 20 = 37$ days so it is also replaced (even though it would have operated satisfactorily for another 9 days). Unfortunately the replacement for A fails in 13 days, but by this time C has operated for 31 days so it is then replaced along with A.

$$\text{Material cost} = \binom{\text{number of}}{\text{breakers}}\left(\frac{\text{cost}}{\text{breaker}}\right) = (28)(\$150) = \$4,200$$

$$
\begin{array}{ll}
\text{Labor cost} = \text{18 single replacements at } (.5\,\text{hr})(\$90/\text{hr}) & = \$810 \\
\qquad\qquad\;\; \text{5 double replacements at } (.75\,\text{hr})(\$90/\text{hr}) & = \underline{\;\;338} \\
& \qquad\qquad 1,148 = 1,148
\end{array}
$$

$$
\begin{array}{ll}
\text{Downtime cost} = \text{18 breakdowns at .5 hr} & = 9.00\,\text{hr} \\
\qquad\qquad\qquad\;\; \text{5 breakdowns at .75 hr} & = \underline{3.75\,\text{hr}} \\
\qquad\qquad\qquad \text{Total} \quad 12.75\,\text{hr at \$300} & = \underline{\;\;3,825} \\
& \text{Total cost} \quad \$9,173
\end{array}
$$

The least-cost policy is to replace each breaker after it fails.

QUEUING MODELS FOR ANALYZING MAINTENANCE SERVICE FACILITIES

18.5   The time required to replace a filter on any of 500 industrial mixers can be considered a constant at 15 minutes per filter. Maintenance records show that the failure rate of filters is distributed according to a Poisson distribution, with a mean of 2 per hour. (a) Find the average number of mixers waiting for a filter replacement. (b) Find the average waiting time of a mixer for repair.

(a)
$$N_{q(c)} = \frac{\lambda^2}{2\mu(\mu - \lambda)}$$

where λ = arrival rate = 2/hr
   μ = service rate = (filter/15 min)(60 min/hr) = 4/hr

$$N_{q(c)} = \frac{2^2}{2(4)(4-2)} = .25\,\text{mixer}$$

(b)
$$T_{q(c)} = \frac{\lambda}{2\mu(\mu - \lambda)} = \frac{2}{2(4)(4-2)} = .125\,\text{hr} = 7.50\,\text{min}$$

18.6   A textile firm uses a cost of \$30 per hour for direct and indirect labor maintenance and estimates downtime costs on any of a large group of spinning machines at \$150 per hour per machine. If breakdowns are distributed according to a Poisson distribution with a mean of four per hour and the mean number of units a worker can service is six breakdowns per hour (distributed exponentially), what is the optimal maintenance crew size?

In the absence of other information, estimate the total maintenance costs (crew + downtime) per hour, beginning with one worker, and increase the crew size until total costs are minimized. The number of units in breakdown is the mean number in the system, N_s:

$$N_s = \frac{\lambda}{\mu - \lambda}$$

where μ = mean arrival rate = 4/hr
   μ = mean service rate (varies depending upon crew size)

For crew size of 1:

$$
\begin{array}{ll}
\text{Crew cost} = \text{1 worker at \$30/hr} & = \$\;\;30 \\
\text{Breakdown cost} = (N_s)(\text{cost/hr}) & \\
\qquad\qquad\qquad\;\; = \left(\frac{4}{6-4}\right)(\$150/\text{hr}) & = \underline{\;\;300} \\
& \qquad\qquad \$330/\text{hr}
\end{array}
$$

For crew size of 2:

$$\text{Crew cost} = 2 \text{ workers at } \$30/\text{hr} = \$\ 60$$

$$\text{Breakdown cost} = \left(\frac{4}{12-4}\right)(\$150/\text{hr}) = \underline{\ \ 75\ \ }$$
$$\$135/\text{hr}$$

For crew size of 3:

$$\text{Crew cost} = 3 \text{ workers at } \$30/\text{hr} = \$\ 90$$

$$\text{Breakdown cost} = \left(\frac{4}{18-4}\right)(\$150/\text{hr}) = \underline{\ \ 43\ \ }$$
$$\$133/\text{hr}$$

For crew size of 4:

$$\text{Crew cost} = 4 \text{ workers at } \$30/\text{hr} = \$120$$

$$\text{Breakdown cost} = \left(\frac{4}{24-4}\right)(\$150/\text{hr}) = \underline{\ \ 30\ \ }$$
$$\$150/\text{hr}$$

The total costs for crew sizes of two and three are so close that other, noneconomic factors should probably be deciding criteria.

Supplementary Problems

18.7 Manchester (England) Woolen Mills has kept records of breakdowns on its carding machines for a 300-day work year as shown in Table 18-14

Table 18-14

Number of Breakdowns	Frequency (in days)
0	40
1	150
2	70
3	30
4	10
	300

The firm estimates that each breakdown costs $65, and it is considering adopting a preventive maintenance program that would cost $20 per day and limit the number of breakdowns to an average of one per day. What is the expected annual savings from the preventive maintenance program?
Ans. $1,800 per year

18.8 Cascade Plastics has a group of molding machines that require breakdown maintenance at a (Poisson-distributed) mean rate of six per day. Each maintenance technician can service a Poisson-distributed average of eight per day. If downtime costs are $400 per 8-hour workday, what size maintenance crew will be the least costly? Maintenance labor costs are $15 per hour.   *Ans.* Two technicians at cost = $480 per day

18.9 In a simulated operation, a firm's maintenance worker received requests for service and provided service during an 8-hour period, as shown in Table 18-15. The maintenance labor cost is $14 per hour, and delay time (when machines are not being operated or repaired but instead are simply waiting for service) is $45 per hour. Find (*a*) the idle-time cost for the maintenance worker and (*b*) the delay-time cost for the machinery.   *Ans.* (*a*) $35 (*b*) $90

Table 18-15

Request Arrival (clock) Time	Required Service Time (hours)
0:00	1.5
1:00	.5
3:30	2.0
4:00	.5
7:00	1.0

18.10 Worldwide Construction Co. has received a large contract for a highway construction project wherein they will be penalized $2,500 per day for each day the project falls behind schedule. Each breakdown of a carryall during the day shift costs an average of $50 in repair and service maintenance costs plus the loss of one-tenth day in completion time. The carryalls can be serviced on an overtime basis during an evening shift (with no loss of production time) at a cost of $80 each. (Assume 10 carryalls.) See Table 18-16.

Table 18-16

Weeks after Maintenance	Probability of Breakdowns
1	.1
2	.1
3	.3
4	.5

(*a*) What would be the expected cost of following a policy of simply waiting until carryalls breakdown to service them?   (*b*) How often should the carryalls be serviced?   *Ans.*   (*a*) $938 (*b*) every 3 weeks

18.11 A vegetable processing plant in the Sacramento Valley has one maintenance crew to service breakdowns in any one of several buildings on a first-call priority basis. Breakdowns occur on an average of $\lambda = 5$ per week (Poissonly distributed) but the crew could service an average of $\mu =$ eight breakdowns per week (negative exponential service times). Find (*a*) % *U*, (*b*) T_s, (*c*) N_s, (*d*) T_w, (*e*) N_q, and (*f*) the probability of the crew finding three breakdowns to worry about at one time. (*Hint*: See Queuing equations in Chap. 15.)   *Ans.*   (*a*) 62.5 percent (*b*) .23 weeks (*c*) 1.67 breakdowns (*d*) .20 weeks (*e*) 1.04 (*f*) .09

18.12 Quick Freeze Foods has a corn line with two stripper saws operating in sequence to cut kernels from corn cobs. Blades on both the primary *P* and secondary *S* saws get dull and must be replaced periodically as shown in Table 18-17.

Table 18-17

	Blade Cost ($)	Installation Cost ($)	Operating Life
Primary	$ 60	70	80 hr
Secondary	40	60	100 hr
Both	100	90	

Should the blades be replaced individually at the end of their operating lives, or should both be replaced every 80 hours?   Make your comparison over an 800-hour period.   *Ans.*   Replace both at 80 hours.

18.13   In response to a customer request for failure-rate data, an instrument manufacturer tested a group of 30 instruments over a 2,000-hour test period and found that four failed. Find (*a*) FR$_\%$ and (*b*) FR$_n$ (in failures per unit per year).   *Ans.*   (*a*) 13.3 percent (*b*) .625 failure per year

18.14   The purification system in a water treatment plant has three components in series (R_1, R_2, and R_3). The component reliabilities for a 3-month period *remain constant* and are as shown in Fig. 18-9. At the end of each 3-month period all components are replaced regardless of the length of service. In the meantime, each time any component breaks down, the cost of downtime and repair is \$300. What is the annual expected cost of downtime and repair?

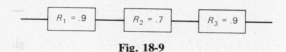

Fig. 18-9

Ans.   \$519.60

18.15   The maintenance manager for a nationwide trucking firm has found that a substantial savings in tire cost can be gained by contracting with a tire manufacturer to replace tires on the entire fleet of trucks at one time. For safety purposes, the manager feels this should be done at the time 15 percent of the tires are worn out. If tire life is normally distributed with a mean of 30 months and standard deviation of 3 months, when should the replacement take place?   *Ans.*   26.9 months

18.16   Pressure relief valves in a chemical plant are known to have a MTBF of 30 years. Assuming the failure rate is constant, what is the likelihood a given value will function, without failure for 10 years?
Ans.   .78

Appendix A

Random Number Table

27767	43584	85301	88977	29490	69714	94015	64874	32444	48277
13025	14338	54066	15243	47724	66733	74108	88222	88570	74015
80217	36292	98525	24335	24432	24896	62880	87873	95160	59221
10875	62004	90391	61105	57411	06368	11748	12102	80580	41867
54127	57326	26629	19087	24472	88779	17944	05600	60478	03343
60311	42824	37301	42678	45990	43242	66067	42792	95043	52680
49739	71484	92003	98086	76668	73209	54244	91030	45547	70818
78626	51594	16453	94614	39014	97066	30945	57589	31732	57260
66692	13986	99837	00582	81232	44987	69170	37403	86995	90307
44071	28091	07362	97703	76447	42537	08345	88975	35841	85771
59820	96163	78851	16499	87064	13075	73035	41207	74699	09310
25704	91035	26313	77463	55387	72681	47431	43905	31048	56699
22304	90314	78438	66276	18396	73538	43277	58874	11466	16082
17710	59621	15292	76139	59526	52113	53856	30743	08670	84741
25852	58905	55018	56374	35824	71708	30540	27886	61732	75454
46780	56487	75211	10271	36633	68424	17374	52003	70707	70214
59849	96169	87195	46092	26787	60939	59202	11973	02902	33250
47670	07654	30342	40277	11049	72049	83012	09832	25571	77628
94304	71803	73465	09819	58869	35220	09504	96412	90193	79568
08105	59987	21437	36786	49226	77837	98524	97831	65704	09514
64281	61826	18555	64937	64654	25843	41145	42820	14924	39650
66847	70495	32350	02985	01755	14750	48968	38603	70312	05682
72461	33230	21529	53424	72877	17334	39283	04149	90850	64618
21032	91050	13058	16218	06554	07850	73950	79552	24781	89683
95362	67011	06651	16136	57216	39618	49856	99326	40902	05069
49712	97380	10404	55452	09971	59481	37006	22186	72682	07385
58275	61764	97586	54716	61459	21647	87417	17198	21443	41808
89514	11788	68224	23417	46376	25366	94746	49580	01176	28838
15472	50669	48139	36732	26825	05511	12459	91314	80582	71944
12120	86124	51247	44302	87112	21476	14713	71181	13177	55292
95294	00556	70481	06905	21785	41101	49386	54480	23604	23554
66986	34099	74474	20740	47458	64809	06312	88940	15995	69321
80620	51790	11436	38072	40405	68032	60942	00307	11897	92674
55411	85667	77535	99892	71209	92061	92329	98932	78284	46347
95083	06783	28102	57816	85561	29671	77936	63574	31384	51924

Source: Paul G. Hoel, *Elementary Statistics,* 2d ed., John Wiley & Sons, Inc., New York, 1966. Reproduced by permission of the publisher.

Areas Under the
Normal Probability Distribution

Values in the table represent the proportion
of area under the normal curve between
the mean ($\mu = 0$) and a positive value of z.

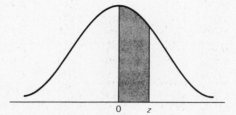

z	.00	.01	.02	.03	.04	.05	.06	.07	.08	.09
.0	.0000	.0040	.0080	.0120	.0160	.0199	.0239	.0279	.0319	.0359
.1	.0398	.0438	.0478	.0517	.0557	.0596	.0636	.0675	.0714	.0753
.2	.0793	.0832	.0871	.0910	.0948	.0987	.1026	.1064	.1103	.1141
.3	.1179	.1217	.1255	.1293	.1331	.1368	.1406	.1443	.1480	.1517
.4	.1554	.1591	.1628	.1664	.1700	.1736	.1772	.1808	.1844	.1879
.5	.1915	.1950	.1985	.2019	.2054	.2088	.2123	.2157	.2190	.2224
.6	.2257	.2291	.2324	.2357	.2389	.2422	.2454	.2486	.2517	.2549
.7	.2580	.2611	.2642	.2673	.2703	.2734	.2764	.2794	.2823	.2852
.8	.2881	.2910	.2939	.2967	.2995	.3023	.3051	.3078	.3106	.3133
.9	.3159	.3186	.3212	.3238	.3264	.3289	.3315	.3340	.3365	.3389
1.0	.3413	.3438	.3461	.3485	.3508	.3531	.3554	.3577	.3599	.3621
1.1	.3643	.3665	.3686	.3708	.3729	.3749	.3770	.3790	.3810	.3830
1.2	.3849	.3869	.3888	.3907	.3925	.3944	.3962	.3980	.3997	.4015
1.3	.4032	.4049	.4066	.4082	.4099	.4115	.4131	.4147	.4162	.4177
1.4	.4192	.4207	.4222	.4236	.4251	.4265	.4279	.4292	.4306	.4319
1.5	.4332	.4345	.4357	.4370	.4382	.4394	.4406	.4418	.4429	.4441
1.6	.4452	.4463	.4474	.4484	.4495	.4505	.4515	.4525	.4535	.4545
1.7	.4554	.4564	.4573	.4582	.4591	.4599	.4608	.4616	.4625	.4633
1.8	.4641	.4649	.4656	.4664	.4671	.4678	.4686	.4693	.4699	.4706
1.9	.4713	.4719	.4726	.4732	.4738	.4744	.4750	.4756	.4761	.4767
2.0	.4772	.4778	.4783	.4788	.4793	.4798	.4803	.4808	.4812	.4817
2.1	.4821	.4826	.4830	.4834	.4838	.4842	.4846	.4850	.4854	.4857
2.2	.4861	.4864	.4868	.4871	.4875	.4878	.4881	.4884	.4887	.4890
2.3	.4893	.4896	.4898	.4901	.4904	.4906	.4909	.4911	.4913	.4916
2.4	.4918	.4920	.4922	.4925	.4927	.4929	.4931	.4932	.4934	.4936
2.5	.4938	.4940	.4941	.4943	.4945	.4946	.4948	.4949	.4951	.4952
2.6	.4953	.4955	.4956	.4957	.4959	.4960	.4961	.4962	.4963	.4964
2.7	.4965	.4966	.4967	.4968	.4969	.4970	.4971	.4972	.4973	.4974
2.8	.4974	.4975	.4976	.4977	.4977	.4978	.4979	.4979	.4980	.4981
2.9	.4981	.4982	.4982	.4983	.4984	.4984	.4985	.4985	.4986	.4986
3.0	.4987	.4987	.4987	.4988	.4988	.4989	.4989	.4989	.4990	.4990

Source: From Paul G. Hoel, *Elementary Statistics*, 2d ed., John Wiley & Sons, Inc., New York, 1966. Reproduced by permission of the publisher.

Appendix C

Binomial Distribution Values

$$P(X|n,p) = \frac{n!}{x!\,(n-x)!}\,p^x q^{n-x}$$

n	X	.05	.10	.15	.20	.25	.30	.35	.40	.45	.50
1	0	.9500	.9000	.8500	.8000	.7500	.7000	.6500	.6000	.5500	.5000
	1	.0500	.1000	.1500	.2000	.2500	.3000	.3500	.4000	.4500	.5000
2	0	.9025	.8100	.7225	.6400	.5625	.4900	.4225	.3600	.3025	.2500
	1	.0950	.1800	.2550	.3200	.3750	.4200	.4550	.4800	.4950	.5000
	2	.0025	.0100	.0225	.0400	.0625	.0900	.1225	.1600	.2025	.2500
3	0	.8574	.7290	.6141	.5120	.4219	.3430	.2746	.2160	.1664	.1250
	1	.1354	.2430	.3251	.3840	.4219	.4410	.4436	.4320	.4084	.3750
	2	.0071	.0270	.0574	.0960	.1406	.1890	.2389	.2880	.3341	.3750
	3	.0001	.0010	.0034	.0080	.0156	.0270	.0429	.0640	.0911	.1250
4	0	.8145	.6561	.5220	.4096	.3164	.2401	.1785	.1296	.0915	.0625
	1	.1715	.2916	.3685	.4096	.4219	.4116	.3845	.3456	.2995	.2500
	2	.0135	.0486	.0975	.1536	.2109	.2646	.3105	.3456	.3675	.3750
	3	.0005	.0036	.0115	.0256	.0469	.0756	.1115	.1536	.2005	.2500
	4	.0000	.0001	.0005	.0016	.0039	.0081	.0150	.0256	.0410	.0625
5	0	.7738	.5905	.4437	.3277	.2373	.1681	.1160	.0778	.0503	.0312
	1	.2036	.3280	.3915	.4096	.3955	.3602	.3124	.2592	.2059	.1562
	2	.0214	.0729	.1382	.2048	.2637	.3087	.3364	.3456	.3369	.3125
	3	.0011	.0081	.0244	.0512	.0879	.1323	.1811	.2304	.2757	.3125
	4	.0000	.0004	.0022	.0064	.0146	.0284	.0488	.0768	.1128	.1562
	5	.0000	.0000	.0001	.0003	.0010	.0024	.0053	.0102	.0185	.0312
6	0	.7351	.5314	.3771	.2621	.1780	.1176	.0754	.0467	.0277	.0156
	1	.2321	.3543	.3993	.3932	.3560	.3025	.2437	.1866	.1359	.0938
	2	.0305	.0984	.1762	.2458	.2966	.3241	.3280	.3110	.2780	.2344
	3	.0021	.0146	.0415	.0819	.1318	.1852	.2355	.2765	.3032	.3125
	4	.0001	.0012	.0055	.0154	.0330	.0595	.0951	.1382	.1861	.2344

Source: Adapted from R. S. Burington and D. C. May, *Handbook of Probability and Statistics with Tables*, 2d ed., McGraw-Hill Book Company, New York, 1970. Reproduced by permission of the publisher.

n	X	.05	.10	.15	.20	.25	.30	.35	.40	.45	.50
							p				
	5	.0000	.0001	.0004	.0015	.0044	.0102	.0205	.0369	.0609	.0938
	6	.0000	.0000	.0000	.0001	.0002	.0007	.0018	.0041	.0083	.0156
7	0	.6983	.4783	.3206	.2097	.1335	.0824	.0490	.0280	.0152	.0078
	1	.2573	.3720	.3960	.3670	.3115	.2471	.1848	.1306	.0872	.0547
	2	.0406	.1240	.2097	.2753	.3115	.3177	.2985	.2613	.2140	.1641
	3	.0036	.0230	.0617	.1147	.1730	.2269	.2679	.2903	.2918	.2734
	4	.0002	.0026	.0109	.0287	.0577	.0972	.1442	.1935	.2388	.2734
	5	.0000	.0002	.0012	.0043	.0115	.0250	.0466	.0774	.1172	.1641
	6	.0000	.0000	.0001	.0004	.0013	.0036	.0084	.0172	.0320	.0547
	7	.0000	.0000	.0000	.0000	.0001	.0002	.0006	.0016	.0037	.0078
8	0	.6634	.4305	.2725	.1678	.1002	.0576	.0319	.0168	.0084	.0039
	1	.2793	.3826	.3847	.3355	.2670	.1977	.1373	.0896	.0548	.0312
	2	.0515	.1488	.2376	.2936	.3115	.2965	.2587	.2090	.1569	.1094
	3	.0054	.0331	.0839	.1468	.2076	.2541	.2786	.2787	.2568	.2188
	4	.0004	.0046	.0185	.0459	.0865	.1361	.1875	.2322	.2627	.2734
	5	.0000	.0004	.0026	.0092	.0231	.0467	.0808	.1239	.1719	.2188
	6	.0000	.0000	.0002	.0011	.0038	.0100	.0217	.0413	.0403	.1094
	7	.0000	.0000	.0000	.0001	.0004	.0012	.0033	.0079	.0164	.0312
	8	.0000	.0000	.0000	.0000	.0000	.0001	.0002	.0007	.0017	.0039
9	0	.6302	.3874	.2316	.1342	.0751	.0404	.0207	.0101	.0046	.0020
	1	.2985	.3874	.3679	.3020	.2253	.1556	.1004	.0605	.0339	.0176
	2	.0629	.1722	.2597	.3020	.3003	.2668	.2162	.1612	.1110	.0703
	3	.0077	.0446	.1069	.1762	.2336	.2668	.2716	.2508	.2119	.1641
	4	.0006	.0074	.0283	.0661	.1168	.1715	.2194	.2508	.2600	.2461
	5	.0000	.0008	.0050	.0165	.0389	.0735	.1181	.1672	.2128	.2461
	6	.0000	.0001	.0006	.0028	.0087	.0210	.0424	.0743	.1160	.1641
	7	.0000	.0000	.0000	.0003	.0012	.0039	.0098	.0212	.0407	.0703
	8	.0000	.0000	.0000	.0000	.0001	.0004	.0013	.0035	.0083	.0176
	9	.0000	.0000	.0000	.0000	.0000	.0000	.0001	.0003	.0008	.0020
10	0	.5987	.3487	.1969	.1074	.0563	.0282	.0135	.0060	.0025	.0010
	1	.3151	.3874	.3474	.2684	.1877	.1211	.0725	.0403	.0207	.0098
	2	.0746	.1937	.2759	.3020	.2816	.2335	.1757	.1209	.0763	.0439
	3	.0105	.0574	.1298	.2013	.2503	.2668	.2522	.2150	.1665	.1172
	4	.0010	.0112	.0401	.0881	.1460	.2001	.2377	.2508	.2384	.2051
	5	.0001	.0015	.0085	.0264	.0584	.1029	.1536	.2007	.2340	.2461
	6	.0000	.0001	.0012	.0055	.0162	.0368	.0689	.1115	.1596	.2051
	7	.0000	.0000	.0001	.0008	.0031	.0090	.0212	.0425	.0746	.1172
	8	.0000	.0000	.0000	.0001	.0004	.0014	.0043	.0106	.0229	.0439
	9	.0000	.0000	.0000	.0000	.0000	.0001	.0005	.0016	.0042	.0098
	10	.0000	.0000	.0000	.0000	.0000	.0000	.0000	.0001	.0003	.0010

Poisson Distribution Values

$$P(X \leq c|\lambda) = \sum_{0}^{c} \frac{\lambda^x e^{-\lambda}}{x!}$$

The table shows 1,000 times the probability of c or less occurrences of an event that has an average number of occurrences of λ.

Values of c

λ	0	1	2	3	4	5	6	7	8	9	10
.02	980	1000									
.04	961	999	1000								
.06	942	998	1000								
.08	923	997	1000								
.10	905	995	1000								
.15	861	990	999	1000							
.20	819	982	999	1000							
.25	779	974	998	1000							
.30	741	963	996	1000							
.35	705	951	994	1000							
.40	670	938	992	999	1000						
.45	638	925	989	999	1000						
.50	607	910	986	998	1000						
.55	577	894	982	998	1000						
.60	549	878	977	997	1000						
.65	522	861	972	996	999	1000					
.70	497	844	966	994	999	1000					
.75	472	827	959	993	999	1000					
.80	449	809	953	991	999	1000					
.85	427	791	945	989	998	1000					
.90	407	772	937	987	998	1000					
.95	387	754	929	984	997	1000					
1.00	368	736	920	981	996	999	1000				
1.1	333	699	900	974	995	999	1000				
1.2	301	663	879	966	992	998	1000				
1.3	273	627	857	957	989	998	1000				
1.4	247	592	833	946	986	997	999	1000			
1.5	223	558	809	934	981	996	999	1000			
1.6	202	525	783	921	976	994	999	1000			
1.7	183	493	757	907	970	992	998	1000			
1.8	165	463	731	891	964	990	997	999	1000		
1.9	150	434	704	875	956	987	997	999	1000		
2.0	135	406	677	857	947	983	995	999	1000		

Source: Adapted from E. L. Grant, *Statistical Quality Control*, McGraw-Hill Book Company, New York, 1964. Reproduced by permission of the publisher.

Values of c

λ	0	1	2	3	4	5	6	7	8	9	10	11	12	13	14	15	16	17	18	19	20	21	22
2.2	111	355	623	819	928	975	993	998	1000														
2.4	091	308	570	779	904	964	988	997	999	1000													
2.6	074	267	518	736	877	951	983	995	999	1000													
2.8	061	231	469	692	848	935	976	992	998	999	1000												
3.0	050	199	423	647	815	916	966	988	996	999	1000												
3.2	041	171	380	603	781	895	955	983	994	998	1000												
3.4	033	147	340	558	744	871	942	977	992	997	999	1000											
3.6	027	126	303	515	706	844	927	969	988	996	999	1000											
3.8	022	107	269	473	668	816	909	960	984	994	998	999	1000										
4.0	018	092	238	433	629	785	889	949	979	992	997	999	1000										
4.2	015	078	210	395	590	753	867	936	972	989	996	999	1000										
4.4	012	066	185	359	551	720	844	921	964	985	994	998	999	1000									
4.6	010	056	163	326	513	686	818	905	955	980	992	997	999	1000									
4.8	008	048	143	294	476	651	791	887	944	975	990	996	999	1000									
5.0	007	040	125	265	440	616	762	867	932	968	986	995	998	999	1000								
5.2	006	034	109	238	406	581	732	845	918	960	982	993	997	999	1000								
5.4	005	029	095	213	373	546	702	822	903	951	977	990	996	999	1000								
5.6	004	024	082	191	342	512	670	797	886	941	972	988	995	998	999	1000							
5.8	003	021	072	170	313	478	638	771	867	929	965	984	993	997	999	1000							
6.0	002	017	062	151	285	446	606	744	847	916	957	980	991	996	999	999	1000						
6.2	002	015	054	134	259	414	574	716	826	902	949	975	989	995	998	999	1000						
6.4	002	012	046	119	235	384	542	687	803	886	939	969	986	994	997	999	1000						
6.6	001	010	040	105	213	355	511	658	780	869	927	963	982	992	997	999	999	1000					
6.8	001	009	034	093	192	327	480	628	755	850	915	955	978	990	996	998	999	1000					
7.0	001	007	030	082	173	301	450	599	729	830	901	947	973	987	994	998	999	1000					
7.2	001	006	025	072	156	276	420	569	703	810	887	937	967	984	993	997	999	1000					
7.4	001	005	022	063	140	253	392	539	676	788	871	926	961	980	991	996	998	999	1000				
7.6	001	004	019	055	125	231	365	510	648	765	853	915	954	976	988	995	998	999	1000				
7.8	000	004	016	048	112	210	338	481	620	741	835	902	945	971	986	993	997	999	1000				
8.0	000	003	014	042	100	191	313	453	593	717	816	888	936	966	983	992	996	998	999	1000			
8.5	000	002	009	030	074	150	256	386	523	653	763	849	909	949	973	986	994	997	999	1000			
9.0	000	001	006	021	055	116	207	324	456	587	706	803	876	926	959	978	989	995	998	999	1000		
9.5	000	001	004	015	040	089	165	269	392	522	645	752	836	898	940	967	982	991	996	998	999	1000	
10.0	000	000	003	010	029	067	130	220	333	458	583	697	792	864	917	951	973	986	993	997	998	999	1000

Appendix E

Present Value Factors for Future Single Payments

Periods until payment	1%	2%	4%	6%	8%	10%	12%	14%	15%	16%	18%	20%	22%	24%	25%	26%	28%	30%	35%	40%
1	.990	.980	.962	.943	.926	.909	.893	.877	.870	.862	.847	.833	.820	.806	.800	.794	.781	.769	.741	.714
2	.980	.961	.925	.890	.857	.826	.797	.769	.756	.743	.718	.694	.672	.650	.640	.630	.610	.592	.549	.510
3	.971	.942	.889	.840	.794	.751	.712	.675	.658	.641	.609	.579	.551	.524	.512	.500	.477	.455	.406	.364
4	.961	.924	.855	.792	.735	.683	.636	.592	.572	.552	.516	.482	.451	.423	.410	.397	.373	.350	.301	.260
5	.951	.906	.822	.747	.681	.621	.567	.519	.497	.476	.437	.402	.370	.341	.328	.315	.291	.269	.223	.186
6	.942	.888	.790	.705	.630	.564	.507	.456	.432	.410	.370	.335	.303	.275	.262	.250	.227	.207	.165	.133
7	.933	.871	.760	.665	.583	.513	.452	.400	.376	.354	.314	.279	.249	.222	.210	.198	.178	.159	.122	.095
8	.923	.853	.731	.627	.540	.467	.404	.351	.327	.305	.266	.233	.204	.179	.168	.157	.139	.123	.091	.068
9	.914	.837	.703	.592	.500	.424	.361	.308	.284	.263	.225	.194	.167	.144	.134	.125	.108	.094	.067	.048
10	.905	.820	.676	.558	.463	.386	.322	.270	.247	.227	.191	.162	.137	.116	.107	.099	.085	.073	.050	.035
11	.896	.804	.650	.527	.429	.350	.287	.237	.215	.195	.162	.135	.112	.094	.086	.079	.066	.056	.037	.025
12	.887	.788	.625	.497	.397	.319	.257	.208	.187	.168	.137	.112	.092	.076	.069	.062	.052	.043	.027	.018
13	.879	.773	.601	.469	.368	.290	.229	.182	.163	.145	.116	.093	.075	.061	.055	.050	.040	.033	.020	.013
14	.870	.758	.577	.442	.340	.263	.205	.160	.141	.125	.099	.078	.062	.049	.044	.039	.032	.025	.015	.009
15	.861	.743	.555	.417	.315	.239	.183	.140	.123	.108	.084	.065	.051	.040	.035	.031	.025	.020	.011	.006
16	.853	.728	.534	.394	.292	.218	.163	.123	.107	.093	.071	.054	.042	.032	.028	.025	.019	.015	.008	.005
17	.844	.714	.513	.371	.270	.198	.146	.108	.093	.080	.060	.045	.034	.026	.023	.020	.015	.012	.006	.003
18	.836	.700	.494	.350	.250	.180	.130	.095	.081	.069	.051	.038	.028	.021	.018	.016	.012	.009	.005	.002
19	.828	.686	.475	.331	.232	.164	.116	.083	.070	.060	.043	.031	.023	.017	.014	.012	.009	.007	.003	.002
20	.820	.673	.456	.312	.215	.149	.104	.073	.061	.051	.037	.026	.019	.014	.012	.010	.007	.005	.002	.001
21	.811	.660	.439	.294	.199	.135	.093	.064	.053	.044	.031	.022	.015	.011	.009	.008	.006	.004	.002	.001
22	.803	.647	.422	.278	.184	.123	.083	.056	.046	.038	.026	.018	.013	.009	.007	.006	.004	.003	.001	.001
23	.795	.634	.406	.262	.170	.112	.074	.049	.040	.033	.022	.015	.010	.007	.006	.005	.003	.002	.001	
24	.788	.622	.390	.247	.158	.102	.066	.043	.035	.028	.019	.013	.008	.006	.005	.004	.003	.002	.001	
25	.780	.610	.375	.233	.146	.092	.059	.038	.030	.024	.016	.010	.007	.005	.004	.003	.002	.001	.001	
26	.772	.598	.361	.220	.135	.084	.053	.033	.026	.021	.014	.009	.006	.004	.003	.002	.002	.001		
27	.764	.586	.347	.207	.125	.076	.047	.029	.023	.018	.011	.007	.005	.003	.002	.002	.001	.001		
28	.757	.574	.333	.196	.116	.069	.042	.026	.020	.016	.010	.006	.004	.002	.002	.001	.001	.001		
29	.749	.563	.321	.185	.107	.063	.037	.022	.017	.014	.008	.005	.003	.002	.002	.001	.001	.001		
30	.742	.552	.308	.174	.099	.057	.033	.020	.015	.012	.007	.004	.003	.002	.001	.001	.001	.001		

Present Value Factors for Annuities

Years (N)	1%	2%	4%	6%	8%	10%	12%	14%	15%	16%	18%	20%	22%	24%	25%	26%	28%	30%	35%	40%
1	.990	.980	.962	.943	.926	.909	.893	.877	.870	.862	.847	.833	.820	.806	.800	.794	.781	.769	.741	.714
2	1.970	1.942	1.886	1.833	1.783	1.736	1.690	1.647	1.626	1.605	1.566	1.528	1.492	1.457	1.440	1.424	1.392	1.361	1.289	1.224
3	2.941	2.884	2.775	2.673	2.577	2.487	2.402	2.322	2.283	2.246	2.174	2.106	2.042	1.981	1.952	1.923	1.868	1.816	1.696	1.589
4	3.902	3.808	3.630	3.465	3.312	3.170	3.037	2.914	2.855	2.798	2.690	2.589	2.494	2.404	2.362	2.320	2.241	2.166	1.997	1.849
5	4.853	4.713	4.452	4.212	3.993	3.791	3.605	3.433	3.352	3.274	3.127	2.991	2.864	2.745	2.689	2.635	2.532	2.436	2.220	2.035
6	5.795	5.601	5.242	4.917	4.623	4.355	4.111	3.889	3.784	3.685	3.498	3.326	3.167	3.020	2.951	2.885	2.759	2.643	2.385	2.168
7	6.728	6.472	6.002	5.582	5.206	4.868	4.564	4.288	4.160	4.039	3.812	3.605	3.416	3.242	3.161	3.083	2.937	2.802	2.508	2.263
8	7.652	7.325	6.733	6.210	5.747	5.335	4.968	4.639	4.487	4.344	4.078	3.837	3.619	3.421	3.329	3.241	3.076	2.925	2.598	2.331
9	8.566	8.162	7.435	6.802	6.247	5.759	5.328	4.946	4.772	4.607	4.303	4.031	3.786	3.566	3.463	3.366	3.184	3.019	2.665	2.379
10	9.471	8.983	8.111	7.360	6.710	6.145	5.650	5.216	5.019	4.833	4.494	4.192	3.923	3.682	3.571	3.465	3.269	3.092	2.715	2.414
11	10.368	9.787	8.760	7.887	7.139	6.495	5.937	5.453	5.234	5.029	4.656	4.327	4.035	3.776	3.656	3.544	3.335	3.147	2.752	2.438
12	11.255	10.575	9.385	8.384	7.536	6.814	6.194	5.660	5.421	5.197	4.793	4.439	4.127	3.851	3.725	3.606	3.387	3.190	2.779	2.456
13	12.134	11.343	9.986	8.853	7.904	7.103	6.424	5.842	5.583	5.342	4.910	4.533	4.203	3.912	3.780	3.656	3.427	3.223	2.799	2.468
14	13.004	12.106	10.563	9.295	8.244	7.367	6.628	6.002	5.724	5.468	5.008	4.611	4.265	3.962	3.824	3.695	3.459	3.249	2.814	2.477
15	13.865	12.849	11.118	9.712	8.559	7.606	6.811	6.142	5.847	5.575	5.092	4.675	4.315	4.001	3.859	3.726	3.483	3.268	2.825	2.484
16	14.718	13.578	11.652	10.106	8.851	7.824	6.974	6.265	5.954	5.669	5.162	4.730	4.357	4.033	3.887	3.751	3.503	3.283	2.834	2.489
17	15.562	14.292	12.166	10.477	9.122	8.022	7.120	6.373	6.047	5.749	5.222	4.775	4.391	4.059	3.910	3.771	3.518	3.295	2.840	2.492
18	16.398	14.992	12.659	10.828	9.372	8.201	7.250	6.467	6.128	5.818	5.273	4.812	4.419	4.080	3.928	3.786	3.529	3.304	2.844	2.494
19	17.226	15.678	13.134	11.158	9.604	8.365	7.366	6.550	6.198	5.877	5.316	4.844	4.442	4.097	3.942	3.799	3.539	3.311	2.846	2.496
20	18.046	16.351	13.590	11.470	9.818	8.514	7.469	6.623	6.259	5.929	5.353	4.870	4.460	4.110	3.954	3.808	3.546	3.316	2.850	2.497
21	18.857	17.011	14.029	11.764	10.017	8.649	7.562	6.687	6.312	5.973	5.384	4.891	4.476	4.121	3.963	3.816	3.551	3.320	2.852	2.498
22	19.660	17.658	14.451	12.042	10.201	8.772	7.645	6.743	6.359	6.011	5.410	4.909	4.488	4.130	3.970	3.822	3.556	3.323	2.853	2.498
23	20.456	18.292	14.857	12.303	10.371	8.883	7.718	6.792	6.399	6.044	5.432	4.925	4.499	4.137	3.976	3.827	3.559	3.325	2.854	2.499
24	21.243	18.914	15.247	12.550	10.529	8.985	7.784	6.835	6.434	6.073	5.451	4.937	4.507	4.143	3.981	3.831	3.562	3.327	2.855	2.499
25	22.023	19.523	15.622	12.783	10.675	9.077	7.843	6.873	6.464	6.097	5.467	4.948	4.514	4.147	3.985	3.834	3.564	3.329	2.856	2.499
26	22.795	20.121	15.983	13.003	10.810	9.161	7.896	6.906	6.491	6.118	5.480	4.956	4.520	4.151	3.988	3.837	3.566	3.330	2.856	2.500
27	23.560	20.707	16.330	13.211	10.935	9.237	7.943	6.935	6.514	6.136	5.492	4.964	4.524	4.154	3.990	3.839	3.567	3.331	2.856	2.500
28	24.316	21.281	16.663	13.406	11.051	9.307	7.984	6.961	6.534	6.152	5.502	4.970	4.528	4.157	3.992	3.840	3.568	3.331	2.857	2.500
29	25.066	21.844	16.984	13.591	11.158	9.370	8.022	6.983	6.551	6.166	5.510	4.975	4.531	4.159	3.994	3.841	3.569	3.332	2.857	2.500
30	25.808	22.396	17.292	13.765	11.258	9.427	8.055	7.003	6.566	6.177	5.517	4.979	4.534	4.160	3.995	3.842	3.569	3.332	2.857	2.500

Equations and Factors
for 10% Interest

n	To find F, given P: $(1 + i)^n$	To find P, given F: $\dfrac{1}{(1 + i)^n}$	To find A, given F: $\dfrac{i}{(1 + i)^n - 1}$	To find A, given P: $\dfrac{i(1 + i)^n}{(1 + i)^n - 1}$	To find F, given A: $\dfrac{(1 + i)^n - 1}{i}$	To find P, given A: $\dfrac{(1 + i)^n - 1}{i(1 + i)^n}$
	$(F\|P)_{10}^n$	$(P\|F)_{10}^n$	$(A\|F)_{10}^n$	$(A\|P)_{10}^n$	$(F\|A)_{10}^n$	$(P\|A)_{10}^n$
1	1.100	.9091	1.00000	1.10000	1.000	.909
2	1.210	.8264	.47619	.57619	2.100	1.736
3	1.331	.7513	.30211	.40211	3.310	2.487
4	1.464	.6830	.21547	.31547	4.641	3.170
5	1.611	.6209	.16380	.26380	6.105	3.791
6	1.772	.5645	.12961	.22961	7.716	4.355
7	1.949	.5132	.10541	.20541	9.487	4.868
8	2.144	.4665	.08744	.18744	11.436	5.335
9	2.358	.4241	.07364	.17364	13.579	5.759
10	2.594	.3855	.06275	.16275	15.937	6.144
11	2.853	.3505	.05396	.15396	18.531	6.495
12	3.138	.3186	.04676	.14676	21.384	6.814
13	3.452	.2897	.04078	.14078	24.523	7.103
14	3.797	.2633	.03575	.13575	27.975	7.367
15	4.177	.2394	.03147	.13147	31.772	7.606
16	4.595	.2176	.02782	.12782	35.950	7.824
17	5.054	.1978	.02466	.12466	40.545	8.022
18	5.560	.1799	.02193	.12193	45.599	8.201
19	6.116	.1635	.01955	.11955	51.159	8.363
20	6.727	.1486	.01746	.11746	57.275	8.514
21	7.400	.1351	.01562	.11562	64.002	8.649
22	8.140	.1228	.01401	.11401	71.403	8.772
23	8.954	.1117	.01257	.11257	79.543	8.883
24	9.850	.1015	.01130	.11130	88.497	8.985
25	10.835	.0923	.01017	.11017	98.347	9.077
26	11.918	.0839	.00916	.10916	109.182	9.161
27	13.110	.0763	.00826	.10826	121.100	9.237
28	14.421	.0693	.00745	.10745	134.210	9.307
29	15.863	.0630	.00673	.10673	148.631	9.370
30	17.449	.0573	.00608	.10608	164.494	9.427
31	19.194	.0521	.00550	.10550	181.943	9.479
32	21.114	.0474	.00497	.10497	201.138	9.526
33	23.225	.0431	.00450	.10450	222.252	9.569
34	25.548	.0391	.00407	.10407	245.477	9.609
35	28.102	.0356	.00369	.10369	271.024	9.644
40	45.259	.0221	.00226	.10226	442.593	9.779
45	72.890	.0137	.00139	.10139	718.905	9.863
50	117.391	.0085	.00086	.10086	1163.909	9.915
55	189.059	.0053	.00053	.10053	1880.591	9.947
60	304.482	.0033	.00033	.10033	3034.816	9.967
65	409.371	.0020	.00020	.10020	4893.707	9.980
70	789.747	.0013	.00013	.10013	7887.470	9.987
75	1,271.895	.0008	.00008	.10008	12708.954	9.992
80	2,048.400	.0005	.00005	.10005	20474.002	9.995
85	3,298.969	.0003	.00003	.10003	32979.690	9.997
90	5,313.023	.0002	.00002	.10002	53120.226	9.998
95	8,556.676	.0001	.00001	.10001	85556.760	9.999
100	13,780.612	.0001	.00001	.10001	137796.123	9.999

Learning Curve Coefficients

% base	70%	74%	78%	80%	82%	84%	86%	88%	90%	94%	98%
2	7.486	5.469	4.065	3.523	3.065	2.675	2.343	2.058	1.812	1.418	1.121
5	4.672	3.674	2.927	2.623	2.358	2.125	1.919	1.738	1.577	1.307	1.091
10	3.270	2.718	2.283	2.098	1.933	1.785	1.651	1.529	1.419	1.228	1.069
20	2.290	2.012	1.781	1.674	1.585	1.499	1.420	1.346	1.277	1.155	1.048
30	1.858	1.687	1.540	1.473	1.412	1.354	1.300	1.249	1.201	1.113	1.036
40	1.602	1.489	1.389	1.343	1.300	1.259	1.221	1.184	1.149	1.085	1.027
50	1.429	1.351	1.282	1.250	1.220	1.190	1.163	1.136	1.111	1.064	1.020
60	1.300	1.248	1.201	1.178	1.158	1.137	1.118	1.099	1.081	1.047	1.015
70	1.201	1.167	1.137	1.121	1.108	1.094	1.081	1.088	1.056	1.032	1.010
80	1.122	1.101	1.083	1.074	1.066	1.058	1.050	1.042	1.034	1.020	1.007
90	1.056	1.047	1.039	1.034	1.031	1.027	1.023	1.020	1.016	1.010	1.003
100	1.000	1.000	1.000	1.000	1.000	1.000	1.000	1.000	1.000	1.000	1.000
110	.9521	.9593	.9665	.9696	.9731	.9764	.9796	.9827	.9855	.9916	.9973
120	.9105	.9239	.9369	.9428	.9492	.9551	.9610	.9670	.9726	.9839	.9947
125	.8915	.9076	.9231	.9307	.9381	.9454	.9526	.9552	.9667	.9803	.9935
130	.8737	.8921	.9104	.9200	.9279	.9359	.9447	.9528	.9609	.9769	.9923
140	.8410	.8640	.8864	.8974	.9084	.9188	.9294	.9399	.9501	.9704	.9903
150	.8117	.8381	.8645	.8776	.8905	.9029	.9156	.9280	.9402	.9645	.9882
160	.7852	.8152	.8452	.8595	.8744	.8885	.9028	.9170	.9309	.9590	.9864
170	.7611	.7938	.8270	.8428	.8591	.8752	.8910	.9067	.9225	.9538	.9847
175	.7498	.7842	.8183	.8352	.8520	.8687	.8854	.9020	.9185	.9513	.9838
180	.7390	.7746	.8103	.8274	.8452	.8624	.8798	.8974	.9144	.9489	.9830
190	.7187	.7568	.7947	.8133	.8322	.8510	.8698	.8885	.9070	.9443	.9815
200	.7000	.7400	.7800	.8000	.8200	.8400	.8600	.8800	.9000	.9400	.9800
220	.6665	.7098	.7540	.7759	.7981	.8201	.8423	.8646	.8870	.9321	.9772
240	.6373	.6835	.7306	.7543	.7783	.8022	.8265	.8508	.8754	.9249	.9748
260	.6116	.6602	.7103	.7349	.7607	.7863	.8123	.8384	.8649	.9182	.9726
280	.5887	.6392	.6915	.7177	.7447	.7717	.7992	.8270	.8550	.9122	.9704
300	.5682	.6203	.6743	.7019	.7301	.7586	.7875	.8161	.8492	.9066	.9684
400	.4900	.5476	.6084	.6400	.6724	.7056	.7396	.7744	.8100	.8836	.9604
500	.4368	.4970	.5616	.5956	.6308	.6671	.7045	.7432	.7830	.8662	.9542
600	.3977	.4592	.5261	.5617	.5987	.6372	.6771	.7187	.7616	.8522	.9491
700	.3674	.4294	.4978	.5345	.5729	.6129	.6548	.6985	.7440	.8406	.9449
800	.3430	.4052	.4746	.5120	.5514	.5927	.6361	.6815	.7290	.8306	.9412
900	.3228	.3850	.4549	.4929	.5331	.5754	.6200	.6668	.7161	.8219	.9380
1000	.3058	.3678	.4381	.4765	.5172	.5604	.6059	.6540	.7047	.8142	.9351

Source: R. W. Conway and Andrew Schultz, Jr., "The Manufacturing Progress Function," *Journal of Industrial Engineering,* vol. 10, no. 1, January–February 1959, pp. 39–54; and Thomas E. Vollman, *Operations Management,* Addison-Wesley Publishing Company, Reading, Mass., 1973, pp. 381–384. Reproduced by permission of the AIIE and Addison-Wesley.

Appendix I

Normally Distributed Random Numbers

	1	2	3	4	5	6	7	8
1	.34	−.25	−.97	−.62	.37	−1.89	−.79	−87
2	−1.09	1.13	.99	.72	−.82	.46	−.41	.35
3	−1.87	.35	−.56	−.53	.91	−.48	1.31	.95
4	1.57	.75	1.20	2.29	.02	.67	−.41	.35
5	2.09	−1.54	1.02	−1.06	.65	−2.05	.73	−1.06
6	.37	.64	1.26	−.39	−.25	.53	.29	−.14
7	.03	−.71	1.08	.53	.28	.37	.27	−1.06
8	1.42	−.41	−.60	.75	−1.02	.91	2.11	.35
9	−.26	.99	−1.09	3.29	−.62	1.23	−1.36	.79
10	.93	.29	−.46	.63	1.84	−.36	.46	−1.00

Index